Communications
in Computer and Information Science 1135

Commenced Publication in 2007
Founding and Former Series Editors:
Phoebe Chen, Alfredo Cuzzocrea, Xiaoyong Du, Orhun Kara, Ting Liu,
Krishna M. Sivalingam, Dominik Ślęzak, Takashi Washio, Xiaokang Yang,
and Junsong Yuan

Editorial Board Members

More information about this series at http://www.springer.com/series/7899

Andrei Chugunov · Igor Khodachek ·
Yuri Misnikov · Dmitrii Trutnev (Eds.)

Electronic Governance and Open Society: Challenges in Eurasia

6th International Conference, EGOSE 2019
St. Petersburg, Russia, November 13–14, 2019
Proceedings

 Springer

Editors
Andrei Chugunov (iD)
ITMO University
St. Petersburg, Russia

Yuri Misnikov (iD)
University of Leeds
Leeds, UK

Igor Khodachek (iD)
Russian Academy of National Economy
and Public Administration
St. Petersburg, Russia

Dmitrii Trutnev (iD)
ITMO University
St. Petersburg, Russia

ISSN 1865-0929   ISSN 1865-0937 (electronic)
Communications in Computer and Information Science
ISBN 978-3-030-39295-6   ISBN 978-3-030-39296-3 (eBook)
https://doi.org/10.1007/978-3-030-39296-3

This Springer imprint is published by the registered company Springer Nature Switzerland AG
The registered company address is: Gewerbestrasse 11, 6330 Cham, Switzerland

Preface

The 6th Annual International Conference on Electronic Governance and Open Society: Challenges in Eurasia (EGOSE 2019) was held during November 13–14, 2019, in St. Petersburg, Russia.

This conference was the result of a joint effort by the eGovernance Center of ITMO University and North-West Institute of Management, branch of Russian Presidential Academy of National Economy and Public Administration (RANEPA).

EGOSE 2019 aimed to address the main issues of concern within the Information Society: e-government, e-governance, and e-democracy. The conference provided a platform for networking and collaboration of eGovernance experts from the whole world.

Through the EasyChair system, 82 full text papers by authors from 12 countries were submitted to the conference. As a result of the double-blind peer review process, the Program Committee selected 32 papers by authors from 8 countries for presentation and publication (acceptance rate 39%). The accepted papers were presented at eight conference sections united by topics:

- Smart City
- Digital Government, Society, and Economy
- Digital Intelligence, Data Science, and Cybercrime
- Social Networking and Media

The conference working days began with plenary sessions conducted by invited key speakers:

Prof. Dr. Marijn Janssen (full professor in ICT and Governance and head of the Information and Communication Technology section of the Technology, Policy, and Management Faculty of Delft University of Technology, the Netherlands) gave a talk titled "Information Sharing in the Digital Age" about various types of information sharing arrangements and mechanisms for ensuring privacy and compliance.

Dr. Andrea L. Kavanaugh (Associate Director, Center for Human-Computer Interaction Virginia Polytechnic Institute and State University, USA) gave a talk titled "Too Small to Fail: Social Networks and Communities Online" analyzing the use of the Internet including social media at the local level and how that connects with regional and national/global use.

November 2019

Andrei Chugunov
Igor Khodachek
Yuri Misnikov
Dmitrii Trutnev

Organization

Steering Committee

Andrei Chugunov	eGovernanace Center, ITMO University, Russia
Igor Khodachek	Russian Academy of National Economy and Public Administration, North-West Institute of Management, Russia
Yuri Misnikov	eGovernance Academy, Estonia, and Institute of Communications Studies, University of Leeds, UK
Dmitrii Trutnev	eGovernanace Center, ITMO University, Russia

Program Committee

Artur Afonso Sousa	Polytechnic Institute of Viseu, Portugal
Olusegun Agbabiaka	Softrust Technologies Limited, Nigeria
Martynov Aleksei	Lobachevsky State University of Nizhny Novgorod (UNN), Russia
Dennis Anderson	St. Francis College, USA
Francisco Andrade	University of Minho, Portugal
Farah Arab	Université Paris 8, France
Mohammed Awad	American University of Ras Al Khaimah, UAE
Maxim Bakaev	Novosibirsk State Technical University, Russia
Alexander Balthasar	Bundeskanzleramt, Austria
Luis Barbosa	University of Minho, Portugal
Anna Bilyatdinova	ITMO University, Russia
Radomir Bolgov	Saint Petersburg State University, Russia
Sunil Choenni	Research and Documentation Centre (WODC), Ministry of Justice, The Netherlands
Andrei Chugunov	ITMO University, eGovernment Center, Russia
Cesar A. Collazos	Universidad del Cauca, Colombia
Shefali S. Dash	National Informatics Centre, India
Saravanan Devadoss	Addis Ababa University, Ethiopia
Subrata Kumar Dey	Independent University, Bangladesh
Behnam Faghih	Technical and Vocational University, College of Bushehr, Iran
Olga Filatova	Saint Petersburg State University, Russia
Enrico Francesconi	ITTIG-CNR, Italy
Miguel J. Galindo	University of Zaragoza, Spain
Despina Garyfallidou	University of Patras, Greece
Carlos Gershenson	UNAM, Mexico
J. Paul Gibson	Mines Télécom, France

Ilias Pappas	Norwegian University of Science and Technology, Norway
Manas Ranjan Patra	Berhampur University, India
Rui Quaresma	Universidade de Évora, Portugal
Aleksandr Riabushko	Office of the Affairs of the Ulyanovsk Region, Russia
Gustavo Rossi	LIFIA-UNLP, Argentina
Alexander Ryjov	Moscow State University, Russia
Michael Sachs	Danube University Krems, Austria
Jenny Marcela Sanchez-Torres	Universidad Nacional de Colombia, Colombia
Adriano Santos	Universidade Federal de Campina Grande, Brazil
Carolin Schröder	Centre for Technology and Society, Germany
Shafay Shamail	LUMS, DHA, Pakistan
Irina Shmeleva	University ITMO, Russia
Rudrapatna Shyamasundar	TIFR, India
Greg Simons	Uppsala University, Sweden
Evgeny Styrin	National Research University Higher School of Economics, Russia
Neelam Tikkha	MMV, RTMNU, India
Dmitrii Trutnev	eGovernance Center, ITMO University, Russia
Mario Vacca	Italian Ministry of Education, Italy
Costas Vassilakis	University of the Peloponnese, Greece
Lyudmila Vidiasova	ITMO University, Russia
Vasiliki Vrana	Technological Education Institute of Central Macedonia, Greece
Wilfred Warioba	Commission for Human Rights and Good Governance, Tanzania
Maria Wimmer	Universität Koblenz-Landau, Germany
Kostas Zafiropoulos	University of Macedonia, Greece
Nikolina Zajdela Hrustek	University of Zagreb, Croatia
Hans-Dieter Zimmermann	FHS St. Gallen University of Applied Sciences, Switzerland
Vytautas Čyras	Vilnius University, Lithuania

Contents

Digital Intelligence, Data Science and Cybercrime

Social Networking and Media

xiv   Contents

Smart City

A Study of the Composition of Smart Urban Decisions from the Point of View of the Population and Authorities. Case of St. Petersburg

I. S. Savenkov$^{(\boxtimes)}$, S. A. Mityagin, and A. I. Repkin

ITMO University, St. Petersburg, Russia
savenkovilya93@gmail.com,
{mityagin, airepkin}@corp.ifmo.ru

Abstract. The article presents results of a study of the problems, needs and ideas about the composition of decisions of a smart city when forming the concept of smart city for St. Petersburg. An independent survey of government officials was conducted. It was done in order to reveal their ideas about the composition of the necessary decisions for a smart city and also to compare results with a similar study for the population. The study of the population of St. Petersburg was carried out by a mass survey and in-depth case studies. As a result, significant differences in expectations from a smart city between these groups of stakeholders are shown. In addition, there were differences in the expectations of citizens with the requirements of international standards. The revealed effects confirm the hypothesis of the need for flexible and adaptive approaches to the creation of smart cities. Smart city should be positioned as an adaptive city for the needs of citizens.

Keywords: Smart City · Value-oriented approach · Urban studies · Human-oriented approach

1 Introduction

We don't currently have the generally accepted definition of "smart city". However, definition of "Smart City" declares approaches to the development of the city and the expected effects that are similar for cities of different types. The Smart City Paradigm covers several ideas. The main ideas are: save resources, create high quality urban environments. It can be achieved through the effective management of urban processes in combination with the open interaction of all stakeholders (for example citizens, business and authorities).

The main feature of smart city technologies is the most stable communication between the knowledge accumulated by mankind and the citizens. Such communication makes possible to reach a new level of energy consumption, create the most comfortable conditions for economic growth and allow us to preserve the environment for future generations. Smart City technologies were introduced in different areas

A. Chugunov et al. (Eds.): EGOSE 2019, CCIS 1135, pp. 3–16, 2020.
https://doi.org/10.1007/978-3-030-39296-3_1

unevenly and independently of each other because organizations or authorities tried to introduce everything at once.

Forester magazine suggests the following definition for smart city: A "city" that uses information and communications technologies to make the critical infrastructure components and services of a city - administration, education, healthcare, public safety, real estate, transportation, and utilities - more aware, interactive, and efficient [3]. Smart city development concepts are being actively studied all over the world (in Russian studies concepts outlined in journal Control Engineering Russia [2] and foreign researches were conducted for Forester [3]).

There are 2 main concepts of building smart cities:

1. Building smart cities from scratch.

The main advantages: the ability to introduce technologies comprehensively, the opportunity to cover full of the urban environment, design of the city is based on technologies (there is no need to adjust technologies for existing design solutions).

Main disadvantages: such cities are private solutions to specific problems (business, science or energy), as a result, they are not attractive for long stays.

2. The introduction of smart technologies in existing cities.

The main advantages: meet the specific "challenges" of the city (only what is needed will be introduced).

Main disadvantages: may have a negative impact on the unique cultural and historical landscape, as well as the atmosphere and needs of citizens.

The main priority is given to the following areas (according to the standards,): citizens involvement, open data, application of creative research talents, administrative services, infrastructure and adaptability of the city.

Currently, the "Smart St. Petersburg" program is being implemented in St. Petersburg. This program is aimed at achieving the goals defined by the social development strategy of St. Petersburg for the period up to 2030 and it is associated with the development, the introduction of widespread use of information and digital technologies in housing and communal services, energy and transport infrastructures, public administration, and public security.

In our study, we propose an approach that will allow assessing the needs of a Smart City by residents and authorities and comparing these needs.

2   The Procedure of Creation of Smart City in St. Petersburg

Activities in the field of smart city have been systematically carried out since 2017 in St. Petersburg. The result of this activity is the concept of the development of St. Petersburg using the technologies of the Smart City (approved at a meeting of the government of St. Petersburg in February 2018) [4]. A priority program and related technology deployment activities are currently being developed using this concept. The activities of the program "Smart St. Petersburg" correspond to the activities of the departmental project of the Ministry of Construction "Smart City" [5]. However, we expect to ensure the introduction of technology in all spheres of life in the city in

St. Petersburg. The figure shows the grouping of functional elements of Smart St. Petersburg in 4 layers.

Sociotechnical functional elements	Public services (electronic)	Interaction with residents	Interaction with organizations	Open data	IOT services	Additional assignment solutions	Security
Industry functional elements	Ecology	Housing and communal services	Urban environment	Health care	Energy		
Intersectoral functional elements	City managment	City informational resources	Informational interaction between the components of Smart City	Information and analytical support	Strategic planning		
Physical communications tools	Resource control sensors	CCTV	Access points to the infrrormation	Communication tools	Data centers	Active elements of urban environment	

Fig. 1. Functional elements of Smart St. Petersburg (Color figure online)

Each layer is highlighted in a unique color, the common features of the layers are divided into 2 blocks (dark green - additional solutions for a smart city and gray - safety).

Layer 1 (pale green). The development of elements of the base layers (physical means of information interaction and intersectoral functional elements) is necessary for the possible development of top-layer elements. The functioning of the elements of this layer ensures the updating of the parameters of the digital image of the city.

Layer 2 (rose). Intersectoral functional elements are binding to the entire infrastructure of a smart city. They define the structure of the digital image as a whole.

Layer 3 (pale orange). Interrelated set of industry functional elements in the hierarchy.

Layer 4 (blue). The layer of social interactions of decisions of the smart city, citizens and the parties implementing these decisions.

The process of introducing smart city technologies in St. Petersburg implies a specific cycle of events each year. The cycle consists of 4 stages (Fig. 2).

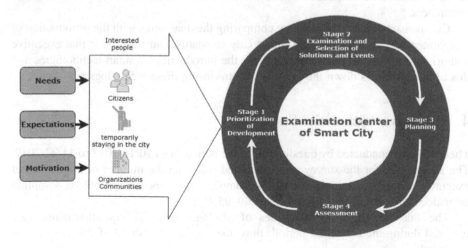

Fig. 2. The order of implementation of Smart City solutions in St. Petersburg

Stage 1. Activities to update the characteristics and parameters of the digital image of the city. Identifying problems and prospects for development based on it.

Stage 2. Selection of projects for inclusion in the smart city in priority areas. Creating a list of projects proposed for implementation as part of Smart St. Petersburg. Preparation for final decision-making by the responsible government authority.

Stage 3. Realization and implementation of projects. The implementation takes place in accordance with the scheme (Fig. 1).

Stage 4. Monitoring, evaluation of target indicators of the effectiveness of the implementation of Smart St. Petersburg and its components.

It is necessary to take into account the capabilities and readiness of citizens and authorities to interact with new technologies, as well as to take into account the needs of both categories because smart technologies require maximum involvement of all participants.

3   Our Approach

To conduct research and comparison we collected data from various sources. Then we implemented them in a form in which they can be compared. City parameters, included in the concept of the development of St. Petersburg using the technologies of the Smart City, were proposed as a single set of parameters for evaluation (Sect. 2, Fig. 1).

The Staff of ITMO University under the coordination of the Committee on Informatization and Communication of St. Petersburg developed questionnaires that were proposed for the passage of an employee of executive authorities. Then algorithms based on convolution and the calculation of the average ranks were applied to this data. In detail, the research algorithm and its results are presented in Sect. 4.

To collect information from the citizens were used 3 organizations: "Beautiful Petersburg", "Our Petersburg" and Urban Research Laboratory of ITMO University. Results and research methods are presented in Sect. 5. We again applied the algorithm based on convolution and the calculation of the average ranks to determine the overall rating from three studies, because in this case we had 3 different ratings with the same parameters.

Comparison of data was made by comparing the final ranks with the introduction of a separate scale based on existing Smart City standards. Our position is that executive authorities and citizens perceive differently the introduction of smart technologies and this ultimately slows down the process of introducing these technologies.

4   Executive Authorities Survey

The study was conducted by questioning in the period from 10/16/2017 to 11/22/2017. The sample size for the survey was calculated based on the number of employees of executive authorities. Sample size – 281 (sample is non-repetitive, stratified, sampling error does not exceed 5%, reliability level - 95,4%).

The study involved 59 authorities of St. Petersburg. 375 questionnaires were received during the collection period; thus, the required threshold of the sample was exceeded.

4.1 Employee Survey Results

In the course of the study, an employee of executive authorities of St. Petersburg were asked whether they were ready for the implementation of the "Smart City" projects, etc. 63% are inclined to readiness, and 37% are more skeptical. In general, 4 out of 5 respondents at least heard something about the "smart cities" project.

In a survey of employees were asked about their expectations from the project "Smart St. Petersburg". The study revealed the prevalence of ideas about the smart city as a system of quality territory management, building an effective dialogue with citizens.

In order to determine the priorities of the project Smart City St. Petersburg, employees were asked to identify 3 priority areas for its development.

Figure 3 presents a ranking of areas reflecting the most important areas for making a breakthrough - quality of life (safety, cultural diversity, health), management (openness, electronic services, dialogue with citizens) and the environment (ecology, energy conservation, urban planning).

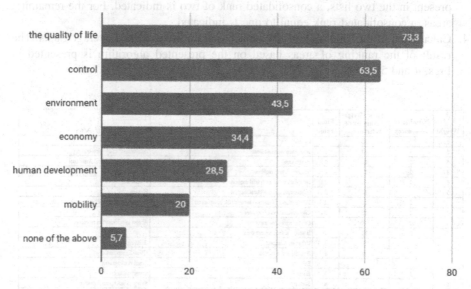

Fig. 3. The results of the survey about areas of development.

4.2 Highlighting Priority Areas for All Surveys

The formation of the final ranks of the directions and areas of the introduction of technologies of the "smart city" from the point of view of executive authorities of St. Petersburg is carried out on the basis of convolution and the calculation of the average ranks of the regions according to all the above lists. It should be noted that priorities are determined for the directions and areas of implementation of the "smart city", and not for projects and proposals. So, the mention of the area is estimated. The number of offers within one area does not affect its priority.

Since the regions and directions are represented in all the considered lists with different compositions, the algorithm of "convolution" of the lists of directions is used with the following weighting:

1. Enter the columns "Metric", "Final rank" and "Weight".
2. Weights are assigned according to the affiliation to the direction indicated in Fig. 3 and, moreover, the weight was determined by the popularity of the areas in the answers in the questionnaires:
- Areas related to population mobility have weight «1».
- Areas related to human development have weight «2».
- Areas associated with the development of economic potential have weight «3».
- Areas associated with the environment have weight «4».
- Areas associated with improved city management have weight «5».
- Areas associated with the direct improvement of the quality of life of the population have weight «6».
- Others have weight «0,5» .
3. For areas present in all three lists, a consolidated rank of three is indicated. For areas present in the two lists, a consolidated rank of two is indicated. For the remaining areas, a consolidated rank equal to one is indicated.
4. Calculation of the final rank of the areas based on the weighted average ranks. The result of the ranking of areas based on the presented algorithm is presented in Figs. 4 and 5.

Weight	Number of references	Metric (Weight * Number of references)	Final rank	Directions	Area
6	2	12	1	Security	Public safety
6	2	12	1	Interaction with residents	Involvement in decision making
6	2	12	1	Health care	Availability of Medical Assistance
6	2	12	1	Interaction with residents	Informing people
5	2	10	2	Information and analytical support	Forecasting
5	2	10	2	Information and analytical support	Planning
5	2	10	2	Informational interaction between the components of Smart City	Exchange of information between the state bodies
5	2	10	2	City informational resources	Resource Accounting
5	2	10	2	City informational resources	Access to information resources
5	2	10	2	Interaction with organizations	
4	2	8	3	Urban environment	Building
4	2	8	3	Housing and communal services	House Equipment
4	2	8	3	Ecology	Waste management
4	2	8	3	Energy	Energy saving
6	1	6	4	Security	Safety in emergency situations
6	1	6	4	Security	Fire safety
6	1	6	4	Interaction with residents	Accounting of complaints and appeals
6	1	6	4	Interaction with residents	Consideration of people's opinions
6	1	6	4	Public services	Service centers
6	1	6	4	Public services	Electronic form
6	1	6	4	Urban environment	Available Environment
6	1	6	4	Security	Safety of buildings and structures
5	1	5	5	Informational interaction between the components of Smart City	The interaction of public authorities with residents

Fig. 4. The list of final ranks by authorities (part 1)

Weight	Number of references	Metric (Weight * Number of references)	Final rank	Directions	Area
5	1	5	5	Open Data	Open services
5	1	5	5	Resource control sensors	
5	1	5	5	Information and analytical support	Analysis
5	1	5	5	City informational resources	Directories and Classifiers
5	1	5	5	Energy	Energy Management
5	1	5	5	Data centers	
4	1	4	6	Access points to the information	Internet access
4	1	4	6	Urban environment	Yard and house territory
4	1	4	6	Urban environment	Improvement of urban environment elements
4	1	4	6	Ecology	Ecology Monitoring
4	1	4	6	Ecology	Reduced environmental impact
3	1	3	7	Economy	Ecosystem of Innovation
1	2	2	8	Access points to the information	Transport equipment
1	2	2	8	Transport	Transport management
2	1	2	8	Education	Education profiling
2	1	2	8	Education	New educational areas
2	1	2	8	Education	Equipment of educational organizations
2	1	2	8	Education	Access to education
1	1	1	9	Tourism	Tourist navigation
1	1	1	9	Tourism	Tourist information
1	1	1	9	Transport	Parking
1	1	1	9	Transport	Roads
1	1	1	9	Transport	Payment systems

Fig. 5. The list of final ranks by authorities (part 2)

Identical ranks are assigned to directions if their final grades are equal. Summarizing information from executive authorities, the most priority directions are:

1. Security
2. Health care
3. Interaction with residents
4. Informational interaction between the components of Smart City
5. City informational resources.

5 Population Survey

All over the world, in the practice of creating smart cities, special attention is paid to citizens as important stakeholders in the organization of a new city management system using information and communication technologies. Given the importance of the opinions of citizens in St. Petersburg, it was decided to conduct a study of the opinions and expectations of citizens about the project smart city of St. Petersburg.

The study was conducted in order to identify the needs of the population in the technologies of the "smart city" (open data, electronic public services and the possibility of involving citizens in solving local problems of the city's life). The study was conducted by staff of ITMO University under the coordination of the Committee on Informatization and Communication of St. Petersburg. The study was conducted in the period 2.11.2017–20.11.2017 using the online questionnaire method. The target group of respondents consisted of active citizens - Internet users. The choice of this target group was determined by the purpose of the study, as well as its belonging to the group of "early followers" of innovation, according to the theory of E. Rogers.

To calculate the sample, data on the size of the general population of 3.36 million people were used (Internet users among the population of St. Petersburg aged 18 years and older). Minimum sample size is 384 people (simple non-repeat sample, 95% accuracy, 5% confidence interval). 421 respondents participated in the survey.

5.1   City Problems

This set of questions was devoted to the study of the opinions of citizens on urban issues in St. Petersburg. Open-ended questions were included in the survey question-naire: "What urban problems do you think exist in St. Petersburg?". The survey was programmed as mandatory for a response, which allowed gathering a wide range of respondents' opinions. A semantic analysis of the detailed answers received was conducted. The results of the analysis are presented in Fig. 6. (data was taken for a category containing more than 1000 hits).

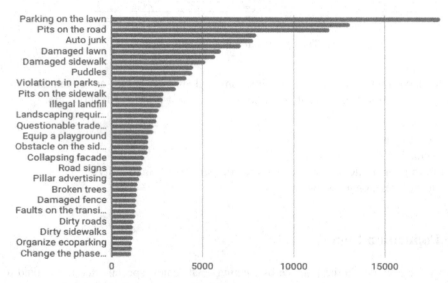

Fig. 6. Diagram of the popularity of subcategories of citizens' appeals

5.2   Smart City

In this questionnaire block, respondents were asked if they know something about the projects of "Smart Cities" and about their expectations of using new technologies in St. Petersburg. According to the results of the survey, it was revealed that almost ¾ of the respondents hear something about such projects, and every fifth person said that he clearly understands how to implement such a project in St. Petersburg.

During the study, optimistic and skeptical expectations of citizens from the implementation of the project "Smart St. Petersburg" were studied. Positive expecta-tions are associated with the following aspects:

- The city will become comfortable for living, European (19.3%);
- Opinions of citizens will be heard, and decisions will be made more effectively (17.6%);
- The authorities will solve the transport problem (15.1%);
- A convenient communications infrastructure will be built (10.1%);
- I expect just something good (5.9%).

Restrained expectations from the project "Smart St. Petersburg" respondents expressed in connection with the fact that:

1. They have no positive expectations due to the experience of other programs (19.3%);
2. There is corruption, a reason for enrichment (8.4%);
3. Expect the failure of the project (5.1%);
4. Authorities considered to slow down the process, "authorities are deaf to citizens" (4.2%)

The transition to questions about ideas and expectations from project implementation was opened for those respondents who showed their awareness of smart cities projects. We collected data from 3 different sources and summarized the results for each survey. Generalization of information from "Beautiful Petersburg", "Our St. Petersburg" and sociological research allowed us to identify priority directions and areas for the introduction of smart city technologies, which are presented on in Figs. 7, 8 and 9 (numbers indicate the final rank in the opinion of respondents).

Sociotechnical functional elements	Public services (electronic)	Interaction with residents	Interaction with organizations	Open data	IOT services	Additional assignment solutions (Transport)	Security
Industry functional elements	Ecology 5	Housing and communal services 4	Urban environment 2	Health care	Energy	1	3
Intersectoral functional elements	City managment	City informational resources	Informational interaction between the components of Smart City	Information and analytical support	Strategic planning		
Physical communications tools	Resource control sensors	CCTV	Access points to the infrrormation	Communication tools	Data centers	Active elements of urban environment	

Fig. 7. Data on the results of the portal "Beautiful Petersburg"

Sociotechnical functional elements	Public services (electronic)	Interaction with residents 5	Interaction with organizations	Open data	IOT services	Additional assignment solutions (Transport)	Security
Industry functional elements	Ecology	Housing and communal services	Urban environment 2	Health care	Energy	4	3
Intersectoral functional elements	City managment	City informational resources	Informational interaction between the components of Smart City	Information and analytical support	Strategic planning		
Physical communications tools	Resource control sensors	CCTV	Access points to the infrrormation	Communication tools	Data centers	Active elements of urban environment	

Fig. 8. Data on the results of the portal "Our St. Petersburg"

Sociotechnical functional elements	Public services (electronic)	Interaction with residents 5	Interaction with organizations	Open data	IOT services			
Industry functional elements	Ecology	Housing and communal services 2	Urban environment 1	Health care	Energy	3 (Transport) solutions assignment Additional		Security 4
Intersectoral functional elements	City managment	City informational resources	Informational interaction between the components of Smart City	Information and analytical support	Strategic planning			
Physical communications tools	Resource control sensors	CCTV	Access points to the infrormation	Communication tools	Data centers	Active elements of urban environment		

Fig. 9. Data on the results of sociological research

5.3 Priority Directions of Implementation from the Point of View of Citizens

The formation of the final ranks of directions and areas of implementation of smart city technologies from the point of view of residents was carried out on the basis of convolution and the calculation of the average ranks of areas for all sources. Thus, the following priority areas for citizens were identified:

1. Urban environment
2. Additional assignment solutions (Transport)
3. Housing and communal services
4. Security
5. Interaction with residents

6 Matching Expectations from a Smart City

6.1 Authorities

The main conclusions based on the survey of executive authorities:

1. A high percentage of employees use information systems (and a high need for unified IP and data digitization).
2. A high percentage of manual drafting of documents (70%).
3. Readiness of the authorities to electronic dialogue with the residents of the city.
4. Awareness of the project smart city is very high (80%).
5. The problems associated with retraining and complexity in managing data flows.
6. Identified priority areas for the project smart city of St. Petersburg in terms of employees: quality of life (safety, cultural diversity, health), management system (openness, electronic services, dialogue with citizens) and the environment (ecology, energy conservation, urban planning) (Fig. 10).

The compilation of information received from the executive authorities allowed us to identify the following priority areas indicated in the figure with the bright green, other colors indicate layers in accordance with the legend to Fig. 1.

Sociotechnical functional elements	Public services (electronic)	Interaction with residents 3	Interaction with organizations	Open data	IOT services	Additional assignment solutions	Security 1
Industry functional elements	Ecology	Housing and communal services	Urban environment	Health care 2	Energy		
Intersectoral functional elements	City managment	City Informational resources 5	Informational interaction between the components of Smart City 4	Information and analytical support	Strategic planning		
Physical communications tools	Resource control sensors	CCTV	Access points to the infrormation	Communication tools	Data centers	Active elements of urban environment	

Fig. 10. Priority areas for changes in the implementation of Smart City according to executive authorities (numbers = Final ranks)

6.2 Citizens

The main conclusions based on the survey of citizens:

1. 94% of citizens prefer to communicate with the authorities using an electronic format.
2. 57% consider Internet calls to be an effective way to solve urban problems.
3. The level of awareness of the smart city project reaches 74.6% of the respondents.
4. Respondents believe that the most acute at the moment are urban problems associated with public transport, roads, parking lots, traffic jams, infrastructure, construction and landscaping. It is expedient to introduce technologies of the "smart city" to solve exactly these problems that concern the citizens.
5. 77% believe that the use of electronic portals can influence political decisions.
6. Citizens consider the priority areas for the Smart St. Petersburg project are: the openness of government, the inclusion of citizens in management, improvement of homes and territories, improvement of the environmental situation and improvement of the quality of life (including solving transport infrastructure problems and development) (Fig. 11).

Sociotechnical functional elements	Public services (electronic)	Interaction with residents 5	Interaction with organizations	Open data	IOT services	(E.e. Transport) 2	Additional assignment solutions	Security 4
Industry functional elements	Ecology	Housing and communal services 3	Urban environment 1	Health care	Energy			
Intersectoral functional elements	City managment	City informational resources	Informational interaction between the components of Smart City	Information and analytical support	Strategic planning			
Physical communications tools	Resource control sensors	CCTV	Access points to the infrormation	Communication tools	Data centers	Active elements of urban environment		

Fig. 11. Priority areas of change in the implementation of Smart City in the opinion of citizens (numbers = Total ranks)

The compilation of information received from citizens allowed us to identify the following priority areas indicated in the figure with the bright orange, other colors indicate layers in accordance with the legend to Fig. 1.

6.3 Standby by Standards

During the study of the ISO 37120 standards [6] and the CIMI index [7], a list of expectations from the introduction of smart city technologies was formed. These expectations should be considered when introducing a smart city in St. Petersburg.

1. Improving the environmental situation
2. Resource Saving
3. Smart traffic management
4. Smart technologies in healthcare
5. Management of information infrastructure of the city
6. Opening of city data
7. Increasing the openness of the government
8. Development of new forms of financial relations in the city
9. Smart urban development planning
10. Improving the improvement of the city (the development of public spaces)
11. Security
12. Smart City Local Solutions Dependent on Territorial Context
13. Formation of positive opinions of residents about the introduction of a smart city.

6.4 Discussion

It can be noted that the respondents of both parties allow mutual dialogue, as well as allow its possibility without full-time participation (electronic form). Both parties understand the subject matter that needs to be addressed, but they see different solutions and related problems in different ways, and there are also some differences in priority areas.

As the study showed, joint decision-making (with the use of citizens and authorities) is necessary for the full implementation of smart technologies. Each citizen, or at least each socio-demographic group of citizens, should be considered as stakeholders because citizens are active participants in the formation of a city in the "smart" paradigm. The success of the introduction of smart city technologies is largely determined by the activity of citizens in using new technologies and the speed at which new behavioral attitudes are formed. However, the policy of forming a smart city and, consequently, determining the composition of technologies and solutions of a smart city are determined by public authorities. In this connection, the issue of overcoming the information barrier and the formation of the image of a smart city, comparable to the representation of citizens is an important task in the development of modern cities.

Despite the difficulties and costs incurred in the introduction of new systems that are able to fully ensure the interaction of people and executive authorities, this approach is the best solution to meet the needs of residents in the framework of a given strategy.

At this stage, results can be used as one of the elements of a decision support system for the implementation of Smart City technologies in St. Petersburg. Our study is limited to the basic parameters of the concept. It is necessary to take into account not just the functional elements of the smart city of St. Petersburg for obtaining detailed results. Each element must be divided into components. In this way, it will be possible to form a better connection between concrete decisions and the opinions of respondents.

To improve this approach and conduct more detailed research, it is planned to link the obtained results with the analysis of profiles of users of social networks (considering their interests and hobbies). Thus, we can get a complete picture for all participants of the process of informatization in the city. Connecting the data collected from social network profiles will allow us to create a powerful analytical device to support decision-making during the process of implementing smart city technologies, based on current research results and constantly updated user profile data.

7 Conclusions

In this paper, we hypothesized that executive authorities and citizens diverge in expectations from smart technologies. Approaches to the implementation of a smart city in St. Petersburg were analyzed. Key areas of change were identified and key concepts of smart St. Petersburg were described. Surveys were conducted on the subject of expectations from a smart city using popular city portals and city committees. The research results were processed and presented in the form corresponding to the terms and formulations of the concept of smart St. Petersburg. The ways of further development of this work and the possible application of current results in city decision making were also identified.

This research is financially supported by The Russian Science Foundation, Agreement № 17-71-30029 with co-financing of Bank Sankt-Petersburg.

References

1. Drozhzhin, Sergey I., Shiyan, Artem V., Mityagin, Sergey A.: Smart city implementation and aspects: the case of St. petersburg. In: Chugunov, A., Misnikov, Y., Roshchin, E., Trutnev, D. (eds.) EGOSE 2018. CCIS, vol. 947, pp. 14–25. Springer, Cham (2019). https://doi.org/10.1007/978-3-030-13283-5_2
2. Bukhanovsky, A.V., Mityagin, S.A., Karsakov, A.S., Vasilev, V.N.: "Smart St. Petersburg": an integrated approach to the introduction of information management technologies for megalopolis. Control Eng. Russ. 1(79), 18–25 (2019)
3. Belissent, J.: Smart City Leaders Need Better Governance Tools: Smart City Governance Brings New Opportunities for Tech Providers. Forrester Research, Cambridge, MA (2011)
4. The law of St. Petersburg dated 12.19.2018 No. 771–164
5. Order of the Ministry of Construction of Russia of October 31, 2018 No. 695 "On approval of the passport of the departmental project for the digitization of the municipal economy - "Smart City"
6. ISO 37120:2018 – Sustainable cities and communities

7. IESE Cities in Motion Index (ST-471-E)
8. Minelli, A., Ruffini, R.: Citizen feedback as a tool for continuous improvement in local bodies. Int. J. Public Sector Manag. **31**(1), 46–64 (2018)
9. Fernandez-Anez, V., Fernández-Güell, J.M., Giffinger, R.: Smart City implementation and discourses: an integrated conceptual model. The case of each year. The cycle consists Vienna. Cities **78**, 4–16 (2018)
10. Sikora-Fernandez, D.: Smarter cities in post-socialist country: example of Poland. Cities **78**, 52–59 (2018)
11. Kumar, H., Singh, M.K., Gupta, M.P., Madaan, J.: Moving towards smart cities: solutions that lead to the smart city transformation framework. Technol. Forecast. Soc. Change 1–16 (2018)
12. Kummitha, R.K.R., Crutzen, N.: How do we understand smart cities? An evolutionary perspective. Cities **67**, 43–52 (2017)
13. Borsekova, K., Koróny, S., Vaňová, A., Vitálišová, K.: Functionality between the size and indicators of smart cities: a research challenge with policy implications. Cities **78**, 17–26 (2018)
14. Bakıcı, T., Almirall, E., Wareham, J.: A smart city initiative: the case of Barcelona. J. Knowl. Econ. **4**(2), 135–148 (2013)
15. Mora, L., Deakin, M., Reid, A.: Strategic principles for smart city development: a multiple case study analysis of european best practices. Technol. Forecast. Soc. Chang. **142**, 1–28 (2018)
16. Alawadhi, S., et al.: Building understanding of smart city initiatives. In: Scholl, H.J., Janssen, M., Wimmer, M.A., Moe, C.E., Flak, L.S. (eds.) EGOV 2012. LNCS, vol. 7443, pp. 40–53. Springer, Heidelberg (2012). https://doi.org/10.1007/978-3-642-33489-4_4
17. Fernandez-Anez, V.: Stakeholders approach to smart cities: a survey on smart city definitions. In: Alba, E., Chicano, F., Luque, G. (eds.) Smart-CT 2016. LNCS, vol. 9704, pp. 157–167. Springer, Cham (2016). https://doi.org/10.1007/978-3-319-39595-1_16
18. Haarstad, H.: Who Is Driving the 'Smart City' Agenda? Assessing Smartness as a Governance Strategy for Cities in Europe. In: Jones, A., Ström, P., Hermelin, B., Rusten, G. (eds.) Services and the Green Economy, pp. 199–218. Palgrave Macmillan UK, London (2016). https://doi.org/10.1057/978-1-137-52710-3_9
19. Monzon A.: Smart cities concept and challenges: Bases for the assessment of smart city projects. In: International Conference Smart Cities and Green ICT Systems 2015, pp. 1–11. IEEE (2015)
20. Braude-Zolotarev, M., Grebnev, G., Yermakov, R., Rubanov, G., Serbina, E.: Interoperability of information systems. Compendium INFO-FOSS. RU, pp. 100–108, Moscow (2008)
21. Level of IT development in Russian subjects, http://minsvyaz.ru/uploaded/files/vopros-2-prezentatsiya.pdf. Accessed 21 Mar 2018
22. Disposal of Government of St. Petersburg № 21-rp 2017/04/14, http://base.garant.ru/43424628/. Accessed 13 Mar 2018
23. Concept of Smart St. Petersburg, http://petersburgsmartcity.ru. Accessed 30 Apr 2017

Simulating Budget System in the Agent Model of the Russian Federation Spatial Development

Aleksandra L. Mashkova[1,2,3]([✉]) [iD], Ekaterina V. Novikova[1] [iD],
Olga A. Savina[1,3] [iD], Alexander V. Mamatov[3] [iD],
and Evgeniy A. Mashkov[1] [iD]

[1] Orel State University Named After I.S. Turgenev, Komsomolskaja St. 95,
302026 Orel, Russian Federation
aleks.savina@gmail.com
[2] Central Economics and Mathematics Institute, Russian Academy of Sciences,
Nakhimovsky Av. 47, 117418 Moscow, Russian Federation
[3] Belgorod National Research University, Pobedy St. 85, Belgorod 308015,
Russian Federation

Abstract. In this paper we present methods, data and algorithms for simulating budget system in the model of the Russian Federation spatial development. We show the place of this task in methodology of our research and give a brief overview of the background results. Key objects of the budget system in the model are the federal budget, regional budgets and extra budgetary funds: pension, medical and social insurance. We determine revenues and expenditures of the budgets and funds on the basis of federal laws, Budget and Tax codes of the Russian Federation. Since the exact reproduction of excise rates and customs duties is problematic due to model aggregation, we calculate model rates of excises and duties for selected sectors on the basis of retrospective data presented on the budget system portal and in the federal input-output table. Structure of the budget expenses in the model was simplified by aggregating expenditure items into major groups correlated with sectors of the economy. Presented algorithm of the budget system simulates interaction of the federal, regional budgets and extra-budgetary funds with agents and organizations in the model. For validation of the budget system algorithms in the model we conduct retrospective modeling for the federal budget and the budget of Belgorod region in 2014.

Keywords: Computer model · Spatial development · Agent-based modeling · Budget system · Tax · Excise · Retrospective simulation

1 Introduction

Spatial development of the Russian Federation is quite disproportional: some regions are overpopulated, which causes environmental, housing and transport problems; others, conversely, suffer from outflow of population. This situation is determined by concentration of science, technology and innovations in large centers and a huge gap in quality of life in various regions. Strategy of the Russian Federation spatial

A. Chugunov et al. (Eds.): EGOSE 2019, CCIS 1135, pp. 17–31, 2020.
https://doi.org/10.1007/978-3-030-39296-3_2

development [26] is aimed at correcting the current situation by improving interregional infrastructure and stimulating new centers of economic activity, which would smooth socio-economic differences between regions.

The task of evaluating alternative policy options for development of territories requires special methods and tools that can integrate accumulated data on the population, economy and social sphere. Policy relevant spatial modeling is an expanding area of research, which has a lot of potential for the evaluation of the socio-economic and spatial effects of major national social policy programs [5].

In our research we construct the agent-based model of the Russian Federation spatial development, which simulates dynamics of population and production in different regions and interrelations between them. Significant part of the model is administrative institutions that implement control actions, such as tax, monetary and investment policies. Crucial element in this context is the budget system, as a key channel of financing federal and regional programs, aimed at developing infrastructure and creation of new centers of economic activity. Simulating of the budget system in the model should take into account the spatial aspect of collection and redistribution of funds at the levels of the federal and regional budgets. Thus, the structure of financing of the spatial development projects would be reflected.

2 Literature Review

Planning and prediction of the spatial development processes, which is studied within the new economic geography, summarizes a number of research tasks of the regional economy through an integrated approach and consideration of macroeconomic factors and interrelations. A number of works is devoted to the empirical studies based on statistical data and to structural modeling based on econometric estimation of the factors, included in existing theoretical models [7, 8, 22].

The main method in our research is agent-based computational economy (ACE) [13, 29], which includes heterogeneity, bounded rationality, non-equilibrium dynamics and direct interactions among economic agents [9]. ACE models are often used to study effects of policies on macroeconomic and spatial dynamics [4], and have already been implemented in different areas of macroeconomic policy such as fiscal [2], monetary [11, 21], macroprudential [1, 3, 19] and labor market policy [18, 23, 25].

One of the most complete ACE models is Eurace simulator, which is designed as an agent model of complex multiple-market economy and incorporates crucial connections between the real economy, credit and financial markets. Different markets are modeled in great detail with, for example, the labor market firms seeking credit, buying capital goods, deciding production levels, advertising and appointing staff, and selling consumption goods, and households applying for jobs, deciding on offers, commuting to work, buying goods, saving with banks, and seeking credit [12]. Dynamics of credit money in Eurace is endogenous and depends on the supply of credit from the banking system and the demand of credit from firms in order to finance their production activity. Eurace model takes into account many factors affecting parameters of economic activity, however, studies based on it do not operate real data from EU countries, they use test environment to observe macroeconomic and social phenomena (for example, abstract 'Country 1' and 'Country 2') [12]. Similarly, in ACE models of separate markets, the study of processes through simulation is conducted on the abstract data sets [11, 18, 19].

Spatial aspect of social policies is usually taken under consideration in regional models, such as microsimulation model for Leeds City Council. The model consists of 715 thousand individuals within households along with their associated attributes and provides a spatial decision support tool for the local council officers. In particular, the system can be used to describe current conditions in neighborhoods, predict future trends in the composition and health of population and conduct analysis to measure the likely impact of policy interventions at the local level [4]. Similar system in Russia was designed for Saint-Petersburg [27].

3 Methodology of Case Study

In our research we combine ACE approach with available open data, constructing the agent-based computer model of the Russian Federation spatial development, which reflects age-sex structure and resettlement of the population, composition of households, regional economic structures, administrative and educational institutions. Research methodology includes the following steps:

1. Reconstructing current territorial and demographic structure of population, administrative and economic system of the Russian Federation in the agent-based computer model.
2. Simulating dynamics of the system through behavior of agents, organizations, regional and state administration.
3. Setting scenario parameters and alternative control actions for the system.
4. Conducting a series of experiments, statistical processing and analysis of the results.

The main task on the first stage is reconstruction of an artificial society for the base year of modeling. 2014 was chosen as the base year, since then the federal input-output table was prepared, which contains crucial information about interrelations in the real economy. Issues of search and integration of the initial modeling data are discussed in [15], reproduction of population structure and economic interrelations – in [16].

The budget system simulation considered in this article belongs to the second stage of the methodology, since it reflects the dynamic aspect of tax and duties collection, payment of transfers to the population, financing of budget organizations and key sectors of the national economy. Also at the second stage algorithms of population dynamics [14], behavior of agents in the areas of education, employment and migration [17], activities of commercial [15] and financial organizations are developed. To verify algorithms on this stage, retrospective modeling for the base 2014 is carried out. Results of retrospective simulation of population and organizations are presented in [16].

3.1   Defining Structure of the Budget System of the Russian Federation

The budget system of the Russian Federation consists of the federal budget, regional budgets and extra-budgetary funds: pension, medical and social insurance. Since the model on a geographical scale is a set of regions, without dividing into smaller components, the local level of the budget is not considered in it. Each budget has revenue and expenditure part defined by the Budget Code of the Russian Federation [6].

Sources of revenues of the federal budget are commercial organizations, the Central Bank; funds, banks and governments of the foreign countries (Fig. 1). Organizations pay income tax, value added tax, excise taxes on manufactured and imported goods, import and export customs duties, tallage for use of natural resources and negative impact on the environment. The Central bank transfers part of its profit, defined in the Federal law on the federal budget (75% of the profit in 2014, 90% in 2015–2016, 100% from 2017). Foreign sources pay interest on loans and duties under the customs agreement between Russia, Belarus and Kazakhstan.

Regional budgets receive taxes on personal income, part of the excises on manufactured goods, tallage for use of natural resources and corporate income tax. For many regions, a significant source of revenue is subsidies from the federal budget.

Extra-budgetary funds are filled by insurance fees from employers (both commercial and budget organizations) and subsidies from the federal budget.

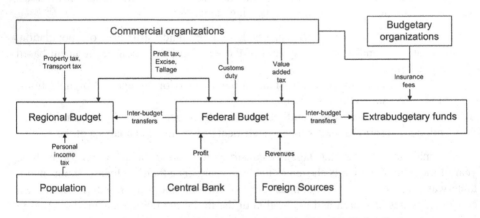

Fig. 1. Revenues of the budget system of the Russian Federation

Recipients of the federal budget in the model (Fig. 2) are ministries and departments, extra-budgetary funds, regional budgets and foreign sources. Ministries and departments provide direct financing of budget organizations and indirect financing of commercial organizations in key industries through the federal target programs. Regional budgets finance budgetary organizations and the regional programs through local departments. Recipients of extra-budgetary funds are individuals (through the system of social transfers) and medical organizations.

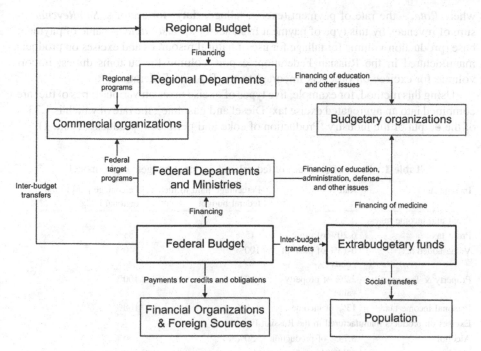

Fig. 2. Expenses of the budget system of the Russian Federation

3.2   Preparation of Initial Data

Revenues of the federal and regional budgets consist of taxes, excises, tallage and customs duties (Table 1). For a number of revenues the payment is divided between the federal and regional budgets. Main information sources on tax rates and benefits for their payment are the Tax Code of the Russian Federation [28] and the Budget Code of the Russian Federation [6], articles and expenditure in a particular year are set in the Federal Law on the federal budget [10]. Retrospective data on the execution of budgets are presented on the Portal of the budget system of the Russian Federation [20].

While the agent model of the Russian Federation spatial development simulates agents and households in detail [14], it aggregates organizations to the sector-region scale, so that one macro-organization 'Sector S in region R' presents a set of real-world organizations in this sector and region. This assumption is due to lack of information about production, employment and financial state of organizations [16, 17], while available data is presented in the regional and sector scale [25]. Due to the accepted aggregation of objects in the model, the exact reproduction of revenue items, and particularly, excise rates and customs duties on specific goods, is quite difficult. To solve this problem, we calculate model rates of excises and duties for the industry, determined on the basis of retrospective data for 2014, presented on the budget system portal [21]:

$$Rate_s = \frac{SumRevenue_s}{BaseValue_s} \tag{1}$$

where $Rate_s$ – the rate of payment (excise, tallage, duty) for sector s; $SumRevenue_s$ – sum of revenues by this type of payment from sector s; $BaseValue_s$ – value of payment base (production volume for tallage for use of natural resources and excises on products manufactured in the Russian Federation; export volume for customs duties; import volume for excises on products imported to the Russian Federation).

Using this method, for example, five types of excise taxes on various types of fuel are combined into an aggregated excise tax 'Diesel and gasoline', the rate of which is 1.33% of the output of the industry 'Production of coke and petroleum products'(Table 1).

Table 1. Rates of revenues of federal and regional budgets in the model

Income item	Rate	Percentage paid to the federal budget	Percentage paid to the regional budget
Profit and income taxes			
Profit tax	6-20% of profit	15%	85%
Value added tax	0-18% of price of goods	100%	0%
Property & Transport tax	2.2% of property value	0%	100%
Personal income tax	13% of income	0%	100%
Excises on products manufactured in the Russian Federation			
Alcohol	6.74% of production volume	50%	50%
Tobacco products	153% of production volume	100%	0%
Diesel and gasoline	1.33% of production volume	12%	88%
Cars and motorbikes	0.95% of production volume	100%	0%
Excises on products imported to the Russian Federation			
Alcohol	6.6% of import volume	100%	0%
Cars and motorbikes	1.44% of import volume	100%	0%
Diesel and gasoline	6.47% of import volume	100%	0%
Tobacco products	52.41% of import volume	100%	0%
Tallage for use of natural resources			
Tallage for hydro-carbon extraction	35.92% of production volume	100%	0%
Tallage for other mineral extraction	7.2% of production volume	40%	60%
Customs duties			
Export of oil and gas	88.72% of export volume	100%	0%
Export of petrochemical	53.23% of export volume	100%	0%

Another complex issue is defining conditions for granting privileges on value added and profit taxes. When determining the average value added tax (VAT) rate for the industry, exceptions described in the Tax Code of the Russian Federation [28] are taken into account; so that industries where VAT is zero (such as medicine, public administration), preferential (food) or partial (where some organizations operate under the simplified tax system and are exempt from VAT) are defined. The average rate of VAT and income tax for each industry is determined by the iterative proportional fitting algorithm based on the actual VAT collected [20], total amount of taxes paid by each industry in the input-output table [24] and the list of exceptions [28].

Some non-tax revenues of the federal budget (revenues from foreign sources, payment for a negative impact on the environment) are not specified in percentage terms, but in fixed monetary terms; such parameters are set on the basis of retrospective data and change in the forecast period in accordance with the expected scenario. The part of non-tax revenues to the regional budget (fines, revenues from municipal property) is calculated as a percentage of tax revenues and is distributed among payers - organizations of the relevant industry.

Revenues of extra-budgetary funds consist of insurance fees paid by organizations for their employees, income from the fund assets and inter-budget transfers (Table 2).

Table 2. Rates and sources of revenues of extra-budgetary funds in the model

Income item	Rate	Source
Pension Fund		
Fees for compulsory pension insurance	22% of accrued salary	Budgetary and commercial organizations
Revenues from the fund assets	31.7 billion RUR	Financial organizations
Inter-budget transfers	2414.6 billion RUR	Federal and regional budget
Social Insurance Fund		
Fees for compulsory social insurance	2.9% of accrued salary	Budgetary and commercial organizations
Revenues from the fund assets	9.1 billion RUR	Financial organizations
Inter-budget transfers	52.1 billion RUR	Federal and regional budget
Compulsory Medical Insurance Fund		
Fees for compulsory medical insurance	5.1% of accrued salary	Budgetary and commercial organizations
Revenues from the fund assets	1.3 billion RUR	Financial organizations
Inter-budget transfers	30.6 billion RUR	Federal and regional budget

Structure of federal budget expenses in the model was simplified by aggregating expenditure items into major groups correlated with sectors of the economy. Expenditure of the federal budget, except from direct inter-budget transfers and repay of the federal debt, is managed by ministries and departments, which, in turn, distribute funds among the recipients. Direct beneficiaries are budget organizations of the industries presented in Table 3. Funding for commercial organizations goes through federal targeted programs with tools of direct subsidies (in the industries 'Transport', 'Agriculture & Fishery', 'Fuel and energy complex', 'Mining', 'Forestry') and government orders ('Water management', 'Road infrastructure', 'Housing and communal services').

Expenditure of the regional budget is managed by regional departments. For each region, the budget has its own distribution structure. Expenditures of extra-budgetary funds include transfers to various groups of the population (pensioners, disabled people, persons on maternity leave, etc.). Rates of transfer payments for the base year of modeling are set on the basis of Federal state statistics service [24] data, and for subsequent years are loaded to the model as scenario parameters.

Table 3. Expenses of the federal budget in the model

Issue	Share in budget expenses, %	Issue	Share in budget expenses, %
Financing of budget organizations in sectors:		Financing of commercial organizations in sectors:	
State administration	6.3	Transport	4.19
National defense	16.5	Agriculture & Fishery	2.65
National security	13.7	Fuel and energy complex	0.44
Environmental protection	0.7	Mining	0.8
Education	4.3	Forestry	0.48
Culture & Cinematography	0.5	Housing and communal services	0.8
Space research	0.55	Road infrastructure	8.07
Physical culture &Sports	0.4	Water management	0.47
Mass-media	0.4	Inter-budget transfers	
Science	3.85	Pension Fund	14.95
Public debt expenses		Social security fund	8.15
Internal debt	2.1	Regional budgets	5.4
External debt	0.7	Compulsory Medical Insurance Fund	3.6

3.3 Algorithms of the Model

The agent approach implies reproduction of interactions of micro-level agents. In the paper [15] interactions of a commercial organization with employees and counterparties are described. Here we consider interaction of model objects that are associated with functions of the budget system. The algorithm presented in Fig. 3 involves interaction of federal, regional budgets and extra-budgetary funds with organizations, agents and each other.

Events of the organizations that are significant for this task are wages payment, followed by payment of fees to extra-budgetary funds; supplies (VAT and excise taxes are paid on imported goods); sales (VAT; excise taxes on goods produced in the territory of the Russian Federation; customs duties on exported goods); payment of other taxes (tallage for use of natural resources, property and transport tax) and calculation of the financial result (payment of income tax). Agents pay personal income tax on wages and profits.

The federal budget receives various tax and non-tax payments, finances departments, which in turn finance budgetary and commercial organizations. Also the federal budget distributes transfers to regional budgets and extra-budget funds, and repays the state debt.

Regional budgets receive taxes, fees and excises from the local organizations and transfers from the federal budget. Further, budgetary and commercial organizations are financed from the regional budget.

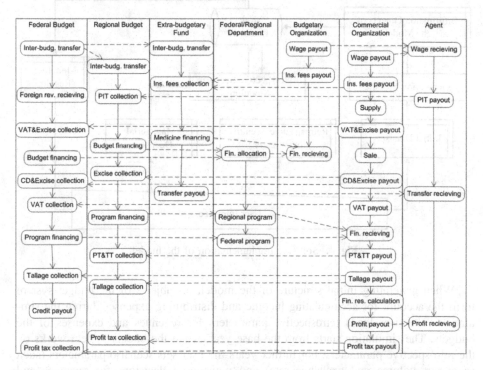

Fig. 3. Interrelation between budget system, agents and organizations in the model of the Russian Federation spatial development (CD – customs duties, VAT – value added tax, PIT – personal income tax, PT&TT – property and transport tax).

Extra-budgetary funds receive insurance fees from organizations, transfers from the federal budget, as well as revenues from the fund assets management. Then, from the fund's expenditures, money is allocated to finance budgetary organizations in the medical sector to pay for health care expenses. Funds also pay benefits, pensions and other social transfers.

4 Empirical Analysis of the Case

The model of the Russian Federation spatial development is being programmed on C# in Microsoft Visual Studio 2015. Figure 4 shows interface of the model and sequence of data processing in it. Initial modeling data sets are loaded in the form of Excel tables, checked for completeness and consistency [16]. In the generation module, initial modeling data is transformed to information objects of the model (agents, households, organizations, administrative institutions). Results of the generation procedure are stored in the model database [15], which is being changed during retrospective or scenario modeling.

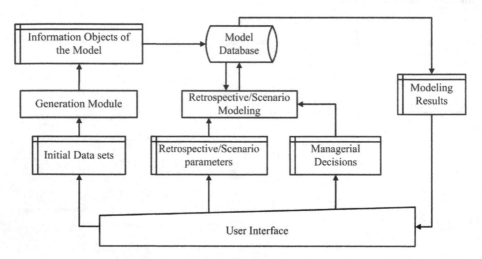

Fig. 4. Software implementation of the model

When generating initial structure of the model, all objects of the budget system form the account for accumulating income and distributing expenses during the simulation. The user loads retrospective parameters for revenues and expenses of the budgets. The simulation starts from the base year, when the budget system works on the retrospective parameters. For further years the user sets scenario parameters (such as export volume and exchange rate) and managerial decisions for revenues and expenses of the budgets (tax and fees rates, structure of the expenditures).

For validation of the budget system algorithms in the model we conduct retrospective modeling for 2014 year. In Table 4 there are presented revenues of the federal budget and budget of Belgorod region in the model, compared with the real data from Portal of the budget system of the Russian Federation [20].

Table 4. Results of the retrospective simulation

Income item	Revenues of the federal budget in 2014 (simulation results)	Revenues of the federal budget in 2014 (real data)	Revenues of the budget of Belgorod region in 2014 (simulation results)	Revenues of the budget of Belgorod region in 2014 (real data)
Profit and income taxes				
Profit tax	420650	420510	12960	12740
Property & Transport tax	–	–	7880	7840
PIT	–	–	13092	12970
Taxes and excises on products manufactured in the Russian Federation				
Value added tax	2184225	2181420	–	–
Alcohol	85930	85930	1100	1100
Tobacco products	314000	314000	–	–
Diesel and gasoline	102500	102500	2580	2580
Cars & motorbikes	16850	16850	–	–
Taxes and excises on products imported to the Russian Federation				
Value added tax	1750350	1750240	–	–
Alcohol	35400	35400	–	–
Cars & motorbikes	18820	18820	–	–
Diesel & gasoline	12680	12680	–	–
Tobacco products	4760	4760	–	–
Tallage for use of natural resources				
Tallage for hydro-carbon extraction	2836800	2836800	–	–
Tallage for other mineral extraction	47820	47820	712	710
Customs duties				
Export of oil and gas	3107610	3107610	–	–
Export of petrochemical	1489390	1489390	–	–
Revenues from the Customs Union	762400	762400	–	–

(*continued*)

Table 4. (*continued*)

Income item	Revenues of the federal budget in 2014 (simulation results)	Revenues of the federal budget in 2014 (real data)	Revenues of the budget of Belgorod region in 2014 (simulation results)	Revenues of the budget of Belgorod region in 2014 (real data)
Other custom duties	104020	104020	–	–
Other revenues				
Income from the state property	417673	445580	610	610
Administrative fees and charges	286920	286920	840	840
Inter-budget transfers	–	–	22700	22700
Other budget revenues	247324	471710	–	160
Total	14246122	14496800	62384	62160

Tax, excise and duties rates were taken from Tables 1 and 2. A number of items of income were set as a set of retrospective parameters, in particular: property income (for the federal budget it consists of income from stocks, income from managing budget assets and profit of the Central Bank; for regional - rental payments); administrative fees (distributed among organizations in proportion to their income); other custom duties (paid by exporting organizations in proportion to the export volume). Other revenues to the federal budget in the model are income of budget organizations, in the real budget these are a number of different items, the total amount of which is less than 3% of the total budget revenues.

Presented in Table 4 results of retrospective simulation show a fairly high accuracy of the revenue part formation of federal and regional budgets in the model. Deviation of total amount of income of the federal budget from the real values was 1.7%; for comparison, the deviation of the forecast values of the federal budget during its formation from its execution was 1.8% according to the portal of the budget system of the Russian Federation [20].

The resulting deviation is due, firstly, to the presence of a certain set of revenues, which cannot be taken into account by the specification of the model and the data presented (for example, when the government sells intangible assets, it is unclear to which industry these assets belonged and who was the buyer); and, secondly, approximation in the formation of the list of tax benefits for various industries. Due to the method described in Sect. 3.2, the excises and duties are reproduced with high accuracy on the base year of the simulation, although some errors may occur in subsequent periods.

For the budget of the Belgorod region, deviation of income for the base year of the simulation is 0.4%.

5 Discussion of Results

The scientific value of the proposed approach is creation of methods for integrating large arrays of real data into social simulation models, which makes it possible to reflect in detail the social institutions existing in the country, in this case the tax and budget system. In practice, this would allow to carry out multivariate scenario calculations in the recreated socio-economic environment to support managerial decisions in the field of spatial development.

Particularly, the budget system, simulated in detail, would allow to reflect directions of financing of the infrastructure projects, aimed at more even spatial development of the country. Since the volumes of financing required for such projects are quite significant, it is necessary to determine the sources and the cost of attracting them through issuing bonds or changing tax rates, and the model is capable of making such estimates.

Calculations on the model are aimed at assessing positive effects of project implementation in relation to production growth, employment and living standards in various regions, as well as sustainability of the budget system in the long-term period during project implementation and the risks of their incompleteness.

6 Conclusions

In this article we presented methods and algorithms of simulating budget system in the agent-based model of the Russian Federation spatial development. Basis for research at this stage were previously modeled population and organizations [14, 16] and algorithms for their interaction [15, 17]. As information sources for the budget system reconstruction we used Tax and Budget codes, federal laws and the official portal. Study of these sources allowed to define components of the budget system and relationship between them; types, rates and sources of revenues to budgets of various levels; volumes and recipients of government transfers and subsidies.

To reproduce mechanisms of the budget system in the model, a number of generalizing assumptions were made, due to the lack of information on some items of income and expenditure budgets of various levels, a large list of tax benefits for various industries, as well as level of aggregation of model objects. Taking these assumptions into account, the model rates of taxes, excise taxes and fees were determined. The budget expenditure items were also aggregated according to the characteristics of the beneficiaries of funding - organizations and residents.

For verification of the developed module, retrospective modeling was performed on the values of the base 2014 year. Comparison of simulation results with the real data for the Russian Federation and Belgorod region showed high accuracy (deviation does not exceed 2%).

For prognostic modeling characteristics of the budget system are loaded to the model as scenario parameters and managerial decisions. Changes in the tax rates and benefits influence on the amount of financing attracted, while distribution of funds among various sectors affect implementation of economic and territorial development programs.

The reported study was funded by RFBR according to the research project № 18-29-03049.

References

1. Alexandre, M., Lima, G.T.: Combining monetary policy and prudential regulation: an agent-based modeling approach. J. Econ. Interac. Coord. (2017). https://doi.org/10.1007/s11403-017-0209-0
2. Arifovic, J., Maschek, M.K.: Currency crisis: evolution of beliefs and policy experiments. J. Econ. Behav. Organ. **82**(1), 131–150 (2012). https://doi.org/10.1016/j.jebo.2012.01.001, http://www.sciencedirect.com/science/article/pii/S0167268112000029. Accessed 29 Nov 2019
3. Ashraf, Q., Gershman, B., Howitt, P.: Banks, market organization, and macroeconomic performance: an agent-based computational analysis. Working Paper 17102, National Bureau of Economic Research (June 2011). https://doi.org/10.3386/w17102, http://www.nber.org/papers/w17102. Accessed 29 Nov 2019
4. Ballas, D., Clarke, G.P., Turton, I.: A spatial microsimulation model for social policy evaluation. In: Boots, B., Okabe, A., Thomas, R. (eds.) Modelling Geographical Systems, The GeoJournal Library, vol. 70, pp. 143–168. Springer, Dordrecht (2002). https://doi.org/10.1007/978-94-017-2296-4_8
5. Ballas, D., Kingston, R., Stillwell, J.: Using a spatial microsimulation decision support system for policy scenario analysis. In: Van Leeuwen. J.P., Timmermans. H.J.P. (eds.) Recent Advances in Design and Decision Support Systems in Architecture and Urban Planning, pp. 177–191. Springer, Dordrecht (2004)
6. Budget Code of the Russian Federation, http://www.consultant.ru/document/cons_doc_LAW_19702/. Accessed 3 Jan 2019 [In Russian]
7. Combes, P.-P., Mayer, T., Thisse, J.-F.: Economic Geography. The Integration of Regions and Nations. Princeton University Press, Princeton, NJ (2008)
8. Davis, D.R., Weinstein, D.E.: Bones, bombs, and break points: the geography of economic activity. Am. Econ. Rev. **92**(5), 1269–1289 (2002). https://doi.org/10.3386/w8517
9. Fagiolo, G., Roventini, A.: Macroeconomic policy in DSGE and agent-based models Redux: New developments and challenges ahead. J. Artif. Soc. Social Simul. **20**(1), 1 (2017). http://jasss.soc.surrey.ac.uk/20/1/1.html
10. Federal Law "On the federal budget for 2014 and planned 2015 and 2016", http://www.consultant.ru/document/cons_doc_LAW_155198/. Accessed 3 Jan 2019 [In Russian]
11. Gatti, D., Desiderio, S.J.: Monetary policy experiments in an agent-based model with financial frictions. J. Econ. Interac. Coord. **10**(2), 265–286 (2015). https://doi.org/10.1007/s11403-014-0123-7
12. Holcombe, M., et al.: Large-scale modeling of economic systems. Complex Syst. **22**, 175–191 (2013). https://doi.org/10.25088/ComplexSystems.22.2.175
13. Lebaron, B., Tesfatsion, L.: Modeling macroeconomies as open-ended dynamic systems of interacting agents. Am. Econ. Rev. **98**, 246–250 (2008). https://doi.org/10.1257/aer.98.2.246

14. Mamatov, A., Mashkova, A., Novikova, E., Savina, O.: Reproduction of dynamics of population of Russian regions using agent modeling. Inf. Syst. Technol. **2**(112), 48–55 (2019). [in Russian]
15. Mashkova, A.L., Savina, O.A., Banchuk, Y.A., Mashkov, E.A.: Using open data for information support of simulation model of the russian federation spatial development. In: Chugunov, A., Misnikov, Y., Roshchin, E., Trutnev, D. (eds.) EGOSE 2018. CCIS, vol. 947, pp. 401–414. Springer, Cham (2019). https://doi.org/10.1007/978-3-030-13283-5_30
16. Mashkova, A.L.: Reconstructing an artificial society on the basis of big open data. In: Supplementary Proceedings of the 7th International Conference on Analysis of Images, Social Networks and Texts (AIST-SUP 2018), vol. 2268, pp. 241–251 Moscow, Russia, 5–7 July 2018
17. Mashkova, A., Savina, O.A., Mamatov, A.: Integrating artificial agent in the simulation model of the Russian federation spatial development. In: Adamov, A., Abzetdin, A. (eds.) The IEEE 12th International Conference on Application of Information and Communication Technologies / AICT 2018: Conference Proceedings, pp. 344–349. Institute of Electrical and Electronics Engineers Inc., Almaty (2018)
18. Napoletano, M., Dosi, G., Fagiolo, G., Roventini, A.: Wage formation, investment behavior and growth regimes: an agent-based analysis. Revue de l'OFCE **124**(5), 235–261 (2012). https://doi.org/10.3917/reof.124.0235
19. Popoyan, L., Napoletano, M., Roventini, A.: Taming macroeconomic instability: Monetary and macro prudential policy interactions in an agent-based model. J. Econ. Behav. Organ. **134**, 117–140 (2017). https://doi.org/10.1016/j.jebo.2016.12.017
20. Portal of the budget system of the Russian Federation, http://budget.gov.ru. Accessed 22 Mar 2019
21. Raberto, M., Teglio, A., Cincotti, S.: Integrating real and financial markets in an agent-based economic model: an application to monetary policy design. Comput. Econ. **32**(1), 147–162 (2008). https://doi.org/10.1007/s10614-008-9138-2
22. Redding, S.J.: The empirics of new economic geography. J. Reg. Sci. **50**(1), 297–311 (2010)
23. Riccetti, L., Russo, A., Gallegati, M.: Unemployment benefits and financial leverage in an agent based macroeconomic model. Econ. Open-Access, Open-Assessment E-J. **7**(42), 1–44 (2013). http://dx.doi.org/10.5018/economicsejournal.ja.2013-42
24. Russian Federation Federal State Statistics Service official website, http://www.gks.ru/wps/wcm/connect/rosstat_main/rosstat/en/main/. Accessed 26 Mar 2019
25. Seppecher, P.: Flexibility of wages and macroeconomic instability in an agent-based computational model with endogenous money. Macroecon. Dyn. **16**(S2), 284–297 (2012). https://doi.org/10.1017/S1365100511000447
26. Strategy of the spatial development of the Russian Federation for the period till 2025, http://static.government.ru/media/les/UVAlqUtT08o60RktoOXl22JjAe7irNxc.pdf. Accessed 27 Feb 2019
27. Sushko, E.: Multi-agent model of the region: concept, design and implementation. Tech. Rep. Preprint WP/2012/292, CEMI RAS (2012), in Russian
28. Tax Code of the Russian Federation, http://www.consultant.ru/document/cons_doc_LAW_19671/. Accessed 3 Dec 2018, [In Russian]
29. Tesfatsion, L.: Agent-based computational economics: a constructive approach to economic theory. Handbook of Computational Economics, vol. 2, chap. 16, pp. 831–880. Elsevier (2006). https://doi.org/10.1016/S1574-0021(05)02016-2, http://www.sciencedirect.com/science/article/pii/S1574002105020162. Accessed 29 Nov 2019

Developing an Effective Model for the Smart City Technology: Implementation as a Part of New Urban Governance

Svetlana Morozova(✉) ⓘ and Daria Maltseva ⓘ

Faculty of Political Science, St. Petersburg State University,
Smolny Street, 1/3, 191124 St. Petersburg, Russia
s.s.morozova@spbu.ru

Abstract. The convergence of information and communication technologies became a determining factor for the increasing importance of smart cities technology implementation in city management. In this article the distinctive characteristics of the smart city concept, problems and new opportunities for urban governance are analyzed. The importance of smart city technology and the complexity of its implementation are highlighted. The network approach and analysis of the most successful global practices in the use of information technologies in urban governance are the benefits of this study and laid the foundation for proposing the desirable conditions for the smart city technology implementation in order to provide its efficiency. As a result these conditions can lay the basis for comparative analysis of the effectiveness of smart city projects implementation in different countries and can be used by local authorities as a strategy for smart city technologies practical application.

Keywords: Public policy · Governance · Network society · Smart city · Information and Communications Technologies · Innovative infrastructure

1 Introduction

In recent decades, public policy problems have become extremely popular due to the growing involvement of various social groups and civic associations in politics. Using the idea of the famous German philosopher and sociologist Jurgen Habermas [1] about the two types of political power, namely, the power of communication, that is generated in the process of public political discourse, and administrative, which is a derivative of the de jure recognition of the state's ruling position, we allocate civic participation, cooperation in the process of developing a common political strategy and co-managing key elements of public policy. Thus, speaking of public policy we imply "the way and the result of public participation in the process of making decisions that are priority for society" [2] or "that sphere of political relations in which the institutions of the state and civil society interact in conditions of relative publicity" [3]. These definitions allude to the concepts of "network communication," "network community," and "network society" which first appeared in the early 1970s and can still be used as a conceptual basis in modern public policy.

© Springer Nature Switzerland AG 2020
A. Chugunov et al. (Eds.): EGOSE 2019, CCIS 1135, pp. 32–40, 2020.
https://doi.org/10.1007/978-3-030-39296-3_3

The next peak of keen interest to network communications and network communities was in the late 1980s–early 1990s, and that was closely related to the revolutionary breakthrough in the development of information technology and the fundamental renewal of media resources. This brings us to the works of Jan van Dijk [4], who defined the network society as a form of society that increasingly organizes social relationships using media networks, to gradually replace or at least supplement social communications. He considered the formation of a network society based on free instant access to media resources (the Internet brings "the entire world" to every house) as an inevitable social process [5].

Researchers increasingly state that network structures contribute to overcoming or at least mitigating many negative trends through equitable communication, opportunities for real citizens to participate in governance, and unhindered access to information flow. They are capable of stimulating production and exchange of new knowledge. On the other hand, the growth of network structures is undoubtedly the consequence of the revolution that has occurred over the last 30 years in the field of information and communication technologies. New technologies provide the possibility for such type of communication that has never existed before [5].

The convergence of information and communication technologies became one of the key factors contributing to the rapid development of smart cities and their influence on social and economic processes.

Based on the network and comparative approaches to urban governance this article proposes desirable conditions for the smart city technology implementation in order to provide the efficiency of this process.

2 Theoretical Framework

The concept of "smart city" is one of the most widespread up to date concepts which contains ideas about the future of the cities and ways their problems should be solved.

According to a number of scientists, the city can be defined as "smart" provided that investments are directed to the human and social capital; and such spheres, traditional for the majority of the cities, as transport and ICT. It is the key to sustainable economic development and quality life intermingled with rational and the most effective management of natural resources based on the assistance of all participants of the city life. As the Spanish economist, the expert in the field of "smart" cities Hermenegildo Seisdedos remarks, the "smart city" concept means the efficiency reached on the basis of intellectual management and integrated by ICT as well as active participation of citizens in the city development [6].

It is important to remark that creating the conditions for city development, providing uniformity of economic and social development of the country's territories due to growth of their own competitiveness becomes a key challenge today. The relations of interaction and cooperation based on the most effective use of limited resources (primarily intellectual) and not the competitive relations play the key role here. "Smart cities" can be defined as the systems integrating the following directions (axes) within uniform city space [7]:

- Smart People;
- Smart Governance;
- Smart Living;
- Smart Mobility;
- Smart Economy;
- Smart Environment.

These 6 axes are based on theories of regional competitiveness, effective use of natural resources, transport mobility and ICT of urban economy, priority formation of human and social capitals, improving the quality of life and also participation of citizens in the city management.

Since the definition "smart city" is still a rather vague concept and is not always used with agreed criteria, it is necessary to consider in more detail those characteristics of "smart city" which are most often mentioned at this subject discussion.

- *Effective innovative infrastructure*

Present conditions make it necessary to use network infrastructure in order to improve economic and political efficiency and to provide cultural, social and city development [8]. The term "infrastructure" in this context indicates development of spheres of business services, housing, rest, mode of life and ICT and also puts in the forefront the idea of a "network city" as the main model of [9]. It emphasizes the crucial role of hi-tech and creative fields of activity in the long-term urban growth. The abovementioned aspects, in addition to the "soft" infrastructure, constitute the core researches of Florida [10]. His main idea is that «today firms are focused on the "creative people" engaging, capable to solve problems more effectively and from a different angle». Even the creative and qualified labor force doesn't guarantee effective functioning of municipal economy, however it is obvious that in the knowledge-intensive economy these factors will promote success of the city development [11].

- *Creation of the comfortable business environment*

It is necessary to use the possibilities of ICT concerning the increase in local welfare and competitiveness that in its turn means integrated, multisector approach to city development on the basis of the system of hierarchically built indicators and the prospect of multilevel planning [12]. It sets a task of ensuring business establishment at the head of the city development which main goal is attracting new investments and enterprises. Data show that business focused cities really prevail among the cities with satisfactory socio-economic indexes. One of the most striking examples of such a "smart city" is Dubai which not only develops as "smart city", but also duplicates the model of city development in the international space in the form of such town-planning projects as Dubai-Malta and Dubai-Kochi.

- *Technological platforms on the basis of wireless sensor networks*

Wireless sensor networks are specific technologies which make it possible to create really "smart cities". The goal consists of creating the distributed network of intellectual sensor nodes, which can measure the parameters for more effective urban management [13]. Data are transmitted over the wireless network in real time to citizens or to the appropriate supervisory authorities. For example, it is an effective way to control automobile traffic to redistribute the traffic load, to regulate the speed and density of traffic flow, to reduce its volume through systems which indicate where there is the next free slot for the parking. Both time and fuel can be saved this way. The joint platforms existing today for data management online, gaining information from sensors, give the chance not only to obtain data from sensors and on their basis to build dynamics, forecasts and to carry out analytical works, but also to provide big transparency of calculations in housing sector.

For example, there are already such platforms as Xively and Wikisensing which simplify interaction between consumers (users) and service providers, allow developers to structure graphics and plans directly on websites, to analyze the incoming information and to send results to appropriate governing bodies essential for their strategic monitoring and management decision making [14].

A smart city, therefore, is a large system connecting many components like the ones described above. It resides in the increasingly effective combination of digital telecommunication networks, ubiquitously embedded intelligence, sensors and tags, and software [15].

3 Statement of the Problem

Modern cities are faced with the challenge of technological development, infrastructure changes, rational use of resources and the attraction of modern technologies in administrative management.

The successful implementation of the "smart city" concept is the practical realization of the intellectual capital in the form of projects and initiatives for urban development carried out in order to maximize the useful resources to attract human capital and technology.

The potential listed above smart city axes is the responsible use of natural resources, the production of innovations as an instrumental resource for city development, efficiency as the ability of the urban system to provide quality public services, and competently interact with private actors and various categories of citizens.

Overall it should be taken into account that today cities are increasingly interconnected, which makes it possible to more efficiently organize a free informational message between them and create an infrastructure that, by networking methods, establishes connections among subjects and optimizes the use of resources. In this case, there is a problem of effective public administration of smart cities.

There are a number of difficulties that public authorities may encounter in carrying out their work:

- organizational (legal and regulatory barriers, lack of coordination and communication between the participants of the "smart city" implementation, lack of necessary labor resources, low level of popularization of the "smart city" concept);
- financial, related to the lack of financial resources and caused by the lack of business models that determine the profitability of investments in smart city projects;

- infrastructural, reflecting the lack of integration of the "smart city" concept in the existing urban development projects, underdevelopment of housing and communal services, transport system;
- technological (low extent of representation of constituent territories of the Russian Federation on the Internet)
- IT skills (lack of employees with integration skills and culture, lack of IT training programs).

In this article we will offer our recommendations on the successful implementation of the "smart city" model in order to improve the efficiency of public administration.

4 Methods

A key feature of the methodology of this article is the combination of network and comparative approaches to urban governance.

Applying a network approach to urban development implies a fundamental change in the management ideology, the transition from the Max Weber bureaucratic model of public administration to the model of public management, which focuses on the criterion of efficiency. This transition is characterized by a gradual departure from the bureaucracy, characterized by hierarchy, autocratic governance, a strict division of labour and responsibility, and executiveness. The new public management aims to improve the efficiency of the public sector by importing successful technologies from the management of commercial organizations. For instance, the state has a budget, production facilities, resources, and shareholders - citizens as consumers of its services.

These subjects interact not only on the basis of the principles of power, coercion and social support, but primarily on the basis of partnership, mutual responsibility and cooperation. The state initiates, stimulates and directs, while striving for the fullest and most qualitative satisfaction of its "shareholders" interests, for the growth of capitalization of budget revenues, and improvement of management technologies.

Relations among the government and citizens are the most significant in urban governance transformation and becomes an element of social engineering in the implementation of smart city technologies.

The comparative approach enabled a value analysis of theoretical substantiations of the smart city concept and global practices of implementing the smart city model in public administration.

5 Discussion

The main difference between the "smart" city and the traditional city lies in their relationship with the citizens. In the usual city services on the basis of ICT can't provide the same flexibly to changes of economic, cultural and social conditions as services in the "smart" city do. Thus, the "smart" city is person-oriented, based on infrastructure of ICT and continuous city development with constant accounting for requirements of ecological and economic sustainability.

Many largest world cities, including New York, Shanghai, Seoul, Singapore, Tokyo, Amsterdam, Dubai, Kochi, Cairo, and Malaga successfully implement "smart" projects today. Considering modern rates of innovations, it is quite probable that in the following decade the "smart city" model will become real and popular strategy of urban development.

Existing projects of the "smart city" differ considerably. Several smart cities initiatives are aimed at environment. The basic concept of a smart city is the use of technology to increase sustainability and to manage natural resources better. Protecting natural resources and related infrastructure is of particular interest [16]. For instance, in Amsterdam a lot of attention is paid to strengthening ecological sustainability on the basis of more rational organization of works, use of the latest technologies to reduce harmful emissions into the atmosphere, more effective use of energy. In other cities measures are taken to transform wide range of city functions to "smart", using everywhere widespread "smart" technologies in all aspects of citizen's life. The examples of such strategy are the project of Deutsche Telekom «T-city» in Germany (begun in 2006) and the City of Electronic Integration project (u-city) in the Republic of Korea (begun in 2004). The Smart Seoul project is carried out for the purpose of an urban management transformation to more "smart" and improvement of life quality.

It should be noted that the "smart city" concept differs in Europe and Asia. European countries generally have a social dimension, while Asia countries have a technological focus. For example, the city of Vienna focuses on the care of diverse populations and balance of public interest. Vienna's strategy represented a broad ranging project incorporating buildings, climate, transport, education, people and administration [17]. The Dubai smart areas are transport; electricity; government services; economic services; infrastructure; communications and urban planning.

Thus, for the successful implementation of the smart city strategy it is necessary to have, first, a progressive, modern institutional environment, a developed infrastructure, including ICT infrastructure and its readiness for innovation, monitoring, data collection, data processing, and management decision making. Secondly, an important condition is the presence of a developed city management system with smart users, a high level of management system readiness for changes, ensuring the consumption of services in the conditions of their digitalization, as well as stimulating its further development.

We have already remarked that the term "smart cities" is rather vague and experts use it for very different processes, but it essentially implies two important aspects: a set of sensors for reception and processing information, developed data collection systems and specialized analytical software; "smart" citizens who are interested in applying smart technologies.

As a possible solution to the previously identified problems, state authorities need to develop the following set of measures: organizational problems can be solved on the basis of the creation of either a project office or a single open platform that coordinates the actions of all participants involved in the implementation of the smart city concept. Infrastructure development can be achieved through the use of various models of public-private partnerships, financing of key projects can be carried out by granting tax preferences, additional attraction of budget funds, banks and funds.

The development and implementation of smart systems can be accompanied by the participation of all stakeholders (urban citizens, local communities, public and non-profit organizations, professional associations, representatives of large, small and medium-sized businesses, representatives of government bodies). The government should act as an initiator of such interactions, ensuring the identification of the interests of all participants and exercising control over their activities.

For the successful implementation of the strategy, it is equally important to prepare citizens for life in a smart city. The public authorities of the city, which seeks to become smart, need to work in the following areas:

1. Applying strategies of informing the citizens at the regional and federal levels, making information on smart cities mechanisms available in popular media and Websites;
2. Providing more opportunities for citizens to get Internet connection and increase wi-fi coverage. The quality and availability of the ICT infrastructure are important for smart cities [7]. ICT infrastructure includes wireless infrastructure (fiber optic channels, Wi-Fi networks, wireless hotspots, kiosks) [18], service-oriented information systems [19].
3. Creating conditions for training citizens how to work in smart city system;
4. Increasing the citizens' motivation to use smart city technologies by using information mechanism and improving feedback. People and communities are components that requires smart cities initiatives to be sensitive in balancing the needs of various communities [15].

One should bear in mind the fact that efficiency of process and improvement of smart city technologies also depend on use of available experience, both domestic and foreign.

6   Conclusion

Let us draw the bottom line. An effective model for the smart city technology implementation is the one, which would comply with the following conditions:

First, it is necessary to ensure the quality and availability of the ICT city infrastructure. The protected ICT infrastructure of the subsequent generations has paramount value for efficient provision of new services in "smart cities" and their availability in the future.

Second, smart governance based on citizen participation is required. Due to this condition it should be responsive and transparent.

Third, there must be "smart" citizens who are interested in applying smart technologies. ICT are the means for "smart city" functioning, but they are ineffective if there are no competent users able to interact with "smart" services. The "smart city" should not only grant access to "smart" devices for all categories of people with different levels of income and different age groups, but also train them to work with these devices. "Smart city" is constructed on the basis of making network of "smart" devices available to all users; meeting the citizens' demand or creating services that bring the highest value.

Fourth, there is need to remove legal and regulatory barriers. Properly built and integrated management system should be created in the city. The numerous systems of the "smart city" will act harmoniously only on the basis of strict observance of uniform standards.

Fifth, it is important to use smart city technologies that are already used successfully both at home and abroad.

Sixth, we conclude that for the effective introduction of smart city technologies, it is necessary to ensure high level of funding for these projects by the city government. However, only the richest cities (Vienna, Dubai) can afford their own individual smart projects. In general, local authorities should use various models of public-private partnerships to fund "smart city" plans.

These conditions can become the basis for comparative analysis of the effectiveness of using the smart city strategies in different countries and can be used by local authorities as a key to implementing smart city technologies.

Acknowledgements. The research and publication is funded by Russian Foundation for Basic Research (Svetlana Morozova) (project № 19-011-00792 "Evaluation of social and political effects of new technologies of urban development in the context of the current stage of the administrative reform of the Russian Federation" and Russian Humanitarian Fund (Daria Maltseva) (project № 17-33-01134 "Strategic Modeling in Space of the Political Competition and System of Public Administration").

References

1. Yu, H.: Sociostructural transformation of the public sphere. In: Public Sphere: Theory, Methodology, Stage Case: Collective Monograph. TsSPGI, Moscow (2013)
2. Arendt, H.: Vita activa, ili o deiatel'noi zhizni [Vita activa, or about active life]. Aleteya, Saint-Petersburg (2000)
3. Belyaeva, N.Yu.: Public policy in Russia: theory and practice. Tena, Moscow (2006)
4. Van Dijk, J.: The Network Society: Social Aspects of New Media. SAGE Publications Ltd., London (2006)
5. Aleinikov, A.V., Kurochkin, A.V., Mal'tseva, D.A.: The information efficiency of new knowledge production in the era of network communications. Sci. Tech. Inf. Process. **45**(1), 22–27 (2018)
6. Caragliu, A., Del Bo, C., Nijkamp, P.: Smart cities in Europe. J. Urban Technol. **18**(2), 65–82 (2011)
7. Giffinger, R., Fertner, C., Kramar, H., Kalasek, R., Pichler-Milanovic, N., Meijers, E.: Smart cities – Ranking of European medium-sized cities. Smart Cities. Centre of Regional Science, Vienna (2007). http://www.smart-cities.eu/download/smart_cities_final_report.pdf. Accessed 10 May 2019
8. Hollands, R.G.: Will the real smart city please stand up? City **12**(3), 303–320 (2008)
9. Komninos, N.: Intelligent Cities: Innovation Knowledge Systems and Digital Spaces. Routledge, New York (2002)
10. Florida, R.: Kreativnyi klass: liudi, kotorye meniaiut budushchee [Creative class. People who change the future]. Classics, Moscow (2007)
11. Nijkamp, P.E.: Pluribus Unum. Research Memorandum, VU University, Amsterdam (2008)

12. Odendaal, N.: Information and communication technology and local governance: understanding the difference between cities in developed and emerging economies. Comput. Environ. Urban Syst. **27**(6), 585–607 (2003)
13. Asín, A.: Smart Cities from Libelium Allows Systems Integrators to Monitor Noise, Pollution, Structural Health and Waste Management (2011). http://www.libelium.com/smart_cities/. Accessed 10 May 2019
14. WikiSensing collaborative sensor data management (2017). http://wikisensing.org/. Accessed 10 May 2019
15. Chourabi, H., et al.: Understanding smart cities: an integrative framework. In: 45th Hawaii International Conference on System Science (HICSS), pp. 2289–2297. IEEE (2012)
16. Hall, R.E.: The vision of a smart city. In: Proceedings of the 2nd International Life Extension Technology Workshop, Paris, France (2000). http://www.osti.gov/bridge/servlets/purl/773961-oyxp82/webviewable/773961.pdf. Accessed 10 May 2019
17. Shichiyakh, R.A., Klyuchnikov, D.A., Balashova, S.P., Novoselov, S.N., Novosyolova, N. N.: Smart city as the basic construct of the socio-economic development of territories. Int. J. Econ. Financ. Issues **6**(S1), 157–162 (2016)
18. Al-Hader, M., Rodzi, A.: The smart city infrastructure development & monitoring. Theor. Empirical Res. Urban Manag. **4**(2), 87–94 (2009)
19. Anthopoulos, L., Fitsilis, P.: From digital to ubiquitous cities: defining a common architecture for urban development. In: Proceedings of the 6th International Conference on Intelligent Environments, Kuala Lumpur, Malaysia (2010)

Citizens' Understanding of Smart City Development: The Case of St. Petersburg, Russia

Lyudmila Vidiasova[1]($\boxtimes$) (iD), Felippe Cronemberger[2] (iD),
Natalia Osipova[3] (iD), and Elena Bershadskaya[3]

[1] ITMO University, Saint Petersburg, Russia
bershadskaya.lyudmila@gmail.com
[2] University at Albany, SUNY, Albany, NY, USA
fcronemberger@alumni.albany.edu
[3] Penza State Technological University, Penza, Russia
O_Natali_V@mail.ru, bereg.50@mail.ru

Abstract. The paper assesses a model for a smart city development based on the citizens' survey results. A survey of 600 Saint Petersburg citizens was conducted to reveal citizens' understanding in three areas: (1) conceptual understanding of smart cities; (2) priority areas for smart city development (3) citizens' attitudes, positive and negative expectations and risks. Correlation matrices were built based on citizens' perceptions of the risk and were separated into technological, management and social categories. Of the ten selected indicators, six belong to the social group, one to the technological group and three to the management group. Findings suggest that (1) social aspects are especially important in smart city initiatives (2) conceptual understanding of smart city is still scarce; (3) awareness on priorities and risks associated to developments at the local government level is more pronounced.

Keywords: Socio-technical systems · Smart cities · Governance

1 Introduction

Smart cities is a topic that continues to attract attention across a variety of domains. While technology and organizational aspects are the most commonly studied covered in literature [1, 2], attention is yet to be given to complex socio-technical constructs that are more deeply connected with public administration challenges. To respond to such necessity, aspects such as governance [3], collaboration [4] and public value [5] are receiving more scrutiny, getting analyzed both in broader and interdisciplinary contexts and empirically. Although research on those elements contribute to framing the debate around what seems to be relevant to smart city development, there is still limited research on citizens' perception and understanding of efforts taking place inside city hall.

By exploring the public of citizens in St. Petersburg, Russia, this paper is concerned with two questions: (1) What do citizens perceive or understand of smart city development? and (2) What seems to matter to them as far as the topic is concerned.

A. Chugunov et al. (Eds.): EGOSE 2019, CCIS 1135, pp. 41–54, 2020.
https://doi.org/10.1007/978-3-030-39296-3_4

This paper also sheds light to an important construct in public administration - trust -, and also explores the extent to which citizens trust the model proposed to the studied city. Data from a survey with 600 Russian citizens and interviews was collected to examine citizens' understanding and perceptions of commonly researched smart city dimensions such as technology and policy. Main findings and implications of this research agenda are presented at the end.

2 Literature Review

2.1 Perceptions on Smart City Initiatives

Cities demonstrate increasing concern with public challenges at the local level. In face of issues related to mobility [6] and emergency preparedness [7], the need for development of efficient and systematic ways of helping public authorities becomes pressing. In such context, information technologies are often considered to play a promising role in delivering solutions and improving urban life [8].

Literature at the intersection of public administration and technology has been acknowledging for quite some time that technological solutions do not necessarily ensure outcomes in public sector projects [9, 10]. In face of the limitations of technological determinism, research on socio-technical factors is gaining volume, especially in fronts such citizens' perceptions of [11], participation [12], policy co-creation [13] and collaborative data analytics [14]. Even within the same municipal limits, expectations on policy and technological initiatives and their outcomes are known to vary in peculiar ways [15]. With the purpose of informing policy-makers and public leadership, who are constantly pressed to design and implement innovative solutions to increasingly intricate problems, it is the responsibility of researchers on local governments to understand the complexity, map nuances and the dynamic of public´s perceptions on different socio-technical phenomena [16].

Research has explored smart cities in different ways, and many constructs have been considered to assess how cities view smart city development. Besides covering what it means to be a smart city [17, 18], research endeavors are now dedicated to understanding what a smart city could mean to people, an agenda that explores levels participation and engagement [19], perceptions on potential risks [20] and trust [21]. As interests in measures of success grows, it becomes critical to evaluate conceptual understanding of smart cities, but also understand perceptions of conceptualization efforts at a more fundamental level [1].

Despite academic and practitioners familiarity with smart cities and related concepts as a research agenda, it is not unreasonable to consider that citizens, those who are destined to benefit from smart city initiatives, may not be well acquainted with the topic [22] and may need to be included in the debate [23, 24]. The risk in not factoring citizens in smart city debates could make research and practice on smart city development susceptible to a normative bias, alienating rather than including citizens, collaborators and public perceptions at large.

2.2 Smart City Development in Russia

Smart city development in Russia is quite a new topic. The introduction of modern technologies in the cities' development of cities is confirmed by the goals and objectives approved by the decree of the Government of the Russian Federation of July 38, 2017 No. 1632-p of the Digital Economy of the Russian Federation [25]. According to this program, 18 municipalities from 15 regions were selected to participate in the pilot program for the Smart City implementation of the Smart City project. In their territories will be tested "smart solutions" contained in the bank solutions "Smart City". The list includes both cities with more than one million citizens and jurisdictions with a population of less than 100 thousand people: Voronezh, Yekaterinburg, Novouralsk (Sverdlovsk region), Novosibirsk, Ufa, Perm, Veliky Novgorod, Yevpatoria (Republic of Crimea), Izhevsk (Udmurtia), Glazov (Udmurtia), Sarapul (Udmurtia), Tolyatti (Samara Region), Sarov (Nizhny Novgorod Region), Yelabuga (Tatarstan), Kotovsk (Tambov Region), Magas (Ingushetia), Satka (Chelyabinsk Region), Sosnovy Bor (Leningrad region) [26].

It's worth noting that much attention in these programs is devoted to technological components counting the following key blocks to be developed in the smart cities: introduction of "smart" utilities, formation of an accessible, comfortable and safe environment for the health of citizens, creation of innovative urban infrastructure, digitalization of construction, digitalization of territorial planning, development of urban transport systems.

At the same time, there are some examples of developed citizens in Russia that deservedly can be called smart. As well as there are several attempts to evaluate smart city development in Russia. The digital life index of Skolkovo Moscow School of Law is calculated for the 15 largest Russian cities (Moscow, St. Petersburg, Kazan, Volgograd, Novosibirsk, Yekaterinburg, Nizhny Novgorod, Samara, Chelyabinsk, Omsk, Rostov-on-Don, Ufa, Krasnoyarsk, Perm, Voronezh) and takes into account seven areas of application of digital technologies: transport, finance, trade, health, education, media, government.

National Research Institute of Technology and communications (NIITS) (Smart cities indicators) created a rating "Indicators of smart cities" The rating is based on data obtained from open sources, and takes into account 26 indicators characterizing the level of development of 7 key areas of the smart city: smart economy, smart management, smart inhabitants, smart technology, smart environment, smart infrastructure and smart finance [27]. Also, some research is devoted to smart city prospects or the barriers revealing. It should be noted that financial resources, technological infrastructure are among mostly mentioned barriers.

Urban development is considered to be an important part of economic growth because 74% of Russian citizens live in them. However as noted in the analytical report of the Center for Strategic Development Northwest [28], at the same time, a comprehensive target scenario of intellectualization and digital transformation for Russian cities is not yet formed. First, in Russian cities (especially large ones), a request has been formed for the introduction of technologies and products of the new generation, which will contribute to the effective solution of the most pressing problems. Secondly, the transition to smart cities is perceived as one of the elements of a larger initiative to form a digital society and economy. Finally, thirdly, the state's position regarding the institutionalization of the topic of smart digital cities is being actively developed (including this area in the implementation of the Digital Economy of the Russian Federation program, creating a specialized working group under the Ministry of Construction of Russia, and forming a number of leading players in smart city development, etc.).

3 Research Design

The incipiency of empirical work on citizen's perceptions of smart city development not only in Russia but in literature asks for a design collects and analyze primary and data. The sociological survey was conducted in the form of a questionnaire in October and November, 2018. There were two purposes. First, to identify the attitudes of St. Petersburg residents to the city program "Smart St. Petersburg". Second, to determine what were the priority directions of the city's development. Lastly, the goal was to establish the level of adaptation of the city's population to new information technologies. The technological dimension, in the opinion of the majority of members of the expert group [29], was confirmed to be of fundamental importance for the implementation of the "smart city" project, which hence justifies its importance to the questionnaires developed.

In accordance with the purpose of the study, the questions in the questionnaire were compiled in a way to obtain information on three main blocks:

- Readiness to use new technologies (indicating the overall level of technology and gadgets penetration into the daily practices of city residents);
- Level of perception of the «smart city» concept (reflecting the level of smart city awareness and understanding of its components);
- Citizens' willingness to participate in urban governance (showing willingness to participate in the smart city and its management, as well as actively use new technologies).

To calculate the sample population, data on population size and age and sex composition were used. The data was obtained on the official website of the Office of the Federal Statistical Service for St. Petersburg and the Leningrad Region. Based on the data on the size of the general population, the sample size for the survey was calculated - 600 respondents. The sampling error does not exceed 4%, the level of reliability was 95%. The sample is representative by sex and age of respondents.

A total of 600 residents belonging to various social, age and gender groups of St. Petersburg were interviewed (Table 1). Confirmatory factor analysis method was used to measure citizens' perceptions in adapting to new technologies. The same framework was used to assess the influence of factors and risks.

The matrix of variables was formed according to survey results and were calculated in the package STATISTICA 12.5. The set of these variables is summarized as risk vectors and divided in dimensions such as technological (indicated T01 etc.), management (Y1 etc.) and social risks (C01 etc.) In the considered method of factor analysis, the risk vector (10) put in correspondence the vector of factors. The values of the pair correlation coefficients for the considered group of indicators

Table 1. The survey sample structure

Age	Male		Female	
	%	No. of respondents	%	No. of respondents
18–25	50,8%	47	49,2%	46
26–35	49,7%	57	50,3%	57
36–45	48,3%	47	51,7%	50
46–55	43,6%	48	56,4%	62
56–65	39,3%	35	60,7%	54
65+	30,0%	29	70,0%	68
Total		263		337

The matrix of variable values was formed according to the table of results of a survey of residents of St. Petersburg and has a dimension of 13×6. The set of these variables is summarized in a risk vector (see Fig. 1 for example). The components of vector coincide with the development indicators of the city. In the considered method of factor analysis, the risk vector (10) put in correspondence the vector of factors $\underline{F01}$:

$$\underline{F02} = (F01; F02; F03; \ldots; F0_k) \tag{1}$$

The ratio between the vectors (1) and (2) is given by a linear functional of the following form

$$\underline{X02} = \{F02\} \cdot \underline{F02}, \tag{2}$$

where $\{F02\}$ - matrix of factor loadings of the indicated group of indicators of possible risks.

$$\underline{X02} =$$
$$(T01; \; T02; \; T04; \; T05; \; Y01; \; Y02; \; Y06; \; C01; \; C02; \; C03; \; C04; \; C05; \; C07)$$

Fig. 1. A vector used to in confirmatory factor analysis.

4 Data and Results

4.1 Conceptual Understanding of Smart City Projects

The level of familiarity with the concept of "smart city" was measured by a questionnaire which contained questions such as "Nowadays, the use of information technologies for effective management of the city environment, which is called the smart city, is becoming quite popular in the world. Are you familiar with such projects? Answers obtained were reported to be of four types (Table 2).

Table 2. Familiarity with the smart city concept.

Answers	No. of respondents	% of responses
Yes, I know what is it	57	9,6%
I've heard something	183	30,5%
I do not know	329	54,8%
No answer	31	5,1%

Findings suggest that less than 10% of respondents are familiar with the "smart city" concept. When asked "What is Smart City for you? Can you list examples of any projects implemented in the direction of the "smart city"?", less than 8%, gave a meaningful answer. The majority of respondents declined to answer. The stimates obtained indicate that information about the "Smart City" project in St. Petersburg has not yet received sufficient dissemination at the level of the urban community, at least to the extent it is possible to assert that people are aware of current smart city developments. The majority of respondents presented not a specific view on smart city image but more a descriptive case of technological city with smart transport, security cameras etc.

4.2 Priorities Assessment in Smart City Projects

Priority areas of implementation for Smart City projects in St. Petersburg used the following criteria:

(1) security and law and order;
(2) ecology;
(3) energy and engineering support;
(4) transportation;
(5) utilities;
(6) landscaping;
(7) territorial development;
(8) health care;
(9) social support;
(10) education;
(11) physical culture and sports;
(12) culture;
(13) tourism;
(14) the economy;
(15) industrial policy and innovation.

Respondents from various groups of the population were asked to assess the priority of the above items, indicating the numbers of each of them in descending order of importance: the first number being the most significant, and the fifth-fifth row (first column), the least. Statistically processed survey results are summarized in Table 3.

Table 3. Citizens' assessment of Smart City priorities

№	1	2	3	4	5	6	7	8	9	10	11	12	13	14	15
1	217	109	18	90	74	13	9	33	17	9	5	3	1	2	0
2	6	87	26	83	121	55	13	64	36	19	7	10	7	2	7
3	2	1	19	36	86	38	14	78	55	24	14	20	8	6	6
4	0	1	0	22	25	24	9	45	37	31	9	16	14	7	9
5	0	1	0	0	15	9	11	20	15	26	4	13	15	8	5
6	1	1	0	0	1	11	4	10	9	12	4	6	6	14	6
7	0	0	0	0	0	1	11	5	4	7	2	5	5	4	5
8	0	0	0	0	0	0	0	10	3	6	1	1	4	5	1
9	0	0	0	0	0	0	0	0	11	0	0	3	0	2	5
10	0	0	0	0	0	0	0	0	0	9	1	0	1	1	0
11	0	0	0	0	0	0	0	0	0	1	9	1	0	0	1
12	0	0	0	0	0	0	0	0	0	0	1	9	0	0	0
13	0	0	0	0	0	0	0	0	0	0	0	0	9	1	0
14	0	0	0	0	0	0	0	0	0	0	0	0	1	7	2
15	0	0	0	0	0	0	0	0	0	0	0	0	0	2	8
Σ	226	200	63	221	322	151	71	265	189	144	57	87	71	61	54
S	1,07	1,51	2,02	2,05	2,35	2,99	3,79	3,21	3,61	4,47	4,81	5,02	5,83	6,77	6,96
Rank	1	2	3	4	5	6	9	7	8	10	11	12	13	14	15

The rows of the tables show the number of respondents who put the industry under the column number in the place corresponding to the row number. The final lines of the tables indicate (a) the total number of Σ respondents who answered this questionnaire; (b) the calculated weighted average estimates of S priorities of selected industries; c) place assigned to the domain.

4.3 Assessment of Risks of Smart City Development

A questionnaire for a survey of St. Petersburg residents in order to assess the severity of risks contained the following question: "What are the threats from the introduction of "Smart City" technologies you can assume?". Residents of the city were asked to assess the possible threats listed in the list (13 risks in total) on a scale from 0 to 5, where 5 is the maximum, 0 is the minimum. The matrix of values was formed according to the table of survey results of St. Petersburg residents. The combination of these variables was summarized in a risk vector. The list of risks was formed from the indicators proposed for assessing the level of threats to the implementation of the Smart St. Petersburg project to the expert group, as well as to the staff of the IOGV. The factor analysis of risks conducted according to the results of a survey of residents of Petersburg included the following indicators and the variables:

T01 - cyber security threats, information systems vulnerability;

T02 - uncontrolled development of artificial intelligence;

T04 - incompatibility of data transmission between Smart Systems and less developed territories;

T05 - outdated architecture for new technologies;

Y01 - inflexibility of power, resistance to the inclusion of citizens in political decision-making;

Y02 - erosion of power, the possibility of social conflicts;

Y06 - complication of the city management processes;

C01 - the disappearance of many professions, and as a result, the growth of unemployment;

C02 - public distrust of new digital technologies;

C03 - strengthening the "digital" gap between "smart" and other cities;

C04 - inequality between citizens due to different ICT competencies;

C05 - preservation of preferences for the use of non-electronic technologies;

C07 - an increase in entry migration to life-saving "smart cities" (variable designations are retained for the purpose of comparability of results)

The eigenvalues of the correlation matrix and the corresponding percentages of the total variation are presented in Table 4. Only three significant factors F01, F02 and F03, have eigenvalues greater than one. The accumulated dispersion of the first three factors makes up approximately 60.3% of the total dispersion. The first factor (F01) in the model revealed the greatest impact on possible risks associated to the smart city project, explaining more than 43.4% of the total variation. The second factor (F02) explains more than 10,1%, while the third (F03), about 6,8%.

According to statistical analysis, three factors are sufficient to explain the effect of the risks taken into account by the *Kaiser-Gutman* criterion; according to the "scree" criterion, the variability of indicators can be explained even by two factors.

Table 5 shows the values of the elements of the matrix of factor loadings $\{F02\}((3))$, calculated on the basis of the matrix of coefficients of pair correlation.

The level of influence of variables (Table 5) on the main factor F01 risk indicators are arranged in the following order:

(1) C07 - an increase in the migration of people to comfortable "smart cities";
(2) C04 - inequality between citizens due to different ICT competencies;
(3) Y06 - complication of city management processes;
(4) C05 - preservation of preferences for the use of non-electronic technologies;
(5) C03 - strengthening the "digital" gap between "smart" and other cities;
(6) C01 - the disappearance of many professions, and as a result, the growth of non-profit;
(7) C02 - public distrust of new digital technologies;
(8) Y02 - erosion of power, the possibility of social conflicts;
(9) T04 - incompatibility of data transmission between Smart Systems and less developed territories;
(10) Y01 - the inflexibility of power, resistance to the inclusion of citizens in political decision-making.

Of the ten selected indicators, six belong to the social group, one to the technological group and three to the management group. Social indicators in the list also occupy the first and second places.

Table 4. The eigenvalues of the correlation matrix

Value number	Eigenvalues of correlation matrix, and related statistics Active variables only			
	Eigenvalue	% total variance	Cumulative eigenvalue	Cumulative, %
1	6,505168	43,36779	6,50517	43,3678
2	1,518959	10,12640	8,02413	53,4942
3	1,025852	6,83901	9,04998	60,3332
4	0,950393	6,33595	10,00037	66,6691
5	0,653706	4,35084	10,65408	71,0272
6	0,636897	4,24598	11,29098	75,2732
7	0,562827	3,75218	11,85380	79,0253
8	0,523087	3,48725	12,37689	82,5126
9	0,505068	3,36712	12,88196	85,8797
10	0,453659	3,02439	13,33562	88,9041
11	0,423592	2,82395	13,75921	91,7281
12	0,396406	2,64271	14,15561	94,3708
13	0,345606	2,30404	14,50122	96,6748
14	0,310443	2,06962	14,81166	98,7444
15	0,188336	1,25557	15,00000	100,0000

Table 5. Matrix of factor loadings of risk indicators

Var.	Eigenvectors of correlation matrix Active variables only								
	Factor 1	Factor 2	Factor 3	Factor 4	Factor 5	Factor 6	Factor 7	Factor 8	Factor 9
1	−0,1209	−0,5056	0,0962	0,4651	0,3262	0,3862	−0,4521	−0,1722	−0,0144
2	−0,1701	−0,4243	−0,1501	0,4583	0,0153	−0,3658	0,5792	0,1875	−0,0687
3	−0,2426	−0,1089	0,3651	−0,3729	0,2882	−0,0520	−0,0520	0,0059	0,1374
4	−0,2055	−0,4157	0,3044	−0,3152	−0,3014	−0,1744	−0,1744	−0,2012	0,1302
5	−0,2252	−0,4169	−0,1068	−0,2650	−0,3820	−0,2290	−0,2290	0,4740	0,1279
6	−0,2492	−0,0158	−0,3771	−0,1924	0,5131	−0,1087	−0,1087	−0,3516	−0,5263
7	−0,2883	0,0751	0,0231	−0,1839	0,3362	−0,0683	−0,0683	0,5774	−0,1336
8	−0,2511	−0,0258	−0,4615	0,1219	0,3360	−0,1772	−0,2290	0,4740	0,1279
9	−0,2511	0,1289	−0,4305	0,0750	−0,2490	0,1079	−0,1087	−0,3516	−0,5263
10	−0,2735	0,0478	−0,1857	−0,1545	−0,1128	0,3362	−0,0683	0,5774	−0,1336
11	−0,2979	0,2135	0,1773	0,1765	0,0787	0,4179	0,3723	−0,2840	0,5594
12	−0,2822	0,2019	0,0449	0,2819	−0,1678	−0,1974	−0,1948	−0,0095	−0,0946
13	−0,2999	0,2146	0,2009	0,1259	−0,1942	−0,0419	−0,1101	−0,2582	0,1359
14	−0,3171	0,1398	0,1418	0,1318	0,0310	0,1880	0,2009	−0,0253	0,0374
15	−0,3155	0,1684	0,2476	0,0760	0,1062	0,1939	0,1393	0,1124	−0,4186

5 Findings and Discussion

Results suggest that understanding of smart cities is diffuse, but somewhat loosely associated to the idea of a city with comfortable living place that improves the quality of life of citizens. Perceptions of the "Smart City" concept by residents of St. Petersburg are sparse, with awareness of constructs related to smart city development projects apparently limited. Findings seem to conform with what is known about the experience of other cities, especially those where smart city development is incipient. The issue could be addressed by holding additional open discussions, organizing advertising campaigns in the press, in the media sphere and policy awareness events. In this regard, great importance is attached to the involvement in online communities.

The level of trust and readiness in the use modern information technologies is estimated on the basis of statistical data on the socio-economic development of St. Petersburg in 2017. Data shows that 80.7% of the population are active users of the Internet; 98.2% of urban organizations use computer equipment, modern information and communication technologies, the Internet; The number of subscriptions of mobile devices or radio telephone (cellular) communication is 2718.9 per thousand people. As per the findings in this paper, the level of technical equipment and the readiness of St. Petersburg residents to use modern information technologies seem relatively higher and similar to indicators of most cities where Smart City projects are actively implemented. The survey results showed that the majority of St. Petersburg residents are active Internet users: they use the Internet every day (42%) or almost always are online (26%). Less than half of the residents surveyed identified themselves as fairly experienced IT users who easily cope with a standard set of new programs for personal needs and job responsibilities (32%).

The level of public confidence in information technologies currently exceeds the median value of the indicator ($3/2 = 1.5$) and is generally satisfactory. The indicator "communication with authorities and their representatives through official pages on social networks" reveals the lowest level of confidence. This low score is not so much due to distrust of information technology, as the general distrust of citizens to the state executive bodies. The all-Russian opinion polls by Russian Public Opinion Research Center (VCIOM) indicate that citizens' approval of state authorities activities usually does not exceed 45%: for the Government 42%, for State Duma- 35%, for the Parliament – 38%.

Within the framework of this model, respondents from various groups of the population were also asked to rate the priority areas of the implementation of the smart city projects. The weighted average estimates of the priority of selected industries are calculated; place assigned to the industry. According to the resulting estimates of S, formed on the basis of a survey of residents of St. Petersburg, the priorities of the implementation of the projects of the Smart City were determined. Respondents indicate that the primary attention should be paid to the following sectors: housing and public utilities (14.7%), health care (12.0%), transport (10.6%), security and law and order (10.3%), ecology (9.1%). Conceptually, within the framework of model No. 1, a comfortable for life city (1) strives for leadership in the field of innovation, cybersecurity and security of information; introduction of a personalized online service of intellectual mobility; digital identifiers for residents using identity verification, the provision of personal data and transactions in both the public and private sectors; creating a system of intelligent traffic management; (2) in the design of residential areas takes into account the factors contributing to the reduction of crime; creating a human-centered transport system and reorganizing industrial zones; (3) in which the prevention of diseases and the formation of a healthy lifestyle; priority is given to the health and comfort of people when planning a city. This is confirmed by the results of the study, so among the examples some respondents identified areas such as participation in city life (interacting with authorities through Internet portals), transportation (smart traffic lights, stops with electronic scoreboards, smart parking), lighting (smart meters), ecology (eco-friendly transport, smart collection and removal of garbage), security (video surveillance), government and social services (e-government services), health care. Comparison of the ranking of the residents with the ranking of the staff of the city administration shows that in 7 cases out of 15 the opinions of the representatives of both groups either completely coincide or differ slightly. In 7 cases out of 15, the difference is 2–3 ranks. Only in one case the difference is significant (higher importance of management risks indicated by the authorities). The consensus observed suggests that people essentially expect similar outputs from endeavors undertaken by local governments.

It is worth noting the low willingness to participate in the management of the city (16%), for example, by filing appeals and initiatives through official portals. Less than one third of participants in the survey indicated readiness to participate in the life of the city, while 26% would not be willing to take part in city government.

Finally, an assessment of the severity of risks during the implementation of the project "Smart Petersburg" was carried out according to the results of the survey of residents of St. Petersburg among the listed threats (13 risks in total) on a scale from 0 to 5, where 5 is the maximum sharpness and 0 is the minimum. Most of the surveyed residents of St. Petersburg in their assessments tend to believe that the greatest obstacle to smart city development in St. Petersburg is social in nature. Independently of questions asked, the study also revealed that citizens value the importance of taking into consideration migration issues in smart city development, an aspect the current research did not focus on. However, this topic could be interesting for elaboration in future.

6 Conclusion and Future

Results presented in this paper bring an overview of three aspects that are worth being observed in smart city development: conceptual understanding of what is taking place; practical understanding of what is or should be taking place, such as priority areas; and risks associated to smart city development initiatives. Those aspects are in line with several existing frameworks for smart city assessment and are useful to guide empirical research.

As far as the St. Petersburg experience is concerned, there are different levels of understanding in the way citizens perceive those aspects. Although many respondents were direct and elaborated on smart city aspects, findings suggest that conceptual understanding remains scattered and vague among citizens. That may have implications to the extent to which public leadership, smart city champions and communication strategists are being effective in conveying the message about smart city development. That is paramount because, public resources are being invested in much of what literature identifies as relevant - technological solutions, for instance -, but relevant constructs(collaborative governance) or means of assessing success(public value) are still unclear or remain unexplored in the light of citizens' expectations.

On the other hand, citizens seem to be more clearly aware of city concerns such as priorities to be addressed and risks to be mitigated. In contrast with the confusion in conceptualizing what smart cities stand for, this paper suggest that people may be more prepared to discuss issues faced by their local governments in more practical terms or in terms they are more familiar with. Observed discrepancies shed light to the importance of understanding meaning systems and information access aspects when designing information management and diffusion strategies to audiences that, as observed, may be quite singular even within the municipal boundaries.

This study is clearly not definitive, nor can speak to different realities, since only one case for smart city development is examined. The path to examine relevant aspects in detail is nonetheless defined and should continue to encourage iterative data collection both on technicalities of smart city development plans, and on citizens' perceptions and understanding of how those plans may affect their lives. The first step is to acknowledge that differences in perceptions exist. The second is to understand the consequences of it. A glimpse of those consequences is presented by the results in this paper, and should be used to inform public leadership and help them in calibrating communication efforts in smart city development.

Acknowledgements. The study was performed with financial support by the grant from the Russian Foundation for Basic Research (project № 18-311-20001): "The research of cybersocial trust in the context of the use and refusal of information technology".

References

1. Gil-Garcia, J.R., Helbig, N., Ojo, A.: Being smart: emerging technologies and innovation in the public sector. Gov. Inf. Q. **31**, I1–I8 (2014)
2. Silva, B.N., Khan, M., Han, K.: Towards sustainable smart cities: a review of trends, architectures, components, and open challenges in smart cities. Sustain. Cities Soc. **38**, 697–713 (2018)
3. Liu, X., Zheng, L.: Cross-departmental collaboration in one-stop service center for smart governance in China: Factors, strategies and effectiveness. Gov. Inf. Q. **35**, S54–S60 (2015)
4. Broccardo, L., Culasso, F., Mauro, S.G.: Smart city governance: exploring the institutional work of multiple actors towards collaboration. Int. J. Public Sector Manag. **32**, 367–387 (2019)
5. Meijer, A.J., Gil-Garcia, J.R., Bolívar, M.P.R.: Smart city research: contextual conditions, governance models, and public value assessment. Soc. Sci. Comput. Rev. **34**, 647–656 (2016)

6. Teslya, N.N., Ryabchikov, I.A., Petrov, M.V., Taramov, A.A., Lipkin, E.O.: Smart city platform architecture for citizens' mobility support. Procedia Comput. Sci. **150**, 646–653 (2019)
7. Gaffney, C., Robertson, C.: Smarter than Smart: Rio de Janeiro's flawed emergence as a smart city. J. Urban Technol. **25**, 47–64 (2018)
8. Alawadhi, S., et al.: Building understanding of smart city initiatives. In: Scholl, H.J., Janssen, M., Wimmer, Maria A., Moe, C.E., Flak, L.S. (eds.) EGOV 2012. LNCS, vol. 7443, pp. 40–53. Springer, Heidelberg (2012). https://doi.org/10.1007/978-3-642-33489-4_4
9. Fountain, J.E.: Building the Virtual State: Information Technology and Institutional Change. Brookings Institution Press, Washington, D.C. (2004)
10. Dawes, S.S.: The evolution and continuing challenges of e-governance. Public Adm. Rev. **68**, S86–S102 (2008)
11. Lytras, M.D., Visvizi, A.: Who uses smart city services and what to make of it: toward interdisciplinary smart cities research. Sustain. Sci. Pract. Policy **10**, 1998 (2018)
12. Novo Vázquez, A., Vicente, M.R.: Exploring the determinants of e-participation in smart cities. E-Participation in Smart Cities: Technologies and Models of Governance for Citizen Engagement. PAIT, vol. 34, pp. 157–178. Springer, Cham (2019). https://doi.org/10.1007/978-3-319-89474-4_8
13. Yu, J., Wen, Y., Jin, J., Zhang, Y.: Towards a service-dominant platform for public value co-creation in a smart city: evidence from two metropolitan cities in China. Technol. Forecast. Soc. Change **142**, 168–182 (2019)
14. Susha, I., Janssen, M., Verhulst, S.: Data collaboratives as "bazaars"? A review of coordination problems and mechanisms to match demand for data with supply. Transform. Gov. People Process Policy. **11**, 157–172 (2017)
15. Vidiasova, L., Cronemberger, F., Tensina, I.: The smart city agenda and the citizens: perceptions from the St. Petersburg experience. In: Alexandrov, D.A., Boukhanovsky, A.V., Chugunov, Andrei V., Kabanov, Y., Koltsova, O. (eds.) DTGS 2018. CCIS, vol. 858, pp. 243–254. Springer, Cham (2018). https://doi.org/10.1007/978-3-030-02843-5_19
16. Janssen, M., Helbig, N.: Innovating and changing the policy-cycle: policy-makers be prepared! Gov. Inf. Q. **35**, S99–S105 (2018)
17. Gil-Garcia, J.R., Pardo, T.A., Nam, T.: What makes a city smart? Identifying core components and proposing an integrative and comprehensive conceptualization. Integr. Psychiatry **20**, 61–87 (2015)
18. Cronemberger, F., Gil-Garcia, J.R., Costa, F.X., Pardo, T.A.: Smart cities depictions in wikipedia articles: reflections from a text analysis approach. In: Proceedings of the 11th International Conference on Theory and Practice of Electronic Governance, pp. 560–567. ACM, New York (2018)
19. de Lange, M., de Waal, M.: Owning the city: new media and citizen engagement in urban design. First Monday, **18** (2013). https://doi.org/10.5210/fm.v18i11.4954
20. Vidiasova, L., Cronemberger, F., Vidiasov, E.: Risk factors in smart city development in Russia: a survey. In: Chugunov, A., Misnikov, Y., Roshchin, E., Trutnev, D. (eds.) EGOSE 2018. CCIS, vol. 947, pp. 26–37. Springer, Cham (2019). https://doi.org/10.1007/978-3-030-13283-5_3
21. Cao, Q.H., Khan, I., Farahbakhsh, R., Madhusudan, G., Lee, G.M., Crespi, N.: A trust model for data sharing in smart cities. In: 2016 IEEE International Conference on Communications (ICC), pp. 1–7 (2016)
22. Vanolo, A.: Is there anybody out there? The place and role of citizens in tomorrow's smart cities. Futures **82**, 26–36 (2016)
23. Capdevila, I., Zarlenga, M.I.: Smart city or smart citizens? The Barcelona case. J. Strategy Manag. (2015). https://doi.org/10.1108/JSMA-03-2015-0030

24. van Waart, P., Mulder, I., de Bont, C.: A participatory approach for envisioning a smart city. Soc. Sci. Comput. Rev. **34**, 708–723 (2016)
25. Order of the Government of the Russian Federation dated July 28, 2017 "1632-p" On approval of the program "Digital economy of the Russian Federation" (2017). http://static.government.ru/media/files/9gFM4FHj4PsB79I5v7yLVuPgu4bvR7M0.pdf
26. Ilyina, I.: Why is it difficult to create smart cities in Russia. Portal IQ. HSE. RU (2016). https://iq.hse.ru/news/%20191493819.html
27. Smart cities indicators. NIITS—2017 (2017). http://niitc.ru/publications/SmartCities.pdf
28. Priority directions for the introduction of smart city technologies in Russian cities. Expert-analytical report. Center for Strategic Development Northwest, Moscow (2018). https://www.csr.ru/wp-content/uploads/2018/06/Report-Smart-Cities-WEB.pd
29. Vidiasova, L., Kachurina, P., Cronemberger, F.: Smart cities prospects from the results of the world practice expert benchmarking. Procedia Comput. Sci. **119**, 269–277 (2017)

The Importance of "Smart City" Characteristics for a City Brand. Comparative Perspective

Revekka Vulfovich(✉)

North-West Institute of Management Branch of RANEPA,
Sredny Prospect VO, 57/43, Saint-Petersburg 199178, Russia
prof_vulf@bk.ru, vulfovich-rm@ranepa.ru

Abstract. Cities in the modern world are competing for resources – material, financial, scientific and, of course, human. They need investors, specialists, labour force for low qualification jobs with low wages and also tourists to adore their beauties and to bring money into the budgets. The important role in the attraction process is played by the city marketing and branding which are also some kind of resources giving new development possibilities and chances in the hard competition. It is a very new trend for modern cities to become "smart" and it is a question if "smartness" makes the city brand more attractive for various user groups or these groups are indifferent to the image of a "smart city" making the decision about the investing into the city, coming to live in this city or choosing the city as a place of interest. The situation gets even more complicated in the regions of mega-cities because of their size and complicated structure. They are not ordinary cities in a "normal" sense of the word but huge agglomerations. To make the agglomeration "smart" and to reflect this characteristic in a brand is a difficult task. The problem is not less important for St. Petersburg than for other European cities and agglomerations.

Keywords: Competition · Resources · Investors · Qualification · Tourists · City marketing · Branding · "Smart city" · User · Indifferent · Mega-cities · Agglomerations

1 Introduction

The city as a phenomenon of the civilization which has been existing for centuries and the urban way of life were spreading since very early times all around the world [1]. But the existence forms of a city have been changing all the time and the presentations of a city's image have been developing with it. In the 21st century we already can not find traditional cities among the largest and most famous ones. Their space form has become disperse and they are now not cities in the traditional meaning of the word but huge agglomerations consisting of dozens and sometimes hundreds of settlements of different size and structure.

But at the same time from outside they are perceived as whole systems with definite features developed in the course of history in the frame of a state and influenced by multiple factors. Space and time – two dimensions critical for a city, its form and

© Springer Nature Switzerland AG 2020
A. Chugunov et al. (Eds.): EGOSE 2019, CCIS 1135, pp. 55–70, 2020.
https://doi.org/10.1007/978-3-030-39296-3_5

functioning – are interacting, intersecting and influencing each other. Results and effects are various and sometimes uninspected. So, to create the image of a modern city and to develop the brand to represent it in the world is a task of high complexity and needs qualified professionals and appropriate instruments.

The new information age gives opportunities to characterize the new city forms in a very detailed and actual presentation and also makes it possible to represent them in such a way that every interested person is able to develop his/her own picture and to make the opinion about the city's opportunities to satisfy his/her personal needs and to evaluate risks for every investor, new citizen, tourist or other "guest". "Smart cities" represent themselves through multiple channels and become leaders in the competition. Their functional potential grows with every new step along the road to really "smart performance" in all spheres critical for a life quality and further development.

City marketing has become a field of theoretical research and practical activity. The creative industries are now working intensively on development of symbolic images in new information modes collecting millions of reviews every hour. Far cities become near and attract interest of people all over the world. Earlier impossible actions are not only fully possible but can be fulfilled with an enormous speed and give an absolute effect.

In this article we analyse different city forms and dimensions, brands matching them and possibilities to improve the city image developing its creative brand. Branding and marketing of St. Petersburg influenced by "smart city" model are examined from comparative perspective.

2   Data and Methodology: The Agglomeration Brands as Complex Communication Systems and Hyperspaces

Data for a large cities brand analyses are taken from surveys. One of the last is the survey made by The Guardian. The comparison is based on two main criteria: the assets and the buzz. The first category is objective and includes climate, infrastructure, institutions, transportation etc. The second one shows the presentation strength, first of all through Internet. The results of the survey are partly expected but some of them seem to be unusual [2].

The first theoretical and analytical question is the question about the dimensions of the territory and population in the analysed systems. E.g. Paris being included into the first four leaders' group with New York City, London and Los Angeles together is not the City of Paris (Ville de Paris – the official name of the commune and the department, about 2mln citizens) but the so called "Large Paris" (Grand Paris) with 12mln inhabitants, including 8 departments and hundreds of communes. Analysing New York, the authors evaluate the territory which they call New York City but being asked about the population number in modern New York every New Yorker says these are 20mln. It means that most modern large cities are agglomerations and their brands include data not only characterizing the city itself but also large territories in the surrounding region.

From the point of view of collecting, structuring and transferring information it means even larger amount of data, more complicated information structure and evaluation of main processes. Big Data as a new phenomenon in the information space allows more objective evaluation and comparison of different cities.

In the above-mentioned survey such cities as Shanghai, Tokyo, Beijing, Sydney, Atlanta and Melbourne are characterized as underperformers. Partly it is connected with a language (for Chinese cities and Tokyo) and partly with the used communication systems. In the information world described in detail by Castells [3] unification of the communication systems is a crucial condition of success. It is compressing space and making the time for all functional processes shorter. As Castells noticed, the space of places is more and more dependent on the space of flows – capital, information, technology, organizational impulses and symbols, pictures and mental constructions' flows. On the crossroad of a space of places and a space of flows the new "smart city strategy" starts to influence the cities' images and new pictures and new brands have to be created. To become the "top-city" or the "challenger" a large city region (agglomeration) needs a real" smart city" development strategy (Fig. 1).

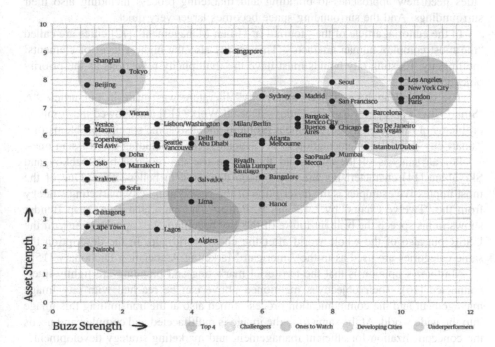

Fig. 1. Guardian "Cities: global city brand barometer". Source: Saffron Brand Consultants [4]

As the analyses methodology we use the systems theory approach which allows to connect "smart city" elements with different dimensions of hyperspace and the comparative approach to the characterization of new tendencies in city branding in the "smart city" context which develops innovative city images. In our monography published in 2001 [5] we formulated the notion of the political hyperspace of a city and metropolitan region as not only a political but also economic and social space which determines the development conditions and life quality as the main objectives and the final effect of this development. In our analysis we used the theory of the 10-dimensional hyperspace of Kaku [6], the theory of social space creation of Lefebvre [7], the information space and society notions of Castells [8] and the ekistics theory of Doxiadis [9]. All these theoretical approaches help to determine the interior flows of agents functionating and interacting in the city with each other. But according to the systems approach developed by Winer [10] and von Bertalanffy [11] in the 20th century most systems are complex structures and are open to interact also with their surroundings. For a space of large agglomerations, it is even more important because of their complex characteristics and intersection of different interests, policies and decision-making mechanisms. One of the most difficult questions for mega-cities and largest agglomerations is the question of balanced policy developed and implemented with the objective to create optimal and unified life quality for the whole agglomeration becoming more and more integrated. But borders of different kinds are not disappearing also in the mind of people evaluating the city realty from outside. That's why cities need new approaches to branding and marketing process including also their surroundings. And the surrounding space becomes larger very quick.

In the editorial article of the "Journal of Urban Management" [12] cities are called "the most complex human artefacts". This means also the highest level of elements' multiplicity. Existing city brands must have the multiplicity reflections as the priority objection.

The detailed analyses of the "smart city" literature was made in our article "A 'Smart City" concept for Russian Cities – Does it Work? [13] and showed the common problems of this new city development problem and also some specific problems of a "smart city" model implementation in post-socialist cities including the Russian ones.

For an analysis of the city brand theory we use the research by Rozhkov and Skryabina [14] characterizing the city brands described in belles-lettres. One of the most impressive examples is the description of the New Vasuki city marketing strategy from the "Twelve Chairs" by I. Ilf and E. Petrov. The main character Ostap Bender shows in his speech the brilliant future of the city becoming the capital not only of the USSR but also of the whole world after the chess world cup. In the description the same categories are used as in the American Marketing Association Dictionary [15].

Martinez's opinion is that the territorial marketing and branding are tightly interconnected [16]. Their objectives mentioned above can be reached with city image management and the communication process aimed also at the transmitting this image into the wide world. At the same time the image is multifaceted and complex and needs the conceptualization for efficient management and marketing strategy development.

Castillo-Villar shows that the city image consists of some interdependent structured knowledge elements (stereotypes and beliefs) which sum up the known facts about the city and also our feelings and emotions connected with different features of the city. It means that they make some combination of cognitive and emotional elements [17]. This allows the individuum to identify the main features in the territorial branding context.

He also describes the territorial branding theory principals in his article. They are at the same time important for the developing of the positive territory image [18]. The main brand features correlate with the image absorbing its identification and differentiation for such purposes as investment, new citizens and tourist's attraction and also at the same time for keeping the citizens satisfaction level and their pride for the city they are living in alive. The territorial brand is important not only for an image development and transmitting but it is also a very significant phenomenon generating powerful positive (they can be also negative under some conditions) influences on the economy, social reality, culture and policy of the territorial entity.

3 Results: City Brand Examples and the Main Consumers of the City Brands

Large agglomerations are some kind of gravity centres in the modern competitive world. Their brands are the markers that give signals to different categories of users. It is important to understand what these categories need to satisfy their needs including information and to create the possibility to attract people needed for different development trajectories and strategies.

The first group are investors bringing to the city capital, initiative, innovation and creating new workplaces. They need large amounts of objective information and services connected with starting business, working out the organization strategy and selecting and recruiting staff. High developed "smart city options" are of great importance for them.

The second group coming to the city is a group of highly qualified specialists invited to improve the personal quality and to give new chances for economic development. Most of them have to work in innovation and creative branches of city economy. The creative image and its reflection in the city brand are of high importance for them. Besides this, they need high quality housing, good ecological surrounding, a high level of social services (healthcare, education for children, possibilities for leisure and sports). They are also not indifferent to the city image as such. In spite of the fact that they have high income they would like to have lower expenses for keeping a high quality of life. The general security and mobility level are very important for them. Often, they leave the city if their expectations in this field do not come true. Such things as climate, geography and even language are not the first priority. They learn quickly if needed and get accustomed to local conditions rapidly.

The third group consists of labour migrants who leave their countries and cities because of a work places lack or danger for their lives and their families. They are workers of different qualification level and mostly do not know any language besides their mother tongue. Housing quality and social services are not very important to them. They know beforehand that they will have only few possibilities to find job and will get low wages. They have years of hard work and low quality of life in future and hope only to ensure better life for their children.

The fourth group is the tourists who come to the city to get new historic, cultural and other experiences, to get rest and pleasure. They need information, new impressions and unusual sensations which they cannot have in cities where they live permanently. Security in a very broad sense (personal, water and food quality, finances and property security, epidemiology and information safety), mobility and expenses comparable with their financial opportunities are very important. Too high expenses make the city for them not very attractive.

The last and in some sense the most important group is the group of permanent citizens who need to be proud of their city and to know that it is an exclusive one. It does not matter if it is some small or middle size city or a huge agglomeration. Information technologies give the opportunity to make the city brand work also for them. Of course, such things as security, mobility and lower expenses for housing and services are for them of great importance (Table 1).

Table 1. Needs of consumers in a "smart city" and city brands (created by the author).

Groups	Smart economy	Smart mobility
Investors	Short time and less efforts to start business, private-public partnership through IT	Low expenses for transportation of raw materials and end products
High qualified specialists	High tech branches, remote work, distant learning	
Creative industries	Car sharing, mobile applications, Internet connections in the public transport	Surveillance network with no blind spots and zero data security, house security systems
Labour migrants	All kinds of jobs also low qualified and with low wages but integrated into the smart economy	Public transport with "smart stops" and other public information resources
The city community tolerant to "migrants"	Sensors helping to make water, electricity and expenses lower. Percentage of the population	

In 2017 the Resonance Consultancy Groupe developed the "Global Ranking of Place Equity" to compare the city brands using six core categories: place (characteristics of natural and artificial surrounding), people (diversity level got through migration), prosperity (GDP per capita, employment level and number of high ranking companies' offices), product (city's institutions in cultural, educational and other fields, attractions, offered services and businesses of different kind including creative industries), programming (the arts, culture and entertainment) and promotion (electronic city representation volume in a form of articles, posts and others). Comparing with the earlier mentioned The Guardian ranking we can say that such categories as place, people, product and programming can be seen as parallels to the assets strength and promotion is comparable with the buzz strength. But principally both rankings try to show how important is the evaluation and the representation of a city for its development and for creating the positive image of the city for the outside world and the creation of an integrative self-identification for citizens. The second objective is not less important than the first. Most of all it is crucial for historic cities with a rich and long way through epochs and events (Table 2).

Table 2. Cities' and agglomerations' brands (2017 [20], *2019* [21]) (created by the author).

Characteristics	St. Petersburg	London	Paris	New York	Berlin	Singapore	Moscow
Territory city	1 439 km^2	1,572 km^2	105.4 km^2	777.93 km^2	891.1 km^2	719.1 km^2	2561,5 km^2
Territory agglomeration	11,600 km^2	8,382 km^2	17,174.4 km^2	34,490 km^2	30,370 km^2	–	5698 km^2
Population city	5, 383, 968	8,787,892	2,141,000	8.550.000	3,748,148	5,664,322	12 615 88
Population agglomeration	5,900,000–6,200,000	13,879,757	12,405,426	20,182,305	4,470,000	–	16 710 000–17 000 000
Place city	39 (*22*)	–	–	–	18 (*74*)	2 (*7*)	42 (*9*)
Place agglomeration	–	10 (*19*)	13 (*16*)	12 (*23*)	–	–	–
People city	78 (*130*)	–	–	–	60 (*93*)	6 (*15*)	72 (*126*)
People agglomeration	–	15 (*12*)	31 (*16*)	13 (*11*)	–	–	–
Prosperity city	49 (*152*)	–	–	–	90 (*86*)	1 (*53*)	18 (*117*)
Prosperity agglomeration	–	23 (*9*)	68 (*2*)	13 (*5*)	–	–	–
Product city	23 (*9*)	–	–	–	10 (*11*)	8 (*28*)	3 (*1*)
Product agglomeration	–	1	1 (*3*)	4 (*10*)	–	–	–
Programming city	18 (*20*)	–	–	–	12 (*14*)	22 (*23*)	6 (*9*)
Programming agglomeration	–	1 (*1*)	2 (*4*)	3 (*3*)	–	–	–
Promotion city	78 (*73*)	–	–	–	5 (*16*)	6 (*6*)	40 (*11*)
Promotion agglomeration	–	1 (*1*)	3 (*3*)	2 (*2*)	–	–	–
Integral Index city	44 (*54*)	–	–	–	13 (22)	2 (*8*)	15 (*6*)
Integral Index agglomeration	–	1 (*1*)	4 (*2*)	3 (*3*)	–	–	–

4 Discussion: The City Brands Reflect the "Smartness". Do They Not?

The first image of Saint Petersburg as the imperial capital, "window to Europe" and first Russian city of European type, created by the strong will of Peter the Great and the first city brand as the brand of the capital in the ancient state getting absolutely new features – the sea country and the active world politics actor – was created by A. Pushkin in his poem "The Bronze Horseman". The abstract devoted to Saint Petersburg brand begins with the words "one hundred years have passed and the young city...."

But in the world of the 21st century the old historic facts, traditions and also magnificent architecture, beautiful sights, museums and other things typical for historic cities are not enough for a success as a magnet for investors and new citizens. "Smart city" models often can connect the past, the present and the future showing all the interest groups that their interests are taken into account when city strategies are developed. All groups need the smart model also when their needs are different.

Many ratings connected with a "smart city" models and their development level are created by different organizations – mostly private because of a high interest to this issue in the business community. They give us the possibility to compare the reality of the two largest and most developed Russian cities with their counterparts in the competition for resources, citizens (first of all, specialists), tourists and labour migrants (the birth-rates are falling in Russia also in 2019 and labour force is decreasing). We have chosen, first of all, European cities (Paris, London and Berlin) because of their high historic and cultural relevance. New York is of a high interest because of its high ranks in many ratings. Singapore is an Asian city and very different from all cities mentioned above but it started its development from a very low development level and has reached extremely high results in many spheres without any natural resources. Another reason for interest in this city is its dimensions – the population size of Singapore is close St. Petersburg numbers. How we can see (Table 3), Moscow's positions are better but St. Petersburg is far behind all other cities. And the ratings IESE: Cities in Motion Index 2018 and 2thinknow: Innovation Cities™ Index: Global 2018 show the lower rank in comparison with 2017 (103, 123) and (93, −18 2017). It signals the citizens and the city organizations and authorities the necessity to analyse and to make decisions according to the real situation if we want to become a "smart city" with the clear and definite strategy also in the IT-technology field and with a high life quality attractive for the world. Also, the touristic brand needs the "smart city" supplement.

In the Russian governance praxis, the agglomeration notion had no normative definition until 2019. The "Strategy of the territorial development in the Russian Federation" [29] was adopted in February 2019. In the document two agglomeration types are marked out. These are large agglomerations with a core-city from 500000 up to 1million citizens, large and extra-large agglomerations with a core-city with the population more than 1 million. The definition seems to be not detailed enough and, in some parts, it does not reflect the existing reality. E.g. in the region of St. Petersburg there are not always borders between settlements in the core of the agglomeration. The definition does not include transport connections among all connection types on the territory. But without them real agglomerations cannot function effectively and the social space with new features cannot be constructed.

Besides that, it is not possible to reach a high integration level without special mechanisms and instruments including strategic planning, territorial marketing. The meta-brand for a whole space is also needed. There are excellent examples of this kind. In the region of New York City (the so called tri-state metropolitan region, population size about 20 millions) about hundred years ago, at the beginning of the 1920s on the initiative of different interest groups (business, local authorities, public organizations, individual citizens) the Regional Planning Association was created as a non-profit organization and it developed the Strategy for the whole region with a very heterogenous law, organizational and social structure and environment. The region had also at that time a very high level of connectiveness in different spheres.

The First Regional Plan was published in 926, the fourth one - in 2017. The tagline as the reflection of the region image and sounding as its brand is "Making the Region Work for All of Us)". The famous "I love NY" is expanded to the whole region with its rich natural resources (forests, bodies of water and so on). The unique culture of New York City has become absolute accessible for all citizens of the region with the intensive transport connections created through implementation of all four Regional Plans. New York as a whole is one of the most secure territories in the USA and

Table 3. "Smart city" development level illustrating indexes (created by the author)

INDEXES	St. Petersburg	London	Paris	New York	Berlin	Singapore	Moscow
Easy Park Groupe 2017 (city) [22]	88 (3,98)	16 (7,18)	19 (7,14)	24 (6,99)	12 (7,39)	2 (7,83)	77 (4,50)
Arcadis The Sustainable Cities Index 2018 [23] (city)	Not included	1	15	14	18	4	58
IESE Cities in Motion Index 2017 [24] (city)	103 (57,46)	2 (98,71)	3 (91,97)	1 (100)	9 (83,40)	22 (79,22)	89 (61,83)
IESE Cities in Motion Index 2018 [25] (city)	123 (42,37)	2 (99,27)	3 (90,20)	1 (100)	11 (76,74)	6 (79,52)	70 (55,50)
Eden Strategy Institute and ONG&ONG Pte Ltd. Top 50 smart city Governments 2018 [26] (city)	Not included	1 (33,35)	46 (22,4)	4 (31,3)	29 (25,8)	2 (32,3)	Not included
Roland Berger The Smart City Breakaway. How a small group of leading digital cities is outpacing the rest 2019 [27] (city)	Not mentioned	2 (73)	10 (63)	Not mentioned	Stadt-land-digital project [28]	4 (69)	Not mentioned
2thinknow Innovation Cities™ Index: Global 2018 [28]	93 (−18 to 2017)	2 (−1 to 2017)	9 (0 to 2017)	4 (−2 to 2017)	14 (+3 2017)	6 (+1 to 2017)	48 (−5 to 2017)

perhaps the only region in the country where you can live comfortably and work effectively without a private car. It gives the possibility to get housing in other parts of the region not only in New York City.

It is very difficult to characterize the agglomerations in Russia. The definition is new and shows not all specific features. The St. Petersburg's agglomeration is mostly defined as the region around the city 60 km in radius. To reach the agglomeration boarder in any direction takes an hour and a half. It is so because of the not enough developed transport infrastructure and low interaction between the city and the Leningrad Region (Fig. 2).

But in future it is possible that the territory size will enlarge and the radius of the agglomeration space will reach 120–140 km. First of all it depends on the economic development and the number of new citizens coming to the city and investors bringing their capital into the region. Already now the city of St. Petersburg needs plots for housing construction, industry development and also for waste disposal. Thousands of city dwellers have their private plots with summer houses ("dachas") in different parts of the Leningrad Region. In summer the number of people living the largest part of time in the Region doubles.

Besides that, the citizens of St. Petersburg with higher income want to have their own houses but not flats. The construction of individual houses inside the city is a rare possibility because of a dense building structure and extreme high prices for plots.

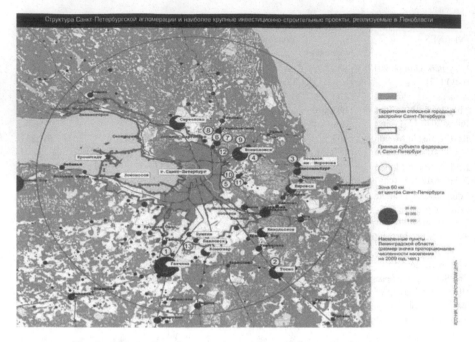

Fig. 2. The St. Petersburg agglomeration with the radius 60 km [30]

The distance 120–140 km from the city will not become an obsticle for choosing a plot there if the roads are good, cars are high speed and all conditions are safe. In this case the agglomeration can get such an outlook.

Many problems are connected with an agglomeration enlargement in the St. Petersburg's region. The first is the problem of political structure. The city and the region are two different autonomous subjects of the Russian Federation. They have their own Status, legislation, governments. Some special features are typical for landscapes and population. The region is not so highly urbanized and the population is used to the life in small cities and country settlements. The expences will grow highly if both subjects become one political entity. Economic development in the region is in some sense more intensive than in the city. In the new autonomus region the position of the city is not clear (it must become a "normal" municipality) but no doubt that the interests of the city will dominate (Fig. 3).

Another question is what features of the region can make the city brand of St. Petersburg more attractive and how the "smart city" projects can be developed and implemented in this situatuation.

In all ratings and researches about "smart cities" we can find only the data about cities itself. All projects are developed for cities and not agglomerations because of the political character of decisions taken about these innovations. Councils and government authorities are responsible for a quality of life in a city. Later the technological solutions can be also implemented in the region around the city. In France new legislation is adopted to create "metropolises" around the main cities in order to develop

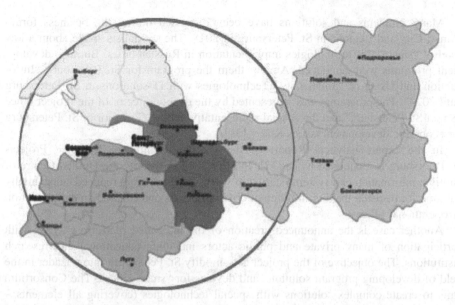

Fig. 3. The St. Petersburg agglomeration with the radius 120–140 km (developed by the author)

also common strategies for a whole region. The main project is of course the "Gran Paris" project. New programms should also include "smart city" elements.

In all cases the core of the agglomeration brand is the image of the core city. But for St. Petersburg many historic places, resorts and recreation areas around the city in the Leningrad Region can be additional attraction places for tourists and other groups coming to the North-West of Russia.

The development of "smart" technologies in the infrastructure (better control of water quality and consumption volumes, electricity consumption), informational maintenance of the transport system, better quality and accessability of administrative services for business and citizens, lower expences for housing and other life quality aspects can give the region a new development mode and better city image which has to be shown for the world (Fig. 4).

Fig. 4. The emblem of the Business-forum in St. Petersburg

Many problems and solutions have been discussed during the business forum "Smart City and Region" in St. Petersburg in 2018. The specialists spoke about a low level of "smart city" technologies implementation in Russian cities. But also development programs were annouced. Among them the program for St. Petersburg "Introduction and Using of "Smart City" Technologies with IT-solutions in St. Petersburg until 2024". The programm was represented by the deputy director of the Project office "Smart St. Petersburg" and the special representative of the Governor of St. Petersburg for economic development issues Kotov [31].

In the expert-analytical Report of the Russian Centre for Strategic Projects St. Petersburg is mentioned twice [32]. In May 2017 in the city the Unified Centre of multiple information city systems started to work. Its functioning reduced substantially the time for decision making in different crisis situations and ensured an early reaction of operational offices.

Another case is the announced creation of the integrated platform CityNet with participation of many private and public actors including educational and research institutions. The objective of the project is to modify St. Petersburg into a leader in the field of developing program solutions and devices for "smart cities". The Consortium aims to create complex solutions with special technologies (covering all elements – program solutions, electronics and including the whole process), business models and also needed laws and other documents. Digital services have to be introduced on this intergrated platform and to create the new branch of city industry (Fig. 5).

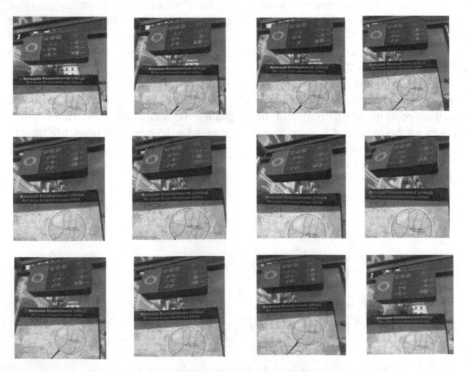

Fig. 5. The "smart bus stop on the Nevski Prospect". 30.05.2019 (photos made by the author)

The perspectives of the "smart city" model development is St. Petersburg are not fully clear. The above mentioned program could not be found on the information resources web sites of the city government. The deadline of the CityNet program have not be defined. The citizens of St. Petersburg do not know exactly what technologies are used today in the city for their sake and comfort [33]. As an example we have analysed the functioning of one smart stop on the Nevsky Prospect during 4 min: 16.14–16.18.

As we can see there are some problems with the information. This type of the bus stops is not the first and the best one. On some stops the scoreboards have been changed two or three times. Some of them do not work at all now. The idea is excellent and such scoreboards can be seen in many cities of Europe. But we understand quite well that if we want to have "smart mobility" for all citizens and tourists all bus stops have to be "smart" and all vehicles in the streets must also be "smart". It means, they need special equipment to be reflected on the scoreboards on the stops and in the mobile application. There is such application for smartphones but there is a problem – not all passengers have smartphones.

The main principle of a "smart city" already mentioned in our article is "the city is for all of us". In the city brand this principle has to be expressed as distinct as possible to be understood by all users: investors, specialists, labour migrants, tourists and citizens.

5   Conclusions

The world becomes more urban steadily. It means that cities are centers of the processes: they concentrate masses of heterogeneous population and have multiple complicated problems. Life quality depends on policy of city authorities and activity of citizens. Last decades brought new tendencies and many cities in the world try to solve problems with a help of new information technoloigies. "Smart city" concepts and models are developed and implemented all over the world. But the results and effects of this development are not always positive. Technology can help to make life quality in the city better but not all problems can be solved with it.

It is possible to save electricity and water with a help of sensors but if not all citizens have access to these facilities sensors can not make their quality of life better. It can seem strange but on the territory of St. Petersburg – the second largest city in Russia – there are settlements without flowing water and central heating. "Smart city" solutions can not be priorities of St. Petersburg at the time because of many other complicated problems which are more important for a quality of life of its citizens.

"Smart housing", "smart infrastructure", "smart healthcare" and other elements of the model are very attractive but we tried to show in our research that they are first of all actual for cities where many problems typical for St. Petersburg and other Russian cities have been solved decades ago or are in a solving process now with a help of more developed systems. For example, Berlin, the city is developing very rapidly with an intensive influence of the Federal Republic of Germany. East Berlin becomes more and more the integral part of a more developed Western city and the Brandenburg Region is developing with them together.

Making decisions about the development of a "smart city" elements in St. Petersburg the city authorities have to balance costs and effects and think about other needs and expences to be done for getting better life quality for all citizens. The citizens with higher income are able to create better life quality themselves getting mobile applications. But other categories of citizens need also healthcare, transportation, facilities and so on. It is not so important for them if the city is "smart" or not. They want to live comfortable and safe in it.

The brand of a "smart city" can help only if the city is already on the higher stage of development and this brand is reflecting the actual situation and not only plans, programs and other declarations of intentions such as the creation of the integrated platform CityNet. It is excellent if St. Petersburg becomes one of the leaders among cities with developed IT-technologies but let us start with "smart" bus stops installing them in all parts of the city and letting them work correctly.

References

1. Wirth, L.: Urbanism as a way of life. Am. J. Sociol. **44**(1), 1–24 (1938). http://www.jstor.org/stable/2768119. Accessed 12 May 2019
2. The world cities with the most powerful brands. https://www.theguardian.com/cities/datablog/2014/may/06/world-cities-most-powerful-brands-get-the-data. Accessed 19 May 2019
3. Castells, M.: The Space of flows. In: The Information Age: Economy, Society and Culture. Vol. 1: The Rise of the Network Society, pp. 407–460. Blackwell, Oxford (1996). https://deterritorialinvestigations.files.wordpress.com/2015/03/manuel_castells_the_rise_of_the_network_societybookfi-org.pdf. Accessed 14 May 2019
4. Cities - global city brand barometer. https://saffron-consultants.com/. Accessed 13 May 2019
5. Vulfovich, R.M.: Governance in Metropolitan Regions: Policy Aspects, 346 p. Publishing of Herzen University, St. Petersburg (2001). (in Russian)
6. Kaku, M.: Hyperspace. A Scientific Odyssey Through Parallel Universes, Time Warps, and the Tenth Dimension, 336 p. Anchor Books Doubleday, NY and others (1994). http://www.unariunwisdom.com/wp-content/uploads/2016/01/Michio-Kaku-Hyperspace-Book.pdf. Accessed 22 May 2019
7. Castells, M.: Op. cit
8. Lefebvre, H.: The Production of Space, 435 p. Blackwell Publishing, Maiden (2007)
9. Doxiadis, C.: Ekistics, the science of human settlements. Science **170**(3956), 393–404. https://www.doxiadis.org/Downloads/ecistics_the_science_of_human_settlements.pdf. Accessed 20 May 2019
10. Winer, N.: Cybernetics or Control and Communication in the Animal and the Machine, 205 p. M.I.T Press, Cambridge (1985). https://monoskop.org/images/5/5a/Wiener_Norbert_Cybernetics_or_the_Control_and_Communication_in_the_Animal_and_the_Machine_2nd_ed.pdf. Accessed 14 May 2019
11. von Bertalanffy, L.: General System Theory. Foundations, Development, Application, 279 p. George Braziller, New York (1968). https://monoskop.org/images/7/77/Von_Bertalanffy_Ludwig_General_System_Theory_1968.pdf. Accessed 29 May 2019
12. Shih-Kung, L.: Toward a general theory of cities. J. Urban Manag. **7**(2), 43–45 (2018). https://www.researchgate.net/publication/326536359_Toward_a_general_theory_of_cities. Accessed 20 May 2019

13. Gribanova, G., Vulfovich, R.: A 'Smart City" concept for Russian cities – does it work? In: 10th International Multi-Conference on Complexity, Informatics and Cybernetics: IMCIC 2019. http://www.iiis.org/bestpapers.asp?year=2019. Accessed 13 May 2019
14. Rozhkov, K.L., Skryabina, N.: How to capture the idea of a place? The case of five Moscow districts. J. Place Manag. Dev. **8**(3), 206–232 (2015)
15. American Marketing Association. Dictionary. https://www.ama.org/resources/Pages/Dictionary.aspx. Accessed 27 May 2019
16. Martinez, M.N.: City marketing and place branding: a critical review of practice and academic research. J. Town City Manag. **2**(4), 369–394 (2011)
17. Castillo-Villar, F.R.: City branding and the theory of social representation/Bitacora 28 (urbano\territorial) - Universidad Nacional de Colombia, Bogotá (1), 33–38 (2018). https://www.google.ru/search?newwindow=1&source=hp&ei=nLU5XKzvOcmMsgHy97fIBw&q=City+branding+and+the+theory+of+social+representation+&btnK=Google+Search&oq=City+branding+and+the+theory+of+social+representation+&gs_l=psy-ab.3..33i160.4935.4935..6955...0.0..0.100.100.0j1......0....2j1..gws-wiz.....0.IwG0w8qJZPY. Accessed 26 May 2019
18. Ibid Safe cities: Using smart tech for public security. http://www.bbc.com/future/bespoke/specials/connected-world/government.html. Accessed 01 June 2019
19. Resonance Consultancy. World's Best Cities. A Ranking of Global Place Equity (2018). http://resonanceco.com/insights/the-2018-worlds-best-cities/. Accessed 29 May 2019
20. Resonance Consultancy. World's Best Cities. A Ranking of Global Place Equity (2019). http://resonanceco.com/reports/2019-worlds-best-cities/. Accessed 28 May 2019
21. Easy Park Groupe 2017. https://www.easyparkgroup.com/smart-cities-index/. Accessed 06 May 2019
22. Arcadis. The Sustainable Cities Index 2018. https://www.arcadis.com/en/united-states/our-perspectives/sustainable-cities-index-2018/united-states/. Accessed 16 May 2019
23. IESE Cities in Motion Index 2017. https://media.iese.edu/research/pdfs/ST-0442-E.pdf. Accessed 12 May 2019
24. IESE Cities in Motion Index 2018. https://media.iese.edu/research/pdfs/ST-0471-E.pdf. Accessed 06 May 2019
25. Eden Strategy Institute and ONG&ONG Pte Ltd. Top 50 smart city Governments 2018. https://static1.squarespace.com/static/5b3c517fec4eb767a04e73ff/t/5b513c57aa4a99f62d168c60/1532050650562/Eden-OXD_Top+50+Smart+City+Governments.pdf. Accessed 02 May 2019
26. Berger, R.: The Smart City Breakaway. How a small group of leading digital cities is outpacing the rest 2019. https://www.google.de/search?eiGrDyXI2nGOaXmwXJ246QCg&q=++Roland+Berger.+The+Smart+City+Breakaway.+How+a+small+group+of+leading+digital+cities+is+outpacing+the+rest+2019.+&oq=++Roland+Berger.+The+Smart+City+Breakaway.+How+a+small+group+of+leading+digital+cities+is+outpacing+the+rest+2019.+&gs_l=psy-ab.12...3654.35901..37566...0.0..0.0.0.......1....1j2..gws-wiz.....0..0i71.IAvNkzTmFl0. Accessed 23 May 2019
27. 2thinknow Innovation Cities™ Index: Global 2018. https://www.innovation-cities.com/innovation-cities-index-2018-global/13935/. Accessed 25 May 2019
28. Strategy of territorial development in Russian Federation. Adopted with the Order of the Government of Russian Federation from 13.02.2019 N 207-o. http://static.government.ru/media/files/UVAlqUtT08o60RktoOXl22JjAe7irNxc.pdf. Accessed 11 May 2019
29. The St. Petersburg agglomeration with the radius 60 km. https://www.google.de/search?q=Санкт-Петербургская+агломерация+картинка&tbm=isch&source=iu&ictx=1&fir=S6Bs42mC_fWyNM%253A%252CsC-_l_zjtG9GNM%252C_&vet=1&usg=AI4_-kQJERcatCpjzcio6rf4OG6dyZZ1ig&sa=X&ved=2ahUKEwjwt. Accessed 26 May 2019

30. The city and the Region: Digital Technologies on the Way for a "Smart Country". Business-forum, 21 February 2019. https://www.content-review.com/articles/46177/. Accessed 07 May 2019

31. The Centre for Strategic Projects. Introduction Priorities of "smart city" technologies in Russian cities. Territorial Development. The Expert-analytical Report, pp. 42–47 (2018). https://www.csr.ru/wp-content/uploads/2018/06/Report-Smart-Cities-WEB.pdf.   Accessed 02 May 2019

32. Drozhzhin, S.I., Shiyan, A.V., Mityagin, S.A.: Smart City implementation and aspects: the case of St. Petersburg. In: Chugunov, A., Misnikov, Y., Roshchin, E., Trutnev, D. (eds.) Electronic Governance and Open Society: Challenges in Eurasia. 5th International Conference, EGOSE 2018, St. Petersburg, Russia, 14–16 November 2018 Revised Selected Papers, pp. 23–24. https://www.springer.com/gp/book/9783030132828. Accessed 28 May 2019

Digital Government, Society and Economy

Existing and Promising Theoretical Approaches to Understanding ICTs Contribution to Anti-corruption Efforts

A Literature Review

Cecilia Strand[1]([✉]) [iD] and Mathias Hatakka[2] [iD]

[1] Department for Informatics and Media, Uppsala University, Uppsala, Sweden
cecilia.strand@im.uu.se
[2] Department of Informatics, Örebro University, Örebro, Sweden
Mathias.Hatakka@oru.se

Abstract. Two theories, often presented as bifurcated, dominate attempts to understand corruption in the social sciences: collective action and principal-agent. Both theories seek to explain when and why corruption happens, as well as how it can be addressed. With the ICT4D field often criticized for being under-theorized, the following study explores which theories are drawn upon to understand ICTs as an anti-corruption tool in developing countries. Through a literature review of 20 years of IS and ICT4D research, the study analyses 19 peer reviewed journal articles' theoretical underpinnings together with methodological approaches as well theoretical contribution. The results find that even if a few studies declare some, often only cursory, theoretical underpinnings and influences, they infallibly fail to present a theoretically informed analytical framework detailing ICTs contribution to anti-corruption. In conclusion, with most of the papers containing no theoretical references, the field is still clearly struggling with theory. The article discusses the benefits with appropriating theory, such as principal-agent and collective action as well as more critical approaches to un-pack ICTs contribution to anti-corruption efforts.

Keywords: Corruption · Principal-agent theory · Collective action theory · ICTs · Anti-corruption efforts

1 Introduction

Corruption is a major development barrier, as it disrupts trade, private and public investments, as well as siphons off precious resources intended for the weakest members of societies. Although corruption typically is more conspicuous in least developed countries contexts, it is present in most places. In Europe, post-communist countries stand out with higher levels of corruption than Westerns Europe [1, 2].

Academic interest in corruption as a multifaceted and complex social phenomena was until the 1980s thoroughly lacking, and primarily coming from scholars engaged in political, sociological, and criminal law research [3]. The lack of reliable data, in particular economic data impaired early research efforts on corruption. Today the field has diversified and the body of research has increased our understanding of both the causes and the effects of corruption on development.

Corruption impacts development adversely by eroding investments away from its intended purposes. Dimant and Tosato's [3] review finds that corruption, including bureaucratic inefficiency impact economic growth negatively by eroding investment climate and/or investment quality, as well as lead to lower levels of foreign direct investment and international trade. It has been argued that "nations cursed with unbalanced, corrupt, unstable or unpredictable governments inevitably fall behind" [4: p.30], because they are unable to provide the required institutional predictability for private investors to be comfortable to invest. In addition to providing a number of obstacles for economic growth, corruption also erodes political legitimacy [3]. High levels of corruption, erodes citizens' general political trust, that is, their trust in elected officials, political parties, public administration, which combined over time can increase political volatility [5]. More recent research argue that corruption also has a negative impact on a society's ability to build the necessary human capital, and thus its ability to tackle development challenges. The phenomena of brain drain, i.e., that highly skilled individuals opt to leave, increases when education and skills does not pay off, which tends to be the case in corrupt countries.

The body of research on causes of corruption are more diverse, as the particular drivers of corruption to a degree is both context dependent and a result of the academic discipline and theoretical lens, i.e., analysis of empirical data is colored by the applied political, historical, social, cultural or institutional lenses.

With corruption identified as a major barrier to development; it has received significant attention and resources from both bilateral and multi-lateral development partners. The importance of the issue and subsequent attempts to develop effective anti-corruption measures has given birth to what has been labeled an 'anti-corruption industry' [6]. However, there appears to be very few cases of real success, i.e., examples of countries that have managed to significantly reduced corruption as a result of external interventions. Furthermore, countries that has managed to decrease corruption levels do not appear to follows a set formula, which limits development partners ability to replicate past successes stories.

With Information and Communication Technologies (ICT) fast proliferation, even in low income settings, it has been repeatedly suggested that ICTs can function as an important tool for anti-corruption efforts. ICTs primary contribution, lies in their ability to address the traditional information asymmetry between government and citizens [7, 8], citizens ability to crowd-source information and that citizens can mobilize to hold officials accountable for lack of services or requests for unlawful fees [9]. Examples such as the flash demonstrations in Manilla, Philippines, were over one million people prompted by text messages besieged one of Manila's main highways in May 2001 to demand the resignation of President Estrada due to corruption provides anecdotal support [10].

ICTs could also facilitate reporting of corruption, by making it easier and more affordable. If systems enable online reporting, i.e., removes the requirement to travel to a police station and allow for anonymous reporting, some key deterrents are removed.

In short, ICTs support multiple important processes, as it facilitates detection and reporting of corruption, which combined creates a non-conducive environment for corruption [8]. Despite, these and others claims, it is however seldom explicated exactly how ICTs contribution should be understood theoretically.

This study seeks to contribute to this under-developed field, and explores which theories are drawn upon to understand ICTs as an anti-corruption tool in developing country contexts. Theory and theory development are seen as essential for expanding our understanding of ICTs across contexts, as well as provide evidence-based guidance to practitioners. "[T]heory guides the process of making sense of complicated and often contradictory real-world phenomena. Theory acts as a lens through which we focus and magnify certain things, while filtering out others things presumed to be'noise'" [11, p. 800].

This study answers the following research questions:

(1) Which theories are drawn upon to understand ICTs as an anti-corruption tool in developing countries?
(2) Does the field engage in informed borrowing of theories such as principal-agent or collective action, or is the field generating novel approaches to understand ICTs role in anti-corruption efforts?

The Information Systems (IS) field's lack of theorization and lack of core theories has been discussed repeatedly [11]. A recent literature review of 143 empirical studies in the closely related Information and Communication Technologies for Development (ICT4D) field, found that chosen theories were often mismatched with the real-world phenomenon the studies claimed to address [12]. ICT4D, is typically concerned with exploring how ICT can facilitate development [13–15] and requires a mix of theories addressing both the nature and complexity of implementing information systems (IS) and development as a process and context [16]. The field of ICT4D is thus inherently multidisciplinary [15].

Albeit the debate concerning whether theoretical inspiration should be drawn from other discipline or organically evolve from the field itself remains unsettled, there appear to be some agreement that better theories are needed [11]. Lyytinen and King [17] argues that the IS field, should remain boundary spanning and seek inspiration from a wide market of ideas. This research subscribes to the notion that theoretical diversity is essential to disciplinary evolution. Adapting theories from other disciplines can thus contribute greatly to our understanding of ICTs [11]. In the light of drawing from other disciplines, two theories warrant some attention, namely *principal-agent theory* and *collective action theory*.

2   Key Theoretical Approaches for Understanding Corruption: Principal-Agent and Collective Action

Two theoretical models dominate research on corruption and anti-corruption efforts: principal-agent and collective action. Although they arguably are often portrayed as bifurcated, others argue they are complementary and that their relative explanatory power is determined by context-specific factors [18]. The following section presents the two models separately, and ends with a non-bifurcated perspective where the two approaches are seen as complementary.

2.1 Understanding Corruption as a Principal-Agent Problem

Historically, corruption research has been dominated by the principal-agent theory [19]. The theory has influenced not only how we understand corruption and its causes, but ways to address it, i.e., anti-corruption programming [20]. The principal-agent theory postulates that corruption occurs when an agent, delegated by a principal, such as government ministers and ministries, or voters to perform tasks on its behalf, such as providing public services; abuses the information asymmetry concerning the agents' tasks and transactions as well as system weakness, such as lack accountability to self-enrich at the expense of the principal's interests. A key feature in the principal-agent theory is an assumption that agents are viewed as rational and that corruption can be addressed by changing the cost-benefit calculation the agents engages in when an opportunity arises.

Another feature of the principal-agents approach is that information asymmetry, i.e., the principle knows less than the agent, which provides the agent with opportunities to pursue interests, which are not aligned with the principal's. So, unless the agent is, or is forced to be, transparent in their service provision and law enforcement duties the principal, including in extension voters, have limited ability to monitor and control the local public officials actions.

The principal-agent theory suggest that corruption is best addressed by diminishing the information asymmetry and build systems that enable the principle to monitor and sanction agents should they deviate from the non-corrupt norm, as well as strengthen external monitoring by supporting for example citizen reporting, whistleblowing and civil society groups with an anti-corruption agenda. Interventions should thus focus on enforcing alignment and detection of deviant agents.

Although the aforementioned system of delegation forms the basis upon which all governments are structured, and the theory hence should be universally applicable; it has been repeatedly pointed out that the theory erroneously assumes that the principal's interest lies in the public good. In systemically corrupt contexts, however, where both the principal and the agent engage in self-enrichment, the theory fails to effectively capture the dynamics of corruption or suggest ways to address it. Furthermore, the results for anti-corruption interventions operating from a principal-agent framework, has produced some mixed results, questioning the theory's relevance across contexts [21].

2.2 Understanding Corruption as a Collective Action Problem

With the principal-agent theory unable to adequately capture corruption in context with systemic corruption, where both principle and agents engaged in self-enriching actions, collective action theory attempts to explain how perceived societal norms hold significant explanatory powers in understanding why individuals both condone and/or engage in corrupt practices. At the core lies an assumption that actions are heavily influenced by expectations of how others may act. Systemic corruption emerges and is sustained when there is an expectation that others will be corrupt. When individuals do not trust that others will not cheat, i.e. secure undue benefits for themselves and their kin, corruption gets perpetuated and hard to eradicate through administrative reforms. The collective action theory postulate that corruption persists because corruption has become an expected behavior. That is, corruption is the norm and not an exception to a norm of integrity. There is thus little to be gained from abstaining from or resisting corruption i.e., act in the interests of the public good, unless others does the same. In a society with systemic corruption, corrupt practices are the most rational response. Persson, Rothstein and Teorell [20], concludes: "Insofar as corrupt behaviour is the expected behaviour, everyone should be expected to act corruptly, including both the group of actors to whom the principal-agent framework refers to as 'agents' and the group of actors referred to as 'principals'" (p. 457). Collective action theory highlights that single and isolated anti-corruption efforts are unlikely to produce the system change that would challenge corruption as a socially acceptable practice. It has also been suggested that collective action inspired intervention should follow a "big-bang" logic to be stand a chance to disrupt deeply rooted norms sanctioning corruption based on the notion that everybody-else-is-doing-it-too [22].

2.3   Understanding Corruption Using Non-bifurcated Approach

Peiffer and Marquette [6], proposes a non-bifurcated approach, where the two theories are seen as complementary rather than opposing, and argues that it is the context in which corruption takes place that determines the relative contribution of the two approaches. The authors even "cautions against any attempt to view the challenges of anti-corruption through only one lens, regardless of context" [6, p. 6]. Walton and Jones [18] also argues that multiple lenses are required to understand real-world cases and how local and national patronage politics is enabled by the lack of vertical monitoring and accountability, as well as norms concerning so called gifting and expectations of resource redistribution. Furthermore, both principal-agent and collective action share a 'blind spot' in the sense that they approach corruption as a problem, which fails to acknowledge that corruption can also be regarded as a problem-solver, especially in contexts where the state and its institutions are weak [6]. We need to recognize that corruption functions "to 'solve' the political problems of maintaining stability, providing access to state services and serving as a mechanism for political redistribution in a challenging environment" (p. 10). By openly acknowledging that corruption is a rational response to a challenging political and social context, the processes that perpetuate corruption are more easily discernable. Unless the political dynamics and the patron-client networks that underpin and enable corruption, is recognized, anti-corruption efforts is unlikely to be successful [6].

In short, corruption needs to be approached using all three perspectives, but that the particular context and its specific circumstances will determine the relative efficacy of the individual approaches. Failure to take into the account the context, may even worsen corruption. Persson, Rothstein and Teorell [20] warns that anti-corruption efforts inspired by a principal-agent approach seeking to increase awareness on corruption, address information asymmetry and enlist citizens as watch-dogs could backfire in contexts with high levels of corruption. If corruption is made to seem as more frequent than it really is for the purpose of raising awareness, it could erode an existing but fragile trust in others [22]. By exposing the level of systemic corruption, individuals may erroneously conclude that everyone else is corrupt and thus be less likely to object to corruption and even become more prone to take part in corruption.

3   Methodology

In this literature review we followed Webster and Watson's method for systematic literature reviews [23]. A literature review is a central academic activity as it provides a ground for "theory development, closes areas where a plethora of research exists, and uncovers areas where research is needed" [23. p.xiii]. It has even been argued that literature reviews are "critical to strengthening IS as a field of study" [23 p.xiv], and essential to the development of IS-theories.

3.1   Literature Search Strategy

This literature review period was limited to the last 20 years, that is, 1999 to 2019. We choose four different sources to identify relevant material. The search term used in all searches was: corrupt* OR bribe* OR graft OR anti-corruption AND Mobile* OR Cell phone* OR ICT OR Information and communication technology.

1. We started by searching for papers in the three highest ranked Information and Communication Technologies for Development (ICT4D) journals (Heeks 2010), ITD (Information Technology for Development), ITID (Information Technology for International Development) and EJISDC (Electronic Journal of Information Systems in Developing Countries). The search in the three top ICT4D journals resulted in seven papers.
2. We searched for paper in Web of Science's five information system categories which covers a broader scope of publication outlets. The search in Web of Science resulted in 62 papers (excluding duplicated from the first search).
3. Thirdly, we used Primo (Peer-Reviewed Instructional Materials Online Database), which is a publication service that includes numerous databases. The search in Primo resulted in 29 papers (excluding duplicated from the first and second search).
4. Finally, we applied the same search strategy using Google scholar which generated some 28 000 suggested sources. We choose to review the first five pages.

The searches in select journals and scholarly databases resulted in 98 items, and google scholar suggested an additional 49 items. Each paper where reviewed for relevance in two steps prior to in-depth analysis and coding. (1) We were only interested in peer-reviewed journal publications, as conference proceedings and book chapters generally has less stringent requirements to include theory. (2) Each abstract was reviewed to ensure that the article addressed ICTs and corruption, albeit it could be a secondary theme. In cases where the abstract failed to provide the necessary information for inclusion, the full text was reviewed.

After excluding all non-peer-reviewed items, conference papers, and journal publications that failed to address ICTs in relation to anti-corruption as a primary or secondary theme, the final sample consisted of 19 journal articles.

3.2   Data Analysis

With an overarching purpose to understand which theories are drawn upon to understand ICTs as an anti-corruption tool in developing country contexts, the 19 papers identified for inclusion were read and coded on five aspects:

1. If the article used theories and if so, did theories have a central role for informing the purpose, analysis and discussion of the results?
2. In the case of theory use, which theories were presented as informing the study?
3. Assessment of theoretical ambitions, i.e. review the existence of attempts to develop new approaches to understanding ICTs role in anti-corruption efforts.
4. Which research design the papers used, type of data and methodology. As theoryeither guides choice of research design and methodology or is developed as result of a more grounded theory approach, this study assumed that theoretical preferencescould be better understood if the study also analyzed the methodological approaches the reviewedresearch used.
5. A summary of the main conclusions relevant to understanding ICTs anticorruption potential.

Each journal article was read in full to identify the role of theory in understanding ICTs as an anti-corruption tool. That is, what aspects or intersections of ICTs, corruption, and constraints of a development context did the theory explore or explain.

4   Results

Each article were coded as either *full integration of theory*, where the chosen theoretical framework was not only presented, but integrated into research design, purpose/hypothesis and the analysis of the result, or *weak reference*, where theories were briefly introduced in the background or literature review of the text, but failed to inform the purpose, analysis or discussion, or as *un-theoretical*, where no theory was identified. The main finding is that theories are poorly used, with most journal articles having no manifest reference to theory (Fig. 1). Eleven out of the 19 articles fail to integrate and draw upon a well-chosen theory's ability to provide structure and/or explanatory power in relation to the subject matter. This result indicates that low levels of theorization, continues to haunt the IS field.

4.1   Manifest, Weak and Latent References to Theories

There are no clear preferences in terms of the theories that do appear in the material. The single article that use theory comprehensively draw upon institutional theory. It is noteworthy that the article that use theory extensively is published by a top journal, with a strong emphasis on theory and theory development.

Articles with weak references to theories draw upon a wide range of theories, such as modernization theory, an undefined trade theory, process virtualization theory, new public management theory and finally two references to principal-agent theory (see [24, 25]). As most of the theories originate from fields other than IS or ICT4D, it can be

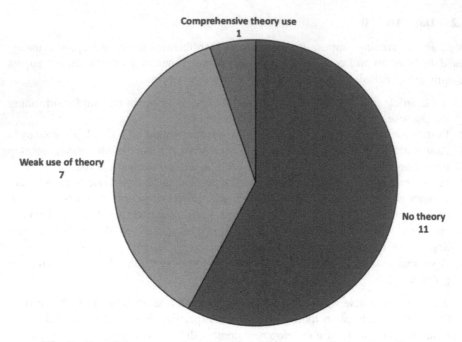

Fig. 1. Use of theory to understand ICTs in relation to anti-corruption efforts

concluded that the field engage in informed borrowing from other social sciences as argued by Webster and Watson [23]. However, as the chosen theory/theories are limited to weak references typically early in the text and not used for analytical purposes, theory plays a limited role. Despite, two references to principal-agent theory, neither article take full advantage of the extensive research carried out in this tradition. No article refers to collective action theory, even if several of the empirical cases are situated in contexts where corruption is systemic.

In addition, it should be noted that although several of the articles did not contain any manifest reference to theory, and subsequently were coded as "no theory", they appeared to have been inspired by theory. The following will serve as an example of principal-agents logic, even if the article contained no reference to the theory. "The use of ICT in the client-administration relationship would reduce corruption levels by limiting direct contact and allow for reconstruction of all of the digital records to apply for a given permit, document, etc." [26: p.199]. The quote indicate that ICTs contribution lies in its ability to increase transparency, remove a corruption bureaucrat, and replace it with a digital platform that treats the user according to pre-programmed rules.

4.2   Research Designs, Methods and Data Sources

In terms of research design and methodological approaches, the reviewed material has a clear preference for a research design consisting of statistical analysis of multi-country data, using secondary data gathered by World Bank, United Nations Developing Program, Transparency International and International Telecom Union (Fig. 2).

Only seven studies rested on primary data gathered for the purpose of the particular study. Few studies, even when using a mixed methods design, included qualitative data, such as interviews and observations. Indeed, only one study included interview material.

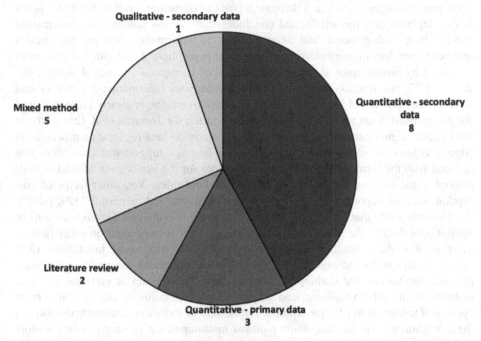

Fig. 2. Methods in ICT and corruption research

Since all mixed methods studies also contained secondary quantitative data, the preference for quantitative data was quite evident.

4.3   Findings in Relation to ICTs as an Anti-corruption Tool

As the reviewed articles span across multiple fields in terms of thematic and geographic focus, the review of main conclusions focused on identifying the existence of reoc-curring themes. Two main themes were identified.

The first theme was named, *assumed effects with unidentified rationale* and comprises of studies assuming that ICTs has an innate anti-corruption effect, albeit that effects are being held hostage, or conditioned on other facts such as political will and rule of law. "[…] empirical findings provide evidence of high corruption inertia in Africa and show that the rule of law is the strongest factor determining the level of corruption. Results reveal that African economies can benefit from the anti-corruption effects of ICT adoption only once a threshold of rule of law is reached. Thus, policies based on the use of the internet and mobile phones are effective in combating corruption in Africa but need to be strengthened by greater law enforcement." [27: p.662].

Under the second theme labeled *transparency supports monitoring and control*, we find the studies with weak or latent references to principal-agent logic. ICTs ability to facilitate information flows with or without government permission, increase transparency and facilitate monitoring as well as replace lower level bureaucrats, i.e. remove selfserving agents, which all should lower corruption-levels. Garcia-Murillo [24] draws upon principal-agent theory as a theoretical point of departure, even if the theory is not fully integrated into the article, and concludes that "across contexts, as government expand their web-presence and allows access to information and provide greater number of services through electronic means, the perception of corruption decreases as measured by businessmen's' perception on level of corruption". principal-agent logic, that is, ICTs contribution lies in its ability to addresses information asymmetry and discretionary powers of agents, as well as facilitate oversight, is clearly present even if the theory itself is not identified a source of inspiration for Terziyan et al. [28] study on the Ukraine higher education system. A country study on land registration processes in Nigeria echoes the same logic. "Generally, our findings suggest that corruption was reduced with the introduction of electronic services for the verification of land records through legal searches and the recertification of land titles. Yet, other forms of corruption, such as nepotism and favouritism, are persistent and increasing" [29: p.290].

The only study that fully utilize theory, bridge the two themes. Through the lens of institutional theory, the study finds that ICTs potential is dependent on other factors, most notably the strength and independence of legal and media institutions [30]. "Overall, the results indicate that legal and media institutions are perhaps the foundational institutions for curbing corruption. When corruption is endemic in these institutions, its adverse effects tend to permeate both business and citizen service systems. Development of e-government can be one of the ways to arrest corruption in these institutions. In contrast, while political institutions are present in every nation, their corruption effects on business and citizen systems are somewhat muted, especially in the presence of strong legal and media institutions. In sum, media and legal institutions tend to be the government's watchdog and enforcer institutions, respectively, and it is therefore imperative that corruption in these institutions be mitigated as a policy measure, perhaps through e-government. Moreover, our results provide initial empirical evidence for the positive role of e-government in mitigating corruption in a nation's service delivery systems for businesses and citizens".

5 Discussion

With corruption identified as a major barrier to development holding back both people, communities and countries, a triangular exchange between academia, practitioners and policy makers is important. Relevant and comprehensive analysis of both qualitative and quantitative data can provide invaluable insights into what factors appear to fuel corruption in particular place, which in turn can inform policy interventions in contexts blessed with a political will to address the issue.

A pertinent question is however, how important is theory in a field that clearly can claim merits by being practice oriented? Although, we concur with the position that research must contain a practice-oriented facet; theory and theory development holds the promise of making knowledge generated in one context transferable to other. Furthermore, theory assists in moving beyond the mere descriptive and enables understanding of not only correlations but causes. In a field that is desperate for solutions, providing insights beyond the detailed descriptive is central. From that perspective, this literature review's findings are troublesome.

As presented earlier, the a-theoretical approach cannot be attributed to the lack of attempts to theorize around corruption as a societal phenomenon, even if those attempts are mainly coming from disciplines outside IS and ICT4D. ICT4D is by its very nature an inter-disciplinary field, and lends itself well to borrowing theories from other disciplines [11]. As already pointed out, ICT4D's multidisciplinary nature, means it can, or perhaps even should borrow theories from several disciplines and engage in cross-disciplinary research [12]. Given this presumed openness to other social science- why this lack of theory? Although this question could only conclusively be answered by engaging with individual authors, there are a few plausible explanations.

Firstly, the type of studies conducted in this field, that is, statistical analysis of multiple countries using secondary data collected by other entities than the researchers themselves may not be conducive to theorization. Statistical analysis will generously provide support for identifying correlations between factors at an aggregated level. Theory building, testing or expansion on the other hand requires in-depth understanding beyond mere correlations in large data samples. Statistical analysis of multi-country data, using fixed entry point to explore the complexities of corruption combined with no or little qualitative data fails to provide the researcher with the in-depth understanding that would enable theory building, testing or expansion.

Secondly, the subject appears to be relatively new. All studies that ended up being included is from 2004 and onwards, with the majority of the studies dated from 2013 or later. Lack of theoretical ambitions and sincerer attempts may thus be reflective of fact that the field is still in a descriptive phase. Descriptive accounts should not be dismissed as unimportant, as detailed and comprehensive descriptions of a phenomenon is fundamental to the research enterprise, and adds invaluable knowledge of the shape, prevalence and potentially nature of the phenomena. But as the exploration of ICTs contribution to anti-corruption efforts widens and deepens, theoretical ambitions should increase. It has been argued that as a field of inquiry develop, "their theories are often placed on a hierarchy from *ad hoc* classification systems (in which categories are used to summarize empirical observations), to taxonomies (in which the relationships between the categories can be described), to conceptual frameworks (in which propositions summarize explanations and predictions), to theoretical systems (in which laws are contained within axiomatic or formal theories) [31]. In its short history, IS research has developed from classification systems to conceptual frameworks" [23: p. xiii]. Lack of theory, may also be a reflection of exciting theories' inability to interpret and explain results from the field, which appears to be inconclusive at times. Or put differently, theories resting on notions of transformative technology for development, are a poor match when ICT fails to deliver, or explain how initial small-scale successes can be scaled to bring about sustainable large-scale benefits.

Thirdly, lack of incentives may contribute. Historically academic output outside the highest ranking journals and in particular conference contributions has not had theorization as a prerequisite for publication. Other key stakeholders with a keen interest in the academic output, most notably development practitioners have not conditioned their interests either on theory building or testing.

Although this study confirms prior studies in terms of the ICT4D and IS field's historically low level of contribution to theory development [32], an exploration of other social sciences attempts to understand corruption may prove to be a meaningful exercise to further our understanding of how ICTs could contribute to anti-corruption efforts. The final section explores some potentially meaningful research directions.

5.1   ICTs in Relation to Principal-Agent and Collective Action Theory

As detailed earlier, social sciences have congregated around two main approaches to understand corruption. This literature review find that principal-agent theory appear to have sparked some interests among IS and ICT4D researchers, albeit the exploration is still in its infancy.

We concur that the principal-agent theory's main propositions intuitively makes sense to explore in relation to ICTs. If we leave aside that in a significant number of contexts, the principle, as in government officials is as corrupt as the agent/s, the theory highlights the importance of transparency and its role in enabling accountability. ICTs does facilitate general access to information and thus increase transparency. In instances where the primary principle, such as government, strive to keep its traditional information monopoly, ICTs can facilitate horizontal crowd sourcing of information and bypass government attempts to control flows of information. Crowed sourced information allows citizens' to performs oversight in the case where both principle, as in elected officials and public servants as in lower level officials, fail to share essential information [33]. ICTs, most notably mobiles allows citizens to not only to share information and consequently threatens government officials' ability to take clandestine decisions outside rules and regulations, as well as mobilize against it. ICTs thus increase the risk of detection, which would be a deterrent in a society where corruption is not socially acceptable.

In contexts, where there is political will to address corruption, ICTs would address the information asymmetry between different levels of government and provide feed-back loops on lower level governments' performance, as well as establish rules-based decision-making systems, which are, if not impossible, at least sufficiently cumbersome to over-ride. In short, ICTs enables (but does not guarantee) accountability, in contexts where there are principles with sufficient interests to challenge corrupt practices. Perhaps it is in the context where there is a minimum level of political will or critical mass of principles, as in civil society and citizens; principal-agent framework is likely to provide a rewarding structure for a systematic exploration of how ICTs would support principles eager for change. But as eluded to earlier, ICTs particular contribution is conditional on a number of factors, with the constellation of principles' and their interest in fighting corruption as well as power to sanction corruption being of particular importance. Whether, the implied logic of principal-agent theory would stand the test of empirical testing, and thus provide guidance on which type of ICTs thatcreate a critical level of transparency and enforceable accountability routines and thus challenge some of the processes that maintains corruption. Principal-agents theory's usefulness to study and understand these and closely related processes, requires multiple single case studies, diligently applying a principal-agent logic to purpose, research design and analysis.

None of the reviewed studies utilized collective action theory to explore how ICTs could be understood in relation to anti-corruption efforts, or begin to support efforts to challenge social practices when entire societies condone and/or engage in corruption. Indeed, this theoretical approach is harder to envision as a single approach, as it would require a portion of unfashionable techno-optimism. But as argued earlier, in a number of contexts where corruption is engrained in every aspect of society, it is complementary to principal-agent theory, as it urges us to be very mindful of the overall corruption contexts.

6 Conclusion

This study sought to explore which theories are drawn upon to understand ICTs in relation to anti-corruption efforts in developing country contexts. The study finds that the field appears to suffer from a theory deficit, as theory is seldom utilized for either structuring research or explaining the phenomena. Furthermore, the study finds that the field fails to take advantage of other social sciences theoretical explorations and most notably the dominant theories, principal-agent and collective action theory. Nor has the field begun to generate novel approaches to understand ICTs as an anti-corruption tool.

Albeit there are several reasonable explanations for the current impasse, it is the authors view that the lack of theorization impairs the fields further advancement and ability to provide important guidance for policy makers and practioners. The remedy lies within academia and its ability to apply some tough-love to its peers. The authors would urge editors and reviewers to discuss their role in allowing journal publication of material with little or no theoretical contribution.

References

1. Batory, A.: Why do anti-corruption laws fail in Central Eastern Europe? a target compliance perspective. Regul. Gov. **6**(1), 66–82 (2012)
2. Jancsics, D.: Petty corruption in Central and Eastern Europe: the client's perspective. Crime Law Soc. Change **60**(3), 319–341 (2013)
3. Dimant, E., Tosato, G.: Causes and effects of corruption: what has past decade's empirical research taught us? a survey. J. Econ. Surv. **32**(2), 335–356 (2018)
4. Andonova, V.: Mobile phones, the Internet and the institutional environment. Telecommun. Policy **30**(1), 29–45 (2006)
5. Engler, S.: Corruption and electoral support for new political parties in central and eastern Europe. West Eur. Politics **39**(2), 278–304 (2016)
6. Marquette, H., Peiffer, C.: Corruption and collective action. DLP Research Paper (2015)
7. Lio, M.-C., Liu, M.-C., Ou, Y.-P.: Can the internet reduce corruption? a cross-country study based on dynamic panel data models. Gov. Inf. Quart. **28**(1), 47–53 (2011)
8. Strand, C., Hatakka, M.: Anti-corruption efforts in national ICT policies. In: Nielsen, P., Kimaro, H.C. (eds.) ICT4D 2019. IAICT, vol. 551, pp. 520–531. Springer, Cham (2019). https://doi.org/10.1007/978-3-030-18400-1_43

9. Gaskins, L.E.: The effect of information and communications technology (ICT) diffusion on corruption and transparency (a global study). Texas A&M International University (2013)
10. Rafael, V.L.: The cell phone and the crowd: messianic politics in the contemporary Philippines. Philippine Polit. Sci. J. **24**(47), 3–36 (2003)
11. Truex, D., Holmström, J., Keil, M.: Theorizing in information systems research: a reflexive analysis of the adaptation of theory in information systems research. J. Assoc. Inf. Syst. **7**(1), 33 (2006)
12. Andersson, A., Hatakka, M.: What are we doing?: theories used in ICT4D research. In: 12th International Conference on Social Implications of Computers in Developing Countries, 19–22 May 2013, Ocho Rios, Jamaica, pp. 282–300 (2013)
13. Heeks, R.: ICT4D 2.0: the next phase of applying ICT for international development. Computer **41**(6), 26–33 (2008)
14. Prakash, A., De', R.: Importance of development context in ICT4D projects: a study of computerization of land records in India. Inf. Technol. People **20**(3), 262–281 (2007)
15. Unwin, T.: ICT4D: Information and Communication Technology for Development. Cambridge University Press, Cambridge (2009)
16. De', R., Ratan, A.L.: Whose gain is it anyway? structurational perspectives on deploying ICTs for development in India's microfinance sector. Inf. Technol. Dev. **15**(4), 259–282 (2009)
17. Lyytinen, K., King, J.L.: Nothing at the center?: academic legitimacy in the information systems field. J. Assoc. Inf. Syst. **5**(6), 8 (2004)
18. Walton, G., Jones, A.: The geographies of collective action, principal-agent theory and potential corruption in Papua New Guinea (2017)
19. Ugur, M., Dasgupta, N.: Evidence on the economic growth impacts of corruption in low-income countries and beyond: a systematic review. In: EPPI-Centre Social Science Research Unit, Institute of Education, University of London (2011)
20. Persson, A., Rothstein, B., Teorell, J.: Why anticorruption reforms fail—systemic corruption as a collective action problem. Governance **26**(3), 449–471 (2013)
21. Johnsøn, J., Taxell, N., Zaum, D.: Mapping evidence gaps in anti-corruption: assessing the state of the operationally relevant evidence on donors' actions and approaches to reducing corruption. U4 Issue (2012)
22. Rothstein, B.: Anti-corruption: the indirect 'big bang' approach. Rev. Int. Polit. Econ. **18**(2), 228–250 (2011)
23. Webster, J., Watson, R.T.: Analyzing the past to prepare for the future: writing a literature review. MIS Q., xiii–xxiii (2002)
24. Garcia-Murillo, M.: Does a government web presence reduce perceptions of corruption? Inf. Technol. Devel. **19**(2), 151–175 (2013)
25. Mahmood, R.: Can information and communication technology help reduce corruption? how so and why not: two case studies from South Asia. Perspect. Glob. Dev. Technol. **3**(3), 347–373 (2004)
26. Szopiński, T., Staniewski, M.W.: Manifestations of e-government usage in post-communist European countries. Internet Res. **27**(2), 199–210 (2017)
27. Sassi, S., Ali, M.S.B.: Corruption in Africa: what role does ICT diffusion play. Telecommun. Policy **41**(7–8), 662–669 (2017)
28. Terziyan, V., Golovianko, M., Shevchenko, O.: Semantic portal as a tool for structural reform of the Ukrainian educational system. Inf. Technol. Devel. **21**(3), 381–402 (2015)
29. Akingbade, A., Navarra, D., Georgiadou, Y., Zevenbergen, J.: A case study of geo-ICT for e-government in Nigeria: does computerisation reduce corruption in the provision of land administration services? Surv. Rev. **44**(327), 290–300 (2012)

30. Srivastava, S.C., Teo, T.S., Devaraj, S.: You can't bribe a computer: dealing with the societal challenge of corruption through ICT. MIS Q. **40**(2), 511–526 (2016)
31. Parsons, T., Shils, E.A.: Toward a general theory of action, New York, for analysis of parsons work, see Victor Lidz (2000), 'Talcott Parsons'. In: Ritzerm, G. (ed.) The Blackwell Companion to Major Social Theorists, pp. 388–431. Blackwell Publishers, Oxford (1962)
32. Sein, M.K., Thapa, D., Hatakka, M., Sæbø, Ø.: A holistic perspective on the theoretical foundations for ICT4D research. Inf. Technol. Devel. **25**(1), 7–25 (2019)
33. Bailard, C.S.: Mobile phone diffusion and corruption in Africa. Polit. Commun. **26**(3), 333–353 (2009)

Analyzing Civic Activity in the Field of Urban Improvement and Housing Maintenance Based on E-Participation Data: St. Petersburg Experience

Sergei Kudinov(✉)📵, Ekaterina Ilina📵, and Aleksandr Antonov📵

Institute for Design and Urban Studies, ITMO University, Birzhevaya Liniya 14, 199034 Saint Petersburg, Russia
{sergei.kudinov, ilinaer, asantonov}@itmo.ru

Abstract. Electronic participation tools are becoming increasingly popular among citizens as a means of communication with the authorities. Residents actively use dedicated websites and mobile applications to send electronic appeals on problems of the urban environment. In some big cities, it can be hundreds of thousands and even millions of messages annually. Big data allows for the analysis of civic activity and subjective perception of the environment by residents.

In this paper, we studied the data of a popular Russian portal called Our St. Petersburg, which provides means for interaction between residents and organizations responsible for the elimination of environmental defects.

A distribution of user activity was built based on the number of messages sent by them, which made it possible to identify groups of the most active participants. We identified the preferences of "activists" and "ordinary residents" among the most popular categories of complaints. It was found that activists are more likely to pay attention to citywide problems (for example, urban environment violations on the streets), while the majority of users are more focused on the problems of housing and communal services related to their apartment and house.

Keywords: Electronic participation · Electronic appeal · Civil society · Civic activity · Urban improvement · Housing and communal services

1 Introduction

In the process of developing systems for interaction between citizens and the state, along with the intensive spread of digital technologies in society, web resources and mobile applications began to emerge, allowing residents to report urban improvement problems to government agencies by electronic means rather than in a traditional way, in the form of a paper letter or personal visit to the authority [1, 2]. There are electronic participation systems all over the world. For example, in the USA, there are multiple portals for submitting electronic appeals [3, 4], the largest and the most popular of them

© Springer Nature Switzerland AG 2020
A. Chugunov et al. (Eds.): EGOSE 2019, CCIS 1135, pp. 88–102, 2020.
https://doi.org/10.1007/978-3-030-39296-3_7

being NYC311 [5]. In Singapore, a platform named OneService submits information on urban environment problems to 11 municipal institutions [6]. Such services are popular in Europe as well, for example a British service named FixMyStreet [7] or a municipal app of the Barcelona City Council [8].

In Russia, e-participation services began to spread in 2010 after this form of communication between citizens and authorities was enshrined in law [9]. Two portals became popular in St. Petersburg: Beautiful Petersburg [10] created by an eponymous social movement [11], and Our St. Petersburg [12], a service organized and maintained by the city administration [13]. A similar service named Our City also exists in Moscow [14]. It was created on the initiative of the mayor and the city government.

Distinctive features of all these portals are the indication by users of the geographical location of the detected problems, their categorization and provision of a channel for delivering information about the problem to the authorized services and authorities [15]. The operating principle of such e-participation services is approximately the same: a user finding a city problem marks a point on the map or indicates an address, selects one of the proposed categories to which the problem relates, attaches a photo of the problem if necessary, after which the service sends the information to the authorities. A website or a mobile application can act as a tool for submitting appeals.

The emergence of such automated systems has facilitated and accelerated the process of filing appeals, making citizens more active in solving urban environment problems [16]. In turn, the number of appeals increased dramatically as such systems became popular. Thus, the base of Our St. Petersburg increased to include 1,500,000 citizens' messages from its creation in 2014 till February 2019. Such amount of data provides great opportunities for automated analytics, including indirect assessment of the quality of the urban environment, and civic activity research [17].

This paper focuses on the analysis of publicly available data on messages of Our St. Petersburg users related to the problems of urban improvement as well as housing and communal services, in order to assess the perception of the urban environment and its problems by society. Studying e-participation data can help to find out where there are systemic problems with the urban environment, where residents pay sufficient attention to the quality of the environment, where there are active citizens or active communities with which the authorities could interact.

In addition, long-term monitoring of continuously updated e-participation databases allows us to observe how the perceived quality of the urban environment changes over time, to assess the dynamics of civic activity more accurately than with traditional methods of sociological research (polls, questionnaires, population censuses), which are usually not conducted with sufficient regularity [18].

2 Related Works

Studying urban environment using data on e-participation of citizens is a particular case of using urban big data in the analysis of social, economic and other processes occurring in the urban environment [19]. For example, data on check-ins in social media was used to determine the nature of difficulties in road traffic [20], as well as to identify the boundaries of vernacular regions in the city [21]. Data on residents traveling by taxi allowed us to study patterns of population mobility and identify anomalies in traffic [22]. Information on real estate prices in the study "Structure of 311 service requests as a signature of urban location" was used to monitor and predict the socio-economic dynamics of territories [18].

The practice of studying urban environment using e-participation tools is still underdeveloped in the Russian Federation. In the world in general, this area of urban research is also just beginning to gain popularity within the framework of the concepts of Smart Cities [23]. In this context, citizens play the role of a kind of sensors that collect city data and route it to the main base [24].

Data on e-participation of citizens is analyzed from the standpoint of improving the work of public authorities [13]; urban processes and the environment are studied with the help of such data: dependence of noise pollution of the urban environment on city development [25], the nature and specifics of offenses in the city [26], as well as modeling socio-economic composition of urban areas [18].

The completeness of data on e-participation available to researchers determines the range of possibilities for searching for dependencies between civic activity of residents and various environmental factors and socio-economic indicators of the city. For example, it was revealed that there is a connection between the existence of local web communities in a limited urban area and civic activity, which is expressed by sending complaints about the state of the urban environment [17].

Limitations can be exemplified by the database of 311 service, which contains no data on the authors of messages, which is why conclusions about activity can only be made in a generalized form: at the level of houses, districts and other territorial units [27]. From this point of view, the database of the Our St. Petersburg portal, which is explored in this work, is of great interest because it contains valuable data on individual users for analysis.

3   Data Source

In 2014, at the initiative of the Administration of St. Petersburg, a service was developed, the main function of which is to provide citizens with the opportunity to quickly send messages about the problems of the urban environment and utilities. In addition, the service provides an opportunity to study technical and economic passports of residential buildings, to obtain information about organizations that manage residential buildings, and about the asset holders of non-residential buildings. The service is implemented as a web portal named Our St. Petersburg and a mobile application named Our SPb. A user can file a message both in person (through the web portal or the mobile app) and with the help of an operator by calling the local number 004.

The user must have an account on the portal in order to file messages in person. When registering, users provide their first name and last name, email address and confirm they have read the terms and conditions. Particular attention should be paid to one of the clauses of the terms and conditions, which states that "the relations arising from the operation of the Portal are not covered by the provisions of the Federal Law

'On The Procedure For Consideration Of Appeals By Citizens Of The Russian Federation'". This means that all messages sent by the user through the service are outside the legal framework of the federal law that regulates electronic participation in Russia and are not subject to mandatory review within 30 days from the date of registration. That is why we do not use the term "appeal" as defined by law — a proposal, statement or complaint sent to a government body—in this study in relation to the Our St. Petersburg portal. However, the portal states that "the message is reviewed in accelerated mode" and "is mandatory for review by the executive authorities of St. Petersburg working with the portal".

All problems that can be fixed with the help of the portal are preset in an organized list (classifier). In the first step, the problem object is selected ("Budget institution", "Water body", "Yard", "Building", etc.), after which subcategories for the selected object become available (for example, "Dangerous trees", "Constructions that interfere with parking", etc. are available for a "Yard" object). Next, the user fills in the message form indicating the location (marking a point on the map or specifying the exact address of the object), describing the problem and mandatorily attaching 1 to 5 photos confirming the presence of the problem.

The submitted message gets the status "Moderation" and should be checked by a moderator within one working day. If the message form was filled in incorrectly or another message had already been submitted for this problem before, the user will get a denial in his/her profile with the reason indicated. If the message form is filled in correctly, a registration number is assigned to it, it is placed on the portal and then redirected to an organization whose competence includes elimination of this kind of problems.

The responding organization either fixes the problem and attaches photos confirming this, or reports the deadlines for elimination and the reason why immediate elimination is impossible. The response generated by the organization is also reviewed by a moderator. In the case of a correct response stating that the problem is solved, the message gets the status "Response received". If a solution is planned in the future, the message gets the status "Intermediate response". The user can see the status of the message and the response in his/her profile.

The user can rate the received response within 10 days by choosing one of the two ratings: "Satisfied" or "Not satisfied". If no rate is provided by the user, the message automatically gets the status "Completed: Automatically". If within 10 days from receiving the response the user decides that the problem is solved and chooses "Satisfied", the message gets the status "Completed: User satisfied with the solution". If the user thinks the problem has not been solved and chooses "Not satisfied", he/she can submit another message for this problem.

If the user reported the problem by calling 004, the message is filled in by the operator with the information from the caller, and other users do not see this message on the Our Saint Petersburg website. However, the caller can view the message using a link sent to him/her in a text message. Requests submitted through operators by calling 004 are processed the same way as messages submitted through the website.

4 Data Collection and Primary Filtering

4.1 Obtaining a Message Database

Much of the data about the messages created on the Our Saint Petersburg portal during its existence is available to any user for viewing, but the structured, machine-readable information about the messages is not open data and is not available in the database export format. At the same time, according to the portal's terms of information use, all materials of the portal can be reproduced without any restrictions on the volume and timing of publication as long as a reference to the source is included. Thus, we decided to perform data scraping of open pages of Our Saint Petersburg.

Regardless of whether the message is available for viewing by any user or not, for each message it is possible to obtain the following data: ID (the number assigned to the message at the time of registration), CATEGORY (the category of the object to which the problem relates), SUB_CATEGORY (subcategory refining the subject of the problem), NAME (a typical description of the reason or nature of the problem), DISTRICT (the administrative area of the city), MO (the municipal district), LATITUDE, LONGITUDE, AUTHOR_ID (message author's account number), AUTHOR (message author's first name and the first letter of the last name, if available), STATUS and STATUS_ID (name and ID of the current status of the message), RAISED_DATE (message creation date) and LAST_UPDATED_DATE (the date when the data on the message was last updated).

In order to obtain the most complete set of data, the maximum existing message number at the time of organizing the data collection (October 2018) was determined. In order to collect the data, a program was developed that repeatedly executed requests for pages with supposed message registration numbers and, in the event of a positive response (the page exists), saved the available information into a CSV file.

As a result, data on 1,275,766 messages from the moment when the portal was created (March 2014) till the moment when the collection program was executed (October 2018) was obtained.

4.2 Preparing Data for Analysis

At the current stage of the study, it was decided to analyze current messages on urban problems in terms of civic activity of users and categories of problems that attract the most attention. For this reason, the data sample was reduced to the last full year—from October 3, 2017 to October 3, 2018.

However, primary data analysis showed that the field RAISED_DATE (message creation date) was not filled for all messages. The creation date turned out to be hidden from third-party users for messages the details of which are only available to its author. Since the exact date of creation of the message is not important for the tasks of the analysis, for the messages with hidden creation dates, it was decided to assign them an approximate date closest to the reliable date. For this, data from the through numbering of messages (ID field) was used: the synthetic date of message creation was extrapolated on the basis of the nearest messages for which there was reliable data on the creation date. As a result, augmented data was filtered by the creation date.

It is important to note that this sample included both messages sent by users themselves through the web portal and the mobile application, and messages created by operators when users phoned 004. However, an important feature of the operators' work with the portal is that no personal accounts are created for phoning users. Messages of such users are assigned to operators' service accounts. Therefore, to ensure correct analysis of civic activity in future, we had to exclude from the sample the accounts of operators representing sets of arbitrary users.

A study of a set of messages which were reliably known to belong to operators' accounts, showed that the AUTHOR field for such messages contained symbol sequences like "…" and "- -." instead of names. In addition, it was revealed that the list of sent messages and the success of their consideration is unavailable for operators' accounts, while regular users' accounts have such an opportunity. As an additional check, the messages probably belonging to operators' accounts were marked on the map to make sure that the geography of the messages does not have high concentration zones and the points are evenly distributed throughout the city, since operators receive calls from all districts of the city.

Based on the identified patterns, operators' accounts were excluded from the sample under study, and the final sample included 345,662 records.

5 Methodology and Experiment

To conduct a civic activity study, the database of urban environment problems in St. Petersburg described in the previous section was analyzed using the Tableau Desktop 2019.1.0 Public Edition [28] and Microsoft Excel 365 (version 1904).

The following tasks were stated:

1. To build the distribution of activity and rank the users by the number of messages they sent.
2. To search for special features in the spatial and categorical distribution of messages of the most active users.
3. To compare the spatial and categorical distribution of messages of groups of the most active users and users who sent a small number of messages.

5.1 User Activity Analysis

In total, 32,309 users were included in the sample under study, who sent messages during the year considered. User activity in this work means the number of messages sent by the user for the period under study.

The study shows that user activity is in a wide range: the most active user sent 8,722 messages, while the average activity is 11 messages per user, the median is 2 messages per user, and about 45% of all users in the year considered sent only one message.

To make data interpretation more convenient, users were ranked by groups depending on their activity. Figure 1 shows the activity of users, on which the horizontal axis of activity has a logarithmic scale with base 2.

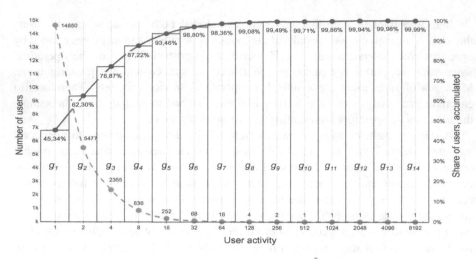

Fig. 1. User activity diagram (Color figure online)

The red dots and the dotted line connecting them reflect the average and upwardly rounded number of users UC who sent the number of messages corresponding to the activity group $g_i \geq 2$:

$$UC_{g_i} = \left\lceil \frac{\sum_{m=1}^{i} UC_m - \sum_{n=1}^{i-1} UC_n}{2^{i-2}} \right\rceil, \tag{1}$$

where $\sum_{m=1}^{i} UC_m$ is the total number of users who sent no more than 2^{i-1} messages, $\sum_{n=1}^{i-1} UC_n$ is the total number of users who sent no more than 2^{i-2} messages.

This approach to the calculation of user activity allows smoothing the unevenness of activity between the key activity values for each group.

As you can see in the diagram, the largest group g_1 represents the users who sent just one message. There are 14,650 such users, and they make up 45.34% of the entire sample. The blue dots on the bars of groups g_i and the solid line connecting them reflect the share of all users who sent no more than 2^{i-1} messages.

As the number of messages sent by each user increases, the number of users in each activity group drops dramatically. So, two messages (group $g2$) were sent by almost 2.7 times less (5,477) users than those who sent one message, 4 messages (group $g3$) were sent by a further 2.3 times less (2,355) users, and so on.

In fact, 80% of users sent no more than 5 messages, 90% of users sent no more than 10 messages. Moreover, only about 1% of users sent at least 100 messages each.

Nevertheless, the total volume of messages of more active users is more weighty than the one-time activity of the majority of users. Figure 2 clearly shows the distribution of the number of sent messages among users.

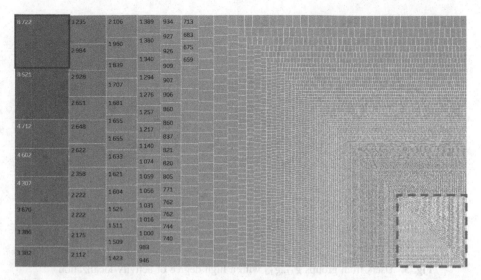

Fig. 2. Activity distribution among users. The red dotted frame outlines the cluster of users who sent one message at a time. The blue solid frame outlines the most active user who sent 8,722 messages. (Color figure online)

Each rectangle reflects a single user, the displayed numbers show the activity value. The larger the size of the rectangle and the more its color is shifted from the red area to the green area, the more messages this user sent.

For subsequent analytics of users' behavioral characteristics, it was decided to simplify the activity groups to two clusters. One cluster of users under the conditional name "residents" consolidated groups $g_1..g_7$. This cluster includes 31,779 users, which makes up about 98% of the entire sample. The most active of these users sent no more than 64 messages for the entire period under study, and in total all the participants in this cluster sent 132,588 messages. The second cluster under the conditional name "activists" consolidated groups $g_8..g_{14}$. It includes the remaining 530 users, which makes up less than 2% of the entire sample. At the same time, in aggregate, the "activists" sent 213,074 messages, which is 1.6 times higher than the total activity of all the "residents".

5.2 Analysis of the Behavioral Characteristics of "Activists"

As part of this research phase, all the messages of the "activists" were marked on a map. A visual analysis of the most active users from groups $g_{11}.g_{14}$ shows that they are characterized by a high degree of localization of activity associated with probable places of residence, work, and regular travel routes. Examples of such users are given in Fig. 3.

Fig. 3. Users from groups $g_{11}..g_{14}$ with a high degree of activity localization

At the same time, several accounts were discovered with a large spatial distribution of activity. For some of them, it can be explained by the peculiarities of the person's business activity, for example, by regular trips around the city (Fig. 4a). But one of the accounts shows atypical activity: the points on the map are evenly distributed between houses in all districts of the city (Fig. 4b). It is most likely that this account is a third-party message aggregator for urban issues.

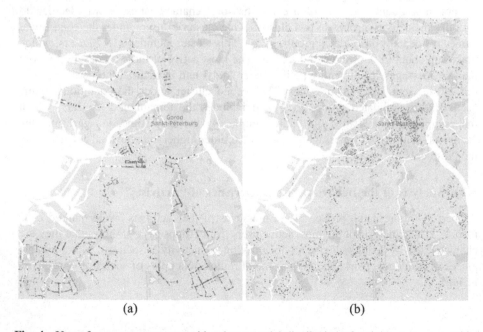

(a)   (b)

Fig. 4. Users from groups $g_{11}..g_{14}$ with a large spatial distribution of activity; a – a user with peculiarities of business activity; b – probably an aggregator account

Also, when analyzing the activity of users from groups g10..g14, a set of at least 9 accounts was found, probably belonging to one user. This is indicated by several facts. First, they all have the same value of the AUTHOR field, which contains the user's first name and the first letter of the user's last name. Second, the AUTHOR_ID values for these accounts indicate that they were created in a row within a short period of time. Finally, a spatial analysis of the distribution of the points of messages created by these accounts indicates a single user behavioral pattern (Fig. 5).

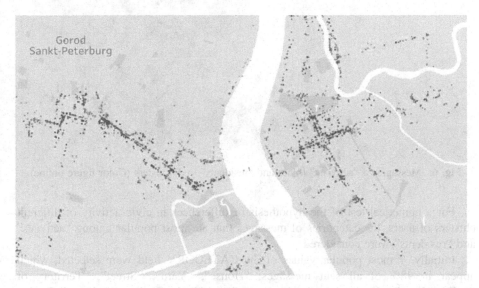

Fig. 5. User activity of the user with multiple accounts (different colors indicate messages sent from different accounts of the same user). (Color figure online)

One of the possible reasons for such user's actions may be the limit on the Our St. Petersburg portal: no more than 30 messages may be sent per day from one account. It is noteworthy that in total this user sent more than 10,000 messages from these 9 "activist" accounts. No more owners of several accounts were identified among "activists".

5.3 Comparison of the Activities of "Residents" and "Activists"

The next task of the study was to compare the behavioral characteristics of the two clusters of users. Two maps were combined (Fig. 6): the messages sent by "activists" (213,074 points) were marked on one, and the messages sent by "residents" (132,588 points) were marked on the other.

A primary visual analysis of the result showed a noticeable tendency: the points of "activists" are mainly located along the grid of city streets, while the points of "residents" are mainly concentrated inside groups of buildings. This tendency is especially clear for peripheral areas of the city.

Fig. 6. Messages of "activists" (blue) and "residents" (red) clusters (Color figure online)

For a numerical test of the hypothesis of differences in civic activity of different clusters of users, the categories of messages that are most popular among "activists" and "residents" were considered.

Initially, 7 most popular values of the CATEGORY field were selected, which appear in 98% of all sent messages: "House", "Yard", "Street", "Territory of St. Petersburg", "Construction", "Apartment" and "Park, Garden, Boulevard, Garden square".

Then the share of messages of each category in the total number of messages of all 7 categories was calculated separately for "residents" and for "activists". For most categories, a significant disproportion in the share between "residents" and "activists" was revealed. To characterize this disproportion, the parameter named balance of interests was introduced as the difference between the absolute values of the shares of "residents" and "activists" for each category. After this, categories were ordered by the mental perception—from private space ("Apartment") to public space ("Territory of St. Petersburg").

In Fig. 7 you can visually assess the focus of attention of the civic activity of "residents" and "activists" by key categories of urban problems. The diagram clearly shows a shift in the balance towards greater activity of the "residents" on issues primarily related to the violation of personal comfort—the categories "Apartment", "House", "Yard". At the same time, the attention of "activists" is more attracted to violations of the urban environment in public places—the "Territory of St. Petersburg" category in general, the "Street" category and the "Facility" category, which include, for example, problems with kiosks, fences, garages.

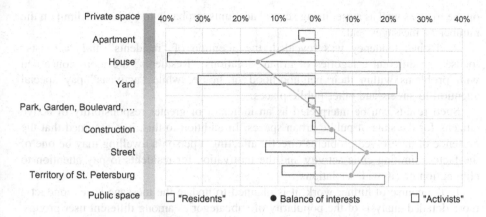

Fig. 7. Balance of interests of civic activity of "residents" and "activists"

This data confirms the hypothesis about the difference in the focus of interests of "residents" and "activists", which was put forward at the stage of expert assessment of the distribution of messages on the map.

6 Conclusions and Further Work

In the course of the study, civic activity of citizens was explored on the basis of electronic participation data obtained from the Our St. Petersburg portal. The prepared database included data on about 350,000 problems of urban improvement as well as housing and communal services, about which more than 32,000 users sent messages within one year from October 2017 to October 2018.

Each message contains not only information about the nature of the problem and its location, but also anonymous information about the account of the author of the message. This made it possible to analyze the activity of individual users. Identifying city areas with an increased activity of citizens is not the only possibility that such information opens up. The study helped to determine that high civic activity is connected not only with the unfavorable state of the urban infrastructure, but also with the presence of individual citizens showing outstanding activity in sending messages about urban problems.

It was found that about 45% of users only sent one message per user, 80% of users sent no more than 5 messages per user, and 90% of users sent no more than 10 messages per user. A logarithmic scale of activity groups was built, on the basis of which users were divided into two conditional clusters: "residents" (users who sent no more than 64 messages) and "activists" (users who sent 65 messages or more). Although the share of "residents" was 98% of the entire sample, 2% of "activists" sent 1.6 times more messages than all the "residents" in total.

Spatial analysis of the messages of "activists" showed a high degree of localization of civic activity around frequently visited places. At the same time, one large account was discovered, a probable aggregator, with an atypical nature of message distribution on the map, as well as a user using several accounts, probably to bypass the limit on the number of messages sent.

A distinct tendency was revealed: the attention of "residents" and "activists" focuses on different categories of urban violations. "Residents" are more concerned with problems within their neighborhood or house, while "activists" pay special attention to streets and other public places.

Such results can be interpreted as an indicator of greater responsibility of active citizens for the state of public urban spaces. In addition to this, it is assumed that the presence of unresolved problems directly affecting a person's dwelling may be one of the factors limiting civic activity and the motivation for residents to pay attention to elimination of citywide violations.

In the course of further work, it is planned to update the message base, conduct a more detailed analysis of the popularity of subcategories among different user groups, perform long-term monitoring of civic activity dynamics among users over time, including searching for and describing cases of residents becoming more active and the dropping activity of users with a large number of previously sent messages.

Acknowledgment. This research is financially supported by The Russian Science Foundation, Agreement №. 17-71-30029 with co-financing of Bank Saint Petersburg.

References

1. Vidiasova, L., Mikhaylova, E.: The comparison of governmental and non-governmental e-participation tools functioning at a city-level in Russia. In: Chugunov, A.V., Bolgov, R., Kabanov, Y., Kampis, G., Wimmer, M. (eds.) DTGS 2016. CCIS, vol. 674, pp. 135–144. Springer, Cham (2016). https://doi.org/10.1007/978-3-319-49700-6_14
2. Choi, B.-Y., Al-Mansoori, M.K., Zaman, R., Albishri, A.A.: Understanding what residents ask cities: open data 311 call analysis and future directions. In: Proceedings of the Workshop Program of the 19th International Conference on Distributed Computing and Networking, p. 10. ACM, New York (2018). https://doi.org/10.1145/3170521.3170531
3. New-York City 311. The Official Website of the City of New York. https://www1.nyc.gov/311. Accessed 01 Jun 2019
4. Moradi, R.: Smarter CRM from a Customer Service Perspective: A Process Evaluation on the City of San José's My San Jose Smartphone Application for City Services. Master's Projects. 591. San Jose State University (2018). https://doi.org/10.31979/etd.pb86-sed4
5. Kontokosta, C., Hong, B., Korsberg, K.: Equity in 311 reporting: understanding socio-spatial differentials in the propensity to complain. In: Bloomberg Data for Good Exchange Conference, New York. arXiv:1710.02452 (2017)
6. OneService Municipal Services Office. https://www.oneservice.sg/aboutus. Accessed 01 Jun 2019
7. FixMyStreet Platform. mySociety Limited. https://fixmystreet.org/. Accessed 01 Jun 2019
8. Bústia Ciutadana. https://ajuntament.barcelona.cat/apps/ca/bustia-ciutadana. Accessed 01 Jun 2019
9. "About the order of consideration of appeals of citizens of the Russian Federation". http://pravo.gov.ru/proxy/ips/?docbody=&firstDoc=1&lastDoc=1&nd=102106413. Accessed 01 Jun 2019. (in Russian)
10. "Beautiful Petersburg". http://krasimir.org/about. Accessed 01 Jun 2019. (in Russian)

11. Kudinov, S.: Using e-democracy mechanisms for civic initiatives for the improvement of the urban environment. In: Proceedings of the International Conference "Internet and Modern Society", St. Petersburg, Russia, pp. 23–24 (2013). (in Russian)
12. The Portal "Our St. Petersburg". http://gorod.gov.spb.ru/. Accessed 01 Jun 2019. (in Russian)
13. Chugunov, A.V., Kabanov, Y., Misnikov, Y.: Citizens versus the government or citizens with the government: a tale of two e-participation portals in one city-a case study of St. Petersburg, Russia. In: Proceedings of the 10th International Conference on Theory and Practice of Electronic Governance, pp. 70–77. ACM (2017). https://doi.org/10.1145/3047273.3047276
14. Our City Moscow. https://gorod.mos.ru/. Accessed 01 Jun 2019. (in Russian)
15. Kandappu, T., Misra, A., Koh, D., Tandriansyah, R.D., Jaiman, N.: A feasibility study on crowdsourcing to monitor municipal resources in smart cities. In: Companion of the Web Conference 2018 on the Web Conference 2018, Lyon, pp. 919–925 (2018). https://doi.org/10.1145/3184558.3191519
16. Chugunov, A., Rybalchenko, P.: Development of the system of electronic interaction between citizens and authorities in St. Petersburg: the experience of "Our Petersburg" portal, 2014–2018. Information resources of Russia, no 6, pp. 27–34 (2018). (in Russian)
17. Kudinov, S., Ilina, E., Grekhneva, E.: Exploring the connection between the existence of local web communities and civic activity: St. Petersburg case study. In: Chugunov, A., Misnikov, Y., Roshchin, E., Trutnev, D. (eds.) EGOSE 2018. CCIS, vol. 947, pp. 334–347. Springer, Cham (2019). https://doi.org/10.1007/978-3-030-13283-5_25
18. Wang, L., Qian, C., Kats, P., Kontokosta, C., Sobolevsky, S.: Structure of 311 service requests as a signature of urban location. PLoS ONE 12(10), e0186314 (2017). https://doi.org/10.1371/journal.pone.0186314
19. Zheng, Y., Capra, L., Wolfson, O., Yang, H.: Urban computing: concepts, methodologies, and applications. ACM Trans. Intell. Syst. Technol. 5(3), 1–55 (2014). https://doi.org/10.1145/2629592
20. Pan, B., Zheng, Y., Wilkie, D., Shahabi, C.: Crowd sensing of traffic anomalies based on human mobility and social media. In: Proceedings of the 21th ACM SIGSPATIAL Conference on Advances in Geographical Information Systems, Orlando, Florida (2013). https://doi.org/10.1145/2525314.2525343
21. Nenko, A., Koniukhov, A., Petrova, M.: Areas of habitation in the city: improving urban management based on check-in data and mental mapping. In: Chugunov, A., Misnikov, Y., Roshchin, E., Trutnev, D. (eds.) EGOSE 2018. CCIS, vol. 947, pp. 235–248. Springer, Cham (2019). https://doi.org/10.1007/978-3-030-13283-5_18
22. Castro, P.S., Zhang, D., Chen, C., Li, S., Pan, G.: From taxi GPS traces to social and community dynamics: a survey. ACM Comput. Surv. (CSUR) 46(2), 17 (2013). https://doi.org/10.1145/2543581.2543584
23. Stratigea, A., Panagiotopoulou, M.: 'Smart' cities as a new paradigm for serving urban sustainability objectives – a view in the mediterranean experience. In: Korres, G., Kourliouros, G., Tsobanoglou, K.A. (eds.) Proceedings of International Conference on Socio-economic Sustainability, Regional Development and Spatial Planning: European and International Dimensions and Perspectives. International Sociological Association, pp. 213–220 (2014)
24. Berntzen, L., Johannessen, M., Böhm, S., Weber, C., Morales, R.: Citizens as sensors human sensors as a smart city data source. In: SMART 2018: The Seventh International Conference on Smart Cities, Systems, Devices and Technologies (2018)

25. Hong, A., Kim, B., Widener, M.: Noise and the city: leveraging crowdsourced big data to examine the spatiotemporal relationship between urban development and noise annoyance. Environ. Planning B Urban Analytics City Sci. (2019). https://doi.org/10.1177/23998083 18821112
26. Solymosi, R.: Exploring spatial and temporal variation in perception of crime and place using crowdsourced data. http://discovery.ucl.ac.uk/1541235/1/PhDThesis_PostCorrectionsFinal. pdf. Accessed 01 Jun 2019
27. Minkoff, S.L.: NYC 311: a tract-level analysis of citizen-government contacting in New York City. Urban Aff. Rev. **52**(2), 211–246 (2015). https://doi.org/10.1177/10780874 15577796
28. Tableau Desktop Public Edition. https://public.tableau.com/s/. Accessed 01 Jun 2019

The Internet in Theory Reevaluated: Theorizing the Role of the Internet in the Political Space

Galina Nikiporets-Takigawa[1,2](✉) ⓘ

[1] University of Cambridge, Sidgwick Avenue, Cambridge CB3 9DA, UK
gn254@cam.ac.uk
[2] Russian State Social University, Vilgelma Pika St. 4, 129226 Moscow,
Russian Federation
nikiporetsgiu@rgsu.net

Abstract. The aim of this paper is to critically reevaluate the capacity of the theories on the internet in politics to grasp the increasing impact of the internet to political space in all countries with rising internet penetration rate. At first, the paper clarifies the current level of the internet coverage around the world and Russia as one of the examples. The influence of the increasing impact of the internet for social spaces and the political space among them in countries with unlimited internet availability is discussed and the conclusion is drawn that the internet influence the political space in the most significant way. Secondly, the paper analyzes the main theoretical approaches to the internet role in politics and draws the conclusion on the shortcomings in the level of the theories and their nationally biased specifics. Finally, it is concluded that the existing theories are incapable to cover the complexity of the effects of the internet on political space. The importance of a macro-theory which can overcome the ideological biases that is characteristic for national approaches to the topic of the role of the internet in politics and can help to analyze the multilayered and controversial influence of the internet on the political space is emphasized.

Keywords: Internet in theory · Internet in politics · Ideologically biased internet theories · National vs global theories · Internet in politics macrotheory

1 Statement of the Problem. Research Design, Methods and Data

The internet coverage and penetration rate is in focus of government and big corporations' interest in many countries around the world, but almost 3 (2937) billion users are accounted for the next twenty countries (Table 1).

These data suggest that when we argue about the impact of the internet to the political space in different countries, we should consider the global specifics of the internet and each national political situation together. In several countries, the idea of the information society theorist D. Bell on ensuring equal access to information for everyone and each social group (or each 'status', since according to D. Bell, in a post-industrial society 'statuses' replace political classes) has not yet been realized. To the greatest extent, this applies precisely to those countries that lead the list in the Table 1.

© Springer Nature Switzerland AG 2020
A. Chugunov et al. (Eds.): EGOSE 2019, CCIS 1135, pp. 103–115, 2020.
https://doi.org/10.1007/978-3-030-39296-3_8

Table 1. Top 20 countries with the highest number of internet users

Country of region	Population as for 2018	Number of internet-users as for 31.12.2018
1. China	1,415,045,928	772,000,000
2. India	1,354,051,854	462,124,989
3. USA	326,766,748	312,322,257
4. Brazil	210,867,954	149,057,635
5. Indonesia	266,794,980	143,260,000
6. Japan	127,185,332	118,626,672
7. Russia	143,964,709	109,552,842
8. Nigeria	195,857,237	98,391,456
9. Mexico	130,759,074	85,000,000
10. Bangladesh	166,368,149	80,483,000
11. Germany	82,293,457	79,127,551
12. Philippines	106,512,074	67,000,000
13. Vietnam	96,491,146	64,000,000
14. UK	66,573,504	63,061,419
15. France	65,233,271	60,451,689
16. Thailand	69,183,173	57,000,000
17. Iran	82,011,735	56,700,000
18. Turkey	81,916,871	56,000,000
19. Italy	59,290,969	54,798,299
20. Egypt	99,375,741	48,211,493

Source: Internet World Stats [37]

In China, the internet is not available for a half of the population; and for the second half, it is limited by the content filtering system developed at the state level. Moreover, the 'old' mass media are still traditionally influential in the PRC. In India, the factor of restrictions and prohibition of free access to the internet is absent, but internet coverage covers only a third of the population [2]. National specifics may also be caused by the most popular access to the internet - via a smartphone or via a computer. For example, in India and in China, smartphones are becoming the dominant way of accessing the internet, which means specific opportunities for political participation [31: 21].

Compared with above-mentioned and many other countries, Russia is much closer to countries with a high rate of 'readiness for the network society', despite the existence of laws restricting the circulation of a certain content on the internet; services that control internet content and prohibit sites that are dangerous from the official point of view; as well as ongoing government initiatives to increase such state-of-the-art restrictions. Such indicators, the so-called NRI indices (index of readiness for the network society) are published in the reports of The Global Information Technology Report for each country. 'Twenty-five leaders from year to year include Australia, Great Britain, Germany, Hong Kong, Denmark, Iceland, Canada, the Netherlands, Norway, Singapore, the USA, Taiwan, Finland, Switzerland, and Sweden. In addition to them, among the leaders in different years were: Japan - 8 times; Korea - 7 times; Austria - 6 times; Israel and France - 5 times; Ireland, Estonia and Luxembourg - 3 times; New Zealand - 2 times; Belgium - 1 time' [28]. Even though the Russian Federation has never been among the leaders of this rating and as of 2016 was just 41st, the Russian citizens mostly have unlimited access to the internet and actively use it. Russia headed to cover the country with the internet long after many other technologically advanced countries, but achieved impressive results in a shorter time. If in 2003, when the Public Opinion Foundation (FOM) began regular measurements of the number of internet users, only 10%, 7%, 3% (monthly, weekly, daily audience) of Russians used the internet, then ten years later, in 2013, they became 59%, 57%, 48% and fifteen years later, in 2018 - 72%, 70%, 64% [15]. The dynamics of the internet coverage in absolute figures is that the number of Russians who use the internet every month jumped from just 3.2 million in 2003 to almost 110 million in 2018. At the state level, the task is to provide 85% with access to the internet by 2020. Russian laws enacted to control internet content and to restrict freedom of the internet use are not so radical as in China and many other countries. In addition, Russia executes the UN resolution, which proclaims access to the internet as a base public value, and disconnecting from the internet as a violation of the human rights.

Russia shares another global trend: the rapid progress in the popularity of the social networks and instant messengers. Russia, due to the great cheapness of service providers, became the site of the unprecedentedly rapid development of mobile internet. In small cities and villages of the vast country, the mobile internet was for a while the only option, as there was no broadband access. In addition, it was Russia that became the birthplace of high-end Russian-language networks and instant messengers: VKontakte, launched in 2006, and Telegram, launched in 2013. The penetration of social networks in Russia as of 2018 is estimated at almost 50% of the population (67.8 million people or 47%), with YouTube and VKontakte lead among networks and are used by 63% and 61% individuals, respectively, of 67.8 million Russians who use social networks and instant messengers. Odnoklassniki (42%), Skype and WhatsApp (38%), Facebook (35%), Viber (33%), Instagram (31%), Google+ (30%), Facebook massager (11%) and Twitch (7%) are less popular social networks and instant messengers in Russia [32]. In general, the top five resources that Russians use every day from mobile gadgets are VKontakte, WhatsApp, Google, Yandex, Instagram [23], and from desktops are Yandex, VKontakte, Mail.ru, YouTube, Google [ibid]. Which means that Russians use the internet for communication and information through two or three social networks and/or instant messengers, a pair of search engines and one email service.

The most popular Russian social network is VKontakte which significantly exceeds the typologically similar Facebook in popularity and is considered the biggest social network in Europe [ibid]. The only rival of VKontakte is YouTube and this is the global trend. In the western countries YouTube, having overtaken by 2018 another Facebook product of WhatsApp and second only to Facebook, ranks first in popularity among all social networks. YouTube users in 2018 is estimated as 1500 million, WhatsApp and Facebook Messenger - 1300 million, WeChat - 963 million, QQ - 850 million, Instagram 700 million, QZone 606 million, Tumblr 368 million, Sina Weibo 361 million, Twitter 328 million, Baidu Tieba 300 million, Skype 300 million, Viber 260 million, Snapchat 255 million, LINE 214 million, Pinterest - 200 million, YY - 122 million, Linkedin - 106 million, Telegram - 100 million [32].

Another feature of the Russian internet, which makes it related to the leading countries with the highest level of the 'readiness for the network society' is a gradual slowdown in the speed of the country's internet coverage, which already started in Russia in 2013. Despite the fact that FOM (Public Opinion Foundation) then confidently predicted annual growth of 6% of the monthly audience, 66.6% in the summer of 2014 and 90% by 2018; the milestone planned for 2014 (66%) was reached only by the summer of 2015, and in 2018 the penetration rate was only 72% [15], but not the planned 90%. Such a phenomenon can be called the achievement of the 'saturation point' when all who wanted to use the internet got access to it. At the same time, this means that the internet from the secondary space of communication, information, organization and leisure activities for intellectual elites [27] turned into a mass space - accessible and necessary for all types of daily human activities.

After describing the pace of the internet coverage in different countries using Russia as an example lets discuss the main effects that expanding internet coverage has on the political space. It is first research question of the paper which we are going to answer with help of the dialectical and systemic method applied to the literature review. Then we will discuss and rethink the existing theoretical and methodological paradigms that explain the role of the internet in politics to prove the hypothesis that they are not able to explain the new political processes that have affected the political space in the information society. The material for answering the research questions are the secondary sources. Empirical base of the research is also data collected for various studies performed by the author in 2011–2018. Among them are data from social networks and instant messengers, as well as polling data from the Levada Center, VTsIOM, FOM and several foreign agencies regarding Internet coverage, the structure of Internet communities, the nature of Internet consumption, and the relative popularity of social networks and instant messengers.

2   Results: The Consequences of the Increasing Internet Coverage for the Political Space

The high rate of internet coverage in combination with the unlimited right to use the internet cause the increasing internet influence on all social spaces and political space among them. Already two generations, whose daily practices are firmly connected to the internet are active in society. This is the generation of millennials, which are also named the 'generation Y' or 'network generation'; and the 'generation Z' or the generation of 'digital people.' Growing up of these generations occur in the 'media-rich house', 'stuffed' with devices and gadgets [1, 21]. The more representatives of these generations come to politics, economics and other social spaces, the more inevitable and obvious the impact on the corresponding social spaces from the internet. The influence of the internet spreads very quickly and in just one generation the internet has changed the ways of perception, use and production of almost all mass media, as well as 'the fundamental nature of communication and attitude to the audience' [14].

The internet becomes a 'special cultural artefact' [13, 14], creating new tradition of 'perpetual connectivity' [16] to communication and information sharing; 'the constant tetheredness to others and to information' [31], or, in terms of language and memes of social networks: the tradition to be 'always on' [3]. The internet has also created rules for multiple self-presentations and interactivity, and a specific communicative space with its own communication logic. The amount of information surrounding the individual has grown critically, access has been simplified and the types and means of obtaining it have changed. The internet also produces the need and/or the ability to obtain new amounts of information, including raw data, and use a fundamentally new methodology for aggregating, storing and processing this data (Big Data). Due to new volumes of information and communication, to which an individual is permanently connected or even tied, the structure of identities has become more complicated: an individual can simultaneously have several identities: national, cultural and ideological [29].

Because of all these influences, the man of 'the Guttenberg galaxy' in the 21st century is practically crowded out by the man of 'the internet galaxy'. Namely, 'human informational', living in a 'global village', possessing informational consciousness, knowledgeable in digital culture, using information technologies and communicating with their help with the whole world, and experiencing tremendous pressure of information - including any misinformation where the truth does not differ from the fake, fake is like the truth and the 'village' is like the 'global theatre' (metaphor of McLuhan who means that the society more produce rather than perceive the information). Since the internet is both a global and national space, all these changes apply to all countries where at the state level the task to provide the population with the internet and to expand the internet coverage is set and implemented, but also reveals national specific characteristics. The globalized space of nation states, in turn, become a 'network state or network frontier' [26], for which criteria and concepts of physical geography are not suitable [17].

In the politics, the internet has the most significant impact, moreover, its influence is important 'in terms of long-term social changes' [Schroeder: 8]. Indeed, blogging became an integral component of the daily practices of the civic activists and political elites in different countries at the turn of the 21st century. Political movements, built on the opportunities offered by social networks and instant messengers, changed the political landscape at the beginning of the 21st century. The internet provides prospects for a fuller representation of the political interests of citizens, for discussion of the political agenda by the government and the public, produces new forms of civic interaction and new forms of political participation [11]. The internet is pushing the media towards greater differentiation, connecting people from above, including more active and targeted communication of elites with the masses, as well as providing more opportunities for participation in politics at the grassroots level. In addition to this, the internet destroys the existing mass media system in countries, defeating the print media and almost defeating television (according to statistics on news consumption and priority sources of information for different countries). It is difficult for traditional media to compete with such advantages of the internet as the ability to reach wider audience with quick and cheap dissemination of necessary information with an option of the effective feedback [7].

Such destruction of traditional mass media has serious political consequences, first of all, for the state, as it loses a reliable conductor of its own decisions and informational support, and has to rely on the completely unreliable and not loyal internet. New media have radically changed the state institutions, how the political leaders communicate with masses, the technologies and methods of conducting the electoral campaign, as well as the civic participation in politics. The dynamic development of social networks, which are becoming even more relevant means of political information and communication, cannot be predicted, and the unpredictability of this development has even more serious implications for politics. Political mobilization and political participation are increasingly linked to the internet and less and less in need of offline forms. Political parties and political organizations use two types of political mobilization and participation: online and offline, with the first in some cases being the only one. New online practices affect structure and the hierarchy of the political movement [24: 154], resources, coordination, information flow. Internet become the major institute of the political mobilization, covering even those countries where face-to-face communication is very important part of the national culture. In different countries of the world, the internet is a 'place and method of protest' - an institution for the opposition political spectrum, where social and political movements for which access to other political institutions and resources is denied, are crystallizes and developed. As history shows, such social and political movements are faster than the rest of society, in the mastering of the newest technologies of their time, adopting their potential. Network social movements, as well as other forms of political participation with the help of the internet, neglect physical territories and borders and become cross-regional and transnational in nature.

The technical ability to overcome attempts to censor the internet means that society has equal opportunities to get acquainted with opposing points of view. However, the internet multiplies the number of points of view so that it makes it difficult to choose. On the one hand, the communicative medium created by the internet, as well as the tradition of the constant connection of the individual to the exchange of communication and information with each other, makes it possible to find like-minded people to discuss this or that information with them. This can facilitate self-selection between the truth and the fake among information flows and various points of view, as well as help to choose the correct interpretation from a collective point of view. The internet is the only one of all sources of information that can quickly expose a fake (and just as quickly throw it into a public field). Consequently, the internet can function as a 'public sphere', which appears to be a critical forum where people come together to freely discuss vital issues for society and work out jointly acceptable solutions (J. Habermas). On the other hand, because of the internet, which does not limit the circulation of content and makes any point of view visible, including radical and extremist, it is possible to choose the radical and extremist point of view as the only correct one and consolidate the individuals around it. These consolidations around different ideas, communications arising on the internet are difficult to control, prevent or stop, since the internet creates an autonomous space for production and exchange of information and communication from government and any other control. The principle of protecting content generated on the internet is inherent in the internet, and new social networks, instant messengers, and filter hackers are created faster than repressive measures and structures designed to restrict this freedom. The internet has transformed the space of political communications so much that it is impossible to control all the institutions, channels and content of communication, as 'the network structures of communication emerging in politics, supported by appropriate electronic-technical devices like the internet, are fundamentally not amenable to information control' [33: 7].

3 Discussion

Thus, the internet introduces into the political space the set of the changes. What theories do we have in the political science to describe these changes?

Influence, role, effects, special significance of the internet in the political space are analyzed with the help of several theoretical approaches. Considering which of them were proposed by researchers to understand the influence of the internet on the political space in the historical continuum, we can distinguish several stages of their development, as well as directions characteristic of the western and non-western (Russia as an example) theoretical approaches.

Western scientists began to study the role of the internet in the political space from the standpoint of the theory of democratization and the habermasian theory of the public sphere and introduced the understanding of the internet as the public sphere of the deliberative democracy which forms the deliberative discussion platform, providing equal access for free discussion of informational occasions, helping to find those who experience similar emotions or similar attitude to a particular informational subject and ready to discuss this or that social and political problem and the way to solve it (Dahlgren; Janssen and Raphaël; Papacharissi; Sinekopova – see more names in [25]). The idea of the internet as a public sphere was further transformed into the idea of the internet as a sphere of 'digital democracy' (Bimber, Blumber and Gurevitch, Iosifidis & Wheeler, Loader, see more in [12]) or 'internet democracy', more precisely, user-generated democracy. With such a democracy, the drivers of democratic transformations are the internet users united in the networks or social groups. This form of democracy is also called 'network democracy' or 'e-democracy' ('e-participation') [4, 5, 10, 30].

All these theories underline the ability of the internet to expand political liberalism and pluralism. Multiplying the number of information and communication fields to which an individual is simultaneously connected, equal access to information and communication for all members of society can develop a plurality of views, and also contribute to the fact that an individual can be a carrier of different political identities. According to the theory of the connection of political stability and cross political identities (S. Lipset], the presence of several political identities and pluralism of political views fosters tolerance. Tolerance, in turn, leads to a decrease in aggression in society, and, consequently, to the political stability of society. In this sense, the internet, strengthening political pluralism and helping individuals to acquire several identities, can function as a 'liberalizer' and 'democratizer' in relation to the political regime. However, these are only opportunities that individuals are free to use or neglect. Therefore, the degree in which this potential of the internet is used depends on the specific society. Moreover, the more the internet coverage becomes widespread, the less one can hope that the influence of the internet will necessarily lead to the victory of the deliberative democracy, which traditionally is carried by liberal-oriented intellectual elites.

At the same time, the internet brings exactly the opposite effect to the development of political liberalism and pluralism. It creates effective opportunities for the authorities to control and manipulate them. Both possibilities are very limited and are not used quite efficiently, but in countries with different political regimes from democracy to authoritarianism they are actively used. The internet also contributes to the emergence of other adverse effects that are undesirable for the interests of various political actors. For example, the internet can lead to political fragmentation, in which ideological opponents never communicate with each other, being united on the internet only with like-minded people. This feature, on the American material, were firstly mentioned by S.J. Rodgers; Wilhelm [6], and has been constantly proved by C. Sunstein in all his works (see the latest [34]).

The internet can also contribute to the emergence of 'network individualism' [38]. Fragmentation can lead to the transformation of the internet into a 'zone of digital war' [18]; which means that the internet is also approached with the theoretical framework of the theory of information wars, in which the internet has become a new and especially dangerous 'weapon'. This theoretical approach together with the point of view of the theory of information wars is actively developed in Russian works on the role of the internet in politics [19]. Other Russian researchers associate the internet with the emergence of a 'special type of political system - 'plurarchy' [20: 203] which is characterized by 'the atomization of political actors who are not able to coordinate the actions and decisions of each other. Such coordination is carried out by moderators or nodal points ('hubs') of this network, which throw in certain content, direct the discussion, i.e., control the political process in the network. Naturally, this state of affairs turns out to be significantly different from the idea of free and sovereign will of the citizens '[ibid].

At the same time, attention is being paid to the new risks for the political system produced by the internet and the inability to control the content that is generated and circulates on the internet. For example, it is argued that the freedom to produce any meaning on the internet and the lack of control over the information impact 'give the process of legitimizing a political system an uncontrollable, spontaneous character due to the deep dynamics of the mentality' [36: 28]. Developing such theories, the researchers emphasize the manipulative potential of internet communication, especially strong because it is hidden under the declaration of freedom of choice and full informational openness of the network society, as well as repeatedly enhanced by large data that gave politicians additional knowledge about their electorate, and therefore help politicians more effectively manipulate the electorate. Thus, such a characteristic of the internet as 'deliberative', its freedom and lack of control, the possibility to deliver 'free and sovereign will of citizens' [20: 203] is called into question.

Another major approach is to understand internet as a new information and communication technology, under the influence of which various changes in the political space occur; or as a new space of political communication (G.L. Akopov, E.A. Markov, S.P. Potseluev, A.I. Solovyev, R. Denton and Woodvard GC; V. Eranti and M. Lonkila; R. Hayes; M. Innes; J. Kietzmann; C. Lampe; N. Luhmann; B. McNair; L. Scissors; A. Smock; D. Wohn; D. Wyld; A.L. Zhan).

M. Castells introduced the theoretical basis for another approach to the internet: as a network connecting individuals with internet communication networks and producing a special type of society - 'network society'. According to Castells, the internet also produced another political phenomenon: 'networked social movements', which 'grow from the acts of communication' [8]. The internet is understood as the reason for the formation and rapid development of the 'network society'. Such a society consists of networks connected by internet communication ('digital communication networks' [9] and gathers together to achieve political aims in form of the 'networked social movements' [ibid: 21]. M. Castells sees the fundamental difference between the 'internet galaxy' in that the entire social (including political) structure of society goes into such networks. The internet within this approach is understood as a network itself, which creates new rules, norms, forms of using information and communication, on which political movements entirely depend. Network social movements are of great research interest, in addition to M. Castells himself, also of F. Flanagin, J. Juris; C. Heldman, J. Thompson, R. Collins; D. Della Porta & M. Diani; H. Flam, D. King; J. Goodwin & J.M. Jasper; D. McAdam; A. Melucci; W.R. Neuman, G.E. Marcus, A.N. Cregler & M. Mackuen; D. Ost et al.

In Russia, the 'network approach' received theoretical and applied development in the works of G.L. Akopov, I.A. Bykov, Yu.V. Irkhin, A.V. Kurochkin and A.S. Sher-stobitov, I.V. Miroshnichenko, O.V. Mikhailova, N.A. Ryabchenko, L.V. Smor-gunov. Based on the approach, the researchers develop as the main subject the innovative political management in a networked society, a network form of government and the implementation of public policy, and the network strategies in political campaigns. In this version of the network approach, the internet is recognized not as the main factor in the formation and development of a network society, but as a tool or technology used in networks for communication between political institutions and civil society, or a form of interaction between civil society and the state alternative to the traditional one. At the same time, the critical importance of networks is emphasized, but the 'network approach' does not emphasize the critical and special significance of the internet, which cause the existence of networks and is itself a network.

In general, even though many important conclusions made about the role and place of the internet, as well as about the functions, elements, characteristics of the internet in the political sphere within the framework of these leading approaches to understanding the internet in politics (as the deliberative public sphere, as a new space of political communication, as a network space) the comparative analysis of the results obtained with their help has not been carried out. The next step has not been taken - the complexity of the evidences of the role of the internet in the political space is not structured and not systematized.

Moreover, the estimates of the role of the Internet in politics periodically range from cyber optimism to cyber pessimism and back [22]. By the second decade of the 21st century, academic discussions recognized that the impact of the Internet on political process and the political system is so complex that they should avoid extremes and dichotomy of 'positive/ negative' assessments [35]. Nevertheless, the dichotomy in the approaches to assessing the role of the Internet is still observed, and the role of the Internet in politics is constantly evaluated in a polar way: either as good or evil. There is also the alarmism of cybersceptics, inclined to exaggerate the threats and challenges associated with the effects of the Internet on the political sphere. Such alarmism is clearly manifested in the Russian tradition of research on the role of the internet in politics. However, the understanding of the internet as a new space of political communication, which is another leading direction in Russian studies of the role of the internet in the political space, relates to the concept of the public sphere, and thus shares the understanding of the possibilities of the internet to create space to express the free and sovereign will of citizens, at the same time autonomous from the state control.

The dichotomy, as well as an excessive focus on the threats that are associated with the internet, also leads far away from the task of comprehensively assessing the role and place of the internet in the political process. National specifics prevents the unification of theoretical approaches and generates ideological-dictated approaches. The attitude to the internet as an instrument, technology, form, space leads to an understanding of its role in the political space as secondary, auxiliary, decorative, as a background, and not as an actor in political space. Such a difference in assessments when using the same approach is because the western researchers, even when they study political situations in countries with regimes which are far from western ideas of democracy, approach the internet in politics as a phenomenon of the western system of developed democracy. Non-western researchers consider the national conditions of developing democracies or nondemocratic regimes in which the internet exists and which determine its functioning.

It is not a coincidence that the deliberation discourse is not popular in Russian studies of the role of the internet in the political sphere. Network social and political movements caused by the internet are also out of the academics' focus. Russian researchers are generally more cautious in their assessments of the leading role of the internet in political process, except for recognizing its large, in the opinion of some researchers, manipulative potential. It is much more popular in the Russian academic context in assessing the role of the internet to talk about the secondary importance of this role, secondary nature, complementarity, subordination of the internet in relation to political institutions and in political processes. For example, the expert discussion of the results of the study 'Institutional problems of mass politics: methodological and theoretical aspects' makes a verdict of the subordinated position of internet activity: 'Even recognizing that internet activity still retains a subordinate position in relation to social forms of participation, it is impossible not to take into account the qualitative transformation of the political space. And the essence of these transformations does not so much reduce the role of the traditional institutions of representation, as it changes the emphasis in their positioning' [11: 4]. Those concepts in which the role of the internet is defined as 'technology' and 'tool' are concepts that emphasize the auxiliary nature of the internet, but not the role of subject and actor.

This is a definite aberration, since those influences that the researchers distinguish, the role they describe, the effects that, in their opinion, bring the internet into the political space, the characteristics of the internet in the political space, which are noted in various studies, much deeper and wider than 'secondary', 'subordination', instrumental, decorative, and more of a determining character than instrumental, auxiliary and subordinate, which in these studies is attributed to the internet.

4 Conclusion

The above-mentioned approaches to the internet (as to the new space of political communication, as well as to the network space, or to the deliberative space) fail to describe the entire impact of the internet on the political space. They do not allow to summarize the role of the internet in the political space in details, look at them together, to structure and systematize them to see the specifics in the complex. Two leading Russian approaches to understanding the role of the internet in politics (as a new space of political communication and as a network space) develop independently of each other. Given the multidirectional effects of the internet on the political space, national and global specifics of this impact, as well as the rapid expansion of this impact, it is necessary to create a theoretical framework that should take into account all the impacts, all their specificities and analyze the functioning of the internet in the politic space dynamics. This task has not yet been undertaken.

Thus, critically rethinking the major in political science theories analysing the role of the internet in politics we can recognize them as inadequate to the current stage of the growing influence of the internet on the political space. This emphasise the importance of the task to create a macro-theory that considers leading political understanding of the role of the internet in politics, can also be transposed from the political space to another social sphere, can also be applicable to any national situation, allowing the escaping dichotomy and ideological bias dictated by the difference in political regimes in a particular country. The political space is wired in Russia and around the world, like any other social space. Therefore, such a theory should be suitable for any national situation.

References

1. A new generation of Internet users. Study the habits and behavior of Russian youth online. https://www.thinkwithgoogle.com/intl/ru-ru/insights-trends/user-insights/novoe-pokolenie-internet-polzovatelei-issledovanie-privychek-i-povedeniia-rossiiskoi-molodezhi-onlain/. Accessed 28 Apr 2018
2. Agur, C.: ICTs and education in developing countries: the case of India. In: Greenhow, C.H., Sonnevend, J.A.C. (eds.) Education and Social Media: Toward a Digital Future, pp. 61–78. MIT Press, Cambridge (2016)
3. Baron, N.S.: Always On: Language in an Online and Mobile World. Oxford University Press, Oxford (2008)
4. Benkler, Y.: The Wealth of Networks: How Social Production Transforms Markets and Freedom. Yale University Press, New Haven (2007)
5. Bennett, L.: Lifestyle politics and citizen-consumers: identity, communication and political action. In: Corner, J., Pels, D. (eds.) Media and the Restyling of Politics: Consumerism, Celebrity and Cynicism, pp. 137–150. Sage, London (2003)
6. Bijker, W.E., Hughes, T.P., Pinch, T.J.: The Social Construction of Technology Systems: New Directions in the Sociology and History of Technology. The MIT Press, Cambridge (2012)
7. Bykov, I.A.: Setevaia politicheskaia kommunikatsiia: teoriia, praktika i metody issledovaniia. SPbGU, Saint Petersburg (2013)

8. Castells, M.: The Internet Galaxy: Reflections on the Internet, Business, and Society. Oxford University Press, Oxford (2003)
9. Castells, M.: The Rise of the Network Society. The Information Age. Economy, Society, and Culture, vol. 1, 2nd edn with a New Preface edition. Wiley–Blackwell (2009)
10. Dahlgren, P.: Media and Political Engagement: Citizens, Communication and Democracy. Cambridge University Press, Cambridge (2009)
11. Expert discussion of the results of 'Institutional problems of mass politics: methodological and theoretical aspects' project (2016). http://www.isras.ru/files/File/publ/Patrushev_Expert_osuzhdenie_04_03_2015.pdf. Accessed 24 Dec 2018
12. Grachev, M.N.: Online-deliberatsiia: razrabotki, issledovaniia i practica. Politicheskaia nauka 1, 280–292 (2013)
13. Hine, C.h.: Ethnography for the Internet: Embedded, Embodied and Everyday. Bloomsbury Academic, New York (2015)
14. Hirshberg, P.: First the media, then us: how the internet changed the fundamental nature of the communication and its relationship with the audience. change: 19 key essays on how the internet is changing our lives (2014). https://www.bbvaopenmind.com/wp-content/uploads/2014/01/BBVA-OpenMind-Book-2014-DataSheet-Change.pdf. Accessed 28 Apr 2018
15. Internet in Russia. Dynamics of internet penetration. Winter of 2017–2018. https://fom.ru/SMI-i-internet/13999. Accessed 28 Apr 2018
16. Juris, J.: Networked social movements: the movement against corporate globalization. In: Castells, M. (ed.) The Network Society: A Cross-Cultural Perspective, pp. 341–362. Edward Elgar, Cheltenham (2004)
17. Kabanov, Y.: Information space as a new (geo) political space: the role and place of states. Comp. Policy 4, 54–59 (2015)
18. Karatgozianni, A.: Digital Cultures and the Politics of Emotion: Feelings, Affect and Techno-Logical Change. Palgrave Macmillan, New York (2012)
19. Kurban, A.V.: Structural model of online information network processes. Strateg. Commun. Bus. Politics 2, 76–84 (2016)
20. Kurochkin, A.V.: Social networks as an instrument of political mobilization: the danger of manipulation and the limits of democracy. Polit. Expertise: PolitEx 8(3), 200–207 (2012)
21. Livingstone, S.: The media-rich home: balancing public and private lives. In: Young People and New Media: Childhood and the Changing Media Environment. SAGE Publication Ltd, London (2002)
22. Loader, B.D., Mercea, D.: Networking democracy? social media innovations and participatory politics. Inf. Commun. Soc. 14(6), 757–769 (2011)
23. Mediascope. http://mediascope.net/services/media/media-audence/internet. Accessed 20 Nov 2018
24. Mercea, D.: Digital prefigurative participation: The entwinement of online communication and offline participation in protest events. New Media Soc. nms.sagcpub.com/content/14/1/153. https://doi.org/10.1177/1461444811429103
25. Misnikov, Y.: How to Read and Treat Online Public Discussions among Ordinary Citizens Beyond Political Mobilisation. Empirical Evidence from the Russian-Language Online Forum. Digital Icons: Studies in Russian, Eurasian and Central European New Media, vol. 7, pp. 1–37 (2012)
26. Morozova, E., Miroshnichenko, I., Ryabchenko, N.: Frontier of the network society. World Econ. Int. Relat. 2(60), 83–97 (2016)
27. Murthy, D.: Towards a sociological understanding of social media: theorizing Twitter. Sociology 46, 1059–1073 (2012)

28. Networked Readiness Index. The Global Information Technology Report» for World Economic Forum (2016). http://reports.weforum.org/global-information-technology-report-2016/networked-readiness-index/. Accessed 20 Nov 2017

29. Nikiporets-Takigawa, G.: Digital debates on Soviet memory in the national identity construction of post-Soviet migrants. In: Smith, S., Opitz, C. (eds.) Negotiating Linguistic, Cultural and Social Identities in the Post-Soviet World Peter Lang, pp. 163–181, Bern (2013)

30. Oudshoorn, N., Pinch, T., Bijker, W.E., et al.: How Users Matter (Inside Technology): The Co-Construction of Users and Technology. MIT Press, Cambridge (2005)

31. Schroeder, R.: Social Theory After the Internet: Media, Technology, and Globalization. UCL Press, London (2018)

32. Social networks in 2018. https://www.web-canape.ru/business/socialnye-seti-v-2018-godu-globalnoe-issledovanie/. Accessed 06 Dec 2018

33. Soloviev, A.I. Political communication: to the problem of theoretical identification. Polis.-2002, no. 3, p. 5–18 (2002)

34. Sunstein, C.: #Republic. Divided Democracy in the Age of Social Media. Princeton University Press (2017)

35. The Oxford Handbook of the Internet Studies. Oxford University Press, Oxford (2013)

36. Timermanis, I.E., Evseeva, L.I., Shipunova, O.D.: Kommunikativnoe prostranstvo legitimatsii politicheskoi sistemy v usloviiach setevogo obshchestva. In: Communicative space of legitimization of the political system in the conditions of a network society. Vestnik RSUH, vol. 6, pp. 26–36 (2015)

37. Top 20 Countries - Internet Users 2018. https://www.internetworldstats.com/top20.htm. Accessed 17 Mar 2018

38. Wellman, B.: Physical pace and cyber place: the rise of networked individualism. Int. J. Urban Reg. Res. 25(2), 227–252 (2001)

The Impact of Open Government
on the Quality of Governance:
Empirical Analysis

Nicole Fuks and Yury Kabanov[(⊠)]

National Research University Higher School of Economics,
St. Petersburg, Russia
nikol.fuks@gmail.com, ykabanov@hse.ru

Abstract. The paper aims at contributing to the debate on whether open government impacts the quality of governance, and if so, identify the causal mechanisms that might be evident to support this impact. Using structural equation modeling, we test the sample of country-level data from 2014 to 2017, assessing the direct effect of open government on the government effectiveness, as well as its indirect effect via the levels of democracy and corruption. Our analysis confirms that open government may have positive effects on the quality of governance, but this effect is moderated by the level of corruption in a country.

Keywords: Open government · Governance · Government effectiveness · Public policy · Structural equation modeling

1 Introduction

Open government, like other ICT–enabled public sector innovations, is normatively meant to lead to a more democratic society, where citizens are empowered to control bureaucracy and participate in public policy-making [1]. Yet, the concept itself is rather multifaceted, and its possible impacts are diverse and currently formulated usually as normative assumptions. According to Meijer et al. transparency (*vision*) and participation (*voice*), being the key components of open government, may have both positive and negative implications to politics and decision–making [2]. Such ambiguity is further complicated by the lack of quantitative empirical analysis and the general immaturity of the field: as revealed by Ignacio Criado et al. open government studies are still dominated by "exploratory-descriptive" and "normative" research [3].

Our paper aims at contributing to the discussion on possible effects of open government with an empirical statistical analysis, focused on the quality of governance. Using the data from the World Justice Project, World Bank and other relevant sources, we conduct structural equation modeling (SEM) to estimate direct and indirect effects of open government on the quality of governance, understood as government effectiveness, and to test existing theoretical assumptions on the role open government plays in increasing democracy and reducing corruption.

The paper is structured as follows. Firstly, we provide a literature review, highlighting the framework and hypotheses of the research. Secondly, we explain the

© Springer Nature Switzerland AG 2020
A. Chugunov et al. (Eds.): EGOSE 2019, CCIS 1135, pp. 116–124, 2020.
https://doi.org/10.1007/978-3-030-39296-3_9

design of the empirical study. Thirdly, we present the results of the study, followed by the discussion of findings and limitations, as well as the outline of some future steps.

2   Open Government Effects: Review and Framework

The major problem arising with quantitative open government research is that of definition and the operationalization of the concept. While the idea of government openness had existed quite long before, information technologies and new solutions (e.g. open data) gave a new impetus for its spread – as a policy and as a trendy term – throughout the globe [3, 4]. Though it is fundamentally about *transparency, participation* and *collaboration*, as was proclaimed by B. Obama in his Open Government Initiative of 2009,[1] and international institutions like the *Open Government Partnership*[2] and the *OECD* [5] seek to establish a sort of common approach, researchers and policy-makers tend to define the concept differently, or prioritize its particular dimensions in different ways [6]. In the case of open government data, several comparative studies have found a substantial variety of policy strategies across the polities [7, 8].

As the concept is hard to grasp in its entirety, scholars usually explore its certain aspects and test their impact on democracy or good governance. For instance, a popular topic is transparency, which is found to be important for government fiscal effectiveness [9] or corruption reduction [10], although the effect is usually nuanced and moderated by other factors. While some authors claim that transparency is a cornerstone of an effective democratic governance [12–14], others warn about possible shortcomings of executive capacity and decrease in citizens' confidence in authorities [11, 15, 16]. Another subject of research is the impact of open government data, which is theorized in its application to transparency, public engagement, economic growth, but the empirical results are usually controversial [17, 18].

In the paper we attempt to take a more holistic view on open government, following Meijer et al. as a synthesis of *vision* and *voice*, where "citizens can monitor and influence government processes through access to government information and access to decision-making arenas" [2, p. 13]. Such a complex definition not only embraces two important dimensions of open government (information and participation), but also corresponds to the approach of the World Justice Project (WJP), assessing government openness according to such criteria as *publicized laws and government data, right to information, civic participation,* and *complaint mechanisms.*[3] It has already been successfully utilized in analyzing the impacts of open government: Lee et al. used WJP Open Government Index to assess the influence of openness on economic prosperity, and found its positive impact via the rule of law and control of corruption as important mediating variables [19].

---

[1] Open Government Directive. 8.12.2009. URL: https://obamawhitehouse.archives.gov/open/documents/open-government-directive.

[2] https://www.opengovpartnership.org/.

[3] https://worldjusticeproject.org/our-work/research-and-data/wjp-rule-law-index-2019.

Following the argument and methodological approach of Lee et al. [19], we seek to find the paths open government may contribute to the quality of governance, which may be direct and indirect. As for the latter, two possible lines of thought derive from the literature. The first one is more *voice*-based and implies that new ICT tools provide new dynamics of governance, leading to greater democratization [20], and open government here is becoming a platform of citizen-government communication, ensuring the democratic governance through information provision and participation [21].

Another path is more *vision*-based. Access to the government data is vital for ensuring transparency and responsibility, as well as ensuring citizens' confidence in government [13]. Some authors claim that open government opens a window of information for citizens about the political decision-making process, thereby strengthening the accountability of politicians [22] and has potential to reduce corruption by stimulating public control [13].

Such paths can be understood twofold. On the one hand, they are meant to be practical mechanisms of open government policy implementation: when open government strategy is in action, citizens acquire more opportunities to participate, which leads to a more democratic political system, and get information to control the government, which leads to the reduction of corruption. Both outcomes are thus positive for the quality of governance. On the other hand, high levels of democracy and low corruption rates can be viewed as necessary conditions that facilitate the implementation of open government: however sophisticated an open government policy is, it is hard to expect visible outcomes for good governance, unless conditions for its implementation are more or less appropriate.

In this regards, we hypothesize that along the *direct effect*, open government may lead to the quality of government via two major paths: through political system democratization due to the increase of public participation (*H1*) and through the reduction of the level of corruption due to government transparency and public access to government information (*H2*). The theoretical model of the study is presented on Fig. 1, which is further statistically tested using the SEM.

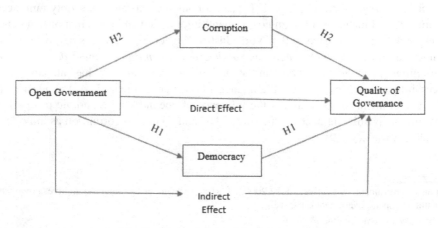

Fig. 1. Theoretical model of the research

3 Data and Methods

In our analysis we use the SEM as a method to examine not only the direct effects, but also the impact of moderating variables. We perform a path analysis, calculating the path coefficients, showing the direction of association between the variables (direct, if the number is positive and inverse, if the number is negative), standard error (SE), p-value, reflecting the strength of association, as well as standardized regression coefficients (standardized regression weights), looking at which it is possible to draw conclusions about the results of the analysis. The analysis is done using R and SPSS AMOS software.

Our dependent variable is the quality of governance, which is operationalized using the *Government Effectiveness* score – a sub-index of the World Governance Indicators (WGI) by the World Bank.[4] This sub-index has been chosen as a relevant proxy to assess the quality of bureaucracy and public policy.

Our independent variable derives from the WJP Rule of Law Index, in particular the *Open Government* score. This sub-index includes four dimensions: *government bills and government data, the right to information, civil participation and complaint mechanisms.*[5] Also two mediated variables are used: *Democracy* corresponds to our first hypothesis and is operationalized using the Freedom in the World data by the Freedom House. The higher the score, the more democratic a country is.[6] To test the second hypothesis about *Corruption* we use the data from the Corruption Perception Index by Transparency International, where countries with lower levels of corruption perception have lower index scores.[7] Due to the data availability, our sample is limited to 2014–2017, with 311 valid country-year observations with full data. Independent variables are taken with a one year-lag to highlight the causality effects. The descriptive statistics is given in Table 1.

Table 1. Descriptive statistics of the variables

Variable	Code	Number of cases	Minimum	Maximum	Mean	Std. Deviation
Quality of governance	WGI_GE	328	−1.6700	2.2000	0.1526	0.8947272
Open government	OGI	328	0.2300	0.8800	0.5447	0.1398925
Democracy	FIW	328	3.00	100.00	66.20	25.53986
Corruption	CPI	311	11.00	92.00	45.87	19,632

---

[4] https://info.worldbank.org/governance/wgi/#home, last access 2019/03/05.

[5] https://worldjusticeproject.org/our-work/research-and-data/wjp-rule-law-index-2019.

[6] https://freedomhouse.org/report/freedom-world/freedom-world-2019.

[7] https://www.transparency.org/research/cpi/overview.

4 Results of the Analysis

Firstly, we ran an exploratory correlation analysis to estimate the association between the variables (Table 2). The results confirm that all variables correlate positively and significantly with each other, proving the relevance of the hypotheses drawn. At the same time, the correlation coefficients are quite high and call for cautiousness in further interpretation of findings due to the multicollinearity problem. The latter is quite common for the WGI and similar aggregate measurements, as they overlap and are usually hardly discernable from each other [23].

Table 2. Results of the pearson correlation analysis

	WGI_GE	OGI	FIW	CPI
WGI_GE	–	,775** (328)	,609** (328)	,895** (311)
OGI	,775** (328)	–	,764** (328)	,827** (311)
FIW	,609** (328)	,764** (328)	–	,696** (311)
CPI	,895** (311)	,827** (311)	,696** (311)	–

Note: ** - correlation is significant at the 0,01 level. Number of cases is in parentheses.

Secondly, we performed the SEM in the version of the Maximum Likelihood Path analysis to estimate direct and indirect effects between the variables. The general overview of the goodness of fit of the model is presented in Table 3. For the indicated degrees of freedom and p-value, the chi-square value for accepting the null hypothesis should be approximately 3,84. In our model the value is higher (4,318), hence we may reject the assumption that the distribution of the real data does not differ from the hypothetical distribution and, therefore, we can further use it for interpretation. Also, to estimate the total value of the model from a statistical point of view, one can refer to the RMSEA parameter, which should be from 0.5 to 0.8 in order for the model to be valuable for analysis. The resulting value is approximately 0.6, which allows us to further use the results of the analysis of this model for interpretation.

Table 3. Goodness of the model fit

Fit statistic	Value
Chi-Square	4,318
Degrees of Freedom	1
Probability Level (p-value)	0,41
RMSEA	0,595

The coefficients obtained from the path analysis are presented on Fig. 2 and Table 4. Several conclusions may be drawn from the output. The direct effect of open government on the quality of governance is not significant, thus rejecting the assumption of direct influence. At the same time, while open government positively and significantly affects the level of corruption (in countries with the higher rate of open government, the level of perceived corruption is lower), and the latter positively affects the quality of governance. Finally, while open government has a positive association with the level of democracy, there is no significant relationship between democracy and the quality of government in this model.

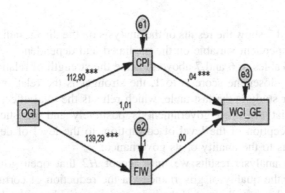

Fig. 2. Path-analysis for model. Note: *** - statistically significant at the level of 0.001.

Table 4. Path analysis results for model. Note: *** - statistically significant at the level of 0.001.

Path	Estimate	S. E.	C. R.	P (p-value)	Standardized regression weights
CPI <— OGI	112, 903	4,401	25,652	***	0,821
FIW <— OGI	139, 291	6,500	21,429	***	0,764
WGI_GE <— CPI	0,036	0,002	17,933	***	0,785
WGI_GE <— FIW	−0,001	0,001	−0,962	0,336	−0,037
WGI_GE <— OGI	1,015	0,338	3,005	0,003	0,159

Table 5. Calculation of standardized direct effect of variables from the model

Standardized direct effect	OGI	FIW	CPI
FIW	0,764	0,000	0,000
CPI	0,821	0,000	0,000
WGI_GE	0,159	−0,037	0,785

Table 6. Calculation of standardized indirect effect of variables from the model

Standardized indirect effect	OGI	FIW	CPI
FIW	0,000	0,000	0,000
CPI	0,000	0,000	0,000
WGI_GE	0,616	0,000	0,000

Table 7. Calculation of standardized total effect of variables from model

Standardized total effect	OGI	FIW	CPI
FIW	0.764	0.000	0.000
CPI	0.821	0.000	0.000
WGI_GE	0.775	−0.037	0.785

Tables 5, 6 and 7 show the results of the analysis on the direct, indirect and general effects of the independent variable on the mediated and dependent.

The score in Tables 5, 6 and 7 above indicate the strength of relationship between the variables: the closer the score is to 1, the stronger is the relationship. The most interesting for our study is the last table, which reflects the total effect. The presented numbers show that the open government is positively and statistically significant related to the perception of the level of corruption, to the level of democracy in the country, as well as to the quality of its governance.

Based on the analysis results we may accept *H2* that open government has a positive effect on the quality of governance via the reduction of corruption, and it is worth noting that the overall effect of the independent variable on the dependent one is quite high (0,775). At the same time, we cannot accept *H1* regarding the positive impact of open government on the quality of government through increasing democracy, since the link is not statistically significant.

5   Discussion

Based on the preliminary analysis we carried out, several conclusions can be drawn. First of all, open government, taken holistically as a combination of information openness and citizen participation, may indeed be considered important for the quality of governance, which corresponds to theoretical expectations. However, this effect is not automatic. Like in the research by Lee et al. when open government did not show a significant direct effect on economic prosperity [19], our analysis has shown that the effect is moderated by other factors. In our case, the corruption reduction has proved to be the path that links government openness and governance quality: countries that adhere to more openness tend to have less corruption (at least on the level of perceptions), which at the same time leads to the increase in government effectiveness. Similarly, we could not confirm our fist hypothesis that openness is linked to quality of government via democracy, though the latter correlates significantly with the open government. This may be an artifact of analysis, but at the same time might be explained by the predominance of *vision* rather than *voice* in open government initiatives. This disbalance was revealed previously [2], and while scholars have recently started to draw more attention to participation issues [3], for decision-makers in many countries, increasing transparency remains the key priority of the open government policy [5, p. 38].

The presented research has several limitations. The first one lies in the data and method employed. Due to the limited data availability, the time period and the range of countries under analysis is limited, and the use of aggregate indices can give only a very basic overview with possible statistical problems (e.g. multicollinearity). Hence, further rigorous statistical analysis is needed to encompass more variables and to enlarge the sample. Qualitative and mixed-method empirical research can also help to find a more nuanced relationship between the observed concepts. The second limitation is the issue of causality: while our model suggests that open government impacts the quality of government and other variables, the causality may also be reversed, as these are more corruption-free and effective democracies that are more eager to implement open government innovations. The problem of causality should also be further addressed on theoretical and empirical levels.

6 Conclusion

Open government research remains a maturing field [3], and further empirical research is needed to test whether its normative implications towards democracy and good governance are supported by evidence. Our study presents an attempt of such research, and it can be generally concluded that open government may impact the increase of the governance quality in terms of effectiveness. At the same time, it has been shown that the relationship between the variables is rather indirect and moderated by other variables (in our case – the level of corruption), which convert published information and citizens engagement facilities into visible governance-related effects. While this finding is in line with previous studies and theoretical expectations, further research is needed to expand the sample and encompass more explanatory models.

Acknowledgement. The research is a part of the project "Strategies and mechanisms of stability in multilevel political systems" within the HSE Program of Fundamental Studies (2019).

References

1. Hansson, K., Belkacem, K., Ekenberg, L.: Open government and democracy: a research review. Soc. Sci. Comput. Rev. **33**(5), 540–555 (2015)
2. Meijer, A.J., Curtin, D., Hillebrandt, M.: Open government: connecting vision and voice. Int. Rev. Adm. Sci. **78**(1), 10–29 (2012)
3. Ignacio Criado, J., Ruvalcaba-Gómez, E.A., Valenzuela-Mendoza, R.: Revisiting the open government phenomenon. a meta-analysis of the international literature. eJournal eDemocracy Open Gov. **10**(1), 50–81 (2018)
4. Yu, H., Robinson, D.G.: The new ambiguity of open government. UCLA L. Rev. Discourse **59**, 178–208 (2011)
5. OECD: Open Government: The Global Context and the Way Forward. OECD Publishing, Paris (2016). https://doi.org/10.1787/9789264268104-en
6. Ruvalcaba-Gomez, E.A., Ignacio Criado, J., Gil-Garcia, J.R.: Discussing open government as a concept: a comparison between the perceptions of public managers and current academic debate. In: Proceedings of the 19th Annual International Conference on Digital Government Research: Governance in the Data Age, Delft, The Netherlands. ACM (2018). https://doi.org/10.1145/3209281.3209320

7. Davies, T.: Open Data Policies and Practice: An International Comparison. SSRN (2014). https://ssrn.com/abstract=2492520
8. Zuiderwijk, A., Janssen, M.: Open data policies, their implementation and impact: a framework for comparison. Gov. Inf. Q. **31**(1), 17–29 (2014)
9. Montes, G.C., Bastos, J.C.A., de Oliveira, A.J.: Fiscal transparency, government effectiveness and government spending efficiency: some international evidence based on panel data approach. Econ. Model. **79**, 211–225 (2019)
10. Lindstedt, C., Naurin, D.: Transparency is not enough: making transparency effective in reducing corruption. Int. Polit. Sci. Rev. **31**(3), 301–322 (2010)
11. Grimmelikhuijsen, S.G., Meijer, A.J.: Effects of transparency on the perceived trustworthiness of a government organization: evidence from an online experiment. J. Public Adm. Res. Theory **24**(1), 137–157 (2012)
12. Brin, D.: The transparent society. Harvard J. Law Technol. **12**(2), 370–385 (1999)
13. Bertot, J.C., Jaeger, P.T., Grimes, J.M.: Using ICTs to create a culture of transparency: E-government and social media as openness and anti-corruption tools for societies. Gov. Inf. Q. **27**(3), 264–271 (2010)
14. Ganapati, S., Reddick, C.: The use of ICT for open government in US municipalities: perceptions of chief administrative officers. Public Perform. Manage. Rev. **37**(3), 365–387 (2014)
15. Halachmi, A., Greiling, D.: Transparency, e-government, and accountability: some issues and considerations. Public Perform. Manage. Rev. **36**(4), 562–584 (2013)
16. Etzioni, A.: Is transparency the best disinfectant? J. Polit. Philos. **18**(4), 389–404 (2010)
17. Ruijer, E.H., Martinius, E.: Researching the democratic impact of open government data: a systematic literature review. Inf. Polity **22**(4), 233–250 (2017)
18. Virkar, S., Pereira, G.V.: Exploring open data state-of-the-art: a review of the social, economic and political impacts. In: Parycek, P., et al. (ed.) Electronic Government. EGOV 2018. LNCS, vol. 11020, pp. 196–207. Springer, Cham (2018). https://doi.org/10.1007/978-3-319-98690-6_17
19. Lee, S.Y., Díaz-Puente, J.M., Martin, S.: The contribution of open government to prosperity of society. Int. J. Public Adm. **42**(2), 144–157 (2019)
20. Ignacio Criado, J., Sandoval-Almazan, R., Gil-Garcia, J.R.: Government innovation through social media. Gov. Inf. Q. **30**(4), 319–326 (2013)
21. Dervin, B.: Information↔ democracy: an examination of underlying assumptions. J. Am. Soc. Inf. Sci. **45**(6), 369–385 (1994)
22. Janssen, M., van den Hoven, J.: Big and Open Linked Data (BOLD) in government: A challenge to transparency and privacy? (2015)
23. Langbein, L., Knack, S.: The worldwide governance indicators: Six, one, or none? J. Dev. Stud. **46**(2), 350–370 (2010)

Gamification as a Trend in the Development of Civic and Political Participation

Olga Sergeyeva[1]([✉]) [iD], Elena Bogomiagkova[1] [iD],
Ekaterina Orekh[1] [iD], and Natalia Kolesnik[2] [iD]

[1] St Petersburg University, Smolnogo st. 1/3 Entrance 9, St. Petersburg, Russia
o.v.sergeyeva@spbu.ru
[2] Sociological Institute of the RAS, a Branch of the FCTAS of the RAS,
7 Krasnoarmeyskaya st. 25, St. Petersburg, Russia

Abstract. The paper analyzes the methods of gamification in the practices of civic and political participation and it identifies research questions about the problems and prospects of this trend of social inclusion. Gamification creates a new experience of political actors, be it a leader, a political consultant or a representative of the masses; a review of the research allows us to clarify the actual "growth points" of social analytics of gamification. Particular attention is paid to cases related to game mechanics of urban participation, immersive journalism and the use of digital resources by political technologists in election campaigns. The analysis of the scientific discussion about urban participatory democracy revealed that the success of these practices is influenced not only by political will of the coordination potential of the local social structure but also by autonomy and financial capabilities of a political organization interested in civil participation and the design of the participation process. The possible examples of immersive journalism and its gamified product, newsgames, in Russian realities are such information resources as "Lentach" and "Meduza". New digital products are actively used by politicians and political technologists at the federal and regional levels. In conclusion, the authors discussed the phenomena of interpassivity.

Keywords: Digital media · Gamification · Participatory culture · Digital engagement · Political alienation · Participatory Budgeting · Newsgames

1 Introduction

Transforming impact of digital media can be seen, among other things, in new forms of civic and political participation. Interactive media embodied in miniature gadgets allows changing the mechanism of citizen mobilization. There is intensively developing a new media trend - gamification or the use of game elements (points, badges, virtual currencies, levels and progress indicators) to motivate participants in social and political interactions, to hold their attention and interest. Political tacticians hope that gamification can withstand political absenteeism, unwillingness to participate in political issues, fatigue, and political frustration.

© Springer Nature Switzerland AG 2020
A. Chugunov et al. (Eds.): EGOSE 2019, CCIS 1135, pp. 125–137, 2020.
https://doi.org/10.1007/978-3-030-39296-3_10

Even though the stimulation of social activity with the help of game elements - ratings, points, awards - existed in social organizations of past time, a real turn towards gamification became possible thanks to the variety of "digital footprints" that accompany most of the actions of a today's user. Due to the global infrastructure of computer networks, "digital footprints" can be converted into points, create activity leader lists, thereby encouraging some actions and restricting others. Thus, by supporting gamification, digital media can form behavioral responses, mobilize a person through the loyalty of the organization where, for example, he scored more points.

Observing the genesis of game projects in the political sphere is an essential subject of critical social analysis because it gives us information about changes in the engagement institutes. Gamification creates a new experience of political actors, whether leader or an average person. Scientific knowledge of gamification in the spheres of politics and civil society lags far behind the spheres of the economy, organization communications, and education. The experience of gamification analytics available from game studies whose thesaurus effectively combines the languages of IT specialists and residents of cultural studies is not systematized enough. Consequently, the article aim is to provide an overview of gamification directions in the practice of civic and political participation, based on which to put questions about the problems and prospects of this trend of social involvement. We attributed the gamification directions to activities of the main political actors, which traditionally include the state, parties, citizens, and the media. We also sought to identify the process in which the game elements were introduced. The logic of our overview of gamification cases is shown in the following diagram (see Fig. 1):

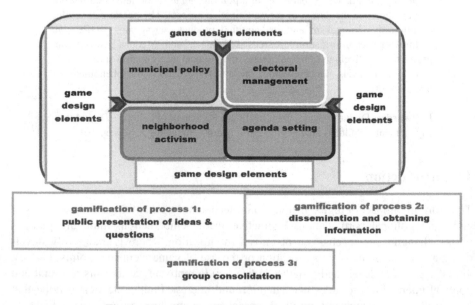

Fig. 1. Visualization of gamification trends in politics

2   Literature Review

The term "gamification" originated in the environment of IT developers and was taken up by philosophers and social scientists. The first mentions of gamification in the scientific bases Scopus and Web of Science relate to 2011. In 2011 in the Russian eLibrary, the term "gamification" is referred in the full texts of two articles only. However, in 2012, Russian publications are containing this term in the title, annotations or keywords. It is now clear that for nearly a decade, an interdisciplinary research field is developing, the focus of which is the manifestation of gamification in various public spheres.

So far, the authors have been competing in their attempts to define gamification, and operating with this concept fluctuates between two primary meanings. First, gamification relates to the widespread adoption and institutionalization of computer games, which affect the everyday life experience and interactions. Secondly, it is considered as the use of game elements (points, badges, virtual currencies, levels and indicators of progress) to motivate participants of any action, increase their activity and retain attention and interest. Researcher and game designer S. Deterding stresses that gamification is not a participation in games, but only some entertainment elements embedded in other social contexts to make non-game products, services or applications more motivating and/or attractive to use [4].

Much progress in the study of gamification practices was made in the areas of marketing and organizational communications. The first books on gamification, "Game-Based Marketing" and "Gamification by Design" by Zichermann were published in 2010 and 2011 [23, 24]. At that time, there was already a practical implementation of the principles of gamification in the form of the Saleforce platform, created in 2007 by "Bunchball" (founded in 2005). In 2010, "Badgeville", which also specializes in software that gamifies business processes, have begun to work. It is these processes associated with the economy - labor, personnel management, consumer behavior - today demonstrate approbation of gamification strategies and theoretical elaboration of these innovations.

The works analyzing the specifics of gamification of political interactions rely a lot on ideas about participatory culture. Digital participation arose where the roles of information users and information creators are intertwined: Web 2.0 gives users a platform for civic expression. Joint games also become such areas [18].

Crowdsourcing is another concept explaining the nature of the policy field in connection with gamification. Crowdsourcing means "transferring work to the crowd," and it is closely related to the idea of a "collective mind" that supports an egalitarian society. Usually, gamers individually seek to a goal, while crowdsourcing unites all this human power to solve one particular problem. According to ideas of well-known media analysts Bogost, Ferrari, and Schweizer gamification of journalism is the case of political crowdsourcing [2]. On the examples of "Wired magazine" projects, they explain the effects of interactive game models, in which many citizens participate, who can offer solutions to the topical issues of current politics.

In addition to the above, it can be stated that the academic vision of policy field gamification has two epistemological branches - positive and critical. The first is presented, for example, in the works of game developer and researcher J. McGonigal. In her book "Reality is Broken: Why Games Make Us Better and How They Can Change the World" she explores the role of games in empowering social and political participation in societies in which people are tired of aggressive, annoying, direct coercion and engagement. Game applications are, in her opinion, the system of "fixing broken reality" [10]. If computer games were first assessed as a way to escapism, then McGonigal explains the participatory game resources with examples, trying to prove that the connections between people do not disappear, but they are regrouping (or, as she writes, "reinventing").

Critical position on the gamification of the policy field denotes the developing trend as libertarian paternalism. Libertarian paternalism implies, for example, that the state gives citizens the freedom to choose, but introduces rules for a limited number of options. People should feel free, but their behavior is regulated. This principle is known to all gamers: the available choice is somewhat limited in most computer games, but with these restrictions, some do good deeds, and some do wrong [16]. Participants can choose only those options that are provided to them. Feature options are embedded in a carefully built selection architecture. Critics of gamification see in it a method aimed not at changing the ideas of a person, but a means of controlling visible behavior. The computer game researcher Bogost expresses bright polemical judgments: gamification is a means of exploitation, perversion, and simplification of the game medium, created by marketers and big business for easy gain [3].

A literature review allows clarifying the current "growth points" of social analytics of gamification. Political issues worked out much less representatively than economic. There is no systematization of gamification cases in the field of politics, and this is important for considering the positive and negative effects.

3   Game Mechanics of Citizen Participation

Disappointment in politics and civil structures, expressed in absenteeism, diminished interest in cooperation and collaboration with neighbors and colleagues, and the avoidance of political news are all global processes. In this context, the tools for increasing the motivation with which the political elites (both governing and opposition), civic activists of any movements try to interest and mobilize citizens for their support to become especially in demand. Political actors view the use of gaming principles and technical resources of digital media as a super strategy to engage.

The level of local policy shows the steadiest trend of gamification. A prime example is a movement of "Participatory Budgeting in Your City," which implies the joint decision of citizens on how to spend public money with the maximum benefit for the local community. Authors analyzing contemporary participatory democracy attribute this practice of budget formation to the number of the most advanced municipal innovations, emphasizing two of its essential characteristics: (1) people intervene in a strategic scope of the power - they begin to control the money; (2) this practice breaks the standards of non-participatory culture that are already entrenched in Western societies and induces new methods of collective action [1, 12, 13].

The summing up of the national examples of Participatory Budgeting in European countries (Spain, Slovakia, Estonia, Germany [8, 9]) in the USA, Canada [17], and Brazil [20] allows us to characterize clearly which game elements are used to activate citizens. We can say that in the game terms, Participatory Budgeting corresponds with the favorite genre of computer games - economic strategies, ideally offering the gamer to feel like a demiurge. Let us remember Tropico 5 (2014) or Cities: Skylines (2015–2018), where the community well-being depend on the gamer's actions. Obviously, in Participatory Budgeting these feelings are not so unambiguous, and the visual component of the gaming environment is far from the graphics of "Tropico 5", but we cannot no take into account the immersion in the pleasure of control. The competition of budget proposals generates more obvious gaming excitement among the actors of Participatory Budgeting. Citizens vote online or in-person for funding ideas, which are reflected in the online table of leading proposals.

The Russian experience of gamification of civic participation at the municipal level is the functioning of the "Active Citizen" as an online platform for voting among Moscow residents on city development. Voting results are implemented either in the adoption of laws of the Moscow city or in departmental decisions. However, calling the experience of "Active Citizen" an electronic referendum, we must bear in mind that the results of the voting have no legal validity, but they are an advisory agent in the choice of government decisions. The actions of the participants of the "Active Citizen" are comparable to the games, because on this platform awards for activity were introduced. The "Online Store of Reword" works here, the bright interface of which is typical for any online store. A voting resident of Moscow, thus, can get gaming pleasure from both promoting his opinion, and from gaining points.

Fig. 2. Screenshot of the "Online Store of Reword", the Moscow project "Active citizen" https://shop.ag.mos.ru/catalog/

The researchers of municipal participatory democracy underline that the success of these practices depends on the balance of four factors: "(1) political will, (2) organizational capacity of the social fabric of a territory, (3) autonomy and financial capacity of the promoter political entity and (4) organizational architecture (or "design") of the participatory process" [1]. Gamification is the design of a participatory process (factor 4) that is expected to be able to "reanimate" the self-organization» of citizens tired of traditional involvement.

4   The Appeal of Issues Through Immersive Journalism

Agenda setting as a process of formation of the ideas about the issues that are important for the political and social life of the country, what decisions should be taken, and which of them are correct and most appropriate, who is responsible for their implementation, etc. is an integral part of modern public policy. Both the political elite and representatives of civil society, as well as the media are involved in this process. «The appeal of issues» is one of the variables influencing the mobilization for participation, which was justified by American researcher Rosenau in the middle of XX century. The term stands for the ability of the organizers of the mobilization campaigns to pick up the questions, the content of which forces to intensify the socio-political perceptions and the personal activity of individuals [15]. One of the modern ways to attract the attention of audiences, which appeared with the development of digital media, is immersive journalism and newsgames as its gamified product. Even though certain game elements were part of the journalist practice for a long time (you can remember crossword puzzles and word search in print newspapers, etc.) newsgames give the audience another, namely, an interactive experience. Newsgames is an interactive format for presenting important political and social events, news, combining the features of a computer game and journalism. This format appeared recently, and its clear comprehension has an even shorter history. In the Web of Science Core Collection database, the first publication on newsgames dates to 2007. Famous game designer and scholar G. Frasca is credited with creating the term newsgames. He focused on editorial games and described these games as political cartoons meets computer simulations. Another researcher I. Bogost «moved the field forward by opening the definition to anything created at the intersection of journalism and gaming» [6].

Currently, the newsgames format is becoming increasingly widespread. Renowned newspapers and magazines like "The New York Times" and "Wired magazine" have featured newsgames on their websites [2]. News Internet media company BuzzFeed's announced the establishment of studio solely for the creation of newsgames [14]. James reports: «American University's JoLT (Journalism Leadership Transformation) program for journalism and game design hosts an online resource of games designed by and for journalists that will be useful for teaching and researching the history of digital technologies and the evolution of emerging media in journalism» [6, p. 379]. The site contains the database, which is a collection of online games, simulations, and interactives created by journalism organizations or with journalistic value. In Russia, the information resources "Lentach" (Lentach (oldlentach) is an online community focused on unusual or political news. For more details see http://lenta.ch/news) and "Meduza"

(Meduza is a Russian-language online publication registered in Latvia, created by the former editor-in-chief of the online edition Lenta.ru Galina Timchenko. For more details see https://meduza.io/) also used the format of newsgames.

In the context of the spread of ideas and practices of participatory government, the inclusion of game mechanics and principles in media communication is designed to overcome both interactive fatigue [19] and reducing of public interest in the political and social life of the country, as well as engage audiences not only in perception, but also in the production of content. Becoming gamers previously «passive» users get a personal experience of perception of information and become accomplices of news creation.

The newsgames format has several features. First, newsgames are distinguished from a usual computer game by using real social, cultural or political events (current or past) as a game space (setting) as well as the images of political leaders, public figures, news heroes, and representatives of different social groups as game characters. So, Plewe and Fürsich consider an example of newsgames, in which gamers will immerse themselves in the everyday reality of refugees and migrants to feel their experience [14]. Current news become a narrative for the game. Second, since potential users of newsgames are large audiences, they need to be quickly and universally accessible for everyone: "Newsgames need to make use of simple or previously existing game mechanics that their gamers are already familiar with" [14, p. 2472]. Also, as a rule, newsgames are posted on the online platforms of media publications. Third, newsgames, offering specific rules, allow the gamer not only to feel like a participant in actual events but also to influence them.

For several years (since 2014), the "Lentach" information resource has used the newsgames format for summarizing and evaluating the results of the year. The idea of these games is that successful actions of the user who turned out to be a participant in the events of the past year can change the present, albeit in virtual reality. The game has the slogan "It is time to change history!". Political and social events that have attracted attention in the past year act as game plots, and the gamer is offered, consistently moving from one situation to another, with the help of game simulations to prevent what happened or affect it. The game assumes the presence of several levels, and the transition to the next level is possible only with the successful completion of the previous one (turn-based game). The characters of newsgames are well-known political figures, such as the President, deputies, governors, etc. However, the user is not invited to take their place, to manage the avatar, he is instead an external observer of situations (view in the game from a third party).

As an example, we can consider playing around a high-profile case of 2018 with deputy L. Slutsky, who was accused of sexual harassment. The plot of the game lies in the fact that somebody's hands symbolizing harassment try to touch the girls-journalists when they interview the deputy. The gamer must prevent harassment by clicking on the hands approaching the journalists (Fig. 2).

Fig. 3. Screenshot of the game «The new year 2019» by the information resource Lentach, https://russia2518.lenta.ch

Visual and sound signals accompany successful or unsuccessful blocking of hands. After successfully passing the level, the game reports that the deputy was punished (which was not) and informs about the changes in social reality that could have happened if everything had happened. Next, the gamer is invited to participate in other events which are the next levels of the game.

Lentach as a resource known for its provocative uses dramatic political events as plots for newsgames, caricature ridiculing them. In this case, the game can be compared with satire. The visual content of newsgames by Lentach is simple and schematic, the process of the game is accompanied by music, which also sets a specific context for immersing and experiencing what is happening on the screen. Newsgame by Lentach does not require special skills or technical equipment from the gamer; success in the game depends on the performance of simple functions. Instead, the user needs a speed of reaction and timely keystrokes.

Another example is the game of the "Meduza" company, which also presumes relatively simple mechanics and contains not only information but also an assessment of current events in Russia. So, one of newsgames by "Meduza", based on the problem of billions of dollars in debt for gas in some regions of Russia, offers the gamer to collect these debts. The mechanics of the game are similar to "Tetris". Money is pouring from the top of the screen, and the gamer needs to manipulate obstacles to get the money into the wallet standing at the bottom. Depending on how much debt the gamer was able to collect, at the end he gets a particular title, for example, «Holy» that has not collected debts (Fig. 3).

In Russia, the potential of newsgames is used primarily by opposition information companies. The very mechanics of the game puts the gamer in the position of a critic of the phenomenon that underlies the game plot. Offering some rather than other situations as elements of the game, the company designates them as necessary and significant, highlighting them from the whole space of problems that can become visible to users, thereby contributing to the agenda setting. The creators of the games determine a specific perspective on the topic. Newsgames contain an explicit or hidden assessment of political and social events, and gamers can only act in conditions that are set by the logic of the game (Fig. 4).

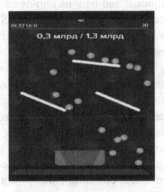

Fig. 4. Screenshot of the game «Collect debts for gas», https://meduza.io/games/soberi-dolgi-za-gaz

5 Election with Gamification

Interestingly, the online space of modern social networks gamifies the field of politics with its technological permissibility, without the need for the additional introduction of game mechanics or game elements. This is due to the presence of accounts of politicians who support active self-presentation online in social networks. The attraction of interest of the electorate is promoted by their comments, photos and video clips; shocking statements and presentations of ambitious projects collect feedback from the audience that can reward politician's posts with "likes" and comments on the posts, along with rewarding the most noticeable comments with "likes". However, there is a complex background behind the innocent likes: firstly, such "likes" can be regarded as a form of statements "for" or "in support", respectively, they perform a legitimizing function. Symbolic approval of posts means approval of political ideas and attitudes. Secondly, "likes", received for the best - the wittiest and accurate - comments, are regarded as a reward (bonuses) and are a pleasure for commentators, and most importantly - encourage all the following comments. People access social networks, are capable of joining political communities and, thus, form a stable connection with the source of pleasure.

Further, thanks to the algorithm of the Internet and social networks and records that are filtered based on individual preferences, a person may have a feeling that many people share his or her position, this can lead a person to share even more statements, comments and likes. Awards in the form of likes in social networks make the very process of participation in support of political statements and ideas pleasant to users. Nevertheless, such "public" political participation causes reasonable skepticism. Political statements and ideas are legitimized without proper consideration, which can create additional problems in the political interaction of elites offline. Nominal involvement in political issues is growing, but the quality of this involvement leaves much to be desired.

The problem of mobilizational appeal is especially acute during periods of election campaigns. During that period of time participation through likes is insufficient for political leaders, so, both traditional and new technologies of voter's involvement are used. Gamification was successfully used by the last US President Barack Obama during his election campaign in 2012, who has connected a social network with the Foursquare function. This network provides users with the ability to mark their location in various places and notify their friends about it. During the campaign Obama's supporters had the "achievement" reward: those who followed the future president in five events organized by the candidate's headquarters became the lucky ones. They received the "Obama for America" badge directly in "Foursquare," and then they could win a dinner with the candidate [7].

Modern political technologists state that the style of political communication is changing towards a more interactive form. According to Morris, the practician of political campaigns today, a political consultant should not only provide a voter with information but also involve him in some attractive activity (participation in ratings, quests, flash mobs, free competitions or in exchange for bonuses) [11].

In Russian politics at the federal and regional levels, more and more often new technologies are used in electoral technologies. In the Russian media this process is referred to as "uberization of politics" or "politics without barriers" - on the principle of open doors. Active involvement of digital products by the new politicians in their campaigns is being considered: sites and accounts of the election headquarters of political parties and social and political organizations, personal sites and pages in social networks, blogs, free applications for smartphones.

The digital resource is used by both representatives of (pro) governmental struc-tures and oppositionists, both politicians of megalopolises and those who live in small municipal settlements. According to D. Gudkov and M. Katz, the "political Uber" created by them for the municipal candidates in Moscow in 2018 "allowed political newcomers to overcome the fear of bureaucracy and conduct their campaign according to the quest rules". As a result, the United Democrats Coalition held 266 candidates for deputies in 62 district councils. D. Gudkov explains this successful result by several factors: the revolution in the minds, the victory of new technologies and progress, the common sense, the existing demand for change, the "coolest headquarters", the support provided from below and self-financing through fundraising [22].

Innovative political strategies were also used at the federal level, for example, in the presidential election campaign of 2018 when one of the candidates K. Sobchak man-aged to build a working network-oriented political party. There were not only tradi-tional but also, and most significantly, digital methods involved in the conducted election campaign. The process of interaction between all the participants in the election process was mediated by an automatic system using a whole set of technical tools. The website of K. Sobchak allowed the candidate's supporters not only to participate in writing the "123 difficult steps" candidate program but to provide financial assistance, receive e-mails, text and voice messages from the candidate and symbolic awards for completed tasks as well.

6   Discussion

Gamification is the reality of today and it is logical to imagine that this process is a result of social changes in contemporary society. In this sense, we are not just talking about trendy technology used by someone for some purpose but also about the ubiquitous trend of our time brought about by certain circumstances. The need to use special mechanisms of involvement in any process is caused by weakening attention, a decreasing interest, a reduction or lack of desire to participate among consumers. It is hard to disagree with Zichermann and Linder that "the classical ways of engaging in the modern world no longer work, given the huge number of distractions that are rapidly increasing" [25, p. 23]. They are echoed by Werbach and Hunter: "traditional ways of motivating customers and employees often do not live up to expectations. The carrots and sticks method does not work anymore and money, social status and the fear of being punished work up to a certain point only" [21].

At first glance, the idea of gamification as a technology used in the sphere of politics is rather transparent: it is assumed that the introduction of game mechanics or game elements will stimulate, involve, allow to overcome the problem of political absenteeism, the person's refusal to participate in politics (management) by that in itself the game brings to man the pleasure - the pleasure of the game. It is crucial to keep in mind that today we are dealing with automated technological games. Automation is manifested in the fact that part of the activity is delegated to the game. As computer games analyst Galloway writes, modern games that are based on program code are active environments that enable gamers to perform actions but also produce actions themselves [5, p. 25]. In addition, by delegating activity to games we delegate passivity to them. Pfaller and Zizek, were the first to have written about the possibility of contemporary media being passive objects instead of man put in that position. In other words, computer games can perform actions for us, but they can also undergo and experience something instead of us [26].

Delegation of passivity or inter-passivity leads to a more accurate understanding of the gamification of political participation. We can discuss a process in which citizen engagement through online resources that automatically count points that assign a place in a rating, allows people not only to act but also to evade action. While in the era of television politics the question was raised about couch activism or weakness of the viewer who was placed in front of the screen, today interpassivity is relevant - when digital media balance activity with a measure of relaxation of a visually involved participant, for example, in a flash mob. Thus, with the spread of gamification the niche of interpassivity can expand raising new questions about political ontology in the digital age.

7 Conclusion

Any game is a system based on the rules and involves the achievement of a quantified result in the form of points, scores, places, etc. Taking on the roles of gamers, users not only follow the logic of game achievements (points, scores, etc.) and seek to influence the result but also enjoy the process of the game, that is an essential part of this format. Digital game projects are being introduced into politics today, both at the national and municipal levels. Game design is incorporated in the agenda setting, citizen science, citizen-sensing, citizen sourcing, public deliberation, participatory budgeting, the preparation of meetings in support of candidate/party. The overview of electoral cases allows us to say that today the interaction of elites and masses is no longer possible without gaming components, while the consolidation of voters through IT platforms give active citizens to feel themselves inside the process continuously.

A distinct track of gamification is the development agenda with the help of immersive journalism. Involvement, participation, immersiveness are the critical characteristics of newsgames. Newsgames are the part of immersive journalism, which is an emerging trend that amplifies the impact of the news on a person by creating a sensory and interactive experience. The goals of this format can be different and range from overcoming interactive fatigue to the economic and political ones.

The trend of gamification in politics is a new challenge for the social sciences, which can raise critical questions about the cultural and behavioral effects of gaming stimulation of activism. Critical emphasis increases the discussion, opposing managerialism, widespread among political consultants.

Acknowledgments. The reported study was funded by RFBR and EISR according to the research project № 19-011-31375.

References

1. Allegretti, G., Antunes, S.: The Lisbon participatory budget: results and perspectives on an experience in slow but continuous transformation. J. Field Actions **11** (2014). http://journals.openedition.org/factsreports/3363. Accessed 31 May 2019
2. Bogost, I., Ferrari, S., Schweizer, B.: Newsgames: Journalism at Play. The MIT Press, Cambridge (2010)
3. Bogost, I.: Gamification is Bullshit. http://bogost.com/writing/blog/gamification_is_bullshit/ 2011. Accessed 31 May 2019
4. Deterding, S., Sicart, M., Nacke, L., O'Hara, K., Dixon, D.: Gamification: using game-design elements in non-gaming contexts. In: Proceedings of ACM CHI 2011 Conference on Human Factors in Computing Systems, pp. 2425–2428. Vancouver, BC, Canada (2011). https://doi.org/10.1145/1979482.1979575
5. Galloway, A.R.: Gaming: Essays on Algorithmic Culture. University of Minnesota Press, Minneapolis (2006)
6. James, J.: Newsgames – journalism innovation through game design. Am. J. **34**(3), 379–383 (2017). https://doi.org/10.1080/08821127.2017.1344074
7. Katz, J.E., Barris, M., Anshul, J.: The Social Media President: Barack Obama and the Politics of Digital Engagement. Palgrave Macmillan, New York (2013)

8. Kersting, N, Gasparikova, J., Iglesias, A., Krenjova, J.: Local democratic renewal by deliberative participatory instruments: participatory budgeting in comparative study. In: Kuhlmann, S., Bouckaert, G. (eds.) Local Public Sector Reforms in Times of Crisis: National Trajectories and International Comparisons, pp. 317–332. Palgrave Macmillan, London (2016). https://doi.org/10.1057/978-1-137-52548-2_18

9. Krenjova, J., Reinsalu, K.: Good governance starts from procedural changes: case study of preparing participatory budgeting in the city of Tartu. Socialiniai tyrimai/Soc. Res. **32**(3), 28–40 (2013)

10. McGonigal, J.: Reality is Broken: Why Games Make Us Better and How They Can Change the World. The Penguin Press, New York (2011)

11. Morris, D.: Vote.com: How Big-Money Lobbyists and the Media Are Losing Their Influence, and the Internet Is Giving Power Back to the People, 3rd edn. Renaissance Books, Los Angeles (2011)

12. Norris, P.: Democratic Deficit: Critical Citizens Revisited. Cambridge University Press, New York (2011)

13. Pateman, C.: Participatory democracy revisited. Perspect. Polit. **10**(1), 7–19 (2012). https://doi.org/10.1017/S1537592711004877

14. Plewe, Ch., Fürsich, E.: Are newsgames better journalism? empathy, information and representation in games on refugees and migrants. J. Stud. **19**(16), 2470–2487 (2018). https://doi.org/10.1080/1461670X.2017.1351884

15. Rosenau, J.N.: Citizenship Between Elections. An Inquiry into the Mobilizable American. The Free Press, New York (1974)

16. Thaler, R., Sunstein, C.: Nudge: Improving Decisions About Health, Wealth and Happiness. Yale University Press, New Haven (2008)

17. The Participatory Budgeting Project. https://www.participatorybudgeting.org/. Accessed 31 May 2019

18. Van Deth, J.W.: Democracy and involvement: the benevolent aspects of social participation. In: Torcal, M., Montero, J.R. (eds.) Political Disaffection in Contemporary Democracies: Social Capital, Institutions and Politics, pp. 101–129. Routledge, New York (2006)

19. Van Oenen, G.: Three cultural turns: how multiculturalism, interactivity and interpassivity affect citizenship. Citizsh. Stud. **14**(3), 293–306 (2010). https://doi.org/10.1080/13621021003731856

20. Wampler, B.: Participatory Budgeting in Brazil: Contestation, Cooperation, and Accountability. State University Press, Pennsylvania (2007)

21. Werbach, K., Hunter, D.: For the Win: How Game Thinking Can Revolutionize Your Business. Wharton Digital Press, Pennsylvania (2012)

22. Zhegulev, I.: Interview of Dmitry Gudkov on the success of the municipal elections in Moscow, the "uberization" of politics and the conflict with Navalny. Medusa Project. https://meduza.io/feature/2017/09/11/my-deputaty-za-nami-narod-kakogo-hrena-u-nas-net-polnomochiy. Accessed 31 May 2019

23. Zichermann, G., Linder, J.: Game-Based Marketing: Inspire Customer Loyalty Through Rewards, Challenges, and Contests. Wiley, Hoboken (2010)

24. Zichermann, G., Cunningham, Ch.: Gamification by Design: Implementing Game Mechanics in Web and Mobile Apps. O'Reilly Media, Sebastopol (2011)

25. Zichermann, G., Linder, J.: The Gamification Revolution: How Leaders Leverage Game Mechanics to Crush the Competition. McGraw-Hill, New York (2013)

26. Zizek, S.: Interpassive subject. Slavoj Žižek. https://zizek.uk/the-interpassive-subject. Accessed 31 May 2019

Conceptual Modeling of the Social Environment for Information Support in Management Processes

Alexey Y. Timonin$^{(\boxtimes)}$ ⓘ, Alexander M. Bershadsky,
and Alexander S. Bozhday ⓘ

Penza State University, Krasnaya Street, 40, Penza 440026, Russia
c013s017b301f018@mail.ru, bam@pnzgu.ru,
bozhday@yandex.ru

Abstract. Currently, there has been growth of the digital economy and the informatization for most social processes. The managing socio-economic systems acquires a new specificity, both in terms of goals and means. Now special importance and prospects are opened up for the application of Big Data, Data Mining and distributed databases. The relevance of this work is to provide information support for the socio-economic management using large amounts of unstructured web-data. The research aim is the formalization of the social environment elements and decision methods of social profiling system. The concepts of social phenomenon, personal and shared social profile are formalized. Conceptual social profile models have been developed to describe the individuals and groups, as well as the complete social environment. The obtained results make it possible to systematize the social environment processes of collecting and analyzing data, providing the possibility of uniting the personal social profiles into groups and carrying out applied researches.

Keywords: Social environment · Social phenomena · Social profile · Graph theory · Set theory · Unstructured data · Big Data

1 Introduction

The modern specificity of managing socio-economic systems is associated with the following important circumstances:

- a sharp increase in the data volumes and the dynamics of its distribution in social media;
- increasing the human factor importance in the conditions of information communications development;
- the emergence of new socio-economic and cultural threats associated with cyber-terrorism, information wars, social entropy in the networks, etc.;
- territorial globalization of sources and distribution channels of information content;
- a strong dependence of the nonlinear social environment on informational influences such as stuffing and fake news, as well as difficulties in forecasting of socio-economic processes development.

A. Chugunov et al. (Eds.): EGOSE 2019, CCIS 1135, pp. 138–151, 2020.
https://doi.org/10.1007/978-3-030-39296-3_11

Thus, decision maker has a problem of scientific, methodological and instrumental re-equipment. Mathematical, informational, algorithmic and technical support is required to enable the gathering, storage, monitoring and analysis of large amounts of heterogeneous data. These data generated by available Internet resources and services (news portals, social networks, personal blogs, forums, etc.). It should provide the possibility of social profiling for individual persons, various groups, social phenomena, events and processes; establishing explicit and hidden relationships between personal and group profiles; detection of causal relationships in the society information field.

This paper is devoted to modeling the social environment as a system for further use in social profiling solutions. The research materials are the unstructured public data of the social environment and its constituent elements. The representation of social environment should be formalized to ensure the possibility of automated computer processing. A set of interacting personal and group social profiles (SP) is object of this work. Research methods based on set theory, semantic networks and metagraph theory.

SP components are divided by nature and roles and highlighting the list of unique attributes. Results should consider all the common people properties. New models will be foundation for methods, that can refer to already collected unstructured heterogeneous data in order to expand the information card. It shouldn't make changes to the SP structure. There should be an opportunity for analyzing the tonality and considering several points of view on the same fact in the finished social profile. It is also required to define a set of quantitative metrics and describe their applicability to the developed models in applied research of society at various levels.

2 Background

Current trend is latest information technologies associated with the collection and processing of Big Data, Data Mining and NoSQL databases. A significant contribution to these areas' development was made by the works of scientists Dean [9, 11], Gemavat [9, 11], Cutting [14], Kafarela [14], Olson [16] and others. Many of them are at the origin of the creation holistic solutions MapReduce, Hadoop, as well as modern data storing methods of varying structure degrees.

Comprehensive modeling of the social profiling process is based on the fundamental works in different science spheres such as social management, unstructured data analysis, graph theory and networks. In particular, this is the work of the authors Moreno [15], Sowa [22], Barabashi [2], Watts [26] and Strogatz [26]. Sociometry [15] offers the necessary basis for the study of relations within society. It contributed methods to obtain information about the real status of a person inside a group, psychological compatibility between group members at the moment and the existing subordination structure. Studies of the "Small world network" [26] phenomenon led to the creation of social networking services (SNS) within the global telecommunications. It strengthened the connectivity of the Internet space. Further it led to a strong people connectivity around the world. In practice, it was found that the structure of the social environment is well described using the scale-free networks [2] theory at different levels.

Currently, the problem of heterogeneous public web-data applied usage is paid attention by many scientists, among which works on the use of socialized data stand out separately: Eskes [12], Roy [19], Bosco [5], Schamp-Bjerede [20]. The processing of unstructured socialized data of a different nature includes also russian scientists: Bolshakova [4], Shmid [21], Suturin [23], etc. Most of these works are aimed at solving specific social analytics tasks. Models for transforming the "black box" into an actor network using the mathematical apparatus of set theory were considered in paper [25]. The obtained results allow to investigate the structural properties of actor networks, including communities of people. However, there are no quantitative studies in the work: the diversity of composite objects parameters is not considered. In the case of the society study, the possibilities of determining priority information and identifying subjective judgments are not displayed. Grebennikov [13] developed an algorithm for determining the movement of the crowd using the Helbing model and a list of individual agents' characteristics. The importance of considered social relationship properties and specific subjective qualities and attitudes is highlighted in this research. Palagin [18] has provided automated models for the processing of natural language using semantic networks [22] and graphs. As a result, the conceptual graph representations partially increased expressive power in the formalization process of unstructured texts on inflectional languages.

The materials of universal describing and studying the social environment are not enough in open access. Their assessment and comparison are difficult with the described authors models. However, a study of existing works showed that their conclusions do not have obvious contradictions between each other. They can be taken as reasoned examples to create a holistic social environment modelling approach. Their ideas influenced the principles of the current work.

3   Social Environment and Its Elements Definition

"The social environment is an aggregate of the material, economic, social, political and spiritual conditions of existence, formation and activity of individuals and social groups" [17]. Scientists traditionally distinguish social macroenvironment and microenvironment. Macroenvironment includes public institutions, culture and economics. This research is important to analyze global social patterns. It can be used in the tasks of socio-economic management at the levels of a region, country or worldwide. The microenvironment describes the immediate a person entourage—family, work, study, etc. The tasks associated with the microenvironment analysis are increasingly popular now. It is due to the availability of detailed social statistical and open biographical information on the Internet. Also, the possibility of a deeper social interaction processes study has a significant impact.

The social environment researches cause some difficulties for analysts. First of all, this is the gathering and processing of a large semi-structured text amounts, geospatial, multimedia and statistical data. The all-encompassing interpretation complexity due to the presence of intricate connections between environmental individual elements. Another problem is the relevance loss of the original data over time. That is caused by the high dynamics of social communications and requires periodic updating of the social environment representation. Such an environment is called a social continuum. The external influences and the human factor value cannot be excluded. Human perception is subjective and limited by the capabilities of his brain. Therefore, different problems (for example, the contradiction of the obtained results, the erroneous interpretation of individual statements, the neglect of implicit interconnections, decision making not on the basis of objective conclusions, but on personal subjective experience, etc.) potentially possible in the study of such a complex system as a social environment.

We proposed to divide social environment data into logically related components to simplify the interaction of decision makers with it. In other words, the social environment is a dynamic data combination of individuals, social groups and phenomena. With such a division, it becomes possible to conduct research on individual environmental components and to define explicitly/implicitly related social structures (in particular, personal social profiles).

Personal social profile (SP or PSP) [8] is a dataset able to characterize the social properties of a person in one way. And besides it should be clearly structured - both for the convenience of human perception and for subsequent automated processing. Based on this definition, the SP consists of structured socialized (defining a specific person) data presented in the form of a heterogeneous semantic network [22]. Methods for solving the social profiling problem are based on the SP model [7] in addition to the social environment model. Personal social profile is the simplest case of social environment items description. That has a single central element - the unique identifier of the key person. As a result, the personal profile has a more understandable structure and the smallest number of implicit relationships between its constituent parts. And the less influence the human factor has on the analysis results.

The SP can include a social group data and considers more general social trends, such as common interests, interpersonal interactions, behavioral patterns. That called group social profile (GSP). It is represented as a set of personal profiles united by several criteria and has an arbitrary number of common properties. Social groups in case of their nature can be specific, explicitly designated or abstract, implicit and determined only by a number of corresponding signs. In view of the above, GSPs analysis is very eligible to management tasks.

It is necessary to describe important facts for a holistic view of an individual, group or social environment in SP compiling process. Such facts may be central objects in the study of the social environment state. They are called the social phenomena or facts (SF). SF represent explicit or indirect information about real world events, ideas and the results of interaction between individuals and their groups in the social environment. For example, social phenomena can be represented by public opinion, innovation, legislative initiatives and events in the management tasks. SFs have distinctive features, such as the occurrence time and place, the involved participants number, the associated real-world objects, the list of related concepts and facts, the descriptive characteristics of this phenomenon, the sources list. They can be grouped by matching properties and divided to comparative samples.

4 Generalized Social Profile Modeling

A personal social profile consists of interrelated a person's social activity static and dynamic characteristics. Also, it includes environment items linked with the analyzed person. They are atomic objects - actants (concepts, events, properties, processes) and predicates. The relationships are determined either "as is" or more detail by considering intonation tonality, weights, etc. The item importance degree depends both on the distance to the central social object (usually analyzed person's ID) and on external factors determining their weight. The tonality analysis of SP elements provides complex mood of the person.

The personal social profile commonly can be described by the formula:

$$PSP = S(X, v) \cup R(Y, u) \cup Q(m+n) \tag{1}$$

where $S = \{S_1, \ldots, S_m\}$ is the set of analyzed person's social objects (themes, events, persons, etc.); $R = \{R_1, \ldots, R_n\}$ is the set of social connections between the person's social objects; m, n are the numbers of social objects and connections, with $m - 1 \leq n$; v, u - weights of social objects and connections; $Q = \{Q_1, \ldots, Q_{m+n}\}$ - the fuzzy set of intonation degrees, depending on the number of social characteristics; X, Y – properties sets (attributes and definitions) of social objects and connections.

The group social profile consists of persons set, taken on a number of similar characteristics (such as status, interests, connections with common objects, etc.). Examples of social groups are: old-age pensioners, amateur anglers, peoples who have ever lived at a certain address. The number of internal connections in a collective SP is greater than the total number of personal SP connections. It since to consider adding the relationships of one person with another. As a result, the GSP will contain a larger number of social objects. Also, it has own unique properties that none of the personal profiles included.

You can find hidden dependencies in GSPs. If one group member has undefined attribute value and others have it approximately the same, then we can conclude that the first one has the same property. For example: the age of students from one class, the general interest area of the conference participants, the presence of the vehicle at the garage cooperative members, etc.

5 Development of a Conceptual SP Model for the Big Data Analytical System

Big Data technologies engaged the methods development for operating a social profiling system. It is necessary to take its advantages on parallel processing of unstructured initial data. But the SP core must remain structured. It is required the disaggregation of social characteristics into semantic categories. Importance degrees must be implemented in the personal identification process. Text is the most complete and understandable for semantics representation. Therefore, all the raw information is reduced to the textual form. Then the integrated model of the social profile will take the form:

$$SE = \{PP, PG, FACT, PDYN\} \tag{2}$$

where *PP* is the static part of the personal SP, *PG* is the static part of the group SP, *FACT* is the description of the connected SF, *PDYN* is the dynamic data. We show it in Fig. 1.

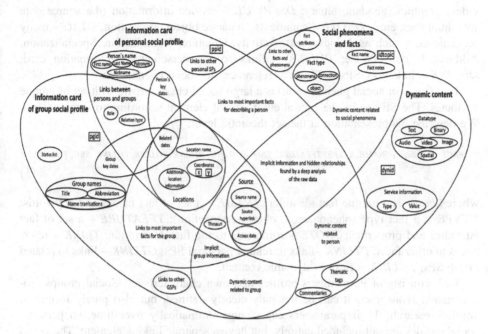

Fig. 1. Representation of social profiles composite sets on the Venn-Euler diagram.

Clearly defined definitions and categories are required to process composite social characteristics. It is needed for an objective interpretation initial information amounts, equivalent expressions and reducing the human factor influence on the social profiling results. Characteristic sets can be presented as dynamic complemented reference books and static thesauruses (explanatory, industry, multilingual dictionaries and glossaries).

A detailed model of the personal social profile considers the data separation into the static and dynamic parts:

$$PP = \{ppid, PNAME, PDATE, PLOC, PLINK, PGLINK, PTLINK, PDLINK, SRC, THLNK\} \tag{3}$$

where *ppid* is a unique social profile identifier; *PNAME* – the set of person's names (full name, pseudonyms, nicknames); *PDATE* – a set of person's key dates; *PLOC* – a set of related geolocations, including names, coordinates, linked dates and additional notes; *PLINK* – the links to other SPs; *PGLINK* – the links to related social groups, social roles and the relationship types are included; *PTLINK* – links to the most significant social phenomena and characteristics for a analyzed person; *PDLINK* – most stable links to the dynamic objects; *SRC* – source references and access dates; *THLNK* – links to thesauri.

Dynamic content is directly SP part not included to the information card. Its integration lets you design adaptive software tools [6] for the decision makers support.

$$PDYN = \{dynid, DATATYPE, DSERVICE, DNOTE, DTAG, PDLINK, DGLINK, DTLINK, SRC, THLNK\} \quad (4)$$

where *dynid* is a unique identifier of a dynamic social object; *DATATYPE* – text, audio, video, graphics, geodata, binary; *DSERVICE* – service information (the source data size, html tags, etc.); *DNOTE* – comments, dynamic object description; *DTAG* – many thematic tags, such as Achievement, Activity, Creature, Organization, Specialization, Address, E-mail, Phone; *PDLINK* – links to the personalized information card; *DGLINK* – links to GSPs; *DTLINK* – references to social phenomena.

Fact (topic or social phenomenon) is a large social characteristic with set of unique attributes. The SF can be the central environment element according to some criteria. We describe his presentation at the set-theoretic level:

$$FACT = \{idtopic, TNAME, TTYPE, TFEATURE, TNOTE, TLINK, PTLINK, GTLINK, DTLINK, SRC, THLNK\}$$

$$(5)$$

where *idtopic* is a unique fact identifier; *TNAME* – a set of fact names and keywords; TTYPE is a fact type (phenomenon, object, connection); *TFEATURE* – a set of fact attributes and properties; *TNOTE* – comments to the fact description; *TLINK* – references to other facts; *PTLINK* –links to related personal SPs; *GTLINK* – links to related group SPs; *DTLINK* – links to dynamic content.

GSP consists of its members profiles and own characteristics. Social groups representation is abstract. It can be not only clearly defined, but also purely formal in applied research. Their parameters can change dramatically over time, so personal social profiles are not included entirely, but have a separate linking element. The group social profile model will take the following form:

$$PG = \{pgid, PGNAME, GTAG, PGDATE, PGLOC, GLINK, PGLINK, DGLINK, GTLINK, SRC, THLNK\} \quad (6)$$

where *pgid* is a unique group identifier; *PGNAME* – the set of group names (official, abbreviation, translation); *GTAG* – a set of tags to describe the group social status; *PGDATE* – key dates of the group; *PGLOC* – a number of group geolocations associated with a social profile, including the name of locations or their coordinates, dates and comments; *GLINK* – links to other group profiles; *PGLINK* – links to group members; *DGLINK* – references to group dynamic attributes; *GTLINK* – links to related SP.

A separate dataset from various dictionaries and reference books is highlighted in the social profile model:

$$THESAURUS = \{def, SEMPROP, VALUE\} \quad (7)$$

where *def* is a concept, definition or term from a dictionary; *SEMPROP* is its semantic relationships, *VALUE* is the meaning of a concept, definition or term.

6   Graph Representation of the Social Environment Model

The SP nodes will be divided into 2 types in terms of graph theory [22, 25]:

- actants are social objects consisting of actors and artifacts (themes, events, communities, locations, parameters, media content, etc.);
- predicates are social relations between actants.

Thus, the conceptual graph is a representation of simple social profile. This methodology has the transforming operations by generalization and specialization. Operations realize the convenience of expressing the statement semantics:

- Copy the original graph.
- Replacing the original graph with the concepts specialization labels by a graph used the vertices labels.
- Combining vertices and edges of two graphs.
- Graph simplification by removing duplicated vertices and the incident edges.

It is possible to research the social micro- and macroenvironment if there are some linked and detailed personal SPs. The social environment is a scale-invariant network [2], capable of continuous expansion. It incorporates a variety of social profiles and phenomena. The social environment allows any actant and multiple interrelations (indirect and hidden as well) be a central object. This is unlike the social profile. The concept of a social environment is closely related to the social network definition. Therefore, the same study methods can be used to it [10].

The social environment has the property of emergence. There are parameters manifested in the environment only, not individual components. The same applies to its elements are sets of smaller social objects. For example, social groups should be considered as monolithic objects with unique parameters into the environment. But they include separate social characteristics from people descriptions, not only a group attribute. Again, people can be members of several social groups and move between them. It leads to a change in the semantics of these groups. Therefore, it is proposed to use the apparatus of metagraphs to describe the social environment (see Fig. 2) [3]:

$$SE = \{EV, SP, ER, SR\} \tag{8}$$

where EV is the vertices set from dynamic content represented by the properties of the social environment; SP is meta-vertices set represented by the SP of individuals, groups and phenomena; ER includes many edges showing the relationship within the social environment; SR is the set of meta-edges between the included social profiles.

There are common calculated metrics of the social environment analysis in the metagraph form [1, 10]:

1. Number of N_{ER} edges, N_{SR} meta-edges, N_{EV} vertices, N_{SP} meta-vertices in the metagraph.

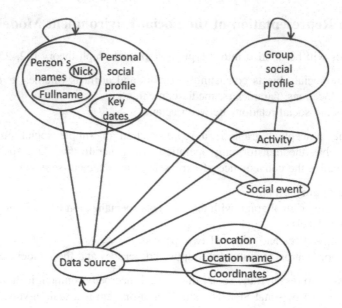

Fig. 2. The structure of the social environment sector in the metagraph form.

2. The input (9) and output (10) degrees are the number of edges and meta-edges incident to the vertices.

$$deg_{in}(x_i) = \sum_j y_{ij} \qquad (9)$$

$$deg_{out}(x_i) = \sum_j y_{ij} \qquad (10)$$

where $x_i \in EV \cup SP$; $y_{ij} = [0; 1]$ – the absence/presence of an edge between two vertices. The vertices degree distribution k accords the power law [2]: $P(k) \sim k^{-\gamma}$, with $\gamma \in [2; 3]$.

3. The graph density (11) is the ratio of existing edges and meta-edges number to their maximal number. This property may take a value greater than one. The society researches show interconnection strength of the social elements in applied tasks. It allows one to isolate individual parts from the social environment for a more detailed analysis. Another application is to compare the state of the social environment at different times. The high-density graph is more difficult to overall analysis.

$$D(SE) = \frac{N_{ER} + N_{SR}}{(N_{EV} + N_{SP})(N_{EV} + N_{SP} - 1)} \qquad (11)$$

4. Eccentricity – the largest geodesic distance between two vertices. Special cases are: the graph diameter (12) is the maximal eccentricity between any two vertices; the graph radius (13) is the minimal eccentricity between any two vertices. In applied

tasks, it allows one to find out the influence of an individual or a phenomenon, the current state and trends of a social group spread.

$$d(SE) = max_i\left(max_j\left(L\left(x_i, x_j\right)\right)\right) \tag{12}$$

$$r(SE) = min_i\left(max_j\left(L\left(x_i, x_j\right)\right)\right) \tag{13}$$

5. Intermediation – the number of paths, including a given vertex. It determines the total number of individual or group connections by selecting the considered SP from the social environment description.
6. The centrality shows the most significant graph vertices. Centrality makes it possible to determine the leaders and most mobile group members, significant phenomena and objects of the social environment, authoritative information sources, etc. in the social management tasks. Let consider three types of centrality:
   a. Closeness centrality (14). The sum inverse of the shortest paths between the vertexes.

$$C_{prox}(x_i) = \frac{1}{\sum_{j=1}^{N_{EV}+N_{SP}} L_{min}\left(x_i, x_j\right)} \tag{14}$$

   b. Degree centrality (15). It is proportional to the links number of the chosen vertex. Also, it is a local characteristic due to consideration only the nearest vertex neighborhood.

$$C_{deg}(x_i) = \frac{deg(x_i)}{deg_{max}} \tag{15}$$

   c. Betweenness centrality (16). It defines the percentage of minimal distances connecting all vertex pairs and transitional vertices. It is a global characteristic of a vertex.

$$C_{betw}(x_i) = \sum_{j<k} \frac{L_{min}\left(x_j, x_k, x_i\right)}{L_{min}\left(x_j, x_k\right)} \tag{16}$$

7. The average path length (proximity) (17) is the arithmetic mean of the distances between the central and other graph vertices. It can show the difference degree of views, living standards, cultural characteristics, the social 'periphery' remoteness.

$$Prox(x_i) = \frac{\sum_{j=1}^{N_{EV}+N_{SP}} L\left(x_i, x_j\right)}{\left|L\left(x_i, x_j\right)\right|} \tag{17}$$

8. The cycle length cl (SE). The graph girth is the smallest cycle in the graph. The graph circumference is the largest cycle in a graph. The property helps to explore the feedback mechanisms and providing homeostasis in communities.

9. Connectivity – the minimal number of edges N_r, whose removal will cause a graph decomposition. This property allows to find key connections and relationships in society.
10. The bridge – the vertex connects separate parts of the social environment graph. The network structure is broken when it is deleted. That leads to the growth of individual nodes. The bridge is used with connectivity in applied management tasks.
11. Balance – the absence of situations "positive interaction between A and B, as well as A and B, but negative interaction between B and C". Balanced networks are more comfortable [10] for actors. It can be useful for the sustainability analysis of social groups and environment.
12. Transitivity – the condition "if there is interaction between A and B, as well as between B and C, then there is an interaction between A and B". It is used to identify implicit patterns and relationships within the social environment.
13. The clusterization coefficient (18) – used to find the nearest neighbors and their interaction (cohesion) degree.

$$CC_i = \frac{2(N_{ER}(x_i) + N_{SR}(x_i))}{deg(x_i)(deg(x_i) - 1)} \qquad (18)$$

The proposed social environment model makes it possible to automate and algorithmize a number of social and economic management tasks [24]. There are some examples: distribution monitoring of the significant opinions, reactions and ideas impacts in society; preventing the threat of crime and assessing the society tension by the territorial and thematic aspects; identifying the social tension causes and actions to reduce it; production management to maximize profits and meet customer requirements; collaborative filtering to promote commercial goods and services; medical and social researches to improve the quality of people life; management of the social environment through the Internet of Things and the Smart City systems, where impersonal statistical GSPs data serve to fine-tune the IT-environment in accordance with the wishes and needs of people.

7 Discussion

The final results are considered as mathematical models of a social environment and its elements. These representations divided into static and dynamic parts. Their practical application areas are the social process management using large unstructured web-data. The listed 13 metrics make it possible to cover most of the current areas of social media analytics. The presented models describe the state of the electronic social environment. Models and methods being developed are compatible with metrics. It is possible to create a universal analytical solution for parallel processing of heterogeneous unstructured social data on their basis.

The system functionality is scaled depending on the tasks to be solved: from the study of an individual - the compilation of a personal social profile, to full-scale studies of the macroenvironment at the regional and international levels. This is achieved through the social environment model decomposition into separate connected blocks, which are efficiently processed using Big Data tools. Some examples: forecasting the consequences of certain innovations and bills; adjusting medical aid by analysis of the patient's activity data. The need of reference books and dictionaries was defined for the full social environment analysis and the subsequent development of a social profiles. The question of the personal social profile representation was considered in the task of analyzing communities and society. An important advantage is the binding lack of the proposed models to specific analytical solutions. There is the possibility of using them with only public data sources.

The further work direction is the methods development and adaptation to the tasks of social profiling and environment state mapping. In addition, the content tonality analysis is necessary for the most accurate people assessment. It makes management decisions easier.

8 Conclusion

The results of this work are the formalized concepts of social phenomenon (SF), personal social profile (PSP) and a group social profile (GSP). They are represented by social profile models of a person or a group and the metagraphic information model of the social environment. They separately highlighted the properties of tonality and significance for each component. This is the requirement of a social profile building system. Fuzzy criteria determine the truth and statement values contained in the social profile raw data. The difference is the possibility of expanding the SP static part without changing the models themselves due to a deeper analysis of the already assembled unstructured content. Another models' difference is the possibility of a quick transition between the society levels: from considering the characteristics of an individual or other social object to analyzing the processes of the macroenvironment. This is achieved by using the methodology of the metagraphs theory.

References

1. Babkin, E.A., Kozyrev, O.R., Kurkina, I.V.: Principles and algorithms of artificial intelligence: The monograph. Nizhny Novgorod Technology State University: Nizhny Novgorod, Russia (2006)
2. Barabási, A.L., Albert, R.: Emergence of scaling in random networks. Science **286**(5439), 509–512 (1999)
3. Basu, A., Blanning, R.W.: Metagraphs and Their Applications. Springer, Boston (2007). https://doi.org/10.1007/978-0-387-37234-1
4. Bolshakova, E.I., Klyshinsky, E.S., Lande, D.B., Noskov, A.A., Peskov, O.V., Jagunova, E. V.: Automatic natural language processing and Computational Linguistics: a Tutorial. MIEM, Moscow, Russia, p. 272 (2011)
5. Bosco, C., Patti, V., Bolioli, A.: Developing corpora for sentiment analysis: the case of irony and senti–TUT (Extended Abstract). In: Proceedings of the Twenty-Fourth International Joint Conference on Artificial Intelligence (IJCAI 2015), pp. 4158–4162 (2016)

6. Bozhday, A.S., Evseeva, Y.I.: The method of reflexive self-adaptation of software systems. In: Proceedings of Higher Educational Institutions. Volga region. Technical science, № 2 (46), pp. 74–86. Publishing House of the Penza State University, Penza, Russia (2018). https://doi.org/10.21685/2072-3059-2018-2-7
7. Bozhday, A.S., Timonin, A.Y.: Design of personal social profile on the basis of public data sources. Sci. J. Progressive Res. Sci. Genesis **1**, 179–181 (2015)
8. Bozhday, A.S., Timonin, A.Y.: Requirements for the type and content of social profile data. In: Topical Issues of Modern Science: Theory and Practice of Scientific Research: Proceedings of the All-Russian Scientific and Practical Conference, pp. 257–260. Publishing House of the Penza State Technological University, Penza, Russia (2017)
9. Chang, F., et al.: Bigtable: a distributed storage system for structured data. ACM Trans. Comput. Syst. (TOCS) **26**(2), 4 (2008)
10. Churakov, A.N.: Analysis of social networks. Soc. Stud. **1**, 109–121 (2001)
11. Dean, J., Ghemawat, S.: MapReduce: simplified data processing on large clusters. Commun. ACM **51**(1), 107–113 (2008)
12. Eskes, P., Spruit, M., Brinkkemper, S., Vorstman, J., Kas, M.J.: The sociability score: app-based social profiling from a healthcare perspective. Comput. Hum. Behav. **59**, 39–48 (2016). https://doi.org/10.1016/j.chb.2016.01.024
13. Grebennikov, R.V.: Development of individual characters when modeling the behavior of the crowd. In: Bulletin of the Voronezh State University. Series: System Analysis and Information Technologies, vol. 2, pp. 107–110, Voronezh, Russia (2008)
14. McAfee, A., Brynjolfsson, E., Davenport, T.H., Patil, D.J., Barton, D.: Big data: the management revolution. Harvard Bus. Rev. **90**(10), 60–68 (2012)
15. Moreno, J.L.: Sociometry, Experimental Method and the Science of Society: An Approach to a New Political Orientation. Beacon House (1951)
16. Olson, M.: Hadoop: Scalable, flexible data storage and analysis. IQT Quart. **1**(3), 14–18 (2010)
17. Osipov, G.V.: Sociological Encyclopedic Dictionary. M-Norma, Moscow, Russia (1998)
18. Palagin, A.V., Krivoy, S.L., Petrenko, N.G.: Conceptual graphs and the semantic networks in natural language processing systems information. Math. Mach. Syst. **1**(3) (2009)
19. Roy, P., et al.: Using social network analysis to profile people based on their e-communication and travel balance. J. Transp. Geogr. 24111–24122 (2012). https://doi.org/10.1016/j.jtrangeo.2011.09.005
20. Schamp-Bjerede, T., et al.: New perspectives on gathering, vetting and employing Big Data from online social media: an interdisciplinary approach. In: International Computer Archive of Modern and Medieval English-ICAME Conference. Trier, Germany (2015)
21. Shmid, A.V., et al.: New Ways of Working with Big Data: The Winning Strategy of Management in Business Intelligence, p. 528. Palmir Publishing House, Moscow (2016)
22. Sowa, J.F.: Conceptual Structures: Information Processing in Mind and Machine. Addison-Wesley, Reading (1984)
23. Suturin, G.S.: The formation of communities on the basis of graph-interests. Curr. Res. Soc. Probl. **1**, 214–218 (2013)
24. Timonin, A.Y., Bershadsky, A.M., Bozhday, A.S., Koshevoy, O.S.: Social profiles - methods of solving actual socio-economic problems using digital technologies and big data. In: Digital Transformation and Global Society. DTGS 2018. Communications in Computer and Information Science, vol. 858, pp. 436–445. Springer, Cham (2018). https://doi.org/10.1007/978-3-030-02843-5

25. Tselyh, A.A., Dedulina, M.A: Graph-theoretic approaches to modeling actor networks in science and technology research. In: Modeling, Optimization and Information Technology. Science Magazine, vol. 6, № 4. Publishing house «MOIT», Voronezh, Russia. (2018). https://moit.vivt.ru/wp-content/uploads/2018/10/TselykhDedyulina_4_18_1.pdf.   Accessed 29 Nov 2019

26. Watts, D.J., Strogatz, S.H.: Collective dynamics of 'small-world' networks. Nature **393** (6684), 440 (1998)

Stage Models for Moving from E-Government to Smart Government

Florian Lemke[1]([⊠]), Kuldar Taveter[2], Regina Erlenheim[2],
Ingrid Pappel[3], Dirk Draheim[3], and Marijn Janssen[4]

[1] Capgemini, Business and Technology Solutions – Public Sector,
Berlin, Germany
florian.lemke@capgemini.com
[2] Socio-Technical Systems Laboratory, Tallinn University of Technology,
Tallinn, Estonia
{kuldar.taveter, regina.erlenheim}@taltech.ee
[3] Information Systems Group, Tallinn University of Technology,
Tallinn, Estonia
{ingrid.pappel, dirk.draheim}@taltech.ee
[4] Technology, Policy and Management Faculty, Delft University of Technology,
Delft, The Netherlands
M.F.W.H.A.Janssen@tudelft.nl

Abstract. The emergence of super-applications is a complete game changer in how future governments will deliver e-services and interact with their citizens. With respect to this, the scope of currently established e-government stage models is exhausted. Therefore, this article proposes a "provident stage" as an extension of the Layne and Lee stage model, that adequately addresses the rapid technological development and evolvement of mobile- and smart-government solutions. We argue that super-applications can drive the transformation of e-government towards a yet unforeseen quality level: smart government. This article discusses that transition process, the influence of mobile government solutions in this as well as emerging citizens' expectations for modern government service delivery.

Keywords: Stage models · E-government (eGov) · Smart government (sGov) · Digital government · Super-applications · Provident services · WeChat

1 Introduction

The daily use of social networking applications on mobile devices has a major impact on how modern societies are connected. For governments, a new era of public service delivery has begun. Governments adopt super-applications to their current repertoire of channels for service delivery. Meeting the citizens' needs is part of the modern idea of citizen-centric service delivery. By combining modern technologies with government services, a greater acceptance and data-driven, *provident services* will be able to entirely change the role of governments in modern societies. Exploring this new phenomenon will help to gain a better understanding of the transition from e-government (eGov) to smart-government (sGov) due to the use of super-applications.

© Springer Nature Switzerland AG 2020
A. Chugunov et al. (Eds.): EGOSE 2019, CCIS 1135, pp. 152–164, 2020.
https://doi.org/10.1007/978-3-030-39296-3_12

Due to the involvement of Big Data and data analytics, proactive government decision-making will reach a new stage of eGov maturity.

Due to rapid technological development and change, existing e-government stage models reached their possibilities to illustrate currently emerging maturity levels of e-government. To address this, we suggest extending common stage models by a *provident stage*, based on the widely acknowledged stage model of Layne and Lee [17, 18]. Our suggested extension is based on evidence from a literature review and, furthermore, evidence from a case study of the super-application WeChat, based on data from Tencent Holdings Ltd. and eight personal open interviews – each 1, 5 h – that we have conducted in the PRC (People's Republic of China). The interviewees have been WeChat users, specialists in the R&D sector, software developers in Beijing, and official WeChat project managers in the WeChat headquarters in Guangzhou.

The technological development put forth the topic of mobile government (mGov). Our research addresses the importance, efficiency and effectiveness of non-state developed applications for the acceptance of e-government services. It aims to verify that super-applications strongly push the transition towards sGov and that they can enthuse citizens with using government e-services. In Sect. 2, we discuss related work regarding the transition from eGov towards sGov. In Sect. 3, we present the case of the Chinese super-application WeChat that exemplifies this rapid development of mobile government solutions. In Sect. 4, we discuss the existing stage model by Layne and Lee and introduce and discuss the suggested *provident stage*. We finish the paper with a conclusion in Sect. 5.

2 Related Works

The existence of synonyms of the term "smart" shows that even a definition that has gained a high level of acceptance in its field of research struggles with alternatives such as, percipient, astute, shrewd and quick. Due to this, they have created a definition of sGov centred on the changes and challenges for public administration and society. "As smart-government, or the organizations and networks within the political jurisdiction (e.g. a city, a town, a nation), will use emerging and nanotechnologies and various innovative strategies to gain a sound understanding of their communities and constitutes (being percipient), they would use that ability to accurately assess situations or people (being astute), show sharp powers of judgement (being shrewd), and then make decisions and respond quickly or effectively (being quick)" [1–4].

The development of smart city initiatives has shown that especially the borders between the terms of smart city and sGov are overlapping. "Therefore, the authors call a city smart when it takes action towards innovation in management, technology, and policy, all of which entail risks and opportunities" [5]. The discussion of attempts to define the sphere of each of the terms has developed two different understandings, which on the one hand state that the term of smart city is only a subset of sGov, and on the other hand scholars see sGov within the smart city nexus.

In smart and sustainable cloud-based ICT meta-architecture, the benefits of sGovs and their actions described by government platforms especially can be evaluated. They show the advantages of sGovs for public administration and citizens as well as stakeholders in the process of open government service delivery. The benefits include lower software development, support, and maintenance costs; provision of higher application portability and interoperability; enhancing smart services; and a shortened time-to-market strategy for services. The involvement of Big Data Management, the Internet of Things (IoT), sensor networks, smart devices, embedded systems, 5G and cloud computing technologies in public administration will allow sGovs to create entirely new ways of governing cities, states or nations. "By introducing new type of knowledge processes such as information collection and processing, real-time forecasting and alerting, collectives and crowd-sourced intelligence, cooperative distributed problem-solving and learning from it" [6, 7], sGovs will reach a new level of interconnection between all kinds of stakeholders for public service deliveries.

Jörn von Lucke [3] has developed a design showing an integrational approach to sGov in public administration. The core of this model shows that cyber-physical systems (CPS) will involve intelligent networking objects such as sensors, actuators, and M2M communication to enhance the development of future public administration. CPSs are heterogeneously networked entities that link and combine real physical objects with digital information and communication systems. These are IT systems as part of devices, structures, or processes that directly detect physical data via sensors and act on physical processes through actuators, but above all that evaluate and store the acquired data. In addition, they can actively or reactively interact with the physical and digital world. For this purpose, they are connected via digital communication devices (M2M) and in global networks. This offers the possibility to use the data and services that are available worldwide [3].

To provide investment security, compatibility, and future viability for governments and stakeholders, the sGov approach must be integrated. The major question in the development of sGov service delivery is to identify what intelligently connected objects the public sector needs and in which CPSs these must be embedded.

As shown in Fig. 1, one must ensure that the objects not only function in a closed ecosystem but that they are also integrated into the Internet of Content (Web 1.0: World Wide Web and Management Networks, Electronic Government), the Internet of Communication (Web 2.0: Social Media, Open Government) and the Internet of Context (Web 3.0: Semantic Web – Big and Open Data, Open Government Data). The design of the Internet of Things (Web 4.0: Smart Ecosystems, Internet of Things, sGov) with its sensor and actuator networks and its services are, from the state's point of view, essential. As one of the last stages, one can define the network communication on a real-time level as the Web 5.0 – the so-called Internet of Thoughts or the Tactile Internet, which supports real-time government.

In his analysis of sGovs, von Lucke [3] has outlined strengths, weaknesses, chances and risks regarding future public administration. Weaknesses of sGov, as he pointed out, are the specific efforts and time for the development of software solutions that requires financial expenses, and insufficient scientific background. Also, its lack of political prioritization, as well as the lack of research and development capacities of new solutions will be considered as weaknesses. Risks that von Lucke's system wanted to eliminate are the lack of creativity and design, the uncertainty of successful implementation, the disruptive nature of changes arising from innovation, the fears resulting from the distorted image of "Glass Citizen", which especially in Germany is

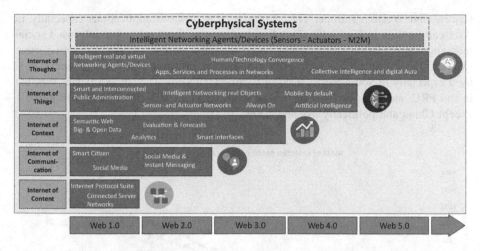

Fig. 1. Integrational approach of sGov solutions and their development.

an issue of privacy, and lack of permanent funding, acceptance, and participation of citizen in early stages.

Chances for sGov are the potential for innovation and the given impulses for society, new intelligent networking of things, services and CPS, increasing efficiency and effectiveness, and in the long run reductions in fees and charges for public administration services. He supports his argumentation with an integrated approach to IT, an intensification of networking and interconnection of agencies, as well as a demand of mission statements by smart authorities, smart management and for smart citizens.

3   The Case of the Super-Application WeChat

The super-application WeChat has been developed in a unique surrounding that is characterized by the Great Firewall, and that can only be found in the PRC. In China, the IT solutions are much more focused on the needs and traditions of the users – the regional-cultural background plays an important role in the development of innovative IT solutions. Surely, the development of emergent technologies will also be performed only within a framework that especially focuses to serve its one-party state that has been ruled by the Chinese Communist Party (CCP) since 1949.

WeChat has been developed towards a social networking application that combines functions such as instant messaging, e-commerce and payment services. In the Western World, government e-services are not supported by applications like WeChat. Applications such as WhatsApp and Facebook will need to be analyzed separately due to their more open and democratic and less government-influenced development. Developing countries especially have shown a greater interest and closer connection to innovation and technological change in the past. The acceptance rates for new technologies are higher than in economically mature and developed countries, e.g. in

Central and Western Europe. The increasing use of those applications especially in Asia can be seen in Fig. 2 [8]. This figure compares the most commonly used social messenger applications in the world based on their number of monthly active users (MAU). These applications are mostly used in certain geographic areas. KakaoTalk is used especially in South Korea, Zalo in Vietnam, LINE in Taiwan and Japan, WeChat in the PRC and Facebook Messenger as well as WhatsApp cover the entire globe – except China and politically isolated states.

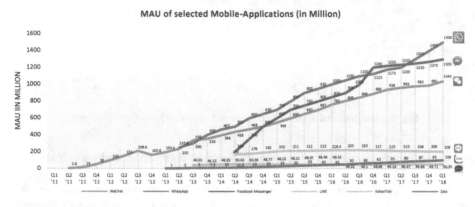

Fig. 2. Monthly active users of mobile application over the past years.

Super-applications enable possibilities to implement services under the idea of Government as a Platform (GaaP). Therefore, they will be able to provide data information for smart cities and innovative administrative government processes.

Sensors can gather various types of data. Smartphones are great examples for this type of data-gathering. The location, temperature, 3D movements, fingerprints, light, atmospheric pressure and even camera sensors with possibilities for face recognition as well as the recognition of handwriting have built into the new types of smartphones. All that gathered information will be used to improve the user-experience and to measure the behaviour of the user. As mentioned in the interviews given by the WeChat managers in Guangzhou, for WeChat this has always been the basic understanding for the development of their application.

In the next step, analytics will be able to predict user preferences and calculate risks of decision-making. Analytics help to define new levels of verification to securely store any kind of information on the user's personal device. "With the mobile Internet extending to IoT in recent years, Chinese Internet enterprises have emerged as the most dynamic actors in the development of IoT, and have been strongly influencing the patterns, models and industrial ecological system of China's IoT development. Major Chinese Internet companies have entered the field of IoT through wearable intelligent terminals, smart home, mobile health care, IoV, security, [virtual reality (VR), artificial intelligence (AI)] and other businesses, and have made rapid development in some of these areas" [9].

One of those examples is the super-application WeChat, which "can communicate with home appliances, toys, routers, wearable devices, sports equipment and other types of smart devices, and help to interconnect intelligent devices and hundreds of millions of Wechat users" [9–11]. With WeChat, not only can people be connected and relationships maintained, but also connections between people and objects or connections between objects can be made. IoT has become reality in China through WeChat. As follows, WeChat will be used to define this new stage of transition of government e-services.

The involvement of data analytics and the implementation of mobile government in the set up, and agile system that can be used on cloud services, also outlines the before mentioned definition of sGov. The developed *provident stage* uses the data that is gathered by governments to better serve citizens' and clients' needs. Hence, this stage plays a major role in the transition process of government. The implementation of emerging technologies and innovation that can be driven by IoT in the public sector, has shown a move towards a more digitalized and more open and interconnected type of government, as outlined in the conducted interviews with interviewees from the R&D sector. This shows that governments will be able to push their transition on the new level, due to the implementation of super-applications to reach the more advanced type of government – sGov.

4 Extending Stage Models from eGov to sGov

The transition of government is a wide term. Due to the involvement of information technologies, governments have been pushed towards the implementation of those technologies. The wide range of possible changes in governments have shown major improvements in organizational structures of government as seen in Fig. 1. eGov has been a way of better serving the citizens using new technologies and through new channels. It has also changed the entire process of services that governments provide and has changed the entire organizational structures of governments.

Several different stage models for eGov have been developed by scholars in the past. Those stages have some basic features in common. "All of them bring to bear a differentiation in describing the development from the simple information service to a more refined one-stop government" [12]. Some scholars especially worth mentioning are Layne and Lee. They offer the general bases of analysing stage models in present work, because it has been the most general but also the most often referenced model over the past years. Several others, such as Hiller and Bélanger [13], Andersen and Henriksen [14], and Klievink and Janssen [15], have been used to shape the right understanding for developing a stage model extension for a new and innovative way of government that is mainly data-driven and proactive.

Various contributions have pointed out problems that need to be overcome to be able to reach the next stage of eGov. Some of them have shown that government officials on lower and higher levels are likely to resist any changes and development in established systems and processes.

Being able to overcome this barrier will drive the transition of government towards a more digitalized and future-oriented government that can have the ability to serve their citizens better than it did ever before. Action areas to become more open and as well predictive are the community engagement and co-production of services, financial investment, automation, collaboration, and governance. To be able to transform government service delivery from eGov to sGov, agencies must collaborate and provide a seamless integrated service delivery across all domains.

4.1 Existing Stage Model by Layne and Lee

Governments do not change for intrinsic reasons but are led by visions of eGov emerging in society. Those visions are shaped by ideas and a new understanding of governance based on a citizens-centred concept instead of a traditional bureaucracy-centred vision. These kinds of visions are driven by a result-centred and market-centred ways that are actively promoting innovation [16].

There are four objectives that describe the change in governments due to the help of information technologies. From an organizational point of view, it can be said, that governments try to internally enhance the cooperation and collaboration between several government divisions among several levels and various locations. The new way of government will also provide better services to external entities such as businesses (e.g. elimination of redundant data collections and their reduction of transaction costs). Focused on the delivery of services to individuals, governments have set their visions to provide services to their citizens that are working to improve the government-citizen relationship that has been difficult in the past. Lastly, from an individual perspective, governments try to improve their internal processes to boost efficiency and effectiveness of their own administration.

Based on those four objectives, scholars have developed stage models, each having a different approach and, therefore, differing in the number of stages.

Layne and Lee [17] have developed their stage model on the basic understanding of eGovernment as a chaotic and unmanageable development of government-citizen interactions. In this sense, they claim the importance of dividing the development into distinguishable stages. Therefore, they have developed the four stages: (1) catalogue; (2) transaction; (3) vertical integration; and (4) horizontal integration.

The integration of government agencies, as described by Layne and Lee, has been unique. "In Layne and Lee this is divided into vertical; cross-hierarchical integration and horizontal; cross-functional integration. The other models do not separate the cross-functional and cross-hierarchical integration from each other" [12, 18].

The model is based on technical, organizational and managerial feasibility. The authors define their model as a framework for an evolutionary phenomenon that is called – eGov.

The first stage of the model delivers static or just basic information by using websites. Besides basic information delivery, the functions of this stage are the publication of documents and the possibility of downloading form sheets. Therefore, this information is of a general nature and mostly pays attention to the agency or department itself. The established online procedures of government departments and their agencies tend to be created in a mainly decentralized way. There will be no interaction between government and citizens and no cooperation among agencies. The move into this stage is initiated by external pressures arising from client (e.g. citizens' and businesses') expectations.

The second stage of the Layne and Lee model extends the previously established possibilities of the catalogue stage. In general, it allows citizens to fill in online forms for governments. This shows that a transaction between government and citizens has been established. For Layne and Lee, this stage represents an internal focus shift that moves agency systems onto the existing websites. Examples of this stage are the renewal of the residence parking permits (e.g. in the Federal Republic of Germany), the renewal of licences, the possibility of paying fines, and checking evidence online (e.g. in the United States of America and the Federal Republic of Germany). A full integration of agency systems has been archived achieved in the next stage of the model. This full integration allows the citizens not only to view information but in addition helps them to post their own information and responses directly into the agency systems. Direct and personal interaction with government officials will be reduced and a greater location-independence can be seen [12, 16, 18].

In the third stage of the model, a vertical integration has been introduced. This stage differs from the other stage models proposed in the literature. The vertical integration most likely focuses on the transformation of the delivered services rather than on the automation of already existing business processes. It describes the process of integration into a vertical cross-governmental way. In comparison to the first two stages, this stage focuses on the development and the integration of agency systems with the help of web interfaces. In addition, the Layne and Lee model focuses on organizational changes. This is highly important to promote the change in government structures using information and communication technologies. In this third stage, the possibility of connecting government agencies on different levels occurs and offers practical functions such as the "integration of local level business license application [that] is being linked to state and government level to obtain an employer identification number [(e.g. in the United States of America)]" [12]. A linkage of local- and state-systems on higher-levels brings this stage to its maturity.

The last and fourth stage of this model describes the horizontal integration and focuses on the integration of systems on the same level of government. Several agencies offer one system for their service delivery to their clients. Even though several agencies deliver different services and functions, the information regarding the client that they have in common can be communicated and shared. A functional example is the possibility for the clients to pay their business fees and taxes to several government entities. This will be possible due to the interconnection of agency systems that makes it possible to divide the payment and deliver it to the right agency [12, 16, 18].

For the Layne and Lee stage model, the importance of outlining the change of organizational structures due to the implementation and interconnection of agency systems shows that the transformation of government systems does not only include the delivery of services that they provide. It also underlines the internal aspect of change that needs to be done to reach the expectations of modern government.

4.2 Extension of Current eGov Stage Model

With the implementation of super-applications in the delivery process of government services, the terms "fast and effective" have taken on a new definition and understanding. It is above the so far seen eGov approach that delivers information and services to their citizens over the Internet. Due to the wide distribution of smartphones all over the world, the Internet has become part of people's lives. The Internet is now accessed directly from the people's pocket and it has become mobile.

All this has made it possible to access government services over the browser on the clients' smartphones and entirely new problems occurred that have questioned the accessibility and verification functions for government e-services. "With a rapid proliferation of smartphones, public smartphone applications have emerged as a new technology and innovative way to achieve smarter government. [...] [G]overnment agencies have followed the trend of the rapid proliferation of public applications without considering how high-level citizen-centric services could be delivered through the public applications" [1]. Therefore, governments had to face the lack of acceptance of their mobile e-services. The use of data that has been given by the clients, has made governments a powerful stakeholder regarding to Internet technologies in a data-driven world.

Data-driven government that will be able to proactively use and deliver information to their clients would be the next generation of government. Sirendi and Taveter even argue that "designing proactive services of e-governance should be seen as the next stage in service design for e-governance. [...] [P]roactive public electronic services should be designed in a way that supports the automation and intelligent processing of already available information to reflect the purpose of meeting the needs of different stakeholders yet maintaining a people-first-policy" [10, 11, 19]. This new type of government is able to serve its people's needs in a better way than they were able to deliver services ever before. At the same time, they will be able to provide decision-making to serve their people even before they know that they need to be served by the government.

Based on this new understanding of government, a new stage for describing this transition of government will follow. In this case, it can be said that due to the rapid growth in demand of government e-services for mobile devices and the occurrence of data-driven government that will be able to proactively serve their citizens and enterprises requires a new stage to define the maturity of governments in the transition process from eGov to sGov.

Therefore, the authors propose an extension of the Layne and Lee stage model, as shown in Fig. 3. This fifth stage extends the existing stage model and focuses on the delivery of this service and the use of government data. This stage will be named as the *provident stage*. Due to the use of analytics and artificial intelligence (AI), a new way of governing citizens will be implemented. Data-driven governments are currently in this stage and they will, on a more mature level of this stage, actively invest in deep data analytics and AI. Its decision-making is based on Big Data and will be able to proactively serve its citizens in the future [7]. The delivery of e-services in this fifth stage supports the use of smartphones and developed implemented mobile government applications.

Considering the use of super-applications in this transition from eGov towards sGov, archiving this stage will be possible by implementing eGov services in daily-

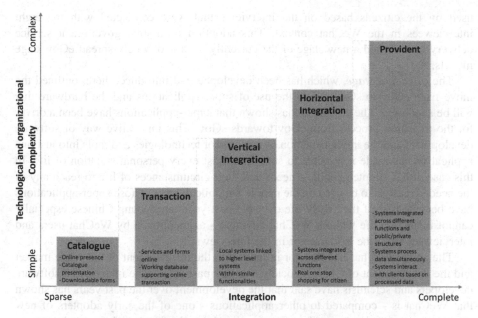

Fig. 3. Extension of the Layne and Lee stage model including the *provident stage*.

used super-applications. In this *provident stage*, organizational structures of government will not be entirely changed anymore. Policy adjustments and new legislative procedures will help to legally connect third-party applications and data-security laws for government databases. Data gathering due to the help of those implemented e-services will offer new possibilities for governments to predict economic changes and movements of society on the long- and short-term scale.

This new way of implementing e-services and analysing the way they input data will surely have an impact on the policy outcomes. By implementing agile delivery procedures that are based on the citizens given data, new ways of customisation for e-services will occur. "In the context of an architecture of consumption, agile delivery is an extremely powerful approach, since it allows the recombination and reuse of standard building blocks, closely customized to user's requirements" [20].

This newly and fully citizen-centric approach for government e-services has become a goal for the delivery of those services. This proposed extension of the Layne and Lee stage model shows that even the general stage model will reach its maturity due to the development of ICT and its implementation by government agencies.

5 Conclusion

The novel idea of combining super-applications and the use of eGov service delivery has shown a remarkable change in the way future governments will deliver and interact with their citizens and country-based enterprises. The case study has addressed new ways of interaction between governments and citizens, which have been developed and used by the citizens based on the interviews that were conducted with the eight interviewees in the WeChat context. This adoption of mobile government service delivery has reached a new stage of the currently used and widely spread eGov stage models.

The *provident stage*, which has been developed and introduced here, outlined the move from eGov to sGov due to the use of super-applications and the hardware that will be supported. The case study has shown that super-applications have been a driver for the transition process from eGov towards sGov. This innovative way of software development and the implementation of new sensor technologies and tools into just one application has made it possible to support almost every personal situation of life. In this case, it has adopted people's needs and their circumstances of life to reach any of the needed reasons to be used on the people's mobile devices. Those super-applications have become part of their daily life over the past years and young Chinese especially cannot imagine a life without WeChat anymore - as mentioned by WeChat users and interviewees from the R&D sector in the interviews.

The application has had a major influence on the development of the entire market and the development of Chinese society over the past years. The interviewed software developers and scientists have said that the development over the past years has shown that WeChat is - compared to other applications - one of the early adopters of new possibilities that technology offers. They outlined that the framework for implementing and adjusting services within the application has always been at the forefront. It has changed online and offline business models, it has created entirely new business models and it was able to implement already existing models.

WeChat's existence has increased the users' ability to easily communicate with friends, businesses, and governments. The implementation of public services in WeChat has created the first steps for governments to directly interact with their citizens over their personal mobile devices. For the interviewed users, this has been revolutionary, but it has not changed the way Chinese sense their government.

This implementation process for eGov services specifically explains the first subsidiary research question that asked for the ways to implement government services though through GaaP based on super-applications. The platforms that have been developed to offer several services on WeChat have created the possibility for individuals from all over the world to develop microblogs, games, remote controls for any kind of hardware in IoT and many other innovative ideas. By using location services, the service delivery has been shaped especially for the users and just offer services that have been available in their area.

The research has outlined that especially with the use of super-applications, the transition process has led towards a mature level of eGov. While introducing a next stage for the Layne and Lee eGov stage model – that has especially been focused on Big Data and proactive service delivery due to Non-Stop-Shops – the use of super-applications on next-generation smartphones has been a driver for this process of transition towards sGov.

Summarized, it can be said that due to this research the understanding of mobile service delivery needs to become part of the policy-making process of Western/European governments and supranational organizations in the near future. Innovative ways of service delivery will guide public administration towards a more interconnected, efficient and effective approach on how to govern a country in the 21st century. Making governments smart will increase the trust and positive attitude of citizens towards governments and their service delivery.

Further research could be conducted to draw out specific cases in Western/ European countries and to underline this next generation move towards smart government. This will push this framework to a more practical level.

References

1. Gil-Garcia, J., Helbig, N., Ojo, A.: Being smart: emerging technologies and innovation in the public sector. Gov. Inf. Q. **31**, I1–I8 (2014)
2. Gil-Garcia, J., Pardo, T., Aldama-Nalda, A.: Smart cities and smart governments: using information technologies to address urban challenges. In: Proceedings of dg.o 2011 – the 14th Annual International Conference on Digital Government Research. Quebec City, pp. 296–297 (2013)
3. von Lucke, J.: Smart government – the potential of intelligent networking in government and public administration. In: Proceedings of CeDEM 2016 – Conference for e-Democracy and Open Government (CeDEM), pp. 137–144 (2016) https://doi.org/10.1109/cedem.2016.22
4. Mellouli, S., Luna-Reye, L., Zhang, J.: Smart government, citizen participation and open data. Inf. Polity **19**, 1–4 (2014). https://doi.org/10.3233/ip-140334
5. Nam, T., Pardo, T.: Conceptualizing smart city with dimensions of technology, people, and institutions. In: Proceedings of dg.o 2011 – the 12th Annual International Conference on Digital Government Research, pp. 282–291. ACM (2011)
6. Recupero, D.R., et al.: An innovative, open, interoperable citizen engagement cloud platform for smart government and users' interaction. J. Knowl. Econ. **7**(2), 388–412 (2016)
7. Sun, Z., Strang, K., Pambel, F.: Privacy and security in the big data paradigm. J. Comput. Inf. Syst. 1–10 (2018)
8. Statista Homepage. https://statista.com/. Accessed 01 May 2019
9. Friess, P., Li, J.: EU-China Joint White Paper on the Internet of Things. EU-China IoT Advisory Group. European Union (2016)
10. Scholta, H., Mertens, W., Reeve, A., Kowalkiewicz, M.: From one-stop-shop to no-stop-shop: an e-government stage model. In: Proceedings of ECIS 2016 – the 25th European Conference on Information Systems, pp. 918–934. AIS (2016)
11. Scholta, H., Mertens, W., Reeve, A., Kowalkiewicz, M.: From one-stop-shop to no-stop-shop: an e-government stage model. Gov. Inf. Q. **36**(1), 11–26 (2019)
12. Persson, A., Goldkuhl, G.: Stage-models for public e-services – investigating conceptual foundations. In: Proceedings of the 2nd Scandinavian Workshop on e-Government, Copenhagen (2005)
13. Hiller, J., Bélanger, F.: Privacy strategies for electronic government, E-government series. Pricewaterhouse Coopers Endowment for the business of Government (2001)
14. Andersen, K.V., Henriksen, H.Z.: E-government maturity models: Extension of the Layne and Lee model. Gov. Inf. Q. **23**, 236–248 (2006)
15. Klievink, B., Janssen, M.: Stage models for creating joined-up government: from local to nation-wide integration. In: Proceedings of the 2008 International Conference on Digital Government Research, pp. 117–123 (2008)
16. Siau, K., Long, Y.: Synthesizing e-government stage models – a meta-synthesis based on meta-ethnography approach. Ind. Manag. Data Syst. **105**(4), 443–458 (2005). https://doi.org/10.1108/02635570510592352

17. Layne, K., Lee, J.: Developing fully functional E-government: a four stage model. Gov. Inf. Q. **18**, 122–136 (2001)
18. Lee, J.: 10 year retrospect on stage models of e-Government: a qualitative meta-synthesis. Gov. Inf. Q. **27**(3), 220–230 (2010)
19. Sirendi, R., Taveter, K.: Bringing service design thinking into the public sector to create proactive and user-friendly public services. In: Nah, F.F.-H., Tan, C.-H. (eds.) HCIBGO 2016. LNCS, vol. 9752, pp. 221–230. Springer, Cham (2016). https://doi.org/10.1007/978-3-319-39399-5_21
20. Brown, A., Fishenden, J., Thompson, M.: Digitizing Government – Understanding and Implementing New Digital Business Models. Palgrave Macmillan, New York (2014)

Cross-Boundary Projects E-Governance as a Method of EAEU Economic Policy Integration

Marina Tsurkan[1,2](✉) (iD), Dokukina Irina[1,2] (iD), and Nadezhda Pilipchuk[1] (iD)

[1] Tver State University, Zhelyabova st. 33, 170100 Tver, Russian Federation
080783@list.ru
[2] Central Russian Institute of Management Branch of RANEPA, Boulevard Pobedy, 5A, 302028 Orel, Russian Federation

Abstract. This study systematizes the notion of the project e-governance as the method of maintaining consistent economic policy between the countries of the Eurasian Economic Union (hereinafter EAEU): the Russian Federation, Belarus, Armenia, Kazakhstan and Kirgizstan. The article defines conceptual space for the category "Cross-boundary projects e-governance for the EAEU countries". The paper analyses project management development in the EAEU countries and union member states, identifies the development trends for the corresponding territories. The benchmarking reveals best experience of the e-governance projects at the state level. The authors propose and justify the EAEU cross-boundary project classification, which specifies and distinguishes the following notions: "EAEU cross-boundary IT projects of first priority" and "EAEU cross-boundary sustaining IT projects". The article outlines the main development elements of the EAEU e-governance development institution: Strategic central project office. That is the organization, created by the Eurasian Economic Commission and dealing with planning and control of the cross-boundary project activity between EAEU members, providing methodological and administrative support that is in charge of creating project oriented project portfolio e-governance system, separate cross-functional projects e-governance system and EAEU programs e-governance system. The authors have worked out a simplified pattern of the proposed cross-boundary projects e-governance scheme in order to conduct consistent economic policy between EAEU countries.

Keywords: Project approach · E-governance · Cross-boundary project · Integration · Project office · EAEU

1 Introduction

To maintain consistent economic policy between EAEU countries we should be constantly searching for new tools, methods and mechanisms, as well as analyzing and improving the current ones. In the public management the project approach has been a common method to conduct consistent economic policy for more than 50 years in many countries, for the transnational unions this method also has always been one of the most popular ones.

In particular, in the European Union (hereinafter referred to as EU) there is an e-governance system for mutual projects on the development of the social sphere in the EU members, for mutual transport infrastructure, for environmental projects [1].

Nowadays the EU is the best example of the transnational projects implementation in the ICT area.

EAEU joint projects can facilitate both mutual economic policy and coordination of actions of all the union members under general methodology, i.e. become a key element of integration within EAEU and collaboration with the third countries.

However, transnational projects implementation calls for modern methods and e-governance institutions which haven't been implemented yet, since they require proper scientific justification.

Project approach research line in terms of EAEU remains nearly intact in Russian and foreign scientific works. Among rare publications the works of Tkachenko E.A. should be emphasized. This author regards mutual projects of EAEU countries as a tool for EAEU joint industrial policy maintenance [2].

The representative of the Presidential state management Academy in the Kyrgyz Republic Kulmatova A.T., investigating the role of the Republic in the EAEU integration projects and pointing out their significance, also specifies that under these projects "Kirghizia can push on to the next level of economic and social development, recover national output and boost national economy" [3].

Beresnev justifies the significance of EAEU infrastructural projects, taking into consideration the economic safety priorities [4].

The works of Karachai and Bolgov are of particular interest for this study. These authors analyze the e-participatory projects within the institutional framework of the e-governance system in the EAEU [5].

In particular, the authors ground advantages of e-test application for migrants, mobile apps use for the foreign citizens, who can pass an assembled examination in the countries of origin.

Authors have compiled a list of parameters for comparison of strategies and programs on development of information-oriented society in the EAEU countries.

However, there are no publications, which regard project approach as the method of consistent economic policy implementation in EAEU countries. There are no studies that systematize the notion of project management development in the EAEU countries, determine possible trends for transnational projects, there are no proposals on creation of unified electronic system for EAEU mutual projects management.

2 Methodology

The primary method of the study is the method of structural levels, proposed by doctor of Economics Karaseva [6]. This method allows to consider project approach as a part of EAEU economic system.

Under project management development analysis in the EAEU countries, the authors performed benchmarking, where they took their own comparison criteria as the reference values to compare the following: the existence of methods and tools for project e-governance, in particular, project management data system for public authorities; existence of national standards in project management, approval of international standard ISO 21500-2014 "Guidance on project management"; existence of project-digital competences development center in public structures, Central project office functioning; project office in public private partnership; experience in implementation of projects.

The authors employed simulation method, statistical analysis method etc. to work out proposals for project approach implementation.

The open data sample under study includes information, obtained from the official sites of the state central banks of EAEU countries, Economic Commission for Europe (hereinafter referred to as ECE), global bulletin repository of the Analytical center, affiliated to the Government of the Russian Federation.

3   Results

3.1   The Conceptual Space for the Category "Cross-Boundary Projects E-Governance for the EAEU Countries"

The notion of e-governance is mainly used in Russian and foreign scientific works in terms of corporate and state management.

New IT technologies in state management help to extend direct communications and feedback between the state and emerging civil society in Russia, stimulate the involvement of various population groups in the country management, including regional management, local communities management, improve the procedures of collection, processing and analysis of data, both on general state of things and on particular directions of development of the Russian Federation and society [7].

Supranatorial transnational management of EAEU countries mutual projects implies wide application of information and communication technologies, a new level of efficiency and convenience for the EAEU organizations and citizens in terms of obtaining services, necessary for mutual projects implementation, as well as information on the process of implementation of these projects and the results.

EAEU transnational projects e-governance should reduce the influence of geographic location of project participants, ensure efficient and less labor consuming management and fundamental change in mutual relations of EAEU representatives; expand the responsibility of public authorities in the EAEU countries for the projects implementation.

EAEU transnational projects e-governance presumes that at least 2 state members should participate in the process: the Russian Federation, Belarus, Armenia, Kazakhstan or Kirghizstan.

3.2   The Project Management Development Analysis in EAEU Countries

The modern project development that is aimed at reaching transnational goals of EAEU countries is now at the initial stage of implementation only in terms of particular question: accomplishment of the EAEU digital agenda up to 2025 in order to create a unified financial market.

Since 2014 the union has been implementing an integrated data system, establishing cross-boundary confidence space, launching project on cross-boundary space development, which provides the opportunity to recognize digital signatures and is focused on electronic workflow management on the territory of the EAEU.

A special project office was created to support business and governmental initiatives of Eurasian Economic Commission members; the first project in this area has been already launched. It is called "Digital tracking of products".

The regulatory base for the implementation of EAEU joint projects in terms of digital transformation includes the documents, approved by the Supreme Eurasian Economic Council, Eurasian Intergovernmental Council, the Eurasian Economic Commission Council and the Eurasian Economic Commission Board. These documents are represented in Table 1.

Thus, within the EAEU there is the so called Regulatory Sandbox – a special legal regime that allows legal entities, who are engaged in developing new financial products and services to conduct experiments, connected with the implementation of such products in the reserved area, without breaking the laws of each particular country.

The project office includes representatives of all the EAEU members, who have advanced skills in the area of project evaluation and analysis. The office experts are supposed to communicate directly with all the similar EAEU structures, which are involved in the project implementation for EAEU members [5].

The notion of "project office" has been recently introduced to the EAEU transnational management, while its synonym "project management office" has been used at the corporate level for 10 years.

"Project management office is a centralized organizational structure, intended for improvement of project management methods and results" [8].

The project management development in EAEU countries is unequal: The Russian Federation is introducing project approach to the public management structures, Kazakhstan and Belarus are successfully applying management in question to public private partnership (hereinafter – PPP); Kirgizia has signed an agreement on implementation of the first PPP project, Kirghizia is effectuating infrastructural projects with the assistance of the Eurasian Fund for Stabilization and Development.

Project management national standards. Currently in Russia there are 4 project management standards (including ISO 21500-2014). The situation in the Republic of Kazakhstan is the same.

The introduction of project approach into the public management system of the Russian Federation implies active participation in the process of project management or project management realization.

To manage projects means to organize and/or to plan them, as well as to control and/or to coordinate material and technical, financial and labor resources during the project cycle. Project management is aimed at reaching the goals of efficient project by means of modern methods, technologies and technical tools in order to obtain the results (to get the products), stipulated by the project [9].

Table 1. Regulatory documents, employed for the implementation of EAEU joint projects in terms of digital transformation

The Supreme Eurasian Economic Council	The Eurasian Intergovernmental Council	The Eurasian Economic Commission Council	The Eurasian Economic Commission Board
Resolution № 12 "Key lines of EAEU digital agenda implementation up to 2025", dated the 11th of October 2017	Resolution № 2 "On implementation of project, named Eurasian industrial cooperation and subcontracting network and technology transfer", dated the 30th of April, 2019	Resolution № 111 "On necessary improvements for initiatives evaluation criteria in the course of EAEU digital agenda implementation", dated the 20th of December, 2017	Resolution of Board № 58 "On the requirements to the set of documents, necessary for project launch in the course of EAEU digital agenda implementation, as well as to project data sheet", dated the 16th of April, 2019
Resolution № 21 "On development of the EAEU digital agenda", dated the 26th of December, 2016	Resolution № 6 "On setting conditions for development of the digital trade ecosystem in the EAEU", dated the 30th of April, 2019		Resolution № 29 "On procedure of submitting information about the initiative in the course of the EAEU digital agenda implementation", dated the 19th of February, 2018
EAEU digital agenda statement	Resolution № 1 "On project implementation tools in the EAEU digital agenda", dated the 1st of February, 2019		
	Resolution № 4 "On Procedure of improving initiatives in the course of EAEU digital agenda implementation", dated the 25th of October, 2017		

Intersectoral interaction project in public structures is a complex of interrelated activities, aimed at constructing and/or reconstructing of infrastructural object in the area that has limited duration and resources and implemented within the framework of meaningful, motivated and profitable interaction of state (municipal), commercial and (or) non-commercial sectors.

The modern implementation tools for the projects in question are public private partnership, concessional legal relations, special investment contracts – SIC (bilateral interaction) and participatory budgeting (bi- or trilateral interaction).

The Russian Federation has started to introduce project approach to the public structures recently pursuant to RF Government Decree, dated 15 of October 2016 № 1050, which later was annulated in virtue of another RF Governmental Decree № 1288, which was adopted at the end of 2018.

This decree has established project activity procedure that sets organizational scheme for project activity management system, stages of launching, preparing, implementation, monitoring and termination of prioritized projects (programs) at the federal level. This procedure should be used at the regional level as well.

In order to fulfil the Decree the project e-governance system in public structures is being developed. It should ensure interaction of the project activity management structures, presented in Fig. 1. The interaction should be at the federal level and involve special modules of "Electronic budget" data system.

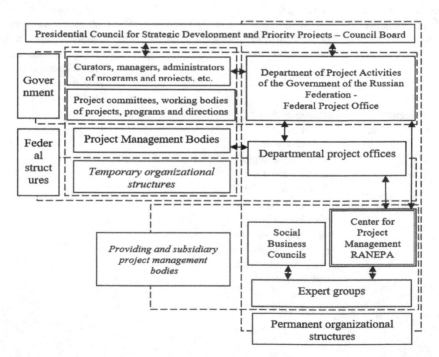

Fig. 1. Interdepartmental interaction under project management system in the Russian Federation, ensured by modules of the "Electronic budget" data system

Nowadays the project offices are being created in the regions and municipalities of the Russian Federation, there are many training programs, aimed at developing project competences for public and municipal servants.

The project management is being implemented in the governmental structures of the Republic of Kazakhstan within the third stage of state modernization. This stage is devoted to technical modernization.

Having analyzed the international experience, the public authorities of the Republic of Kazakhstan have devised a pattern for electronic project development, which should facilitate the implementation of additional measures, targeted at boosting the economy.

"Project management department coordinates and provides methodological support for the state agencies that are involved in project management implementation. The responsibilities of this department also include automated project implementation monitoring, analytical support for setting and reaching target values, established by public authorities, as well as studying of project management international experience and its proper application" [9].

The project management department resorts to the national information analysis system for the project management. It is called "Project office". It can be used by the employees of enterprises that are related local councils (akimats), industry agencies ministries and joint stock National welfare fund "Samruk-Kazyna".

Public private partnership projects are being commonly implemented in Kazakhstan. In 2011–2014 the amendments to the law of the Republic of Kazakhstan "on concessions" were made. This law stipulates several new legal and financial mechanisms: types of concession agreements; tenders, consisting of several stages (one or two); protection from state concessional liabilities sequestration; direct arrangements with creditors etc.

In 2015 in Kazakhstan a brand new law on PPP was adopted. It was drafted with the assistance of PPP center experts – project office for projects of this type.

This new law supposes deregulation in different areas of PPP implementation, extends the list of PPP participants, increases the impact of private sector on launching and planning of public private partnership projects [10].

Kazakhstan business community also has experience in project management. For instance, construction industry leader Bi-Group Company is one of the best in terms of implementation and use of calendar network planning and project implementation deadline monitoring in data systems.

The first public private partnership agreement was celebrated in Kirghizia and was connected with the healthcare – it was called "Hemodialysis services in Bishkek, Osh and Jalal-Abad". Nowadays there are 15 public private partnership projects in Kirgizia with the total cost over 165 mln. dollars.

Belarus started to evolve project approach within public private partnership in 1991. The PPP development in the Republic of Belarus is carried out according to government activity program of the Republic of Belarus in 2011–2015. The program claims that the PPP has been one of the key directions of the governmental activity in the Republic of Belarus for five years.

Thus, the Republic of Belarus has implemented regulatory system for the public private partnership, has established institutional environment for implementation of corresponding projects, has determined pilot projects. All the PPP experts have prominent digital project competences.

There is an interdepartmental infrastructural coordination Council in the Republic, which, in fact, is the state project office for public private partnership. Besides, in Belarus exists Permanent Committee of the Union State, which can carry out transnational projects of the corresponding union countries in order to reach its own goals.

As for Armenia, there the project approach is implemented as a part of infrastructural projects of the Eurasian Fund for Stabilization and Development. The first project is the construction of the road tunnel "North-South" (the southern part of the tunnel). The second one is the improvement of irrigation systems which is dotted, but is carried out almost in all the parts of Armenia, implying both modernization and repair of existing and construction of new irrigation systems. Many agricultural projects are to be realized soon.

However, we should point out that the main EAEU development institution is the Eurasian Development Bank (EDB), which is the managing tool of the Eurasian Fund for Stabilization and Development.

Some results of the conducted research of EAEU project management development are compiled in the matrix, presented in Table 2.

Table 2. Project management development matrix in the EAEU countries

EAEU member comparison base	Russia	Kazakhstan	Belarus	Kirghizia	Armenia
The use of data systems to implement project management in public sector	+	+	–	–	–
The existence of national standard for project management	+	–	–	–	–
Approval of ISO international standard 21500-2014 "Guidance on project management"	+	+	–	–	–
The existence of digital project competences development center in public structures	+	+	–	–	–
Central project office functioning	+	+	+	–	–
Project office functioning with regard to PPP	–	+	+	–	–
Project development experience	+	+	+	+	+
Project implementation experience	+	+	–	–	–

It is obvious that the transnational projects implementation implies elaboration of unified methodology for project e-governance and this can be fulfilled within ISO 21500-2014 "Guidance on project management". The approval of this standard in Belarus, Kirghizia and Armenia will facilitate Eurasian integration and EAEU collaboration with the third countries by means of mutual projects implementation.

3.3   Transnational Projects Implementation Lines in EAEU Countries

The transnational projects implementation lines in EAEU countries can be identified, regarding the purpose of establishment of this union: to create unified product, operation, service, capital and labor market. Common cross-market needs also should be considered.

However, it is worth mentioning that nowadays in the EAEU countries common market is being emerged, and it differs from the unified one in the level of integration. The unified market should have identical rules for all the members, while the activity of EAEU market members these days can only be coordinated, if the control on the part of national legislation is preserved.

To the unified and common product, operation and service market in the EAEU belong: common financial market, unified service market, transport integration, cross-border trade, common pharmaceuticals market, common power market.

As for e-governance, we should emphasize once again that in the EEC there is a special project office which deals with the EAEU digital agenda on financial market, the first project in this area is already on the way, it is called "Digital tracking of products". It is to be accomplished in 2025. This project is focused on the common financial market development.

Besides, the "Single window" technology and preliminary electronic reporting tools boost the cross-boundary trade. These tools provide data about products, imported to the EAEU.

The information exchange was checked under the testing of the pilot program, devoted to developing of special alerting system for detecting products that don't comply with the EAEU technical standards.

Such a system implies creation of common information resources, involving corresponding state services and agencies to share the data about the detected cases of dangerous goods circulation within the EAEU with the further possibility to submit this information to whom it may concern.

3.4   EAEU Transnational Projects' Classification

Taking into account EAEU countries economic policy on developing mutual markets, we suggest that in this case the following transnational projects should be implemented: aimed at satisfying the needs of particular EAEU market and those, aimed at ensuring proper functioning for the whole market – cross-market projects. However, each group can implement infrastructural, IT and complex projects (Fig. 2).

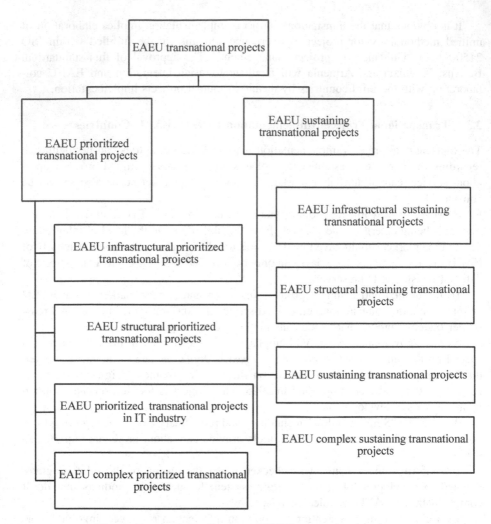

Fig. 2. Proposed classification of EAEU transnational projects.

According to this classification the project "Digital tracking of products", focused on the common financial market development, belongs to EAEU prioritized transnational projects in IT industry.

The project "Development and implementation of the unified system of money remittance on the territory of the EAEU for labor migrants of the state members" will belong to the same group, if launched

Money transfers from labor migrants are of utmost importance for the economies of the "small" countries of the EAEU. The average transfers/GDP ratio for the last five years has made up 16,6% and 29,5% for Kirghizia and Armenia respectively.

Russia is the main donor for these countries, it accounts for 59% and 97% of all the money transfers to Armenia and Kirghizia respectively. EAEU sustaining transnational project can be the project on development and implementation of unified procedure for the market members, when the infrastructural transnational market is launched.

The project "Development and implementation of the unified system of delinquent acts prevention, regarding antitrust on EAEU cross-boundary market" will belong to EAEU sustaining transnational project.

The EEC is in charge of this project. It is EAEU antitrust agency that deals with quelling violations, committed by economic entities, individuals and non-commercial organizations – residents of the EAEU member states, regarding general competition rules. This applies to violations that can have a negative impact on competition on transnational markets.

In particular, the proposed project should be dedicated to the prevention of power abuse on the part of the economic entity or collective dominance abuse.

3.5   EAEU Strategic Central Project Office Organizational Scheme

As we have already mentioned, the first EAEU project office has already been established in the EEC in order to support and work out digital project initiatives, aimed at developing financial market. The project office includes the representatives of all state-members. However, this is not enough to carry out e-governance of project activity elements for the whole range of transnational projects.

If we use project approach to maintain consistent economic policy between EAEU countries, then we should establish Strategic central project office, which will be able to evaluate and analyze any proposed projects that are aimed at developing of EAEU unified markets.

There are several types of project offices:

"Basic project office – provides support and consultations, carry out training.
Managerial – prepares project leaders.
Strategic – manages project portfolio" [11].

Under EAEU Strategic central project office we mean the structure, affiliated to the EEC, which plans and controls transnational project activity of the EAEU members, provides methodological and administrative support, deals with developing of project-focused e-governance system for project portfolios, cross-functional projects programs, implemented in the EAEU countries.

The proposed organizational scheme for EAEU Strategic central project office is presented in Fig. 3.

The expert groups for particular transnational EAEU market should also include government agencies experts of all EAEU members and business communities.

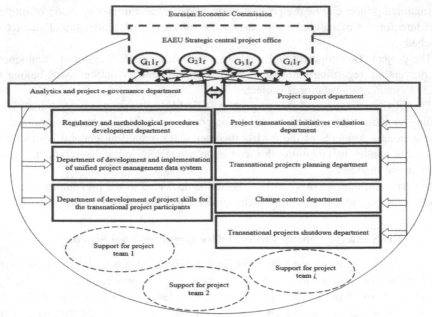

Gi – Team of experts for particular transnational EAEU market

Fig. 3. Proposed organizational scheme for EAEU Strategic central project office.

3.6 Pattern for EAEU Transnational Projects e-Governance

Figure 4 presents simplified pattern for implementation of transnational projects e-governance in the EAEU countries that will help to maintain consistent economic policy.

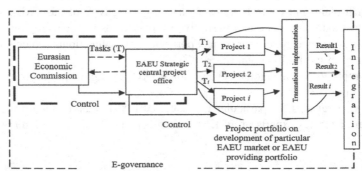

T*i* – tasks on development of particular EAEU market or on cross-market functioning support in EAEU

Fig. 4. Simplified pattern for implementation of transnational projects e-governance in the EAEU countries

To make the proposed pattern come true, we should obviously implement project information management system that is to operate for joint projects. The proper functioning of such system should be ensured by the following modules: project certification; program management; project portfolio management; contract management; project initiative management; management of non-project activities; meeting management; management of orders; time management; performance management; personnel management; management of financial performance of the project; managing risks, problems and open questions; project reporting; generating analytical reports on projects and monitoring; change management; knowledge base management; storage of project documents.

4 Conclusions

The conducted research permits us to conclude the following:

- The level of project management development in the EAEU countries is unequal, nowadays Russia and Kazakhstan have the best experience in this area and besides, they are gaining mutual experience in the implementation of transnational project that forms part of the digital agenda for financial market development;
- It is obvious that the transnational projects implementation implies elaboration of unified methodology for project e-governance, and this can be fulfilled within ISO 21500-2014 "Guidance on project management". The approval of this standard in Belarus, Kirghizia and Armenia will facilitate Eurasian integration and EAEU collaboration with the third countries by means of mutual projects implementation;
- The transnational projects implementation lines in EAEU countries can be identified, regarding the purpose of establishment of this union: to create a unified product, operation, service, capital and labor market. Common cross-market needs also should be considered.
- To systematize the notion of transnational projects that can be regarded as tools for maintain consistent economic policy in the EAEU region, this paper suggest classification, according to which the transnational projects can be divided into prioritized and sustaining. These can be further divided into infrastructural, structural, IT or complex;
- EAEU prioritized transnational projects are those, connected with issues of particular EAEU market;
- EAEU sustaining transnational projects are implemented to ensure proper functioning of the whole market, cross-market projects;
- to develop mutual project e-governance, we should establish EAEU strategic central project office which should become a part of EEC.
- Simplified pattern for implementation of transnational projects e-governance in the EAEU countries, as well as organizational scheme for EAEU Strategic central project office have been elaborated under the study. They serve to maintain consistent economic policy between EAEU countries;
- The expert groups for particular transnational EAEU market should also include government agencies experts of all EAEU members and business communities.

– This topic can be further developed in different ways, in particular, the methods and methodology of EAEU projects e-governance, based on the unified public private partnership principles, should have a proper scientific justification.

References

1. Millan, M., Salvador, R., Mantilla, E., Artinano, B.: Meteorology and photochemical air pollution in southern Europe: experimental results from EC research projects. Atmos. Environ. **30**(12), 1909–1924 (1996)
2. Burinov, M.A.: Digital government as the key factor for regional state management upgrade. Soc. Ski. Philos. **1**(22), 123–129 (2013)
3. Lomovtseva, O.A., Kuzmina, L.R., Golodova, A.A.: Project office as a key factor for municipal formation and city industry development. Volgogr. State Tech. Univ. News **1** (211), 79–85 (2018)
4. Beresnev, F.A.: EAEU infrastructure projects implementation, involving economic safety priorities. In: International Research to Practice Conference, pp. 138–141 (2015)
5. Karachay, V.A., Bolgov, R.V.: Electronic participation projects in the EAEU electronic management system. Eurasian Law J. **7**(98), 215–221 (2016)
6. Karaseva, L.A.: Role of structural levels method in economic system study Tver state university Bulletin. Ser. Econ. Manag. **15**, 25–33 (2012)
7. A common EAEU Digital Agenda would be implemented and a common financial market would be created by 2025. Eurasian Economic Commission. http://www.eurasiancommiss ion.org/ru/nae/news/Pages/3-04-2018-4.aspx. Accessed 20 June 2018
8. Strokovich, A.V.: Project management: study guide (2011). http://uchebnik-online.net/book/ 103-upravlenie-proektamiuchebnoe-posobie-strokovich-av.html. Accessed 04 May 2018
9. Project management: study guide/under the general editorship of I.I. Mazur, 2nd edn., p. 664. Omega-L (2004)
10. Project management: Ministry for the national economy of the Republic of Kazakhstan. http://economy.gov.kz/ru/pages/proektnoe-upravlenie. Accessed 14 June 2018
11. Legislation: Kazakhstan Public-Private Partnership Center. http://kzppp.kz/%D0%B7%D0% B0%D0%BA%D0%BE%D0%BD%D0%BE%D0%B4%D0%B0%D1%82%D0%B5%D0% BB%D1%8C%D1%81%D1%82%D0%B2%D0%BE. Accessed 18 June 2018
12. Krylov, A., Temchina, M.: Guidelines for project management implementation in municipal and regional structures, p. 10

Semantic Business Process Modeling as the Key to Interoperable Public Services in Seamless E-Government

Yu. Akatkin⊙ and E. Yasinovskaya⁽⊠⁾⊙

Plekhanov Russian University of Economics,
36 Stremyanny per., Moscow 117997, Russia
{u.akatkin, elena}@semanticpro.org

Abstract. Essential for digitalization all-as-a-service model causes the shift of state priorities from a simple provision of public information to the delivery of high-quality and efficient public services. This aspect brings a particular importance to the reengineering of public administration procedures aiming to provide public services at a new level. In this paper we propose the approach to the design and modernization of public services, as well as related business processes, which combines existing modeling methods with the enterprise architecture frameworks to ensure semantic interoperability not only at the data models level but using executable models of public service. We represent the method of public services development as semantic business processes in the context of enterprise architecture together with the results of its pilot implementation and evaluation.

Keywords: Digital government · Digitalization · Semantic interoperability · Data-centricity · Model-oriented approach · Information sharing · Business process modeling · Semantic business process

1 Introduction

The expansion of public services provided jointly by various public administrations and subordinate organizations, introduced the paradigm of seamless government prescribing the behavior of government agencies as a whole for the best respond to the needs of citizens and businesses based on collaboration and networking between the government units [1]. The implementation of this paradigm is based on the reorganization of administrative procedures to eliminate obstacles to cross agency interaction [2].

The example of this approach application is the Swiss eGovernment BPM Ecosystem. This BP modeling environment gives the basis for modernization of interagency cooperation. It uses government strategies for BPs modeling, as well as business models and development models to define the functions requiring interaction between the internal and external services of various agencies. At the same time it considers the service-oriented architecture principles which are of key importance for the enterprise architecture implemented in Swiss eGovernment [3].

© Springer Nature Switzerland AG 2020
A. Chugunov et al. (Eds.): EGOSE 2019, CCIS 1135, pp. 179–193, 2020.
https://doi.org/10.1007/978-3-030-39296-3_14

"Business process (BP) is a set of one or more linked procedures or activities which collectively realize a business objective or policy goal, normally within the context of an organizational structure defining functional roles and relationships" [4]. By analogy with the general definition of modeling, here and hereinafter we consider business process modeling as a method to research BPs using their models, as well as a direct building and studying of models describing actually existing and designed BPs to determine or improve their characteristics, rationalize ways of developing them.

BP modeling covers various aspects of enterprise activities: participating organizations, governing documents, compliance of administrative actions with legal norms [5, 6], establishment of roles and positions, use of resources, time frame and dependencies of administrative procedures, document and information exchange between different stakeholders and roles working together in processes, etc. However, the use of BP modeling techniques in public administration works only if the management, the involved departments, and the units responsible for the technological implementation, work closely with each other and achieve a common understanding in process-oriented interaction [2].

Unfortunately, in Russia, the ideas of business processes modeling in the public sector have not found practical application. There are some statements, including proposals for the implementation of Government process management (GPM) - the management approach of "engineering communication processes between the state and societies focused on the fullest possible satisfaction of the needs of service consumers" [7]. Some researchers [8] as well as the authors [9] suggested using BPNM for the e-transformation of state and municipal services and succeeded to implement these principles in reformation of some administrative procedures. However, in most cases, the procedure was formal and had nothing to do either with the development or "new work strategies, the actual process design activity, and the implementation of the change in its complex technological, human, and organizational dimensions" [10], or with "the redesign of business processes utilizing IT to bring about a quantum leap in performance" [11].

To implement the principles of digital economy (openness, data-centricity, customer-centricity) digital public services should follow the concept of "open world"[1], where any person (or system) can find and use all its elements in any place at any time. Semantic interoperability becomes an important condition of an open interaction.

We consider reasonable to support semantic interoperability at the stage of public service development via preserving the domain semantics of modelled business processes. This approach provides the association of concepts and requirements, formalized in data models, with the elements of the business process we use in BP models (e.g. workflow, role, events models and others). Consolidation and alignment of the entire set of models based on the domain ontology synthesized during the development stage allows building an executable model of a business process, where all the elements can get unambiguous interpretation in the context of the domain.

---

[1] https://www.dataversity.net/introduction-to-open-world-assumption-vs-closed-world-assumption/.

2 Methods

To develop the Method of Semantic Business Processes Modeling for Public Services we applied Design Science Research Methodology for Information Systems Research (DSRM) [12]. DSRM incorporates principles, practices, and procedures required to carry out research in information systems and meets three objectives: it is consistent with prior literature; it provides a nominal process model for doing DS research; and it provides a mental model for presenting and evaluating DS research in information systems. DSRM ensures the existence of clear links and a smooth transition between the design and development of our method as well as its application or evaluation in the pilot case study and future works.

DSRM includes six activities: problem identification and motivation, definition of the objectives for a solution, design and development, demonstration, evaluation, and communication (Fig. 1).

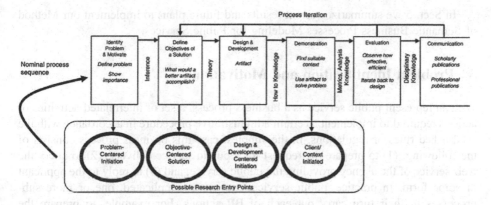

Fig. 1. DSRM process model

This paper represents our research and covers the following DSRM activities we made to develop the Method of Semantic Business Processes Modeling for Public Services (Method).

1. *Problem identification and motivation.* At this stage we conducted the review of current experience in business modeling and its application in public administration procedures to identify the problem and define our motivation (Sect. 3).
2. *Objectives for the solution.* Conducted research together with service oriented and data-centric approaches helped us discover the following objectives of this work:

   - To combine semantic methods of interaction with the business modeling solutions to achieve semantic interoperability.
   - To facilitate the modeling of semantic business processes using various semantic models.

   We suggest our Method as the way to realize these objectives.

3. *Design and development.* We determined the basic approach of using international standards and frameworks together with the business modeling languages and tools to develop the Method (Sect. 4.1). The implementation of this approaches gave the foundation for the suggested Method (Sect. 4.2).
4. *Demonstration.* To demonstrate the power of the suggested Method we conducted a special research in collaboration with the Federal state budgetary institution "National Medical and Surgical Center named after N.I. Pirogov" of the Ministry of Healthcare of the Russian Federation. This pilot case study we shortly represent in this paper (Sect. 4.3).
5. *Evaluation.* Pilot project gave us positive results. Primary evaluation showed the necessity to continue our research aiming to choose modern tools for semantic business process modeling and to extend implementation area.
6. *Communication.* At first stages we published a detailed research and suggested the Method in our book [13] to get expert opinion. We represent it in this paper in order to start the discussion during EGOSE 2019 and use more opportunities for further implementation.

In Sect. 5 we summarize current results and future plans to implement our Method of Semantic Business Processes Modeling for Public Services.

3   Problem Identification and Motivation

We can represent public service as a business process, a set of interrelated activities or actions required to implement a certain administrative procedure in accordance with the established rules or regulations. In the simplest case this business process consists of the following: (1) to prepare the request for a public service delivery, (2) to query the web-service of the agency providing the public service, and (3) to reply to the applicant in some form. In practice, public services are more complicated, one or more sub-processes in their turn carry out each of BP actions. For example, to prepare the response we need to request documents from various departments, to check information about the applicant, to decide whether to provide the service or to reject the request, and then to inform the applicant.

Various methodologies and notations for business processes modeling are applicable for the development of public services, e.g. Business Process Model and Notation (BPMN), Cognition enhanced Natural language Information Analysis Method (Cog-NIAM), eXtended Business Modeling Language (xBML), UML Behavior Diagrams, Event-driven Process Chain (EPC), as a part of Architecture of Integrated Information Systems (ARIS), Icam DEFinition for Function Modeling (IDEF0 и IDEF3).

The most common of them is BPMN [14]. An expressive notation of BP modeling, understandable to both technical specialists and business users is one of the main advantages of BPMN. Great practical importance to BPMN brings the fact that unlike other notations it allows (with some limitations) to create executable BP models.

Relevant works of foreign and domestic researchers show the possibility of using BPMN for public services development [8, 15–18]. In 2011–2013, the team, headed by the authors, developed and successfully tested a production prototype of the Public

Service Preparation System. This system covered main stages of public service development and implementation using BPMN to build up a single information environment based on a unified data model [9].

Despite the positive implementation experience, we should point BPMN does not support all activity modeling aspects, but only for those that are applicable to business processes. As noted in BPMN 2.0 specification (OMG), "this means that other types of modeling done by organizations for business purposes is out of scope for BPMN. Therefore, we point the following aspects that are out of the scope of this specification:

- Definition of organizational models and resources;
- Modeling of functional breakdowns;
- Data and information models;
- Modeling of strategy;
- Business rules models" [14].

The inability of particular languages and process modeling notations to represent all aspects of the activity concerns not only BPMN, but also other notations. A number of papers consider and justify this challenge [19–21]. "This gives reason to conclude that process modeling should be carried out simultaneously in several notations, so that each particular model could reflect a limited set of properties of the modeled phenomenon, and all together they would give a complete and comprehensive understanding of the modeled reality" [22].

To form a complete and consistent set of models is one of the key tasks in building an enterprise architecture. According to ISO R 15704:2008 (4.3.3–4.3.5)[2], standard enterprise architectures and methodologies can be based on common elements of enterprise design and modeling. Such common elements that ensure the consistency of the enterprise's views, in the order of increasing formalization, are dictionaries, metamodels and ontologies.

The use of "particular enterprise models" (reusable standard models) in building the architecture gives the user the opportunity to reuse concepts that are common to many enterprises and, consequently, improve the efficiency of modeling. In the process of architecture building, these models are adapted to the requirements of a specific enterprise. The Open Group Architecture Framework [23] supports this logic in the design and management of enterprise architecture. This framework is used in the construction of European Interoperability Reference Architecture[3].

The joint use of models relating to various aspects of the organization activity in BP modeling was the subject of a series of studies [24–27] in the past fifteen years. The main goal of these studies is to ensure business experts accurately understand the essence of the information used during the development of BP models as well as to provide a correct machine interpretation of data in their further reuse. This creates a basis for semantic interoperability during the joint execution of business processes by various systems. To achieve this goal, we suggest extending the semantics of BP model

---

[2] ISO 15704:2000. Industrial automation systems – Requirements for enterprise-reference architectures and methodologies, https://www.iso.org/standard/28777.html.

[3] https://joinup.ec.europa.eu/solution/eira.

by setting the semantic links between entities used in BP modeling and their similarities in other semantic models that describe the enterprise activity domain.

In 2007–2008 the European project SUPER[4] set the methodology and tools for semantic annotation of BP. This project applied an ontology stack for business processes modeling.

Thus, semantic annotation allows simultaneously to retain the benefits of BPMN and to achieve semantic interoperability of the executable process model. For semantically annotated BP models we use the term semantic business processes, and their management has got the name of SBPM (Semantic Business Process Management) [27].

At the same time, the scope of the mentioned studies remains outside a very important problem. It is the completeness and consistency of semantic description based on a set of models describing the business process domain. Each of these models has its own meaning, i.e. it conveys a certain semantics, but setting a connection between the semantics of different models requires special efforts. Moreover, in modeling notations and methods, such association, as a rule, is either absent (not entailed), or has significant limitations (predetermined links composition/direction, a high level of abstraction).

Even though the existing modeling methods have a long period of development and implementation, they are well-established and effectively cope with their tasks, the notations used for the design still focus on brevity/clarity of graphic primitives and their interrelation. None of them considers that a digital service exists (developed and executed) in a heterogeneous information environment and may be required for the provision of another digital service.

From the point of the architectural approach models reflect the requirements and views of various stakeholders involved in the design, implementation and use of a business process. In this case, to achieve the completeness and consistency in the set of models we consider the requirements and consolidate the views of interested parties. Semantic approach, in its turn, does not use this advantage, thus it significantly limits the possibility to create business processes oriented on the modernization of public administration procedures as well as to meet the requirements of digital economy.

The problem of completeness and consistency is also relevant for the public service design, since we use a wide range of models for both designing the service and providing it to the consumer. Each of these models formalizes one or another aspect describing the public administration activity during the public service provision:

- *Workflow model* describes the elements of a business process reflecting the transfer of documents, information or tasks from one participant to another to perform actions according to a set of guidelines.
- *Organizational (Role) model* reflects the internal structure of BP participants/ executors, control flows, as well as the task distribution and the specific features of performance management.

---

[4] Semantics Utilized for Process Management within and between Enterprises: Using semantics for managing processes within and between enterprises, https://www.oasis-open.org/committees/download.php/15916/Super-use-case.pdf.

- *Event model and/or state model* describes the set of states and transitions that causes the change of the service status.
- *Domain model* formalizes the body of knowledge relating to the service domain, represented as an object model or ontology.
- *Data models, exchange models* integrate sets of concepts for describing data and relationships between them, as well as the constraints imposed on data.
- *The conceptual service model* unifies the description of public services based on the use of open standards.

To solve this problem, we propose to consolidate the architectural approach, the construction of a single information environment and semantic methods within a unified Method of Semantic Business Processes Modeling.

4 Methods of Semantic Business Processes Modeling for Public Services

4.1 Basic Approach to Semantic Business Process Modeling

Models describing the business process domain belong to different segments of the enterprise architecture. The area of use determines the semantics of each model and the application of architectural methodology provides the completeness and consistency of the entire set of models. For example, Architecture Development Method in TOGAF provides checking of completeness, internal consistency and correctness of the architecture models at the step "GAP analysis" when building Business Architecture (Phase B), Information Systems Architectures, including Data Architecture and Applications Architecture (Phase C), as well as Technical Architecture (Phase D) [23].

As a rule, to achieve the completeness of stakeholders' requirements fulfillment it is common to establish the links between model elements and requirements further then subsequently evaluate the scope of requirements. Well-known methods that solve the problem of comparing and consolidating models are good enough to ensure the consistency [28].

The use of these methods allows constructing a generalized model of the BP domain—*the applied ontology of the business process*—an ontology model based on the BPMN metamodel, which serves to describe the domain of the business process. The applied BP ontology provides the description of the semantics and the interlinks of BP elements with the elements of other applied models (i.e. traceability), coordinating and combining semantic models representing various aspects of the business process.

The applied BP ontology can use the mechanisms provided for by the architectural methodologies for cross-model associations. For example, TOGAF offers a way to integrate architectural models based on Content Metamodel (CM)[5], which defines the formal structure and connections of all elements developed within an architecture, such as a process or application. CM is a basic model with a minimum set of functions. It can be extended during the design/configuration of a particular enterprise architecture.

---

[5] Chapter 30. Content Metamodel, http://pubs.opengroup.org/architecture/togaf9-doc/arch/.

We suggest using CM TOGAF with the following extensions for building an applied business process ontology:

- service extension required to combine the information about external services used in the performance of a business process;
- process modeling extension for combining the event model and/or state model in the applied BP ontology;
- data extension using to separate the logical and physical elements of the applied BP ontology based on domain, data and exchange models;
- consolidation of infrastructure extension for consolidating the elements of models representing the implemented tools, programs and other software within the applied BP ontology.

When using the TOGAF Content Metamodel we extend applied BP ontology with CM entities. In this case we can use CM entities as generalizing types for the elements of applied BP ontology. This means they can perform root elements in the type hierarchy of applied BP ontology. Otherwise we can use CM entities as additional classification types that add the context provided by the applied BP ontology to the elements of architectural models.

The basis for the described approach to providing a semantically complete and non-contradictory business process description is a combined use of semantic annotation and architectural methods. Regarding public services this means that their development should be carried out in the context of enterprise architecture construction and reengineering of business processes in the public administration entity providing the service. Providing semantic description of a public service is highly important for semantic interoperability of public service models. Since they are created at the intersections of various domains and executed in a heterogeneous environment of information systems interaction. The latter is due to the fact that public service is not only provided directly to the final consumer, but it can also form a new public service based on existing ones. The use of existing public services by third-party consumers in the development and execution of their own business processes predetermines the logic of designing public services using Semantic Web principles and technologies.

To achieve semantic interoperability, as well as to ensure the completeness and consistency of the public service semantic description we suggest using semantic annotation based on the applied BP ontology. For this purpose, we associate the elements of the applied BP ontology, corresponding to CM TOGAF entities, with the matching elements of BPMN using equivalence relation; we establish generalizing and/or classifying connections of applied BP ontology elements with the entities of other models in accordance with SKOS, and relationships between the elements in applied BP ontology in accordance with CM TOGAF.

4.2 Semantic Business Processes Modeling for Public Services

We suggest implementing the described approach in the following Method of Semantic Business Processes Modeling for Public Services. In accordance with the proposed Method, the development and implementation of a public service passes 4 stages (see Fig. 2).

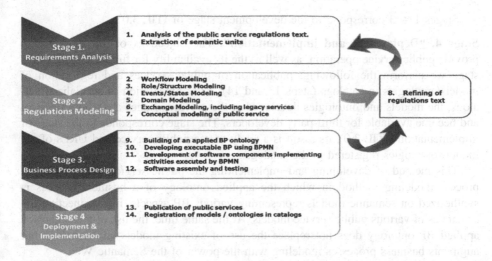

Fig. 2. The stages of public service development and implementation

Stage 1. "Requirements Analysis". The objective of this stage is to form the terminological basis of the applied BP ontology and semantic rules for controlling the content of the business process using the available benchmark data. The stage includes one step: "Analysis of the text containing rules and administrative procedures, regulating the public service (hereinafter – regulations). Extraction of semantic units" (step 1). As a result of this stage, we form the sets of vocabularies describing the semantics of a public service and relationships both between these vocabularies and their elements.

Stage 2. "Regulations Modeling". The goal of this stage is to develop the models formalizing workflow, organizational structure and roles, events and/or states, together with domain and exchange models, including the models for legacy services, a conceptual public service model (steps 2 ÷ 7). In the process of modeling, it may be necessary to refine the regulations text (step 8). The result of stage 2 is a set of models that fully describes the public service regulations, as well as refined regulations text, sets of vocabularies and links where applicable.

Stage 3. "Business Process Design". The purpose of this stage is to develop the public service software. This stage contains the following steps (9 ÷ 12): building of an applied BP ontology; developing executable BP using BPMN; development of software components implementing the activities executed by BPMN (BPMN 2.0); software assembly and testing. During the development of an executable BPMN, we trace the elements the applied BP ontology to BPMN elements. If steps 9 or 10 reveal the need to improve the regulations, we return to refining the regulations text (step 8). After this refining, we must repeat the stages "Requirements analysis" and "Regulations modeling". The result of this step is the software ready for installation and use.

Stages $1 \div 3$ correspond to the development stage of ITIL 3.0^6.

Stage 4. "Deployment and implementation". The objectives of the stage are to provide public service operation, as well as the its availability for further reuse. At this stage we perform the following: publication of public services and registration of models/ontologies in catalogs (steps 13 and 14). After registration in specialized catalogs, the models and ontologies developed at the previous stages are ready for reuse and become available for third-party developers. The stage corresponds to the stage of implementation (ITIL 3.0), its result is a ready-to-use public service and URLs of the models/ontologies registered in the catalog.

This method of developing and implementing the public service uses a business process modeling method in which the applied ontology of a business process is synthesized on semantic models representing various BP aspects, interconnecting the semantics of various public service models. At the same time, the use of the suggested applied BP ontology does not replace the use of existing models and notations but augments business processes modeling with the power of the Semantic Web.

The key features of the proposed Method are:

- **Use of the semantic approach in public service design**
  Semantic interoperability of public services is based on semantic consistency and completeness of models representing the various aspects necessary for designing, executing or improving the service. Semantic interoperability makes possible the reuse of public service during a third-party service/business process performance.
- **Consolidation of various models using applied BP ontology**
  Design and development of complex systems includes the representation of the system and its environment using various models containing their own semantics. It is necessary to determine the models for the development of public services, as well as to ensure the alignment and interconnection of their semantics by comparing and linking elements of different models, harmonizing the conceptual apparatus. The high-level applied business-process ontology combines elements and a set of relationships and provides semantic consistency and completeness, forming the basis for semantic interoperability.
- **Development of semantic business process based on applied ontology**
  We extend the description of the business process by semantic entities associated with the applied BP ontology. Such semantic annotation provides the possibility of representing the business process available for the reuse and accessible for an unambiguous interpretation by other participants of interaction.

4.3 Pilot Case Study. Modeling Business Processes for Digital Health Services

We used the proposed Method of Semantic Business Processes Modeling for Public Services as solution in the joint research of Plekhanov Russian University of

---

^{6} https://www.axelos.com/best-practice-solutions/itil.

Economics and Pirogov National Medical Center[7] on the theme "Development of semantic business processes modeling methods for digital health on the example of medical specials search". This work is important for the development of digital public services. There is no doubt that the possibility to choose the specialist with a required qualification, available at the right place and time, using necessary equipment etc. should extend such a priority public service as "Appointment to the doctor".

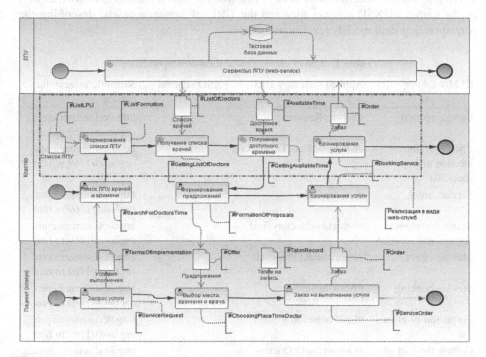

Fig. 3. Business process "Search of MD" in BPMN (http://www.semanticpro.org/articles/business_process_search_of_md_in_BPMN.html)

In accordance with the proposed Method, at stage 1, we analyzed regulatory documents, medicine standards, descriptions of service provision regulations, participating organizations and interacting information systems, prepared by medical specialists in order to form the set of core vocabularies.

Then, at stage 2, we designed workflow, organizational role models and event model based on the highlighted requirements. We also developed domain model and exchange models for information systems and services of testing environment as well as a conceptual model of the search service. We published developed models and existing Digital Health standards in the Center of Semantic Integration[8] semantic assets

---

[7] http://www.pirogov-center.ru/english/about/.

[8] http://csi.semanticpro.org/catalog/en.htm.

catalogue in order to model the basic business process for Digital Health Services following our method.

At stage 3, we designed an applied ontology and modeled the business process of searching and choosing a medical specialist using BPMN. Figure 3 represents the result of BP modeling.

Table 1 lists the elements of BPMN schema and indicates the entities of the developed domain data model we used to describe the search process in BPMN, as well as the names of XSD schema files and the URL of semantic assets, describing the corresponding data models (exchange models).

Table 1. List of elements and their correspondence

BPMN Object	Applied Ontology URI	XSD schema	Semantic asset in the catalog
Service request	#ServiceRequest		http://csi.semanticpro. org/asset/1769.ru.htm
Choice of time, location and specialist	#ChoosingPlaceTimeDoctor		http://csi.semanticpro. org/asset/1769.ru.htm
Service order	#ServiceOrder		http://csi.semanticpro. org/asset/1769.ru.htm
Search for clinics, doctors and schedule	#SearchForDoctorsTime		http://csi.semanticpro. org/asset/1769.ru.htm
Making offers	#FormationOfProposals		http://csi.semanticpro. org/asset/1769.ru.htm
Service booking	#BookingService		http://csi.semanticpro. org/asset/1769.ru.htm
Formation of clinics list	#ListFormation		http://csi.semanticpro. org/asset/1769.ru.htm
Getting the List of Doctors	#GettingListOfDoctors		http://csi.semanticpro. org/asset/1769.ru.htm
Getting the List of schedule slots	#GettingAvailableTime		http://csi.semanticpro. org/asset/1769.ru.htm
Terms of Service	#TermsOfImplementation	TermsOf Implementation. xsd	http://csi.semanticpro. org/asset/1778.ru.htm
Offers	#Offer	Offer.xsd	http://csi.semanticpro. org/asset/1816.ru.htm
Appointment Record	#TalonRecord	TalonRecord. xsd	http://csi.semanticpro. org/asset/1802.ru.htm
Order	#Order	Order.xsd	http://csi.semanticpro. org/asset/1809.ru.htm
List of Clinics	#ListLPU	ListLPU.xsd	http://csi.semanticpro. org/asset/1824.ru.htm
List of MDs	#ListOfDoctors	ListOfDoctors. xsd	http://csi.semanticpro. org/asset/1823.ru.htm
Available appointments	#AvailableTime	AvailableTime. xsd	http://csi.semanticpro. org/asset/1825.ru.htm

To simplify visualization, we do not display the common part of URI – http://pirogov-center.ru/semantic/ontologies/2018/9/ontology/DigitalHealth in Fig. 3 and Table 1. The full URI, for example, for a Service Request (#ServiceRequest) is: http://pirogov-center.ru/semantic/ontologies/2018/9/ontology/DigitalHealth#ServiceRequest.

At stage 4, we launched the developed business process in the testing environment BP execution.

Thus, we implemented the proposed Method of Semantic Business Processes Modelling for Public Services in case study. For further evaluation of this solution we represented the Method for checking and got an approval from domain experts and medical specialists. Implementation results will make the basis for the digital services modeling.

5   Current Results, Future Works and Conclusion

The paper highlights the issues of business process modeling. It represents the approach to semantic business processes modeling necessary for the design of digital public services. Proposed Method of Semantic Business Processes Modeling for Public Services consolidates architectural models, semantic data models and business processes. The authors show the results of the case study reflecting the demonstration, approbation and obtained expert evaluation of the proposed method.

Creating an effective methodology for reengineering and modeling of public services using semantic models of business processes, as well as implementing software tools for its application, is very important for the achievement of higher stages of e-government development (for example, digital government). In the nearest future the government and public administrations will have to face a new level of business integration. It will require not only reengineering of business processes, but also implementing them promptly. However, in public sector it has a certain difficulty [29].

The use of the proposed Method of Semantic Business Processes Modelling for Public Services can increase the readiness of e-Government systems for changes. In our opinion it will enable a qualitative assessment of the public service performance level together with the degree of their citizen-centricity.

The results obtained in the framework of the conducted research our research team plans to develop in the following directions:

- creation of applications and services based on the use of semantic models to provide semantic interoperability of heterogeneous information systems;
- implementation of an interpretable description of business processes in BPMN notation using semantic бкаassets for the development of public services;
- application of the suggested Method of Semantic Business Processes Modeling for Public Services for the digital transformation of public administration.

References

1. Estevez, E., Fillottrani, P., Janowski, T.: From E-Government to Seamless Government. http://citeseerx.ist.psu.edu/viewdoc/download?doi=10.1.1.610.9660&rep=rep1&type=pdf. Accessed 29 Nov 2019

2. Comission of European Communities: Commission Staff Working Paper, Linking up Europe: the Importance of Interoperability for eGovernment Services (2003). http://ec.europa.eu/idabc/servlets/Doc2bb8.pdf?id=1675. Accessed 29 Nov 2019

3. Walser Konrad, Schaffroth Marc BPM and BPMN as integrating concepts in eGovernment – the Swiss eGovernment BPM ecosystem. https://www.academia.edu/3141363/BPM_and_BPMN_as_Integrating_Concepts_in_eGovernment-The_Swiss_eGovernment_BPM_Ecosystem. Accessed 29 Nov 2019

4. Sensuse, D.I., Ramadhan, A.: The relationships of soft systems methodology (SSM), business process modeling and e-Government. Int. J. Adv. Comput. Sci. Appl. 3(1), 179–183 (2012). http://thesai.org/Publications/ViewPaper?Volume=3&Issue=1&Code=IJACSA&SerialNo=28. Accessed 29 Nov 2019

5. Simon, C., Olbrich, S.: Integration of legal constraints into business process models. In: Irani, Z. (Hrsg.) Transforming Government: People, Process and Policy, vol. 2. Emerald, Bradford (2007). https://www.emeraldinsight.com/doi/abs/10.1108/17506160710752002

6. Snellen, A., Zuurmond, I.: From Bureaucracy to Infocracy: Management through information architecture. In: Tyler, Z., Snellen, A. (Hrsg.) Beyond BPR in Public Administration – Institutional Transformation in an Information Age, pp. 205–224. IOS Press, Amsterdam (1997)

7. Korotkov, A.V.: BPM and GPM in e-government. Round table "VRM in Russia: a new round of development", Moscow (2010). http://www.myshared.ru/slide/186947/. Accessed 29 Nov 2019. (in Russian)

8. Kulikov, G.G., Gabbasov, R.K., et al.: Application of the principles of system engineering and BPMN to the process of transfer of state and municipal services in electronic form with the organization of interdepartmental electronic interaction. In: Vestnik of Ufa State Aviation Technical University, vol. 17, no. 5(58), pp. 12–19 (2013). https://elibrary.ru/item.asp?id=20924115. Accessed 29 Nov 2019. (in Russian)

9. Akatkin, Y.M.: Provision of electronic services in the regions of Russia: training system. Inf. Soc. 4, 29–40 (2013). http://emag.iis.ru/arc/infosoc/emag.nsf/BPA/98e0632a2d7675a8442 57c2a0046c798. Accessed 29 Nov 2019. (in Russian)

10. Davenport, T.H.: Process Innovation: Reengineering Work Through Information Technology. Harvard Business School Press, Boston (1993). http://huigensingh.com/wp-content/uploads/2016/10/Innovatie-artikel.pdf. Accessed 29 Nov 2019

11. Thong, J.Y.L., Yap, C.S., Seah, K.L.: Business process reengineering: the case of the housing development board in Singapore. J. Manag. Inf. Systems. 17(1), 245–270 (2000). http://repository.ust.hk/ir/Record/1783.1-24583. Accessed 29 Nov 2019

12. Peffers, K., Tuunanen, T., Rothenberger, M.A., Chatterjee, S.: A design science research methodology for information systems research. J. Manag. Inf. Syst. 24(3), 45–77 (2008). https://doi.org/10.2753/MIS0742-1222240302

13. Akatkin, Y.M., Yasinovskaya, E.D.: Digital transformation of public administration. DataContract and semantic interoperability, M.: LENAND (2019). (in Russian)

14. Business Process Model and Notation (BPMN) Ver. 2.0.2. https://www.omg.org/spec/BPMN/2.0/PDF. Accessed 29 Nov 2019

15. Cognini, R., Falcioni, D., Maccari, M., Polzonetti, A., Re, B.: Scrivania: Public services execution and Semantic Search. In: The 2014 International Conference on e-Learning, e-Business, Enterprise Information Systems, and e-Government, Session: E-Government and issues of interest to Government. Relevant Agencies, and Public Administration (2014). http://worldcomp-proceedings.com/proc/p2014/EEE2928.pdf. Accessed 29 Nov 2019

16. Corradini, F., Falcioni, D., Polzonetti, A., Re, B.: Innovation on public services using business process management. In: 2011 International Conference on E-business, Management and Economics. IPEDR, vol. 25, Singapore (2011). http://www.ipedr.com/vol25/6-ICEME2011-N00010.pdf. Accessed 29 Nov 2019

17. Koznov, D., Samochadin, A., Azarskov, A., Chevzova, J.: Towards e-government services in Russia. In: Proceedings of the International Conference on Knowledge Management and Information Sharing, pp. 294–301 (2011). http://www.math.spbu.ru/user/dkoznov/papers/KoznovKMIS2011.pdf. Accessed 29 Nov 2019

18. Koznov, D.V., Azarskov, A.V., et al.: Model-oriented method of specification of public services. Bulletin of St. Petersburg University Ser. 10, vol. 4 (2012). http://www.math.spbu.ru/user/dkoznov/papers/egov_serv2012.pdf. Accessed 29 Nov 2019. (in Russian)

19. Penicina, L.: Linking BPMN, ArchiMate, and BWW: Perfect Match for Complete and Lawful Business Process Models? http://ceur-ws.org/Vol-1023/paper15.pdf. Accessed 29 Nov 2019

20. Ramani, S., Kumaraswamy, Y.S.: The role of business process model in customer centric eGovernment system. Int. J. Comput. Appl. **72**(12), 13–23. https://doi.org/10.5120/12545-9003. https://pdfs.semanticscholar.org/dfb2/8bba66b0c614f80741133879f3ae284bb479.pdf. Accessed 29 Nov 2019

21. Fyodorov, I.G.: Overcoming the deficit of expressive ability of business process modeling languages. Bus. Inform. **3**(37), 62–71 (2016). https://bijournal.hse.ru/2016-3%20(37)/196777200.html. Accessed 29 Nov 2019. (in Russian)

22. Fyodorov, I.G.: Adaptation of Bunge–Wanda–Weber ontology to the description of executable business process models. Appl. Inform. **10**(4(58)) (2015). http://www.applied informatics.ru/r/articles/article/index.php?article_id_4=1814. Accessed 29 Nov 2019. (in Russian)

23. Open Group Standard Homepage. TOGAF Version 9.1 Document Number: G116. http://pubs.opengroup.org/architecture/togaf9-doc/arch/. Accessed 29 Nov 2019. ISBN: 978908 7536794

24. Fengel, J.: Semantic model alignment for business process integration Dublin Institute of Technology College of Engineering and Built Environment. Thesis for the degree of Ph.D. (2014). https://arrow.dit.ie/cgi/viewcontent.cgi?article=1015&context=builtdoc. Accessed 29 Nov 2019

25. Di Francescomarino, C., Ghidini, C., Rospocher, M., Serafini, L., Tonella, P.: Semantically-aided business process modeling. In: Bernstein, A., et al. (eds.) ISWC 2009. LNCS, vol. 5823, pp. 114–129. Springer, Heidelberg (2009). https://doi.org/10.1007/978-3-642-04930-9_8. Accessed 29 Nov 2019

26. Lin, Y.: Semantic annotation for process models: facilitating process knowledge management via semantic interoperability. Norwegian University of Science and Technology. Thesis for the degree of Ph.D. https://pdfs.semanticscholar.org/c27e/e0fdc6b6ff5a8582d155 6e6feebde93eb6aa.pdf. Accessed 29 Nov 2019

27. Wetzstein, B., Ma, Z., et al.: Semantic business process and product lifecycle management. In: Proceedings of the Workshop SBPM 2007, Innsbruck, CEUR Workshop Proceedings (2007). http://ceur-ws.org/Vol-251/paper1.pdf. Accessed 29 Nov 2019. ISSN 1613-0073

28. Kudryavtsev, D.V.: Practical methods of mapping and integration of ontologies. Seminar "Knowledge and Ontologies *ELSEWHERE», XI National Conference on Artificial Intelligence KII-08, Dubna (2008). http://www.raai.org/conference/cai-08/files/cai-08_paper_226.doc. Accessed 29 Nov 2019. (in Russian)

29. Kasemsap, K.: The Roles of Business Process Modeling and Business Process Reengineering in E-Government. https://www.researchgate.net/publication/298083834_The_Roles_of_Business_Process_Modeling_and_Business_Process_Reengineering_in_E-Government. Accessed 29 Nov 2019

Forward Value Creation and Digital Government: Solving the Cost-Benefit Paradox?

Lasse Berntzen[1($\boxtimes$)], Marius Rohde Johannesen[1],
and Kim Normann Andersen[2]

[1] University of South-Eastern Norway, 3603 Kongsberg, Norway
{lasse.berntzen,Marius.Johannessen}@usn.no
[2] Copenhagen Business School, Howitzvej 60, 2000 Frederiksberg, Denmark
andersen@cbs.dk

Abstract. While adoption of new technologies and supply of online services are in focus of measuring uptake of online services in maturity models, measurement of direct and indirect outcome and value creation for the internal and external end-users are only marginal addressed. Based on three vignettes from Norway, this paper argues that the importance of cost overrun is overestimated in the short run, while long-term benefits, as well as indirect benefits, are underestimated in public sector it-projects. We present a set of propositions for future government digitalization projects, bringing attention to the involvement of internal and external users, and bringing focus to balancing short term and long term direct and indirect costs.

Keywords: eGovernment success · Citizen-centric · Digital transformation · Public sector · Cost-benefit

1 Introduction

This paper contributes to the conceptualization and measurement of eGovernment success. While eGovernment research has been rich on failures of eGovernment [1, 2], there has been less attention to good practice and use of appreciative inquiry methods. Still, at practitioner-oriented conferences such as the Bled Conferences and the Norwegian NOKOBIT conferences, there has been a continuous interest and sharing of projects and approaches on how to manage IT projects. Also, a range of research activities supported and disseminated through, for example, the EU and national funding schemes such as the National Science Foundation, and Norwegian Research Council have generated a massive pile of research. Despite the openness and intentions to share the findings from the projects, there has been a disjointed development in the academic eGovernment focused environment and the more practitioner-focused environment.

The first European Conference on eGovernment was held in 2001 [3], the first International Conference on eGovernment was arranged in 2002 [4]. Both conferences had eGovernment success as important topics, and since then almost two decades of

© Springer Nature Switzerland AG 2020
A. Chugunov et al. (Eds.): EGOSE 2019, CCIS 1135, pp. 194–206, 2020.
https://doi.org/10.1007/978-3-030-39296-3_15

eGovernment research has addressed the success of eGovernment applications. As societies and public values are not constant, the criteria for success have changed over time.

The field of eGovernment is based on public sector transformation, digitalization, citizen-centric services, and public value creation. The concept of public value has been discussed since the time of ancient Greece, but the current public value debate started with Mark Moore's book Creating public value: Strategic management in government. Moore defined the government's role as that of creating public value, but what constitutes public value changes over time [5, 6], hence the need for ongoing research into value creation in eGovernment.

In this paper, we present an overview of existing research on value creation and eGovernment success and discuss how the concepts of transformation, digitalization, citizen-centric services, and public value creation influence our ideas about what constitutes success. We present findings from three Norwegian cases that illustrate how the framework fits with current real-world projects and put forward six propositions on how to forward the value creation for internal and external stakeholders.

2   Prior Research

2.1   Measurement of Success

Many researchers have addressed the measurement of success in eGovernment solutions. In the early years of eGovernment provision of services was seen as a success in itself. Researchers looked for available services and used their existence to benchmark between countries, regions, and municipalities.

Other researchers measured maturity by addressing the system and data integration, as well as organizational transformation. For example, Layne and Lee [7] coined a framework that included four different levels of maturity. The framework is visualized in Fig. 1. The first level was cataloging (presentation of information) online, e.g., static web pages. The second level contains interaction, where citizens can submit forms or comments. The third level addresses vertical integration, where the front-end system (web application) was connected to back-office systems. The fourth level, horizontal integration, is reached when the system communicates with other systems across organizational boundaries to create value for the user. The model was later enhanced by Andersen and Henriksen [8]. Their Public sector Process Rebuilding (PPR) model includes strategic ambitions of the use of ICT in government and focuses on activities and citizen centricity.

Most benchmarks between countries used an approach of scoring the maturity of a number of services governments. Such benchmarks were made by Accenture, Brown University, and the United Nations several consecutive years [9].

Holzer and Kim [10] proposed the following indicators of eGovernment success:

- Information dissemination, means and methods
- Two-way communication, the nature of relationship
- Services that will be available to the citizen or any stakeholder
- Integration

- Political participation, to what extent the citizens will be involved in the political matters, and how it would affect it
- Security, how secure transactions will be
- Usability, how usable (easy to use) will the transactions be and if they are user friendly or not

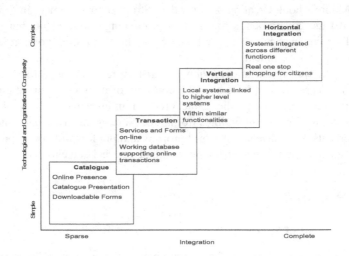

Fig. 1. The Layne and Lee eGovernment maturity model.

Almarabeh and AbuAli [11] argued that two critical requirements are needed for eGovernment success: availability (24 × 7) and accessibility. They also point out the need for a well-trained and motivated workforce, and the need for building trust between different organizational entities.

Bouaziz and Chaabouni [12] emphasized eGovernment as a multidimensional concept and proposed a set of criteria to evaluate the success of eGovernment projects. Their research is based on semi-structured interviews with 51 team-members involved in eGovernment projects in Tunisian government agencies. Two categories are used: Product success and project management success. Product success includes adoption and use by customers, adoption and use by government agencies, satisfaction of stakeholders, site content, usability of sites and systems, impacts of project, and achievement of project objectives. The project management success includes schedule, budget, and technical features.

Roman [13] used a different set of dimensions to evaluate success in eGovernment: Security, functionality, and transformation. Success is dependent on performance along all three dimensions.

Abu Nadi [14] researched success factors for eGovernment adoption in Saudi Arabia. He listed the following eGovernment success factors found in the literature: usage of change agents to encourage eGovernment usage; security; privacy; improving ICT infrastructure suiting eGovernment uses on G2C and G2G levels; encouraging laws and policies related to eGovernment usage; implementing pilot eGovernment/

traditional project; benchmarking; IT training and education; eGovernment marketing; tangible verification; ease of use, and usefulness. Based on focus groups, interviews and a survey with government officials and users, he ended up with the following nine success factors for Saudi Arabia: improving ICT infrastructure, improving ICT services, improving technology literacy, planning and conducting a comprehensive eGovernment awareness program; enforcing technical and legal procedures to protect eGovernment stakeholders; benchmarking; developing user-friendly, organized, will supported eGovernment websites; provision of high quality and low fees services; and provision of hardcopy of e-transactions' status.

Another way to measure success is to look at actual use, e.g., the number of users, the number of transactions. In some cases, it is appropriate to look at uptake as a percentage of a total, e.g., the number of electronic submissions compared to the number of non-electronic submissions. Finally, success can be measured from user feedback, where the users report on importance, availability, and accessibility.

2.2 Government Objective: User-Centric Digital Transformation

The transformation of the public sector can be traced back to the new public management paradigm, which might be characterized a global megatrend in modernizing the public sector organizations since the introduction in the 1980s [15]. The idea behind new public management is to transform the public sector based on ideas from the private sector. A significant development is to see citizens as customers, not as clients. The new public management emphasized measuring user satisfaction of services and creating user-centric services [16].

Digitalization of the public sector aims to make more efficient services. Digitalization relieves employees from simple tasks, so they can focus on more complex tasks. For end-users, digital solutions are available 24 h, seven days a week. Digitalization also brings opportunities for more transparency. Information can be shared cost-effectively. The possible savings from self-service are high. The city of Copenhagen, Denmark estimated the cost of a physical visit by a citizen to Euro 20, the cost of a telephone call to Euro 10, and self-service through the Internet to Euro 0.5 [17].

In the white paper "Digital Agenda for Norway" [18], the government outlines its policy for a digital transformation of the public sector. One of the key objectives is to create a citizen-centric mindset in government. To the user (the citizen), public services should be presented as coordinated and complete. Many public services involve several agencies and levels of government, but with a user-centric mindset, this should not have any consequences for the user, as (s)he expects one single point of entry and one streamlined process. Information sharing is another key element of the policy, and literature finds that services not designed with a user-centric perspective often have a much lower adoption rate [19]. Citizen centric services imply that services are built around the citizen. The problem is that eGovernment services are not always seen to benefit the citizens. It is, therefore, crucial to include citizens in the development process in order to make better and more efficient services as seen from the user perspective.

Usability testing is essential in user-centric government [20]. However, in government projects, the stakeholders can be many and diverse and have interests that do not necessarily align. There can also be significant differences between the objectives of citizens using the system and the government officials handling the case. This presents an additional challenge for user-centric government [21]. Despite this strong focus on user-centricity, eGovernment projects have often been focused around the service being delivered, and citizen needs have not been taken sufficiently into account [22].

2.3   Public Value Creation

Public value creation is about creating value for the citizens. The value is measured by, for example, time-saving, availability through difference proximities and devices, accessibility, and quality of services. There are several competing definitions of what constitutes public value. For example, public value can be seen as a multi-dimensional construct, focusing on both outcomes, culture, and processes. Typical concrete values could be better public services, increased accountability and trust in society and government, or the long term solving of social problems and decreasing socio-economic divides [23]. However, others claim that in order to find what constitutes public value at any given time and in different contexts, it is necessary to examine the deliberation between elected representatives, government officials, citizens, organizational and business stakeholders [24]. Hence, a public value perspective will change over time, and the measures we apply to examine success changes with them.

Empirical research on public values should take account of a broad range of stakeholders, but within and outside of government [25], and some even call for co-production of services, where citizens are included in creating the services they use [26]. This view aligns well with the current user-centric focus in eGovernment and strengthens our argument that a public value perspective can be useful when measuring eGovernment success.

3   Research Design

The objective of this paper is to examine existing research on value creation in eGovernment and apply this to empirical data in order to create a framework for eGovernment success; to address the objective we have conducted three case studies of successful eGovernment projects in Norway, and compared the respondents' ideas on why the projects were successful with literature.

Our study is exploratory; an exploratory case study is a suitable method to address the "how" research questions and understand the phenomenon in its natural context. Our study is also interpretive, as the data collection was not guided by pre-assumptions from literature or theory, and the theory guided our analysis of the empirical findings [27].

We collected data for the case in August/September 2018 and in April/May 2019. The collected data consists of white papers and reports from government and interviews with key personnel in the three cases. For vehicle registration transfer our key informant is working in The Norwegian Public Roads Administration. Other informants include one car sales representative and two recent users of the solution. For electronic prescriptions, the key informants were two general practitioners (medical doctors), one pharmacist, and two prescription users. For tax return statements, the key informants were the research group of the tax authority (e-mail communication) and five users of the service.

The authors have used the three services on several occasions, and we have compared notes on our experiences, as well as supplementary informal interviews with colleagues and friends who are also users of the three services in order to verify our findings and own experiences.

After data collection, we reviewed literature on eGovernment success and public value and compared the cases with findings from literature. This allowed us to create the six propositions presented in Sect. 5.

4 Three Vignettes from Norway

4.1 Vehicle Registration Transfer

The Norwegian Public Roads Administration's vehicle and license registry has been digital since 1980. As part of the government focus on digitalization of the public sector, the system was scheduled for renewal in the 2010s. The project has been split into seven smaller projects and is scheduled to be completed in 2021. The original software, written in Cobol, has been updated and converted to Java and service-oriented architecture, and new functionality is being added. The Autosys project is among the largest ICT projects in the Norwegian public sector, and the main driver is the Norwegian government's plan for digitalization. The project team has worked hard to show the benefits of digitalization in the Norwegian Public Roads Administration, and while we were not able to get any numbers, the respondent hinted that savings in terms of both cost and resources have been significant.

One deliverable of the project is the digitalization of a paper-based and manual process for vehicle ownership transfer. There are millions of vehicle sales and ownership transfers each year, involving citizens, car dealerships, and other public agencies such as police and customs. Previously, selling a car involved sending papers and signatures to the Public Roads Administration. This process was time-consuming and confusing for customers and costly for car dealerships and the local road administration offices handling the paperwork. A problem appeared when one of the parties, for some reason, did not submit the transfer registration form.

The new, digital solution has simplified the process by creating a guided step-by-step process that is completed entirely online. The seller and buyer of a vehicle both have to sign in using their electronic ID and confirm the transfer of ownership. Once this is done, the process is over. For most cases the process is fully automatic, saving a lot of time and resources.

From a user-centric perspective, the case is compelling for several reasons. The respondent from the Norwegian Public Roads Administration points out that self-service is an ideal for public sector digitalization projects, and the back-end interoperability between systems saves a lot of work for case handlers, sellers and buyers alike. While the underlying Autosys system is the same as it was in 1980, the process of transferring ownership has been simplified. This simplification of processes is central to many of the ongoing digitalization projects in Norway, as it is more cost-efficient.

The respondent emphasizes that the most important success criteria of the project have been project management, systems development methodology, and a value-based management perspective. Using Prince 2, agile development methods, and standardized procurement contracts have allowed the project to run smoothly despite the many stakeholders involved. Private sector development and consultancy companies, various offices of the Public Roads Administration and other government agencies such as police and customs.

From a value-based management perspective, user-involvement has been stressed as one important value. Users have been identified as both internal and external. Internal users include case handlers, first-line responders in the regional offices, as well as offices from more specialized areas such as dangerous goods road transport. External users – employees and managers from car dealerships as well as private citizens-as-car-buyers have been involved in several iterations of usability testing. In total, the respondent claims that between 100 and 150 people have been involved in a user-centric development process.

The change of ownership system has also been part of the Norwegian plain language project, another part of the overall digitalization plan for Norway [28]. Using plain language in the change of ownership process has significantly reduced the number of calls and e-mails to local offices, as users find the process and language of the new system easier to understand.

Finally, in terms of user numbers and user evaluation, the respondent would not share numbers and figures, as these are found only in reports used internally in the Autosys project and not available to the public. Instead, he talked about challenges related to the Norwegian "digital first choice" policy, where users are encouraged but not required to use digital solutions. This has led to many users preferring the old manual processes, which in turn lessens the potential benefits of the system. This is confirmed by a study of digital mailboxes comparing Sweden, Denmark, and Norway's different approaches to digitalization. In Denmark, citizens are required to use digital services unless they have health-related reasons for not doing so. In Norway, citizens can opt-out with no explanation, while in Sweden they must opt-in. User numbers show that Denmark's approach is the most effective when it comes to benefits realization and user numbers, but also shows that this approach leads to more resistance and less satisfied users [29]. From a user-centric perspective, this could indicate that "first choice" is a better approach than "no choice", as practiced in Denmark.

4.2   Electronic Prescriptions

Before electronic prescriptions were established, the medical doctor issued a prescription on paper. The patient had to deliver this at the pharmacy and wait for the preparation of the medication. Errors happened because the prescription was in handwriting, and sometimes difficult to decode. There was also some misuse since some patients visited several pharmacies to get multiple doses.

The concept of electronic prescriptions was raised in 1997 by a government-appointed committee to examine the general conditions for sale of medicines [30]. The committee pointed out that electronic prescriptions would make prescriptions safer by making the medical doctor aware of other medicines used by the patient, of possible duplicate prescriptions, and maximum and minimum dosages. The medical doctor could also get information about similar products with a lower price.

Development of electronic prescriptions started in 2004 with an allocation of NOK 40 million in the Government's Fiscal Budget. The Ministry of Health and Care argued that electronic prescriptions would lead to faster and more secure transfer of prescriptions between the medical doctor and the pharmacy. Electronic prescriptions would also make control of prescriptions simpler, more effective, and less resource-consuming [31].

A pilot was launched in May 2008 in the municipality Stor-Elvdal. After four months, the municipality withdrew from the pilot. Municipal officials blamed the system as slow, faulty and incomplete. The company developing the system claimed that the system became more complex than initially anticipated [32].

The plan was to implement electronic prescriptions on national level before 2010.

The system for electronic prescriptions started trials in 2010, and the first release on national level happened in June 2011. Most general practitioners were connected during 2013, and since then hospitals and dentists have been added to the user base.

The new system connects the medical doctor to a national system for prescriptions. The patient can then go to any pharmacy to pick up the medication. The system provides better quality since the errors from hand-writing were removed. The system also provides better protection against misuse.

Citizens can access a history of their prescriptions through a personalized web page using one of several authentication methods.

In a press release from 2015, the minister of health and care, Mr. Bent Høie made the following statement: "To create a health service where the patient is in the center, good ICT solutions must be present".

Despite the problems encountered during the early trials, the current solution is effective for both users and health professionals. At the same time, the quality has improved with less chance of errors being made. Some concerns have been made about privacy, since more health personnel have access to prescriptions, but they are bound by the general confidentiality regulations for health personnel.

4.3 Tax Return Statement

One of the most popular services is the electronic tax return statements. When electronic tax return statements were introduced, citizens could fill in the necessary data and submit it to the tax authorities. The electronic tax return statement won some prices for eGovernment solutions about ten years ago. However, the development has continued, and the tax authority now collects almost all information needed without the involvement of actions from the individual taxpayers. It is no longer necessary to sign the tax return statement (Introduced in 2008). If no modifications are made, the tax return statement is regarded approved by silent consent. The tax authorities have embraced user-centric development, and "user needs" is the most used tag in their development blog [33]. For each iteration of the tax return service, users are invited to test and provide feedback on the solution. The latest version, introduced in 2019, had more than 400 people volunteer to beta-test the solution, and their input was used when finalizing the version.

Table 1 shows the increased use of the tax return statement solution. The numbers were provided by the research group of the Norwegian Tax Administration. Previous to the electronic submission process, the submission of tax return statements involved large amounts of work for the citizens. Citizens had to collect all the information from various sources, check the completeness of the information, and submit a paper-based form with attachments. The electronic solution collects all the information from employers, banks, the national register of properties, and other sources.

Table 1. Tax return statements

	Internet	SMS	Phone	Total
2003	544,000	191,000	378,000	1,113,000
2004	675,346	219,237	294,442	1,189,025
2005	1,255,536	276,006	269,542	1,801,084
2006	1,471,739	341,816	226,218	2,093,773
2007	1,538,025	365,454	194,642	2,098,121
2008	962,743	112,077	55,155	1,131,076
2009	870,000	–	–	870,000
2010	868,514	–	–	868,514
2011	856,396	–	–	856,396
2012	939,910	–	–	939,910
2013	870,270	–	–	870,270
2014	1,110,122	–	–	1,110,122
2015	1,177,822	–	–	1,177,822
2016	1,164,881	–	–	1,164,881
2017	1,230,364	–	–	1,230,364

The citizens only have to check the information and fill in missing data. This can be tax deductions for commuters, properties in foreign countries, and other data not available to the tax authorities. What used to be hours of work is now reduced dramatically. The uptake of the electronic solution may be a clear indicator of success. The tax authorities receive almost no tax return statements on paper. The system is effective both for users and tax authority employees. The few concerns raised have been about tax-payers not checking their numbers for possible errors.

5 Six Propositions on How to Forward the Value Creation for Internal and External Stakeholders

The three vignettes from Norway illustrate well how different projects unfold in the public sector. While there are many IT project and program management books that provide guidelines and check-box tools on how to manage strategic, tactical, and operational aspect of public sector IT-projects, we will in this section formulate six propositions about how to bring the value creation forward when planning, developing, and running IT-projects in the public sector. Thus, our propositions are extensions to the body of IT project and program literature. Also, the propositions add the conceptualization of maturity of digitalization of government by bringing attention to the involvement of internal and external users and bringing focus to balancing short term and long term direct and indirect costs. We have formulated six propositions aiming for developing a research agenda to be explored by the research community and practice.

Proposition 1: Involvement and inclusion of external users in the early phases of project scoping and visions for the IT project minimize the risk of projects benefitting only the internal users

This is perhaps the most visible factor of the three vignettes. All three are concerned with user-centric development and includes stakeholders in various phases of the development process. Norwegian government agencies are cooperating on a common set of principles for user-centric service design, where user-involvement is central. Further, our findings indicate that plain language is an important part of user involvement. All three examples report that much work has gone into creating a language that end-users find easy to understand.

Proposition 2: Factoring in long term benefits will bring attention to the motivation why the IT projects are developed by the public sector

Proposition 3: Having less focus on short term costs of IT projects will reduce IT project overhead costs

Governments are under pressure to become more cost-effective and efficient. This can sometimes be translated into a strong focus on short-term project costs, as the media often coves budget overruns and project issues. As our three examples show, benefits often appear over time. There is often a gap between implementation and realization of public value and economic benefits. For example, the public roads administration started their digitalization process in the 1990s and had to live through several failures before the current project organization found its form. In the short term, it would have been easier to retire the entire project. However, over time, the project matured and started delivering public value. E-prescriptions were also criticized for being over budget and time but are now regarded to be a huge success.

Proposition 4: Bringing value to the end-users needs to be in focus when justifying and evaluating the IT project

In government projects, literature shows that end-users (stakeholders) have different and sometimes competing needs. In our three examples, project management has attempted to balance different interests and needs, while simultaneously having a strong focus on developing value objectives and realizing these. The defined value objectives vary between projects but is often a mix of economic (cost savings for both citizens/organizations and government) and citizen-centric (ease of use, less red tape) values.

Proposition 5: In general, projects need to have a scope and output that can be evaluated and when possible shared with other parts of government

Having a coordinating role in government can help government organizations learn from each other's mistakes and contributes to an increasing level of professionalism in IT projects. In Norway, the directorate for public administration and ICT (DIFI), the language council and others have a coordinating role, inviting managers from different agencies to meet and learn from each other. Over time this leads to the government becoming more competent in managing IT projects. Further, the municipal and regional coordinating entity KS has recently launched a platform for sharing services, projects, and best practices across regional and municipal governments. Finally, our three examples show the importance of clear objectives and evaluation criteria, that also measure success over time.

Proposition 6: Projects should address transparency, privacy, and trust.

The three eGovernment solutions described above are regarded as successes, but the few critical comments raised is about transparency, privacy, and trust. The vehicle transfer application has no documented issues related to transparency, privacy, or trust. The signing is done using the same digital id used for banking applications. The fallback solution is to use a paper-based form, but this is hardly used. There have been some privacy concerns about the electronic prescriptions since the records are accessible for all health personnel using the service. It is, however, possible to limit access to, e.g., one specific pharmacy. This may be an option for patients having privacy or trust-related problems with the service. The objections towards the tax return statement service have to do with the potential of citizens neglecting to inspect the information provided by the tax authority, and thereby missing possible tax-deductions. It seems this problem is merely theoretical since there are no reports of the opposite.

6 Conclusions

While adoption of new technologies and supply of online services are in focus of measuring uptake of online services in maturity models, measurement of direct and indirect outcome and value creation for the internal and external end-users are only marginally addressed. Based on three examples from Norway, this paper highlights that the importance of cost overrun is overestimated in the short run, while long-term benefits, as well as indirect benefits, are underestimated in public sector it-projects.

This study examines three successful applications of eGovernment in Norway. All three services have been driven by the intent of the government to provide citizen-centric services by use of information and communications technology, as well as traditional objectives related to efficiency and effectiveness. All respondents confirm that the user experience has been important for the projects, and data suggests that projects need to handle the tension between long-term benefits and short-term costs, public value as well as evaluation and sharing of results. Our paper presents six propositions, which extends IT and program literature by emphasizing maturity over time as an essential factor. The propositions form the basis of a research agenda for further research in the area of public value creation in government IT projects.

References

1. Heeks, R.: The impact of e-government failure. Institute for Development Policy Management (IDPM), Manchester (2003)
2. Gammage, M.: Why your IT project may be riskier than you think. Harvard Bus. Rev. **89** (11), 22 (2011)

3. Remenyi, D., Bannister, F. (eds.): Conference Proceedings: European Conference on e-Government, MCIL (2001)
4. Traunmüller, R., Lenk, K. (eds.): EGOV 2002. LNCS, vol. 2456. Springer, Heidelberg (2002). https://doi.org/10.1007/978-3-540-46138-8
5. Moore, M.H.: Creating Public Value – Strategic Management in Government. Harvard University Press, Cambridge (1995)
6. Benington, J., Moore, M.H. (eds.): Public Value: Theory and Practice. Palgrave Macmillan, London (2010)
7. Layne, K., Lee, J.: Developing fully functional e-Government a four stage model. Gov. Inf. Q. 18(2), 122–136 (2001)
8. Andersen, K.V., Henriksen, H.Z.: E-government maturity models: extension of the Layne and Lee model. Gov. Inf. Q. 23(2), 236–248 (2006)
9. Berntzen, L., Goodwin Olsen, M.: Benchmarking e-Government – a comparative review of three international benchmarking studies. In: Takahashi, Y., Berntzen, L., Smedberg, Å. (eds.) The Third International Conference on Digital Society (ICDS 2009), pp. 77–82. IEEE (2009)
10. Holzer, M., Kim, S.-T.: Digital governance in municipalities worldwide (2005): a longitudinal assessment of municipal websites throughout the world. E-Governance Institute, National Center for Public Productivity, Rutgers University (2006)
11. Almarabeh, A., AbuAli, A.: General framework for e-government: definition, maturity challenges, opportunities, and success. Eur. J. Sci. Res. 39(1), 29–42 (2010)
12. Bouaziz, F., Chaabouni, J.: Criteria for assessing the success of e-government projects. In: Gil-Garcia, R. (ed.) E-Government Success Factors and Measures: Theories, Concepts, and Methodologies, pp. 273–288. IGI Global, Hershey (2013)
13. Roman, A.V.: Delineating three dimensions of e-government success: security, functionality, and transformation. In: Gil-Garcia, R. (ed.) E-Government Success Factors and Measures: Theories, Concepts, and Methodologies, pp. 171–192. IGI Global, Hershey (2013)
14. Abu Nadi, I.: Success Factors for eGoverment Adoption – Citizen Centric Approach. Lambert Academic Publishing, Saarbrücken (2010)
15. Christensen, T., Lægreid, P. (eds.): Transcending New Public Management - The Transformation of Public Sector Reforms. Ashgate Publishing, Farnham (2007)
16. Røvik, K.A.: Trender og translasjoner - Ideer som former det 21. århundrets organisasjon. Universitetsforlaget (2007)
17. Kjensli, H., Nordli, M.-B., Richardsen, L., Pettersen, C.B., Wilthil, S.E.: eKommune 2012 - lokal digital agenda. Kommuneforlaget (2008)
18. Norwegian Ministry of Local Government and Modernization: Meld. St. 27 (2015–2016) Report to the Storting (white paper): Digital agenda for Norway - ICT for a simpler everyday life and increased productivity (2016)
19. Bertot, J.C., Jaeger, P.T.: The E-Government paradox: Better customer service doesn't necessarily cost less. Gov. Inf. Q. 25(2), 149–154 (2008)
20. Bertot, J.C., Jaeger, P.T., Grimes, J.M.: Using ICTs to create a culture of transparency: e-government and social media as openness and anti-corruption tools for societies. Gov. Inf. Q. 27(3), 264–271 (2010)
21. Axelsson, K., Melin, U., Lindgren, I.: Exploring the importance of citizen participation and involvement in e-government projects: practice, incentives, and organization. Transform. Gov.: People, Process Policy 4(4), 299–321 (2010)
22. Anthopoulos, L.G., Siozos, P., Tsoukalas, I.A.: Applying participatory design and collaboration in digital public services for discovering and re-designing e-Government services. Gov. Inf. Q. 24(2), 353–376 (2007)

23. O'Flynn, J.: From new public management to public value: paradigmatic change and managerial implications. Aust. J. Public Adm. **66**(3), 353–366 (2007)
24. Stoker, G.: Public value management: a new narrative for networked governance. Am. Rev. Public Adm. **36**(1), 41–57 (2006)
25. Hartley, J., Alford, J., Knies, E., Douglas, S.: Towards an empirical research agenda for public value theory. Public Manag. Rev. **19**(5), 670–685 (2017)
26. Bryson, J., Sancino, A., Benington, J., Sørensen, E.: Towards a multi-actor theory of public value co-creation. Public Manag. Rev. **19**(5), 640–654 (2017)
27. Yin, R.K.: Case Study Research and Applications – Design and Methods, 6th edn. Sage Publications, Thousand Oaks (2017)
28. Johannessen, M.R., Berntzen, L., Ødegård, A.: A review of the Norwegian plain language policy. In: Janssen, M., et al. (eds.) EGOV 2017. LNCS, vol. 10428, pp. 187–198. Springer, Cham (2017). https://doi.org/10.1007/978-3-319-64677-0_16
29. Jansen, A.J., Berger, J.B., Goldkuhl, G.: Differences in secure digital post in the Scandinavian countries. In: Tambouris, E., et al. (eds.) Electronic Government and Electronic Participation, vol. 12, pp. 110–121. IOS Press, Amsterdam (2015)
30. Norwegian Official Reports NOU 1997:6. Rammevilkår for omsetning av legemidler (General conditions for sale of medicines) (1997)
31. Aftenposten (newspaper) 07.10.2004. Elektronisk resept
32. Kommunal Rapport (newspaper), 19 September 2008
33. Norwegian Tax Authority: beta.skattetetaten.no. http://beta.skatteetaten.no. Accessed 15 July 2019

Features of the E-government Technologies Introduction in the Medical Care in the Suburban Areas

Alexandr I. Repkin⬡, Nataliya Yumaeva,
and Sergey A. Mityagin⁽✉⁾⬡

ITMO University, Saint Petersburg, Russia
mityagin.spb@gmail.com

Abstract. The paper describes theoretical peculiarities of e-government technology introduction in suburbanized areas in the medical care of the population. The purpose of the paper is to analyze the causes, factors, characteristics and conditions of the introduction of e-government technologies in the suburban areas. The distinctive features in the needs of the population of urbanized areas of their behavioral attitudes when accessing e-government services. The study is based on the example of medical services provided to the population in the framework of the public health system in Russia.

Keywords: Value-based management · E-democracy · E-government · Suburban area · Medical service

1 Introduction

At the present time it is possible to observe an uprise of technical and technological conditions for the migration of urban population to suburban areas. Traditionally, cities become the drivers of economic growth and new stages of the industrial revolution, as they provide better resource utilization in comparison with other forms of territorial organization of economic activity.

Obviously, the second and the third industrial revolutions were primarily a result of innovative accomplishments of the cities. However, the achievements of these revolutions are transforming big cities into agglomerations, which are being increasingly formed by means of suburbanization. On one side, accomplishments in the spheres of construction, transportation, energy and water supply and IT-revolution have provided the possibility of mass supply of living conditions with a city comfort level at a distance of dozens kilometers from a city center, and at the same time keeping an inextricable connection with a city. On the other side, the process of suburbanization remained characterized by problems associated with the territorial remoteness from the service centers of the city. Including medical services. Similar problems are noted in studies [1]. Moreover, it is argued that the suburbs are not only not improve, but on the contrary, worsen the quality of life of its inhabitants [3].

An important feature of the provision of public services in the field of medicine and health care is the need for the physical presence of a person to obtain the appropriate

A. Chugunov et al. (Eds.): EGOSE 2019, CCIS 1135, pp. 207–216, 2020.
https://doi.org/10.1007/978-3-030-39296-3_16

services. This is necessary in the case of medical services related directly to treatment. And it is desirable for activities related to the issuance of supporting documents and certificates. For this reason, in the sub-urbanized territories, which are characterized by territorial remoteness, two issues need to be addressed simultaneously: first, ensuring the availability of medical care and quickly determining its need; second, reducing the need for physical visits to health facilities without the need. This increases the risk of dealing with neglected and acute medical problems. This situation is considered in several studies [5].

E-government technologies, which realize new method of citizens' and public authorities' interconnection in the context of government services rendering via active application of information and communication technology, are an important factor determining the suburbanization process dynamics.

2 Suburbanization Tendencies

Historically the process of mass suburbanization started in countries and cities with high rates of economic and technical progress. In the USA, Western Europe and Japan this process refers to the middle of the XX century. In Russia mass suburbanization began between the centuries XX и XXI because the required conditions were achieved only by that moment. The common causes of suburbanization were, on the one hand, the formation of demand, primarily from the sharply grown middle class, who wants to live in more comfortable housing and social conditions, on the other – the technological progress that made the production of elements of suburban real estate mass and competitive in comparison with urban conditions [6]. Thus, in the US, the factors of suburbanization were: transport policy (mass motorization), housing policy (each family – a separate house), tax policy (stimulating the development of marginal territories), industrial policy [7]. In Western Europe (London and Paris), suburbanization has been developing since the 20s of the twentieth century. Already in the 30s–40s, the number of residents of the Central city began to decline, and the suburban areas to grow rapidly. The social composition of the population is dominated by the middle class. In contrast to the United States, less share of single-family homes and more - townhouses. In Japan, the trend of suburbanization, close to European trends, are developing in the 70–80-ies of the twentieth century [8–10].

In Russia, mass suburbanization begins at the turn of the XX and XXI centuries. In addition, as a pre-urbanization can be estimated seasonal suburbanization (permanent residence in the countryside in the warmer months) and pendulum suburbanization (accommodation throughout the year partly out of town, partly – in the Central city). It can be assumed that in the future some of these citizens will become permanent residents of the suburbanized territories.

It is possible to define the following peculiarities of Russian suburbanization:

1. local nature (remarkable suburbanization tendencies can be found only in Moscow and Saint Petersburg);
2. catching-up development (half-a-century delay from the developed countries gives an opportunity to take into consideration the accumulated international experience);
3. allotment segment (horticultural and gardening areas occupying considerable space in suburban territory);

4. special territory (military bases, proving grounds, restricted objects).

Saint Petersburg agglomeration is specific because it has the biggest in Russia quantity of towns bordering to the metropolis. These are residency towns (Pushkin, Pavlovsk, Gatchina, Petergof, Lomonosov, Strelna) and towns-satellites (Zelenogorsk, Kolpino, Krasnoye Selo, Kronstadt, Sestroretsk, Vsevolozhsk).

3   Features of Electronic Medical Services in Suburban Areas

Suburbanization processes in Russia make an agglomeration management even more complicated because of the features, presented in Table 1.

Table 1. The features of agglomeration management in medical services.

№	The formulation features	Relevance to health services	Problems in the provision of medical services
1.	An area of the object of management increases	High	Difficulty in personal visits to medical institutions
2.	The variety of legal status of land is increasing	Low	Possibility of mobile medical services only
3.	Quantity of administration levels increases	High	The problem of administrative subordination of medical organizations
4.	The need to address many issues manually residents	Low	Getting medical services requires high motivation
5.	Remoteness of the objects of management and managing organizations increases	High	The need to allocate significant time to apply for the service
6.	Length and costs of communications increase	Neutral	Obtaining medical services in electronic form requires appropriate infrastructure
7.	Discontinuity of an urban environment appears	Low	Possibility of mobile medical services only
8.	Living conditions in multistory city and low-rise suburb form different requirements towards goals of authorities	High	The problem of administrative subordination of medical organizations
9.	Interests and psychology of a traditional and a suburban citizen differ a lot	Neutral	Getting medical services requires high motivation
10.	A conflict between economic management of an agglomeration (municipality) and administrative management (city) is typical	High	Difficulty in obtaining medical services outside the region of residence
11.	Suburban life style undergoes the urbanization process	Neutral	Requirements for medical services in suburban areas are increasing
12.	Nature undergoes geourbanization	Neutral	Nature is one of the sources of medical risks

E-government technologies can contribute to solution or at least alleviation of the majority of problems caused by these features. Internet technologies, which provide communication quality, availability of information and various kinds of labor on a level, comparable to urban standards, have become a powerful factor of suburban areas suburbanization.

However, suburbanization simultaneously creates new problems for participants of this process. An important role in the solution of these problems is played by forms of interaction between government and citizens, performed via IT and e-government technologies particularly. In modern medicine, the transition to modern information technology provides several new features and integration with digital diagnostic systems [14]. The use of medical information technology offers many advantages. Other studies have recorded additional time allotted to the computer by doctors after the installation of this system [17], electronic document management [18] and electronic medical records [19]. The system of automatic reminders of patients about procedures, taking medicines and the process of treatment of the disease is cost-effective [20–23]. All three forms were effective, but phone and text reminders were slightly more effective than doctor reminders.

It is noted [24] the importance of the possibility of systematization and centralized storage of information about patients in the form of a complete digital image. Often this image is called "electronic medical card". Electronic medical card – a single electronic database of medical data about the patient [27, 28]. It turned out that the time spent by doctors with documentation in children's and adult departments has significantly decreased [29, 30].

Thus, it is noted that among the significant problems in the provision of medical services in suburban areas is their remoteness, which makes it difficult on the one hand to provide prompt services, on the other hand complicates even the regular settlement of medical organizations by people. Another problem is administrative subordination, which in the absence of acute clinical condition does not allow to apply to the nearest city hospital. The solution to these problems can be the use of modern information technologies, which on the one hand can reduce the time to receive medical services, and on the other to ensure the unity of information resources in hospitals, regardless of administrative charges.

4   A Study of Demand for E-government Services in Medicine on the Example of the St. Petersburg Agglomeration

To illustrate this paper, we will examine rendering of government services in Saint Petersburg multifunctional centers of public and municipal services.

Figure 1 represents a layout scheme of Saint Petersburg territories which can be classified as suburbanized ones. The division is made by municipal districts.

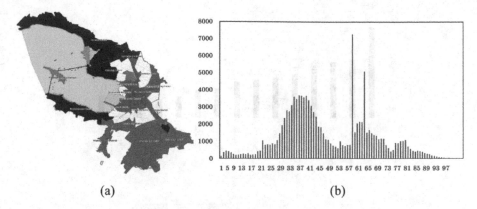

(a)   (b)

Fig. 1. (a) Layout scheme of suburbanized territories of Saint Petersburg; (b) An age structure histogram of government services applicants.

In Fig. 2 dedicated to research of target applicants of government services in Saint Petersburg, it was specified that the largest number of applications were received from citizens at the ages of approximately 33 and 58.

The spikes in this histogram show the need in certain government services for citizens of a particular age. In this respect, it is important to consider the age structure of the citizens of the suburbanized territories. Figure 3 shows the scheme of primary residence of citizens at the ages of 33 and 58 on the territory of Saint Petersburg.

Fig. 2. Scheme of primary residence of citizens.

Thus, territories, classified as suburbanized, are primarily inhabited by people aged 50–60 years. Because of distance barriers multifunctional centers of public and municipal services are used less frequently than the e-services Portal. This fact confirms general conclusions about importance of the introduction of e-government technologies in suburbanization process.

As part of the field study, 840 people in the districts living in the suburban areas of St. Petersburg were interviewed.

Most of the negative cause problems of quality of medicine, noise, as well as traffic jams and pits on the roads.

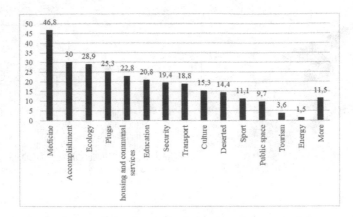

Fig. 3. Priority areas of development of the city according to residents of the study areas.

The development of medicine, first, means an increase in the number of network medical institutions and specialists (Table 2). More clinics and doctors – a clear measure, and structural reforms, such as the development of the insurance system and the private sector, almost no one considers.

Equipment of medical institutions more concerned about the people in suburban territories, but in most the people in the center also more active than the inhabitants of the sleeping area.

Table 2. The main directions of development of the sphere of medicine according to residents.

The wording of the problem	In the middle of the city	Suburban area	Urbanized territory
Improve the equipment of polyclinics and hospitals	62,2	52,5	78,2
Increase the number of doctors	60,3	59.6	61.3
Increase the number of clinics and hospitals	40,4	39,0	42,8
Develop private medicine	8,1	7,7	8,8
Else	21,1	22,8	19,6

The development of medicine, first of all, means an increase in the number of network medical institutions and specialists.

Let us consider how the process of obtaining a medical certificate by the patient now (Fig. 4) and the processes of obtaining a certificate with the help of the service "Medical certificate" with or without electronic signature (Figs. 5 and 6).

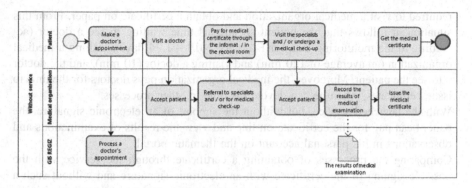

Fig. 4. Business process of getting help now (without service)

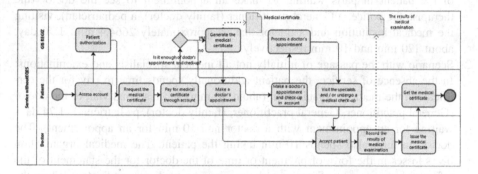

Fig. 5. Business process of obtaining electronic medical certificate without electronic signature

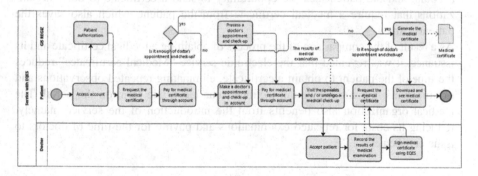

Fig. 6. The business process of getting electronic medical certificate with an electronic signature

After analyzing the business processes, we can draw the following conclusions in two scenarios:

1. Scenario with the passage of all medical specialists and examinations:
   With the service launched, the patient could immediately obtain a medical certificate in electronic form on the portal, while without the service, the patient is

required to visit a medical organization and obtain a certificate on paper. From this situation, it follows that the patient spends his time waiting to see a doctor (according to the monitoring data for February 2019 – 1.74 days), visiting a medical organization (an average of 120 min) and visiting a doctor (10 min), and the doctor – to see the patient. Moreover, the medical organization pays doctors for the time to issue certificates, when he can devote his time to other processes.

With the launched service, but without the support of an electronic signature, the patient can pay for the certificate on-line and view the results of examinations and observations in his personal account on the thematic portal.

Comparing the processes of obtaining a certificate through the service with the possible signing of the certificate with an electronic signature and without such a possibility, it was found that in the first case the patient does not need to visit the doctor, and hand – take the patient. Service with an electronic signature saves time of the patient in parts waiting to make an appointment to see the doctor (the therapist, the police, a General practitioner (family doctor), a pediatrician), visiting the medical institution and a doctor that is approximately 2664,4 min: 1.76 day, about 120 min and 10 min respectively.

2. Scenario with the passage of initially not all medical specialists and examinations: In the absence of service, the patient additionally spends time to pay for the certificate in the medical organization (about 30 min) and a second visit to the doctor (General practitioner, General practitioner, (family doctor), pediatrician) (1.74 days waiting for an appointment with a doctor and 10 min for an appointment). The doctor, in turn, also spends 10 min taking the patient. The medical organization bears losses in the form of payment of time of the doctor for the statement of the reference, an expense of paper and the press of medical certificates. When the service is implemented, the patient has access to a certificate in the personal account, and the patient has the opportunity to send a certificate to other organizations that require a medical certificate from the patient, which also saves the patient's time.

As a result of the comparison of the process of obtaining a medical certificate and its issuance, it was revealed that the electronic service "Medical certificates" reduces the time of the patient to obtain a certificate, eliminating repeated observations and examinations, transferring certain actions to an electronic form on the portal. The medical organization also benefits from the introduction of the service, namely, reducing its costs for repeated examinations and paying for the time of doctors to issue certificates.

5 Conclusions

The level of introduction of e-government technologies in terms of government services rendering is an essential factor in the process of an urban population suburbanization. It can contribute to the acceleration of the suburbanization process by means of creation of services available, comparable to urban standards, or, on the contrary, slow the process. The present study shows the initial formulation of the problem. Authors in future publications plan to review the effectiveness of public service delivery in the suburb areas considering the presence and absence of a full transfer of public services in electronic form.

The presented results demonstrate the demand for high-quality medical services by residents of suburban areas. This demand is likely to grow, as the quality of services provided by residents will approach the urban one with an increase in the number of residents of the suburbs. At the same time, the problems of suburban areas can be compensated to some extent by optimizing the processes of providing medical services. And the introduction of new technologies for the formation of a single database, leveling the impact of different administrative subordination of medical organizations.

Acknowledgements. This work is financially supported by the Ministry of Education and Science of the Russian Federation, Agreement #14.575.21.0161 (26/09/2017). Unique Identification RFMEFI57517X0161.

References

1. Homsy, G.C., Warner, M.E.: Cities and sustainability: polycentric action and multilevel governance. Urban Aff. Rev. **51**(1), 46–73 (2015)
2. Duany, A., Plater-Zyberk, E., Speck, J.: Suburban Nation: The Rise of Sprawl and the Decline of the American Dream. North Point Press, Macmillan, New York (2011)
3. Government Services Portal of Russian Federation. https://www.gosuslugi.ru/
4. Summary of the sample survey "the Influence of behavioral factors on the health of the population". Federal state statistics service (2008). http://www.gks.ru/free_doc/2008/demo/zdr08.htm. Accessed 07 Apr 2018
5. Poudel, S.K., et al.: District health service management. J-GMC-N **12**(01), 75–78 (2019)
6. Suburbanization and improving the quality of life in the United States: from suburbs to outlying cities (2016). https://urban.hse.ru/suburbanization/. Accessed 07 Apr 2018. (in Russian)
7. McCrory, J.: The Edge City Fallacy. New Urban Form or Same Old Megalopolis? (2016). http://johnmccrory.com/selected-writings/the-Edge%20City-fallacy/. Accessed 07 Apr 2018
8. Hayden, D.: A Field Guide to Sprawl. W. W. Norton & Co., New York (2004)
9. Freilich, R.H., et al.: From Sprawl to Sustainability, Smart Growth, New Urbanism, Green Development and Renewable Energy. https://encrypted.google.com/books?id=2hET5BF4jDYC&printsec=frontcover&source=gbs_ViewAPI#v=onepage&q&f=false. Accessed 07 Apr 2018
10. Lewinnek, E.: The Working Man's Reward: Chicago's Early Suburbs and the Roots of American Sprawl. Oxford University Press, Oxford (2014)
11. Glaeser, E.: Triumph of the City, p. 400. The Random House, New York (2011)
12. Duany, A., Plater-Zyberk, E., Speck, J.: Suburban Nation: The Rise of Sprawl and the Decline of the American Dream, p. 293. North Point Press, Macmillan, New York (2011)
13. Garreau, J.: Edge City: Life on the New Frontier, p. 548. Anchor books, New York City (1991)
14. Remezkova, V., Gutkovich, V., Spirina, M.: Russia's way to suburbanization: Moscow and Saint Petersburg experience. Urban Stud. Pract. **1**(1), 24–37, 27 (2016)
15. Agha, L.: The effects of health information technology on the costs and quality of medical care. J. Health Econ. **34**, 19–30 (2014)

16. Yen, K.: Time motion study in a pediatric emergency department before and after computer physician order entry. Ann. Emerg. Med. **53**(4), 463 (2009)
17. Asaro, P.: Effects of computerized provider order entry and nursing documentation on workflow. Acad. Emerg. Med. **15**(10), 911 (2008)
18. Tierney, W.: Physician inpatient order writing on microcomputer workstations: effects on resource utilization. J. Am. Med. Assoc. **269**(3), 379 (1993)
19. McDowell, I.: A randomized trial of computerized reminders for blood pressure screening in primary care. Med. Care **27**(3), 297 (1989)
20. McDowell, I.: Computerized reminders to encourage cervical screening in family practice. J. Fam. Pract. **28**(4), 422 (1989)
21. Rosser, W.: Use of reminders to increase compliance with tetanus booster vaccination. CMAJ **146**(6), 915 (1992)
22. McDowell, I.: Comparison of three methods of recalling patients for influenza vaccination. CMAJ **135**(9), 994 (1986)
23. Rosser, W.: Use of reminders for preventive procedures in family medicine. CMAJ **145**(7), 811 (1991)
24. Apkon, M., Singhaviranon, P.: Impact of an electronic information system on physician workflow and data collection in the intensive care unit. Intensive Care Med. **27**(1), 128 (2001)
25. Overhage, J.: Controlled trial of direct physician order entry: effects on physicians' time utilization in ambulatory primary care internal medicine practices. J. Am. Med. Inform. Assoc. **8**, 364 (2001)
26. Pizziferri, L.: Primary care physician time utilization before and after implementation of an electronic health record: a time-motion study. J. Biomed. Inform. **38**(3), 183 (2005)
27. Poissant, L.: The impact of electronic health records on time efficiency of physicians and nurses: a systematic review. J. Am. Med. Inform. Assoc. **12**(5), 510 (2005)
28. Maslove, D.: Computerized physician order entry in the critical care environment: a review of current literature. J. Intensive Care Med. **26**(3), 168 (2011)
29. Ballermann, M.: Impact of a critical care clinical information system on interruption rates during intensive care nurse and physician documentation tasks. In: MEDINFO, Amsterdam, 275 p. (2010)
30. Goorman, E.: Modelling nursing activities: electronic patient records and their discontents. Nurs. Inq. **7**, 7 (2016)
31. Management Consulting: Rendering of government and municipal services rendering in Saint Petersburg multifunctional centers of public and municipal services, May 2015

Protest Activity on Social Network Sites:
A Method of Citizen's Engagement Assessment

Alexander Sokolov$^{(\boxtimes)}$ ⓘ, Alexey Belyakov ⓘ,
and Alexander Frolov ⓘ

Demidov P.G. Yaroslavl State University, Yaroslavl, Russia
alex8119@mail.ru

Abstract. Internet activism is one of the fastest growing phenomena in modern political practice. Due to the specifics of interaction within virtual networks, new forms of expression of public opinion have appeared, the role of an individual in the formation of the information agenda has increased significantly, and the time for information dissemination and feedback has been reduced. In this regard, the goal of this study was to create and test a methodology for assessing the involvement of users of social network sites in protest actions and campaigns on example of the "Voters Strike" action. I was possible to see that users, in many respects, played a significant role in the increased attention paid to the action both by the government and the media, and by the population. As a result of the study using the author's methodology, it was possible to establish that, despite the high number of reactions, the overall involvement in the protest action "Voters Strike" was at a low level. From this we can conclude that the level of involvement depends on the ability of the initiator of protest activity to maintain a high level of user interest. Also, it was revealed that there is a significant difference between user activity and their involvement.

Keywords: Internet · Social network sites · Protest · Engagement assessment

1 Introduction

Modern social-political processes are a complex system of interrelated relations between different actors. Over the past 10 years these processes have undergone significant transformation through the introduction and development of ICT. So the need to take into account and analyze the products of ICT development that directly affect the nature of social-political relations in modern civil society has appeared.

The internet activism as a phenomenon has begun to attract special attention in Russia since the mid-2000s, when young people in countries with fairly closed and authoritarian regimes began to discover the "world wide web". Using the Internet as an opportunity to exchange and transmit information that wasn't on state television channels, active young people gradually learned to communicate and organize collective actions in a virtual environment. With the appearance of social network sites communication opportunities have increased greatly: the circle of like-minded people has expanded. Such a breakthrough in the organization of communication has become a catalyst for the use of social network sites in protest campaigns. Thus, social network

© Springer Nature Switzerland AG 2020
A. Chugunov et al. (Eds.): EGOSE 2019, CCIS 1135, pp. 217–242, 2020.
https://doi.org/10.1007/978-3-030-39296-3_17

sites have allowed every dissatisfied person to realize himself in a community that unites people with similar contradictions in the awareness of themselves and their own situation. United in larger groups, these communities became the epicenter of growing of public discontent; they found leaders who could activate the participants for active actions. The result was an event that went down in history as "the Arab spring". It should be noted that during "the Arab spring" social network sites were used rather as a means of communication and mobilization of offline activists and also as the channel of dissemination of information about the tragic events of December 18, 2010. Gradually, with the large introduction of social network sites in social and political processes, activity in social network sites began to acquire more significant features, drawing the attention of not only researchers of protest activity and Internet activism, but also real political and public actors. Today social network sites are also the environment of protest activity in the virtual space. Such activity attracts more and more attention of researchers, who, in turn, use different methods to analyze it.

Therefore, there is a growing need for the preparation and testing of methods for assessing the effectiveness of the use of social network sites in protest campaigns: assessing the level of user involvement, the level of their activity, as well as the effectiveness of methods of involvement. Despite the comprehensive introduction of ICT in modern social-political relations, the scientific development of this topic is still not high enough. Such a phenomenon can be explained, firstly, due to the dynamics of changes in the studied sphere. Thus, researchers of the Arab spring, Occupy actions, color revolutions and the wave of protests in Russia in 2011–2013 gave a significant role to the problems of the role of social network sites. However, over time the functionality of social network sites has changed greatly, new forms of information transfer and new platforms, which rapidly gain popularity, such as Instagram, have appeared. At the same time, there is a significant increase in trust of social networks and information on the Internet, which also requires special attention from researches.

Under these conditions, the role of new methods of analysis of social network sites, offering a comprehensive approach to the study of social and political activity in the virtual space, is significantly increase. In addition, the role of monitoring of social network sites, as well as the analysis of the activity of social network sites users in order not to miss the growth of the conflict and to respond quickly to the problems and complaints of users, is increasing.

2 Theoretical Approach

According to one version, social network sites as a phenomenon within the Internet were first mentioned by the American sociologist Howard Reinhold, who created his website "Electronic minds" in 1996, which, according to Reinhold himself, was a virtual public center of the community he created on the Internet. Later, he also identified several fundamental advantages of social networks and gave them a definition.

"A virtual community is a group of people who may or may not meet each other in person, exchanging words and ideas through electronic message boards and networks. Like any other community, it is also a meeting of people who adhere to a certain social contract and have certain interests" [1]. This definition of social network sites makes it possible to see in a set of computer programs and online components of the Internet a complex system of building communication between individuals with the expectation that over time they will be able not only to communicate and transmit information independently, but also to unite into communities based on internal rules and acting on the principles of self-regulation. Thus, professional journalist and analyst Will Kenton emphasizes that social network sites are an online tool for interaction with other people who have common interests, experience or interact in real life [2]. In domestic studies social network sites are given, in general, a similar definition. Thus, Steinberg defined social network sites as network communities and the members of these communities have the opportunity to exchange views, thoughts, emotions without any formal restrictions and create a basis for friendly relations based on common interests [3].

Social network sites, which are one of the most popular sites on the Internet today, create additional opportunities for communication between people, but in the virtual space. Thus, Uspensky in his book notes that each subscriber of such social network sites has the ability to communicate with any subscriber of a similar network both on his own behalf and on behalf of the group [4]. Therefore, we can say that social network sites and the Internet in general form the following types of communication: user – means of communication (computer); user-user; one user – group of users; group of users – one user; group of users.

Such a diversity of communication allows to create a unique environment, which provides that the person who is in it, will not only be better informed, but will also be in a state of constant readiness to react to a particular message, information, action. For modern political communication feedback time can play a crucial role because it reduces not only the time of dissemination of information, but also the response time, which allows you to correct mistakes quickly and not to give reasons for the appearance of discontent when it comes to initiating of protest campaigns. The diversity of types of communication makes an interactive function of social network sites. It is also the main reason for the popularity of social network sites among politicians and public figures around the world.

The development of networked Internet technologies against the backdrop of the crisis of traditional political institutions leads to the fact that citizens (first of all, young people) are increasingly reorienting to new channels of communication and forms of activity that, as Joe Kahne and Katie Cohen point out, cannot but be taken into account [5].

Shirky argues that the Internet and social networks have changed political activities of individuals by greatly facilitating the search and mobilization of supporters [6]. Tafouchi's research suggests the formation of strong and long-term ties between protest activists through communication in social networks [7].

Equally important is the way the protest is interpreted in the media and social media: as a rejection or as a legitimate way of articulating dissatisfaction of citizens with the existing socio-political situation and encouraging social change [8].

Research focuses on the various roles of social networks. In some cases, attention is focused on their socializing function and the process of reconciling private and public interests [9], in others - on their ability to spread information about protests in order to engage and increase the number of activists [10].

It is possible to indicate several basic tools of the impact of social media on protest activity: the mobilization of information and news, assistance in coordinating actions, developing a sense of belonging to events, an exchange of views [11].

Other studies focus on the political component of the activity of users of social network sites. Thus, Bronnikov speaks about the formation of decentralized non-hierarchical network relations [12]. This is due to the fact that political and public communication is moving to social network sites. The reasons for this transition the researchers indicate the widespread use of the Internet, convenience, availability and speed of information exchange [13]. The increasing role of the Internet and social network sites in particular is connected, among other things, with increasing public confidence in these sources of information. Thus, according to the VCIOM study, in 2017 32% of the Russian population receives information from Internet sources and social network sites.

The development of social network sites influenced the protest activity greatly. To understand the essence of this phenomenon, one should turn to the definition of protest activity. Thus, Konevskaya defines the protest activity as "the involvement of citizens in various forms of protest, including mass protest actions, i.e. the implementation of the protest potential in specific behavioral forms, an open form of mass behavior of social community through which dissatisfaction and demands about the changes in processes taking place in the society are expressed" [14]. Therefore, protest activity can be understood as an expression of social, political or economic demands of citizens, various groups and other subjects of social and political relations.

In this case, we can distinguish several subjects:

• Situational protest societies that arise in connection with the aggravation of the crisis in public life, affecting the interests of the population.
• Organized protest movements, characterized not so much by massive participation but by the frequency of protest actions, the organization of the main body and periphery and territorial coverage.
• Mixed types that can occur for the short term to achieve certain goals by the leaders of the protest movement.

This typology can also relate to protest actions partially or completely taking place in social network sites. Thus, many protest actions in social network sites at the initial stage of their development can be attributed to situational ones because they are developed as a reaction of users to social and political information appearing in the Internet space. Such actions include protest communities against the import of garbage from Moscow to the regions of Russia, protests against the system "Platon" and others. Gradually, with the increase in the number of users and the lack of proper response from the authorities, such protest communities gain a stable main body, choose opinion leaders and become organized. This is often due, among other things, to the intro-duction of political actors to these movements, which allows these actions to become mixed and so they can be used for certain purposes (a striking example of such situation is the infiltration of a representative of the Communist party Alexander Vorobyov to protest actions against the import of garbage in Yaroslavl).

Sokolov and Frolov note that the new media allowed the protests to develop with great speed and attract the attention of the world community [14]. To a great extent that kind of attention is connected with the fact that the Internet in the form of such platforms as social network sites removes the restrictions faced by activists of protests in the real space.

In addition, after the protest actions in the Arab countries, numerous Occupy actions and the events in Russia in 2011–2012, it became obvious that social network sites can also be used as a tool for coordinating the actions of protesters. Such a coordination center does not have a physical embodiment, it can have several entry points and many exit points of basic information, and also it connects thousands of users without the need of direct contact, which makes it impossible to close it or entice it to the side of pro-government structures. Thus, despite the closing of the regional headquarters of public and political figure Alexei Navalny, his initiatives still attracted a lot of people because the coordination center of all activity was not in physical embodiment(building, office, broadcasting center), but in the virtual one as webpages in social network sites and, even in the case of arrests and removal of the main initiator from the coordination of the protest, the "virtual headquarters" continued to work thanks to the closest supporters who had access to the webpages of Navalny. Therefore, protest activity in social network sites has a number of advantages in comparison with activity in an offline environment. These advantages, in particular, make Internet activism a more universal and complex tool for expressing social and political interests of the population.

A special vision on protests and protest activity has developed in foreign scientific thought. Thus, the idea of protest activity from the point of view of the theory of collective behavior is of interest. Dementieva, generalizing theoretical approaches to the theory of collective behavior, gives it the following definition: "Relatively spontaneous and unorganized behavior of a group of people responding to an uncertain or threatening situation" [15].

Within the framework of the presented study, protest activity is considered as a special form of activity in social network sites. Protest activity in social network sites is an expression of the protest potential of the population in online platforms using specific forms of activity for these platforms, determined through the involvement of users.

Involvement of users of social networks is one of the necessary indicators to assess the effectiveness of modern social-political campaigns and actions. It should be noted that there is no precise definition and generally accepted rules of what should be understood by the involvement in social-political or protest activity in social networks If we proceed from the concept of involvement and its interpretation from the point of view of the Russian language, the most accurate and broad definition is given by the Efremova dictionary: involvement is derived from the verb to involve i.e. to encourage someone to something, or to participate in something. Thus, involvement in the context of this work can be understood as the motivation of users to participate in a protest campaign or action through activity in social network sites. In addition to the above interpretation, there are other definitions of the word "involvement". So, in the Dahl dictionary the meaning of the word "involve" is presented as coercion to any action or participation in something that, in the opinion of the authors may not be applicable to participation in the social network sites because coercion presupposes the existence of certain relations, and leverage between the object and the subject of enforcement that is difficult to achieve in social network sites because of the specificity of relations between users. In addition, there is an interpretation of involvement as a seduction to something that is also not applicable to social network sites because the subject of involvement often does not have the resources using which he could seduce the object i.e. the user of social network sites.

From the point of view of political science "involvement" is more often understood from the point of view of the theory of political participation. Thus, O. Yu. Kuzin notes that the concept of involvement is used in political literature in two meanings. In the first case, the term is almost synonymous with political participation because it is used to describe the general state and degree of involvement of citizens in political and social activities. In the second case, involvement is understood in a narrower sense: as the purposeful activity of certain actors in the political process and the functioning of civil society, aimed at the inclusion of citizens in political or civil activity, as well as a set of means and methods of such inclusion.

Thus, based on different understandings of the word involvement, we can give the following definition of the involvement of social network sites users in protest activity – a purposeful, intellectual activity aimed to inducing, including users of social network sites in protest activity in social network sites, as well as a set of means and methods of such inducement. This definition formed the basis of the methodology for assessing the activity of users of social network sites and their involvement in protest campaigns and actions.

It is worth noting that for a long time virtual activity was either not evaluated or methods of evaluation of protest activity, which were previously applied to traditional forms of expression of protest activity, were applied to Internet activism. Baranova points out such a problem. She notes that only statistical data are often used to analyze and predict protest activity, and on their basis various "protest indexes" are formulated [16]. Such an approach is certainly not suitable for such a rapidly changing environment as social network sites. In this regard, realizing that conventional methods of analysis are not suitable for virtual reality, the scientific community, as well as the experts in political analysis came to new methods of analysis of protest activity on the Internet and social network sites.

Thus, in the process of searching for methods that can give relevant indicators in the analysis of social network sites, the methods most often used in marketing research, political and sociological analysis were used. One of the approaches to online analysis is suggested by Ushkin. His position is that the mechanisms of marketing analysis are directly or indirectly present in all social network sites [17]. In particular, targeting analysis that allows you to choose from an existing audience the audience that meets the criteria of the study. This approach allows the researcher to effectively distinguish from the many thousands of users of social network sites certain audiences on the basis of age, marital status, professional characteristics and daily interests. Thus, this method is a rather variable method of descriptive statistics, allowing the researcher to analyze social relations in relatively homogeneous groups. Demonstrating the results of this method, Ushkin gave an example of targeting analysis of the community "Svobodniye novosti" in the social network site Vkontakte in 2012–2014. As a result of the study he was able to determine that during this period the audience of the community was strongly delocalized: the majority of users were residents of Moscow and St. Peters-burg, which suggests that the audience of this public does not declare the views of the entire virtual community, despite its number.

Another approach to the analysis of virtual communities is network analysis. It is generally accepted that online interactions often have a network organization, and electronic communication can be represented as a network of senders and recipients of information [18]. Considering the possibility of assessing the interaction of users in social network sites, a specialist in modern technology of media communications Bernie Hogan notes that users of such resources are encouraged to create special connections. These connections are often called "friend," "buddy," or "partner." Such statuses represent mutual relations, which are the edges of the network, and qualitative characteristics by sex, age, place of residence, etc. are the knots on the basis of which such a connection occurs [19]. The development of ICT has allowed to conduct a broadscale network analysis showing the features and areas of interaction of tens and hundreds of thousands of users of social network sites. For such an assessment spe-cialized analytical programs capable of processing large amounts of information are used. Such an analysis gives an idea, for example, of the links between the subscribers of a politician, as well as the way he communicates with his audience. Also, such studies allow to create a map of user interactions, forms of their interaction, as well as to determine the leaders of public opinion, the main body of the network i.e. the most active users, as well as those who take an active part in the interaction within the network. In social-political studies such an analysis allows to classify the active par-ticipants of social-political initiatives, to determine the main points of their interaction, to assess the strength of the links between the participants and the direct initiators of protest campaigns.

Despite the wide possibilities of network analysis, it, to a greater extent, gives an idea of the characteristics of the general summation of users of social networks. For a deeper analysis of the qualitative indicators of protest activity in social network sites such methods as the analysis of the tone of the text, expressed in relation to the author to a particular subject of evaluation can also be used [20]. In addition, within the framework of political analysis it is accepted to apply such approaches as content analysis, intent analysis, narrative analysis, discourse analysis [21]. The summation of these methods used in the framework of one technique can give a more complete picture of the course of a protest action or campaign, the qualitative data of its audience and key topics of discourse.

If it is necessary to transfer qualitative indicators into quantitative aspect methods of multidimensional scaling are often used. As noted by A. Yu. Trusova, in multidimen-sional scaling the role of the source of information is played by experts who subjectively perceive and evaluate quality indicators [22]. Such an assessment allows to transfer such qualitative indicators as "level of involvement", "level of activity", "impact on involvement", etc. in the format of quantitative indicators setting coefficients.

Methods of quantitative indicators analysis, which include statistical data, time characteristics, the number of users and their reactions (likes, reposts, comments, etc.), complement the methods of assessing qualitative indicators. Also, such methods include index analysis, which is very popular among independent researchers and large public and private sociological agencies. Today the generally recognized indexes, which are most often referred to by researchers include: the human development index, the index of polity by Ted Robert Gurr, the index of democratization of Tatu Van-hanen; the globalization index from "Foreign Affairs" & A. T. Kearney and the transformation index Bertelsmann [23].

Despite the fact that each of the above mentioned indexes has unique features, takes into account different indicators and the system of calculations, most of them have similar features. Thus, most of them are based on the method of expert assessments, statistical methods and methods of data collection and content analysis [24].

It should be noted that the above mentioned indexes in general show different methods of analysis of the social-political situation, without affecting the processes taking place in virtual reality, which, as defined in this work, has a great influence in modern society. That is why there is a need to create and use methods of index analysis of social-political relations and processes taking place on the Internet and social net-work sites. For the analysis of such indicators various software can be used, the work of which is based on the processing of a large array of open data from social network sites.

Within the framework of this work, a method of analyzing the activity and involvement of subscribers in protest activity in social network sites will be presented. The author's method lies in the combined assessment of quantitative indicators of subscribers' activity and qualitative analysis of methods of their involvement in protest activity through social network sites. The protest action "Voters' Strike", which took place in Russia on the eve of the presidential elections in 2018, was chosen as an empirical base and approbation of the method.

3 Research Methodology

The aim of this study was to create and test a methodology for assessing the involvement of users of social network sites in protest actions and campaigns on the example of the campaign "Voters' Strike". It should be noted that in order to achieve the goal, it was necessary to create a methodology that would meet the modern requirements for the analysis of social and political campaigns, would have a suffi-ciently high degree of accuracy and would also allow to assess the past or present protest action holistically. In addition, the methodology required universality: it should be simple enough and use universal evaluation indicators to enable those who use it to analyze not only federal activity widely discussed by the public, but also local actions and campaigns at the local and regional levels.

In this work, the event-analysis method was used as a tool for processing a large array of information. The standard matrix for this method was modified to adapt to social networks sites. In addition, the task was to determine the specifics of conducting a protest campaign, the methods and tools of involvement used in it. Since the protest action "Voters' Strike" was a chain of interrelated actions of the actor and reactions of the actors of influence, it was necessary to use a method that allows to evaluate each of the individual events in the context of the entire action. In this regard, the choice was made in favor of a case study because it, in contrast to the most common method of situational analysis, is more adapted to analyze the situation in dynamics.

Since the goal of this work is, among other things, to assess the involvement of users of social networks in protest activity, it is necessary to translate qualitative indicators into quantitative ones. The most common method to achieve this task is the construction of indices. It should be noted that during the creation of the author's index, attention was paid to taking into account all activities, however, it was suggested that different reactions in different degrees express the user's involvement in protest activity, therefore, it was necessary to determine the weighting factor for each of the reactions. It was also decided to conduct expert interviews in which it was proposed to determine the expression of the degree of involvement for each of the types of reactions. The final indicators were applied in the construction of the author's index.

The protest action "Voters' Strike", which took place in Russia on the eve of the presidential elections of 2018, was chosen as an empirical base and testing of the methodology. The source of empirical data was quantitative data on the activity of users from Alexey Navalny's social networks, indicators of Alexey Navalny's activity in social networks, qualitative characteristics of materials published during the "Voters' Strike" campaign, and expert assessments.

For the collection of quantitative data used Internet resource Popsters. With its help, three social networks selected for analysis collecting of information on user's activity: likes, reposts, comments, hashtags, subscriptions, views, and also on Alexey Navalny's publication activity (the number of materials per day, the number of publications by days of the week and time of day etc.). For each of the selected pages, the time frames were set from December 25, 2017 to March 17, 2018. The service allowed us to isolate all materials released during this period, after which, using the integrated tools, we calculated the quantitative indicators. For the analysis of quantitative data, an Event Analysis method was applied. This method is most often used to analyze the situation with the use of the media, however, an example of this method shows that it is also suitable for social networks. The matrix of the event-analysis was created in the Microsoft Excel, the above-mentioned quantitative indicators were entered, separated according to the relationship to the object of study (Alexey Navalny and users of social networks). The data were entered into the matrix, the total number of reactions, the total number of publications, and the ratio of the total number of reactions to the total number of subscribers were counted. The collected quantitative data allowed us to make preliminary conclusions about the activity of subscribers, about the activity of Alexei Navalny, as well as about the dynamics of coverage of the strike action of voters in social networks.

The collection of high-quality empirical data took place by selecting all materials published on the pages of Alexei Navalny on social networks. Of all the publications, the published ones were highlighted in the periods designated by the greatest and least active subscribers. In these materials, the following characteristics were distinguished: the type of material, the method of involvement in the activity of subscribers, the number of reactions to the material, the topic raised by the post, as well as its relationship with the action "Voters' Strike". The obtained data were summarized in matrices and analyzed using the case-study method, which allowed to evaluate the dynamics with the help of what tools, managed to attract the most attention of the audience, which topics most caused the backlash of social network users, and also give a general description of each of selected periods.

Expert assessments were collected through personal and telephone interviews of 10 representatives of state authorities, media representatives, the scientific community, as well as civil society activists. Experts were asked to respond to a number of questions related to the possibilities of using social networks in protest actions and campaigns, the risks of this activity, and to assess on a ten-point scale how much this or that type of activity expresses the involvement of a social network user in protest activity. The obtained data was used in the preparation of the Index of involvement of users of social networks in protest activity as weights.

The application of the method can be described in stages in the following sequence.

At the first stage of application of the method it is supposed to conduct event-analysis of the protest action. Event-analysis is a technique consisting of the collecting and processing of factual information in order to create a clear picture of what is happening in a clear time sequence [25]. Carrying out this type of analysis gives an idea of the total number of reactions, the number of subscribers at a particular moment, as well as in different periods of the action. Thus, it is possible to identify the main stages of involvement of users of social network sites in the protest action and campaign. Therefore, after analyzing the quantitative criteria of "Voters' Strike" campaign, four webpages in social network sites, where the most active coverage of the protest action took place, were selected. In the analyzed webpages publications in the period from 25.12.2017 (the beginning of the action "Voters' Strike") to 17.03.2018 (the actual end of the action) were allocated. Posts were divided into 4 categories: posts containing text information and photos not related to the action directly, videos not related to the action directly, live broadcasts and all materials related to the action. After determining the number of posts and their distribution by categories, the total number of likes, reposts, comments, subscribers, impressions and publications with a thematic hashtag was calculated every day for each of the social network sites. With the help of the online service Popsters each day of the action was analyzed for the presence of the above mentioned criteria, which were recorded in the general table. Based on the results obtained, it was found that during the campaign Alexey Navalny posted in total 583 publications on his webpages in social network sites. These actions were responded 80732606 times including: 7118662 likes, 111635 reposts, 1488109 comments, 72009405 impressions, 15046 publications with a thematic hashtag "#Невыборы2018", "#Забастовкаизбирателей", "#28января". The total number of subscribers on four pages was 3018009, which is quite high for a public and political figure in modern Russia. At first sight, the scale of involvement of social network sites subscribers in the campaign seems to be quite high. However, based on the data obtained through the analysis of Alexei Navalny social network sites, it was estimated that the number of subscriber actions exceeds the total number of subscribers by 26 times. Thus, on average, each subscriber responded to publications 26 times, which is quite low, taking into account that the campaign lasted in total 83 days, and the number of publications during this time reached 583. That is, one subscriber reacted only to 4.45% of all publications. This criteria demonstrates the main drawback of Internet activism – the inconstancy and ambiguousness of the assessment. On the one hand, the total number of reactions in social network sites allows to speak about a high degree of interest in the subject of social-political action, on the other hand, the percent of active subscribers is too small to talk about the large involvement of users in the action.

The next stage of implication of the method is case-study. This method is a deep study of a single situation and its development over time [26]. This method allows us to describe, characterize and compare the different periods of the protest action through its main actors and the objectives of the impact. It can also be used to determine the specifics and results of the social-political actor and his followers' actions in social network sites. Thus, within the framework of the study of the protest action "Voters' Strike", 4 main stages were identified; they were marked either by the greatest activity of users or the greatest activity of the organizers of the action in social network sites. These periods were: the First period – 25–26 December, 2017. This period can be described as the beginning of the action. The second period – 28–29 January, 2018. The first major event in the framework of the action "Voters' Strike" is carrying out protests in more than 100 cities of the country. The third period is February 8, 2018. The second major event in the framework of the action is the announcement of the beginning of the recruitment of independent observers in the headquarters of A. Navalny, as well as the publication of a video investigation related to the scandal with Anastasia Vashukevich. The fourth period is 14–15 March, 2018. The last days before the election, marked by a large number of publications and activity of subscribers.

The main analyzed characteristics were allocated for each period:

- Actor's action goals;
- Total number of actions for the period;
- Number of content types (for Alexei Navalny);
- The correlation of the number and types of reactions to the number of publications (by subscribers);
- The main methods used to engage subscribers (by Alexei Navalny);
- The most interesting publications (by subscribers);
- Impact of additional factors.

The analysis was carried out on the basis of data obtained during the event-analysis on the number of total actions and reactions (Table 1), the number of content types (Table 2) and types of reactions (Table 3).

Table 1. The ratio of actor actions and user reactions

Date	A. Navalny's actions	The number of subscribers' reactions	Relation of activities to reactions
25.12.2017	12	6345198	528767
26.12.2017	8	756742	94593
28.01.2018	12	4403531	366961
29.01.2018	11	3118888	207926
08.02.2018	18	2559988	232726
12.03.2018	9	11288437	627135
13.03.2018	12	2288388	190699
14.03.2018	23	2056097	89396
15.03.2018	15	1712753	190306

Table 2. Types of content and their number for the study period

Date	Text posts in social network sites	Publication of investigations and other videos	Live broadcasting	Information materials about the passage of campaign
25.12.2017	4	2	3	3
26.12.2017	3	3	0	2
28.01.2018	0	0	5	7
29.01.2018	3	0	0	9
08.02.2018	2	7	3	4
12.03.2018	4	2	0	3
13.03.2018	5	2	0	5
14.03.2018	5	5	0	13
15.03.2018	4	2	2	8

Table 3. Total number of user reactions during the study period

Date	Likes	Reposts	Comments	Views	The amount of publications with thematic hashtag "Невыборы", "Забастовка" "28 января"
25.12.2017	523488	6191	137585	5677818	116
26.12.2017	50933	4685	10589	690368	167
28.01.2018	298076	860	72285	4030677	1633
29.01.2018	213145	1696	31772	2872146	129
08.02.2018	159369	606	22004	2377580	429
12.03.2018	545155	4293	93758	10645109	122
13.03.2018	170737	3016	29662	2084819	154
14.03.2018	127563	2604	15639	1910162	129
15.03.2018	104531	999	18011	1589121	91

At the third stage, an expert interview is conducted to clarify the specific characteristics of the evaluation of protest activity in social network sites, as well as to
determine the weighing coefficient of different types of activity, depending on their
importance in assessing the involvement and activity of users of social network sites.10
professionals in the field of civil activity and work on the Internet (specialized government officials, civil society activists, scientists) became the experts. To do this,
experts were offered a scale from 1 to 10 for each type of reactions, where they chose
one option, based on their understanding of the importance of a factor to assess the
involvement of users in the protest action in social network sites. Expert assessments
were distributed as follows (Table 4):

Table 4. Expert evaluation of reaction types

	Likes	Reposts	Comments	Views	Hashtags	Subscribers
Expert 1	7	9	8	5	7	9
Expert2	3	7	5	3	7	6
Expert3	7	6	9	6	5	8
Expert4	8	9	9	7	2	6
Expert5	2	8	7	3	6	2
Expert6	3	6	8	4	6	8
Expert7	4	8	9	2	5	7
Expert8	4	5	4	3	3	3
Expert9	7	8	8	2	2	9
Expert10	3	7	6	2	3	5
Average number	4,8	7,3	7,3	3,7	4,6	6,3
Coefficient	0,48	0,73	0,73	0,37	0,46	0,63

Thus, it can be seen that according to the experts' opinion the greatest involvement is provided by reposts and comments, as a way of direct participation of users in the dissemination and discussion of information. Lookups have the least impact because they do not reflect the real intentions of the viewer.

The fourth stage involves the use of data obtained in the event-analysis and expert survey, which will be used to create an index of involvement of users of social network sites in protest activity. Index is an integral tool of quantitative and qualitative description of political reality in general and protest activity in particular [20]. Within the framework of this research the meaning of author's index is also defined. The index of social network sites subscribers' involvement is a derivative of quantitative criteria and expert assessments used to determine the level of social network sites subscribers' involvement in the protest on the basis of their activity expressed in likes, reposts, comments, lookups, publications with a thematic hashtag and the total number of subscribers on the official web-page of the protest campaign or the initiator of protest activity for a certain period of time.

Index (W) is based on the following variables:

- Le – multiplication of the total number of likes (L) on the official web-pages of the protest activity and the weighing coefficient (e) assigned by the results of the expert survey. This variable shows the most generalized type of user support of a protest action or campaign.
- Ce – multiplication of the total number of comments (C) on the official web-pages of the protest activity and the weighing coefficient (e) assigned by the results of the expert survey. This variable evaluates the level of personal involvement of users by publishing their own opinions on the protest action or on the general discourse.
- F – the total number of subscribers (F) on the official web-pages of the protest activity. The indicator of support, estimated as the desire to join the action and receive the latest information about its progress.

- Re – multiplication of the total number of reposts (R) on the official web-pages of the protest activity and the weighing coefficient (e) assigned by the results of the expert survey. The variable reflects the desire to share information about the action or information related to it with friends and subscribers.
- He – multiplication of the total number of publications with the thematic hashtag (H) in social network sites and the weighing coefficient (e) assigned by the results of the expert survey. This variable reflects the desire of the users of the social network sites to demonstrate their involvement to the protest action or campaign by publishing their own posts with hyperlinks pointing to the action or campaign.
- P – the total number of posts during the study period. This variable shows the activity of the initiator of the protest campaign in social network sites. It allows to estimate the correlation of the total number of publications with the reactions of subscribers.
- t – the number of days in the study period. One of the most important variables because it takes into account the time period of the action and the distribution of the actors' actions by days, weeks, etc.

The formula of the index of social network subscribers' involvement in protest activity is the following:

$$W = \frac{Le + Ce + Re + He}{PF} \Big/ t \tag{1}$$

As a result, we get the level of involvement in the protest in numerical expression. This number reflects the amount of subscribers, one way or another motivated to activity within the protest action. The larger the given number was, the more active subscribers acted in the studied period of time.

Thus, the application of this technique allows us to consider a single protest campaign in terms of involving users of social network sites in protest activities. Due to the variety of methods used, this technique allows not only to assess the involvement of users in the protest activity throughout the campaign, but also to analyze different periods of the protest campaign. On the basis of the methodology recommendations for analogous campaigns and strategies for analogous social-political actions in social networks can be developed. In addition, the method allows to study the principles of involvement of users of social network sites in various activities to prevent the increase of social tension on the basis of the strengths and weaknesses of such campaigns.

4   The Results of Data Gathering

Based on the data obtained in the analysis of Alexei Navalny social network sites a number of regularities in his work with social network sites were found:

1. The largest number of publications during the protest action «Voters' Strike» was published in the social network Vkontakte. This is due to the popularity of this network, on the one hand, and the type of content and the ability to add content from other sources, on the other hand. In addition, we can assume that such an

abundance of content in Vkontakte is explained by the need in a platform that can constantly maintain the attention of the audience, as it is impossible to do in YouTube and it is rather difficult to do in Facebook. The distribution of publications on webpages in social network sites (see Fig. 1).

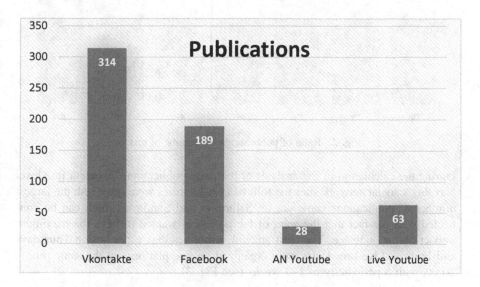

Fig. 1. Number of publications on social networks

2. The most common type of content is text and photo materials. They make up a little more than a half of all publications for the study period – 254. Such a number of publications is connected with the fact that a significant part of the material was posted in social network sites Vkontakte and Facebook, where this type of content is the main. However, it can be explained by the fact that such information is easier to perceive when viewing news feeds, if the publication has a bright picture and a small amount of text (see Fig. 2).

The graph shows that in the most used by Navalny social network the bulk of text messages fell on very short (up to 160 characters, marked in blue) and medium (from 160 to 1000 characters, marked in green) texts. It allows to speak about the concentration of information in small texts, which could also lead to the need to increase the number of posts to convey all the necessary information to subscribers. The increase in the number of long text messages at the weekend can be explained by the fact that Navalny and subscribers have more time both for the dissemination of information and for its perception, i.e. reading.

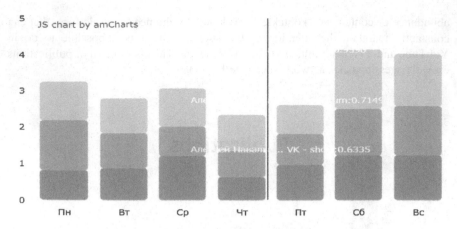

Fig. 2. Ratio of publications by volume of text

3. During the calculation of the analysis of the daily publication of content in Alexei Navalny's social network sites the following regularities were observed: the largest number of publications came out on Saturdays and Sundays, which can be connected with the fact that the team of the politician wanted to have the maximum impact on his audience. The least amount of publications came out on Thursdays and Fridays. Live broadcasts were organized on one platform, at the same time – 20:00, with a periodicity of 1–2 weeks (see Fig. 3).

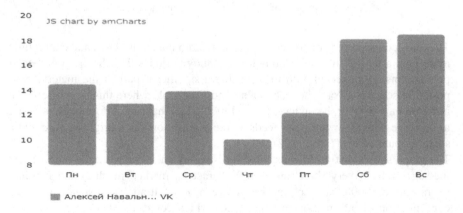

Fig. 3. Distribution of publications by day

4. There is no clear correlation between the key events of the protest action «Voters' Strike» and the number of publications in Alexey Navalny's social network sites. Thus, the largest number of publications – 23 was published on March 14, 2018, when there were no significant events occurred directly for the action. On the other hand, significant moments, such as the beginning of the protest action, all-Russian protests on January 28 and the announcement of the beginning of the formation of teams of observers were covered less (see Fig. 4).

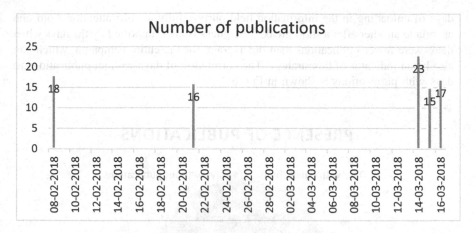

Fig. 4. Number of publications in the study period

5. Unlike the number of publications, the number of reactions from subscribers depends on significant events. So, the publications on February 8 related to one of the investigations of the Anti-corruption Foundation were marked by the greatest number of reactions – 11288437, the second period in the number of reactions – 6345198 was noted during the beginning of the action, 4403531 reactions were recorded on the day of the protests on January 28 (see Fig. 5).

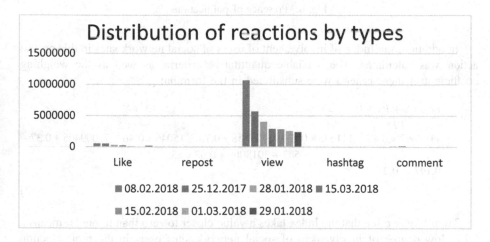

Fig. 5. Distribution of reactions by types

6. In addition, it should be noted that according to the results of the event-analysis Alexei Navalny and his team take a day off every 7–14 days, it is confirmed by the periodicity of days when there were no publication at all or there were only 1–2 publications in social network sites of the public and political. These breaks in publications can be given another explanation: the team of Alexei Navalny arranged

days of unloading in the information field purposefully to shift attention from one agenda to another after a short break. This guess is also supported by the days when there were fewer publications than the average for the entire campaign, which can also be an indicator of this strategy. The correlation of days without publications to days with publications is shown in Fig. 6.

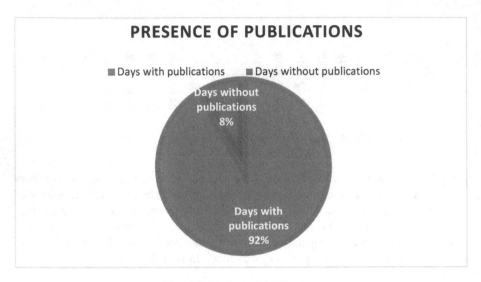

Fig. 6. Presence of publications

In addition, the Index of involvement of users of social network sites in this protest action was calculated. The available quantitative criteria, as well as the weighing coefficient of these criteria were substituted in the formula:

$$
\begin{aligned}
W &= \frac{Le + Ce + Re + He}{PFt} \\
&= \frac{7118662 * 0.48 + 111635 * 0.73 + 1477858 * 0.73 + 15046 * 0.46 + 72009405 * 0.37}{583 + 3018009 * 0.63 * 83} \\
&= 0{,}197 = 0{,}2
\end{aligned}
$$

(2)

Therefore, we see that the Index takes a value closer to zero than to one, it means a fairly low degree of involvement of social network sites users in the protest action «Voters' Strike». Based on this indicator, we can see that, despite the large number of reactions (more than 80 million), at a ratio of the total number of publications distributed by days and the total number of subscribers, this number of reactions is not an indicator of high activity.

The index method allowed to express a qualitative indicator of the involvement of users of social network sites in protest activity in quantitative terms, which allows to make more accurate conclusions, as well as to judge the degree of effectiveness of the methods of user involvement used within the framework of the action under consideration. To do this, the analysis of the main stages of the protest action was made; as a result it became possible to establish the following:

The first stage – December 25–16, 2017

This period was emphasized because it is in fact the beginning of the action. These days, the name of the action was formed, goals and objectives were set, hashtags were introduced, and users of social network sites were notified with an appeal to join mass protests.

During this period the key task for Alexei Navalny and his team was to attract everyone's attention to the procedure of refusal to register a public and political figure as a presidential candidate. During this period his active supporters were broadcasting his speech in the CEC of Russia live; also they urged to support him in social network sites with the thematic hashtags. During this period 20 publications were made, and most of them fall on December 25, 2017. The fact that users of social network sites reacted 3243921 times to the posts during this period is also significative. And most of it again falls on December 25. It should be noted that on December 25 there were than 260 thousand reactions for every post, the average number of reactions per post on December 26 is slightly more than 107 thousand. It is connected, first of all, with the fact that users of social network sites reacted to the "fresh" information submitted in the format of the live broadcast more actively. In addition, an important factor of the high activity of Alexei Navalny subscribers and other users of social network sites was a resonant statement, which was the beginning of the protest action. The statement about the beginning of the "Voters' Strike" was released in the format of a video on Alexei Navalny's channel in Youtube. The release of this video cannot be called accidental. Based on the fact that it was released on the same day as the refusal of registration, it can be assumed that Navalny's team had prepared for the beginning of the protest action in advance, therefore, approached the survey from a professional point of view. However, the sharp decline in activity the day after the announcement of the beginning of the action, as well as the average activity of users up to the next stage, suggests that during this period there were no active actions on the part of the organizers of the action and the work was carried out in a daily routine.

Thus, the analysis of the first stage of the protest action "Voters' Strike" makes it clear that the beginning of the action was due to the mass distribution of video urging to boycott the elections and due to the bright provocative headlines. However, the organizers could not support the level of involvement and support that A. Navalny received on the first day. It can be assumed that this is due to the fact that the beginning of the action on January 25 was marked by too rapid dissemination of information, as a result, in the following days it was addressed by fewer people because the basic information was given on the first day.

The second stage – January 28–29, 2018

This stage is important because on January 28 there was the first large event in the framework of the protest action – protests against the elections in more than 100 cities of Russia. Announced at the very beginning of the "Voters' Strike" it attracted attention and all the information publications about the action were concentrated on it in the period from December 26 to January 27. Communication strategy in this period can be defined as: maximum involvement of users of social network sites in the offline event through live broadcasts. So, in this period 5 h of live broadcasts with direct inclusions from different cities of Russia were made. In addition, during this period, other web-pages of Alexei Navalny published text materials about the protests, as well as the opinions of Navalny regarding the protests, the arrest of one of the leaders during the live broadcast and also about his own detention. At this stage, the maximum number of publications with a thematic hashtag was recorded – more than 1,700, which is explained by the direct presence of users of social network sites at protests. It can be assumed that this number was even bigger because part of the posts was deleted by the users sometime after the completion of the action. In addition, attention is drawn to the fact that a large activity of subscribers was recorded the day after the protests. This may be due to the fact that on this day the exact information about the reasons for the detention of several initiators of the protests including Alexei Navalny and one of the leaders of live broadcast became known. In addition, users of social network sites were attracted by videos about the results of the action, released on the main channel of Alexei Navalny. However, a decreasing level of overall involvement should be noted, the evidence is the low rates of likes, reposts and comments compared with the previous stage. The presence of a large part of Alexei Navalny's subscribers in social network sites directly at protests could cause low activity in social networks. Since many of the subscribers directly participated in the protests, they could not have the desire to discuss and talk about this event.

Thus, one of the key indicators of the second stage of the campaign is the sharply increased number of publications with thematic hashtags, which is explained by the desire of users of social network sites to join the group of protesters and to indicate their presence at the protest or its support with hashtags. It can also be the reason of low activity of subscribers in the format of likes, reposts and comments. In addition, there is a tendency of reducing the interest of both Alexei Navalny and his subscribers to disseminate information on Facebook. If during the first stage subscribers of Alexei Navalny made more than 35,000 actions, then in the second stage their number was slightly more than 5500 with an equal number of publications.

The third stage – February 8, 2018

Despite the short duration this stage is characterized by the largest number of reactions from subscribers, the beginning of a campaign to train independent observers at the headquarters of Alexei Navalny, as well as the publication of a video investigation of the scandal with Anastasia Vashukevich. The total number of publications in this period is 18. However, most of them are only indirectly related to the campaign and are devoted to three topics: the salaries of presidential candidates, the publication of ballot papers in the public domain and the scandal with Anastasia Vashukevich. Although, despite this the greatest activity was recorded in this period. The total number of reactions is 11288437. Most of them are connected with watching videos in YouTube. This is primarily due to the resonance that was caused by the scandal with Anastasia Vashukevich and a well-known businessman. The activity of subscribers connected with the reaction to the video devoted to this scandal leads to the conclusion that the most popular publications among users are publications on acute topics affecting the private interests of famous personalities. In addition, analyzing the publication in Alexei Navalny's social network sites it was concluded that the attention of subscribers was attracted primarily due to the proven format of video investigations, which gave the viewer a large amount of negatively colored information about the current government and presidential candidates in a concise and ironic form with a lot of borrowings from the network Internat. Also, to spread video materials into other networks in the text of the video there were requests to share it with friends and relatives, so that they know who they are going to vote for. All these actions have provided a high number of lookups and likes, but the number of comments and reposts does not indicate a clear desire of users of social network sites to express their opinion on these topics. Thus, it can be seen that the increase in the activity of social network sites users can be associated not so much with the direct coverage of the action, but with the original presentation of the most relevant topics with an emphasis on negative, sometimes artificially inflated features. It is also worth noting that during this period an enlistment of observers was announced, but publications on this topic did not collect a large number of materials. It places in question the desire of Alexei Navalny and his team to attract really as many people as possible, or the disinterest of users of social network sites in this type of public activity. However, the high interest of users of social network sites in acute topics leads to the conclusion that it is necessary to take into account the possibility of focusing the audience's attention on acute issues for their involvement.

The fourth stage – March 12–15, 2018

This stage, in fact, draws a line under the two-month work on the involvement of social network sites subscribers in the protest action "Voters' Strike". During this period, there is a high activity of Alexei Navalny, as well as a high activity of his subscribers in social network sites. It should be noted that by this period the action again shifted the vector of development: from the recruitment of voluntary observers to urging to boycott the elections as not effective and illegitimate.

It should be noted that by the beginning of this period users of social network sites began to lose interest in the theme of the action, which is proved by a significant decrease in activity. Several factors could be the reason for it:

1. There was an overabundance of information about the upcoming elections in both traditional and new media. An active pro-government campaigning in order to attract users to the elections as well as information campaigns of presidential candidates was conducted in the network simultaneously with the main opposition campaign of Alexei Navalny. All this provided a glut of information agenda and could cause a negative perception of the entire agenda related to the elections.

2. Low activity of Navalny's team in this period, which was marked by the number of publications below the average per day. During this period, there were also no loud and resonant topics that Navalny's team could use as reasons to criticize the current government with an emphasis on boycotting the elections.

Despite these factors, a week before the elections Navalny's team renewed its attempts to return the interest of social network sites users to the "Voters' Strike" protest action by re-changing the rhetoric from a recruitment of observers to control the transparency of the elections to urging to boycott these elections; that was initially declared at the beginning of the campaign.

During this period, the largest number of publications informing subscribers about the goals and objectives of the "Voters' Strike" was recorded - 21. The total number of reactions is 4252879. Most of them are the materials in Vkontakte; it also suggests a redirecting of communication with users in favor of the network involving the widest distribution of publications due to the ability to make reposts to friends' communities, as well as to share with friends and subscribers. However, despite the wide media campaign, posts in Alexei Navalny's social network sites had 340708 likes, which is the average for this campaign, 4300 reposts were made, posts were commented 47541 times and looked up 4782308 times, which is also the average. Also about 258 publications with a thematic hashtag were made. The most valued publications among subscribers were the videos released on Alexei Navalny's official channel, where he once again explained his position on the elections of 2018 and urged the audience to boycott them. In addition, during this period the activation of Vkontakte subscribers was seen; they were active in the discussion; however, the discussion was more about the elections themselves, but not about the campaign to boycott them. It is also worth noting that there was a complete absence of changes in Facebook, where before the elections users' activity was seen, but the overall activity of Alexei Navalny's subscribers remained at the lowest level among the four webpages under consideration. Low user activity can be attributed both to the impact of the factors mentioned above and to the absence of sensitive subjects in publications during this period. It is also worth noting that live broadcasts on the channel "NavalnyLive" were unsuccessful. They collected the lowest number of reactions during the whole action. This may be due to the fact that Alexei Navalny himself did not take part in them, which just before the elections could be assessed ambiguously.

The meeting of the head of the CEC with Alexei Navalny became a positive information occasion for the action "Voters' Strike". These publications have become the most valued by subscribers in social network sites. It is possible to assume that popularity of these publications is connected with the well-known person presence in them that is especially sharply perceived just before the elections because of this person's status.

Thus, in the final part of the campaign, we see a short-term increase in the interest of the "Voters' Strike" due to the mass dissemination of information, as well as the appearance of additional information. However, the very next day the activity of users fell significantly despite the preservation of a significant number of publications. In addition, the problem with the decrease in user activity as a whole was not solved, which was indicated in the period from February 9 to March 11.

Based on the analysis of the dynamics of the action "Voters' Strike" we can draw the following conclusions:

1. There is no clear relationship between the activity of subscribers and the number of publications, which can be seen in the periods between the main selected stages and the example of the last stage of the action.
2. The greatest activity is shown by subscribers of the social network site Vkontakte due to the variety of possible forms of its expression.
3. Viewings are the main activity in YouTube and they cannot be unambiguously assessed as an objective indicator because viewing a video means only viewing it, and not unambiguous approval or support.

4. The use of tools to influence the visual perception of the audience of social network sites can be used to increase their activity because it encourages leaving a like and sharing a bright image or video.
5. In social networks there is a tendency for a rapid loss of interest in a particular topic of there is no sufficient information to initiate an active discussion, the desire to share or join anything.
6. Due to the specifics of the audience of the social network sites the involvement of users may fail as it was in the considered action on Facebook.
7. A great influence on the involvement of subscribers has the binding of publications to the significant events of the protest or events close to it.
8. Offline campaigns with the possible participation of active users of social network sites can be accompanied by the active use of thematic hashtags.
9. Live broadcasts are an effective tool to engage users of social network sites in the event only when the main person of the action is involved in this broadcasts.
10. It is possible to attract the attention of users of social network sites not only by covering the course of the action, but also during the preparation of loud and controversial materials about the most current agendas, which are most often discussed by the public.

Thus, the application of the method gave a fairly complete picture of the action "Voters' Strike" in social network sites. It was found that, despite the large number of subscribers and reactions, the real activity of users was at a low level. This is primarily due to the fact that the peak activity of users of social network sites fell on a few days, while during the rest of the days users lost interest in the action. It is connected primarily with the fact that in the considered periods significant for the action events took place or information resources of the campaign was supplemented by another equally controversial topic.

5   Discussion

Approbation of the method presented in the paper allows us to draw several conclusions about it. The positive aspects of the method have already been described above and include complexity, ease of use, and the versatility of the data used. If we pay attention to the shortcomings and weaknesses of the proposed methodology, we should pay attention to the results of the index analysis of the "Strike of Voters" protest action. A low involvement rate shows us what needs to be expanded, revealed and specified in terms of user's engagement. In particular, it seems possible to supplement the method with an analysis of the tonality of comments, which introduces an additional indicator of the attitude of users to the protest action and campaign. In addition, one of the weaknesses of the method is the emphasis on all users of social networks, while the most active users are often subscribers of groups and personal pages of actors, which requires isolating them and their reactions from the total number to specify the overall picture of activity, divide the activity of subscribers and all other users. In this regard, the authors of this method are faced with the need to select and use more accurate tools for analyzing social networks.

Also, it was concluded that it is necessary to obtain additional information about the work of the method by testing it at protest actions and campaigns at the regional and local levels. In particular, the authors expect a number of difficulties associated with the fragmentation of local protests and their accumulation around several centers, rather than one, as was presented during the paper. In this regard, there may be additional requirements for the analysis of social networks, the number of sources of empirical data may increase, which, in turn, may lead to significant differences between the activity and involvement of subscribers. It is also difficult to determine the user's territorial affiliation and establish their direct connection with protest activity in the region, which may require additional network analysis of protest activity in the regional segment of social networks. However, regional protests with several centers of activity are of great interest because the method will allow not only to assess the overall activity of subscribers in the region, but also the activity of subscribers of individual activity centers, which will allow comparing them, identifying real leaders of public opinion, as well as the motivation, recruitment and involvement mechanisms that they use.

From the above, it can be concluded that the method is quite complex, however, to specify the results obtained, as well as to expand the range of possible directions for the study of protest activity, it can be supplemented with the following components: an analysis of the tonality of comments and an index of tonality of the comments of users of social networks, involved in the protest campaign, network analysis to identify the relationship between subscribers and protest organizers in social networks, improvement of software for analyzing social networks, modifying the index of involvement of users of social networks, taking into account the data obtained as a result of tonality analysis and network analysis.

6   Conclusions

Summarizing all the above mentioned, it should be emphasized that social network sites, in fact, have occupied a significant place in social and political relations. Due to the specifics of interaction within virtual network sites, new forms of expression of public opinion have appeared, the role of an individual in the formation of the information agenda has significantly increased, the time for dissemination of information and receiving feedback has decreased. On the example of the campaign "Voters' Strike" it was possible to see that users, in many ways played a significant role in the increased attention to the action both from public authorities and the media and from the population. Despite the fact that the level of involvement in general was at a low level, the fact that more than 70 million users viewed the materials related to the action indicates a significant role played by social network sites in the information support of the action.

In addition, on the example of the action "Voters' Strike" we have seen that social network sites can be one of the tools of organization and implementation of protest activity and can be used as a coordination platform linking supporters and associates with each other without taking into account such restrictions as location, age, gender, social status, etc.

Such opportunities of social network sites make studies related to protest activity in the virtual space even more popular because the risks of increasing of social tension and the rate of its increase from the latent stage to the conflict one are rising. That is why the importance of research, that reveals the forms of protest campaigns, the level of involvement in them, as well as the degree of dependence of the activity of users of social network sites on the actions of certain social-political actors, is increasing. The presented method is applied to these techniques.

As part of study the goal was achieved – a methodology for assessing the involvement in the protest activity in social network sites was created and tested. As a result of the study it was found that despite the high number of reactions, the overall involvement in the protest action "Strike of Voters" was at a low level. This result was gained with the help of the author's method. Using these results it can be concluded that the level of involvement depends on the ability and capability of the initiator of the protest activity to maintain a high level of interest of users. Moreover, to ensure this interest, it is not necessary to increase the number of published materials, which was proved during the event-analysis. In addition, the level of involvement is also influenced by: the use of methods of direct involvement of users in an offline activity, as well as carrying out live broadcasts and using controversial topics to attract attention.

Also, it was found that there is a significant difference between the activity of users and their involvement. Thus, within the action "Voters' Strike" the total activity of more than 3 million users was manifested in more than 80 million reactions, which indicates a high activity of the users. However, the involvement of users in the action, based on its duration and the number of published materials, is at a low level, which the results of event-analysis and index-analysis showed. Thus, we see that the involvement of users in the protest activity in social network sites is a more subtle and complex characteristic than the protest activity in its quantitative expression, which suggests the need for more detailed analysis, development of more accurate methods for assessing the factors that affect both the increase in user activity and maintaining it at a consistently high level.

Acknowledgements. The study was funded by RFBR according to the research project № 17-33-01022 ОГН "Modeling and indexing of protest activity in the subjects of Russian Federation".

References

1. Rheingold, H.: Virtual communities - exchanging ideas through computer bulletin boards. J. Virtual Worlds Res. (S.l.) **1**(1). https://journals.tdl.org/jvwr/index.php/jvwr/article/view/293/247. Accessed 11 May 2019
2. Investopedia: Social Networking Service. https://www.investopedia.com/terms/s/social-networking-service-sns.asp. accessed 13 May 2019
3. Steinberg, I.: Live and virtual social support networks: analysis of similarities and differences. Sociol. J. **4**, 85–103 (2009)
4. Uspensky, I.V.: Internet Marketing. Textbook. Izd-vo SPGUEiF, SPb. (2003)
5. Cohen, C., Kahne, J.: Participatory Politics: New Media and Youth Political Action. MacArthur Research Network on Youth and Participatory Politics, Chicago (2012)

6. Shirky, C.: Here Comes Everybody: The Power of Organizing Without Organizations. Penguin Press, New York (2008)
7. Tufekci, Z.: The medium and the movement: digital tools, social movement politics, and the end of the free rider problem. Policy Internet 6(2), 202–208 (2014)
8. Travaglino, G.A.: Social sciences and social movements: the theoretical context. Contemp. Soc. Sci. 9(1), 9 (2014)
9. Valenzula, S., Arriagada, A., Scherman, A.: The social media basis of youth protest behavior: the case of Chile. J. Commun. 62, 299–314 (2012)
10. Rutherford, A., Cebrian, M., Dsouza, S., Moro, E., Pentland, A., Rahwan, I.: Limits of social mobilization. Proc. Nat. Acad. Sci. 110, 6281–6286 (2013)
11. Bennett, W.L., Segerberg, A.: Digital media and the personalization of collective action: social technology and the organization of protests against the global economic crisis. Inf. Commun. Soc. 14, 770–799 (2011)
12. Bronnikov, I.: Modern features of the Russian internet audience as a participant of political communication. PolitBook 2, 44–59 (2013)
13. Sokolov, A., Maklashin, I.: Features of the internet space as a platform for interaction. Authority 12, 60–62 (2013)
14. Konivskay, O.: Methodological approaches to the study of protest activity of the population. In: Issues of Modern Jurisprudence: Collection of Articles on the Materials of the LVI International Scientific-Practical Conference vol. 12, no. 51, pp. 85–94. SIbaK, Novosibirsk (2015)
15. Dementieva, I.: Study of protest activity of the population in foreign and domestic science. Probl. Dev. Territ. 4(66), 83–93 (2013)
16. Baranova, G.: Methods of analysis of protest activity of the Russian population. Sociol. Res. 10, 143–152 (2012)
17. Ushkin, S.: Protest communities in social networks: three years of observations. Monitoring 6, 112–118 (2014)
18. Hogan, B.: Analysing Social Networks Via the Internet. http://individual.utoronto.ca/berniehogan/Hogan_SAGE_Internetworks_RC1.pdf. Accessed 13 May 2019
19. Smirnova, O., Petrov, A., Babijchuk, G.: The main methods of analysis used in the study of social networks. Mod. Inf. Technol. Educ. 3(1), 151–158 (2016)
20. Alasania, K.: Methods of analysis of political texts. Electron. Sci. Ed. Almanac Space Time 1(10), 1–8 (2015)
21. Trusova, A.Y.: Multidimensional scaling of the structure of society. Bull. SamSU. 66, 62–71 (2008)
22. Frolov, A.: Methods of index research of civil activity for the regions of the Russian Federation. Knowl. Underst. Skill 4, 184–193 (2016)
23. Yaroslavtseva, A.O.: Comparative ratings and indices as tools for measuring political stability. Vestnik RUDN. Ser.: Polit. Sci. 2, 103–114 (2012)
24. Maltseva, A., et al.: Using the methods of event-analysis to investigate processes in the labour market. Internet J. Sociol. Sci. 3(12), 1–9 (2012)
25. Gerring, J.: What is a case study and what is it good for? Am. Polit. Sci. Rev. 2(98), 341–354 (2004)
26. Sokolov, A., Palatnikov, D.: Protest activity: experience of index analysis. Soc. Hum. Knowl. 1(13), 29–37 (2018)

Multi-agent Approach to Modeling
the Dynamics of Urban Processes
(on the Example of Urban Movements)

Danila Parygin(✉) ⓘ, Andrey Usov, Sergey Burov,
Natalia Sadovnikova ⓘ, Pavel Ostroukhov, and Alena Pyannikova

Volgograd State Technical University, Lenina Avenue 28,
400005 Volgograd, Russia
dparygin@gmail.com, usovandrey2013@gmail.com,
sergey.burovic@gmail.com, npsn@ya.ru,
ostropas123@gmail.com, ata343@mail.ru

Abstract. The choice of effective management decisions by city administrations on infrastructure development and resource allocation requires awareness of the processes that are going on. At the same time, the data for analyzing the situation are expensive and only a few cities in Russia can afford to purchase them. In this regard, the purpose of this study, conducted by UrbanBasis Robotics, was the development of methods for constructing an evolving model to assess the state of complex geographically distributed systems, taking into account the constantly occurring changes. It was decided to focus on the description of the dynamics of subject-object interaction at the micro level within the system as a key component of the concept of creating such a model. The concept of building the model includes a well-proven multi-agent approach. The paper provides a detailed overview of the trends in the use of multi-agents and their relevance for modeling the behavior of people and other mutually-influencing objects and processes. The principles for constructing models of changing the state of complex geographically distributed systems that take into account the dynamic properties of their constituent objects are formulated by the authors. The proposed method allows working with events of a measurable scale at the level of interactions between actors (subjects and objects) and their environment. The set of actors behavior models forms an integral model of the macro level. Software solutions for the implementation of this approach are structured in the form of a modular platform for multi-agent modeling of interactions in an urban environment. The practical result of this stage of research was the development of a client-server solution for modeling the states of complex systems in the tasks of analysis the movements and the interactions within an urbanized space. The OpenStreetMap online map data for a fragment of a real urban area is used as a template for the basis for movement. The simulation of the visualization is presented on the website of the live.urbanbasis.com project in the public domain.

Keywords: Multi-agent approach · Movement dynamics model · Urban mobility · Life activity model · Urbanized area · Urban environment · Complex urban system · Geographically distributed system · Actor · Agent based model

A. Chugunov et al. (Eds.): EGOSE 2019, CCIS 1135, pp. 243–257, 2020.
https://doi.org/10.1007/978-3-030-39296-3_18

1   Introduction

Optimization of conditions for the implementation of life activity support processes using the urban infrastructure network is today one of the most important issues for growing cities. City administrations and planners are focused on researching statistical data, opinion polls, data from specialized sensors, counters, video cameras, and other ways to account for the movement of people in space (walking, traveling on private cars or public transport) to make decisions on the development of infrastructure and resource allocation. Models and forecasts of the situation development are built on the basis of these data [1].

However, such studies and their subsequent analysis are extremely expensive and time-consuming. Over the past five years, the Moscow government has spent more than 500 million rubles on the purchase of geodata about the movement of people from mobile operators. This information is used to optimize the support of life activity processes and improve the urban environment [2]. But not many cities in Russia can afford such expenses. Therefore, it takes several years to conduct a comprehensive analysis of the state, for example, in the urban transport system that makes the created models inadequate and eventually leads to multiple local expenses [3]. Attempts to reduce monitoring expenses by using only surveys or sensors in public transport create a fragmentary picture, because cover only part of the population or territory [4].

A wide range of tasks related to the study of flows in the urban environment and a high cost of data for their study with the inevitable need to extrapolate them to get a complete picture of the situation at each point in time require the creation of solutions for integrated predictive modeling [5]. In this regard, the purpose of this study was the development of methods for constructing an evolving model for assessing the state of complex geographically distributed systems, taking into accounts the ongoing changes. At the same time, it was decided to focus on describing the dynamics of subject-object interaction at the micro level in the system as a key component of the concept of creating such a model.

2   Analysis of Existing Solutions for Modeling the Dynamics of Changes in the System Based on a Multi-agent Approach

The use of agent-based approach in modeling complex systems looks most promising in the presence of incomplete data on the environment, the needs of residents and their interaction with each other in the life activity process [6]. Multi-agent systems integrate all modern approaches in the field of the distributed information systems, artificial intelligence, software and allow to implement new level models of behavior and self-organization [7]. Formulating basic rules of interaction and necessary properties of agents, actor-subjects and actor-objects, helps to receive accurate (in some approach) model, which will present different city processes or all set of life activity of a determine city, and will promote to find out a weak points and regularities.

2.1 Modeling of Movements in a Given Spatial Conditions

Applications of multiagent modelling are widely spreaded in the sphere of mobility organization and traffic management. There are a number of the applications, such as ARCHISIM, SimMobility Freight, TRANSIMS, MIRO, Tangramob, ITSGIS and MobiSim, which is intended for the solution of problems of transport systems modeling [8]. It allows to predict traffic flows changes in case of routes correction by means of comparative experiments.

There is a set of different parameters of activity of the city movement, which is monitored at the simulated changes, such as overcome distances by participants of the movement, emissions of carbon dioxide and level of use of resources, transit time, expenses [9] and etc. The persons making decisions can estimate as overall effectiveness of mobility in a city system, as the separate industries, by using such applications.

For example, institutions (suppliers, carriers and recipients) and drivers of cargo vehicles act as agents in a freight transportation modeling. Their actions take place at the strategic, tactical and operational levels: from the choice of enterprises location and structure of a vehicles park before daily interaction at the organization of freights delivery with a planned routes [10]. At the same time independent individual behavior of agents allows to form dynamics of a whole modelled system [11].

Multiagent platforms, such as GAMA, MadKit, Jade, Repast, NetLogo, are the alternative decisions for existing functionality and application [12]. Often it is programs with open source code, libraries and development environments. It includes basic components for creation of agents from any data set (including data of GIS), import the diverse data, usage of available cartographic data, performance of large-scale modeling with millions of agents, the 2D/3D instruments for visualization. At the same time, high-level and intuitively clear agent programming languages, such as cross-platform NetLogo or GAML [13], are used for compliance to requirements of specific issues. Such platforms can be multiple-purpose as GAMA, or specialized as MATSim which provides tools for modeling of traffic flows by modelling of certain car with the theory of queues. But the main thing that it implements a key advantage of multiagent modeling for city tasks, namely opportunity to work at microlevel for creation of steering strategy in compliance with operational parameters of streams and the environment in the complex social and technical territorial distributed systems [14].

The movement of people in an urban environment is an even more variable and weakly formalized system of interactions than transport descendants. Many socio-economic conditions affect the actions of an individual and groups of people of different sizes. And in this case, the potential of multi-agent modeling of their behavior in spatial environments can be fully revealed [15]. Existing research and development for multi-agent modeling of people's movement processes is represented by a wide range of solutions.

First of all, agent models allow studying the behavior and interaction of people in the case of local unforeseen situations. The models help to estimate the number of people who can be saved in case of emissions of toxic substances in industrial production [16] and the effect of human movement on the transmission of infectious diseases in a typical environment on a local scale [17]. Researchers from ITMO University under the leadership of A.V. Bukhanovsky investigated the spread of acute respiratory viral diseases and influenza epidemic in St. Petersburg, taking into account the movement of agents around the territory and their joint location in buildings [18], and also created a large-scale micro-stimulation of a realistic traffic flow of 41,000 private vehicles in Amsterdam during a working day based on OpenStreetMap [19]. Engineering Informatics Group at Stanford University have been investigating human and social behavior during emergency evacuations for many years; they model queuing, competitive and herd behavior [20]. Such approaches are also used in everyday commercial practice, for example, Professor Shingo Takahashi developed a technology to identify the causes of crowds in public places based on the results of multi-agent modeling of the individuals behavior. This technology was used to eliminate queues at the city airport and allowed to detect 4 times more causes of crowds compared with expert analysis [21].

It may be noted the qualitative theoretical and practical study of the issues of modeling movements in given spatial conditions. Existing solutions are firmly embedded in the workflow of environmental planners, transportation engineers, and are successfully used to analyze scenarios and organize coordinated movement of people in a certain infrastructure configuration. Successes in solving local problems led to research and creation of complex models of human behavior.

2.2 Modeling a Life Activity of Communities

In general, the study of the social phenomenon of the crowd with multi-agent modeling formed the basis of a number of complex technological solutions. At the same time, the university development programs from around the world compete with commercial programs like Vissim, SimWalk, Anylogic. So, the Department of Geoinformation Systems and Seodesy of Kharkov University of Municipal Economy has developed an experimental software environment for creating, modifying, executing and visualizing GIS-based model of pedestrian agent flows in urban conditions, at public events or in transport hubs [22]. A crowd simulation library based on refillable set of mental strategies PEDSIM allows to simulate and visualize large-scale indoors and outdoors evacuation and use pedestrian dynamics in third-party software solutions [23]. The expanded platform of interactive modeling of dynamic heterogeneous behavior of crowd was developed at the University of North Carolina with the usage of personal lines theory, syndrome of adaptation and fields of navigation Menge. It provides basic components for researches of the movement, collisions, space acceleration and other properties in tasks from architectural planning to management of artificial and intellectual characters in games and movies. Menge developers supposed, that their work will lead to creation of community of independent research groups which will broaden the platform with the plug-ins [24]. The MARS group (Multi Agent Research and Simulation) of the Hamburg University of Applied Sciences, which develops the distributed and scalable environment for transdisciplinary and city multiagent modeling, adheres to the similar concept of development. The MARS Urban project of simulation is devoted to modeling of traffic flows in the large cities, which is based on multimodal approach, considering interferences different types of participants of traffic and open data, such as OpenStreetMap [25].

The idea about a possibility of a global research of dynamics of human behavior with the help the multiagent of systems for city planning became a world trend in recent years and promotes increase in expectations [26, 27]. Approach to modeling of city processes from below to up and from interaction of individuals to subsequent emergence of social and physical macrostructures has to help to understand various problems of development whether it's a growth of slums and distribution of traffic flows or change of demography, urbanization and ability of infrastructure to cope with these calls [28]. It can become a basis for studying of cause and effect relationship in city systems and people use modes of city spaces if use in combination with big data on geography of the interacting parts. The example of global approach is expanded traffic simulator with open source code InterSCSimulator [29], which is able to model millions of agents with use of real map of the big city. Each agent of the simulator corresponds to the certain actor (the car, hospital, the gas pipeline, other).

It is possible to summarize the analysis of the existing trends in the development of systems for multi-agent modeling of the life activity of people in the city. So it should be noted basic requirements for their development [30], which include ensuring productivity for effective simulation of thousands of agents on a large map, scalability in performing HPC and modularity for distributing tasks of development participants. In addition, it is necessary to talk about the obvious advantages of open source code and the implementation of network access both at the level of creating such platforms and at the stages of operating models in online mode, without which it will be difficult to implement projects of end-to-end simulation of urban processes. It was decided by the UrbanBasis Robotics division of the urban computing laboratory of UCLab to start developing an open online platform for micro-modeling the dynamics of processes in an urbanized space guided by these principles and experience of world practice in the implementation and application of multi-agent systems.

3 Approach to Micromodeling of Processes in Complex Urban Systems

Life activity conditions in cities are constantly changing quantitatively, due to the emergence of new buildings or fluctuations in population, and qualitatively, due to obsolescence of infrastructure or variation in the composition of the population and many other factors. The urban environment is a developing ecosystem in which different spheres of human life merge. The process that provides the diverse needs of residents is interrelated and has a constant multi-directional influence on each other and on the urban base as a whole. Assessment and making informed decisions in such conditions requires the definition and measurement of the occurring impacts, the identification of dependencies between different actions of individual or social groups. So it is necessary to create a system capable of detecting and working out the maximum possible number of alternative scenarios for effective management of the urban environment, timely response to changes, forecasting with the aim of preventing negative consequences.

The implementation of such a system requires the determination of a wide range of parameters of the influence of objects of the urban environment, the natural conditions of the territory, the states of the infrastructure subsystems, the characteristic of people life activity features, etc. However, the comprehensive formalization of the processes and properties of the real world is laborious, especially with a high degree of detail, and is associated with a number of technical and organizational problems. It is often impossible to unambiguously determine the place of objects in the model. Some scopes of life do not have enough data to systematically describe their properties. At the same time, many subsystems, on the contrary, are difficult to isolate due to deep interconnection with adjacent processes. All this necessitates to search for a new approach in solving the problem.

The following principles were formulated based on the identified limitations for constructing state changing models of complex geographically distributed systems that take into account the dynamic properties of their constituent objects:

- The main components of the model are actors (subjects and objects) and the conditionally static environment of their interaction:
  - The subject is an actor who is in a certain state, changing over time under the influence of the determinants that characterize it and as a result of its interaction with the environment, living and non-living objects.
  - The object is an actor reflecting the existence of living organisms (except humans) and artificial creatures (of natural or industrial origin) with limited free will.
  - The environment is a generalized view of the space in which subjects and objects interact, or a complex remainder consisting of objects not previously identified as separate actors (this is not used in the ideal case of a full system description).
- Modeling the existence of each individual subject is performed in the framework of a short-term or long-term scenario, due to its low-level (property) or high-level (role) state producing certain needs, which manifests itself in the form of actions described by a set of rules.
- The basis for building the model should be a modular structure of the means of implementation, which allows extending descriptions of roles, properties and behavior patterns to clarify actions and reactions in the interaction between subjects, objects and the environment (SOE).
- If possible, real statistical data should be used in the modeling process to specify the initial conditions for the interaction of SOE, and in all cases of informational gaps the model should generate realistic parameters.
- The model should support continuous micro-stimulation of the dynamics of changing the parameters of SOE.
- At any time, it should be possible to fix the state of the running simulation as the sum of the actor's actions vectors and the statistics of changes in the SOE macro model.

3.1   The Structure of Platform for Multi-agent Modeling of Interactions in an Urban Environment

It was decided to implement the designated principles of modeling using a multi-agent approach to determine the influence of each individual person on the state of the processes in the city. This approach, based on the description of only local interactions of actors (agents), determined by their goals and parameters, will allow studying the macro model of life activity of the population throughout the urban environment, as well as the specific conditions of those spheres of life that will be involved in modeling.

The agent in the developed system is a model of a person (an actor possessing free will) or other essences of a living and artificial origin. All of them are participants of conditionally dependent dynamic interaction and are capable of transporting material and non-material resources. Certain sets of actions and relationships are components of subsystems of life activity support in cities.

Each sphere of human life activity or urban process, which can be distinguished as a separate subsystem, will be a separate module, the general structure of which is shown in Fig. 1. The module determines the roles, properties and actions of agents associated with its specificity, is responsible for managing and changing the relevant parameters of the actors and the environment, and also accumulates data on their state in the aspect of the implemented sphere of life activity. This structure allows to dynamically connect new modules to the project, as well as run simulations with different sets of modules to more accurately locate and verify interdependencies. At the same time, modules implement two types of tasks: a direct impact on changing the behavior of agents or the performance of service functions and data exchange with other modules (for example, calculating the route of movement from one point to another).

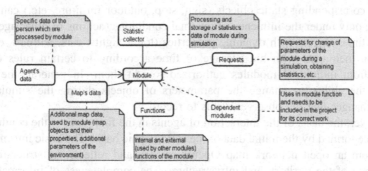

Fig. 1. Description of conditionally detachable subsystem as a separate module.

It is necessary to make maximum use of publicly available data on various areas of city life to increase the reliability of simulation results, for example, on the number of working population, age and gender composition, level of education, etc. An algorithm, which generates the missing values for the parameters of agents in the model based on the data available to it was created for the full description of a particular sphere of life activity due to the limited of real data.

A similar situation is associated with the transforming conditions of the urban environment, caused by large-scale transformations such as changes in the structure of buildings, construction of new roads, construction of new infrastructure facilities, and local events related to the repair of communications, accidents, temporary restrictions on access, etc. A mechanism for editing a running simulation using variable parameters and graphical tools was formed to account for such influences in the model.

Each of the modules of the system collects associated data on the state of the model during operation. This data will be used to analyze the state of complex urban systems. On the other hand, continuous visualization of the dynamics of changes in real time on a digital map of the city is realized based on them. The implemented interaction interface with simulation is designed to provide convenient work, both for developers and researchers involved in the analysis of simulation results, with different levels of training.

3.2   Urban Environment as a Space of Conditions for Agents Interaction

The interaction space of agents in the model is formed by a map of real terrain with areas of different types selected on it. In addition, the agents themselves create for each other a dynamically changing landscape with a certain set of properties. People, animals, traffic lights and road signs, other movable objects and infrastructure elements at each moment of time form new environmental conditions that are unique for each specific agent.

Certain modules are responsible for managing the various elements of the "landscape". Each agent modeling an environmental actor is represented by a set of parameters unique to a given type of objects and spatial coordinates as a property of all objects without exception. The module responsible for managing a specific type of objects can change their parameters, delete and add new units of objects. At the same time, the corresponding static objects (sign, stop, outdoor furniture, etc.) can change their state only under the influence of external conditions (actions of other agents). At the same time, objects with dynamic properties (traffic lights, cars, animals, etc.) can change on their own with the passage of time according to certain rules or upon requests from individual modules authorized to edit them. In general, the system provides the ability to change the parameters of objects during the simulation to identify changes that the observer wants to record.

However, the basis of the interaction of agents in the first place is the conditionally static space formed by the initial data of the cartographic basis. The basic information is loaded from an open network map OpenStreetMap and reflects the structure of the organization of the territory and infrastructure. The completeness of information can vary for different localities from specifying the location of buildings, structures and the road network to data on public transport stops, shops, the appointment of individual buildings. In general, this is the minimum necessary and sufficient spatial information for the initial level of modeling of life activity in conditions close to real. Even a simple division of the environment into three classes (as will be shown on the example implementation in part 4) – roads, buildings, other territory - will allow to simulate the flow of people with reference to the space of a particular city.

3.3   Modeling of Interactions in the System

The system supports two levels of interaction. The interaction of agents with the environment and with each other, as well as the interaction of modules with the database of environmental parameters and with each other.

All entities in the system interact with the environment on the basis of a single principle. Each agent has certain geographical coordinates and, if necessary, can request the parameters of the urban environment for recalculation/verification of its own parameters and conditions for the transition from one state to another.

Modules interact with each other by requesting the necessary information or performing functions related to another module. For example, all modules that work with the location of agents refer to the "Movements" module to determine the available agent movements relative to the urban space, simulate the traffic situation, and obtain motion parameters associated with the actions performed.

The interactions between agents are the most complex in the system. This is due to the fact that such interactions are determined by the parameters of the urban environment, the current properties of the interacting entities themselves, as well as the high-level influences of all the modules currently connected. The modules determine on what grounds and by what rules the interaction of agents will occur. A mechanism for connecting and polling all components to evaluate the current and next state of agents was developed taking into account the desire in the system to maximize the separation of the structure, to provide the modules with full interaction of agents with following all roles, properties and actions (see Fig. 2).

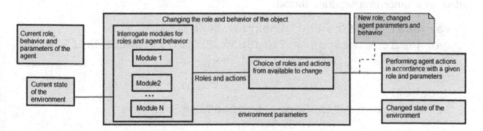

Fig. 2. Defining and dynamically changing the roles, properties and actions of agents.

It was necessary to introduce a scale of priorities for the execution of prescriptions to form a scenario of behavior, choose an action or a rule for its implementation based on a set of defining roles and properties. Arbitration is used in every situation where several modules in one period of time issue a recommendation to change agent parameters. In this case, first, comparisons are made of the significance of the modules within a single weighted system. The analysis of changes induced by the modules is performed in case of equality of the priority values. The scale of priorities is formed in such a way that, in the general case, contributes to the continuation of the normal functioning of agents with the subsequent striving for development and improvement.

4   Implementing a Client-Server Solution for Modeling Movement in a Conditions of Urban Environment

This section briefly describes the architecture of the software package that builds and runs a simulation with the selected modules and parameters. The formalization of an abstract module, defining the main functions and data necessary for the integration of new program components is also presented.

C# language and .NET Core technology are used for implementation of the modeling process which takes place on a cross-platform server (main platform – OS Linux, CentOS). Multithreading is used to search for paths on the map.

Client application is browser oriented (on its basis an Android application was also created) and is a classic bundle HTML/CSS/JavaScript. The visual part of the client that performs the graphical display of the map is implemented using the OpenLayers library.

The server stores a list of clients, a link to the list of objects (actors) on the map, a timer and "HttpListener". Each client has its own connection and role (presently "user" and "admin").

HttpListener waits and handles the connection of new clients in a separate thread. The client is added to the list after connecting, and a separate thread ("HandleClient") is created to work with it, which avoids a delay in sending messages to the server.

The main function of the server is "Update". Sending the state of the model from the server to all connected clients is carried out in this function, with a preliminary conversion of data into the Json format (see Fig. 3, left). The "Update" function is called on a timer in a separate thread:

```
var startTimeSpan = TimeSpan.Zero;
var periodTimeSpan = TimeSpan.FromMilliseconds(150);
UpdateTimer = new Timer((e) =>
{
Update();
}, null, startTimeSpan, periodTimeSpan);
```

Client-server interaction is carried out via the WebSocket protocol. Next event uses to get and display the server status:

```
websocket.onmessage = function(evt) { ... }
```

This event calls the "SetCharacters (JSON.parse (evt.data))" function, which changes the "Source" (data source) of the "charactersLayer" (map component). As a result, the actors appear on the map at the same coordinates where they are located on the server.

The system of commands is used for remote control of the server state (Fig. 3, right). Command format:

```
*command name*#*parameter 1 name*:*parameter 1*, *parame-
ter n name*:*parameter n*
```

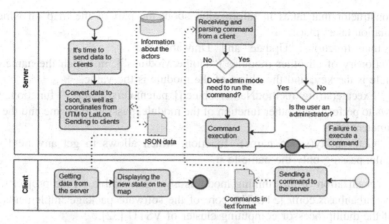

Fig. 3. The order of client-server interaction when updating the visualization status (left) and performing user requests to change the simulation parameters (right).

The program loads all modules from the project folder (Fig. 4) with each new launch. Further, the update ("Update") and data retrieval for drawing ("DrawableData") functions are called for each module. Simulation launch parameters are stored in the settings file "settings/Presets" in xml format.

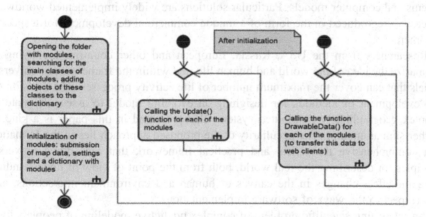

Fig. 4. The procedure for running the simulation.

Each module is based on an initially defined universal structure. The formed functional framework is, in fact, a template for building new modules and is designed to provide transparent project extensibility for implementing more realistic interactions in the model. So the module should include:

- A constructor that takes in information about the part of the map on which the simulation takes place.
- Two main functions: "Update" and "DrawableData".
- A dictionary of all other modules ("anotherModules"), in which the name of the module is the key, and the object of the module is the value.
- The "Execute(string methodName, object[] patemeters = null)" function, which allows to perform any other function of the module, passing the name and the list of parameters to it.
- The "GetProperty(string name)" function, which allows to get any field of the module, passing only the name to it.

The visualization of the running model is always available on the project website http://live.urbanbasis.com/ [31]. The core of the software package implements simulation at the multiprocessor computing cluster of VSTU [32].

5   Discussion

To create a fairly extensive model of a complex system based on micromodels of processes of indivisible inherently actors, is a feasible task at the modern technological level. Social, psychological, economic and other features of human life activity, as well as the processes of functioning of the infrastructure components of environment in many of its aspects are developed with the help of modern means of creating software systems and computer models. Particular solutions are widely implemented worldwide or "easily" reproduced in the form of a unique commercial development for a specific customer.

Researchers from the USA, Russia, European and other countries are trying to summarize the idea of the world and human life in it within the framework of universal models that can cover the maximum number of life activity processes. The decision on the development of methods for designing an evolving model to assess the state of complex geographically distributed systems that presented in this paper is a kind of another similar attempt. The peculiarity of the proposed approach lies in the formation of a comprehensive theoretical and practical framework that lays down universal principles for describing the real world, both from the point of view of understanding cause-and-effect changes in the canvas of human and environment interactions, and with respect to the ways of software implementation.

An interesting scientific problem of complex predictive modeling of people's lives has obvious practical benefits for the development of smart cities. The change in the quality of service that the infrastructure that knows about the needs of users can offer, stimulates the continuation of research in this direction. Now this knowledge is accumulated by commercial companies and administrative institutions around the world, and knowledge remains essentially closed to people. The development of such a project, which forms an idea about the life activity of the population that open to any user, is, among other things, a tool for balancing the interests of an open information society in the right to independence of personal information.

6 Conclusion

The study of the laws of development of complex systems underlies the formation of management strategies that ensure the achievement of the required values of quality indicators. Purposeful change in the behavior of systems, the creation of new ways to control the operation is possible in the context of awareness of the process and their consequences. Modeling is the only alternative to real data for a comprehensive analysis of the state of the system in various circumstances. Modeling does not guarantee complete protection against possible mistakes in making decisions, but allows identifying various problems, analyzing the consequences of choosing, and predicting the development of situations.

The development of an open platform for modeling the behavior of an unlimited number of subjects whose interactions will produce a single, developing model of the population life activity in the environment of particular cities is the goal of the research being conducted. Thus, it becomes possible to simulate and study the macro models of integrated urban systems, built on the basis of micro models of life activity scenarios of individual agents. At the same time, it is possible to reasonably answer the questions of the class "what will happen if …" on many levels at once: from assessing the local problems of organizing the urban environment to balancing the processes at the level of life activity support subsystems and the city as a whole.

The system solves a limited range of tasks on modeling urban processes at the current stage. The platform prototype implements simulation with the "Work", "People" and "Move" modules. However, the proposed approach to building a model allows and suggests its further scaling to account for the specifics of new objects and processes. The platform will describe in more detail and realistically the existing situation in the city regarding various spheres of human life activity as a result of the development and connection of new modules, and the observed simulation will become a source of information for studying various processes in the city. The event flow generated in the model will enrich data with spatial reference of the GIS decision support system [33], and the prepared specifications and platform APIs will provide an opportunity for anyone who wants to refine the components of interaction between the subjects of interest by creating new roles, properties, actions and behavioral rules.

Acknowledgments. The reported study was funded by Russian Foundation for Basic Research (RFBR) according to the research project No. 18-37-20066_mol_a_ved, and by RFBR and the government of the Volgograd region of the Russian Federation grant No. 18-47-340012_r_a. The authors express gratitude to colleagues from UCLab involved in the development of Live. UrbanBasis.com project.

References

1. Parygin, D.S., Sadovnikova, N.P., Shabalina, O.A.: Information and analytical support for city management tasks. Volgograd (2017). (in Russian)

2. Trunina, A.: Moscow Mayor's Office spent ₽516 million to purchase data on the movements of citizens. https://www.rbc.ru/politics/04/03/2019/5c7cd5fe9a794760d9cfb900. Accessed 30 Apr 2019

3. Parygin, D.S., Aleshkevich, A.A., Golubev, A.V., Smykovskaya, T.K., Finogeev, A.G.: Map data-driven assessment of urban areas accessibility. J. Phys. Conf. Ser. **1015**, 042048 (2018)

4. Ustugova, S., Parygin, D., Sadovnikova, N., Finogeev, A., Kizim, A.: Monitoring of social reactions to support decision making on issues of urban territory management. Procedia Comput. Sci. **101**, 243–252 (2016)

5. Maitakov, F.G., Merkulov, A.A., Petrenko, E.V., Yafasov, A.Y.: Development of decision support systems for smart cities. In: Chugunov, A., Misnikov, Y., Roshchin, E., Trutnev, D. (eds.) EGOSE 2018. CCIS, vol. 947, pp. 52–63. Springer, Cham (2019). https://doi.org/10.1007/978-3-030-13283-5_5

6. Parygin, D., Nikitsky, N., Kamaev, V., Matokhina, A., Finogeev, A., Finogeev, A.: Multi-agent approach to distributed processing of big sensor data based on fog computing model for the monitoring of the urban infrastructure systems. In: SMART-2016, Proceedings of the 5th International Conference on System Modeling & Advancement in Research Trends, pp. 305–310. IEEE (2016)

7. Petrin, K.V., Teryaev, E.D., Filimonov, A.B., Filimonov, N.B.: Multi-agent technologies in ergatic control systems. Izvestiya YFU, Tekhnicheskiye nauki **104**(3), 7–13 (2010). (in Russian)

8. Nguyen, Q.T., Bouju, A., Estraillier, P.: Multi-agent architecture with space-time components for the simulation of urban transportation systems. Procedia Soc. Behav. Sci. **54**, 365–374 (2012)

9. Tangramob: an agent-based simulation framework for validating urban smart mobility solutions. http://www.tangramob.com/. Accessed 21 Mar 2019

10. Alho, A., Bhavathrathan, B.K., Stinson, M., Gopalakrishnan, R., Le, D.-T., Ben-Akiva, M.: A multi-scale agent-based modelling framework for urban freight distribution. Transp. Res. Procedia **27**, 188–196 (2017)

11. Mikheev, S.V.: Network-centric management based on micro and macro transport flows. Softw. Syst. **31**(1), 19–24 (2018). (in Russian)

12. Mezencev, K.N.: Multi-agent simulation in netlogo software. Autom. Control Tech. Syst. **1**, 10–20 (2015)

13. GAMA Platform. https://gama-platform.github.io/. Accessed 16 Mar 2019

14. Transport modeling and forecasting: VISUM vs MATSim. http://transspot.ru/2017/05/18/transportnoe-modelirovanie-i-prognozirovanie-visum-vs-matsim/. Accessed 02 Feb 2019

15. Camillen, F., et al.: Multi agent simulation of pedestrian behavior in closed spatial environments. In: IEEE Toronto International Conference Science and Technology for Humanity. IEEE (2009)

16. Salze, P., et al.: TOXI-CITY: an agent-based model for exploring the effects of risk awareness and spatial configuration on the survival rate in the case of industrial accidents. Cybergeo Eur. J. Geogr. (2014). Systems, Modelling, Geostatistics, document 692. https://doi.org/10.4000/cybergeo.26522. http://journals.openedition.org/cybergeo/26522

17. Pizzitutti, F., Pan, W., Feingold, B., Zaitchik, B., Álvarez, C.A., Mena, C.F.: Out of the net: an agent-based model to study human movements influence on local-scale malaria transmission. PLoS ONE **13**(3), e0193493 (2018)

18. Sloot, P.M.A., et al.: Supercomputer simulation of critical phenomena in complex social systems. Sci. Tech. J. Inf. Technol. Mech. Opt. **16**(6), 967–995 (2016)

19. Melnikov, V.R., Krzhizhanovskaya, V.V., Lees, M.H., Boukhanovsky, A.V.: Data-driven travel demand modelling and agent-based traffic simulation in Amsterdam urban area. Procedia Comput. Sci. **80**, 2030–2041 (2016)
20. Chu, M.L.: A computational framework incorporating human and social behaviors for occupant-centric egress simulation. Ph.D. thesis, Department of Civil and Environmental Engineering, Stanford University, Stanford, CA (2015)
21. How did Fukuoka Airport learn which measures would be effective in reducing queues. https://www.pvsm.ru/issledovanie/311754. Accessed 12 Mar 2019
22. Patrakeev, I.M.: Geospatial technologies in the modeling of urban systems. HNUGH (2014). (in Russian)
23. PEDSIM - Pedestrian Crowd Simulation. http://pedsim.silmaril.org/. Accessed 08 Apr 2019
24. Crowd and Multi-agent Simulation. http://gamma.cs.unc.edu/research/crowds/. Accessed 10 Apr 2019
25. Hüning, C., Wilmans, J., Feyerabend, N., Thomas Thiel-Clemen, T.: MARS – a next-gen multi-agent simulation framework. https://mars-group.org/wp-content/uploads/papers/MARS%20-%20A%20next-gen%20multi-agent%20simulation%20framework.pdf. Accessed 23 Apr 2019
26. Heppenstall, A., Malleson, N., Crooks, A.: "Space, the final frontier": how good are agent-based models at simulating individuals and space in cities? Systems **4**(1), 9 (2016)
27. Omarov, B., et al.: Agent based modeling of smart grids in smart cities. In: Chugunov, A., Misnikov, Y., Roshchin, E., Trutnev, D. (eds.) EGOSE 2018. CCIS, vol. 947, pp. 3–13. Springer, Cham (2019). https://doi.org/10.1007/978-3-030-13283-5_1
28. Crooks, A.T., Patel, A., Wise, S.: Multi-Agent Systems for Urban Planning. https://pdfs.semanticscholar.org/bd22/4781639a891435b2477584886a9902ea0ad9.pdf. Accessed 10 May 2019
29. Santana, E.F.Z., Lago, N., Kon, F., Milojicic, D.S.: InterSCSimulator: large-scale traffic simulation in smart cities using Erlang. In: Dimuro, G.P., Antunes, L. (eds.) MABS 2017. LNCS (LNAI), vol. 10798, pp. 211–227. Springer, Cham (2018). https://doi.org/10.1007/978-3-319-91587-6_15
30. Malinowski, A., Czarnul, P., Czuryło, K., Maciejewski, M., Skowron, P.: Multi-agent large-scale parallel crowd simulation. Procedia Comput. Sci. **108**, 917–926 (2017)
31. Live Urban Basis Automaton. http://live.urbanbasis.com/. Accessed 01 June 2019
32. Multiprocessor computing complex (cluster). http://evm.vstu.ru/index.php/labs/hpc-lab/about-hpc. Accessed 12 May 2019. (in Russian)
33. Ustugova, S., Parygin, D., Sadovnikova, N., Yadav, V., Prikhodkova, I.: Geoanalytical system for support of urban processes management tasks. Communications in Computer and Information Science **754**, 430–440 (2017)

E-Government as a Tool in the Fight Against Corruption: Case of Azerbaijan

Igor Chernov, Niyazi Niyazov, Galina Niyazova,
and Radomir Bolgov[(✉)]

Saint Petersburg State University, 7-9 Universitetskaya Emb.,
St. Petersburg 199034, Russia
igor_chernov@mail.ru, niniyazi@yandex.ru,
rbolgov@yandex.ru, st007794@spbu.ru

Abstract. The paper deals with the influence of e-government implementation on the struggle against corruption in Azerbaijan. We draw a conclusion that e-government implementation within the existing governing bodies can decrease corruption only to the certain point, corresponding the level of "overwhelming computerization" of the population.

Keywords: E-government · Open government · Corruption · Anti-corruption efforts · Azerbaijan

1 Introduction

In terms of ICT development social and political reality is changing gradually. E government is viewed, first of all, as a tool of effective governing bodies and as a way of strengthening control over the citizens. On the other hand, civil society perceives e-government as a tool of direct political influence on the governance, where the government implements the demands of the majority of voters. It is obvious that e-society is characterized by political mobility and new abilities for counteracting such conventional drawbacks of bureaucratic apparatus as corruption.

In this research we use the term "corruption" in the narrow sense, meaning "corrupt practices", e.g. "forms of bribery". "Bribe" is considered as "money etc. offered to procure (often illegal or dishonest) action or decision in favor of giver" [30]. Being broadly defined (for instance, as "the abuse of public office for private gain" [17]) this term, in our opinion, not only becomes massive and indefinite, but overshadows the very fact that there are two parties participating (and often interested) in corruption.

The purpose of our research is to define possible boundaries of influence of new ICT tools usage on the elimination of corruption in governing bodies' activity. We investigate the effects of ICT use on corruption at the national level in Azerbaijan.

The hypothesis of the study is the following: e-government implementation within the existing governing bodies can decrease corruption only to the certain point, corresponding the level of computerization of the population.

The hypothesis is tested using secondary data analysis and a certain volume of primary data, collected by the authors. Empirical foundation of the research is formed

A. Chugunov et al. (Eds.): EGOSE 2019, CCIS 1135, pp. 258–269, 2020.
https://doi.org/10.1007/978-3-030-39296-3_19

by a wide range of sources and literature, found in publicly available sources. Moreover, the authors of the research deem it necessary to rely upon the interview given by a number of citizens of the Azerbaijani Republic. It was a questionnaire designed to create an objective viewpoint on the problem studied.

2 Theoretical and Methodological Framework of Research

In the XXI century a great amount of researches studying the role of new ICT in tackling corruption appeared. Among them we should mention Gronlund [19], Twinomurinzi and Ghartey-Tagoe [32], Davis and Fumega [15], Ahiabenu [2], Ben Ali and Sassi [7], Kossow and Dykes [24] and many others and, for instance, documents of Organization for economic cooperation and development [25] and ADB [1]. Moreover the problem was discussed on the platform of international academic conferences [14].

However we tend to agree with Bhattacherjee and Shrivastava [9] stating that 'while prior studies have demonstrated that ICT is an important tool in reducing corruption..., they provide little explanation as to how ICT influences corruption and when does it work best'. It is difficult, on the other hand, to accept their idea 'ICT use reduces corruption by increasing the certainly and celerity of punishment for corruption' [9]. We consider that the conventional "deterrence method", aiming at revealing potential bribetaker, on the one hand, is not effective (in China, for instance), and, on the other, is nor connected with ICT development (both western and eastern medieval deterrence methods of bribetakes were much efficient than modern ones).

E-government is "a form of organization that integrates the interactions and the interrelations between government and citizens, companies, customers and public institutions through the application of modern information and communication technologies" [21].

Thus we prefer to use the linguo-communicative approach as new development of structural and functional approach principles, coined by Tolcott Parsons. The linguo-communicative approach as neo-structuralism turns out to be an alternative to social constructivism [26].

All people, living in a society, use the communication code (language). This code plays cognitive and communicative role and thus structure person-to-personal interaction, forms linguo-communicative networks, e.g. creates the society as a complex of these nets and interactions. There are no "state" and "society" as independent from human objects of the physical world. There realm is constructed by communicative and cognitive functions of the language. Communicative function of the language forms the society as social realm, while cognitive function gives it a label of "an object". Social reality is objective facts, but these facts emerge and exist only as communication between individuals.

In summary, "we call the e-society a virtual set of individuals engaged in different types of relationships, exchanging information and knowledge, with technological access and use". I.e. the e-society, anyhow, is a subset of the traditional society, which has always been existing by communications means. 'E-society can be described as a reality, which emerged through new information and communication technologies that have the potential to change the interaction and interrelations between the different actors within and between communities" [34].

Methodology of our research is based on theoretical approach. Methodology of linguo-communicative approach is based on the communicational function of the language, i.e. implies consideration of all social entities as linguo-communicative communities.

In terms of the linguo-communicative approach the e-society as an objective (accessible to observation) fact exists solely and exclusively as a steady linguistic communication system between the individuals, which inevitably has lingual, rather than physical or spatial boundaries. This communication and the system of stable relations between the individuals during the communication process are called the e-society. Thereby, when we reason about emergence and existence of the universal e-society, in fact, we observe the process of constant interaction and overlapping of a multitude of existent e-communities built up on various and multilingual linguo-communicative communities.

Empirical foundation of the research is formed by a wide range of sources and literature, found in publicly available sources. Moreover, the authors of the research rely upon the interview given by a number of citizens and public servants of the Azerbaijan.

3   Results of Research

3.1   Struggle Against Corruption in Azerbaijan: Cultural and Historical Background

Struggle against corruption for many years has been the core task of governments of majority of global players, including those members who have entered the international community more recently. It is necessary to mention here the states formed on the ruins of the Soviet empire. Relying on the data given by the established "Transparency International" all states can be divided into three groups: the first one is formed by the states where corruption in economy and social life is low, the second one is characterized by the activity aimed at tackling corruption with fluctuating outcome, the third one is characterized by the corruption existing in freedom.

The states of the first group are Lithuania, Latvia, Estonia and, to a great extent, Georgia. In the second group the most powerful state in Belarus, ranking 68th out of 180. It is followed by Armenia (ranking 107th), Moldova, Azerbaijan, Kazakhstan, Uzbekistan (being 122th). Ukraine (ranking130th), Russia and Kyrgyzstan (ranking 135th) and Turkmenistan (ranking 167th) are in the third group [12]. To give the objective evaluation of the processes studied it is necessary to underline the level of corruption in the countries close to Azerbaijan but not being a post-Soviet states. It is Turkey, ranking 81th and Iran, ranking 169th [12].

When one looks at these figures for the first time one may think that government s of the second and the third group states take no measures aiming at problem solution or the measures taken are of demonstrational and declarative character. Accepting this point of view we tend to encourage the scientists studying expansion of corruption in post-Soviet states take into account a set of points which are usually ignored as insignificant and unessential.

In our opinion, one of these is the problem of mental perception of corruption by a certain social, national or religious group. In some cases, all the mentioned levels of corruption join together and form unpredictable and irrational attitude to corruption on the part of a certain individual or society as a whole.

However, it is highly unlikely that corruption phenomenon could be explained by cultural reasons only. Corruption is a universal phenomenon, it has no nationality, it is based on objective social and economic and political factors. Moreover, the emerging of the forms of perception mentioned is caused by historical experience understood by the populace as customs and traditions.

After the WW2 and the death of Stalin the Soviet system, constructed to meet the demands and wished of the only person, turned to be ineffective, especially in economic sphere it failed to meet the demands of people in consumer goods. However, in the beginning of 1960s the USSR took the leading position in space exploration and various weapons inventory.

This system misbalance led to corruption not only in social sphere but in the system of state and party governing across the USSR, including Azerbaijan.

Commodity shortage caused voluntarily alienation in favour of the seller of the money above the price set by the state. This phenomenon was typical for many parts of the USSR, but only in the South Caucasus people really wanted to participate in this activity. This was the first display of grassroots corruption ultimately involving all the population of the republics. The second component was presented by money alienation in favour of public sector workers – teachers, doctors, social service representatives, junior and middle-ranking law-enforcement officers, whose official salary didn't coincide with real minimum subsistent level of the time. In Azerbaijani language the term for such alienation was coined. It was "Şirinlik", literally meaning «Sweet». Later the word «Şirinlik» was used permanently in such cases and the population itself didn't accept such behavior as immoral, considering that they show "Hörmət" ("Respect") to those, whose work was not appreciated by the state.

It is necessary to take into consideration that these words "Şirinlik" and "Hörmət" differ much from widely known "tips", because the amount of money paid could exceed the official salary of the mentioned groups of civil servants.

Surprisingly, comparing with the conventional concept of corruption, "Şirinlik" was given for the civil servant to carry out his job in time carefully, and not to violate the law promoting the interests of bribegiver.

Shaping this corruption system contributed to making "Şirinlik" the real basis for "Dolce vita" of high ranking officials, who got their assignment sheltering the activity of their subordinates helping the population with the problem solution.

3.2 Implementing E-Government and Struggle Against Corruption in Azerbaijan

In 1990–2000s being influenced by US experience many countries start thinking about the necessity to implement "the e-Government" [18], but Azerbaijan was not one of the state to follow the tendency. One of the reasons was that revenues received from "oil strategy" were spent on modernization of this very oil industry, on improvement of the old infrastructure and on military modernization because of unsettled Karabakh conflict. By 2010–2012 Azerbaijan had manages to success in fulfilling all these tasks. Nevertheless, the head of the state realized that to be successful they should pay attention to tackling inner policy problems, the greatest of which was corruption. It was essential to break the vicious circle on interrelations between officials and citizens and to get rid of the words "Şirinlik" и "Hörmət".

It was not until the perception of the Internet as a part of casual life, like radio or TV, by the Azerbaijani people that the solution to the problem became affordable. According to the International Telecommunication Union (ITU), in 2000 the number of people using the Internet was 0.15 unit, in 2005 – 8.03, in 2010 – 46.00, by the end of 2017 – 79.00 [13].

The spread of the Internet allowed the state to take a set of important measures, aiming at struggling against corruption.

In July 2012 the Presidential decree on establishing "ASAN xidmət" (ASAN service), as part of the State Agency for Public Services and Social Innovations under the President of the Republic of Azerbaijan.

According to Azad Jafarli, the head of the State Agency for Public Services and Social Innovations under the President of the Republic of Azerbaijan, the word "ASAN" stands for "Azerbaijan Service and Assessment Network", and the word "asan" means "simple" and "easily". It is obvious that this coincidence is intentional, because its creators wanted citizens to understand that with this service they would probably get aid without "Şirinlik" and "Hörmət". Besides, the following goals of the service were articulated the reduction of additional expenditure and time, provision of tactful attitude and ethic norms treating the population, enforcing respect to state structures, transparency and struggling against corruption, expansion of e-service employment.

ASAN service started its work in January, 2013. In February 2013 deputy head of the State Agency for Public Services and Social Innovations under the President of the Republic of Azerbaijan Anar Guseinov was interviewed by well-known Azebaijani journalist Kamal Ali. He stated that "there are such organizations in Georgia, Russia, Estonia and Kazakhstan, but Azerbaijani is the first in the row, because it managed to join 23 services of other departments. In Georgia there is Public Service Hall, dealing with issuing identity cards and other legal documents. Every month the service conducts 10 thousand transactions – operations with documents. Since 15th of January ASAN service has delivered service to more than 21 thousand people" [31].

Demand for the new service provide the expansion of ASAN xidmət network simultaneously with the expansion of quality and quantity of services mobile service receptions are being organized. The latter turned out to be possible only after the expansion of using of the Internet, where ASAN is functioning.

By September 2013 the number had been 475.000 clients in 14 regions of Azerbaijan [4]. By 2016 ASAN mobile service receptions delivered aid in Bilasuvar [28], Tovuz [29] and other regions of the state. According to the latest data, the number of applicants is increasing sharply.

The following table (Table 1) shows the increase in the number of services delivered, created on the basis of the data, drawn up by the Intelligent Monitoring System of ASAN service itself [22].

Table 1. Number of services delivered by ASAN

ASAN service	2013	2014	2015	2016	2017	2018	2019
Central (stationary)	842785	2607781	3568180	5143807	5654933	6710904	698388
Mobile	57798	65580	259863	532396	367522	379076	5354

Implementation of ASAN service made it necessary to use e-signature. This service was named ASAN Imza which means "easy signature" and opened access to e-service through mobile devices. At the first stage foreign residence would get this permanent ASAN Imza [3].

At first sight it may be considered irrational to let the foreigners use e-signature, but at the time Azerbaijan started to pay special attention to development of tourist sector.

Multiple cultural and sport events, carried out in the state, demanded the cardinal change in visa issue for foreign tourists. It was possible to solve the problem in ASAN service. The new ASAN-visa started to issue e-visas online. There are three steps for getting e-visa. As for the term there are two variants – standard and urgent.

While e-trade was expanding globally the necessity of e-signature usage became clear. As Azerbaijan carries on trade with European countries, it was essential to create e-signatures which will be acknowledged by the EU. In December, 2018 Transport, Communication and High Technology under-Secretary Elmir Velizade during the roundtable discussion devoted to e-identity in e-trade stated that his department was especially interested in acknowledgement of e-signature in other states, particularly in European ones. Thus domestic legislation in the sphere of e-signature is created on the ground of European directives.

Wide spread of e-signature contributes not only to e-trade and digital economy but also turns out to be an essential term for information society development. Theorists state that "e-government and ICT infrastructure development are in top priority in Russia, Kazakhstan and Belarus. However programs and directives of the mentioned states don't imply such components of information community as e-identity, residence registration and ICT in civil society. Nevertheless, these components are present in programs and strategies of other post-Soviet states (particularly, Moldova, Azerbaijan, Kyrgyzstan, Tadzhikistan)" [10].

One more step was made when «ABAD» [20] – Ailə Biznesinə Asan Dəstək (literally, ASAN Support to Family Business) was established in September, 2016. The Azerbaijani word "abad" means "equipped with modern conveniences".

Effectiveness and transparency of ASAN-xidmət turned this service in the only in the state with the exception for the regions of the country which are not covered by the work of ASAN-service [8]. For instance, in the beginning of 2019 ASAN service was proclaimed to issue e-social benefits, it will contribute to struggling against corruption in the vulnerable social sphere.

As it was already stated the expansion of ASAN-service abilities is directly connected with the expansion of the Internet across the country. Thus, Azerbaijani authorities invest heavily in this sector of economy.

According to the Minister of Communication and Information Technologies in 2004–2015 Ali Abbasov, "in 2004–2010 annual rate of development of ICT sector was 30–32%. During the period IT sector was expanded six times, the volume of export – five times, 1.8 bl dollars were invested in the project" [27].

The existing on the common global e-space made it possible for the Azebaibaijani people all over the world use possibilities of ASAN-xidmət through "e-government" website. Corresponding amendment to the previously passed decree was made in January, 15 2019 [23].

Being a success in delivering e-service on its territory, tackling corruption, Azerbaijan tends to share the results with its foreign partners. The first state to cooperate with Azerbaijan in this sphere was Afghanistan, which for a long time was trying to rearrange peaceful life with the help of the international community.

In the beginning of January 2019 the first service center Asan-Khedmat (the same for Azerbaijani ASAN-Xidmət) started to deliver service in this state. It is stated that "the memorandum of understanding signed by the two states imply that ASAN-services with deliver technical support in all the aspects of the initiative. This includes soft decisions, enchange of strategic and legal papers, support in organizing structure and training modules and methodology".

The official Asan-Khedmat website is similar to that of Azerbaijan, although the number of servicer delivered is much lower than in ASAN-Xidmət [5]. Nevertheless, we hope that in the nearest future Afghanistan will succeed in improving the experience.

Meanwhile, Azerbaijani specialists start to involve other resources to struggle against corruption including space ones.

In 2009 Azerbaijan stated its desire to launch its own satellite. In two years the state open joint stock company Azercosmos was established. The new institute aimed at launching national telecommunication satellite AzerSpace, monitoring and using it. The launching took place on February, 3 2013, by the beginning of 2019 the state have already gotten three satellites in orbit [6]. The main task of the third satellite is to expand the territory of the country covered with the Internet, including delivering internet to hundreds of schools, especially in isolated highland areas.

The growing number of Azerbaijani satellites made it possible to observe illegal building activity, which traditionally employs corruption. It was announced that the project carries out the survey every five days and analysis the changes of the earth surface. It helps to prevent illegal building activity and illegal land usage.

The rise of digital technologies in struggle against corruption led to another innovation. In the beginning of January 2019 President of the Republic of Azerbaijan I. Aliev was present at the opening "Real Estate Services of the State Committee on Property Issues". It was proclaimed that the company is delivering 40 services through e-government website. The service e-issue will stop communication between the official and the citizen. The person possessing e-signature can apply for any service through e-government website and gets the result in his profile on this website.

Thus, one of the spheres where officials were able to gain power by just ignoring will soon be out of the area of their influence. That will probably have e great impact on the development of Azerbaijani society.

3.3   Level of Corruption and Level of Computerization

Figure 1 shows that during a certain period of time expansion of the access to the Internet and thus to services and products of ASAN influenced the perception of corruption in Azerbaijan.

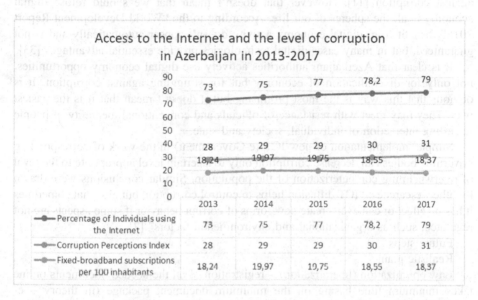

Fig. 1. Access to the Internet and the level of corruption in Azerbaijan in 2013–2017.

We may assume that the decrease of corruption perception level in 2018 in Azerbaijan is linked to slowing down of the Internet expanding in the regions of the state. Unfortunately, we don't possess objective information about the Internet and other telecommunication services published by the International Telecommunication Union to check our idea.

4   Conclusion

Conducting this research we referred to «Digital Planet 2017» , aiming at revealing relevant analytical information on the issue. However in the part named «Digital Evolution Index 2017» , in the section «Scores And Rankings» we not only failed to find information about Azerbaijan, that may be considered logical taking into account the scale of the state in the global economy, but were surprised to find out that the Caspian sea doesn't exist anymore and Azerbaijan has overland boundaries nor only with Russia, bur with Kazakhstan and Turkmenia. To tell the truth, the very presence of such maps in the issue, devoted to digital development at least puzzles [16].

We make this remark intentionally to show that the very existence of accessible digital data (digital cards, for instance) doesn't guarantee the creation of an objective world view.

As for our research, we can't state that the usage of digital technologies and services automatically solves the corruption problem. On the contrary, in 2018 «Transparency International» data showed that despite all the achievement, implementation of new digital services, Azerbaijan made a step backward in struggling against corruption [11]. However that doesn't mean that we should refuse digital economy in all the spheres of our life. According to the "World Development Report 2016", benefit from digital economy activity doesn't appear automatically and is not guaranteed, but in many cases digital technologies provide essential advantages [33].

It is clear that Azerbaijani authorities actively use digital economy opportunities, not only for diversification of economy but for struggling against corruption. It is obvious that this way is the most promising but it doesn't mean that it is the easiest way. They may meet with resistance of officials and conventional mentality of people regarding interaction of individual, society and state.

Simple implementation of new ICT (e-Government) in the work of corresponding governing bodies can decrease corruption only to a certain level appropriate to the level of overwhelming computerization of the population. Similar conclusions were drawn by other researches: "ICT diffusion helps to control corruption but also that sometimes it has no effect or can even create new forms of corrupt behavior if some aspects are not regulated, such as organizational and environmental factors" [7].

Future steps:

Realistic plan:

Law optimization (liberalization) – registration of all the needed documents online takes minimum time basing on the minimum document package (in theory – e-passport, e-signature).

Corruption legalization: fast speed should be officially compensated to state budget (commercial state services development).

Idealistic plan:

Enforcement of citizen's right to gain information (all state institutions are transparent) and functioning of such mechanisms as Crowdsourced reporting, Online corruption reporting (direct report about corruption cases), Issue reporting (direct report about problems with service in state agencies) in the framework of e-Government, creation of alternative non-state public linguo-communicative network, aiming at corruption revealing.

Establishment of direct link with citizens. Modernization of state governing, creation of "ideal state" as linguo-communicative network (such mechanisms of e-Government as Transparency portal, Open data portal, Service automation, Online service [15]), where the following scheme will work: decision making center – computerized mediator on ICT (e-Government) – citizens (e-Society). Decision making center needs no bribes. It may lead to liquidation of bureaucracy.

The question is if Asia needs it, if government machinery will work, if at will be possible for state linguo-communicative network to survive.

According to the western approach, to change the situation drastically the authorities should advance further democratization of public life, civil society establishment, budget expenditure transparency etc. Definitely, all this tasks are right and universal, but they don't take into account the mentality of majority of citizens who used to live in Soviet era. Even 28 years after the collapse of the Soviet Union they live with double standards regarding their respect of law and their accountability to the state. Depending on his or her own interest a citizen can violate law, explaining it by the necessity, but when his or her rights are violated he appeal to the law.

Theoretically it is possible to change the attitude through civil society establishment, however in practice it takes decades and long-term educational activity. Moreover, it is essential that population should get rid of behavior patterns, influenced by the history, customs and traditions.

Any attempts to break social attitude to corruption in Azerbaijan by law enforcement system strengthening or by officials' revenue increases could do little to abolish "Şirinlik" and "Hörmət".

This problem is unlikely to be solved. Nevertheless, future generations and, more precise, future knowledge will do much to defeat "Şirinlik" и "Hörmət".

References

1. ADB: Technical assistance for support for implementation of the second governance and anticorruption action plan. Manila (2008)
2. Ahiabenu, K.: Fighting corruption using ICT (2016)
3. ASAN Imza от ASAN Xidmet. http://vzglyad.az/news/5505/asan-imza-от-asan-xidmet-.html. Accessed 29 Nov 2019
4. 'ASAN Xidmet' served 475,000 citizen. http://www.today.az/news/society/126437.html
5. Asan-Khedmat. http://asan.gov.af/Eng/. Accessed 29 Nov 2019
6. Azerbaijan to launch third satellite. https://www.azernews.az/business/130156.html. Accessed 29 Nov 2019
7. Ben Ali, M.S., Sassi, S.: The role of ICT adoption in curbing corruption in developing countries. In: Kaur, H., Lechman, E., Marszk, A. (eds.) Catalyzing Development Through ICT Adoption, pp. 37–50. Springer, Cham (2017). https://doi.org/10.1007/978-3-319-56523-1_4
8. Bəzi xidmətlər alternativsiz olaraq "ASAN xidmət"də göstəriləcək. https://oxu.az/society/294937?_ga=2.18275833.1118515188.1547848501-1857880355.1547848501. Accessed 29 Nov 2019
9. Bhattacherjee, A., Shrivastava, U.: The effects of ICT use and ICT Laws on corruption: a general deterrence theory perspective. Gov. Inf. Q. **35**(4), 703–712 (2018)
10. Bolgov R., Karachay V.: E-governance institutions development in the eurasian economic union: case of the russian federation. In: ACM International Conference Proceeding Series. 9th International Conference on Theory and Practice of Electronic Governance, ICEGOV 2016, pp. 374–375 (2016). https://doi.org/10.1145/2910019.2910044
11. Corruption Perception Index 2018. Summary table (2018). https://transparency.org.ru/research/indeks-vospriyatiya-korruptsii/rossiya-v-indekse-vospriyatiya-korruptsii-2018-28-ballov-iz-100-i-138-mesto.html. Accessed 29 Nov 2019

12. Corruption Perceptions Index (2017). https://www.transparency.org/news/feature/corruption_perceptions_index_2017. Accessed 29 Nov 2019
13. Country ICT Data (until 2018). Percentage of Individuals using the Internet. https://www.itu.int/en/itu-d/statistics/pages/stat/default.aspx. Accessed 29 Nov 2019
14. Chugunov, A.V., Bolgov, R., Kabanov, Y., Kampis, G., Wimmer, M. (eds.): DTGS 2016. CCIS, vol. 674. Springer, Cham (2016). https://doi.org/10.1007/978-3-319-49700-6
15. Davis, T., Fumega, S.: Mixed incentives: adopting ICT innovation in the fight against corruption. Practical participation. Draft working paper for U4 Anti-corruption resource centre (2013)
16. Digital Planet 2017. How competitiveness and trust in digital economies vary across the world. https://sites.tufts.edu/digitalplanet/files/2017/05/Digital_Planet_2017_FINAL.pdf. Accessed 29 Nov 2019
17. Ear-Dupuy, H., Serrat, O.: Fighting corruption with ICT: strengthening civil society's role. In: Knowledge Solutions. Asian Development Bank, pp. 797–811. Springer, Singapore (2017). https://doi.org/10.1007/978-981-10-0983-9_86
18. Gil-Garcia, R.J., Martinez-Moyano, I.J.: Exploring E-Government Evolution: The Influence of Systems of Rules on Organizational Action. https://scholarworks.umass.edu/cgi/viewcontent.cgi?article=1016&context=ncdg. Accessed 29 Nov 2019
19. Gronlund, A.: Using ICT to combat corruption. Increasing transparency and fighting corruption through ICT: empowering people and communities. SPIDER ICT 4D Series 3 (2010)
20. Haqqımızda. http://abad.gov.az/az/about. Accessed 29 Nov 2019
21. IDT-HSG Center of Excellence for Electronic Government. http://www.electronic-government.com. Accessed 29 Nov 2019
22. İntellektual Monitorinq Sisteminin. HESABATLILIQ MODULU. http://vxsida.gov.az/statistics/. Accessed 29 Nov 2019
23. Konsulluq xidmətlərinin göstərilməsində şəffaflığın artırılması məqsədilə "Azərbaycan Respublikasının Prezidenti yanında Vətəndaşlara Xidmət və Sosial İnnovasiyalar üzrə Dövlət Agentliyinin fəaliyyətinin təmin edilməsi haqqında" Azərbaycan Respublikası Prezidentinin 2012-ci il 5 sentyabr tarixli 706 nömrəli Fərmanında dəyişiklik edilməsi barədə Azərbaycan Respublikası Prezidentinin Fərmanı. https://president.az/articles/31531. Accessed 29 Nov 2019
24. Kossow, N., Dykes, V.: Embracing Digitalisation: How to use ICT to strengthen Anti-Corruption. Deutsche Gesellschaft für Internationale Zusammenarbeit (GIZ) GmbH (2018)
25. Organization for Economic Cooperation and Development: Fighting corruption: what role for civil society? The Experience of the OECD, Paris (2003)
26. Parsons, T.: About social systems (2002)
27. Salaeva, A.: Over 20 years, about $1.8 billion has been invested in the ICT sector of Azerbaijan – Minister. http://1news.az/news/za-20-let-v-sektor-ikt-azerbayzhana-investiro vano-okolo-1-8-mlrd—ministr. Accessed 29 Nov 2019
28. Səyyar ASAN Biləcəriyə gedir. https://sputnik.az/news/20161012/407331177/seyyar-asan-xidmet-bileceri.html. Accessed 29 Nov 2019
29. Səyyar ASAN xidmət Tovuzda. http://www.azadliq.az/xeber/81632/seyyar-asan-xidmet-tovuzda/. Accessed 29 Nov 2019
30. Sykes, J.B. (ed.): The Concise Oxford Dictionary of Current English, 7th edn. Clarendon Press, Oxford (1982)
31. The glass walls of the building "Asan Hidmet" are a symbol of the transparency of the structure's work. https://az.sputniknews.ru/life/20130228/298567289.html. Accessed 29 Nov 2019

32. Twinomurinzi H., Ghartey-Tagoe K.B.: Corruption in developing countries and ICT: the urgent need for work systems to precede e-government. In: Proceedings of the 11th International Conference on Social Implications of Computers in Developing Countries, Kathmandu, Nepal, May (2011)
33. World Development Report 2016: World Bank Digital Dividends (2016). http://documents.worldbank.org/curated/en/224721467988878739/pdf/102724-WDR-WDR2016Overview-RUSSIAN-WebRes-Box-394840B-OUO-9.pdf. Accessed 29 Nov 2019
34. Youth Forum Jeunesse. Policy Paper on the youth perspective on e-society. Adopted by the council of members. Torino, Italy, 13–14 November 2009. On the basis of Understanding e-democracy developments in Europe, Scoping Paper CAHDE (2006) 2E, Council of Europe

Elaboration of Information System of Infrastructure Development of the Northern Sea Route

Sergey Semenov[1], Olga Filatova[1(✉)], Alexey Konovalov[2], and Galina Baturova[2]

[1] The Russian Presidential Academy of National Economy and Public Administration, Prospekt Vernadskogo, 82, 119571 Moscow, Russia
o.filatova87@gmail.com
[2] MIREA - Russian Technological University, Prospekt Vernadskogo, 78, 119454 Moscow, Russia

Abstract. The water area of the Northern Sea Route and the arctic zone of Russia has rather serious development limitations, connected with rather low level of information and communication support. Information and communication limitations have negative influence on the possibilities of the social and economic development of these territories. The most serious limitation seems to be low level of the security as a consequence of lack of information about the changes and limitations of monitoring and communication systems.

The article justifies the need of creation of information system of infrastructure development forecasting along the routes in the waters of the Northern Sea Route in the context of global climate change. The system will be made to support decision making for the infrastructure development of the Arctic zone of Russian Federation that is the key macro region of the country playing a very important role in the social and economic development of Russia. The authors show the key factors, which determine the main requirements to the information and communication system in the Arctic zone and the main features of this system.

Keywords: Russian Arctic · Information system · Northern Sea Route · Development of infrastructure

1 Introduction

Documents of strategic planning of the Russian Arctic contain the statement that economic development and life in this macro region are closely connected with the Ocean, sea transport and functioning of the Northern Sea Route (NSR) [1]. The majority of the settlements in the Russian Arctic are situated on the arctic seashore or near it and in the lower reaches of the rivers flowing into the Arctic Ocean. Disruption of the work of maritime transport, late delivery of fuel, food and other goods to the Arctic because of the short terms of Arctic navigation leads to social and economic consequences (including threats to the lives of people living and working in the region). Climate changes and movement of economic activity in the shelf zone of the Arctic

A. Chugunov et al. (Eds.): EGOSE 2019, CCIS 1135, pp. 270–282, 2020.
https://doi.org/10.1007/978-3-030-39296-3_20

seas increases the role of the sea in the social and economic development of the Russian Arctic. The seaside character of the macro-region distinguishes its natural economic cycles from the "continental" North of Russia and determines the peculiarity of aquatic territorial economic complexes/clusters formed here on the continental shelf and in the coastal zone and oriented on the Northern Sea Route. The NSR (as the Transsiberian railway) is the basic latitudinal transportation route of Russia. Latitudinal routs are the basic communication lines in the country. The perspectives of the development of the whole country depend on the quality of these communications.

Today, both national latitudinal transport and communication lines (Trans-Siberian Railway and Northern Sea Route) do not meet the requirements of trucking industry of XXI century. To achieve strategic goals of national security and economic development of Russia modern transport should meet the goals of the development of territories and waters of the Russian Arctic, Siberia and the Far East. The development of such transportation network implies the inclusion of the high-latitude trans-Arctic transport and transit sea route from Murmansk to Petropavlovsk-Kamchatsky in the Russian transport system and the further use. This route is the North transport corridor, based on the Northern Sea Route with meridional river and railway communications, as well as the airport network. Such transportation frame should interconnect two latitudinal routs with the help of the building up of the meridional communications. This communication design builds so called transportation and communicative network which is the basis of the development of the Arctic zone of The Russian Federation.

The effective functioning of the whole transportation and communicative network needs the possibility of regular cargo transportation through latitudinal and meridional corridors.

So The Northern Transport Corridor should be able to provide a regular route from Murmansk to Petropavlovsk-Kamchatsky – through the Arctic between two extreme non-freezing ports in the West and in the East. Such Northern Transportation corridor can become the regular and the shortest intercontinental transport sea line with unique competitive features [2]. Unique nature and forecasted possibilities of this arctic route make it very attractive for large-scale domestic and international transportation. But in this case the security issues of this route and its information and communicative support become especially important.

We think that the existing information and communication infrastructure does not fully provide the development of the Northern Sea Route and the whole Arctic region. The achievement of these goals needs the information system of the prediction of the infrastructure development along the Northern Sea Route. It demands special decisions in information and communicative sphere. Now there are no such decisions. This fact hinders the development of transport infrastructure of the Northern Sea Route. Because social and economic development of Arctic is closely connected with the development of transport communicative problems create barriers to the sustainable development of territories of the region. The goal of our article is to identify the main criteria for creating an information system for forecasting the development of infrastructure along Northern Sea Route. To achieve this goal, we analyze the climatic and technical factors, comparing them with the plans of social and economic development. The main research questions are:

- What algorithm of actions is needed to predict the development of infrastructure of the Northern sea route?
- What should be the basic features of the information system of forecasting of the environmental influence on various types of industrial and social infrastructure?
- What are the main characteristics of the model of such information system?

2 Methodology

Our article is divided into two main parts:

In the first part, we analyze the actual conditions of the development of Arctic. For the analysis we use open data about ecological, technical and socio-economical aspects of the development of information and communicative infrastructure of the Arctic territories. We choose these aspects because they allow coming to conclusion about the perspectives of the sustainable development of the Arctic and to elaborate the information support system that will take in consideration sustainable development issues.

In the second part, on the basis of the identified specifics of the conditions of development of the Arctic territories, we propose a conceptual framework for creating an information system for forecasting development the Northern sea route. We present the structure of the model of the information system for the environmental assessment considering its influence on industrial and social infrastructure and criteria for ranking indicators. Consistent implementation of the proposed steps with the use of ranking criteria will allow predicting the development of infrastructure of the northern sea route.

3 The State of the Information Support of the Processes of the Research, Development and Use of the Arctic Territories

The fragility and vulnerability of the Arctic nature require the development of resource-saving, energy-efficient technologies that do not cause irreparable environmental damage when developing the richest natural resource base of the macro-region. This will require modern, environmentally compatible technologies and advanced production, highly qualified personnel with competence in the field of environmental safety and sustainable development. Quality of infrastructure of urban territories will ensure the framework of reliability of these territories and the basis for consolidation of new personnel and new production opportunities for development. In this regard, we agree with the statement of one of the key UN-habitat publications that cities and urban areas have a key role to play in addressing the effects of climate change [3].

Currently, the Arctic region is undergoing climatic changes that affect all components of the environment, including aquatic ecosystems, the water balance of river basins, cryogenic processes, etc. The research [4] presents Russian evaluation of the climate change in the Arctic. The research [5] presents the evaluation of the permafrost degradation in Canada. The state and the development of various types of infrastructure in the Arctic are connected with natural risks. The special features and the dynamics of formation of the vulnerabilities of the climate systems in the Arctic are presented in the work [6] in association with adverse hydrological processes: floods, congestion and blockages, ice formation, etc. Permafrost is one of the main factors influencing the processes of flow formation. The processes of formation of groundwater flow also have the opposite effect on the distribution of permafrost by increasing heat fluxes through advection, as well as through convective transfer. The problems of spatial development, temperature and hydrological changes are presented in the researches [7, 8]. Climate warming and permafrost degradation are expected to lead to the transformation of the hydrological cycle in the Arctic and subarctic zones, including changes in the dynamics of soil moisture, intensification of groundwater and surface water, seasonal redistribution of water balance elements [9].

Arctic territories develop in the circumstances of active natural changes without understanding of the value and circumstances of these changes. It is assumed that the degradation of the permafrost zone will lead to a transition from the predominance of surface runoff to the subsurface, which is confirmed by hydrological and geochemical data at the southern border of the permafrost zone [10]. During the recession of permafrost, water exchange between surface and groundwater, groundwater flow, including the movement of water in soils, supra-permafrost, sub-permafrost and minimal river flow, increases. Direct and indirect evidence of such changes is observed in various cold regions of the world. The confirmation of such conclusions can be seen in the works: [9] – the example of Canada, [11] – the example of Europe, [12] – general situation in the Arctic, [13] – North America, Alaska. In the researches [14, 15] the authors made a comparative analysis of the calculations for three generations of models of changes for a significant number of indicators in relation to various macro-regions of the world. Other models also exist – as usual they demonstrate special features of the influence of hydrometeorological, hydrological, cryolitological, ecological and other parameters on certain types of infrastructure in the Arctic. Particularly the problems of acclimatization [16], new approaches to the synoptic climate classification [17], the influence of the climate changes on the economy and especially on tourism [18, 19]. We present these specific data to demonstrate the statement about very significant and poorly predicted changes in vast territories, which are beginning to be more actively developed and involved in the socio-economic turnover. Dynamic and poorly studied changes determine increased requirements for information and communication and analytical support of economic activity in this region. In addition, the climatic features and weak infrastructure provision of the territory impose additional restrictions and requirements on information and communication support of the development of territories.

We do not highlight foreign experience, because except the Russian Federation we practically do not have any example of the country with significant experience of communications in the Arctic seas in the same circumstances. On the other hand there are different information and geoinformation systems that widely use the experience of each other and that have already shown the performance on developed urban territories. But in this field no one can show the good experience of the information support of low urbanized territories. Next we will make the necessary review of existing systems that demonstrate the current situation.

Today, geo-information systems (GIS) provide substantial assistance in economic decision-making. Dewberry elaborated GIS-application TerraGo GeoPDF that allows all involved in emergency response to receive data from GIS Hurricane Evacuation Studies including through mobile devices. New geoinformation instrument uses data from the system of monitoring and analysis of hazardous phenomena. Dewberry elaboration plays an important role: transmits the data processed by the geographic information system directly to field workers, other individuals and organizations who may not have access to GIS capabilities. In practice TerraGo GeoPDF allow you to receive geographic data using mobile devices, as well as exchange maps and snapshots. GeoPDF makes possible to compile multiple layers in PDF, insert coordinates, hyperlinks and view various visual information.

US Department of the Interior launched GIS called Interior Geospatial Emergency Management System (IGEMS) that should help federal, regional and local authorities when making decisions about preparing for an emergency. Data is available to public. GIS allows you to continuously monitor and analyse the development of natural hazards. Reference data and base maps are coupled with current information coming in close to real time. IGEMS uses data from various government agencies, such as the Geological Survey, the National Meteorological Service, and other authoritative sources that have direct access to information about natural hazards. Now it is possible to integrate this heterogeneous information, to provide access to important data to public. The IGEMS web service for monitoring events can run on smartphones and has three base maps: normal administrative, street map and satellite. Various information layers allow you to see on the map information about approaching earthquakes, floods, hurricanes, the boundaries of forest fires, volcanic eruption zones etc. The power of nature is displayed both in corresponding numbers, and more clearly and accessible to a non-expert - in color. Except improving emergency response, such systems help to prevent public panic. XtremeGIS uses information of meteorological web-service AccuWeather, which allows you to monitor the movement of storms and assess precipitation in specific regions. XtremeGIS software also uses geoservice ArcGIS Online and analytical instrument Esri. As a result XtremeGIS can show what office buildings, production sites, logistics and transportation hubs could be threatened by a storm. This allows you to take measures to evacuate staff and protect property in time.

International insurance company Guy Carpenter&Company launched the service GC CAT-VIEWSM that uses geospatial analytical instruments for natural disaster damage assessment. CAT-VIEWSM is made for specific data analysis, received from satellites, manned and unmanned aircraft platforms, social networks, field workers reports and other sources. The system is able to analyze pictures, compare data for different period of time and determine the damage.

The Ministry of Interior affairs of Japan use the big data analysis to give information about evacuation during disasters in time. Such a system more effectively informs people about evacuation plans during natural disasters, such as floods and landslides. The system gathers statistical data about different natural hazards and user's data from social networks. These data allow providing more exact and personalized information based on the user's location and the level of danger. During disasters such as tsunamis and earthquakes, rescuers use geolocation information from smartphones and other mobile devices during evacuation. The information is distributed by traditional information channels (radio and television) and by Internet and mobile networks.

The Russian Arctic can be characterized by extreme natural conditions: low temperatures during all year, long polar night and long polar day, frequent magnetic storms, strong winds and blizzards, dense fogs, monotonous arctic deserts and tundra, permafrost, high dynamics of climate change in recent decades. Negative influence of social and economic factors strengthens natural extreme conditions. Among these factors we can name transport inaccessibility, high production costs and cost of living, small size of the economy and tendencies to its monopolization, isolation and dispersion of settlement.

From the social point of view it is important that there are factors of natural discomfort lack of solar radiation and violation of the customary non-arctic residents of circadian rhythms (alternation of day and night). The cycle "polar day - polar night" not only affects the well-being and efficiency of a person, but also causes additional costs to cover any economic activity.

The goal mentioned in the documents of strategic planning of social and economic development of the Russian Arctic adopted by the President of the Russian Federation and by the Government of Russian Federation is to increase Russia's presence in the Arctic region and intensify economic activity in the region. Strategic documents set tasks of full-scale infrastructure development, not only updating and modernizing existing facilities, but also creating new ones [20]. In the same time the lifecycle of the infrastructure makes tens, and in some cases, hundreds of years (ports, railways, airports, etc.). This influences on demands on the forecasting and planning horizons. In turn, the impact on the environment as a result of infrastructure development requires consideration when making public management decisions.

In order to reduce economic costs, increase the resistance of the infrastructure framework of the macro-region to the possible negative climate processes, it is already necessary to take appropriate response measures and adapt to the observed and predicted climate changes. These problems should be solved together: adaptation measures should be included in the programs of social and economic development of regions and different sectors of the economy of the Russian Arctic. Climate change is not only scientific or ecological problem, but also economic. Adaptation measures directly influence the development of energy, agriculture, forestry and other sectors of the economy, affect the international trade in energy resources and technologies. Therefore, solving this problem directly affects the socio-economic and political interests of the Arctic and extraterritorial countries. Taking into account the size of the territory, geographical location, economic structure, demographic problems and foreign policy interests global climate change makes in Russian Arctic the situation which implies the need for an early formation of a comprehensive and balanced approach of the state to climate issues and related issues based on a scientific analysis of environmental, economic and social factors.

This situation makes actual tasks of interconnection of environmental indicators with indicators of infrastructure development on a macro regional scale in the interests of long-term forecasting of the development of industrial and social infrastructure.

There are two possible solutions:

1. Inertial - using of existing and emerging information departmental/industry, national and global information systems and networks;
2. Active - creation of an automated system of support of the economic and social infrastructure in the difficult climatic conditions of the Arctic.

The system analysis of the current state of information support for the processes of studying, developing and operating the Arctic territories and resources in the Russian Federation allows us to make the following conclusions:

– Information systems and networks in this area are in most cases fragmented, and information resources of these systems and networks are not properly systematized and not unified in terms of their formats.
– Decision makers involved in forecasting the development of infrastructure in the Russian Arctic often do not have access to integrated, complete and accurate information about environmental parameters and long-term forecasts of climate change in the Arctic.
– Standards (protocols) of informational interdepartmental interaction of existing and new information systems and networks are not fully developed.
– Competent distributed user access to departmental paper and electronic information resources in this area is limited in access time (calculated in days).
– Some relevant information resources are only paid.
– The completeness and relevance of information does not fully meet the requirements of a modern public administration system.

Named circumstances make the realization of the first (inertial) solution of the tasks of the infrastructure development difficult. The simple quantitative build-up of the existing information networks in the Arctic does not solve the tasks of the insurance of its infrastructure security. So, today it is necessary to create an automated system to support the economic activities and social infrastructure in the Arctic climatic conditions.

In this part of the article we have summarized the most significant factors that form the environment of uncertainty, the high risks in the implementation of economic and transport tasks for the development of territories. The review of publications allows concluding that, in our opinion, the most significant factor that can reduce these uncertainties and risks is the information support of the system of forecasting changes related to the development of territories. Such an information system should have a number of specific characteristics that take into account the diversity and, possibly, different directions of the changes. It should consider: the possibility of the formats unification, the possibility of the interdepartmental interaction and connection with other information systems, providing twenty four hours every day user access, the ability to provide the most complete information. In the next part we will show our vision of conceptual framework of the creation of the information system of the insurance of the industrial and social infrastructure security in the Arctic.

4 Conceptual Framework of Creating an Information System for the Infrastructure Security in the Waters of the Northern Sea Route

Long-term forecasting of the social and economic development of the Russian Arctic involves ranking indicators of the state of the environment according to the degree of their influence on various types of industrial and social infrastructure [21]. The indicators summarized after aggregation may become input parameters for modeling and creating an automated system to support economic and social infrastructure in the climatic conditions of the Arctic.

The structure of the model of an information system designed to forecast the influence of the environment on various types of industrial and social infrastructure in our opinion should include 8 steps or iterations of the consequent actions for such evaluation.

- Step 1: the collection and systematization of primary digital data in various areas of knowledge about the natural environment of the Russian Arctic into a database. In fact, at this stage we get the primary data of those or other forms of accounting and instrument control (temperature, wind speed, icing, depth, etc.)
- Step 2: the calculation of private quantitative indicators and indicators using existing mathematical models. Here we can get evaluative values in dynamics including some expected results based on trends.
- Step 3: ranking and prioritizing quantitative indicators and indicators are carried out using specially developed prioritization criteria and ranking methodology. On this step there should be identified the most important indicators taking into account the trends identified on the previous stage and the risks formed by the combination of the effects of various factors.
- Step 4: obtained and properly ranked indicators are aggregated into integral ones with determination of the range of their thresholds. On this step we get valid indicators of the potential risks for the infrastructure.
- Step 5: scenario modeling of possible risks, costs, damages and losses of infrastructure facilities based on existing models, taking into account global climate change models, models of operational, short- and medium-term forecasting of the dynamics of natural processes and a preliminary estimate of the cost of preventive measures and the "domino" effect. Here we can rank the level of risks and considering its ranking the mechanism of its compensation should be activated. For example considering the level of risks different preparation and compensation measures could be activated: from temporary staffing of the important objects to the mobilization of the military units and the declaration of emergency mode.
- Step 6: determination of integral indicators of possible risks, costs, damages and losses for infrastructure facilities with the calculation of threshold values. On this step the need of the organizational and resource support of the actions that can compensate the expected infrastructure damage countermeasures appears except the organizational, technical and technological risk management.
- Step 7: adaptation for individual sectors of the economy and social sphere and for different stages of the life cycle of infrastructure facilities by the matrix method.

Here for the solution of the extremal problems the mechanism of sectoral and inter-sectoral cooperation should be activated for the compensation of the infrastructure problems (energy, transport, construction industry, medicine etc.).

- Step 8: development and justification of recommendations for incorporation of the results of modeling in regulatory and methodological documents: strategic planning documents, building codes and regulations etc.

The mentioned sequence of actions affords to move from the particular qualitative indicators to the integral indicators that can help to produce recommendations on the actions for the insurance of the infrastructure sustainability. Eight named steps make the basis of the rational attitude to the current situation and preventive actions. Unfortunately, though the existing information systems give information about par-ticular indicators which are very important for the infrastructure risks accounting they do not afford to solve two fundamental tasks: first – they do not afford to unite the information resources in the integral system for the complex reflection of the data necessary for the decision making. The second – they do not afford to use the scattered data in the integral system of infrastructure security management organization.

Of course, the various parameters of the environment affect different types of infrastructure and the infrastructure facilities themselves. The same parameter will be critical for one object or activity, but completely neutral for another. But the proposed logic of the evaluative actions affords to consider the indicators not in isolation but taking into account their complex impact on infrastructure.

All natural and climatic parameters should identify common properties, allowing evaluating their complex impact on infrastructure development in general. These properties include the specifics of the macro-region, on the one hand, and to mention how a particular climatic phenomenon can damage the infrastructure - on the other. The specifics of the Arctic include both the specifics of complex climatic conditions that place particular demands on materials used in the construction/reconstruction of infrastructure objects adapted to the Arctic climate, architectural solutions, etc.

So, the criteria for ranking indicators of the state of the environment according to their degree of influence on various types of industrial and social infrastructure may be the following:

- The criteria considering the specifics of the arctic climatic conditions (briefly: extremity)
- The criteria considering the specifics of the long-term development of infrastructure in the Arctic (briefly:localization)
- The criteria considering the assessment of the extent and degree of possible damage to the integrated development of infrastructure from a natural climatic phenomenon (briefly: consequences).

From the three named criteria the extremity of the climatic conditions is the most important (has the highest priority) in planning of the actions and in the evaluation of the influence on the industrial and social infrastructure. The importance of this criteria is the highest not only because of the extremal values of indicators of climatic con-ditions (temperature, the wind speed, soil permafrost, glaciation of the objects and others), but also because a huge range of changes in these values. All technologies, materials and constructions for Arctic demand especially high safety resource.

5 Discussion

We proposed an approach to the creation of the structure of the model of an information system to forecast the influence of the environment on various types of industrial and social infrastructure of the NSR which is made for digitalization (or partial digitalization) of predicting the development of the infrastructure of the Northern sea route. The result of such a project can be a new level of information support for the implementation of public policy in the Arctic, the solution of scientific, technical, economic, social and other tasks in the field of studying, mastering and using territories and resources. In our opinion the fact which has especially high importance is that the complexity, low knowledge and high risks of the creation of transport and communicative infrastructure in the Arctic limits the usage of the unique capacities of this territory for the transport and communication development of the world trade. High security of the arctic route could attract significant traffic flows, relevant investments, and activate international cooperation. The technical and technological solutions adopted as part of the creation of the system have commercial potential, since they automate operations that significantly reduce the costs of construction and operation of infrastructure and reduce damage from natural hazards. In general, the results of the model implementation are characterized by a significant multiplicative effect, which is largely determined by the complexity and versatility of the proposed approaches. The effectiveness of implementation of the model can be shown in the improvement of indicators characterizing the state and dynamics of the infrastructure development of the Russian Arctic. The implementation of the proposed recommendations in the work will ensure the achievement of the strategic objectives of the state policy of the Russian Federation in the Arctic related to building up technological potential, introducing necessary information and communication solutions into the economy and social sphere of the macro-region. The possible disadvantage of the structure of the model could be the errors in scenario risk, costs and losses modeling and adaptation of the indicators for special sectors of economy and elaboration of recommendations for statutory acts because these aspects are difficult for automatization and demand expert evaluation. This disadvantage can be compensated by the quality of selection of experts and the number of expert evaluations and the application of the method of quantificative evaluation. We would especially like to mention that information and communication development support will positively affect all aspects of the security of the development of the territory and northern sea route. We think that risk reduction can stimulate international cooperation in the development of the northern sea route, increase investment attractiveness, communication, resource and energy projects in the Russian Arctic.

6 Conclusion

Recently, there has been an exponential growth of decision support information and communication systems in various industries and spheres of life. Such systems are becoming more efficient, reliable and popular. They are used in public administration including strategic planning [7]. There are dozens of information systems and networks in special areas of knowledge (first of all in hydrometeorology, hydrology, permafrost, ecology, etc.). They can be departmental, national, or global (created by international organizations). Information resources in these systems are fragmentary (by frequency, coverage, detailing, comparability, etc.). In most cases such systems are not aggregated, they also are not adapted to accounting when forecasting long-term infrastructure development, and the information systems and networks themselves are weakly interconnected. There are no unified source data formats. On the other hand, industry information systems and networks in which information resources that describe infrastructure development are generated are functioning and developing. The tasks of linking environmental indicators with indicators of infrastructure development on a macro regional scale in the interests of long-term forecasting were set and resolved non-systematically and irregularly. It should be also mentioned that the object of research itself - the Russian Arctic - was "outlined" only in 2014 with the approval of the Decree of the President of the Russian Federation from May 2, 2014 No 296 "On land territories of the Arctic zone of the Russian Federation" [20].

In our research we propose the structure of the model of an information system of assessment of the state of the environment according to its influence on various types of industrial and social infrastructure. Such information system is necessary for the reduction of risks of the development and operation of the Northern sea route. Structurally it should include data gathering and evaluation of the indicators of the state of the natural environment in terms of their impact on the infrastructure and includes 8 steps: 1 - collection and systematization of primary data on the natural environment; 2 - calculation of quantitative indicators; 3 - the ranking and the prioritization of quantitative indicators; 4 - aggregation of ranked indicators in integral indicators; 5 - scenario modeling of the risks, costs, and damages to infrastructure; 6 - definition of integrated indicators of possible risks; 7 - adaptation of indicators for individual sectors of the economy and social sphere; 8 - development and substantiation of recommendations on accounting of results in regulatory documents. We also propose tree criteria of ranking indicators of the state of the environment that should be considered in the perspective model of the information system: extremity, localization and consequences. These criteria allow evaluating complex impact on infrastructure development. As possible directions of future research on the information systems for the prediction of the infrastructure development we find the following: possibilities and problems of digitalization of the use of this model, analysis of application cases in order to improve the proposed information system.

So, the realization of the information system of forecasting according to proposed structure will improve the information support for the realization of the projects in the Arctic and the solution of scientific, technical, economic and other tasks in the field of studying, sustainable development and using the territories and resources of the Russian Arctic. Infrastructure risks reduction will increase the attractiveness of the Arctic territories and projects for them and stimulate international cooperation in the Arctic.

References

1. Postanovlenie Pravitel'stva RF ot 21.04.2014 №366 (red. ot 29.03.2019) «Ob utverzhdenii gosudarstvennoy programmy Rossiyskoy Federatsii «Sotsial'no-ekonomicheskoe razvitie Arkticheskoy zony Rossiyskoy Federatsii». [Decree of the Government of the Russian Federation of 21.04.2014 №366 (ed. from 29.03.2009) "On approval of the state program of The Russian Federation "Socio-economic development of the Arctic zone of the Russian Federation"]
2. Baturova, G.V., Konovalov, A.M., Semenov, S.A., Folomeeva-Vdovina, S.B.: Severnyy transportnyy koridor kak integrator mezhdunarodnogo sotrudnichestva v Arktike – Teoriya i praktika morskoy deyatel'nosti, spetsial'nyy vypusk «80 let s nachala planomernogo izucheniya i razvitiya Sevmorputi» (Tezisy dokladov Mezhdunarodnoy nauchno-prakticheskoy konferentsii). – M.: SOPS. pp. 12–15 (2013). [Baturova G.V., Konovalov A.M., Semenov S.A., Folomeeva-Vdovina S.B. Northern transport corridor as an integrator of international cooperation in the Arctic. Theory and practice of Maritime activities, special issue "80 years since the beginning of systematic study and development of the Northern sea route" Abstracts of the International scientific-practical conference. M. CSPF – pp. 12–15 (2013)]
3. Urban Resilience Enhancer: Climate Action. Electronic resource. https://unhabitat.org/urban-resilience-enhancer-climate-action/. Accessed 03 June 2019
4. Alekseev, G.V., Radionov, V.F., Smolyanitskiy, V.M., Fil'chuk, K.V.: Rezul'taty i perspektivy issledovaniy klimata i klimaticheskogo obsluzhivaniya v Arktike. Problemy Arktiki i Antarktiki 64(1), 262–269 (2018). https://doi.org/10.30758/0555-2648-2018-64-3-262-269. [Alekseev G.V., Radionov V.F., Smolyanitskiy V.M., Fil'chuk K.V. Results and prospects of climate research and climate services in the Arctic. Problems of Arctic and Antarctic. 64(1). 262-269 (2018)]
5. De Grandpré, I., Fortier, D., Stephani, E.: Degradation of permafrost beneath a road embankment enhanced by heat advected in groundwater. Can. J. Earth Sci. 49(8), 953–962 (2012). https://doi.org/10.1139/e2012-018
6. Soldatenko, S.A., Alekseev, G.V., Ivanov, N.E., Vyazilova, A.E., Kharlanenkova, N.E.: Ob otsenke klimaticheskikh riskov i uyazvimosti prirodnykh i khozyaystvennykh sistem v morskoy Arkticheskoy zone RF. Problemy Arktiki i Antarktiki 64(1), 55–70 (2018). https://doi.org/10.30758/0555-2648-2018-64-1-55-70. [Soldatenko S.A. Alekseev G.V. Ivanov N. E., Vyazilova A.E., KHarlanenkova N.E. On the assessment of climate risks and vulnerability of natural and economic systems in the Arctic marine zone RF. Problems of Arctic and Antarctic. 2018. Volume 64. N1. P. 55-70]
7. Fetisov G.G., et al.: Problemy prostranstvennogo razvitiya: metodologiya i praktika issledovaniya. M.: SOPS (2012). [Fetisov G.G., Granberg A.G., Glaz'ev S.YU., Vashanov V.A., Konovalov A.M., Mikheeva N.N., Razbegin V.N., Pilyasov A.N. Problems of spatial development: research methodology and practice. M. CSPF, 2012]
8. Holmes, R.M., et al. Climate change impacts on the hydrology and biogeochemistry of arctic Rivers. In: Goldman, C.R., Kumagai, M., Robarts, R.D. (eds.) Climatic Change and Global Warming of Inland Waters: Impacts and Mitigation for Ecosystems and Societies. Wiley, Chichester (2012). https://doi.org/10.1002/9781118470596.ch1
9. Connon, R.F., Quinton, W.L., Craig, J.R., Hayashi, M.: Changing hydrologic connectivity due to permafrost thaw in the lower Liard River valley, NWT, Canada. Hydrol. Process. 28, 4163–4178 (2014). https://doi.org/10.1002/hyp.10206

10. Sjöberg, Y., et al.: Thermal effects of groundwater flow through subarctic fens: a case study based on field observations and numerical modeling. Water Resour. Res. **52** (2016). https://doi.org/10.1002/2015wr017571
11. Harris, C., et al.: Permafrost and climate in Europe: monitoring and modelling thermal, geomorphological and geotechnical responses. Earth Sci. Rev. **92**, 117–171 (2009). https://doi.org/10.1016/j.earscirev.2008.12.002
12. Hinzman, L.D., Deal, C.J., McGuire, A.D., Mernild, S.H., Polyakov, I.V., Walsh, J.E.: Trajectory of the Arctic as an integrated system. Ecol. Appl. **23**(8), 1837–1868 (2013). https://doi.org/10.1890/11-1498.1
13. Jepsen, S., Voss, C., Walvoord, M., Minsley, B., Rover, J.: Linkages between lake shrinkage/expansion and sublacustrine permafrost distribution determined from remote sensing of Interior Alaska, USA. Geophys. Res. Lett. **40**, 882–887 (2013). https://doi.org/10.1002/grl.50187
14. Knutti, R.: The end of model democracy? Clim. Change **102**, 395–404 (2010). https://doi.org/10.1007/s10584-010-9800-2
15. Reichler, T., Kim, J.: How well do coupled models simulate today's climate? Bull. Am. Meteorol. Soc. **3**, 303–311 (2008). https://doi.org/10.1175/bams-89-3-303
16. De Freitas, C.R., Grigorieva, E.A.: Role of acclimatization in weather-related human mortality during the transition seasons of autumn and spring in a termally extreme mid-latitude continental climate. Int. J. Environ. Res. Public Health. **12** (2015). https://doi.org/10.3390/ijerph121214962
17. Dixon, P.G., et al.: Perspectives on the synoptic climate classification and its role in interdisciplinary research. Geogr. Compass **10**(4), 147–164 (2016). https://doi.org/10.1111/gec3.12264
18. Li, H., Goh, C., Hung, K., Chen, J.L.: Relative climate index and its effect on seasonal tourism demand. J. Travel Res. (2017). https://doi.org/10.1177/0047287516687409
19. Li, H., Song, H., Li, L.: A dynamic panel data analysis of climate and tourism demand: additional evidence. J. Travel Res. **56**(2), 158–171 (2017). https://doi.org/10.1177/0047287515626304
20. Ukaz Prezidenta Rossiyskoy Federatsii ot 2 maya 2014 goda № 296 «O sukhoputnykh territoriyakh Arkticheskoy zony Rossiyskoy Federatsii» (s izmeneniyami ot 27 iyunya 2017 goda № 287). [The decree of the President of the Russian Federation from may 2, 2014 № 296 "About land territories of the Arctic zone of The Russian Federation (with the changes from June 27 2017, N 287)]
21. Arktika: zona mira i sotrudnichestva / Otv. red. - A.V .Zagorskiy. - M.: IMEMO RAN (2011). [Arctic: zone of peace and cooperation. Zagorskiy, A.V. (ed.) - M.; IWEIR RAS (2011)]

Online Tools for Self-assessment: Case of Russia

Mikhail Bundin$^{(\boxtimes)}$, Aleksei Martynov , and Aleksei Pozdnyshov

Lobachevsky State University of Nizhny Novgorod (UNN),
Nizhny Novgorod 603950, Russia
mbundin@mail.ru, avm@unn.ru, nafl978@rambler.ru

Abstract. The use of information technologies for government or public administration (e-government) is an inherent and key element of any modern information society. It is difficult now to find a sphere where the IT would not be used. In Russia, one of the most conservative areas for the use of information technologies was the sphere associated with the implementation of state and municipal control and supervision functions. However, the State Program on Reforming Control and Supervisory Activities adopted in 2016 announced the necessity for widespread use of new information technologies in implementing state control and supervising. As a result, some of Russian state control and supervisory authorities introduced special electronic services and tools for online self-assessment, which are now actively promoted and serve for the organization of control and supervisory activities, partially displacing its traditional forms and methods. The paper provides a brief overview of existing practice of using electronic services for state control and supervising and suggests to introduce a set of regulatory principles for e-inspection tools.

Keywords: E-government · Public administration · State control · E-inspection · Self-assessment

1 Introduction

Since the beginning of the first decade of the 21st century, Russia has been trying to introduce new information technologies in various spheres of public administration. The most well-known and successful e-government projects were the "open government" system and e-services government portal (gosuslugi.ru) [1]. In the last few years, great importance is given to the digitalization of the economy with the adoption of the Strategy of Information Society Development in the Russian Federation for 2017–2030 years [2] and the National Program "Digital economy of the Russian Federation" [3]. These documents underline a special role of the "digital economy" in Russia.

Those changes also impact inevitably Russian public administration system. In 2016 the Council for Strategic Development and Priority Projects headed by the President of the Russian Federation approved a new Federal program "Reform of Control and Supervisory Activities" (implementation period – up to 2025) [4]. This

A. Chugunov et al. (Eds.): EGOSE 2019, CCIS 1135, pp. 283–292, 2020.
https://doi.org/10.1007/978-3-030-39296-3_21

document replaced the Action Plan ("Road Map") to improve control and supervisory activities in the Russian Federation for the period 2016–2017 [5].

These strategic documents envisage an active and wide introduction in the sphere of state control and supervising of new information technologies.

The "Road Map" was destined to modernize and update exiting mandatory requirements that are to be verified during state inspections, as well as to ensure the availability of information about them for business entities. The result of this work should be:

- detecting and eliminating of obsolete, duplicative and redundant mandatory requirements that are to be checked during the state monitoring and supervising activities;
- forming and making available for business entities a set of legal documents containing mandatory requirements for control and supervising (for each type of it) and their regular updating;
- publishing of the lists of mandatory requirements (checklists), as well as their regular updating on official websites of state control and supervising authorities.

In addition, state control and supervising authorities should introduce an analytical system to summarize and analyse their control and supervisory practice as well as to publish the results as open data on their official websites.

The Roadmap specially stressed that improving the efficiency of control and supervisory activities and the transition to new principles of its organization is impossible without a comprehensive and integrated solution. Thus, it was noted that forming of an effective risk assessment and management system needs inevitably a special online software solution (an information system/a tool) that could collect and effectively operate the data on previous inspections. This electronic tool should be fully integrated with already existing governmental portals and systems: federal register of state and municipal services (functions), federal portal for e-services (gosuslugi.ru), governmental automated information system "Administration", departmental information systems of state control and supervisory bodies.

Moreover, in the framework of ongoing reform a special attention is made on introducing new e-services (online services) helping business entities and individuals to clearly understand and check their compliance with existing legal requirements.

2   Methodology

The authors used quantitative and qualitative analysis of existing Russian and some foreign publications in open sources in international and Russian science-citation databases. Considering more practical dimension of the presented research the main emphasis was made on analysis of current practice of implementing online self-assessment tools and services, statistical and analytical data from governmental portals and sites, regulatory documents in the sphere of e-government and online state and municipal services.

3   Literature Review

A brief review of the existing practice of e-government technologies and the current directions of its development demonstrates that the use of information technologies for the implementation of control and supervisory activities is still insufficiently studied in both Russian and international practice [6–8]. The analysis of existing databases of scientific citation used to search for information (Scopus, Web of Knowledge, Russian Science Citation Index) rather demonstrates the focus of modern research on other issues. In addition, it is worth noting that a widespread use of audit and consulting services in foreign countries and their almost limited distribution in Russia largely explains exactly the interest in the study of the Russian practice of using online services for state control and inspection.

As an example of similar solutions, the authors can name online services - a certain calculator, for example, used for the inspection of vehicles in the UK [9] or Self-Assessment Tool of Australian Skills Quality Authority used for Registered Training Organizations [10], which are similar rather to the express-assessment service operated by the Emergencies Ministry of Russia (see Sect. 6).

Meanwhile the practice of use of different self-assessment tools/instruments (SATs) is widely used for different cases where a check for compliance is needed or there is necessity for evaluation/assessment. In most of cases those tools represent a certain questionnaire – a checklist that can be downloaded and be passed offline whether an electronic online form to fill in and obtain a result. As an example - Employment/S Pass Self-Assessment Tool (SAT) of the Ministry of Manpower of Singapore [11], the Self-Assessment Tool (SAT) of the European Commission [12].

4   Regulatory Framework for Self-assessment Online Tools

The above mentioned "The Reform of Control and Supervisory Activities" was followed by adoption of the Standard for the comprehensive prevention of violations of mandatory requirements (hereinafter – the Standard for comprehensive prevention) [13].

Section 5.7 of it is devoted to the creation of interactive services that provide interaction with controlled entities, including tools for self-examination and voluntary confirmation of compliance by them. Those services initially are to be used for self-examination and self-assessment and should be integrated with the official site of the executive body on the page where other information on prevention of violations of mandatory requirements is usually posted. The executive body should provide different types of interactive tools (self-examination/self-assessment) for each type of control or inspection activity with a precise list of requirements that are to be checked in each case.

In addition, for each type of state control (supervision) at least one interactive service for self-examination and self-assessment should provide a possibility of self-examination and self-assessment without passing through electronic identification and authentication (revealing its identity).

The Standard of comprehensive prevention establishes that interactive services without identification or authentication are created in the form of a Questionnaire (a checklist) that helps to identify the corresponding level of risk of under-control entities. That could be done as a list of relevant to the control/inspection questions ("electronic inspector") or in the form of a checklist with corresponding indicators of risks followed by violation of mandatory requirements ("express-assessment").

The Standard of comprehensive prevention stipulates that questionnaires (checklists) for evaluation of the actual level of risk of controlled entities represent themselves a set of parameters relating to the general and specific characteristics of the organization and data obtained from previous control/inspection activities, influencing and (or) potentially able to influence their compliance with mandatory requirements. Each parameter is subject to self-assessment by the controlled entity on a given scale (for example, a five-point scale, or, depending on the nature of the questions, a mixed scale can be applied using possible answers to the questions). The total score obtained by the controlled entity is calculated automatically taking into account a specific weight of each parameter as a risk factor for non-compliance with mandatory requirements, and shows the actual level of risk of non-compliance of the controlled entity with the requirements.

The control and supervisory authority selects the parameters according to the results of its previous law enforcement practice regarding them as typical direct and indirect causes and conditions for violations of mandatory requirements by the controlled entities (for example, the frequency of employee training courses; the technical condition of the equipment used at the production facility; the total number of cases when controlled entities were brought to responsibility for non-compliance with mandatory requirements for the last two years, etc.). Inside each type of state control (supervision) activity, the questionnaires are specified according to possible risk groups or categories of controlled entities.

Thus, according to the Standard of comprehensive prevention "electronic inspector" is nothing more than an electronic form of a checklist with control questions, which are available for filling in online. The answers allow the under-control entity to determine its level of compliance with the mandatory requirements and/or identify timely possible violations of mandatory requirements.

The automated processing should allow the under-control entity to receive a full list of requirements where a possible incompliance was detected. The software tool "electronic inspector" should also signal to the user any case of incompliance or missing answer to a control question and provide with a link where an information about possible risks for the controlled entity in case of the detection of this possible violation by the control or supervisory authority could be found - "a calculator of risks". The calculator of risks gives an eventual and plausible consequences - sanctions which an entity may face in case a real state control or inspection occurs.

5   E-Inspector for Labor Control

Now, the interactive online service "e-inspector" [14] is introduced and actively used in Russia only for implementation of state labor control and inspection.

The service was developed within the framework of the "Concept of Improving of the Efficiency of Ensuring Compliance with Labor Legislation (2015–2020)" [15] as a special electronic tool having information and consulting character. The service is mainly addressed to employers for self-verification of their compliance with the requirements of labor legislation. The employees could possibly use it if they presume a violation of their rights by current employer. The tool should ensure the transparency of the audit of labor legislation by state labor inspectors, clarifying the existing requirements that are checked for compliance during inspections and provide users with clear information about the audit's procedure.

The checklists integrated into the "e-inspector" service are based on existing legal requirements from Russian Labor Code and other legal acts. They mostly include questions on the most important mandatory requirements that limits the inspection's scope.

In 2018, the Ministry of Labor and Social Protection issued special Guidelines for employers on usage of voluntary self-assessment electronic services for checking the compliance with labor legislation requirements [16]. This document contains a common definition of "electronic inspector", which is understood as an electronic online tool that allows the employer to check his compliance with requirements of labor legislation and in case of detected inconsistencies to receive recommendations for their correction before an assumed inspection by the Federal Service for Labor and Employment would take place and also containing legal grounds for state inspection and necessary application forms to fill in.

The same document establishes that the self-assessment service is located on "onlayninspektsiya.rf" (transliteration from Russian, English version is not available).

Service "e-inspector" provides certainty and transparency of the audited norms of labor legislation and helps to understand the requirements that are imposed by state labor inspectors during real inspections as well as giving an information and algorithm of its procedure.

The set of basic principles of "e-inspector" functioning is:

- network interaction between the participants;
- variability (meeting the needs of users to provide and receive information about violations of labor legislation and the recommended ways to correct them);
- one and single visual and technological space for all users;
- comfortable and understandable space;
- possibility to get an efficient "feedback" between the operator of the e-service and its users;
- possibility of personalization of user interfaces (the use of a detailed user dossier and the creation of a personal account).

The Guidelines for employers for self-assessment with labor legislation requirements describe in detail the algorithm of the usage of "e-inspector" tool: registration, creation of a personal account, general description of working interface of electronic services provided and specified personal account services, analysis of typical cases (employment; change and termination of the employment contract; responsibility of the parties to the employment contract; protection of personal data; working time and rest time; remuneration etc.).

The recommended procedure for carrying out a self-assessment test suggests for an employer to designate an entitled person, normally an experienced professional from HR-division with a higher education (having a degree in Law or Economics) and relevant competence.

When choosing a checklist for self-assessment procedure, the user should take into consideration that the tool is destined to check for compliance with the labor rights of each individual employee's case and not for the whole employer's organization.

The filling in of the "e-inspector" checklist is followed by two possible options. In case of absence of plausible violations of the labor legislation the system not only indicates it to the user but also sends the result to the competent authority – the Federal Service for Labor and Employment in order to take measures to encourage a *bona fide* employer (to exclude it from control and inspection plan or postpone its inspecting for later).

The results are provided in the form of an act of verification of compliance by the employer of labor legislation, including a list of violations of labor legislation or simply a notification of full compliance (if no violations were detected).

In case of detection of the inconsistency with the labor legislation the employer receives a list of measures and practical recommendations for corrections of the detected violations with providing samples of necessary documents. The employer shall fix them and bring its organizational and management documentation in accordance with the requirements.

As a result of the audit, the user of the service "electronic inspector" has the opportunity to:

(a) print out the verification act and get the history of self-assessment results with recommendations for correcting possible violations;
(b) return to the list of typical labor situations that are in the scope of state control or audit;
(c) pass other checklist for another labor situation available for selection.

6   Online Express-Assessment Tool

The Emergencies Ministry of Russia introduced in 2017 a new online service "express-assessment" that could be also regarded as a self-assessment electronic online tool [17]. The service is destined to help the controlled entity independently and within minimal time limit to detect plausible violations or risk factors that could be a ground for an unscheduled inspection.

The service also includes a checklist of indicators of possible violations of obligatory requirement formed basing on existing practice of state control and audit measures analysis.

Electronic forms with indicators of risk of violation of obligatory requirements are created in the form of a checklists developed on the basis of indicators of risk of violation of the obligatory requirements and approved by federal executive body.

After getting through the checklist, the system provides the user with the information on presence or non-presence of risk factors in this particular case as well as possible solution how to correct the detected problems in order to comply with the legal requirements. The service has also a 'calculator' for estimating plausible sanctions amount in case of state inspection would be in present.

Thus, the "express-assessment" tool allows business entities and individual entrepreneurs to estimate possible sanctions or to make sure that they are acting correctly. This service includes mainly checklists for anti-fire and emergency situation protection requirements.

The tool provides also a possibility to grade the objects of state inspection according to several parameters (number of floors in the building, absence of a certain number of fire exits, number of everyday visitors who could possibly be present inside, etc.). All the objects are classified into fives risk categories: "high", "significant", "medium", "moderate" and "low".

In total, according to general statistics, there are about 3 million objects controlled or inspected by the Russian ministry of emergency situations and more than 125 thousands of them are rated as "high" risk.

7 General Results and Statistics

In the end of 2017, the number of visitors and users of "e-inspector" service for labor legislation self-assessment increased up to 3.58 million and about 25 millions of views were registered in total. On December 31, 2017, about 302 000 of self-assessment checklist tests were passed and more than 216 000 violations were revealed (initially in 2017 - 124 500 self-assessment tests and 79 100 violations). According to the special calculating tool on eventual risks of non-compliance the use of "e-inspector" tool by employers helped them to avoid plausible penalties in the amount of 6.77 billions of roubles (~ 100 million \$) [18].

During 2018 new data services were introduced interconnected with the use of "e-inspector", now the tool provides also the data on consultations given ($\sim 80\,000$ in total). The services represent itself a sort of a FAQ tool with a possibility to form your own question to the authority if the answer was not found among reviewed practical cases. The latter are usually taken also from another interactive consulting service – "on-duty online inspector", that represents an on-line consulting tool operated by the officers of the Federal Service for Labor and Employment and open for employers and employees. In 2018 a total number of consultations amounts to 242 000. According to the general statistics of the portal the use of "e-inspector" tools and the "onlineinspection" service helped to restore labor rights in more than 3.2 million cases [18].

The Program of comprehensive prevention [19] notes that currently the most popular online services of the "online inspection" portal are: "report the problem", "on-duty online inspector" and "e-inspector".

The document also notes that the service "e-inspector" enables employers to carry out a self-examination or self-assessment on compliance with the requirements of labour legislation at any time and absolutely free. During the audit, the representative of the organization (an entitled person) fills in the smart checklists and receives a result on the absence or existence of violations of labor legislation requirements.

The service "e-inspector" and "onlineinspection" portal are constantly updated and revised by introducing new checklists variable for different practical cases and situations. In 2017 there were 175 situations-checklists for self-assessment and in 2018 another 25 are to be introduced into the "e-inspector" service [18].

In addition, Russian labor inspection launched in 2017 a special mobile application available both for Android and iOS – "I-inspector" [20], which allows users to access their personal profile at "onlineinspection" portal and to declare to the territorial body of Russian labor inspection serious violations of labor rights: no fence on the construction site, builders working without personal protective equipment, concealment of accidents and violation of the prescribed order of their investigation, delays in paying salary or social security, compensatory or other obligatory payment.

Assuming the existent practice and the results of their use the "onlineinspection" portal and "e-inspector" tool provide the necessary conditions for compliance with labour legislation and reducing violations in this area, as well as increase the effectiveness of state control and supervising activity in this sphere. The introduction and use of these services helped also to reduce significantly possible risks and eventual financial losses for business entities and to some extend to decrease administrative pressure on employers.

The whole practice of use of "onlineinspection" and "e-inspector" services demonstrates a new vector in control and supervising activity and prevention of labor violation that could be expanded to other domains. Unfortunately, the "e-inspector" service can't be used for verification of compliance with the requirements of labor legislation in respect of state or municipal public servants.

Currently, only The Emergencies Ministry of Russia expressed clearly its intention to introduce similar project "e-inspector" in addition to "express-assessment" tool in its current practice but it is only in the stage of development.

Unfortunately, there could not be found any information or a feedback from other state control and supervisory bodies of the Russian Federation and it is impossible to evaluate future perspective of use of similar online tools by them.

8   Conclusion

The emergence of self-assessment electronic online tools for implementing control and supervisory activities should be regarded in the whole as a positive practice. Here again it is worth noting the extreme conservatism of this sphere in Russia. The problem of redundancy, duplication and inconsistency of control and inspection requirements remains one of the most emergent. The search for clear and transparent mechanisms that will allow the under-control entities to comply with and the inspection bodies to focus on the more risky areas is still a vital issue. The practice of using online tools for self-assessment despite some obviously positive results is still far from to be perfect – in fact it is about episodic cases in Russia and not a systematic general approach for now. There is still a lot of work to be done to ensure that the legal requirements checked by various control and supervisory bodies are to be harmonized. Nevertheless, a positive tendency becomes already obvious and the statistics of the use of the "e-inspection" tool shows positive dynamics.

The analysis of the main directions of introduction of new information technologies in the state control and supervisory activities in Russian and current practice of use of "online-inspection" tool allow to suggest some basic principles for online support of state control and supervising:

(1) information is provided free of charge;
(2) lawful use of open data, including: the use of open data only for legitimate purposes; the obligation not to distort open data when using them; the obligation to maintain a reference to the source of information when using open data;
(3) limited access to the information on control and supervisory activities - only authorized bodies and their officials have the right to include and operate the records resulting control and supervisory activities;
(4) variability of access to information, there should be a possibility to access some online services without passing an authorization process to state information systems of various subjects of control and supervision;
(5) integration including full integration and sharing data with other state information systems and platforms allowing for interdepartmental cooperation in the field of control and supervision;
(6) reliability and timeliness of data obtained and of entered information on control and supervisory activity. That may help to form a one and single register for all control and supervisory activities performed. The data should be updated within 10 working days period after a state control or audit procedure ended;
(7) reliability of information on checked legal requirements included in online checklists with exact requirements asked for compliance during real state control and supervisory procedure in present;
(8) attention given to the feedback receiving after using online service "e-inspector".

References

1. Public Services Portal of the Russian Federation. https://www.gosuslugi.ru/foreign-citizen?lang=en. Accessed 22 July 2019
2. Strategy for the Information Society Development in Russian Federation 2017–2030, Federal Government of Russian Federation. http://static.government.ru/media/files/9gFM4FHj4PsB79I5v7yLVuPgu4bvR7M0.pdf. Accessed 22 July 2019
3. Federal Program "Digital Economy in Russian Federation", Federal Government of Russian Federation. http://static.government.ru/media/files/9gFM4FHj4PsB79I5v7yLVuPgu4bvR7M0.pdf. Accessed 22 July 2019
4. Federal program "Reform of Control and Supervisory Activities" (implementation period – up to 2025). http://static.government.ru/media/files/vu4xfkO2AdpTk1NaJN9gjDNtc69wa5fq.pdf. Accessed 22 July 2019
5. The Action Plan ("Road Map") to improve control and supervisory activities in the Russian Federation for the period 2016–2017. http://government.ru/rugovclassifier/587/events/. Accessed 22 July 2019
6. Yildiz, M.: E-Government research: reviewing the literature, limitations and ways forward. Gov. Inf. Q. **24**(3), 646–665 (2007)

7. Batley, R., Mcloughlin, C.: The politics of public services: a service characteristics approach. World Dev. **74**, 275–285 (2015). https://doi.org/10.1016/j.worlddev.2015.05.018.eg

8. Bertot, J., Estevez, E., Janowski, T.: Universal and contextualized public services: digital public service innovation framework. Gov. Inf. Q. **33**(2), 211–222 (2016). https://doi.org/10.1016/j.giq.2016.05.004

9. Site-assessment calculator. https://www.gov.uk/government/publications/site-assessment-calculator. Accessed 22 July 2019

10. Australian Skills Quality Authority. https://www.asqa.gov.au/standards/self-assessment-tool. Accessed 22 July 2019

11. Ministry of Manpower of Singapore. https://www.mom.gov.sg/eservices/services/employment-s-pass-self-assessment-tool. Accessed 22 July 2019

12. European Commission. https://ec.europa.eu/growth/tools-databases/escss_en. Accessed 22 July 2019

13. Standard for the comprehensive prevention of violations of mandatory requirements. http://static.government.ru/media/files/vu4xfkO2AdpTk1NaJN9gjDNtc69wa5fq.pdf

14. Electronic inspector. https://онлайнинспекция.рф/inspector/prechecks?category_id=popular. Accessed 22 July 2019

15. Concept of Improving of the Efficiency of ensuring compliance with labor legislation (2015–2020). http://static.government.ru/media/files/vu4xfkO2AdpTk1NaJN9gjDNtc69wa5fq.pdf. Accessed 22 July 2019

16. Guidelines for employers on usage of voluntary self-assessment electronic services for checking the compliance with labor legislation requirements. http://www.consultant.ru/document/cons_doc_LAW_294585/. Accessed 22 July 2019

17. Automation of control and supervision activities. http://www.mchs.gov.ru/dop/Reforma_knd/avtomatizaciya_nadzora. Accessed 22 July 2019

18. General statistics on "e-inspector" and "onlineinspection" services use. https://онлайнинспекция.рф/statistics. Accessed 22 July 2019

19. Program of comprehensive prevention of labor violations. http://rulaws.ru/acts/Prikaz-Rostruda-ot-19.07.2018-N-407/. Accessed 22 July 2019

20. For iOS: https://itunes.apple.com/ru/app/a-inspektor/id1185854875?l=en&mt=8. Accessed 22 July 2019, for Android: https://play.google.com/store/apps/details?id=com.inspector.mobile&hl=ru. Accessed 22 July 2019

Digital Intelligence, Data Science and Cybercrime

Natural Language Processing of Russian Court Decisions for Digital Indicators Mapping for Oversight Process Control Efficiency: Disobeying a Police Officer Case

Oleg Metsker[1], Egor Trofimov[2(✉)], and Sofia Grechishcheva[1(✉)]

[1] ITMO University, Saint Petersburg, Russia
olegmetsker@gmail.com, sofiagrechishcheva@gmail.com
[2] All-Russian State University of Justice, Moscow, Russia
diterihs@mail.ru

Abstract. This article describes the study results in the development of the method of natural language processing (NLP) of semi-structured Russian court decisions to improve the quality of knowledge extraction describing legal process. Improving the accuracy of information retrieval from electronic records of court decisions was achieved with using combination of TF-IDF and latent semantic analysis. As a result, the word combinations of facts of offenses and procedural facts that may affect the decision-making of the court are identified. The applicability of the results is shown on the example of development a decision tree ML model of the appointment of arrest or fine punishment if disobeying a police officer. Automated mapping of court decisions texts on Russian language is also possible use for the development of artificial intelligence systems and new generation decision support systems in law domain.

Keywords: Natural language processing · Artificial intelligence · Law

1 Introduction

This study is aimed to develop intelligent methods for managing the processes of digitalization of law-making and law enforcement, for development of artificial intelligence systems in the field of law, and for designing the system requirements for this process. Moreover, the objectives of the study includes the development of a high-performance solutions to support IT infrastructure of electronic management processes and the electronic state. One of the main task to achieve this aim is a development of the method for automatically layout of court decisions texts based on artificial intelligence technologies. The task of the algorithm is automated to extract key entities (indicators) from semi-structured data for further creation of prognostic and descriptive models for analyzing the effectiveness of control and surveillance activities.

The natural language processing, or NLP is the one of the tool that organizes unstructured or semi-structured data, to extracts specific information from it [1, 2], which is necessary for further goals, and to use this data in process of digitalization [3]. Semi-structured data or texts are everywhere: fiction, science articles, paper and electronic

© Springer Nature Switzerland AG 2020
A. Chugunov et al. (Eds.): EGOSE 2019, CCIS 1135, pp. 295–307, 2020.
https://doi.org/10.1007/978-3-030-39296-3_22

media, legal documents, etc. In particular, we are interested in law texts such as court decision, laws and others.

As it was mentioned above, court decision texts have a semi-structured form. To work with such data written on the natural language the natural language processing, or NLP is used. NLP is a class of methods for data structuring and data extraction [1, 2] and use it in computational processes [3]. In the second part of the study, the related papers are reviewed. Applying NLP to court decision data can detect indicators of the effectiveness of the application of legislation in general and, in particular, control and surveillance activities, which can speed up the work of administrative staff, improve quality of lawmaking and reduce the cost of law enforcement.

The originality of this approach is in the fact that the developed methods and the software provide structuring and layout of court decision texts and recognize the entities in the Russian language. Also, the software recognizes terms' semantics based on their part of speech and document class they belong to.

2 Problem Definition

The digitalization of administrative processes creates opportunities for analysis based on methods of artificial intelligence [4]. However, data from government information systems has a semi-structured form. The most significant information that describes law processes contains in texts written on natural language. Such methods like text mining, data mining, process mining offer great opportunities for better understanding of the processes and their optimization. However, there is an inequality between quality of methods and collected data as those methods define requirements to data structure. Moreover, a great number of laws and their constant modifications demands automated tracking in terms of tools of automated layout: pattern application, text-mining methods have an unsatisfactory short-term benefits. For database analysis of court decisions it is necessary to take into account a fact that laws have been changing and one case can be considered in different ways in different timelines.

An intuitive understanding of the law technical features different types of court acts and processing a sufficient number of court acts indicate that the content of court acts as and array of big data holds a great potential for automating the process of summarizing judicial practice and developing a support system for making court decisions based on predictive models and latent semantic analysis.

However, such data are stored in texts written in the natural language. To apply modern approaches of artificial intelligence it is necessary to structure this data. The development of the tools for automated analysis of semi-structured data of court decisions is a significant science task.

3 Related Works

For the current moment, three general approaches to the text analysis have been formed [1, 5]: keyword, or Linguistic-focus approach; machine learning, or Statistics approach; hybrid approach. The main feature of the first approach is the existence of the given in advance dictionary (the knowledge base), containing words and phrases. This approach uses special rules known as grammars to define the semantics. The most widespread grammars are represented in Backus-Naur form [6] and its modifications. The second approach was formed due to grammar complexity. It is a nontrivial matter to create the grammar that covers the whole language [3]. It uses statistic theory: words are interpreted as independent characteristics to construct the statistic model. Then, the machine learning is realized to get the relationship between them. On practice, the Statistics approach is often supported by the first one. The hybrid approach has many features of key-word approach. Each of them are responsible for the certain step of the text analysis (about it is further below). However, some of those steps use the machine learning to reduce disadvantages of both approaches [5].

According to the linguistic theory, there are several levels of the linguistic knowledge [1]:

- morphology (words and meaningful parts of them);
- syntax (structures of phrases and sentences);
- semantics (the meaning of words, phrases, sentences);
- pragmatics (the impact of the context and information source's intend);
- discourse (paragraphs and texts).

The morphology is responsible for combination of morphemes (roots, suffixes, prefixes, endings). For example, a word with the same root can be a noun, an adjective, a verb and so on. There are free morphemes (prefix over-) that can exist as such without other morphemes; there are connected morphemes (most of suffixes) that do not have any meaning as such. There are also word-formative morphemes that change the words' part of speech. The morphemes are crucial in analysis of EHRs, especially in terms of chemistry or medical procedures. The majority of NLPs in law do not maintain such detailed analysis. Instead of it the regular expressions and the knowledge bases are used to classify words.

The main objective of the syntax is the classification of words on the part of speech feature. That sort of information, as a rule, is indicated in a law lexicon (a dictionary). Take into consideration that part of speech has subclasses, for example, plural and singular forms. Moreover, syntax is responsible for detecting lexemes or, in other words, stable phrases. In analysis of EHRs, lexemes play significant role – many laws and drug titles are lexemes. One more biomedical syntax feature is abbreviations of all kinds: skipping critical in the general language structural elements such as subject and predicate. Verbs and adjectives are often dropped too. In NPLs, the syntax can be embodied with a help of a lexicon and grammars. The regular expressions and circumstances (stochastic) context-free grammars and sometimes dependency grammars are used.

The semantics is responsible for the meaning and interpretation of words, phrases and sentences. In law NLPs, the semantics is limited by meanings of certain words or lexemes, which can be extracted from the knowledge base. In most cases, these classes are enough to get the semantics as long as text is restrain by its subject area. If the lexicon do not contains some of words, it is useful to turn to its morpheme to determine the word's role in the sentence. The semantics of a sentence is defined based on the regular expressions and classes related to tokens. In more complex NLPs, the context-free grammars are used.

The pragmatics is responsible for the context and the meaning that the original source puts in a text. Sentences form a text, semantics of which is an objective of the discourse. To set up the relationship between sentences NLPs use the relational expressions.

There are some studies of text analysis of court decisions base on several languages. These studies are related to text analysis of court decisions on human rights [7]. There are also studies where the German court decision definitions are analyzed based on semantics and language structure [8]. However, works related with Russian lawmaking are hardly identified. Thus, gained result are significant in terms of NLP and at the same time in terms of law and administrative science and electronic state science.

4 Methods

For the processing of court decisions, a combination of TF-IDF and latent semantic analysis methods was used. Finally, the results were validated and interpreted by experts.

4.1 TF-IDF

The concept of TF-IDF, or Term Frequency (TF) and Inverse Document Frequency (IDF) is a widespread technique of calculating weight or importance of the term in the corpus of documents [9]. Based on that idea, the TF-IDF was adjusted to form n-gram terms. The TF-IDF concept is based on such terms like information entropy and expected mutual information [10] and can be denoted the following way [9]:

Let $D = \{d_1, .., d_m\}$ is a corpus of documents, $T = \{t_1, .., t_k\}$ is a corpus of terms contained in D. Then TF-IDF is a matrix $n \times m$, which is formed the following way:

$$TFIDF(t, d, D) = \frac{n(t_i)}{n(t|t \in d_j)} \times \log \frac{m}{|\{d_j \in D | t_i \in d_j\}|},$$

(1)

where $n(t_i)$ – the frequency of a term t_i in document d_j.

TF-IDF is generally used for the text classification in machine learning algorithms, as it transforms text into matrix. Also, TF-IDF calculates weights of the term in the current document among all corpus of documents; that property is frequently used for feature extraction [10]. In this work, TF-IDF is used to form n-grams (see Sect. 2.3).

4.2 Latent Semantic Analysis

Latent semantic analysis, or LSA is a method of the analysis dependencies between features [11]. The latent semantic analysis applied to texts gives a pack of words which behave similarly. Using these words, we get rid of unimportant features. In practice, LSA is based on matrixes operations from linear algebra, precisely, singular value decomposition, or SVD [11]. The main idea of SVD is detecting more informative rows and less informative ones. The concept of SVD can be denote the following way:

Let A be a real $m \times n$ matrix, where $m \geq n$. Then the following matrixes production is called singular value decomposition:

$$A = U \cdot \Sigma \cdot V^T, \qquad (2)$$

where U is a unitary m $\times$ m matrix; $\sum$ is a diagonal real non-negative m $\times$ n matrix; V is a unitary n $\times$ n matrix [12, 13].

LSA uses SVD in terms of reduce dimensions of text vectors. Moreover, it is considered that LSA shows the context similarity of key words. It makes LSA one of the text classification method.

Let we have an input D, which consist of n number of texts, d. Let L is a list of words, or n-grams, which are extracted from D, and the length of L is n. Then the matrix A in terms of LSA is a matrix of n text vectors with m dimensions, where each dimension equals an integer number of inputs of a word l in a document d. The word l is responsible for the row, and a document is responsible for a column. The m $\times$ m matrix U shows the dependency between words, or n-grams with each other, or in other words term-to-concept matrix. The n $\times$ n matrix V shows the document-to-concept dependency. Finally, the diagonal m $\times$ n matrix $\sum$ can be described as concept strengths appearing in descending order [14].

5   Natural Language Processing of Court Decisions

5.1   Open Government Data Collection

The resource of court decisions database of Russian government automated system was collected into three datasets:

- Civil cases (6,845,122 number of cases)
- Cases of administrative offenses (4,444,562 number of cases)
- Criminal cases (3,302,665 number of cases)

For this study, the dataset with administrative decisions was used. One of the most popular articles (13.5%) in administrative cases is article 19.3 (Disobedience to the legal order of the police officer, the Federal security service officer, the Federal state control officer in the field of migration of the Russian Federation).

5.2   Pipeline of Natural Language Processing of Court Decisions

Using the developed method it is possible to define common features of the analysis of the natural language. The majority of NLP method of the Linguistic-focus approach have next functional blocks [2, 3, 6, 7]:

- parsing;
- text segmentation;
- tokenization;
- classification;
- mapping;

As a result, the marked texts of court decisions are obtained with an understanding of what the essence of the administrative process is reflected in them. On the basis of marked texts it is possible to train machine learning models depending on what scale and relationships need to be analyzed or predicted.

5.3   Data Preprocessing

At the first step, the texts of court decisions were divided into introductory, motivational and result parts. The second step is to convert JSON format to Parquet to increase the speed of processing and reading date frames. Further, from the texts removed special characters, forms of words were brought to normal. Then n grams are formed using the following methods.

5.4   TF-IDF Matrix Result

The problem of forming n-grams was solved by using a concept of TF-IDF. It calculates weight of a term in a document for whole dataset. To create n-grams, the algorithm calculates TF-IDF for different pairs, triples, etc. of words based on sklearn library function TfidfVectorizer. Then, the most significant n-grams are filtered and used for the rest steps of the algorithm (Fig. 1).

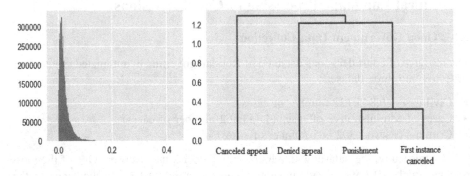

Fig. 1. TF-IDF results in the analysis of the texts of court decisions

As a result, a matrix of proximity of words in various court decisions has been developed. Documents from the appeal were analyzed separately from the first instance. Also analyzed separately the decision on the appointment and abolition of punishment.

5.5   Latent Semantic Analysis of Court Decisions

In the course of the study, we received confirmation that depending on the document in which the term is located, its weight may be different (Fig. 2).

	Administrative punishment	Termination of proceedings	Remain unchanged	Termination of proceedings
Police officer	164.0	116.0	89.0	126.0
Defiance of legal requirements	47.0	52.0	40.0	38.0
Official duty	51.0	52.0	37.0	45.0
Public order	42.0	30.0	40.0	43.0
Public order protection	44.0	30.0	32.0	36.0
Perfomance of duty	0.0	1.0	0.0	3.0
Impede execution	27.0	33.0	21.0	18.0
Draft of a protocol	29.0	39.0	39.0	24.0
Report	13.0	7.0	13.0	14.0
Foul language	15.0	7.0	12.0	13.0
Car	9.0	7.0	40.0	10.0
Patrol car	10.0	4.0	7.0	42.0
Explanation	10.0	8.0	13.0	18.0
Detention	16.0	6.0	13.0	13.0
Clarification	8.0	5.0	10.0	17.0
Subject to termination	0.0	36.0	0.0	22.0
Alcohol intoxication	22.0	4.0	4.0	6.0
Lack of evidence	0.0	21.0	2.0	17.0
Refuse medical examination	3.0	1.0	1.0	0.0
Technical means	1.0	15.0	2.0	9.0
Refuse	13.0	6.0	14.0	17.0
Take actions	0.0	8.0	0.0	0.0

(Term weight scale: 0, 40, 80, 120, 160)

Fig. 2. The most common terms and weight in the texts of court decisions about disobeying a police officer cases

Latent-semantic analysis of the category of decisions on the appointment of an administrative fine in General shows a lower frequency of the use of terms than in other categories of judicial acts: (1) decisions on the termination of proceedings (in the first instance); (2) decisions made in the order of revision of decisions of judges (second instance). This pattern shows that the court of first instance sets out in more detail the motivational part when it makes a decision to terminate the proceedings on an administrative offense, since in this case the court does not agree with the legal position of the official who previously drew up the protocol on an administrative offense in this case. The canceled cases of first instance also have a more detailed motivational part than the decisions of the courts of first instance on the appointment of administrative punishment, but the LSA shows that in this case the courts of second instance pay more attention to the verification of compliance with procedural requirements at the previous stages of the proceedings on administrative law (Table 1).

Table 1. Example of LSA fact classification table.

Fact	Class
Police officer	Factual circumstance
Defense of legal requirements	Factual circumstance
Official duties	Factual circumstance
Public order protection	Factual circumstance
Public safety	Factual circumstance
Performance of duty	Factual circumstance

(continued)

Table 1. (*continued*)

Fact	Class
Obstruction of performance	Factual circumstance
Order requirement	Factual circumstance
Make a report	Procedural fact
Report	Procedural fact
Foul language	Factual circumstance
Patrol car	Factual circumstance
Explanation	Procedural fact
Detention	Procedural fact
Explain	Procedural fact
Subject to termination	Procedural fact
Alcohol intoxication	Factual circumstance
Medical examination	Procedural fact

5.6   Indicators Facts Classification

To mark court decisions, a classification of entities (type of tokens) has been developed, which reflect legal processes. Entities in judicial acts in cases of administrative offenses may be classified as follows as shown in the example:

1. Parameters of the case (introductory part):
1.1. In the name of the Russian Federation
1.2. Type of act
1.3. Subject of administrative jurisdiction
1.3.1. Authority or organization
1.3.2. Judge or officer:
1.3.2.1. Position
1.3.2.2. Full Name
1.3.2.3. Status in progress
1.4. Address of the subject of administrative jurisdiction
1.5. Date of the act
1.6. Place of the act
1.7. Type of proceedings
1.8. Administrative Offense Act:
1.8.1. Name of the law:
1.8.1.1. Kind of law
1.8.1.2. Title of law
1.8.1.3. Date of adoption of the law
1.8.1.4. Law number
…

2. Participants in the case (introductory, descriptive, motivation and resolution parts)
2.1. The person in respect of which the proceedings are conducted in the case of an administrative offense

2.2. Victim
2.3. Legal representative of an individual
2.4. Legal representative of a legal entity
2.5. Defender
2.6. Representative
2.7. Commissioner under the President of the Russian Federation to protect the rights of entrepreneurs
2.8. Witness
2.9. Understood
2.10. Specialist
2.11. Expert
2.12. Translator
2.13. Prosecutor
2.14. The official authorized to make the Protocol on administrative offense
2.15. The official who made the decision in the case of an administrative offense
2.16. The head of the body that issued the decision in the case of an administrative offense
2.17. The official who sent the case of an administrative offense to the judge
3. The way to participate in the court:
3.1. Personal
3.2. Video conferencing
4. Procedural facts
…
5. The credentials of the officer
…
6. Factual circumstances of the case (descriptive and motivational parts)
6.1 Aggravating circumstances
6.2 Extenuating circumstances
…
7. Evidence (descriptive and reasoning part)
…
8. Sources of evidence (descriptive and motivational parts)
…
9. Laws
9.1 Federal laws
9.2 Local laws
…
10. Punishments
10.1 Administrative penalties (operative part)
10.1.1 Penalties
10.1.2 Suspension of activities
10.1.3 Arrests
…
11. The basis of the termination of the proceedings (the reasoning and the operative part)
…

Classification can be implemented in software in the form of ontology, the form of manuals, in the form of knowledge bases, web-services, depending on the task. The interface to the knowledge base must be defined by the infrastructure and the scale of the project. In our case, the shared data is stored in the Parquet files in the HDFS storage.

5.7 Mapping of Court Decision Text

As an example, the following is an excerpt of the marked text on administrative violation in accordance with the article 19.3:

«Примерно в <Time>20.00<\Time> Исламов <Fact>находился_возле<\Fact> и <Fact>оказал<\Fact> <Fact>неповиновение_законным_требованиям<\Fact> <Official>сотруднику_полиции<\Official> <Fact>остановиться<\Fact> и <Fact>пройти_в_патрульную_машину<Fact> для <Process>доставления</Process> в <Body>районный_суд</Body> для <Process>рассмотрения_дела</Process> об <Process>отмене</Process> условно-досрочного освобождения. Исламов свою <Fact>вину_признал</Fact>. Исламов совершил <Offence>административное_правонарушение<\Offence>, что подтверждаться <Evidence>материалами_дела<\Evidence> - <Evidence>рапортом<\Evidence> <Official>заместителя_начальника<\Official> <Body>ООУП_ПДН<\Body> <Body>отдела<\Body> <Body>МВД_России<\Body>, <Official>водителем-полицейский<\Official> <Body>отдела<\Body> <Body>МВД_Россия<\Body>. Исламов находился около <Fact>дома<\Fact>, <Fact>увидев<\Fact> <Official>сотрудников_полиции<\Official> <Fact>пытался_скрыться<\Fact>. Не <Fact>реагировал<\Fact> на <Fact>требование<\Fact> <Official>сотрудников_полиции</Official> <Fact>остановиться<\Fact>. В деле представлен <Evidence>протокол<\Evidence> <Process>административного_задержания<\Process> по <Offence>административному_правонарушению<\Offence>, <Evidence>справка<\Evidence> <Fact>нахождение<\Fact> Исламова в состоянии <Fact>алкогольного_опьянения<\Fact>, <Evidence>акт<\Evidence> <Process>медицинского_освидетельствования<\Process> о <Fact>нахождении<\Fact> Исламова в состояние <Fact>алкогольного_опьянения<\Fact>. Оценив <Evidence>совокупность_ доказательств<\Evidence> <Official>судья<\Official> квалифицировал <Fact>действие<\Fact> Исламова как <Offence>административное_правонарушение<\Offence>, <Law>предусмотренное_КоАП<\Law> <Fact>неповиновение_законному<\Fact> <Fact>требованию<\Fact> <Official>сотрудника_полиции</Official> <Fact>связанное_с_исполнением<\Fact> <Fact>обязанностей_по_охране<\Fact> <Fact>общественного_порядка<\Fact> по обеспечению <Fact>общественной_безопасности<\Fact>, а также <Fact>воспрепятствование_исполнению<\Fact> <Fact>служебных_обязанностей<\Fact>. В качестве <Fact>обстоятельств_смягчающих<\Fact> наказание является <Fact>признание_вины<\Fact>, а <Fact>обстоятельств_отягчающих<\Fact> наказание - <Fact>совершение_правонарушения<\Fact> в <Fact>состоянии_опьянения<\Fact>, <Fact>повторное_совершение<\Fact> <Offence>правонарушения<\Offence> в течении года. С учетом_изложенного <Official>судья<\Official> считает необходимым назначить административное наказание в виде <Punish-mentType>административного_ареста<\PunishmentType> <> <Law>руководство вуясь_КоАП<\Law>»

Thus, it was possible to identify in the text the circumstances of the case, the procedural circumstances in accordance with which the court decided.

6 ML Model of Disobeying of a Police Officer

On the basis of the mapped data of court decisions, a model of sentencing in the form of arrest or a fine for an offence under article 19.3 for disobeying police officers was developed. The task was to determine the circumstances affecting the severity of the punishment (Fig. 3).

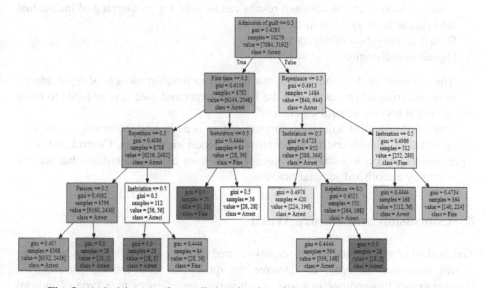

Fig. 3. A decision tree for predicting the size of the penalties under article 19.3

The decision tree was trained on the target "type of administrative punishment", showed significant results of 90% ROC curve. First of all, the tree has the right structure, in which a variable set of factual circumstances of the case (above) leads to variations in the appointment of the type of punishment (below). Secondly, the decision tree has the potential to expand by detailing the quantitative indicator of punishment (the size of the administrative fine, the term of administrative arrest). Third, the decision tree is successfully developed and interpreted on the basis of structured data obtained as a result of natural language processing of judicial acts texts. In General, this shows that the method of decision tree in combination with automated markup of texts of judicial acts has good prospects for the development of a decision support system and develop of predictive models.

7 The Applicability of the Results

As a result of the study, the solutions that can be used in the process of software development for:

1. Structuring and automatic markup of legal texts;
2. Analysis of the effectiveness of norms improvement of law-making and law enforcement;
3. Development of knowledge base of intellectual administrative-legal and criminal control systems;
4. Development of descriptive and predictive models of law enforcement and lawmaking.
   The methods of intellectual information technologies translation for the development of empirical bases of legal Sciences, which contributes to e-science, are obtained. Moreover, the obtained results can be used for prototyping of intellectual information legal systems in the field of:
5. Digital investigation (evidence);
6. Digital administration.

The obtained models and results can be used to develop models of legal administrative and criminal processes. On the basis of structured data it is possible to carry out oversight process control efficiency.

The development of a decision support system is necessary for its implementation in the activities of both courts and control and supervision bodies. Control and oversight officers need a tool that will prevent them from making decisions that are not supported by established judicial practice.

8 Conclusion and Future Work

The method of syntax analysis of semi-structured data in court decisions and mapping it was developed in order to improve the quality of data models for tasks of E-government. Proceedings in cases of administrative offences as a type of judicial process is traditionally considered to be a simplified version of judicial proceedings, which is based, in particular, on such principles as efficiency and economy. These principles are implemented, in particular, in the fact that the proof of the Commission of an administrative offense is quite simple and is based on the Protocol on administrative offense as the basic evidence produced by an objective and competent official.

Understanding the regularity of court decisions allows us to identify: judicial acts that have atypical content, which is a marker of deviation (for example, the motivation of a judicial act in violation of uniform judicial practice); the actual circumstances of the case, procedural facts and other entities that are in correlation with the results of the outcome of the case (administrative punishment, cancellation) or are in correlation with the type of the court decision in the appeal (refusal to satisfy the complaint, change of the decision, cancellation). The presence of indicators allows as to automate the generalization of judicial practice, configure predictive models and develop a system for support judicial decision-making.

Further research is possible in the direction of expanding the classification for criminal cases and for civil cases. It is also possible to detail the existing classification.

Acknowledgements. This research is financially supported by The Russian Science Foundation, Agreement #19-11-00326.

References

1. Friedman, C., Elhadad, N.: Natural language processing in health care and biomedicine. In: Shortliffe, E.H., Cimino, J.J. (eds.) Biomedical Informatics, pp. 255–284. Springer, London (2014). https://doi.org/10.1007/978-1-4471-4474-8_8
2. Doan, S., Conway, M., Phuong, T.M., Ohno-Machado, L.: Natural language processing in biomedicine: a unified system architecture overview. In: Trent, R. (ed.) Clinical Bioinformatics. Methods in Molecular Biology (Methods and Protocols), vol. 1168. Humana Press, New York (2014). https://doi.org/10.1007/978-1-4939-0847-9_16
3. Friedman, C., Rindflesch, T.C., Corn, M.: Natural language processing: state of the art and prospects for significant progress, a workshop sponsored by the National Library of Medicine. J. Biomed. Inform. **46**(5), 765–773 (2013)
4. Metsker, O., Trofimov, E., Sikorsky, S., Kovalchuk, S.: Text and data mining techniques in judgment open data analysis for administrative practice control. In: Chugunov, A., Misnikov, Y., Roshchin, E., Trutnev, D. (eds.) EGOSE 2018. CCIS, vol. 947, pp. 169–180. Springer, Cham (2019). https://doi.org/10.1007/978-3-030-13283-5_13
5. Kreimeyer, K., et al.: Natural language processing systems for capturing and standardizing unstructured clinical information: a systematic review. J. Biomed. Inform. **73**, 14–29 (2017)
6. Backus, J.W.: The syntax and semantics of the proposed international algebraic language of the Zurich ACM-GAMM conference. In: Proceedings of the International Conference on Information Processing, New York, pp. 125–131 (1959)
7. Aletras, N., et al.: Predicting judicial decisions of the European court of human rights: a natural language processing perspective. PeerJ Comput. Sci. **2**, e93 (2016). peerj.com
8. Stephan, W.: Linguistic description and automatic extraction of definitions from German court decisions. In: LREC (2008)
9. Aizawa, A.: An information-theoretic perspective of tf–idf measures. Inf. Process. Manage. **39**(1), 45–65 (2003)
10. Dey, A., Jenamani, M., Thakkar, J.J.: Lexical TF-IDF: an n-gram feature space for cross-domain classification of sentiment reviews. In: Shankar, B.U., Ghosh, K., Mandal, D.P., Ray, S.S., Zhang, D., Pal, S.K. (eds.) PReMI 2017. LNCS, vol. 10597, pp. 380–386. Springer, Cham (2017). https://doi.org/10.1007/978-3-319-69900-4_48
11. Sidorov, G., et al.: Syntactic N-grams as machine learning features for natural language processing. Expert Syst. Appl. **41**(3), 853–860 (2014)
12. Golub, G.H., Reinsch, C.: Singular value decomposition and least squares solutions. In: Bauer, F.L. (ed.) Linear Algebra. Handbook for Automatic Computation, vol. 2. Springer, Heidelberg (1971). https://doi.org/10.1007/978-3-662-39778-7_10
13. Shlens J.: A tutorial on principal component analysis: derivation, discussion and singular value decomposition. In: Derivation, Discussion and Singular Value Decomposition (2003)
14. Yalcinkaya, M., Singh, V.: Patterns and trends in building information modeling (BIM) research: a latent semantic analysis. Autom. Constr. **59**, 68–80 (2015)

Using of Automatically and Semi-automatically Generated Diagrams in Educational Practice

Evgeny Patarakin$^{(\boxtimes)}$ ⓘ and Vasiliy Burov

Moscow City University, Moscow, Russia
patarakined@mgpu.ru

Abstract. Maps and diagrams have long been used by science and education. The results and achievements of geography, astronomy, biology, economics have always been presented in the form of maps. Modern methods and tools of network science allow to deeper understand collaboration because relations between agents of activity are represented as a map. For many collaborative educational systems maps of relations between agents and activity products are built automatically. However, these diagrams are not used in educational practice as tools for better learning. The paper provides examples of how the diagrams were used in educational practice in order to support a group reflection of collaborative activities.

Keywords: Collaboration · Learning analytics · Visual storytelling · Sociograms

1 Introduction

We are increasingly able to work with complex social problems through methods and tools of network science. Network science views social systems as many heterogeneous actors who connected through different types of edges. To study these types of systems is used the set of analytic tools named Social Network Analysis [1]. Social network analysis is used in various spheres. This is especially successful in the field of team games that is close to collaborative learning [2–4]. However, tools of social network analysis are rarely used to support collaborative learning practices [5] and collaborative networking activities practices. This is due not so much to the lack of data or the lack of available visualization applications, but to the fact that the participants in network practices are perceived by the organizers of the practices not as a team, but as individual actors - students or users. In this work, we consider the various cases of network collaboration through the framework of the activities of a team consists of many players that interact working towards a common goal. The coach of this team can use simple methods of analytics based on the data on collaboration as well as on the methods of creating static graphs and dynamic models to understanding process of team collaboration and to increased team performance.

The source materials for the research include logs of computer activities.

We will understand complex systems only if we develop a deep understanding of the networks behind them [6]. A working definition of social network science is the study of network representations of social phenomena leading to predictive models of

© Springer Nature Switzerland AG 2020
A. Chugunov et al. (Eds.): EGOSE 2019, CCIS 1135, pp. 308–319, 2020.
https://doi.org/10.1007/978-3-030-39296-3_23

these phenomena [7]. Deep understanding of collaboration may begin with making maps of our social worlds [8]. A sociogram is a powerful analysis tool, helping us identify structural properties that otherwise would not be obvious in numeric data. Network science and sociograms methodology help us to analyze and discuss situations that develop during a network collaboration in different domains. Social Network Analysis uses various concepts to evaluate different sociograms properties like centrality, connectivity, cliques, etc. [9].

We can use data analytics to create a network of relationships, which develops as a result of collaborative actions. Today's world often sees digital literacy as collaboration skills used to create and reuse digital objects. Through the practice of making, we develop productive agency [10, 11] that encourages us to act, take control of our lives, and develop our own capabilities. Currently, there are many sites for diverse digital making for both adults and children. Modern learning environments are putting software in the hands of children to participate in different types of digital collaborative remixing. Scratch, Pencil Code, Alice, and many others are low-threshold programming environments that make it easier for novices to develop games and interactive stories that can easily be shared with others. In our opinion, the diversity of these practices can be seen as a team-based working that can be supported by team coaching. Network metrics can help a coach to obtain information about the team's process. For example, high density led to increased team performance. On the contrary centralized interaction led to decreased team performance.

2 Agent-Based Modeling of Collaboration

Team coaching augmented by network metrics involves introducing both the coach and the players to the basics of network science. Introducing students and teachers to the network science may begin with the study of maps [12]. For this purpose we can use the combination of agent-based modeling and network analysis [13]. Agent-based modeling permits the desired richness of behaviors and attributes that might bridge the gap between agent-nodes and the real world. As Epstein wrote in his trilogy [14–16] about generative social science, artificial society modeling allows us to grow social structures and demonstrate that certain sets of microspecifications are sufficient to generate the macrophenomena of interest. A famous example of simple actions that actors perform over objects of actions is Termites model [17]. To understand how we can benefit from collateral records we have modified the original text of Termites model by adding new variables and rules. We have inserted a variable called list WIKILOG where turtles make records of their actions [18]. Our next model was implemented in StarLogo Nova environment and its source code is available on the Internet https://www.slnova.org/patarakin/projects/691186/.

There are two breeds of agents in the artificial world of this model. The first breed is for actors or football players. These agents fulfill the following rule: If there is a ball nearby, then you need to turn in the direction of the ball and take a step forward. The second breed is for balls. These agents fulfill the following rule: If there is an actor within two steps, then write to the log-file ID of this agent and ID of yourself and move in the opposite direction from the agent. The procedures governing the ball are shown in the Fig. 1

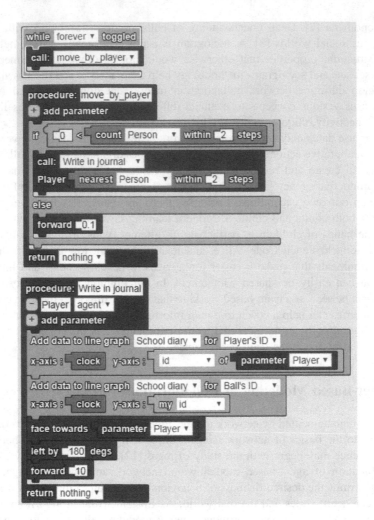

Fig. 1. The procedures governing the ball

Before launching the model, the user can select the number of players and the number of balls that will be used in the game. In this example, there were 300 players and 7 balls in the artificial community. After a few minutes of playing, the recordings were converted to a network diagram (Fig. 2). The edges connect the players and the balls they touched during the game. Even such a simple model allows you to receive different network structures, depending on how far the players see and how far the balls move.

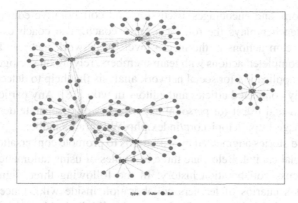

Fig. 2. Network of game players and balls

3 Automatically Generated Diagrams

Various forms of network collaboration may be reduced to a general scheme that allows to analyze and compare the participants' activities. Rephrasing Bruno Latour, we may state that with each editing, remixing and modification of digital objects, all students get an opportunity to improve the learning process. Every action of an agent towards an object leads to the formation of a link between them. If the agents perform action over one and the same object, they become agents of the collaborative activity, indirectly linked with one another by the mutual object of activity.

There is a variety of software tools that have been developed to support the analysis of network structures. In our work, we have chosen a tool that allows us to easily identify the stable patterns in the field of collaborative work, as well as to track and analyze the dynamics of sociograms, to select the participants among stable patterns for their targeted management. Our learning analytics application is based on the R language and Graphviz open source graph visualization software.

4 Three Vignettes with Automatically and Semi-automatically Generated Diagrams

In this section, we consider various situations of collaborative network activities as team activities.

4.1 Wikigrams

Inside the wiki, there are special category tags with which users mark pages with similar topics. Categories are often used to organize collaborative activities. Users working on pages with similar topics form a team. The goal of the team's work on the educational wiki project is to create a collective hypertext consisting of many inter-connected pages. As a rule, the denser the network of participants' interactions, the better the work will be done. The teacher who organizes the work on the project, in every way supports and encourages discussion and collaborative editing of pages. In this sense, the teacher plays the role of a team coach. The coach can evaluate the effectiveness of team actions at the macro level by network metrics. The coach can discuss already completed actions with team members, relying on sociograms. We have created a simple application for social network analysis that help to detect and visualize cliques of densely connected articles and editors in wiki [18]. Any participant can take graphs initial text and use it for personal experiments on a separate designated Wikigram Sandbox page http://letopisi.org/index.php/WikigramSandbox.

We have used stories augmented by wikigrams to promote conversation about social structure and social capital. Below are three examples of using automatically generated diagrams to discuss collaboration history. In the following three vignettes, we will discuss different scenarios of learners collaboration inside wiki. Once, one teacher, acting on a wiki under a nickname "Professor Pchyolkin", decided to write a collective fairy tale with his students. He prepared the pages for possible heroes of this tale and tagged these pages with a general category tag. Then the teacher invited students to work on a common fairy tale. As a rule, an individual student worked on a separate page under the supervision of the teacher. There were only 3 cases when the students independently invented their own characters and worked on the pages of these characters on their own. As a result of such an organization of activity, a relationship map was formed - a proto-narrative describing cases of centralized control (Fig. 3). For all such cases, it is obvious that without a key player, nothing on the playing field would have happened, and there are almost no connecting elements between the participants.

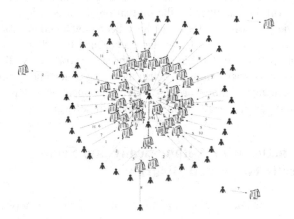

Fig. 3. Different families of novice programming environments.

The second time, Professor Pchyolkin decided to collect descriptions of important things that a person must do before he turns 14 years old. The professor created a template for describing these cases and several pages with examples. After that, the Professor only observed how the activity developed on the field designated by him. New unexpected growth points of new unrelated practices began to appear on the map. For example, at the top of the map were practices related to younger students, and at the bottom of the map were environmental practices (Fig. 4).

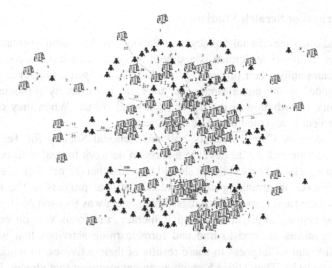

Fig. 4. Diagram of the category "100things"

For the third time, Professor Pchyolkin created a page and a MakeR category and invited participants to collect materials related to makers' activities in this category - recipes for creating toys, tips on working with pieces of fabric. This time, the Professor acted as a metadesigner and did not seek to be at the forefront. He invited not only students, but also his colleagues to participate in a network project. As a result of such an organization of activity, a map is formed, the center of which is not the key player - the organizer, but the main connecting object of activity. In addition, we see several such objects, around which teams of participants are united. Of particular interest is the figure of the participant on the left side of the screen. This player's enthusiasm for editing pages is indicated by the thickness of the edit arrows—he edited his pages 88 and 129 times (Fig. 5).

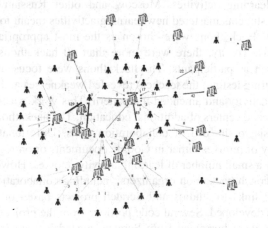

Fig. 5. Diagram of the category "MakeR"

4.2   Sociograms of Scratch Studious

Today's world often sees digital literacy as collaboration skills used to create and remix digital objects. To remix at Scratch is a simple process. Scratch has a community site where users can publish their projects. When Scratchers open a project at the website and "look inside" at the underlying code, they are immediately presented with the option to remix via a button in the upper right-hand corner. When they click on the button, the project is reposted at the site as a remix.

In 2018, Moscow City University and the National Society for Technology in Education joined their efforts to develop a Russian network to deal with new learning activities shaping 21st-century skills. It should be noted that the network organizers had years of experience in arranging social and educational projects at the interface of educational policies and learning activities. This project was focused on digital literacy of all the 21st-century skills, and in digital literacy, the focus was on collaboration skills. The organizers decided to find and form learning activities that would shape students' ability and willingness to share results of their activities, to work as a team, and to distribute tasks. They chose Scratch as an environment that already had tools to arrange and monitor such activities. It should be noted that the Scratch environment affected the strategy of collecting project guidance materials, which were shaped like Scratch projects. The project brought together Scratch hackathons and schoolchildren's Collaborative Challenge competitions. Hackathons and competitions use templates—prototypes of learning activity scripts. The first educational script is a description of learning activity, which includes a sequence of actions. Each act is described as an answer to the How to… question. There were a number of such initial author's learning activity scripts. All of them were posted on Letopisi.org in the ScratchHackathon section. The scripts were described and the list of links to the scripts was posted in the summary entry at http://letopisi.org/index.php/Scratch/HowTo/Hackathon.

At the third stage, the teachers being organizers of school workshops and hackathons were given ready-made guidance materials in the form of a document and a collection of wiki articles. When the teachers arranged school and extracurricular activities, a lot of them additionally tested proposed training scripts and created their own remixes of learning activities. Moscow and other Russian cities welcomed hackathons, where students mastered new learning activities meant to develop network collaboration skills. Hackathons were chosen as the most appropriate format to find innovative solutions. Totally, there were more than 90 hackathons with more than 4,000 schoolchildren as participants. The hackathons were focused on collaboration skills and tools. During testing, the teachers revealed weaknesses and uncertainties in a proposed learning activity and amended the pattern. This work was conducted mostly on-site—in schools and centers of additional education. The hackathons and workshops gave most emphasis to the use of collaboration tools. Unfortunately, the teachers created the majority of remixes either in Google documents or on regional wiki pages. We could find only a small number of learning activity remixes. However, there were a lot of reports of Scratch-hackathon organizers, including collaboration stories, photos of participants and links to studios and Scratch projects based on learning activity scripts the teachers developed. Several code portions from the projects teachers created to hold hackathons were borrowed from Scratch, posted in wiki as visual code and included in a general collection of learning activity guiding materials. During the hackathons and workshops, the schoolchildren switch to their own learning activity, which takes some elements from an educational script and tests it for real. 339 teams of participants managed to finish the work and implement the entire learning activity sequence. The teachers that prompted collaboration between the teams rated the proportion of teams that managed to finish the work and submit it to competition to the total number of participants at appr. 60%. Basically, the losses were due to teamwork complexity, the participants found it difficult to come to terms, to divide their roles and responsibilities. At the final stage, the jury members assessed not only the final project, but also studio materials, remix trees, i.e. to what extent team members' activities complied with the developed learning activity script. The learning activities that helped the students to get the best competition results were discussed with the teachers who arranged them. It is interesting that the organizers focused on various aspects of collaboration tools. For example, the organizers of the winners' works in the senior age category from Pskov gave the highest priority to the remix tree tool. All high school students from Pskov used remixes in their works and tracked partners' activities via remix tree.

Scratch studio brings users together in a team. The team strives to create a common project consisting of a series of remixes. The denser the connections between the studio participants, the better they will do the joint work. The contest organizers play the role of team coaches and they encourage the creation of remixes and discussion of individual projects. The project organizer, in the role of a trainer, can discuss collaborative activities using sociograms.

Since all productive networking systems have common principles, we assume that a similar apparatus may be used for building sociograms based on an analysis of the actions performed by the Scratch community members (scratchers) within studios built for their collaboration. For experiment purposes, we have gathered data on member activities in a number of Scratch studios and generated collaboration sociograms based on the data. An example of such sociograms is shown in Fig. 6.

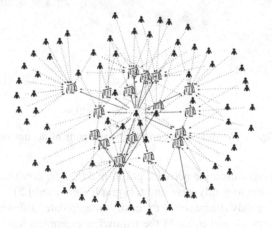

Fig. 6. Sociogram of a Scratch studio

4.3   Sociograms of Crowdsourcing Activities

Preobra.ru - collaborative environment for improvement educational policies [19]. In the Preobra.ru teachers perform the following actions with parts of document: Writing, Voting, Commenting, Answering. The team of participants has the goal of making the document more understandable, simple and interconnected. The greater the density of interaction between the participants, the better they will represent the activities in various parts of the document, the more effectively they will fulfill the task. Moderators of discussion of each educational policy encourage and support the interaction of participants. One of the tools that support such activities may be sociogram. In the final revision of the latest federal educational standards in 2019, 5563 participants took part. The activity of the participants was divided into sections of the document as follows (Fig. 7)

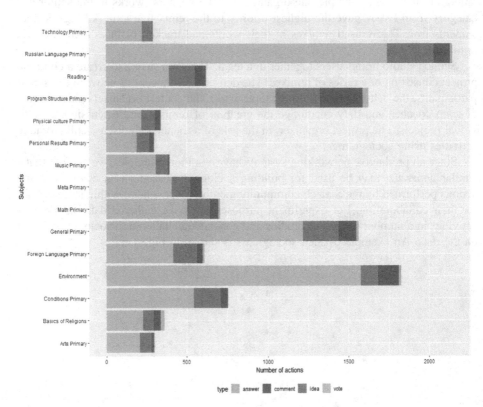

Fig. 7. Numbers of action in different parts of documents

The same data were used for network graph making. To construct sociograms, the language R and its libraries tidyverse and tidygraph were used [20, 21]. The tidygraph package provides a tidy framework to easily manipulate different types of data, including graph, network and trees. In the following example visibility of nodes were changed according to their values of centrality. One of the famous type of scores that determine centrality is the pagerank algorithm.

```
routes_tidy %>%
    activate(edges) %>%
    filter(type ! = "vote") %>%
    activate(nodes) %>%
    filter(!node_is_isolated()) %>%
    mutate(centrality = centrality_pagerank()) %>%
    filter(centrality > 0.0005) %>%
    ggraph(layout = "fr") +
    scale_shape_manual(values = c(16))+
    geom_node_point(aes(colour = type), size = 4) +
    geom_edge_link(aes(), colour = 'grey', alpha = 0.8) +
    scale_edge_width(range = c(0.1, 1)) +
    geom_node_text(aes(filter = (centrality > 0.002), label = NodeID)) +
    ggforce::theme_no_axes() +
    theme(legend.position = "bottom")
```

There are 3739 nodes and 12345 edges in the network. For diagram on the screen we have filtered edges and nodes several times. The final result is shown in the Fig. 8.

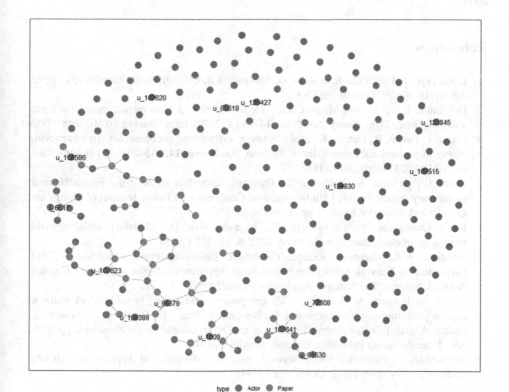

Fig. 8. Sociogram of Preobra (sector of primary education)

5 Discussion

Modern methods and tools of network science allow to deeper understand collaboration because relations between agents of activity are represented as a map. For many collaborative educational systems maps of relations between agents and activity products are built automatically. However, these diagrams are not used in educational practice. We believe that social reflection can be triggered by sociograms. Visual storytelling augmented with sociograms does not result in immediate changes in users' behavior. However, we observe that the participants begin to compare the social structure of the various projects and discuss them on the basis of sociograms. As a rule, they do not operate with network concepts of centrality and connectivity but easily master the terms of key players and groups derived from these concepts. Therefore, power of data visualization helps them to understand the structure of collective activity.

6 Conclusion

The results presented in this paper can be used to form network literacy, which is part of modern computational thinking. For modern students, working in collaborative teams, the ability to read sociograms is as important as the ability to read and write texts.

References

1. Luke, D.A.: A User's Guide to Network Analysis in R. UR. Springer, Cham (2015). https://doi.org/10.1007/978-3-319-23883-8
2. DeChurch, L.A., Mesmer-Magnus, J.R.: Measuring shared team mental models: a meta-analysis. Group Dyn. Theory Res. Pract. 14, 1–14 (2010). https://doi.org/10.1037/a0017455
3. Gama, J., Passos, P., Davids, K., et al.: Network analysis and intra-team activity in attacking phases of professional football. Int. J. Perform. Anal. Sport 14, 692–708 (2014). https://doi.org/10.1080/24748668.2014.11868752
4. Kröckel, P., Piazza, A., Neuhofer, K.: Dynamic network analysis of the Euro2016 final: preliminary results. In: 2017 5th International Conference on Future Internet of Things and Cloud Workshops (FiCloudW), pp. 114–119 (2017)
5. Huerta-Quintanilla, R., Canto-Lugo, E., Viga-de Alva, D.: Modeling social network topologies in elementary schools. PLoS ONE 8, e55371 (2013)
6. Barabási, A.-L.: Network Science. Cambridge University Press, Cambridge (2016). Committee on Network Science for Future Army Applications, National Research Council: Network Science. The National Academies Press (2005)
7. Mehra, A., Borgatti, A., Soltis, S., et al.: Imaginary worlds: using visual network scales to capture perceptions of social networks. In: Borgatti, S., Brass, D., Halgin, D., Labianca, G., Mehra, A. (eds.) Contemporary Perspectives on Organizational Social Networks, pp. 315–336. Emerald Group Publishing Limited, Bingley (2014)
8. Wasserman, S., Faust, K.: Social Network Analysis: Methods and Applications, 1st edn. Cambridge University Press, Cambridge (1994)

9. Schwartz, D.L.: The productive agency that drives collaborative learning. In: Dillenbourg, P. (ed.) Collaborative Learning: Cognitive and Computational Approaches, pp. 197–218. Elsevier Science/Permagon (1999)
10. Schwartz, D.L., Lin, X.: Computers, productive agency, and the effort after shared meaning. J. Comput. High Educ. **12**, 3–33 (2001). https://doi.org/10.1007/BF02940954
11. Börner, K., Palmer, F., Davis, J.M., et al.: Teaching children the structure of science. In: IS&T/SPIE Electronic Imaging, p. 724307. International Society for Optics and Photonics (2009)
12. Fontana, M., Terna, P.: From Agent-based models to network analysis (and return): the policy-making perspective. University of Turin (2015)
13. Epstein, J.M., Axtell, R.: Growing Artificial Societies: Social Science from the Bottom Up. The Brookings Institution, Washington, DC, USA (1996)
14. Epstein, J.M.: Generative Social Science: Studies in Agent-Based Computational Modeling. Princeton University Press, Princeton (2007)
15. Epstein, J.M.: Agent_Zero: Toward Neurocognitive Foundations for Generative Social Science. Princeton University Press, Princeton (2014)
16. Resnick, M.: Turtles, Termites, and Traffic Jams: Explorations in Massively Parallel Microworlds. MIT Press, Cambridge (1997)
17. Patarakin, E.D.: Wikigrams-based social inquiry. In: Levin, I., Tsybulsky, D. (eds.) Digital Tools and Solutions for Inquiry-Based STEM Learning, pp. 112–138. IGI Global, Hershey (2017)
18. Burov, V., Patarakin, E., Yarmakhov, B.: A crowdsourcing model for public consultations on draft laws. In: Proceedings of the 6th International Conference on Theory and Practice of Electronic Governance, pp. 450–451. ACM, New York (2012)
19. Wickham, H., Grolemund, G.: R for Data Science: Import, Tidy, Transform, Visualize, and Model Data. O'Reilly Media Inc., Sebastopol (2016)
20. Tyner, S., Briatte, F., Hofmann, H.: Network visualization with ggplot2. R J. **9**, 27 (2017)

Designing Effective Chatbot Solutions
for the Public Sector: A Case Study
from Ukraine

Yulia Petriv, Regina Erlenheim, Valentyna Tsap$^{(\boxtimes)}$, Ingrid Pappel,
and Dirk Draheim

Information Systems Group, Tallinn University of Technology,
Akadeemia tee 15A, 12619 Tallinn, Estonia
{yulia.petriv, regina.erlenheim, valentyna.tsap,
ingrid.pappel, dirk.draheim}@taltech.ee

Abstract. The goal of this paper is to identify the concerns of various stake-holders as well as limitations and enablers that affect the design of chatbots in the public sector. We are looking into a case from Ukraine, the LvivCityHelper bot solution, and describe the surrounding conditions and factors that determine the chatbot performance. The outcomes of the study are based on a comprehensive analysis of the state of the art and twelve interviews with experts who are involved in the LvivCityHelper bot project. The derived data is then exhibited as an exhaustive interpretation of stakeholders' concerns on various aspects of chatbot application in public e-services. The key findings from the interviews are compared with existing work, and inclusive and exclusive crucial factors in effective chatbot services are defined. Finally, we provide suggestions and rec-ommendations on how to fill the detected gaps that may improve the design, implementation and functioning of chatbot solutions that serve citizens' needs.

Keywords: Chatbot · E-services · Service design · Participation

1 Introduction

Democratic societies are shaped by interactions between citizens and governments. Traditionally, the role of citizens has been quite passive, and citizen's primary activity was mainly limited to participation in elections. In recent years, however, modern democracies have started to recognize the importance of active engagement of citizens in decision-making processes. Enhanced civic engagement relies on information and collaboration, therefore, governments should aim to ensure that citizens are enabled with means to enhance their participation [16]. Two-way communication is equally important in public service design. Engaging citizens in co-production of public ser-vices helps to achieve effectiveness and build citizen satisfaction by increasing trust and developing a sense of "ownership" of the provided services [21].

In the Ukrainian society, the lack of an effective two-way communication between government and citizens leads to growing mistrust and dissatisfaction. Public author-ities tend to operate in organizational silos, and slowly respond to the needs of citizens

© Springer Nature Switzerland AG 2020
A. Chugunov et al. (Eds.): EGOSE 2019, CCIS 1135, pp. 320–335, 2020.
https://doi.org/10.1007/978-3-030-39296-3_24

with regards to openness and transparency. Negative experiences of citizens and businesses in Ukraine with the government as a service provider may shape a negative opinion on its credibility and capability to deliver quality public services [14]. To prevent this, we suggest that the Ukrainian government should look into the adoption of new tools to inform and engage citizens in decision-making processes, including those related to public service design.

One possible solution to enhance communication between citizens and government is to use chatbots as an additional channel of communication. Chatbots are conversational agents that are designed to simulate a human-like conversation with a user on a certain domain or topic using natural language [34]. Chatbots became a popular communication tool in the public sector due to the development of natural language processing (NLP) that improved the quality of conversations, rise in use of messaging applications and also due to a growing demand for a better customer service [17].

Chatbots have many potential benefits for governments, as they allow for better service discovery and information and save manpower expenses by delivering service 24/7 [9]. Chatbots also encourage public participation by collecting feedback from citizens. This feedback can be later used for decision-making purposes as evidence of citizen's needs. Chatbots allow to fully utilize the potential of open data. Citizens will be encouraged to utilize chatbot as a tool to extract particular knowledge from open data and react to it in a form of feedback.

At the same time, public authorities have to understand that chatbots are designed to cater to the needs of a specific group of people in a specific organization [34]. This means that when designing a chatbot for public service one needs to prioritize stakeholders and their needs over the technology.

The LvivCityHelper bot solutions serves as a unique case worth investigating. Current developments in Ukraine create a setting where implementation of such innovation is influenced by a combination of political, economic, technological and societal factors. Morever, due to the relative novelty of chatbot solutions in public sector, especially in Ukraine, it is a notable opportunity of learn lessons from one of the country pioneer projects applying this technology.

Therefore, within this research, we aim to determine what the concerns of stakeholders are as well as what the major limitations in and enablers of the chatbot development in public sector are. We will also distinguish the most significant factors affecting chatbot design. Moreover, having provided the outcomes of our analysis, we will suggest our vision on the future of these solutions.

In Sect. 2, we delve into the state of the art. In Sect. 3 we explain our research methodology. In Sect. 4, we describe the case of the LvivCityHelper chatbot solution. In Sect. 5, we present our analysis of the interview outcomes. We proceed with a discussion of the main results in Sect. 6 and finish with a conclusion in Sect. 7.

2   State of the Art

This section provides an overview of the state of the art in the field of chatbot solutions application in public sector.

Recent advancements in Artificial Intelligence and Machine Learning and increased digital presence of governmental institutions introduce new possibilities to use of chatbots in public sector. In [15], five use cases of chatbots in public sector were identified: answering requests (e.g. responding to frequently asked questions), filling out and searching documents (e.g. filling out petitions and appeals), routing requests (e.g. classifying request and forwarding person to right office), translation (e.g. real-time translation of public information) and drafting documents (e.g. using Natural Language Generation AI to draft documents based on data).

Adroutsopoulou et al. suggested that advanced intelligent chatbots powered by natural language processing, machine learning and data mining technologies should be used as a "new "richer" and more intelligent digital channel of communication between citizens and government" [2].

Implementation of chatbots in public sector faces a number of challenges, stemming from nature of public sector and from technology itself [6]. The first challenge is that public service is restricted by existing legislation when it comes to regulating the status of public employees. The automation brought by AI-powered chatbot may lead to restructuring or eliminating some processed that are usually executed by certain categories of officials - this means that officials themselves may potentially become reluctant to support this technology. Legislation also affects availability of data. Public sector is limited by privacy legislation in its work, and often cannot use data from private sources [7]. This limits the possibilities of chatbot development. Another issue is accountability. Data analysis can serve as a basis of evidence-based decision making in public field. This may cause an effect in political processes on different levels. Therefore, political will (or rather unwillingness) of public sector officials may appear as an obstacle. The last challenge is equal service provision. This requires the chatbot design to take into account factors like (a) digital divide (b) interests and needs of various categories of citizens (c) neutrality of developers of AI systems to prevent bias [7].

The technological factors affecting introduction of chatbots are predominantly related to data quality, management, availability and intake [7]. Relevant data needs to be available at all times, effectively structured, integrated and updated. Updates are essential due to technological advancements and changing platform-specific requirements (e.g. changes in privacy and data protection policies). This also applies to IT infrastructure being updated [7]. Digital divide also affects the adoption of chatbots, as lack of technical skills, lack of access to high-speed internet connection and smartphones will chatbot acceptance, particularly, in the field of finance or those that deal with sharing their personal information, as research suggests [19, 33].

2.1 Factors Affecting the Introduction of Chatbots in the Public Sector in Ukraine

Legislation on Public Service and e-Service Development. In an effort to improve state of public service provision, Ukrainian government defined priority services to be digitized listed in the Decree on adoption of Concept of development of system of electronic services in Ukraine [8]. The Concept includes a three-stage implementation process aiming to develop an effective system of electronic services in Ukraine to satisfy the interests of physical persons and legal entities though development and support of transparent, accessible, secure, anti-corruption, least expensive, fast and convenient electronic services [8]. Neither this Concept nor other Ukrainian legislation mention notion of proactive or invisible services - services initiated by the state itself rather than by the citizen. Government also does not have any set guidelines on online communication and digital presence. This means that although various institutions might be represented in social media (usually Facebook and Twitter), they are not seen as official channels and are not obliged to follow unified rules on information provision for citizens.

The Law on Electronic Trust Services in Ukraine provides a simplified definition of electronic service or e-service as any service provided through information communication system. This definition includes any administrative or other public services provided to physical persons or legal entities in digital form. This means that e-services in Ukraine are often focused on service delivery, not taking into account service mediation - that is, there is a larger focus to achieve the overall goal of providing a service rather than improve the quality of technology that allows to mediate this service. Additionally, although the number of public e-services in Ukraine is constantly growing in recent years, these services largely rely on existing outdated business processes and paper-based interactions. This means that despite the efforts new e-services will continue to carry administrative burden and be subject to corruption [29].

Ukraine also lacks legislation with regards to public digital registers as the draft of respective law is still being under parliamentary review [32]. This creates an obstacle for effective use of state data and for designing integrated e-services based on them [30]. Lack of interoperability between registries negatively affects quality of data that chatbot uses to respond to citizens. In addition, lack of policy with regards to communication of public authorities with citizens using digital channels, means that public authorities might be discouraged from integrating chatbots to their official social media accounts.

A unified state portal of administrative services in Ukraine that provides a list of services available for citizens and businesses. At the same time still remains limited, and majority of these services only provide information about the service rather than allow user of this service to digitally identify itself in order to receive service fully online. This is due to the fact that majority of e-services in Ukraine still remain at first or second level according to the maturity model defined in the Concept mentioned above [29].

With regards to introduction of chatbots in public sector in Ukraine, legislative barriers will serve as limitations to integration of chatbots since many services are not digitized. An improved legislation and sharing the best practices with regards to policy on e-services between various countries and organizations could increase trust in technology and serve as a prerequisite for wider adoption of new technology, like chatbots, in public sector [4].

Social and Cultural Barriers. Culture shapes perception of desirability and value of services due to its influence on citizen's attitude towards others and society [13]. Based on Hofstede's approach, Ukraine remains a centralized country, in which there is an acceptance of unequal distribution of power [10]. This means that organizations tend to follow a strict hierarchy, and political willingness will be one of the key factors to affect development and implementation of new technology like chatbots. As members of a feminine society, Ukrainians tend to stand out less from the crowd and highly value caring for others. Therefore, new e-services are often evaluated on a basis of their value to a society as a whole, rather than on their profitability [13]. An example of such value-centricity over profitability is that Ukrainian government has prioritized many social services as the first services to be digitized in the Concept of development of system of electronic services in Ukraine mentioned before [8]. Therefore, authors presume that chatbot value in public sector may also be evaluated against its societal value. Tendency to avoid uncertainty affects development of public e-services in Ukraine due to high reliance on detailed planning [10]. Business processes in public organizations tend to be restrained by regulations, as it was already mentioned before. Lack of flexibility may negatively affect service design process of chatbot that relies on iteration, co-production and user-centricity. As a collectivist society, Ukrainians rely on relationships when obtaining information or engaging negotiations. This follows that public authorities in Ukraine must establish a trustful and authentic communication style to motivate citizens to use new technology like chatbot (Ibid.).

Lack of trust to public authority is also among factors that negatively affect e-participation process [20]. In Ukraine, state institutions have the lowest level of trust among other institutions (−63% in 2018), which negatively affects perception of trustworthiness of chatbot as a service [12]. A survey about attitudes of Ukrainians to e-services has shown that 79,3% of respondents do not know about existence of public e-services, and only 29% of respondents trust e-services, whereas majority (64%) remains skeptical about their use [31]. This means that chatbots in public sector in Ukraine may not be considered trustworthy by citizens, which would negatively affect their use and development.

Technology and Infrastructure Barriers. Technological advancements affect public sector and urge them to adapt to respond to the needs of citizens. Ukraine remains behind European countries when it comes to digital skills. For example, according to Google Consumer Barometer survey (2018), only 66% of Ukrainians had access to Internet (48% of which daily), whereas in Estonia this number is 82% and 72% respectively. At the same time, the data is not true for all categories of Ukrainians. Among younger generation (under 25), 98% have Internet access, and 89% access Internet daily.

Development of e-government services in Ukraine faces a number of technical and infrastructural obstacles according to expert survey conducted by [5]. The experts noted insufficient financing, lack of IT qualifications among public employees, inconsistency in information systems and low computer literacy of citizens among the problems among the negative factors. Additionally, organizational silos and lack of interoperability as well as outdated data infrastructure has been marked as the most common barriers with regards to adoption of new e-services.

Chatbot development and use in public sector is largely affected by technical infrastructure in place and digital skills of both citizens and public officials [18]. Familiarity with the technology affects trust and encourages use [1]. Ukrainian government must invest in both technical infrastructure (to ensure availability of fast-speed Internet in certain areas, availability of computers and other technology in public libraries and recreational areas that can be accessed by citizens) and digital skills training (to ensure that citizens and public officials know how to use technology) to increase quality of e-services and ensure trust among various groups of citizens [5].

2.2 Application of Chatbots in Ukraine

Despite those factors negatively affecting the development of e-services in Ukraine, there have been a few examples of successful introduction of chatbots in public sector. The most famous example is Opendatabot that currently has over 300 000 users (as of December 2018), with 40 000 daily requests in chatbots [24]. Opendatabot uses open data to monitor changes in registry of Ukrainian companies and changes in judicial registry. It is available on four platforms: Skype, Telegram, Facebook Messenger and Viber, and offers free and paid accounts options with different level of access to various services. The founder of Opendatabot has stressed on the importance of collaboration with government with regards to open data: "Public authorities do not publish data on time, this data is often unstructured, is in a wrong format, etc. We all have to collaborate with state at all times" [11]. Opendatabot provides an example of successful implementation of chatbot that uses open data due to its popularity among people. The author believes that popularity of service is closely linked to overall desire for increased transparency and openness of government in Ukraine, and convenience of chatbot due to its availability on many messaging platforms has encouraged many citizens to use chatbot as the preferred tool to access open data.

Another popular chatbot in Ukraine is RailwayBot that allows users to monitor tickets, check schedule and even purchase tickets of national railway transportation company - Ukrzaliznytsia (Укрзалізниця). The chatbot is available on Facebook Messenger and Telegram. At the moment, RailwayBot team received investment from Ukrzaliznytsia to integrate chatbot with other services and improve its functionality. The author believes that popularity of RailwayBot is attributed to its convenience as compared to the official website of Ukrzaliznytsia. The chatbot allows monitoring of tickets, which eliminates the need to manually check if the new tickets have appeared in the system [28].

We believe that successful examples of chatbot implementation in public sector in Ukraine serve as a precedent for a wider use of chatbots. Citizens perceive chatbots as a convenient tool to interact with government or state-owned enterprise. It can be also assumed, that despite the limitations described in the previous chapters, citizens are encouraged to use chatbots as they seem to better address their needs.

3   Methodology

We use a single case-study method to conduct research. 12 semi-structured interviews were conducted. We have selected interviewees with a variety of backgrounds in order to achieve depth and comprehensiveness of outcomes to address our research objectives. Such backgrounds included public sector representatives (both public officials and NGO members directly cooperating with public authorities), members of the LvivCityHelper bot team, and private sector representatives. The interviews took place in March 2019. All interviews were conducted face-to-face. The language of interviews was Ukrainian, except one that was conducted in Russian. Interviews were recorded and later transcribed into text and translated into English prior to further analysis. Interviewees were provided with the copy of transcripts in order to correct, clarify or expand particular answers, and thus ensure the validity of the study [26]. Section 5 will provide more details on the positions of interviewed experts.

The interviews were first analyzed using quasi-statistical approaches. Quasi-statistical methods are similar to quantitative methods and help identify macro topics. These methods have been used to analyze stakeholder's concerns [25]. According to Runeson and Höst (2009), editing approaches "include few a priori codes, i.e. codes are defined based on findings of the researcher during the analysis" [27]. These approaches allowed to look into detail of the biggest concerns of stakeholders as they help to understand them semantically. This analysis reflected on important remarks according to each stakeholder's group.

Interviews were analyzed using Nvivo 12. This allowed organizing interviewees' responses for better comparison and categorization in thematic analysis) [3]. Simultaneously, the limitations of the software product still required a manual data interpretation to better understand patterns in interviewees' responses.

4   The Case of LvivCityHelper Bot

This section provides an overview of the case study of LvivCityHelper bot with an emphasis on formulating main problems the project faced during its introduction and current development. The case study was chosen because chatbot is a relatively new service and current scientific literature mostly focuses on technical side of the technology. There is a need for a comprehensive research on practical cases, particularly with regards to the application of chatbots in the field of public sector.

4.1   Overview of the Project

In 2018, a second Open Data Challenge organized as a part of USAID/UK project "Transparency and Accountability in Public Administration and Services" with support from State Agency for E-government in Ukraine and in partnership with Eastern Europe Fund and 1991 Open Data Incubator.

20 projects were selected as finalists to participate in a 2-months accelerator program [23]. Among the winners was LvivCityHelper bot - a fast and easy-to-understand solution to obtain publicly available data of the city of Lviv.

The project team declared the mission of LvivCityHelper as "making finding information from Lviv City Council just as fast and easy, as it would be from a colleague or a friend" [22].

The project was presented to the general public and became available for testing on September 12, 2018 [36]. Initially, the chatbot was only available in Telegram, but, as of February 2019, the chatbot is also available for Facebook users [36].

At the moment, LvivCityHelper bot project team consists of 3–5 full-time employees (some developers are engaged in the project on part-time basis) of Lviv Communal Enterprise "Center of Information Technology" of the City. LCE CCIT is also responsible for Lviv Open Data Portal that contains information from different departments and offices of Lviv City Council and other institutions of Lviv in an open data format. Altogether LCE CCIT collaborates with 105 data owners and categorizes data into 18 different groups, from budget to healthcare [35]. Chatbot uses data from Open Data Portal to answer citizen's requests, and some of the chatbot team members are also actively engaged in work of Open Data Portal. As a communal enterprise, LCE CCIT has established communication with data owners that provide data to Open Data Portal; this ensures the availability and the quality of data that is used by chatbot.

In an interview of the project team to 1991 Open Data Incubator, the team explained the motivation behind the project being the lack of understanding how to use Open Data Portal by the general public. The team saw their main task in "designing a convenient way to obtain answers to urgent typical questions".

LvivCityHelper bot's goal is to enable convenient use of open data by Lviv residents and visitors. Currently, four main categories are available according to the official page of LvivCityHelper bot on Facebook and official Telegram channel @LvivCityHelper bot:

a. Infrastructure and its improvement:

- arrival time of public transportation;
- transport schedule for various types of transport based on route number;
- repairs of roads and pavements, educational establishments, playgrounds, buildings and networks based on the street name;
- maintenance of houses based on a street name and a house number.

b. Education:

- contact information of kindergartens, schools, and out-of-school establishments based on name of educational establishment;
- information about acceptance to first grade of secondary school based on residence.

c. Permissions. This category allows users to check information from register of conditions and limitations on construction in the city and to check permits for summer terraces based on address. It also provides link to Lviv City hotline Facebook page and to Lviv City Council official website with a form to file an electronic appeal. This is used to simplify complaint process for citizens and enhance their political participation using digital solutions.

d. Structure of Lviv City Council. This category allows to search contact information of various departments and offices in Lviv City Council and its employees based on last name, position, field of work or full name of department.

5   Outcomes of Interview Analysis

This section explains how we interpreted the collected empirical data from the conducted interviews. The accumulated total length of interviews is 6:34:32.

We divide the outcomes in three blocks on the basis of the quasi-statistical approach (see the description in Sect. 3).

Interviewees were divided into three groups:

- members of LvivCityHelper bot: (1) project manager, deputy director, LCE CCIT; (2) open data analyst, LCE CCIT; (3) software developer, LCE CCIT;
- private sector specialists: (1) managing director/co-founder; (2) project manager; (3) business development manager; (4) node.js developer; (5) founder of Chatbots. Studio;
- public and non-governmental service representatives: (1) head of Smart services and communication bureau of IT office in Lviv City Council; (2) chief specialist of E-governance bureau of IT office in Lviv City Council; (3) project manager of e-Democracy lab of PARD NGO, former member of Public council at SEGA; (4) founder of NGO "Institute of Innovative Governance", Public Information Assistant at UN office in Ukraine.

Three interviews with LvivCityHelper bot team (sector A) were conducted to get a first-hand opinion about limitations and enablers that affected the chatbot development in their public service. Another five interviews were carried out with private sector (sector B) representatives who are directly engaged in chatbot development in various positions. This allowed to get a better understanding of how the chatbot service design process is affected when working with the public sector. Lastly, four interviews were conducted with public and non-governmental sector (sector C) representatives to get a better understanding of limitations and enablers that affect the development of chatbot in the public sector from the public sector perspective. The interview questions were slightly adjusted for each sector to better reflect on their experiences.

Table 1 displays the result of the quasi-statistical approach on stakeholders' concerns using matrix coding query in Nvivo 12. Each node is created based on the interview questions and each number in the cell is divided by the number of column population (shown in each column name) to compare equally. The number in a cell indicates the number of tim8es stated for the node during the interviews. Hence, it can be seen that the greater the number, the higher the interest of each stakeholder. For better visualization, the result is displayed on a green scale.

Table 1. Result of quasi-statistical approach on stakeholders' concerns.

Node	A : sector:= LvivCityHelper (3)	B : sector:= Private (5)	C : sector:= Public&NG (4)
Effect of technology on decision making	1,7	1,2	3,5
Communication	2	0,6	1,5
Chatbots in Ukraine	/	/	/
Popular chatbots	1	0,8	0,8
Factors affecting the introduction	/	/	/
Technical limitations	2	2,4	1,5
Responsibility and political will	1	0,6	2,3
Marketing and interest of citizens	0,7	1,2	4,5
Local changemakers	0,7	0,6	1,5
Legislation	0,3	1,6	2,3
Finances	1	1	1,3
Digital divide	0,7	0,4	3,5
Decision-making process	0	2,6	0
Data privacy	0,7	1	1
Factors affecting the development of technology	/	/	/
Technical capacity	1,3	1,6	0,3
Teamwork and project planning	3,7	2,8	1
Specifics of platforms used	8	0,8	0
Quality of open data	3,7	1	0,8
Political will	0,3	0,6	0,3
Marketing and UX	2,3	3,2	1
Financial	1	0,2	0,5
Collaboration with other organization	4,3	0,2	1

It is clear from Table 1 that the concerns of each stakeholder are well dispersed. We will further explore significant comments related to the top 3 cells (marked dark-green) for each sector and nodes to classify them as limitations or enablers. Table 2 shows the distinguished concerns that are grouped by sector and node. The last column contains an attribute (i.e. "E" for "enabler"; "L" for "limitation") for each of the concerns.

The qualitative analysis allowed to highlight some of the factors mentioned by interviewees that did not get assigned with a high value, though we found them worth to be noted. The experts have stated that among one of the limitations is an incomplete legislation on data protection and privacy. If the regulation does not define any sanctions if rights or obligations are violated hence there is no sense to adhere to it. Further comment related to the legal field concerns a need for a regulative mechanism similar to GDPR. However, as there is no legislation on data protection on a national level, it also causes low awareness of public on security of data and how their data is handled in general. A technical limitation has been noted since there are difficulties in processing and recognition of Ukrainian natural language. With regards to enablers, an initiative in implementing innovative solutions as chatbots that comes from a few politicians is both beneficial for public who receive value services as well as the former who improve their image and PR. Lastly, volunteers were distinguished as enablers due to their significant help in developing chatbot solutions.

We proceed with interpreting and discussing the findings, its applications, and solutions in the next section.

Table 2. Results of semi-quantitative and semi-qualitative analysis of interviews.

Sector	Node	Item	Type
A	Specifics of platform used	Service expansion	E
		Ease of use	E
		Limited functionality	L
	Marketing & UX	Expansion of market	E
		Lack of evaluation methods	L
	Collaboration with other organizations	No unified format for data sharing	L
		Unsynchronized update of data	L
		Communication issues	L
		Use of open data	E
B	Marketing & UX	Data-driven decision making	E
		No guaranteed user feedback	L
	Teamwork & Project Planning	Human-centered approach	E
		Agile approach	E
		Uncertainty	L
		Public vs. Private sector motivation gap	L
	Decision-making process	Lack of common vision in public sector	L
		Speed	L
		Mere following of trends	L
C	Technology impact on decision-making	Quick problem identification	E
		Complexity	L
		Communication bridge for citizens and	E
		Low trust for new technology	L
	Marketing & citizens interests	Affinity with other services	E
		Low awareness due to early adoption stage	L
		User value	E
	Digital Divide	Growth of internet users	E
		Lack of resources	L
		Low education level	L

6 Results and Discussion

In this section, we are providing an aggregated set of results received from the analysis of theories found in literature and interview. We present the holistic view of these findings dividing them into limitations and enablers. At the same time, we are indicating which of them are inclusive (both mentioned in theories and by practitioners) and exclusive (mentioned either in theories OR by practitioners). The difference between the exclusive enablers and limitations we identify as a gap and suggest potential solutions on filling them.

Starting with limitations, we can see that both sources of evidence include the following: limited accessibility, digital divide, lack of technical skills and education; lack of trust and low awareness; level of infrastructure development; common vision of technology and innovation and their adoption manifested in governmental policies and strategies.

The limitations mentioned only in theories are organizational silos, lack of agility, grasping stakeholder interests, lack of service design thinking, costs, cultural values, lack of data-driven approach. The empirical data suggests such limitations as timely update of data between multiple organizations; limited user feedback; manual data processing; motivation; lack of effective penalty; weak personal data protection and data privacy; affinity with other services.

With regards to the enablers, the following ones overlapped: service expansion; changemakers, influencers and volunteers; positive perception of innovations and promising user trends; technology acceptance; addressing user needs by offering value-added service; open data initiatives. The enablers exclusively mentioned in theories are the financial advantage; collaborations via public sector; political support. The empirical data suggests autonomous market expansion; human-centered approach; quick problem identification with data-driven decision making; agile approach; increasing number of Internet users.

Having identified the gaps in the exclusive factors, we ascribe the differences foremost to the inherent features of the chatbot solution in the studied case and its specifications. The chatbot technology is still new and its application in public sector is limited. Another aspect which is specifically attributable to our case is legal. The current regulations do not define any effective penalties when it comes to personal data protection and privacy. We have also noticed that theories point out the lack of agility, design thinking, and data-driven approaches, however, in practice, those approaches are taken into consideration. Moreover, some theoretical suggestions as organizational silos, costs, cultural values, and financial advantage are, at least, in the LvivCityHelper bot case, not always of particular importance.

To fill in the gaps outlined, we firstly suggest ensuring a timely update of data across multiple organizations. Creating a central database could address the existing problem. As an alternative or a temporary measure prior to introducing a central database, a notification system on the updates in datasets could be implemented. Therefore, it is recommended to consider of how data flow will operate already at the stage of designing a service. Uniform maintenance of data should also be considered at the design phase.

We then point to the problem of limited user feedback when an answer to a question of why the user has quit the chatbot is being sought. This means that although chatbot is perceived as a two-way communication tool, such two-way interaction is only limited to active interaction. User will always have a right to quit without providing feedback on "why". From the perspective of stakeholders, it is important to understand why it happened. Therefore, a service cannot be improved accordingly. As a recommendation, chatbot providers should seek alternative ways to receive feedback from users, like surveys or user interviews.

The next issue to address is manual data processing. This means even though theory highly recommends data-driven approach and praises advancement in chatbot technology, chatbot developers still lack effective tools to collect and analyze feedback of users. We are recommending to stay updated on the advancements in the given segment of technology accustoming them to the existing solutions.

Moving forward, attention should be paid to the matter of a careless decision to introduce chatbot. This happens because chatbots are perceived as somewhat of a buzzword. The decision to adopt is rarely based on market research, but rather on the idea of popularity and trend. The interviewees have even indicated that sometimes the service owner simply disappears and no longer supports the project, as there is lack of responsibility in public sector with regards to results of public service performance. This needs to be avoided to maintain citizens' trust. Therefore, we suggest that information about service owner should be more transparent in order to improve accountability of project.

The fifth finding is difficulty of understanding of concepts interlinked with chatbot. Advance in technology means that regular citizens cannot precisely evaluate the need for and the benefits of chatbot, like data-driven decision making, due to complexity of technology. This makes it difficult for citizens to estimate the value of technology. People might be reluctant to use it, as they would simply not understand it. We suggest that government may consider investing in improving digital skills of citizens and prioritize combating the digital divide. In addition, chatbots should also contain guidelines on their functionality.

The sixth finding is autonomous expansion of the market. If launching a chatbot is backed up with a market research of demands and needs, there is a lesser need for advertisement to gain new users. It is supposed that cost of marketing to increase awareness of users, particularly right after the launch, may be reduced as the number of users will naturally grow.

The last finding is affinity with other services. The introduction of chatbot will help automate and accumulate responses for repeated questions and simultaneously improve the efficiency of other services applying the learned patterns. This may also contribute to cost reduction.

We can conclude that exploring a practical case a LvivCityHelper chatbot solution has contributed several new insights on the possible ways to improve the design and implement such solutions in the public sector. Lessons learned from this particular case study can be of use to the stakeholders of other ongoing and/or future projects. The examined gaps in literature in practice also point to areas worth looking into from the research perspective. It is also important to note the holistic perspective of these limitations and enablers where their sum has a greater impact whereas the effect of each factor in isolation may be lower.

7   Conclusion

As we aimed this research to answer the questions of how to design a chatbot for public service, we have conducted a case study of LvivCityHelper bot. The analysis of existing work and empirical data has helped us illustrating and filling the gaps between practice and theory in terms of limitations and enablers of the development of chatbots based on stakeholders' concerns.

The identified gaps are dependent on the contextual and country-specific factors as well as the inherent features of the implemented chatbots. It is also important to point out again the definitive role of legal framework that facilitates the functioning of these innovative solutions, especially, as we learned, in case of Ukraine.

Having studied the LvivCityHelper bot and its stakeholders' opinions, it was discovered that there is rather a small difference between most aspects of the theory. Though some previous work points out finances, cultural values as limitation factors, it turned out to be of lesser importance in practice. Stakeholders rather acknowledge the requirement of effective legislation for unified and smooth process for development and provision of chatbot service; complete user feedback; market research; consideration of digital divide effect, etc.

Having condensed the experts' responses, we have extracted seven findings, i.e. features of chatbot in terms of limitations and enablers, which are recommended for further consideration of stakeholders when designing a chatbot in public service.

References

1. Alsaghier, H., Ford, M., Nguyen, A., Hexel, R.: Conceptualising citizen's trust in e-government: application of Q methodology. Leading Issues E-Government **1**, 204 (2011)
2. Androutsopoulou, A., Karacapilidis, N., Loukis, E., Charalabidis, Y.: Transforming the communication between citizens and government through AI-guided chatbots. Gov. Inf. Q. **36**(2), 358–367 (2019)
3. Auld, G.W., et al.: Development of a decision tree to determine appropriateness of NVivo in analyzing qualitative data sets. J. Nutr. Educ. Behav. **39**(1), 37–47 (2007)
4. Batura, O., Evas, T.: Information society goes east: ICT policy in the EU's eastern partnership cooperation framework. In: Kerikmäe, T., Chochia, A. (eds.) Political and Legal Perspectives of the EU Eastern Partnership Policy, pp. 39–57. Springer, Cham (2016). https://doi.org/10.1007/978-3-319-27383-9_4
5. Bershadskaya, L., Chugunov, A., Dzhusupova, Z.: Understanding e-government development barriers in CIS countries and exploring mechanisms for regional cooperation. In: Kő, A., Leitner, C., Leitold, H., Prosser, A. (eds.) EGOVIS/EDEM 2013, pp. 87–101. Springer, Heidelberg (2013)
6. Capgemini. Unleashing the potential of Artificial Intelligence in the public sector (2017). https://www.capgemini.com/consulting/wp-content/uploads/sites/30/2017/10/ai-in-public-sector.pdf. Accessed 29 Nov 2019
7. Centre of Public ImpactDestination Unknown: Exploring the impact of Artificial Intelligence on Government (2017). https://publicimpact.blob.core.windows.net/production/2017/09/Destination-Unknown-AI-and-government.pdf
8. Decree of Cabinet of Ministers of Ukraine on adoption of Concept of development of system of electronic services of Ukraine, 16 November 2016 (2016). https://zakon.rada.gov.ua/laws/show/918-2016-%D1%80/ed20161116#n15. Accessed 29 Nov 2019
9. Haptik. How the Government can leverage the power of chatbots for public services (2018). https://haptik.ai/blog/how-government-can-use-chatbot/. Accessed 29 Nov 2019
10. Hofstede Insights. Ukraine. Country Comparison (2019). https://www.hofstede-insights.com/country-comparison/ukraine/. Accessed 30 Apr 2019

11. Ivankin, A.: How to create a cool chatbot and not fail: 8 tips from experience of Open DataBot (2017). https://ain.ua/2017/06/29/kak-sozdat-klassnogo-bota-i-ne-oblazhatsya-8-sovetov-iz-opyta-opendatabot/
12. KIIS. Trust to social institutes, December 2018 (2018). https://www.kiis.com.ua/?lang=ukr&cat=reports&id=817&page=1. Accessed 29 Nov 2019
13. Kim, S., Lee, J.: E-participation, transparency, and trust in local government. Public Adm. Rev. **72**(6), 819–828 (2012)
14. Lee, J., Kim, H.J., Ahn, M.J.: The willingness of e-Government service adoption by business users: the role of offline service quality and trust in technology. Gov. Inf. Q. **28**(2), 222–230 (2011)
15. Mehr, H., Ash, H., Fellow, D.: Artificial intelligence for citizen services and government. Ash Cent. Democr. Gov. Innov. Harvard Kennedy Sch., no. August, pp. 1–12 (2017)
16. Meier, A.: EDemocracy & EGovernment: Stages of a Democratic Knowledge Society. Springer, Heidelberg (2012). https://doi.org/10.1007/978-3-642-24494-0
17. Morgan, B.: What is a chatbot, and why is it important for customer experience (2017). https://www.forbes.com/sites/blakemorgan/2017/03/09/what-is-a-chatbot-and-why-is-it-important-for-customer-experience/. Accessed 29 Nov 2019
18. Myeong, S., Kwon, Y., Seo, H.: Sustainable e-governance: the relationship among trust, digital divide, and e-government. Sustainability **6**(9), 6049–6069 (2014)
19. Nam, T., Sayogo, D.S.: Who uses e-government?: examining the digital divide in e-government use. In: Proceedings of the 5th International Conference on Theory and Practice of Electronic Governance, pp. 27–36. ACM, September 2011
20. Nyman-Metcalf, K., Repytskyi, T.: Exporting good governance via e-Governance: Estonian e-Governance support to Eastern partnership countries. In: Kerikmäe, T., Chochia, A. (eds.) Political and Legal Perspectives of the EU Eastern Partnership Policy, pp. 81–100. Springer, Cham (2016). https://doi.org/10.1007/978-3-319-27383-9_6
21. OECD. OECD Public Governance Reviews Estonia: Towards a Single Government Approach. Organisation for Economic Co-operation and Development (2011). https://www.riigikantselei.ee/sites/default/files/content-editors/Failid/oecd_public_governance_review_estonia_full_report.pdf. Accessed 29 Nov 2019
22. Open Data Blog. @LvivCityHelper, NORA, MyCity та Playseek про якість відкритих даних, MVP та відсутність часу. http://blog.1991.center/opendata/odchallenge4?fbclid=IwAR2HdXuO0b8wqEcAkt_tXQsEIyibJX9D7raR22qvpHBdTZ0kedZpnpSIUz4. Accessed 10 Apr 2019
23. Open Data Challenge. https://odc.in.ua/. Accessed 29 Nov 2019
24. OpenDatabot (2018). https://opendatabot.ua/blog/278-happy-new-year-2019. Accessed 29 Nov 2019
25. Robson, C.: Real World Research, vol. 3. Wiley, Chichester (2011)
26. Runeson, P. (ed.): Case Study Research in Software Engineering: Guidelines and Examples. Wiley, Hoboken (2012)
27. Runeson, P., Höst, M.: Guidelines for conducting and reporting case study research in software engineering. Empirical Softw. Eng. **14**(2), 131 (2009)
28. Sapiton, M.: Railwaybot has attracted first investment. The project is having talks with "Ukrzaliznytsia" (2018). https://ain.ua/2018/09/24/ooo-chatbot/
29. TAPAS: Report on Current state and perspectives of development of state digital information resources. (Звіт "Стан та перспективи розвитку державних електронних інформаційних ресурсів") (2017). http://tapas.org.ua/en/components/eservices/. Accessed 29 11 2019
30. TAPAS: Roadmap for development of national interoperability (2017). http://tapas.org.ua/en/components/eservices/systems

31. Tsap, V., Pappel, I., Draheim, D.: Key success factors in introducing national e-Identification systems. In: Dang, T.K., Wagner, R., Küng, J., Thoai, N., Takizawa, M., Neuhold, E.J. (eds.) FDSE 2017. LNCS, vol. 10646, pp. 455–471. Springer, Cham (2017). https://doi.org/10.1007/978-3-319-70004-5_33

32. Verkhovna Rada. Draft Law of Ukraine #8602 on state electronic registries (2018). http://w1.c1.rada.gov.ua/pls/zweb2/webproc4_1?pf3511=64437. Accessed 29 Nov 2019

33. Wang, Y.D., Emurian, H.H.: An overview of online trust: concepts, elements, and implications. Comput. Hum. Behav. **21**(1), 105–125 (2005)

34. Zhou, M., Huang, J.: Knowledge extraction from online discussion forums. U.S. Patent No. 7,814,048. Washington, DC: U.S. Patent and Trademark Office (2010)

35. Lviv's Open Data. About the Project (2019). https://opendata.city-adm.lviv.ua/about. Accessed 29 Nov 2019. [in Ukrainian]

36. Yaremko, A.: The presentation of the Chatbot in Telegram @LvivCityHelper in Lviv today (2018). https://city-adm.lviv.ua/news/city/lviv-changes/254905-s-ogodni-u-l-vovi-prezentuyut-chatbot-u-telegram-lvivcityhelper. Accessed 29 Nov 2019. [in Ukrainian]

Information and Analytical Support
for Countering Crimes in the Sphere of Illegal
Banking Activities by Operational Divisions
of Department of Internal Affairs

Daria Vasilievna Shcherbakova[1](✉) (iD)
and Oleg Anatolyevich Firsov[2](✉) (iD)

[1] Russian Presidential Academy of National Economy and Public
Administration (RANEPA), North-West Institute of Management,
199178 Middle Avenue of Vasilevskiy Island, 57, Saint Petersburg, Russia
daria.ranepa@gmail.com
[2] St. Petersburg University of the Ministry of Internal Affairs of the Russian
Federation, 198206 Pilyutova Street, 1, Saint Petersburg, Russia
firsov.olega@gmail.com

Abstract. The problem of information support of the operational-search activity of the subdivisions of the ES (economic security) and CC (countering corruption) on countering illegal banking activities is due to the fact that the information files of law enforcement, state and supervisory bodies in the database format are not sufficient for a variety of reasons efficiently and not fully, in spite of the fact that the information generated by them is capable of becoming the most important full data on legal entities and individual entrepreneurs and the features of their financial and economic activities. It is indisputable that in order to productively solve the tasks of countering illegal banking activities, an operational worker needs to have relevant and reliable information about the object of operational interest and the subject of the crime itself.

The problem outlined above can be solved either by means of creating a departmental system for analyzing financial and business activities, which is quite expensive, or by using existing information and analytical systems, which requires solving the issue of the basis for access to relevant information resources.

Keywords: Tax evasion · Value added tax · Managed data

1 Introduction

Crimes in the financial and credit sphere occupy a special place in the structure of economic crime due to the accumulation and turnover in this area of a significant amount of money. The insufficiently perfect legal regulation of the procedure for carrying out financial transactions allows transferring significant amounts of money to the shadow sector and enables attackers to receive significant criminal income in a relatively short period [1]. The social danger of illegal banking activity is that it largely forms the circulation of money resources uncontrolled by the state, which undermines the basic principles of market economic relations and creates a threat to the economic security of the state. Crimes that contribute to the outflow of financial resources from the banking sector hinder the implementation of investment projects and adversely affect the implementation of legal financial transactions [2].

Due to a significant reduction in the mass of cash in circulation, substantial savings and increased state control over financial flows occur, leading to a decrease in the level of corruption, the development of an electronic payment system, transparency of the economy, an increase in the state's economic and social stability, financial literacy and legal income population [3].

Crimes in the financial sector, incl. under Art. 172 of the Criminal Code of the Russian Federation is closely connected with tax crime, which causes significant damage to the stability of the credit and financial system of the state as a whole. For non-payment of taxes in the first half of 2018, 1,700 criminal cases were opened, 49 billion rubles of damage were identified, of which 24 billion rubles, they were able to compensate during the pre-investigation and investigation of the criminal case [4]. Illegal cashing and withdrawal of funds to the shadow sector, including abroad, are among the most dangerous threats to the financial security of the state. A distinctive feature of the crimes of the category under consideration is their detailed planning, continuous improvement of the schemes of committing a crime, including using the latest achievements of science and technology. In particular, when carrying out illegal banking activities, electronic keys, passwords, and ciphers are used to manage settlement accounts, which provide exclusive access to their management, the Bank-Client, Bank-Online, and remote banking service payments system, etc. there are automated systems that allow the client to carry out information interaction with the bank in the remote access mode and does not require his personal participation in relations with bank employees. Similarly, activities are organized for the formation and submission of tax reports of organizations involved in illegal banking activities. All these circumstances contribute to the concealment of criminal activity and in their essence exclude the possibility of further identification of criminals as direct participants in criminal activity.

Detection of crimes in the credit and financial sphere, including those related to the implementation of illegal banking activities, is carried out mainly by the units of the Ministry of Internal Affairs (hereinafter - the Ministry of Internal Affairs) and the Federal Security Service (hereinafter - the FSB) of Russia within the framework of their exclusive tasks and powers Law No. 144 of August 12, 1995 "On Operational-Search Activity" (hereinafter - "OSA") and relevant legislative acts of the Russian Federation. In this case, the key to timely detection of such crimes is to obtain in the process of operational-search activity objective and reliable information about the signs of a crime being prepared, committed now or already committed, that is, information that is the result of criminal actions and indicating with more or less probability the event of the crime, the persons who may be involved in it, the place and the manner in which it was committed, as well as other circumstances important for the offense disclosure [5]. In the operational-search opposition to economic crime, largely, the level of information and analytical support for operational-search activity influences the result of such opposition [6]. Internal Revenue Service bears the responsibility to anti-money laundering in the

USA. The IRS includes the investigation unit which has the FBI support to investigate crimes of tax laws. In Russia investigative procedures are held by divisions on DIA. This structural subordination limits the access of investigators to the databases of the tax authorities. For example, in France this is solved by special units which are part of regional tax authorities to ensure interaction with the police.

In the conditions of the development of technical innovations, in order to most effective forms and methods of combating illegal banking activities, in our opinion, employees of operational units should have the right of access to all modern information and analytical resources created as state institutions (tax and customs services, the central bank of the Russian Federation, the Federal Service for Financial Monitoring, etc.) and private organizations. Author's experience of investigative activities allows us to conclude the police officers do not have access to the necessary information within the framework of economic crimes investigation and the experience of interaction with tax authorities is evidence of the delay in the investigation of crimes due to bureaucratic delays.

2 Discussion

Information support is an integral part of both forensic and operational-search, criminal and procedural support of the process of identifying, disclosing and investigating tax crimes. It is obvious that any state is the owner of a vast array of data on citizens and legal entities (and often not only about their own, but also about others). Government agencies will still give odds to any private company with regard to the huge amount of data that is managed [7]. Public authorities, unlike data holders in the private sector, tend to oblige people to provide information, rather than convincing or offering something in return [8]. Therefore, they will continue to collect and accumulate huge amounts of data.

The Russian public administration system is characterized by the implementation of information systems of all kinds for the accumulation, storage and processing of data in all areas of public administration. In Russia, the possibility of using big data technology (Big Data, hereinafter - DB) at the state level is unconditionally realized. However, some government agencies are already quite successfully using these technologies. For example, the Russian tax authorities for processing electronically submitted value added tax returns (hereinafter referred to as VAT), purchase books and sales books, and records of invoices issued and received use the technological base "Automated System for Monitoring VAT Reimbursement 2" (Further, ACS VAT-2) [9].

For the first time, an automated system for monitoring the payment of value added tax was tested in 2013, but a more complete and productive VAT ACS was introduced by the tax service and began to be used from January 2015. The established task of the software is to automate the desk audits of the VAT tax returns, monitor the operations subject to VAT, and identify organizations that do not pay VAT. Thus, ACS VAT-2 currently allows, based on an analysis of the activities of all taxpayers, to identify gaps in the chains of payments. However, such identification is not in itself sufficient to recover tax arrears. It only gives the tax authorities information on which organizations appear to have committed tax violations. Further identification of offenses is in the so-called manual mode [10]. In fact, the "ACS VAT-2" system tells us where to look, but it does not exempt from the need to prove the fact of a person's wrongdoing.

Prior to the implementation of the program, the investigation of cases lasted a very long time. Thus, on April 26, 2019, the Primorsky District Court of St. Petersburg issued a decision on a high-profile criminal case on the creation of a criminal community (OPS) specializing in major financial frauds connected with the illegal return of VAT. Criminal case under two articles of the Criminal Code - Art. 210 (creating a criminal community and participation in it) and Part 4 of Art. The Investigative Committee of Russia (TFR) initiated 159 of the Criminal Code of the Russian Federation (fraud committed by an organized group on a large scale) back in February 2014. As follows from the case materials, the criminal community, the purpose of which was the illegal refund of VAT, has operated on a large scale in St. Petersburg since 2008 and consisted of several divisions - financial, legal and coordination. Counsel A. Swede, according to the materials of the case, headed one of them. The responsibilities of its structure included the registration and re-registration of companies, search for nominee directors and control over them. According to investigators, a lawyer led another division, lawyer T. Makarova. Its functions included the production of forged accounting documentation and tax returns for VAT. The scheme involved about 40 one-day companies. On their behalf, nominal managers filed declarations with the tax inspectorates for VAT refunds on fictitious transactions [11]. The investigation of frauds with VAT lasted more than a year. The materials of the case with the indictment were sent to the court only in September 2015.

The essence of the ACS VAT is that it automatically increases the control ratios of the indicators of VAT returns, which reveals discrepancies (gaps) when the buyer claimed a deduction and the supplier did not calculate the tax. CC ACS compares the data of tax returns, invoices, books of purchases and sales books of different taxpayers in order to identify inconsistencies of the data reflected by the seller with the data of the buyer. The system uses 84 risk criteria, including such as tax burden, profitability, taxpayer for 3 years, arrears of taxes and fees, information about the founders, the director. The system distributes all VAT payers into three groups of tax risk: high, medium, low, which are respectively reflected in the colors: red, yellow and green. The low risk group (green) includes sustainable taxpayers who have been operating for a long time, pay VAT, and have assets and staff. The high-risk group includes taxpayers who pay taxes in the minimum amount; do not have the resources to conduct the declared commercial activity. The middle risk group includes organizations that make mistakes in the details of financial documents. The system allows you to save invoices, tax returns of VAT payers, information about transactions, creating a tax history of companies. The taxpayer must include in the VAT declaration information from purchase books and sales books. The data from his book are automatically reconciled with the data of all its suppliers and customers, which is one of the reasons to assume that it is assumed that the alleged transactions in the financial and economic activities of the taxpayer. This helps tax authorities to separate bona fide taxpayers from unscrupulous, thereby reducing the number of attempts to reduce VAT illegally from the budget of the Russian Federation.

If there are discrepancies in the chain of relations between suppliers and buyers of goods specified in their tax reports, the program signals this to the taxpayer and within 5 days, the taxpayer must eliminate such discrepancies. If the tax reporting is not adjusted, the reasons for the discrepancies are already clarified by the tax inspector in the course of desk audits, followed by a decision on the validity or non-validity of the value-added tax declared to be reduced from the budget [12]. The effectiveness of ACS VAT is evident in terms of the speedy detection of errors in the chains of relations between taxpayers and helps to cover 100% of counterparties.

The special feature of VAT is that the taxpayer, based on the quarterly results, determines the difference between the tax received from customers (that is, calculated on taxable transactions) and the tax transferred to their suppliers (tax deduction on VAT). If the amount of VAT tax deductions exceeds the total amount of tax calculated on taxable transactions, the resulting difference is refundable (refundable) to the taxpayer from the budget after conducting a desk tax audit of the VAT tax return filed by him. So in order to obtain an unjustified tax benefit on VAT (positive difference in VAT), criminals included in the tax deductions deliberately imaginary transactions for the acquisition of goods, works and services with a formally legitimate organization (hereinafter FLO). To identify such inaccurate information on transactions with FLO and aimed primarily ACS VAT.

For example, formally - a legitimate organization from a chain of suppliers formally buys goods and sells to another company, value added should be subject to VAT, but one-day tax does not pay, and anonymous letters are cashed out for cash received on the accounts; the company, which bought the goods, claims VAT for reimbursement [13]. ACS VAT will check operations and if the company declares VAT deductible or refundable, its counterparty must reflect the transaction in which VAT has been paid in its book and pay tax; if there is none, the system will immediately detect it. Chains of imaginary transactions are lined up among dozens of companies, and only one (formal organization) of the participants in the chain does not pay VAT. Previously, only an in-depth on-site tax audit could reveal it; now the ACS VAT immediately calculates all tax breaks and establishes a formally legitimate organization that did not pay VAT. In addition, "ACS VAT-2" allows you to compare not only the data on the accrued and paid VAT, but also to simulate taxpayer avoidance schemes used by the taxpayer.

According to the head of the Federal Tax Service (FTS) M. Mishustin, the use of the VAT-2 ACS made it possible to reduce the number of VAT claims by high-risk organizations by almost eight times. In the field of view of tax authorities, first, those companies that exceed the criterion of 89% of VAT deductions fall. These data indicate that today the vector of work has changed: inspections of enterprises are carried out not by a random sample, but in relation to those who have a high risk of using illegal tax optimization schemes. In the zone of attention increasingly began to fall into the big players. This was largely the result of a change in criminal law in 2016, when threshold values for unpaid taxes were increased, from which criminal liability arises. This largely explains the growth of the damage established and reimbursed during the investigation.

In addition, it is impossible not to dwell on the shortcomings in the operation of the VAT-2 ACS, one of which is the lack of information in the system on tax payment to the budget, since it only contains data presented in tax reports. Thus, there is a bypass scheme for the software complex ACS (CC ACS). It comes down to the inclusion of additional links in the chain, i.e. participants who ultimately lead to a "one-day firm" stating the full amount of VAT to payment in the tax return, but not paying it to the budget. In the new tax period, instead of this "one-day", another is included in the chain.

The report "The tree of relations" allows you to identify and "one-day firms" and beneficiaries. Such information about the inclusion of "one-day firms" in the chain of financial and economic relations for tax service employees is, at a minimum, a reason for conducting a pre-screening analysis, the results of which make a decision on the advisability of appointing and conducting questionable transactions in a taxpayer-beneficiary tax audit. At the stage of such an analysis, the tax authority, in addition to information from the ACS VAT, can analyze information about the financial flows of the beneficiary of suspicious transactions and interrelated organizations, which makes it possible to obtain preliminary information about formally legitimate organizations involved in illegal activities and estimated amounts of underpaid taxes and fees, or VAT amounts claimed for deduction from the budget for imaginary transactions [3]. Accordingly, at the pre-screening analysis stage, the tax authority may not only develop an optimal plan for organizing a field tax audit, but also conclude that there are signs of a crime under Art. 199 and art. 159 of the Criminal Code of the Russian Federation (hereinafter the Criminal Code of the Russian Federation) (regarding the illegal refund of VAT) in the activities of the management of a legal entity - the beneficiary of suspicious transactions. Such results of the pre-audit analysis, if presented in a timely manner (before the start of the GNP (field tax audit) and conducting public tax control measures) could serve as a sufficient basis for the operational units to combat the economic crimes of the internal affairs bodies (hereinafter - DIA) in the framework of the implementation of the powers provided by the law "On the OSA" for documenting illegal activities provided for in Art. 198-199.2 of the Criminal Code, classified in accordance with Art. 151 of the Criminal Procedure Code of the Russian Federation (hereinafter - the Code of Criminal Procedure) to the jurisdiction of the Investigative Committee of the Russian Federation, as well as the crimes provided for by Art. 172 of the Criminal Code of the Russian Federation under investigation to the investigation of the DIA.

In our opinion, one of the advanced information technologies used by the FTS of Russia and the main source of operatively important information about organizations that do not pay VAT, about formally legitimate organizations involved in the process of illegal banking activities today, it is necessary to recognize the software package of automated pay control VAT - CC ACS "VAT-2".

At the same time, the current legislation does not explicitly provide for the obligation of tax authorities to notify the Department of Internal Affairs of the results of pre-screening analysis, established facts of tax violation and possible prospects for conducting a field tax audit, leaving the issue of notification of possible violations of legislation at the discretion of the tax inspector [14].

Semenov [15] defines informational interaction between tax authorities and internal affairs bodies. In his opinion, this is a long-term systematic exchange of information, which is carried out for the purposes of the activities of these bodies by strictly defined regulatory legal acts in ways and in strictly defined forms while respecting state, commercial and tax secrets.

So in accordance with Part 3 of Art. 82 of the Tax Code of the Russian Federation Tax authorities, customs authorities, internal affairs bodies, investigating authorities and management bodies of state extra budgetary funds of the Russian Federation, in the manner determined by agreement between them, inform each other about their materials about violations of legislation on taxes and fees and tax crimes, measures taken to curb them, tax inspections conducted by them, and also exchange other necessary information in order to fulfill the tasks assigned to them.

Art. 4 "Cooperation agreements between the Ministry of the Interior of the Russian Federation and the Federal Tax Service" dated October 13, 2010, stipulates the procedure and forms for their interaction, including the mutual information exchange of information, including in electronic form, of interest to the Parties and directly related to the implementation tasks and functions assigned to them by legislative and other regulatory legal acts of the Russian Federation.

The Order of the Ministry of Internal Affairs of Russia and the Federal Tax Service of Russia of June 30, 2009 "On Approving the Procedure for Interaction between Internal Affairs Agencies and Tax Authorities to Prevent, Identify and Prevent Tax Offenses and Crimes" approved the "Instruction on the Procedure for Interaction between Internal Affairs Agencies and Tax Authorities when Organizing and Conducting tax audits"; "Instruction on the procedure for sending internal affairs bodies to the tax authorities when identifying circumstances that require actions related to the powers of the tax authorities to decide on them" and "Instruction on the procedure for sending materials by the tax authorities to internal affairs agencies when identifying circumstances that allow assume a violation of the legislation on taxes and fees, containing signs of a crime "In this case, the last Instruction on the procedure for sending materials to tax authorities and to the internal affairs bodies when identifying the circumstances that allow to assume the violation of the legislation on taxes and fees, containing signs of a crime, has become invalid in accordance with the Order of the Ministry of Internal Affairs of Russia N 1144, FTS of Russia N MMV-7-2/774 @ of 11.11.2011, in view of changes in the criminal procedure legislation, in accordance with which, from January 15, 2011, criminal cases of crimes under Art. 198-199.2 of the Criminal Code referred to the jurisdiction of investigators of the Investigative Committee of the Russian Federation.

At the same time, the pre-investigation check on the facts of the commission of crimes under Art. 198-199.2 of the Criminal Code of the Russian Federation, which later, as a rule, becomes the reason and the basis for making a procedural decision on initiating a criminal case is still carried out by the units of economic security and anti-corruption of the Ministry of Internal Affairs (hereinafter - ES and CC). At the same time, in practice, reports of the tax service in rare cases become the reason for the start of such pre-investigation checks.

In addition, the information resource of the ACS VAT contains information that can greatly facilitate the activities of the operational units of the internal affairs bodies in identifying crimes provided for by Article.172 of the Criminal Code of the Russian Federation.

The problem of using ACS VAT in the activities of operational units is that direct access to this system is only provided to tax officials, and therefore, analytical information can be obtained from the system only upon request or as part of field or office audits with the FTS. Taking into account the foregoing, in order to exercise their authority to document economic crimes (including Article 198-199.2, 172 of the Criminal Code of the Russian Federation) and to timely identify and document such criminal units of the Electro technical Department and the CC of the Ministry of Internal Affairs of the Republic of Kazakhstan, and in particular, departments to counteract tax crimes need to have prompt access to such a state information resource as ACS VAT.

Obviously, the receipt of information from the ACS VAT on requests sent by mail contributes to red tape when conducting follow-up inspections, the loss of relevance of information due to the long arrival of a long time from the date of the request to the time the initiator received the answer (up to 30 days), the loss actions to document crimes. In addition, the information provided by the tax authority upon written requests may contain only electronic information (on electronic media in the form of tables XL) of the 8th and 9th sections (sales books and purchase books) of tax declarations for VAT checked, but the possibilities of the ACS system VAT on the formation of a tree of connections are not available for their representation of ATS in electronic form. So, an objective picture of connections and counterparties of a taxpayer under review for ATS within the framework of the execution of requests (including in electronic form) for a particular legal entity is not available.

Resolving the issue of promptly obtaining relevant and necessary ATS information from the ACS VAT is possible only by setting up an electronic document flow between the tax service and ATS, or by organizing a workplace in the departments of the ES and DIA CC with connecting the categorized computer equipment to the ES ACS VAT, which will allow the operative within the bounds of their functions of detecting and documenting economic crimes in real time, Actual and relevant information in relation to the audited, including forming and analyzing the tree of connections of the audited legal entity.

It should be noted that the work on the modernization of the CC ACS VAT continues in the plans for its synchronization with the databases of the customs service, the Central Bank of the Russian Federation, Rosfinmonitoring, and the Civil Registry Office. So the latest version of the CC ACS "VAT-3", actively being introduced into the work of the tax authorities in the country, already allows you to identify schemes with the participation of one-day firms, the system includes information from the calculated center of the Central Bank of the Russian Federation. In the near future, it is planned to integrate the system with the database of the Federal Customs Service of the Russian Federation and the Federal Financial Monitoring Service. Another innovation will be an analysis of the chain of relations, not only between legal entities and individual entrepreneurs, but also with the participation of individuals who are not individual entrepreneurs. In addition, the new CC will monitor the compliance of data received from cash registers and sales books.

Thus, the updated program will be able to monitor the entire path of passage of goods (works, services), tax returns, invoices, as well as income and expenses of taxpayers on bank accounts, identify VAT amounts not paid to the budget and interdependent persons, that is, have, all the possibilities to prevent tax minimization schemes. Moreover, if the system detects signs of the use of a tax evasion scheme, it will automatically generate a report that will be a sufficient basis for carrying out verification activities as part of investigative checks on documenting criminal activity against a beneficiary. The direct access of police officers to this report will raise the efficiency of their work.

3 Conclusion

In modern conditions of use by taxpayers of various schemes of tax evasion and illegal VAT refunds from the budget, the use of information and analytical systems to identify facts indicating a violation of the established procedure for conducting financial and economic activities is of particular importance. In view of the implementation of global reforms in our country related to the development of the digital economy, work on creating information and analytical systems is actively carried out in tax and customs authorities. Some information generated by the Federal Tax Service of Russia is publicly available, which allows for the operational verification of data on a legal entity, its relations with other business entities, whether they have signs of a formally legitimate organization, etc. However the biggest part of information is available only with an appropriate request authorized bodies. At the same time, the main task of introducing information technologies into tax administration is to ensure the "inevitability" of fulfilling the obligation to pay taxes, to make taxation more transparent with the help of new technologies.

The establishment of electronic workflows between the operational divisions of DIA and tax authorities or the direct access formation authorized police officers to databases of tax authorities, in particular to the program "ACS-VAT", will allow to respond quickly and identify illegal banking activities and also to make impartial assessment after the investigation. Timely exposure of these crimes allows calling guiltiest to account without giving them the time to hide traces of the crime in order to avoid a punishment.

References

1. Rusanov, G., Pudovochkin, Y.: Money laundering and predicate offenses: models of criminological and legal relationships. J. Money Laundering Control 21(1), 22–32 (2018)
2. Klochko, A., Logvinenko, N., Kobzeva, T., Kiselyova, E.: Legalizing proceeds from crime through the banking system. Criminol. J. Baikal Natl. Univ. Econ. Law 10(1), 194–204 (2016)
3. Chernadchuk, V., Chernadchuk, T., Klochko, A.: Financial control as a means of cognition of the financal activities: theoretical and legal aspects. J. Adv. Res. Law Econ. 8(8), 2383–2390 (2017)
4. Mazenkova, K.: SKR: Nalogovy`x prestuplenij stalo men`she, no ushherb po nim—bol`she (2018) [TFR: Tax crimes became less, but the damage on them—more]. Federal`noe agentstvo novostej, [in Russian]. https://riafan.ru/1107801-skr-nalogovykh-prestuplenii-stalo-menshe-no-usherb-po-nim-bolshe. Accessed 25 May 2019

5. Artemov, N., Arzumanova, L., Boltinova, O., Salamova, S., Sitnik, A., Jin, C.: Liability for violating financial legislation: criminal law and criminological characteristics of financial crimes. Russ. J. Criminol. **11**(4), 717–730 (2017)
6. Shcheglov, E.: Znachenie informacionnogo obespecheniya pri vzaimodejstvii operativny`x podrazdelenij po linii nalogovy`x prestuplenij v processe preduprezhdeniya, vy`yavleniya i rassledovaniya nalogovy`x prestuplenij (2011). [The importance of information support in the interaction of operational units in the field of tax crimes in the process of prevention, detection and investigation of tax crimes], Vestnik Voronezhskogo instituta MVD Rossii, no. 3, pp. 79–85. [in Russian]
7. Sukhodolov, A., Spasennikov, B., Shvyrev, B.: Digital economy: electronic monitoring of offenders and the assessment of its economic feasibility. Russ. J. Criminol. **11**(3), 495–502 (2017)
8. Channov, S.: Bol`shie danny`e v gosudarstvennom upravlenii: vozmozhnosti i ugrozy` [Big data in public administration: opportunities and threats]. Zhurnal rossijskogo prava **262**(10), 111–122 (2018). [in Russian]
9. Rodygina, V.: Cifrovizaciya nalogovogo kontrolya NDS: pravovy`e posledstviya i perspektivy` [Digitalization of value added tax control: legal implications and prospects]. Finansovoe pravo **9**, 29–32 (2018). [in Russian]
10. Timoshenkoto, V.: Sovershenstvovanie kontrolya za ischisleniem i uplatoj NDS na baze "ASK NDS-2" [Improving control over the calculation and payment of VAT on the basis of "ASK VAT-2"]. Pravo i e`konomika **11**, 61–65 (2017). [in Russian]
11. Litovchenko, V.: NDS oformili srokami [VAT is issued by a timing]. Kommersant, (In Russ.) (2019). https://sledcom.ru/press/smi/item/1344224/. Accessed 25 May 2019
12. Semenikhin, V.: Nalogovy`e proverki [Tax audit]. Moscow: Gross-Media: ROSBUX (2017). [in Russian]
13. Soloviev, I.: Nalogovy`e prestupleniya: specifika vy`yavleniya i rassledovaniya [Tax crimes: specifics of detection and investigation]. Moscow: Prospect. (in Russ.)
14. Samarukha, V., Samarukha, A., Samarukha, I.: Problems of counteracting tax crimes. Russ. J. Criminol. **12**(2), 199–210 (2015)
15. Semenov, A.: O nekotory`x voprosax razvitiya e`lektronnoj sistemy` vzaimodejstviya organov vnutrennix del i Federal`noj nalogovoj sluzhby` [About some questions of development of electronic system of interaction of law-enforcement bodies and Federal tax service]. Taxes Taxation **6**, 49–56 (2009). [in Russian]

Streamlining Governmental Processes by Putting Citizens in Control of Their Personal Data

Raf Buyle[1(✉)], Ruben Taelman[1], Katrien Mostaert[2], Geroen Joris[2],
Erik Mannens[1], Ruben Verborgh[1], and Tim Berners-Lee[3]

[1] imec IDLab, Ghent University, Ghent, Belgium
raf.buyle@ugent.be
[2] Informatie Vlaanderen, Flemish Government, Brussels, Belgium
[3] Department of Computer Science, University of Oxford, Oxford, UK

Abstract. Governments typically store large amounts of personal information on their citizens, such as a home address, marital status, and occupation, to offer public services. Because governments consist of various governmental agencies, multiple copies of this data often exist. This raises concerns regarding data consistency, privacy, and access control, especially under recent legal frameworks such as GDPR. To solve these problems, and to give citizens true control over their data, we explore an approach using the decentralised Solid ecosystem, which enables citizens to maintain their data in personal data pods. We have applied this approach to two high-impact use cases, where citizen information is stored in personal data pods, and both public and private organisations are selectively granted access. Our findings indicate that Solid allows reshaping the relationship between citizens, their personal data, and the applications they use in the public and private sector. We strongly believe that the insights from this Flemish Solid Pilot can speed up the process for public administrations and private organisations that want to put the users in control of their data.

Keywords: Personal data · Decentralisation · GDPR · Solid · Linked Data

1 Introduction

With the introduction of the General Data Protection Regulation (GDPR), the European Commission has provided a legal framework that aims to empower individuals in taking control of their personal information [10]. Such control is not necessarily a disadvantage to parties processing personal information: when used properly, GDPR can actually facilitate data flows that used to be much more complicated. GDPR, however, is mostly known for its complex legal effects on European companies dealing with large-scale personal data and may cost them significant resources in order to achieve and maintain legal compatibility. While international and multinational companies also have to respect GDPR rights for European data subjects, even when they do not have a physical European presence, several large players are—to put it lightly—slow with a correct adoption of GDPR. This has created a perverse reverse effect, where European companies that try to respect GDPR become less preferred as business

© Springer Nature Switzerland AG 2020
A. Chugunov et al. (Eds.): EGOSE 2019, CCIS 1135, pp. 346–359, 2020.
https://doi.org/10.1007/978-3-030-39296-3_26

partners, losing revenue to non-European companies that are more "relaxed" with GDPR adoption [14].

Not all organisations that are subject to GDPR have questionable or malicious intent: some of them experience genuine difficulties in trying to adhere to the legal obligations. This is definitely the case for local, regional and national governments, which need personal data to provide the services their citizens require. Governmental structures consist of multiple layers, and every layer consists of its agencies with their own data needs and processes that have grown historically. As a result, citizen data is spread across many places in many copies, leading to complex legal questions as well as numerous inconsistencies and repeated requests for data that is already present in other government administrations. These governments are a demanding party for a legally compliant technical solution to simplify all of their data needs.

The majority of data processes at the government level nowadays essentially aim to tackle the problem of how to move data as frictionless as possible from point A to B. Not only does this create a lot of technical challenges between the many different points, it also becomes a complex legal matter when a governmental "data train" needs to pass by stations A, B, C, and D, where B and C are not legally allowed to see all of the data that A and D can. As such, complex processes exist to verify precisely what the access rights of B and C are, and to then reintegrate their results when pushing the data to D. A telling example is a low-emission zone (LEZ) in which certain vehicles are not allowed in a city centre, or only under certain conditions, because they emit too many harmful substances. In Flanders, a vehicle is linked to a natural person. When entering a LEZ, federal information linking the license plate to the owner is combined with regional data indicating whether a person has a disability; finally the data is processed and the decision whether the vehicle is allowed is passed on to the city.

The Solid ecosystem [2, 15, 21] provides an answer by proposing a personal data pod for every citizen, such that all of their public and private data remains in one place. Instead of moving data between A and D, each of the agencies asks for permission to view a highly specific part of the data. That way, data does not have to be moved around, and GDPR compliance can be assessed automatically for every single data request. Control over personal data in our online and offline lives is a trending topic and therefore researched intensely [7, 16, 17, 19, 20, 22, 23, 26]. The key concept is that people can choose where they store their personal data, which build upon the principles of decentralisation. Blockchain is regularly referred to in this context as a solution for the management of personal data [7, 26]. Blockchain is a way for different parties who do not know each other to come to an agreement without the need for a referee or a trusted third party. This principle is essential, for example, for organising payments without a central bank or central manager, as the decentralised digital currency Bitcoin does [5]. Blockchains replicate data across many nodes. However, often, initiatives use Blockchain when this trusted third party is not required at all. If you have a central player or if the different parties trust each other, then you don't need a blockchain. Also, the immutability character of Blockchain, which implies that data cannot be deleted, might be a challenge in the context of article 17 of the GDPR that gives people the right to erase their personal data [7, 8].

In this article, we explore the perspectives of control over personal data, and discuss two particular use cases that we have implemented using Solid. Solid provides a Web-based ecosystem that builds upon open standards and conventions [24]. According to Harrison, Pardo and Cook [12] an ecosystem is a metaphor often used to "convey a sense of the interdependent social systems of actors, organisations, material infrastructures, and symbolic resources that must be created in technology-enabled, information-intensive social systems" [p. 900]. A telling example of digital ecosystems are open data ecosystems [25]. Open Data refers to the obligation of the government to make their non-privacy-sensitive and non-confidential data freely available on the Web [13]. The open data reusers depend on the data and metadata from the data providers, while the providers depend on the feedback of the reusers to increase the data quality [18, 25]. Albeit all the actors in the open data ecosystem are interdependent to develop their business efficiently and effectively, public administrations and policymakers are in the best position to bootstrap these open government ecosystems [12]. Zuiderwijk, Janssen & Davis state that the open data ecosystem challenges are related to "policy, licenses, technology, financing, organisation, culture, and legal frameworks and are influenced by ICT infrastructures" [25]. The challenges of open data ecosystems, which rewired the "one-way street" into a "bidirectional communication", could be paralleled to the challenges to put the citizen in control of their personal data [12, 18]. By applying the Solid ecosystem approach to two high-impact use cases, the Flemish Government aims to build up the skills and capacity to put the citizen in control.

This article is further structured as follows. In the next section, we present the challenges that we aim to tackle. After that, we explain the basics around Solid in Sect. 3. Next, in Sect. 4, we discuss our approach for tackling the challenges using Solid, followed by a discussion of our implementation in Sect. 5. Finally, we conclude and present our lessons learned in Sect. 6.

2 Challenges

Local and regional governments in Flanders, the northern federated state of Belgium[1], aim to empower citizens in reusing their personal information online in different contexts such as public services, banking, health insurance, and telecom providers. Governments are often the custodian of authoritative personal data, such as a domicile address or medical information, which are administered by public administrations in various information systems. Government administrations in Flanders share and reuse authoritative personal data between their various back-office applications to reduce the administrative burden for citizens [3], which is an implementation of the European 'once-only principle'[2]. However, public administrations are struggling to put the citizen in control.

---

[1] https://www.vlaanderen.be/en/discover-flanders.

[2] https://ec.europa.eu/digital-single-market/en/news/ministerial-declaration-egovernment-tallinn-declaration.

A first challenge is that government administrations struggle to keep personal data such as email addresses, telephone numbers or bank account numbers up to date. As some citizens rarely have contact with their government, personal data is often outdated in the various information systems.

A second challenge concerns to allow citizens to reuse their data in a different context, such as a diploma when applying for a new job. The GDPR regulation 2016/679 states that *"In order to ensure that consent is freely given, consent should not provide a valid legal ground for the processing of personal data in a specific case where there is a clear imbalance between the data subject and the controller, in particular where the controller is a public authority and it is therefore unlikely that consent was freely given in all the circumstances of that specific situation."* (European Commission, 2016, Article 43). To put it differently, the relationship between a government and a citizen is commonly considered as an imbalanced relationship, since the government wields more power than their citizens[3]. Therefore, a consent given by a citizen to reuse the authoritative data managed in government information systems in the private sector, cannot be considered as freely given [8, 9]. Sharing data between government administrations in Europe is not based on a given consent, but has a specific lawful basis.

Therefore, our main research question is: how governmental processes can be streamlined by putting citizens in control of their authoritative personal data, within the context of the GDPR regulation? This research question has two perspectives. On the one hand, how can citizens share their data with government administrations? On the other hand, how can citizens reuse their data stored in government information systems in a different context?

This project evaluates how the decentralised principles of Solid [2, 19, 21, 24] can tackle these hurdles. Solid is an ecosystem that enables individuals to store data in their data pods. This gives users true control over their data, as they can choose where their data resides, and who can access it. The outcome, based on the principles of Linked Data and decentralisation, is valuable for putting the user back in control with respect to public administrations and private organisations.

3 Solid

Solid [2] is a Web-based ecosystem that separates data from their applications, by providing people with their *personal data pod*, in which they can store data independently of the applications that they or others use to access that data. People can decide at a granular level which actors and applications can read from or write to specific parts of their data. The contrast with current application architectures is illustrated in Fig. 1: instead of depending on a few applications that act as a gatekeeper of the data of large groups of people, the citizen is put in control of their personal data.

---

[3] https://ec.europa.eu/info/law/law-topic/data-protection/reform/rights-citizens/how-my-personal-data-protected/can-my-employer-require-me-give-my-consent-use-my-personal-data_en#references
.

Applications need to request access from the citizen in order to be able to operate on their data.

Importantly, Solid is not an application or platform, but a protocol: a collection of open standards and conventions. It builds upon existing Web standards, including the Linked Data stack [2], which can be implemented by anyone.

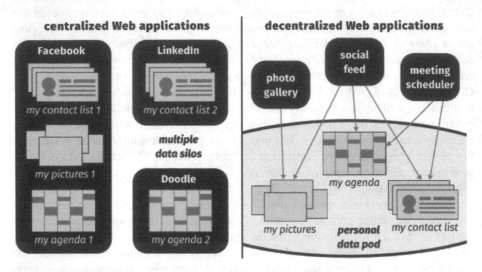

Fig. 1. Current applications are a combination of app and data. Thereby, the app becomes a centralisation point, as all interactions with that data have to go through the app. By introducing the concept of a personal data pod, Solid pushes data out of applications, such that the same data can be managed with different applications. This removes the dependency on a centralised application, as data can be stored independently in a location of the citizen's choice.

A data pod is a personal storage space that can exist anywhere on the Web, such as on your server, a shared community server, or a government-provided storage space. Within this data pod, the owner has full permissions regarding data creation, editing, and control management. The owner can decide to give specific permissions to other people, such as allowing family members to see their holiday pictures or allowing colleagues to read conference notes. Also, people, organisations and applications can post a request to the public inbox of a pod to gain access to personal data. Within Solid, people have at least one data pod for themselves, but they can additionally have multiple other pods, for instance, for home data, work data, medical data, etc.

Whereas typical centralised applications require users to store their data within the application, Solid turns this around by making data personal and allows users to use any application on top of their data after granting explicit access. While simple applications work with just a single data pod, the real power of Solid becomes clear when applications *combine data* from multiple data pods, giving way to *decentralised applications*. For example, social network applications on Solid can store personal information such as posts, friends, comments, and likes in a personal data pod, while their visualisation will require combining data across different data pods. This solves two essential problems. First, data no longer needs to be *copied* in different applications, since applications will point to the single copy. Second, as a consequence thereof, synchronisation problems no longer occur: because there is only one copy of the data, applications can no longer have inconsistent versions of data.

Solid enables several capabilities that are typically missing in the current centralised Web applications:

- **Independent identity**: people choose how they are identified and where their identity resides. In Solid, a personal identifier (WebID) is a URL[4].
- **Control over data**: people can grant and revoke fine-grained access permissions to specific parts of their data.
- **Choice of application**: the danger of vendor lock-in is avoided as data can flexibly be used by different applications.

For our purposes, Solid solves the aforementioned "data train" problem, precisely because data does not move anymore between different government agencies. Instead, each government agency goes directly to the original source of the data, which is the data pod of the citizen. This addressed the problem of multiple copies and synchronisation, as well as the GDPR question of which agency has the right to access what data attributes of a citizen since each agency makes an individual request to the data pod. As such, the many processes focused on transporting data from one hop to the next, will be refocused on reading and writing data from a pod.

4   Approach: Exchanging Personal Information Using Solid

In this section, we explain our approach for allowing citizens to share information with their government and vice versa using Solid. We first start by explaining the requirements of this approach. After that, we discuss two real-world scenarios that make use of this approach: (1) citizens sharing data, such as contact preferences (e.g. email address, telephone number), stored in a pod and (2) reusing authoritative government data in the private sector, such as diplomas, where the citizen keeps the diploma that has been digitally signed by the university and the government holds an indelible copy.

4.1   Requirements

For our use cases, we assume that all citizens can be identified uniquely with a globally unique Uniform Resource Identifier (URI), referred to as a WebID[5]. This WebID points to a Linked Data document with more details about the citizen, in particular, a pointer to the personal data pod. Furthermore, we assume that all government departments and organisations have a WebID and data pod. An overview of the required components can be seen in Fig. 2.

---

[4] Solid uses the WebID-OIDC specification for authentication: https://github.com/solid/webid-oidc-spec.

[5] https://www.w3.org/wiki/WebID.

Typically, Solid data pods have a public inbox where anyone can post messages for the owner, where the messages can then only be read, modified, and removed by the owner. We assume this convention is met for all data pods, as we make use of this functionality for the communication between users.

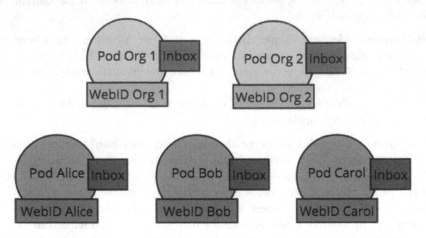

Fig. 2. The required components for our use cases. All governmental organisations (first row), all citizens (second row) have a data pod, WebID, and inbox.

4.2 Use Case: Citizens Sharing Personal Information

The Flemish government has developed a digital assistant that offers an integrated user experience when citizens interact with the different government administrations. A telling example is to provide citizens with notifications regarding the status of their public service, via a preferred channel. As the majority of the citizens have few digital interactions with their government, compared to interactions with the private sector, contact information and information about their preferences are often outdated. Therefore the roles are swapped, and the citizen's pod becomes the source for primary contact information and preferences. This use case addresses the first challenge and avoids that users have to keep their data up-to-date in the various portals of public and private organisations, which has an impact on the timeliness of the data.

We use an email address to illustrate this use case, which applies to any personal information.

Preconditions: Citizen Alice (A) can be identified uniquely by her WebID. Also, A has a personal online data store (pod), hosted on a Solid Server (S). Likewise, organisation (O) has a WebID and a pod.

Use Case 1.1: Share personal data. A authenticates to O, using secure delegated access. After successful authentication, A can grant O access to her email address by adding the WebID from O. O can read the email address from the pod after successful authentication. Extension: A can withdraw O the access to her email address.

Use Case 1.2: Manage personal data. A authenticates to her pod, using secure delegated access. After successful authentication, A can add her email address to her pod via a user interface. Extension: A can modify or delete her email address.

Use Case 1.3: Request access to personal data. O posts a request to the public inbox of A to gain access to the email address of A. After seeing this request, A grants O read access to her email address and send a notification to the public inbox of O. O receives the notification with a link to the original request. O can now read the email address from A.

4.3   Use Case: Citizens Sharing Authoritative Information

Governments aim to empower citizens to reuse their personal information, stored in authoritative data sources on different governmental levels. Telling examples are sharing a diploma when applying for a new Job as can be seen in Fig. 3, or obtaining information about their income and government depths when applying for a loan. This use case evaluates a student that obtains a certificate from the university and addresses the second challenge. As a citizen cannot give the government consent to share their data with private partners, we put the user in control by storing the diploma in the citizens' pod. To put it differently, in the context of GDPR, the data subject becomes the controller of the data. This scenario indicates that Solid allows reshaping the relationship between citizens', their authoritative data and the applications they use in the public and private sector. If the citizen becomes an authentic source, legal agreements must be made to ensure that the authorities have easy access to the data. If the citizen refuses, the government can exercise this right as it does today in the tax context [1].

Preconditions: citizen Alice (A) can be identified uniquely by her WebID. Also, A has a pod, hosted on a Solid Server (S). Likewise, university (U) has a WebID and a pod. An employer (E) of A also has a WebID.

Use Case 2.1: registering as a student. A registers as a student at U, and has to provide her WebID. This will allow the university to send certificates after graduating.

Use Case 2.2: maintaining provenance until graduation. U maintains the whole provenance chain until the graduation of A. The provenance chain describes the history of a digital asset, in this case, a diploma, via a time-ordered sequence of provenance records. This includes all followed courses, grades, teachers, … This information is not publically accessible, only A has read access to this.

Use Case 2.3: obtaining a certificate. A asks for a (summarised) copy of the certificate, so that she can share it with third parties. U will produce a summary of this certificate (not including the whole provenance chain), and send this to the inbox of A's data pod. This certificate is digitally signed by U using asymmetric encryption.

Use Case 2.4: sharing a diploma. Now that A has a copy of her diploma in her inbox, she can share it with anyone. For example, she can publish this on her data pod and give read access for her employer's WebID.

Use Case 2.5: checking the validity of a diploma. If E wants to check if the diploma of A is valid, E has to check the signature of U on this diploma. E does this by extracting the signature from the diploma, determining the authority (U). This can be done using existing document signing mechanisms, such as XAdES [4].

Fig. 3. Authoritative government data on diplomas, valuable for reuse in the private sector.

5   A Digital Assistant for Flemish Citizens

In this section, we discuss the implementation of our approach into 'Mijn Burgerprofiel'[6] (My Citizen Profile), which is a smart digital assistant for Flemish citizens [3] with an overview of all their authentic information and status information of their interactions with the government. The authentication method of My Citizen Profile depends on whether the citizen is using services that process information under GDPR. The European security standard[7] 'electronic IDentification, Authentication and trust Services' (eIDAS) defines a substantial degree of confidence in the claimed or asserted identity of a person to substantially decrease the risk of misuse or alteration of the identity[8]. Users can access personal data via the My Citizen Profile by using their

---

[6] https://overheid.vlaanderen.be/mijn-burgerprofiel.

[7] https://www.eid.as/home/.

[8] http://eur-lex.europa.eu/legal-content/en/TXT/?uri=CELEX%3A32014R0910.

Belgian electronic identity card via a smart card reader or via their mobile phone, with a SIM card and their installed itsme® application[9].

As an example, we elaborate on the first use case that was discussed in the previous section, namely citizens sharing personal information (e.g., an email address). We leave the other use case as future work. As mentioned in Sect. 3, Solid detaches application from data. As such, the implementation of our approach requires two components: (1) storage for data pods, and (2) an application for viewing and using relevant personal information. We discuss both components hereafter.

5.1 Storage for Data Pods

For our implementation, we make use of the Node Solid Server (NSS)[10] (version 5.0.1) to create and host data pods. If the user already has a pod, this can be used to share personal information. NSS implements the required specifications to allow users to register for a WebID and data pod, after which the server hosts this data pod and allows interaction using the Web Access Control specification[11]. NSS allowed us to create Solid pods for any citizens and governmental organisations. As such, the government provides data pods for all citizens by default. However, if citizens desire more control over their pod, they can choose to host a data pod themselves, for example by running NSS privately on their server.

5.2 Application for Interacting with Personal Information

In order to allow governmental organisations to request access to specific information of a citizen, or to view the actual information when access has been granted, we extended My Citizen Profile, where all Flemish citizens have a profile. Currently, this information is stored centrally within the databases of My Citizen Profile. For this work, we created a modified version of My Citizen Profile that instead stores information within the data pod of each citizen. The Flemish Government that hosts My Citizens Profile is a governmental organization, will also have one WebID, just like each citizen.

For our use case, we focus on storing the email address of a citizen. To achieve this, we implemented three components: a Solid linker, an email extractor, and an email visualizer. These components will be explained hereafter.

5.3 Solid Linker

Within the profile settings of My Citizens Profile, we added a field where people can link their account with any Solid WebID, as can be seen in Fig. 4. This involves logging in with any WebID via a pop-up window. By default, each profile is linked with the default government-provided WebID.

5.4 Email Extractor

If a citizen has a valid Solid WebID linked to its My Citizens Profile account, the application can attempt to extract its email address by following the links to the file in its data pod that contains an email address. Based on a WebID, the email extractor component can determine the URL through which the file is available in the user's data pod. With this URL, the extractor will perform an HTTP GET request, together with the authentication token of My Citizen Profile WebID.

If My Citizen Profile has been granted read-access to this file by the citizen, the content of this file will be returned; otherwise an authorisation error will be returned by the data pod of the citizen. If no errors were encountered, the email extractor component will return the discovered email address.

5.5 Email Visualizer

On the personal My Citizen Profile overview page, a field is added that shows the email address of the user if this could be found. For this, the email extractor component is invoked based on the WebID that is linked to the current user. This information is always extracted on-the-fly, which means that this fact is never stored on any other location other than the citizen's data pod. This also means that when the citizen modifies the value, that My Citizen Profile, and any other authorised organizations, will be able to see the updated value immediately. This visualizer can be used in automated processes, such as sending reminders on, e.g., upcoming elections.

Fig. 4. The front-end design of the Digital Assistant, including the citizen's consent for reusing data from their personal data store.

6 Conclusions

In this paper, we presented insights on the implementation of Solid in the Region of Flanders. The Flemish government adapted the My Citizens Profile to be interoperable with the Solid ecosystem to put the citizen in control of their data. We addressed two compelling challenges; firstly that government administrations struggle to keep personal data up to date, and secondly to allow citizens to reuse their data stored in government information systems in a different context. This initiative demonstrated that the Solid ecosystem provides an answer to the challenges by proposing personal data pod for every citizen, which enables them to share their data.

New avenues for future research include investigating methods to keep the most recent version of a (summarised) copy of the authoritative data, such as a domicile address, in the users' data pod. This should ensure that the information that is shared by citizens with the private sector is always up-to-date. Another obvious extension to this research is to inform the user with the nature of the given consent to reuse data from their pod, including: the identity of the reuser, the purpose, the fact that data only will be used for automated decision-making, and/or information whether the consent is related to an international transfer of data [6]. This concept is referred to as 'informed consent' and could be implemented as a set of templates in combination with the users' preferences, which should be exchanged through a standardised vocabulary [11]. Also, all actions should be logged transparently in the pod, including access to data, data modifications, giving consent and revoking of the rights, comparable to expenses on our bank account [24]. This fine-grained and structured log can also be used to detect anomalies and data breaches by using machine learning algorithms. To complete, future research should certainly focus on the different challenges of open government ecosystems applied to the Solid ecosystem, more specific on policy, the role of the different actors and sustainable economic models.

Solid builds upon existing Web standards and methods such as Linked Data and decentralisation, therefore Solid can be seen as process innovation rather than technological innovation. As the Flemish My Citizen Profile also builds upon Web standards, including the Linked Data stack, integration with Solid pods was straightforward. We have used an email address to illustrate this case, but the intention is to broaden this to all personal data. The right as a citizen to have control over personal data could be paralleled with other basic needs. However, it is a challenge to ensure that people have at least one data pod. The Flemish Government provides a guaranteed, uninterrupted and minimal supply of electricity, gas and water for household use[12]. This principle could be extended by offering the citizens a free amount of data storage at a supplier of their choice.

We expect that the insights from this Flemish Solid Pilot can speed up the process in public administrations and private organisations that face the same complexity when trying to put the user back in control.

---

[12] https://www.vlaanderen.be/vlaamse-overheid/persberichten/recht-op-minimumlevering-elektriciteit-gas-en-water.

References

1. Staatsblad, B.: Wijzigingen met betrekking tot de onderzoeksmiddelen van de administratie (2011). https://www.ejustice.just.fgov.be/cgi_loi/change_lg.pl?language=nl&la=N&table_name=wet&cn=2011041406. Accessed 09 July 2019
2. Berners-Lee, T., Verborgh, R.: Welcome to Solid (2019). https://rubenverborgh.github.io/Solid-DeSemWeb-2018/#title. Accessed 09 July 2019
3. Buyle, R., et al.: Semantics in the wild: a digital assistant for Flemish citizens. In: Proceedings of the 11th International Conference on Theory and Practice of Electronic Governance, pp. 1–6. ACM (2018). https://doi.org/10.1145/3209415.3209421
4. Cruellas, J.C., Karlinger, G., Pinkas, D., Ross, J.: XML advanced electronic signatures (XAdES). W3C Recommendation (2003). http://www.w3.org/TR/XAdES. Accessed 09 July 2019
5. Decker, C., Wattenhofer, R.: Information propagation in the bitcoin network. In: IEEE P2P 2013 Proceedings, pp. 1–10. IEEE, September 2013
6. de Montjoye, Y.A., Wang, S.S., Pentland, A., Anh, D.T.T., Datta, A.: On the trusted use of large-scale personal data. IEEE Data Eng. Bull. **35**(4), 5–8 (2012)
7. Esposito, C., De Santis, A., Tortora, G., Chang, H., Choo, K.K.R.: Blockchain: a panacea for healthcare cloud-based data security and privacy? IEEE Cloud Comput. **5**(1), 31–37 (2018)
8. European Commission: Regulation (EU) 2016/679 of the European Parliament and of the Council of 27 April 2016 on the protection of natural persons with regard to the processing of personal data and on the free movement of such data, and repealing Directive 95/46. Official J. Eur. Union (OJ) **59**(1–88), 294 (2016)
9. European Commission. Guidelines on Consent under Regulation 2016/679 Luxembourg: Publications Office (2018). https://ec.europa.eu/newsroom/article29/item-detail.cfm?item_id=623051. Accessed 09 July 2019
10. European Commission. It's your data – take control. Luxembourg: Publications Office (2018). https://ec.europa.eu/commission/sites/beta-political/files/data-protection-overview-citizens_en.pdf. Accessed 09 July 2019
11. Fatema, K., Hadziselimovic, E., Pandit, H.J., Debruyne, C., Lewis, D., O'Sullivan, D.: Compliance through informed consent: semantic based consent permission and data management model. In: Proceedings of the 5th Workshop on Society, Privacy and the Semantic Web - Policy and Technology (PrivOn2017), Vienna, Austria (2017)
12. Harrison, T.M., Pardo, T.A., Cook, M.: Creating open government ecosystems: a research and development agenda. Future Internet **4**(4), 900–928 (2012). https://doi.org/10.3390/fi4040900. MDPI AG
13. Janssen, M., Charalabidis, Y., Zuiderwijk, A.: Benefits, adoption barriers and myths of open data and open government. Inf. Syst. Manag. **29**(4), 258–268 (2012). https://doi.org/10.1080/10580530.2012.716740
14. Jia, J., Jin, G.Z., Wagman, L.: The short-run effects of GDPR on technology venture investment (No. w25248). Natl. Bureau Econ. Res. (2018). https://doi.org/10.3386/w25248
15. Mansour, E., et al.: A demonstration of the solid platform for social web applications. In: Proceedings of the 25th International Conference Companion on World Wide Web, pp. 223–226. International World Wide Web Conferences Steering Committee (2016). https://doi.org/10.1145/2872518.2890529
16. Mun, M., et al.: Personal data vaults: a locus of control for personal data streams. In: Proceedings of the 6th International Conference on Emerging Networking Experiments and Technologies, p. 17. ACM (2010). https://doi.org/10.1145/1921168.1921191

17. Narayanan, A., Toubiana, V., Barocas, S., Nissenbaum, H., Boneh, D.: A critical look at decentralized personal data architectures. arXiv preprint arXiv:1202.4503 (2012)
18. Pollock, R.: Building the (Open) Data Ecosystem, 11 March 2011. http://blog.okfn.org/2011/03/31/building-the-open-data-ecosystem/. Accessed 9 July 2019
19. Solid. Welcome to Solid (2019). https://solid.inrupt.com/. Accessed 09 July 2019
20. Van Kleek, M., OHara, K.: The future of social is personal: the potential of the personal data store. In: Miorandi, D., Maltese, V., Rovatsos, M., Nijholt, A., Stewart, J. (eds.) Social Collective Intelligence. CSS, pp. 125–158. Springer, Cham (2014). https://doi.org/10.1007/978-3-319-08681-1_7
21. Verborgh, R.: Ruben Verborgh on data & privacy. Imec Mag. (2019). https://www.imec-int.com/en/imec-magazine/imec-magazine-january-2019/back-to-the-future-how-we-will-regain-control-of-our-personal-data. Accessed 09 July 2019
22. Vescovi, M., Perentis, C., Leonardi, C., Lepri, B., Moiso, C.: My data store: toward user awareness and control on personal data. In: Proceedings of the 2014 ACM International Joint Conference on Pervasive and Ubiquitous Computing: Adjunct Publication, pp. 179–182. ACM (2014). http://dx.doi.org/10.1145/2638728.2638745
23. Whitley, E.A.: Informational privacy, consent and the "control" of personal data. Inf. Secur. Tech. Rep. 14(3), 154–159 (2009). https://doi.org/10.1016/j.istr.2009.10.001
24. Yeung, C.M.A., Liccardi, I., Lu, K., Seneviratne, O., Berners-Lee, T.: Decentralization: the future of online social networking. In: W3C Workshop on the Future of Social Networking Position Papers, vol. 2, pp. 2–7 (2009)
25. Zuiderwijk, A., Janssen, M., Davis, C.: Innovation with open data: essential elements of open data ecosystems. Inf. Polity 19(1, 2), 17–33 (2014)
26. Zyskind, G., Nathan, O.: Decentralizing privacy: using blockchain to protect personal data. In: 2015 IEEE Security and Privacy Workshops, pp. 180–184. IEEE (2015). https://doi.org/10.1109/spw.2015.27

Approaches to Analysis of Factors Affecting the Residential Real Estate Bid Prices in Case of Open Data Use

Dmitry Boiko[1], Danila Parygin[2(✉)] [iD], Oksana Savina[2],
Alexey Golubev[2], Ilya Zelenskiy[2], and Sergey Mityagin[3]

[1] GeoClever, Barrikadnaya Str. 1B, 400074 Volgograd, Russia
d.boyko@geoclever.ru
[2] Volgograd State Technical University,
Lenina Ave. 28, 400005 Volgograd, Russia
dparygin@gmail.com, ax.golubev@gmail.com,
ilyhaspmarine@gmail.com, nov1984@yandex.ru
[3] ITMO University, Birzhevaya line 14, 199034 Saint Petersburg, Russia
mityagin@itmo.ru

Abstract. Determining the procedure and approaches to automating real estate appraisal is an important condition for improving e-government on the basis of one of the key economic sectors throughout the state. The paper discusses a set of approaches to the analysis of factors affecting the pricing of objects that offer in a market of residential real estate. The components of the process of working with source data on real estate objects in Russia are described. Ways of extraction a structured description of particular factors, source data geocoding, merging data from various sources with the subsequent normalization of data for some factors are suggested. Testing of the proposed solutions was carried out on the basis of data sets for the Volgograd region: downloads from the ad placement site for the period from January to December 2018, data from the ReformaGKH website, the OpenStreetMap mapping project and the depersonalized information of the Unified State Register of Real Estate. Approaches to the analysis of physical (year of completion, type of object by period of construction, area of premises, number of floors of a building and floor of an apartment) and spatial characteristics of real estate objects were proposed and tested. The location quality factor is taken into account in the form of an integrated assessment of the results of the analysis of the density map of social infrastructure objects location. In general, the work offers step-by-step instructions on the formation and analysis of the information base, indicating specific sources and methods for calculating valuations, applicable for any region of Russia.

Keywords: Real estate · Pricing factor · Physical characteristic · Spatial factor · Object evaluation · Apartment · Data preprocessing · Data normalization · Dataset · Geocoding · Urban infrastructure · Open data · Bid price

© Springer Nature Switzerland AG 2020
A. Chugunov et al. (Eds.): EGOSE 2019, CCIS 1135, pp. 360–375, 2020.
https://doi.org/10.1007/978-3-030-39296-3_27

1 Introduction

Making informed decisions on managing the development of urbanized areas requires consideration of complete and current information on the organization of the space and infrastructure of a particular city. The urban environment has a rich stock of information. City data are presented in open access, in specialized databases and cadastres, in the form of ready-made reports and implicitly, as a stream of transactions of residents in the process of their life activity [1]. However, the situation is such that the data cannot be effectively used to support decision making due to fragmentation, heterogeneity, lack of structuring tools and processing methods for solving specific tasks [2]. This leads to a loss of data relevance, the impossibility of integrated accounting of current conditions and obtaining forecast estimates.

For example, for the Russian real estate market is the actual question of rational use of urban areas. In the central areas of cities is typical residential buildings of the third quarter of the last century. This situation is connected with the historical conditions of the development of cities in different years and is caused by the solution of the current tasks of that period, but the transformation of the real estate market under modern principles is required today. The discrepancy between the cost of capital construction projects and land located under them slows down economic processes. However, it is necessary to be guided by weighted information on the technical condition of buildings and utilities, the market value of real estate objects, the perception by stakeholders of key consumer expectations factors, etc., in order to make an informed management decision on reconstruction.

The lack of development and limitations to the use of existing methods of automating the analysis of pricing factors and models for evaluating real estate objects does not allow for proper verification of the profitability and effectiveness of territorial development projects. Potentially, the use of open data and information support of their intellectual processing should contribute to the formation of adequate to this time processes of life activity conditions management [3].

Residential real estate objects are in the highest demand market. In view of this, the conducted research is aimed at studying the economic component of this sphere, due to particular pricing factors of the market value of residential real estate. Formation and testing of approaches based on real conditions of working with available information will increase the understanding of all components of the processes in this area and solve the issues of inefficient management of the housing stock in Russia.

2 Methodological Tools of Cost Factors Analysis for the Purpose of Residential Real Estate Valuation

World practice in the field of real estate appraisal approaches the choice of suitable methods depending on the objectives of the assessment, the number of evaluated real estate objects and the amount of data available on them. The main concepts for determining the value of objects are individual and mass assessments of real estate [4].

Individual assessment is aimed at assessing a particular property on a specific date. Mass assessment is a systematic assessment of a group of real estate on data for a certain period, through the use of statistical analysis and standard calculation procedures [5]. Mass methods are used in the case of a large number of different assessment objects, grouping and classifying them. Both individual and mass appraisal of real estate objects is based on the calculation of three basic approaches [6]:

- Cost – reflects the required costs for the construction of the property.
- Comparative – the market value is determined by adjusting the analogue object in comparison with the subject property.
- Profitable – involves the study of the capitalization of income brought by the object during the period of operation.

A comparative approach is one of the key, especially when carrying out a mass assessment. This approach includes a number of specialized methods. Appraisers prefer the sales comparison method based on the analysis of sales transactions [7], which implies the existence of a certain amount of statistics on sales of similar objects.

Similar objects are characterized by a close location and comparable basic characteristics. However, differences in the quality of repairs performed, the number of bathrooms or other factors may not be taken into account. Such simplifications are due in part to the availability of usually limited information for large samples of objects. On the other hand, the final result of evaluation based on a group of analogues gives the average value (median) of prices, and the sought value is a specific indicator attributable to any property from the specified group of objects.

Of course, there are many factors that, one way or another, affect the assessment. In different classifications their meaning will be different. Researchers from Vilnius, for example, provide a list that includes both basic elements such as building age and number of rooms, and more exotic indicators of the area's criminality, clean air, well-groomed territory, lack of noise, drug addicts and alcoholics on the streets, and beauty of architecture [8]. Such factors, in spite of an objective and intuitive interpretation of the conditions that form the price of an object, in practice cannot be centrally and remotely determined for a large territory. And if the identification of the unique qualities of objects in an individual assessment is a mandatory criterion, then in a mass assessment only the main pricing factors have to be taken into account.

The approaches applied with an increase in the number of objects to be evaluated are largely based on the development of standard methods and techniques for statistical analysis. Most of the results obtained should be within the range of the average deviation from the real sales prices when checking the resulting models. And the assessment must meet existing professional standards in terms of model quality criteria. The standards of the International Association of Tax Appraisers directly indicate the average deviation values of dispersion coefficient for different objects types [9].

Rethinking the applied approaches to the assessment came with the development of new technologies for working with information. Specialists in this field are transformed into online agencies, and assessment methods include big data tools, artificial neural networks, and various means of intellectual data processing to take into account the widest range of cost factors [10]. Although often when building econometric models, the calculation of estimates of model parameters and the significance of the estimates obtained is still carried out in MS Excel [11].

Another pivot point for pricing research at the international level was the development of approaches to the analysis of the spatial characteristics of real estate objects [12]. Experts and researchers consider various ways of taking into account the location of objects, as well as variants of the initial data that can be interpreted to assess the spatial component [13]. In general, pricing issues have undergone a significant evolution at the national and supranational levels in developed countries. So, the statistical service of the European Union requires from the member-countries the formation of housing price indices based on the unified methodology [14].

The basis for the application of any tools are the initial data that quantitatively and qualitatively characterize real estate objects in terms of their location, size, main structural systems, etc. Modern research methods, including those using machine learning, are demanding on qualitative data. For example, in European countries, a systematic approach to the accumulation of information and an inventory of the infrastructure and property complex is organized at a high level, but current, high-quality and timely data is still expensive material [15]. In Russian practice, sources of such data are government and commercial information systems containing analytical and factual information on objects:

- Ads from services like Avito [16] and Domofond [17], containing the bid prices and the most complete public information about real estate objects.
- Public cadastral map of Rosreestr [18].
- Electronic trading platforms with information on public bidding at the federal [19] and municipal levels.
- Information about the monitoring of the real estate market [20].
- Official data of the territorial bodies of the Federal State Statistics Service [21].
- Analytical information about the price situation in the real estate market [22].
- Commercial research conducted in regional real estate markets [23, 24].

However, it must be stated that the openness of all these sources of information is relative [25]. Collecting the required amount of data on the proposals for a sufficiently large group of objects identical in characteristics, which could be considered as a homogeneous sample, is fraught with considerable difficulties. In this regard, the work on the project is actually divided into two equivalent stages. Operations such as the collection of particular properties of objects, the preprocessing of all existing data sets, normalization, must necessarily be preceded directly by the analysis of pricing factors. And information on residential real estate, which was in focus of the study, is presented in open data in an acceptable volume, unlike other types of objects.

3 Preprocessing and Normalization of Data on Real Estate Objects

Studies were conducted on real estate objects of the Volgograd region. A preliminary analysis showed that the initial information for a comprehensive study of the characteristics of residential real estate in general is presented in sufficient volume and in a form ready for automated processing [26]. However, the implementation of the main task of the study is hampered by a number of technical and organizational problems described in the previous section.

First of all, the available data on real estate objects are in a fragmented and multi-format state. A set of preprocessing measures should precede the stage of their analysis to assess pricing factors. The study of the state of the information base made it possible to identify the need for the following key procedures:

- Data on some characteristics of objects are presented in the form of an unstructured description in a natural language, requiring purification from related information and formalization of presentation.
- The spatial reference of an object is performed by specifying an address and geo-coordinates, but this basic information is often presented in a different format or is incomplete, which requires geocoding the entire source data set.
- A pool of information distributed across multiple sources complements a single list of real estate objects that need to be enriched with disparate data.
- Part of the characteristics of objects has a large scatter of values, it is noisy with incorrectly entered or single instances of data, and therefore it is necessary to normalize the information database in some parameters.

3.1 Extracting a Structured Description of Particular Factors

The Tomita-parser tool [27] developed by Yandex was chosen to solve the problem of obtaining data on the characteristics of real estate objects presented in an unstructured description in a natural language (in the present case, Russian). Support for various linguistic features, for example, the ability to check the concordance of words by gender, number and case, self-assignment to unknown words of the necessary grammatical characteristics, etc. can be distinguished among the advantages of this tool.

The mechanism of context-free formal grammars (CF grammar) underlies the work of Tomita. These grammars describe the rules for the formation of chains of words in texts and their interpretation as facts – structured data fields. The desired characteristics of the property (the state of the object and its address) acted as such facts in the conducted study. Accordingly, its own CF grammar describing the rules for the derivation of those chains of words by which these characteristics can be represented in the text was written for each of the characteristics.

Figure 1 shows a fragment of a grammar describing the rules for inference of chains. In this example, Tomita should interpret such chains as the name of the street on which the property described in the text is located.

```
StreetShort -> (StreetIm) (Initials) StreetNameNoun<gram="род">;
StreetShort -> (StreetIm) (Initials) StreetNameNoun;
StreetShort -> StreetNameNoun<gram="им">;
StreetShort -> StreetNameAdj<qnc-agr[1]> StreetW<qnc-agr[1]>;
```

Fig. 1. Fragment of CF grammar for street name.

Tomita parser returns an XML tree containing information about the data extracted from each processed text as a result of the work. An example of a visual presentation of the results of the Tomita-parser is presented in Fig. 2.

A wrapper program module designed to start the Tomita parser and process the XML tree received at its output was written in Python 3. The module adds information obtained as a result of parsing the XML tree to the description of the corresponding object as additional data fields. Figure 3 shows an example of the results.

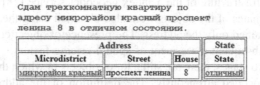

Сдам трехкомнатную квартиру по адресу микрорайон красный проспект ленина 8 в отличном состоянии.

Address			State
Microdistrict	**Street**	**House**	**State**
микрорайон красный	проспект ленина	8	отличный

Fig. 2. An example of a visual representation of the work of Tomita-parser.

Both desired characteristics were successfully extracted from unstructured descriptions of objects in natural (Russian) language as a result of the described actions. Property addresses were obtained for more than ninety thousand source advertisements for real estate properties. Information about the state of objects in the format of assessments "excellent", "good", "normal", etc. was obtained for 35,268 objects.

```
{'description': 'сдам трехкомнатную квартиру
по адресу микрорайон красный проспект
ленина 8 в отличном состоянии',
'microdistrict': 'микрорайон красный',
'street': 'проспект ленина',
'house_number': '8',
'state': 'отличный'}
```

Fig. 3. An example of the results of the wrap program.

3.2 Source Data Geocoding

The geocoding task is one of the most important, since solves several problems with existing data. The spatial reference for each property in the existing disparate sets is indicated usually in the form of only geo-coordinates or addresses recorded in a different format. So it is necessary to ensure the linking of several data sources that contain various kinds of information. Then the following actions require execution:

1. Reduction of address fields to a common format.
2. Geocoding of addresses and coordinates.
3. Exclusion of duplicate objects.

It is necessary to bring all data sources to a single form, i.e. standardize field names, before proceeding to geocoding. This task can be done in semi-automatic mode, since each data source has unique and common fields and was solved in two steps. First, the extraction of addresses from natural language texts was performed for the declaration files, as described above in Sect. 3.1. Next, a manually created dictionary for converting titles was used. In general, it can be written in json format as follows:

{"Description": "text", "Geocode": "coord", "Phone Number": "phone", ...}

At the second stage, the address information was reduced to a general form. A pass through all the data was made for this. The address of each element has been re-encoded from a scattered format into a general view. Such an operation can be performed using the infrastructure of the Yandex geocoder service [28]. The approximate values of the coordinates of the objects were also obtained using the geocoder in cases where the data contained only the address. The presence of object coordinates is a key condition for the subsequent assessment of spatial pricing factors.

After the first two stages, there are still a lot of objects in which the address is either not specified or geocoded erroneously. The definition of the address was also performed by the Yandex geocoder using the coordinates specified in the data.

Verification of several fields on their partial or complete identity was performed to identify duplicate data in the third stage of work with the addresses of objects. Address fields, phone numbers and descriptions served as such markers. In addition, only the most recent records in which there is data on the floor, area, floors number of the building were preserved in the presence of repetitions.

3.3 Merging Data from Various Sources

The project information pool included data from state automated information systems and third-party network resources. The sources included the following datasets:

1. The data were downloaded from sites for placing ads for the period from January to December 2018, a total of 146,429 objects of various types.
2. Depersonalized information from the Unified State Register of Real Estate (USRRE) in the Volgograd Region, which included information on 728,174 residential and commercial real estate.
3. The list of apartment buildings with the main characteristics, located in the Volgograd region, as well as services/works on the overhaul of common property in them according to the state system "ReformaGKH" [29] in the amount of 10,647 pieces.
4. Map data from the OpenStreetMap project [30], describing 202,903 infrastructure objects of all types in the Volgograd Region.
5. Separate lists of social infrastructure (medical and educational institutions), prepared by the relevant departments.
6. Stopping points according to Yandex.Maps [31], Google Maps [32] and 2GIS [33].
7. The database of the Federal Information Address System (FIAS) [34], and some other state classifiers and reference books.

The data from the first three sources needed to be combined into a single structure after geocoding. This task of combination could be done in several ways:

1. By unique numbers (FIAS, cadastral number, OKTMO, etc.) or their combination.
2. By "informal" parameters (address, coordinate, floors number, etc.) or their combination.

The second method was used to conduct data fusion in view of the completeness features of information from some sources. Python 3 and the pandas library were used for faster data processing. The main idea of this method was to successively cut off unsuitable elements using a list of parameters. Search by certain parameters of elements from the first source was carried out in similar sections of data of the second source. At the same time, the data on the number of floors in the building, the year of construction and the walls material indicated in the advertisements were prioritively checked and corrected according to the USRRE data. As a result, a list of 97,688 residential real estate objects in the Volgograd region was obtained at the exit, enriched with a full list of characteristics from all available sources.

3.4 Normalization of Data on Particular Factors

However, the formed base required another stage of purification and normalization. The following criteria were selected for final data preparation in this study:

1. Only objects with full address down to the house number.
2. Only objects with non-empty fields (price, area, floor, etc.).
3. Objects are combined into classes by area.
4. Removal of extreme emissions by price, area, number of floors, and other, quantitative and qualitative parameters.
5. Delete the first and last percentiles of the data.

Python and the pandas library were also used to normalize the data. As a result, the final base for analytical processing was formed after data normalization. The volume of the sample after normalization became 33,704 objects.

4 The Approach to Analysis of Pricing Factors

The formation of the value of the property due to the use of various approaches to real estate valuation. On the one hand, the selection of the main factors affecting the price of the property can be carried out by an expert method [35] with a survey of a large number of experts who are familiar with the pricing process in the residential real estate segment. On the other hand, the determination of pricing factors is possible based on the analysis of market information [36].

The described study is based on normalized data on the residential real estate market of the Volgograd region, which contain objective information about the state of the real estate market and the main preferences of direct market participants (sellers and buyers). All this is necessary for the formation of pricing models. The used statistical comparative analysis of the normalized data of the bid prices allows to establish the influence of the parameters of real estate objects on their market value, as well as to predict the emerging trends in the development of the residential real estate market.

4.1   Identification and Analysis of the Pricing Factors Applicability

The cost of residential property is influenced by many factors that differ in the degree of direct impact. There are factors that are not directly related to the property, but have a strong indirect effect on the bid price formation. Pricing, as shown by a comparative analysis of the market for transactions in residential real estate, is influenced by external, local and internal factors that characterize the consumer properties of the studied objects and the environment of their functioning [37].

The main objective of the study was to select those pricing factors that are taken into account in the evaluation process for the selection of analogous objects. Significant pricing parameters were selected from those contained in the text of ads (market information), state registries and factors of the local environment. The following classification of factors is proposed to use according to the studied approach:

1. The primary factor (fundamental) – microdistrict in which the property is located, transport accessibility, distance from the city center, the state of adjacent territory.
2. The secondary factor – a residential house (apartment location), its physical characteristics: year of construction, walls material, building type, its condition, number of floors (the floor of object), presence of an elevator in the building.
3. The tertiary factor – the physical parameters of a residential premises (room, apartment, house): total/living area, number of rooms, ceiling height, the presence of a balcony or loggia, condition of the interior.

4.2   Analysis of the Influence of Objects Physical Characteristics

The total number of pricing factors for any property is very large [38]. Factors whose change has a negligible effect on the adjustment of the transaction price are excluded from consideration in the sensitivity analysis process. The applied approach to analyzing the physical characteristics of the objects will be demonstrated using the example of one secondary (apartment floor) and one tertiary (apartment/room area) factors.

The study of the dependence of the specific bid price on the value of the area factors/number of floors of the premises is at the basis of the approach used. These factors, as a rule, underlie the regression analysis used to establish the market value.

The classification reflecting the main dimensions of the total area presented in the ads was developed at the first stage of the analysis. The entire set of residential premises (apartments) available on the market of the Volgograd region can be divided on the basis of the provisions of [39] into thirteen classes according to the total area of objects ("class" – sq.m–sq.m): "0" – 0–28; "1" – 29–38; "1.5" – 39–44; "2" – 45–53; "2.5" – 54–56; "3" – 57–65; "3.5" – 66–70; "4" – 71–77; "4.5" – 78–84; "5" – 85–96; "5.5" – 97–103; "6" – 104–109; "7" – 110–1000.

The presented classes are conditionally reflect the approximate number of living rooms. So the class "0" characterizes the total area of a studio apartment or a room in a dormitory. Classes "1", "2", etc. can be identified in a similar way. The presence of objects of different periods of construction on the market, heterogeneity of objects by type of housing and space-planning decisions necessitated the inclusion in the list of classes of intermediate subgroups "1.5", "2.5", etc.

The area interval specified in the class "7" takes into account all objects of extreme size that are present on the market. This class is not considered in further research.

A graph reflecting the dependence of the price of a residential property on its total area was built at the second stage on the basis of normalized information. The following conclusion can be made on the basis of the data presented (Fig. 4): the market bid price of the object increases as the total area of the residential real estate increases.

Analysis of the median values of the specific indicator of the price of a residential property for each of the selected classes is characterized by inversely proportional dependence on the object area (Fig. 5). Thus, the classical principle of real estate valuation confirms: than larger the area of the object, then lower the price of the object.

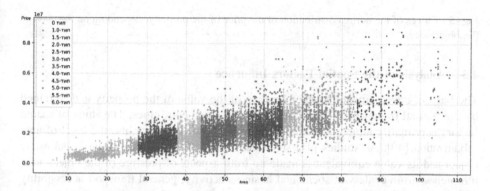

Fig. 4. The dependence of the price of residential premises in apartment buildings from the area of these premises.

The factor of influence of the floor object location on the price is due to the following dependency: the price of the object located on the extreme floors (first/last) is significantly lower than the price of the object located on the other floors. The matrix of coefficients (Table 1), reflecting the dependence of the number of floors of the location of the residential property and the price of the object, was built on the basis of this relationship. The coefficient represents the ratio of the average unit price of apartments located on the N floor of M-storey apartment houses to the average unit price of apartments located on all floors of the M-storey apartment houses. The obtained coefficients can be used to adjust the prices of similar objects within the framework of a comparative approach to valuation.

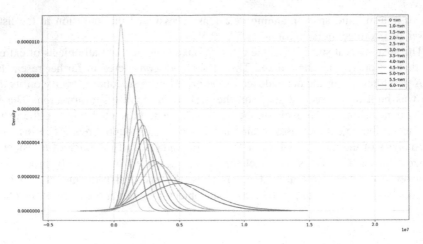

Fig. 5. Curves of the normal distribution of the price of the property, depending on the class of the object area.

4.3 Analysis of the Spatial Factors Influence

The basis of development and the formation of the value of the property is determined by the "spatial framework" – the boundaries of settlements, cities. The study of spatial factors is primarily aimed at studying the organization of space and the level of area urbanization [40]. As studies [41] show the impact of spatial factors on a real estate object and its value equivalent is made up from aspects of prestige of the object area, remoteness from centers of social and business activity, general transport accessibility and quality of the surrounding environment, creating comfort or discomfort of stay.

It should be talk about the limited information on the placement of key facilities (public transport stops, schools, kindergartens, clinics, shopping facilities, public catering facilities) that characterize spatial data, in open access. This is due to often not updated information in public systems, incomplete information on fully open services and inaccessibility for automatic data processing from commercial network resources. However, access to a fairly extensive set of sources of spatial data, as already described above, was obtained in the research process.

The approach used was to identify local centers of attraction based on an analysis of the distribution density of objects of the socio-economic infrastructure (Fig. 6). Conventional weights characterizing the degree of accessibility of public facilities for residential properties located in their areas of influence were measured for local centers of attraction. Spatial indices L were calculated for each object by the formula:

$$L = \frac{\sum_{i=1}^{n} \frac{w_i}{d_i^2}}{n} \tag{1}$$

where

i – the ordinal number of the local center of attraction;

n – the number of local centers of attraction;
w – the weight of the local center of attraction;
d – the distance from the local center of attraction to the object

The distance to the city center has been added to this factor.

The identified areas of concentration of objects of socio-economic infrastructure indicate an increased level of quality of life of the population in these areas. This, in turn, can be considered as a positive trend for the growth of the cost of residential real estate located near these local centers. In addition, the influence of spatial factors on the formation of the value of the property is confirmed.

Table 1. Matrix of coefficients.

Number of floors (M)	Floor apartment location (N)								
	1	2	3	4	5	6	7	8	9
1	1.0000	0	0	0	0	0	0	0	0
2	0.9833	1.0178	0	0	0	0	0	0	0
3	0.9842	1.0061	1.0225	0	0	0	0	0	0
4	0.9817	1.0371	1.019	1.0086	0	0	0	0	0
5	0.9754	0.9823	0.9938	1.0806	1.0317	0	0	0	0
6	0.9705	0.9647	1.0039	1.037	1.0219	0.936	0	0	0
7	1.0604	0.8915	1.0258	0.7943	1.0727	1.1435	0.9972	0	0
8	0.9747	1.0139	1.0206	1.0178	1.0146	1.0132	0.996	0.9941	0
9	0.9389	0.9962	1.0327	1.0212	1.0283	1.0181	1.0512	1.0154	0.9927

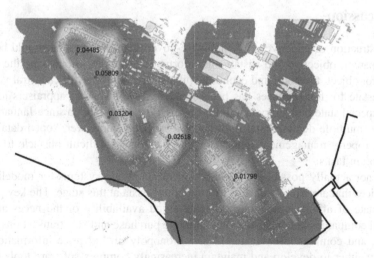

Fig. 6. Heat map of the infrastructure placement density (on the Volzhsky city example).

It was decided to present the results of the analysis in the form of a price map. The proposed method of price zoning is based on the existing boundaries of cadastral quarters. The average unit price (rubles/sq.m), according to the existing analogues, is calculated within quarter and is represented as a color gradation on the map (see Fig. 7). This approach involves the use of zoning results for analytical purposes, for example, to build monitoring systems for the administration [42].

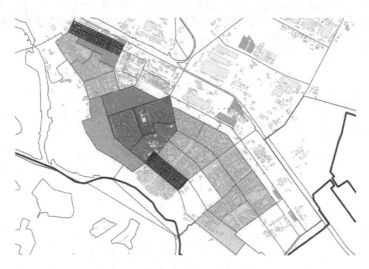

Fig. 7. Fragment of the price zoning map of the territory (on the Volzhsky city example).

5 Discussion

The construction of effectively functioning e-government institutions should be based on transparent, objective and sustainable information tools for monitoring the state of the control object, territory, and economic pillars. The authority for cadastral valuation of real estate for tax purposes has been transferred from market appraisers to newly created special state budgetary institutions in each region of Russia since January 2017. However, multiple departmental information bases and, moreover, "open data" in the field of property management remain for many regions a difficult obstacle to solving the valuation tasks.

It is not actually possible to construction of automatic systems for modeling real estate prices that are equally effective throughout Russia at this stage. The key problem of this state of affairs is imaginary openness and availability of the necessary data. Financial companies hide statistics on real estate purchase and sale transactions in their archives, and commercial websites form a monopoly on bid price information. It is necessary either to develop and maintain increasingly complex software tools for data collection [43], or to buy information from intermediaries.

Detailed information on apartment buildings, socio-economic infrastructure and other information that is important for determining the various parameters of objects is stored separately on the level of a variety federal, regional and municipal operators of data. Moreover, part of the information is accessible from the outside only on request with the receipt of data via non-automated communication channels.

In such conditions, the role of data analysts is extremely large throughout this research process. Only a professional can set the correct vector of calculations and restrictions with such a wide variety of conditions and influence factors, especially at the stage of developing technologies and approaches to the use of specific data sources on residential real estate objects.

In this regard, this study has a special methodological value for the countries of the Eurasian region, due to the same initial state and multiple attempts to transform the industry of assessment and accounting for the real estate market. The demonstrated potential of analyzing the data available to a wide range of specialists and their actual state outlines the range of research possibilities. In this paper, actually step-by-step instructions on the formation and analysis of the information base, indicating specific sources and methods for valuations, applicable for any region of Russia are proposed.

6 Conclusion

The paper describes the results of the study, reflecting the components of the process of working with the initial data on real estate objects from the stage of their preprocessing to obtaining valuations of particular factors affecting the residential real estate bid prices. The study of the applicability of the identified pricing factors to analyze their impact on the value of objects was carried out on the basis of the information base obtained from open sources. Two groups of pricing factors were identified. There are the (internal) characteristics of the objects, such as the type of object by period of construction, the area of rooms, the number of floors of the building, etc. As well as there are spatial factors those are taken into account in the form of an integrated assessment of location quality. Approaches to the analysis of the studied factors have been proposed and tested, and conclusions have been made about the appropriateness of their use, taking into account the degree of influence on formation the final price of offer for real estate.

The development of approaches to an objective assessment of development indicators and the use of territories in conditions of a high potential of modern information processing means has a special scientific and practical significance. The expected results, aimed initially at the tasks of monitoring complex geographically distributed urban systems, will make it possible in the future to develop full-fledged tools for informed management decision-making on various aspects of spatial and infrastructural development of cities.

Acknowledgments. The reported study was funded by Russian Foundation for Basic Research according to the research project No. 18-37-20066_mol_a_ved. The authors express gratitude to colleagues from UCLab involved in the development of OS.UrbanBasis.com project.

References

1. Parygin, D.S., Sadovnikova, N.P., Shabalina, O.A.: Information and analytical support for city management tasks. Volgograd (2017). [In Russian]
2. Ustugova, S., Parygin, D., Sadovnikova, N., Yadav, V., Prikhodkova, I.: Geoanalytical system for support of urban processes management tasks. In: Kravets, A., Shcherbakov, M., Kultsova, M., Groumpos, P. (eds.) Communications in Computer and Information Science, CIT&DS 2017. Communications in Computer and Information Science, vol. 754, pp. 430–440. Springer Cham (2017). https://doi.org/10.1007/978-3-319-65551-2_31
3. Mashkova, A.L., Savina, O.A., Banchuk, Y.A., Mashkov, E.A.: Using open data for information support of simulation model of the Russian Federation spatial development. In: Chugunov, A., Misnikov, Y., Roshchin, E., Trutnev, D. (eds.) EGOSE 2018. CCIS, vol. 947, pp. 401–414. Springer, Cham (2019). https://doi.org/10.1007/978-3-030-13283-5_30
4. Ozerov, E.S.: Economic Analysis and Real Estate Valuation. Saint Petersburg (2007)
5. Sternik, G.M., Sternik, S.G.: Property Market Analysis for Professionals. Ekonomika Publishing, Moscow (2009). [In Russian]
6. Gryaznova, A.G., Fedotova, M.A.: Real estate valuation. Fin and Stat, Moscow (2008)
7. Mirzoyan, N.V.: Valuation of real estate. Moscow (2005). [In Russian]
8. Burinskienė, M., Rudzkiene, V., Venckauskaite, J.: Models of factors influencing the real estate price. In: 8th International Conference on Environmental Engineering (2011)
9. International Association of Assessing Officers. https://www.iaao.org/. Accessed 21 Apr 2019
10. Kirzhner, E.: Big Data Applications in Real Estate Analysis. https://codeburst.io/big-data-applications-in-real-estate-analysis-502accc54dc8. Accessed 10 Jan 2019
11. Sanina, L.V., Sherstyankina, N.P., Bergen, D.N., Dashkevich, P.M.: Modeling of the price for flats at the regional market of real estate (at the example of Irkutsk region). In: Proceedings of Universities Investment Construction Real estate, vol. 7, no. 3, pp. 27–41 (2017)
12. Hill, R.J., Scholz, M.: Can geospatial data improve house price indexes? A hedonic imputation approach with splines. Rev. Income Wealth **64**(4), 737–756 (2018)
13. Chica-Olmo, J., Cano-Guervos, R., Chica-Rivas, M.: Estimation of housing price variations using spatio-temporal data. Sustainability **11**(6), 1551 (2019)
14. Housing price statistics - house price index. https://ec.europa.eu/eurostat/statistics-explained/index.php/Housing_price_statistics_-_house_price_index. Accessed 17 July 2019
15. Constantinescu, M.: Machine-Learning Real Estate Valuation: Not Only a Data Affair. https://towardsdatascience.com/machine-learning-real-estate-valuation-not-only-a-data-affair-99d36c92d263. Accessed 14 July 2019
16. Avito. https://www.avito.ru/. Accessed 18 Jan 2019
17. Domofond.ru. https://www.domofond.ru/. Accessed 22 Nov 2018
18. Public cadastral map. https://pkk5.rosreestr.ru/. Accessed 07 Nov 2018
19. The official website of the Russian Federation for posting information on tendering. https://torgi.gov.ru/. Accessed 26 Feb 2019
20. Federal Service for State Registration, Cadastre and Cartography. https://portal.rosreestr.ru/. Accessed 29 Nov 2018
21. Federal State Statistics Service. http://www.gks.ru/. Accessed 25 May 2019
22. Official statistics. https://fedstat.ru/. Accessed 19 Feb 2019
23. Real Estate Website. https://regionalrealty.ru/. Accessed 14 Apr 2019
24. Real Estate Market Indicators. https://www.irn.ru/. Accessed 20 Mar 2019

25. Karyagin, M.E., Romanov, V.A.: Russian large cities' open data: problems of innovative development. In: Proceedings of the International Conference on Electronic Governance and Open Society: Challenges in Eurasia (EGOSE 2016), pp. 120–125. ACM, New York (2016)
26. Parygin, D.S., Malikov, V.P., Golubev, A.V., Sadovnikova, N.P., Petrova, T.M., Finogeev, A.G.: Categorical data processing for real estate objects valuation using statistical analysis. J. Phys.: Conf. Ser. **1015**(032102) (2018). IOP Publishing
27. Tomita-parser. https://tech.yandex.ru/tomita/. Accessed 17 Nov 2018
28. Geocoder. https://tech.yandex.ru/maps/geocoder/. Accessed 30 Jan 2019
29. Housing and Communal Services Reform Fund. https://www.reformagkh.ru/. Accessed 04 May 2019
30. OpenStreetMap. https://www.openstreetmap.org/. Accessed 03 June 2019
31. Yandex.Maps. https://yandex.ru/maps/. Accessed 11 Mar 2019
32. Google Maps. https://www.google.ru/maps/. Accessed 01 June 2019
33. GIS. https://2gis.ru/. Accessed 29 May 2019
34. Federal Information Address System. https://fias.nalog.ru/. Accessed 08 Apr 2019
35. Ferlan, N., Bastic, M., Psunder, I.: Influential factors on the market value of residential properties. Eng. Econ. [Инженерная экономика] **28**(2), 135–144 (2017)
36. Treece, K.: Comparative Market Analysis. https://fitsmallbusiness.com/comparative-market-analysis/. Accessed 16 Mar 2019
37. Goodwin, K.: Location: Physical and Environmental Factors in Real Estate. https://www.propertymetrics.com/blog/2017/12/12/location-physical-and-environmental-factors/. Accessed 27 Dec 2018
38. Punshon, B.: What influences a property's value?. https://www.finder.com.au/what-influences-a-propertys-value. Accessed 11 Apr 2019
39. Set of rules 54.13330.2011 "Residential apartment buildings". http://docs.cntd.ru/document/1200084096. Accessed 31 Mar 2019
40. Alonso, W.: Location and Land Use: Towards a General Theory of Land Rent. Cambridge University Press, Cambridge (1964)
41. Bertaud, A., Renaud, B.: Cities without land markets: location and land use in a socialist city. http://alainbertaud.com/wp-content/uploads/2013/06/Cities_without_Land_Markets_Russian_Version.pdf. Accessed 15 Feb 2019
42. Parygin, D., Sadovnikova, N., Kalinkina, M., Potapova, T., Finogeev, A.: Visualization of data about events in the urban environment for the decision support of the city services actions coordination. In: SMART-2016, Proceedings of the 5th International Conference on System Modeling & Advancement in Research Trends, pp. 283–290. IEEE (2016)
43. Cherkesov, V., Malikov, V., Golubev, A., Parygin, D., Smykovskaya, T.: Parsing of data on real estate objects from network resource. In: Proceedings of the IV International Research Conference "Information Technologies in Science, Management, Social sphere and Medicine" (ITSMSSM 2017), vol. 72, pp. 385–388. Atlantis Press (2017)

Secrecy of Telecommunications as a *Sui Generis* Limitation for Data Circumvention in Russia's Digital Economy: Statement of Problem and Directions for Development

Vladislav Arkhipov[1]([✉]) [iD], Ruzanna Akhobekova[2],
Roman Amelin[3] [iD], Sergey Channov[4] [iD], and Victor Naumov[5] [iD]

[1] Saint Petersburg State University, 13B Universitetskaya Embankment,
Saint Petersburg 199034, Russia
vladislav.arkhipov@dentons.com
[2] Russian State Academy of Intellectual Property, Miklukho-Maklaya Street,
55a, Moscow 117279, Russia
ruzanna.akhobekova@dentons.com
[3] National Research Saratov State University named after N. G. Chernyshevsky,
83 Astrakhanskaya Street, Saratov 410012, Russia
ame-roman@yandex.ru
[4] The Russian Presidential Academy of National Economy and Public
Administration, 23/25 Sobornaya Street, Saratov 410031, Russia
sergeychannov@yandex.ru
[5] Institute of State and Law of the Russian Academy of Sciences,
10 Znamenka Street, Moscow 119019, Russia
victor.naumov@dentons.com

Abstract. This paper provides a legal overview of the Russian secrecy regulations in one of the areas, namely communication secrecy, taken as a representative example to which big data technologies may be especially relevant if applied to analysis of masses of information that is sensitive, but at the same time very promising if processed by the big data instruments. The main legal challenge for processing of this information on a large scale is not only personal data laws, but also very special secrecy regimes of their kind. The authors analyze the applicable rules, heavily focus on detailed analysis of the voluminous case law, and provide argument for the directions of development of legislation that may enable more infusion of "open" big data technologies into these areas. The directions are focused around re-defining of legal concepts in this area, providing formal certainty of the definition of personal data and explicit recognition of anonymization techniques employing removal of "linking codes". The authors use formal legal method and discuss the topic from the domestic legal perspective; hence, it may be useful, *inter alia*, for comparative legal research.

Keywords: Privacy · Information law · Telecommunications secrecy · Personal data · Identification · Semantic limits of law

© Springer Nature Switzerland AG 2020
A. Chugunov et al. (Eds.): EGOSE 2019, CCIS 1135, pp. 376–395, 2020.
https://doi.org/10.1007/978-3-030-39296-3_28

1 Introduction

1.1 Scope, Purpose and Methodology of the Paper

This paper presents the findings of a legal research focused on telecommunication secrecy as a legal concept used in the legislation of the Russian Federation. Hence, the perspective provided in this paper is limited to the subject matter and methodology used in legal (juridical) science, namely such branches of it as general theory of law and information law. Furthermore, this paper is focused on certain narrow aspects of telecommunication secrecy, which have been rarely researched so far in sufficient detail in specific modern context, i.e. what kind of information is included into this concept in current regulatory environment and what are the general limitations and perspectives for its economic circumvention. More "traditional" issues, such as e.g. human rights perspective or lawful intercept problems, are excluded from the scope of this paper. Thus, this paper seeks to answer the following questions in relation to Russian law: what do existing rules provide on the kinds of information covered by communication secrecy, on the grounds for providing this information to third parties, on relation of this concept with the concept of personal data, and what could be the ways to facilitate information circumvention in the context of big data. By the "context of big data" the authors mean the economy based on usage of the informational technologies that rely on processing of extremely large volumes of various data, most often indiscriminately from legal point of view. In this context, economy actors strive to achieve maximum economic benefit that such information may provide irrespective of whether the source information constitutes some kind of confidential information, e.g. certain kinds of personal data or communication secrecy. From formal point of view, regulation of big data technologies constitute integral part of digital economy incentives, and that is why they are related to digital economy from legal perspective (please see Sect. 1.2 for additional references in respect of both big data context and digital economy regulatory incentives).

The main thesis of this paper is that telecommunication secrecy is a sui generis limitation for commercialization of data in digital economy that has to be adapted to the modern realities. Because of the fact that telecommunications form part of the core infrastructure of electronic governance and open society, the limitations established by the regime of telecommunication secrecy are relevant to a broad spectrum of areas of concern, including but not limited to open government data, citizen centered e-government, smart cities, social media etc. The purpose of the paper is to remediate the existing gap in the relevant literature that focuses more on personal data and often neglects similar yet special limitations.

Consequently, the main cognition method used by the authors is so-called "formal legal (dogmatic) method", developed in general theory of law. This method is a special cognition method in legal sciences, and it implies two parts: the "deductive-axiomatic" and the "hypothetical-deductive". The deductive-axiomatic part implies performing the analysis of current legal rules (both statutory and elaborated in course of court practice) with conditional acceptance of their provisions as axioms by means of using various methods of legal interpretation (grammatical, logical, systemic, functional etc.). The hypothetical-deductive part implies forming a hypothesis of the result of legal interpretation, which is then confirmed or disproved with the same instruments. The formal legal method as a whole allows answering two questions: (1) what the regulation of social relationships is at a given instant and (2) in which cases there is no formal certainty of legal rules (or there is a gap in legislation). One of the most recent studies that contains a concise summary of this method of cognition is the research performed by Timoshina [1]. The use of formal legal method explains the usage and amount of legislative acts and court decisions referred to in this paper.

It is important to note that this paper emerged as an offset of a larger research performed, inter alia, by part of the authors of this paper (Naumov, Arkhipov, Akhobekova): the research project "Determination of the Scope of Data Comprising Bank Secrets, Communication Secrets, Medical Secrets, Commercial Secrets and Other Kinds of Secrets and Procedure of Their Transfer to Third Parties" (2018) [2] of more than 400 pages, performed under the assignment of Skolkovo Foundation as a part of research projects within the Digital Economy of the Russian Federation Program, featuring 11 jurisdictions within its scope (the materials are publicly available by the link provided). This larger research also involved the use of special "comparative legal method" (the legal phenomena of the same level but relating to different legal systems are compared in order to identify similarities and differences between them), developed in general theory of law by a number of authors including Van Hoecke [3].

Since this paper has strict limitation by volume, it is not possible to share the full scope of comparative research results to the degree that a critical reader would find sufficient. Nevertheless, some of the findings are included into the conclusion of this paper by reference. Consequently, the previously mentioned limitation is also a reason why this paper focuses on Russian law only. This implies the limitations of its own: the formal legal concepts that exist on micro-level of national legal systems, such as the Russian telecommunication secrecy regime, are defined by general framework of each respective national legal system. Thus, referring to non-Russian literary sources that relate to similar formal legal concepts of foreign legal systems existing on micro-level would be of little use for developing national legislation without detailed and extensive systemic comparative research, which is not in the purpose of this paper. However, the analysis of telecommunication secrecy as a micro-level legal phenomenon of the Russian legislation presented in this paper would be helpful for those foreign readers who are performing their own comprehensive comparative research.

1.2 Literature Review in Relation to the Paper

Telecommunication secrecy by itself has been a subject of research for quite a long time almost all over the world. However, the relevant publications are mostly focused on general regulatory and human rights aspects, such is e.g. the state of privacy as such or legal aspects of law enforcement surveillance, while the topic of technical legal aspects of information circumvention in the age of big data is covered indirectly or incidentally. The amount of sources demonstrating this could be voluminous; therefore, we provide just a few examples by means of reference [4–8]. It should also be noted that in foreign literature the concept and term "telecommunication secrecy" is not often used as a sui generis concept and is most commonly associated with a part of the general notion of "privacy" [9, 10] which is a fundamental concept in many Western jurisdictions that is historically based on the approach of Warren and Brandeis as reflected in their article of 1890 [11], and further elaborated by other researchers [12]. By way of comparison, in Russia the approach is different since the positive law of the Russian Federation lacks general notion of privacy, and operates with various kinds of secrecy and special information regimes. Some of them can be associated with a "privacy-like" concept of "inviolability of private life", but generally speaking, as Dmitrik puts it, "in domestic legislation the approaches of 'inviolability' and 'control' are mixed" [13, p. 54]. This makes it difficult to consider Russian concept of secrecy of telecommunication as a direct analogy of foreign concept of "privacy" or its clear counterpart, prevents using of simple comparative legal method that implies comparison of legal rules at micro-level, and explains why it makes sense to provide an up-to-date snapshot of the modern Russian regulation of this topic which is exactly one of the purposes of this paper and which could be useful for foreign readers who delve into this topic. We also have to emphasize that purpose of this paper is to consider special regime of telecommunication secrecy in the aspect of circumvention of big data. The foreign literature related to big data mostly focuses on the aspects of personal data and not always differentiates between general privacy concepts, personal data concept and telecommunication privacy often mixing it [14, 15], which is normal for the Western approach, but not fully applicable in respect of Russia.

Concerning domestic literature, the situation is to certain extent similar, with the exception that the Russian authors, of course, recognize the highlighted differences in general attitude to the concept of "privacy" as formal legal concept. The discussion of the communication secrecy is often limited to theory of law and constitutional law aspects [13]. In some cases, authors consider high-level considerations regarding principles of law [16]. There is also a number of publications focused on technical legal aspects, including those of access of law enforcement authorities to the telecommunication data [17]. Each of these contexts are important, but do not consider the matter in a very specific context of limitations for circumvention of data interrelated with personal data, which is exactly the focus of this paper.

In part of the literature review, we have to draw special attention to the issue of persona data. Nowadays it almost goes without saying that there is a conflict between incentives of various business agents to commercialize big data they collect and principles of personal data legislation, and that such conflict is not yet resolved. Several foreign authors pose this or closely related problems as well [14, 15]. As regards the domestic literature, what Savelyev, wrote back in 2015 remains true: there is an apparent contradiction between the context of big data and personal data regulation based on the EU model. In particular, big data is not compatible with the principle of limitation of personal data processing by a purpose defined beforehand, with the idea of informed, specific and aware consent as the principal instrument to make processing of personal data legitimate, and with the assumption that anonymization of personal data actually guarantees their actual anonymity [18]. Facilitating use of big [user] data requires certain improvements to the personal data legislation such as ensuring transparency of operations with such data starting from the stage of their collection, "red tape reduction" in part of consents and privacy management, developing new adequate methodology for anonymization of personal data and easing of processing of anonymized data, introduction of self-regulation mechanism and providing new effective ways to protect their rights to personal data subjects [19]. Savelyev suggests developing a new concept of regulating data turnover based on a complex approach that would take into consideration personal data legislation, civil legislation and legislation on protecting of competition [20]. From methodological standpoint it should be noted that we rely on Savelyev's definition of big data in application to legal aspects, namely definition of big data as a "complex of instruments and methods of processing of structured and non-structured data of huge volumes from different sources that are subject to constant updates in order to improve the quality of management decisions, creating new products and gaining competitive edge" [18, p. 47]. Both personal data and the data which constitutes telecommunication secrecy form potential sources for big data.

The outline and references provided above accurately convey the main focus on personal data legislation that is predominant in current debate in Russian professional and expert field related to what changes in the national legislation are required in order to facilitate commercialization of data, especially in view of the priorities that were initially set forth by the Program "Digital Economy of the Russian Federation" (now a national program) [21, 22] and Strategy of the Development of Informational Society of the Russian Federation for 2017–2030 [23], which are focused, inter alia, on regulatory attention to big data technologies. Consonant problems are considered by other authors who look into the personal data regulation under other angles [24, 25]. However, we have to admit and emphasize that personal data is not the only kind of normative regulation that is applicable to the information with the impact that efficient commercialization of data is put under question. As Savelyev correctly mentions, personal data legislation emerges in the late second half of XXth century because technologies allowing automated personal data processing emerged and posed substantially new threats that required new privacy regulations in addition to the existing ones [19]. At the same time, what is currently kept in the background of the existing discussion is that personal data legislation is not the only limiting factor for developing of data commercialization technologies. The "old" privacy rules on secrecy are still in effect and, in most cases, they act as sui generis rules that impose additional obligations and barriers on participants of the digital economy.

This particular aspect of relation of the secrecy regulation to digital economy has been so far rather neglected in the modern context of discussion in Russia. Yet it presents very apparent and hard challenge to the relationships in question. The selection of the secrecy of telecommunication as the research topic is important and it forms a representative subject of analysis for two reasons: first, it presents a proliferate area for dogmatic legal analysis based on legislation and court practice, and second, this area is of especial relevance for digital economy context since telecom companies form a backbone of the digital economy infrastructure. Furthermore, by way of example, IDC consistently highlights growth of big data market and puts emphasis on the role of telecommunication companies and their capacity in commercializing user data [18, 26].

2 Regulations and Practice Regarding the Communication Secrecy

2.1 Definition and Principles

One of the main problems of using information available to telecommunications operators is likely that the legislation does not define what constitutes information covered by communication secrecy. Such uncertainty makes further use of any information relating to subscribers and their communications difficult.

The concept of communication secrecy is indicatively mentioned in the Russian Constitution (Article 23) [27], the Law on Communications (Article 63) [28] and the Law on Postal Communications (Article 15) [29]. According to those laws, communication secrecy means privacy of correspondence, telephone conversations, postal, telegraph and other messages transmitted over telecommunications networks and postal communication networks.

The principles for determining which information is covered by communication secrecy are not specified in the legislation. Nevertheless, an interpretation of the applicable laws and regulations and case law together makes it possible to formulate the following principles:

1. Any messages are covered by communication secrecy regardless of the technical means used to transmit them.
2. The list of information covered by communication secrecy is not exhaustive.
3. The basic criterion for technical information and personal data to be covered by communication secrecy that can be formulated despite the ambiguous case law is the possibility that any details of communication, including its existence, participants and other circumstances might be divulged if that information is disclosed.

2.2 Which Kinds of Information are Covered by Communication Secrecy

Analysis of the legislation and case law shows that they treat the following information as being covered by communication secrecy:

1. The content of any messages regardless of how they are transmitted (via postal communication networks, via telecommunications or the Internet), including any enclosures, documents or information attached to such messages [29], (Russian Federation Constitutional Court Judgment No. 25-P of October 26, 2017 [30]).
2. The content of telephone conversations, namely any information that can be transmitted, preserved or established with the help of telephone equipment (Russian Federation Constitutional Court Ruling No. 345-O of October 2, 2003 [31]).
3. Information about postal money transfers (Article 63 of the Law on Communications [28]).
4. Information about messages and about postal items transmitted over telecommunications networks and postal communication networks, in other words, metadata (Article 63 of the Law on Communications) [28]. Interestingly, only the content of

such messages was initially protected by communication secrecy. The scope of information was gradually expanded and began to include different types of metadata [32].

Now the most controversial topic is the issue of what constitutes metadata and technical information covered by communication secrecy. The applicable laws and regulations do not contain a complete list of such information and the term communication secrecy is defined using descriptive categories. The case law on this issue is not uniform.

Analysis of Russian case law allows us to determine the list of metadata and technical information covered by communication secrecy as follows:

– data about incoming and outgoing signals connecting telephone devices of specific telecommunications users [31, 33];
– data itemizing subscribers' bills stating the date and time of all connections made, their duration and subscriber numbers, and also the subscriber device identification number (IMEI), data about connections between specific subscribers (date, time and duration), and IP addresses to the extent they make it possible to identify communications of telecom services users [34–36];
– information about email addresses, including the email addresses from which users collect mail, the email addresses users use for correspondence and to which correspondence is forwarded [32, 37].

It is interesting to look separately at case law over treating various types of technical information as being covered by communication secrecy. As already noted, the case law on whether subscriber numbers and other subscriber device identifiers (including the mobile phone serial number (IMEI), the IMSI number, dynamic or static IP address of a device on the Internet, the unique data network equipment identifier (MAC address) are covered by communication secrecy is ambiguous.

However, we can note that generally the courts specifically treat IMEIs as information covered by communication secrecy [31, 33–35, 38, 39], although diametrically opposed decisions can also be found [40].

The case law on whether IP addresses are covered by communication secrecy is not so clear. The courts most often do not consider IP addresses information covered by communication secrecy because that information relates to the subscriber's personal data [41, 42].

There are diametrically opposed decisions on the issue of whether email addresses are covered by communication secrecy [37, 43].

However, considering the latest decisions from the Russian Federation Supreme Court, we can conclude that the case law is developing in such a way that the determining factor for one or another type of technical information, including subscriber numbers, IMEIs and IP addresses being covered by communication secrecy is whether the information is requested with regard to the subscriber's communications or separately. For example, neither static nor dynamic IP addresses themselves, without being linked to users' communications, are covered by communication secrecy (although the Federal Service for Supervision of Communications, Information Technologies and Mass Media [Roscomnadzor], for example, treats static IP addresses as personal data).

This legal position is confirmed by an RF Supreme Court judgment that stated the following: "The courts reasonably proceeded on the basis that by providing intelligence and surveillance authorities with data about a user of communication services determined both by a static IP address (allocated by a telecommunications operator as a fixed address assigned to the user's end user equipment when the Internet access services agreement is concluded), and by a dynamic IP address, the telecommunications operator does not encroach on the communication secrecy protected by law" [44]. At the same time, such information may be protected as personal data. But if we are talking about providing an itemization of calls and other details of communication, then IMEIs, subscriber numbers, IP addresses and the like are considered information covered by communication secrecy.

The case law also shows a distinction between information comprising a communication secret and information about users of communication services, especially if that information is requested not in connection with messages transmitted by those users. As a rule, the courts and other government authorities do not treat information about subscribers and services provided, for example, subscribers' full names, information about connections to Internet resources, etc. as being covered by communication secrecy [42, 45].

Yet, even in this case, as the evolving court practice shows, the basic determining criterion for treating one or another type of information as being covered by communication secrecy is whether or not the information is associated with users' communications. If personal information of subscribers/users of the communication services requested in connection with subscribers'/users' communications, e.g., itemization of calls, then such information may be covered by communication secrecy.

Here it is worth recalling the administrative case against a local telecommunications operator, MGTS (a subsidiary of one of Russia's largest telecommunications operators, MTS PJSC). MGTS was subjected to administrative liability under Article 14.1 of the Administrative Offenses Code [46] (doing business in violation of the terms of a license) for providing information about subscribers, including subscribers' search queries, URLs visited by subscribers, the subject matter of information posted by subscribers on the Internet resources they visited, and a subscriber's IP address sufficient to generate an advertising profile needed to provide the subscriber with targeted ads [47].

2.3 The Procedure and Conditions for Providing Third Parties with Information Covered by Communication Secrecy

We can note the following regarding the procedure and conditions for providing third parties with information covered by communication secrecy.

First, the cases and procedure contemplated by the legislation for providing third parties with information covered by communication secrecy generally have to do with the restrictions established for public law purposes. In particular:

1. Information covered by communication secrecy can be provided only on the basis of a court order in the scope and on the grounds provided for by federal laws, unless federal laws stipulate otherwise (Article 23(2) of the RF Constitution [27], Article

63(3) of the Law on Communications [28], para. 14 of RF Supreme Court Plenum Judgment No. 8 of October 31, 1995 [48]);

2. The main sources of law specifying the procedure for issuing a court order to provide information covered by communication secrecy are the Criminal Procedure Code [49] and the Law on Intelligence and Surveillance Operations [50]. The Criminal Procedure Code details the conditions for investigators to access various information covered by communication secrecy (Articles 185-186.1 of the Criminal Procedure Code). The Law on Intelligence and Surveillance Operations covers the procedure and grounds for accessing information covered by communication secrecy when conducting intelligence and surveillance operations. The authorities conducting intelligence and surveillance operations receive access to the information if there is a court order (Articles 8 and 12 of the Law on Intelligence and Surveillance Operations).

3. Therefore, the basis for providing information covered by communication secrecy is a court order, which must be reasoned and substantiated, which the higher courts have said on numerous occasions (rulings of the RF Constitutional Court, RF Supreme Court and European Court of Human Rights).

4. Information covered by communication secrecy cannot be provided to third parties on grounds other than under a court order (with the exception of the cases contemplated by federal laws). And the law does not make exceptions for either affiliates or auditors, or for other third parties, which is supported by the case law [34].

The Law on Communications [28] envisions that information about a subscriber can be provided to third parties only with the subscriber's consent, unless it is provided to authorities performing intelligence and surveillance operations or the Federal Security Service (FSB). The rules for obtaining such consent are set out in the Personal Data Law [51]. As stated above, information about a subscriber is also treated as personal data.

Second, however, the legislation does not establish special rules or norms determining how to transfer (including across borders) information covered by communication secrecy to commercial entities.

This is likely connected with the fact that the telecommunications operator (person or entity providing postal or other services) is essentially not the legal owner or user of the information covered by communication secrecy. This concerns in particular the content of the messages themselves.

It is worth mentioning here one of the most important court decisions concerning communication secrecy, where the Russian Federation Constitutional Court (the "RF Constitutional Court") expressed important legal positions that could be very important for the use of communication secrecy in big data.

We are talking about Russian Federation Constitutional Court Judgment No. 25-P of October 26, 2017 [30]. One Mr. Sushkov filed a complaint with the RF Constitutional Court that the provisions of Article 2(5) of the Law on Information [52] do not comply with the RF Constitution to the extent they allow the right holders of mail and other similar services (in the case in question, Mail.ru LLC) to be considered the owners of any information and messages that are sent by the users of those services.

The basis for filing the complaint was the preceding litigation that considered the issue of the legality of Mr. Sushkov's dismissal in connection with his disclosure of the employer's trade secret by sending messages containing the employer's trade secret to his personal email address. The courts found the dismissal lawful, as sending a message to a personal address may be considered disclosure of information because the entity supporting that service becomes the owner of the information sent in the message.

The RF Constitutional Court accepted the complaint and consider the following issue: "… the provision of law that is understood in the law enforcement practice as making it possible to consider the person who provides email services the owner of the information contained in the electronic messages received or sent by the users of those services" [30]. The RF Constitutional Court made the following important findings when it considered Mr. Sushkov's complaint:

1. In accordance with the Law on Information, the person providing electronic mail services is not the owner of the information contained in the electronic messages received or sent by the users of those services.
2. It is the user of the mail services/sender of the electronic messages who is the owner of the information.
3. The status of a mail service (or other entities providing similar services on the Internet) is similar to the status of telecommunications operators although the Legislation does not state this specifically. Therefore, entities providing these services and other organizers of dissemination of information on the Internet are required to ensure communication secrecy, and take technical and organizational steps to prevent disclosure.

Here it is also interesting to recall the case of Burkov v. Google [53]. The essence of the dispute was that a user of the Gmail mail service filed a lawsuit against Google LLC, believing that his right to communication secrecy had been violated because the right holder of the service was reading his correspondence. The user made this assumption based on the contextual advertising he was shown and that contained elements corresponding to the content of the claimant's email correspondence.

In Google LLC's opinion, the claimant's right to communication secrecy had not been violated because it is a robot that views the electronic messages and compiles the ads on that basis. Also, Google LLC does not actually provide postal services and does not publish the ads, which are placed and set by users of the AdWords service.

In the dispute, the court agreed with the claimant's arguments and held Google LLC liable on the basis of the following:

"On February 21, 2014, when reading his electronic mail from the mailbox with the address '*****@gmail.com', B. discovered that the ad slogans were based on the text of an email, and it follows from the screenshot of the electronic message that both the ad and the email were in the national language using the Cyrillic alphabet. The respondent did not dispute this fact.

Therefore, the panel of judges finds that the respondent Google LLC in performing its obligations to third parties under advertising agreements and effectively placing it in its Google product segment conducts monitoring, inter alia, of email messages, and places those ads, inter alia, in the private correspondence of Russian Federation users of the Google product based on the results of monitoring a specific user of the product" [41].

Thus, according to these court decisions, telecommunications operators are not only not the owners of information covered by communication secrecy, but also cannot use that information even with the help of automation.

This is the major difference between communication secrecy and other types of professional secrecy, for example, doctor-patient confidentiality and banking secrecy, where most information comprising those types of secrets is communicated to banks and/or healthcare institutions for the purpose of providing services (treatment). In other words, banks/healthcare institutions are precisely the legal users of that information. It only remains to determine the limits of that use. Telecommunications operators, on the contrary, should not have access to the messages, telephone conversations, etc. themselves in order to provide the services: it is enough to have subscribers' personal data alone.

In this regard, it is logical that the legislation does not contain special norms about rules for obtaining and administering consents to provide third parties with information covered by communication secrecy. Nevertheless, some provisions of the legislation imply it is possible to access such information with the subject's consent. For example, the Law on Intelligence and Surveillance Operations provides for the possibility of eavesdropping on conversations on the written request of persons whose life, health and property are endangered (Article 8 of the Law on Intelligence and Surveillance Operations) [50].

There are also no special detailed rules in the Russian legislation on the form of consent to use a communication secret. However, various rules for providing communication services and the Law on Communications [28] provide that information about subscribers may be provided only with the subscribers' written consent.

The last thing worth noting is that, considering the specific nature of information covered by communication secrecy, disclosure of this information in the form of open source data or otherwise is not provided for by the legislation. Subscribers' consent is even required to publish information about them in a publicly accessible database of telecommunications operators' subscribers (Article 53(2) of the Law on Communications [28]).

2.4   Summary Conclusions in the Context of the Research: The Context of Personal Data

The dogmatic analysis of the normative rules and their interpretation by the case law suggests three relevant conclusions in the context of this paper that are directly exposed by the above paragraphs or are implied therein:

1. The legislation on communication secrecy forms a special set of rules that cannot be considered as a part of personal data legislation and, therefore, form a sui generis limitation for data circumvention.
2. The scope of data that can constitute communication secrecy (from the contents of the message that is naturally personalized by the fact that it is tied to a certain sender and recipient) corresponds to the definition of personal data ("any information relating to directly or indirectly identified or identifiable individual") [51] which leads to a situation where different sets of rules apply to the same set of data. It can

also be noted that this kind of situation was revealed in respect of most of the countries that comprised prior multi-jurisdictional research (especially including EU jurisdictions, such as e.g. Germany or Spain) [2, pp. 334–448].

3. In terms of potential access to the data by third parties, the rules on communication secrecy (a) do not provide instrument for expressing will of the individuals (even if each of the participants of the communication agrees to such access), and (b) in current interpretation by courts, these rules prevent using of automated and anonymous analysis of the information contained within the messages. Each of these aspects does not fit the logic of the personal data legislation that allows both things and provides instruments for them – this discussion is even more acute in a situation where functional interpretation of legal rules does not allow to identify what should be considered as lex specialis in this situation, where by default each area in question is a lex specialis in its own right.

In total, three points mentioned above give a situation where, to put it simply and exaggerate slightly but without breaking internal logic, (1) there are two different sets of legislation, which (2) regulate relationships about the same value (data), and (3) provide contradicting rules.

There can be two major theories explaining this situation.

First: there, nonetheless, should be a mistake, and these two sets of legislation have different subject-matter (like, in case of property, civil code regulates ownership while criminal code is focused on making citizens to avoid forceful distribution of property without will of all interested parties, but does not protect ownership per se).

Second: there is no mistake, and current situation presents a unique case of transition where "old" rules that emerged on previous stage of technological development are going to be replaced by new, more modern rules, yet the "old" rules have not yet been abolished and co-exist with the new ones.

The first theory seems not corresponding to the facts: both personal data and secrecy legislation have actually the same subject matter, which is protecting privacy of individuals [13]. In the light of this, the second theory seems more sound indeed, because the secrecy of communication can actually be seen as a set of rules based on the "old" principles that relate to pre-automated processing of personal data. Therefore, based on the second theory the digital economy context calls for not just aligning the legislation of personal data with the modern realities, but also aligning the secrecy legislation with the personal data legislation. The ways these two can be aligned are suggested in the section below.

3 Proposals Based on the Research Results

In light of the empirical material, we believe it possible to formulate the following basic conclusions and related proposals concerning possible areas for developing legislation and practice in these fields to be applied in the Russian legal system in order to facilitate commercial use of big data technologies in the area of telecommunications (please note that such kind of alignment logically comes before any discussions on whether such kind of commercialization could be used in compliance with the protected values, because it is more aimed to reach formal certainty of legal rules). That being said, please note that while this paper focuses on the communications secrecy only (otherwise it would be impossible to delve deep enough into the problem and maintain the formal limits of the paper), it indeed forms representative material, and similar problems are found in other secrecy regimes. The proposals suggested in this paper have been first formulated in the preceding research [2] that is quite recent, and the relevant academic discussion of these proposals in application to specific legal problem of the Russian legislation and in the specific meaning conveyed by this particular paper are yet to be formed in the literature.

3.1   Eliminating Formal Uncertainty in Statutory Concepts

As it is demonstrated by means of application of the formal legal method based on review of the Russian legislation and case law, the concepts of various types of secrets as set forth and used in Russian legislation and practice are not clearly defined, which leads to disputes over whether specific information falls under one or another type of secret. Even in those cases where certain types of information covered by a certain type of secrecy are listed in the laws and regulations in sufficient detail, the list is not exhaustive. The general lack of uniformity in interpreting definitions is confirmed by the case law. At very high level of generalization, similar problem exists in other jurisdictions within the scope of preceding research as well, but, from formal legal perspective at micro-level they take different forms [2].

Although it is hardly possible to create a universal and "once and for all" established specific definition for each type of secrecy, what can be done is to establish at the regulatory level the principle that one or another type of information is treated as the relevant type of secret. Based on the example of communication secrecy, the information being related to the act of communication (information identifying a specific message and circumstances in which it is transmitted) could act as such a principle. The methodology for identifying principles could be based on the idea of the cases in which a secrecy subject's rights could be violated by the method directly corresponding to the nature of the relationship. It is both admissible and necessary when developing such specific regulatory definitions to consider case law and other law enforcement practice. And it should be borne in mind that even if there are separate defined approaches reflected in the law enforcement practice, including acts of the Russian Federation Constitutional Court, such positions in the Russian legal system cannot replace the provisions of federal law in terms of legal effect. Accordingly, it is advisable to introduce these amendments at the level of federal legislation defining the various types of secrets (Article 63 of the Law on Communications [28], et al.).

We can note as a separate possible area for further discussion that in the Russian Federation there are currently no uniform general rules regulating the institution of secrets as such. The only regulatory act that considers this issue in a systematic way continues to be the Russian Federation President's Decree No. 188 of March 6, 1997 (version of July 13, 2015) "On Approving the List of Information of a Confidential Nature" [54] that was adopted more than 20 years ago and naturally does not account for the subsequent substantial development of law and practice. In order to ensure uniform legal regulation of the various types of secrets and administration of the law in this area we believe in future it could be advisable to follow the approach of establishing the general concept of "secret" at the level of the Law on Information (as a variety of confidential information defined in Article 2(7) of the Law on Information) [52] and to define the legal status of "owner of the secret" (obladatel' tainy) by analogy with "owner of information" (obladatel' informatsii) (Article 6 of the Law on Information) [52].

3.2 Restructuring the Formal Concepts of Secrecy in Relation to the Concept of Personal Data

The preceding research shows that in jurisdictions that rely mainly on the European model of regulating personal data relations there is often a lack of certainty as to how personal data and various types of secrets correlate [2]. The most general approach is that these two concepts are conmingled in a way described above in Sect. 2.4 of this paper. This is connected, first of all, with the possibility of broadly interpreting the term personal data in general ("any information relating to a directly or indirectly identified or identifiable individual" according to Article 3(1) of the Personal Data Law) [39], and secondly with the ambiguity of specific components of that term in the context of comparing it with the legal treatment of various types of secrets, in particular, the term "indirectly" from the definition above. Two aspects of this problem are therefore apparent: (1) the rules on the respective secret and on personal data simultaneously apply to the same set of data, which could present considerable difficulty in practice; (2) it is unclear whether information in certain cases can be a secret but not be personal data.

The recommendation is to adopt a legal position that personal data is the "umbrella term" for each specific type of secret, so that the legislation on secrecy – in part related to individuals – would be incorporated into personal data legislation as the most advanced one. According to the general rule of effective legislation (including considering European examples), both legislation on a type of secret and legislation on personal data may simultaneously apply to the same set of data. At the same time, considering that in a digital economy the legal procedures related to processing information need to be simplified in certain cases, and, in some instances, the secrecy regime may already provide enough protection, it should be admissible to establish in the Personal Data Law a rule making it possible to restrict the "absolute right" to personal data and, for those purposes, empowering the Russian Federation Government to set forth, at the level of a statutory act, necessary modifications to the personal data legislation (entirely or in part) in respect of the information protected by the rules on a type of secret and/or to clarify the criteria according to which the information can or cannot be considered as certain secret (as a subnotion of personal data, if we follow this new model) in the specific case.

3.3 Improving Legal Rules on Anonymization of Data and Establishing Clear Treatment of Anonymized Data

The research suggests that subsequent economically viable circulation of data received under a secrecy regime (and, as a rule, the associated personal data regime) is possible only if those regimes are first "lifted," however this can be done only if the information is anonymized [2]. Otherwise, it will be difficult for data to subsequently circulate in big data format due to the requirements to the relevant consents; the requirements are numerous and difficult to follow on the current technological level. At the same time, it is still possible to obtain consents and it seems necessary in cases where "targeted" information has economic value. However, only "irreversible anonymization" will make it possible to achieve these goals, while "reversible anonymization" can be considered a way of protecting information, not changing the legal treatment of the information. The objectives of processing large volumes of irreversibly anonymized information, which no longer falls under the regime of personal data or any secret (because there is no formal certainty for such qualification) cannot be achieved under the current regulations.

The key recommendation in this case is to establish at the level of the Law on Information (considered as the legal regulatory act establishing the general rules both for personal data and for various types of secrets, including subject to the aforementioned proposals) the concepts of "reversible anonymization of information" and "irreversible anonymization of information" or terms outwardly similar to them. When defining these concepts, to consider that "reversible anonymization" implies that it is possible to restore the original information, as intended in Roscomnadzor Order No. 996 "On Approval of the Requirements and Methods for Anonymization of Personal Data" of September 5, 2013 [55]. That order envisions that anonymized personal data will still be complete, structured, relatable, preserve its semantic integrity and continue to apply. It also emphasizes that anonymization of personal data is intended to protect the data from unauthorized use (that is why it is "reversible anonymization of information"). "Irreversible anonymization of information" implies on the contrary that it is not possible to restore the relatability of the information to a specific person, and, considering international experience, requires that "linking codes" in the information's content be deleted. The Law on Information also needs to specify that irreversibly anonymized information is no longer treated as personal data or any applicable secret. Such information can still be subject to the general provisions on confidentiality under a contract, and, all else being equal, such information can, for example, be the subject of civil commerce as a database. Irreversible anonymization can have economic value in those cases where big data needs to then be used for analytical purposes and not for "targeted" messages to data subjects.

From the legal drafting perspective, enshrining "irreversible anonymization" with regard to personal data will also require amendment of Article 3 of the Personal Data Law [51]. That article defines anonymization of personal data as actions that result in it becoming impossible to determine whether personal data belongs to a specific personal data subject without the use of additional information. It will also be necessary to amend other provisions of that law in which anonymization ("reversible anonymization") is considered as "processing of personal data." This recommendation also correlates to the aforementioned recommendations as "irreversible anonymization" by deleting "linking codes" implies that the information will no longer be indirectly relatable to that individual.

4 Conclusion

Big data technologies are some of the most in-demand and promising technologies in the world today. Many companies in Russia are also expressing interest in big data. However, the Russian legislation still lags behind the technological and is ill-equipped for the use and commercialization of big data. Moreover, many areas of legislation could present a serious obstacle to the high-scale commercial use of big data technology.

One of those areas is legislative restrictions on the use of different types of confidential information, so-called secrets. Russia is one of the most regulated jurisdictions in the world in terms of limits on the use of information. For example, there are more than 30 different types of secret (taina). The most valuable for commercial use in big data is information covered by such types of heavily regulated secrecy as communication secrecy (taina svyazi), banking secrecy (bankovskaya taina) and doctor-patient confidentiality (vrachebnaya taina).

This provides an overview of the legal regulation of confidential information treated as communication secrecy, taken as a representative example, and proposes several ways of amending legislation that would facilitate use of big data technology. The viewpoint expressed in this article is intentionally limited to purely legal aspect of the problem hence the proposals relate mostly to considerations of legal technique, e.g. internal contradictions or formal unclarity revealed in statutory texts, including by means of analyzing case law.

This paper considers a problem of reconciling a number of regulations limited to restricting circumvention of information to the modern context of big data technologies. On the one hand, these limitations that emerged during the period where modern information society technologies were not present, do form a barrier for development of new emerging bid data instruments. On the other hand, these requirements did not appear out of nothing and retain their relevance to the constitutional ideals of protecting individual secrecy which can be historically associated with the famous wording of the right "to be let alone", coined by Judge Cooley and popularized by Warren and Brandeis [11, p. 195]. Yet they should conform with the more advanced principles of regulation, the ones of personal data, as far as it comes to individuals, which can be seen as the next step in development of privacy rights. As it is mentioned in studies, the secrecy rights and personal data rights could be seen as passive and active sides of the same protected value [12]. The proposed development direction lies in search for balance.

What such a balance, as this paper suggests, implies as the most important step is eliminating uncertainty of both personal data, consistently indicated by the researchers from the adoption of the relevant federal law [57], and secrecy regimes by means of restructuring of legal connection between them so that secrecy would be considered as a part of personal data regime to the extent it concerns individuals rights. Additionally, the balance could be achieved by introducing special legal rules for anonymization techniques employing destruction of "linking codes" so that the information concerned becomes anonymized irreversibly and therefore has insignificant chances to affect someone's life. Moreover, in the grand scheme of things, and from the standpoint of legal theory, it seems to be no longer absurd or inappropriate to highlight the conflict between formerly developed rules and modern necessities of big data. The latter have long left the experimental stage and now have easily identifiable "social currency value", a concept that stems from theoretic sociology [58] that neatly describes what can and what cannot be regulated by law from common sense perspective [59, 60], whether we consider them from economic, or from other social value perspectives. The problem of legitimate use of data related to individuals, in general, is relevant for most of the areas of digital economy, including e-governance [61]. The problems related to improvement of the legislation on secrecy, including secrecy of communications, are currently raised on the federal level in new format, corresponding to the modern technological environment, by the officials involved in implementation of the national program "Digital Economy of the Russian Federation" [62], the integral part of which was the initial research that gave a rise to this article. In the context of this paper, this can be seen as at least indirect validation of the proposals formulated.

References

1. Timoshina, E.: Theory and sociology of law of L.I. Petrazycki in the context of classical and postclassical legal understanding. Dissertation for seeking of the degree of Doctor of Legal Sciences. Institute of State and Law of the Russian Academy of Sciences, Moscow (2013). (in Russian)
2. Arkhipov, V., Akhobekova R., Naumov V., et al.: Determination of the scope of data comprising bank secrets, telecommunication secrets, medical secrets, commercial secrets and other kinds of secrets and procedure of their transfer to third parties. Skolkovo Foundation, Moscow (2018). http://sk.ru/foundation/legal/m/sklegal03/22588/download.aspx. Accessed 2019 July 24. (in Russian)
3. Van Hoecke, M.: Methodology of comparative legal research. Law Method, 1–35 (2015). https://doi.org/10.5553/REM/.000010. Boom Juridische Uitgevers, Hague
4. Jones, M.: It's about time: privacy, information lifecycles, and the right to be forgotten. Stanford Technol. Law Rev. **16**, 101–154 (2012)
5. Reidenberg, J.: The data surveillance state in the US and Europe. Fordham law legal studies research paper no. 2349269 (2013). https://ssrn.com/abstract=2349269. Accessed 2019 July 24
6. Obar, J., Clement, A.: Internet surveillance and boomerang rooting: a call for Canadian network sovereignty. In: TEM 2013: Proceedings of the Technology & Emerging Media Track – Annual Conference of the Canadian Communication Association, pp. 1–10, https://ssrn.com/abstract=2311792. http://dx.doi.org/10.2139/ssrn.2311792. Accessed 2019 July 24
7. Bhatia, G.: State surveillance and the right to privacy in India: a constitutional biography. National Law School India Rev. **26**(2), 127–158 (2014)
8. Leenes, R., Koops, B.-J.: 'Code' and privacy – or how technology is slowly eroding privacy. Michigan Telecommun. Technol. Law Rev. **12**(1), 115–188 (2005)
9. Solove, D., Schwartz, P.: Information Privacy Law, 6th edn. Wolters Kluwer, New York (2018)
10. Bygrave, L.: Data Privacy Law: An International Perspective, 1st edn. Oxford University Press, Oxford (2014)
11. Warren, S., Brandeis, L.: The right to privacy. Harvard Law Rev. (5), 193–220 (1890)

12. Rodotà, S.: Data protection as a fundamental right. In: Gutwirth, S., Poullet, Y., De Hert, P., de Terwangne, C., Nouwt, S. (eds.) Reinventing Data Protection?, pp. 77–82. Springer, Dordrecht (2009). https://doi.org/10.1007/978-1-4020-9498-9_3
13. Dmitrik, N.: Limits of legal regulation in digital age. Inf. Soc. (3), 47–58 (2018). (in Russian)
14. Wachter, S., Mittelstadt, B.: A right to reasonable inferences: re-thinking data protection law in the age of big data and AI. Columbia Bus. Law Rev. (2), 494–620 (2019)
15. Stalla-Bourdillon, S., Knight, A.: Anonymous data v. personal data – a false debate: an EU perspective on anonymization, pseudonymization and personal data. Wisconsin Int. Law J. **34**(2), 284–322 (2017)
16. Pleshanov, A., Fetisov A.: The role of principles of legality and fairness in ensuring the implementation of the right to privacy of communication: material and procedural legal aspects. Arbitr. Civil Process (12), 58–60 (2018). (in Russian)
17. Ismailov, C.: Operative investigation events that limit constitutional rights to secrecy of correspondence when searching for missing people: problems of implementation and ways for improvement. Russian Investigator (20), 40–44 (2016). (in Russian)
18. Savelyev, A.: Problems of the application of personal data legislation in the era of big data. Law J. High. School Econ. (1), 54–61 (2015). (in Russian)
19. Savelyev, A.: Directions of regulation of big data and protecting privacy in new economic realities. Law (5), 122–144 (2018). (in Russian)
20. Savelyev, A.: Towards the concept of data regulation in the digital economy. Law (4), 174–195 (2019). (in Russian)
21. Decree of the Government of the Russian Federation of 28 July 2017 No. 1631-p "On Approval of the Program 'Digital Economy of the Russian Federation'" (lost its effect), "ConsultantPlus" legal reference system. (in Russian). Accessed 2019 July 24
22. Passport of the National Program "Digital Economy of the Russian Federation", approved by the Presidium of the Council of the President of the Russian Federation on Strategic Development and National Projects, Protocol of 24 December 2018, No. 16, "ConsultantPlus" legal reference system. (in Russian). Accessed 2019 July 24
23. Decree of the President of the Russian Federation of 9 May 2017 No. 203 "On the Strategy of Development of Information Society in the Russian Federation for 2017–2030", "ConsultantPlus" legal reference system. (in Russian). Accessed 2019 July 24
24. Tereshchenko, L.: State control in the area of personal data protection. Law J. High. School Econ. (4), 142–161 (2018). (in Russian)
25. Sergeev, A., Tereshchenko, L.: Big data: in the search of place in the system of civil law. Law (11), 106–123 (2018). (in Russian)
26. IDC forecasts revenues for big data and business analytics solutions will reach $189.1 billion this year with double-digit annual growth through 2022, 4 April 2019. https://www.idc.com/getdoc.jsp?containerId=prUS44998419. Accessed 2019 July 24
27. The Constitution of the Russian Federation of December 12, 1993, "ConsultantPlus" legal reference system. (in Russian). Accessed 2019 July 24
28. The Federal Law of July 7, 2003 No. 126-FZ "On Communications", "ConsultantPlus" legal reference system. (in Russian). Accessed 2019 July 24
29. The Federal Law of July 17, 1999 No. 176-FZ "On Postal Communications", "ConsultantPlus" legal reference system. (in Russian). Accessed 2019 July 24
30. The Russian Federation Constitutional Court Judgment No. 25-P of October 26, 2017, "ConsultantPlus" legal reference system. (in Russian). Accessed 2019 July 24
31. The Russian Federation Constitutional Court Ruling No. 345-O of October 2, 2003, "ConsultantPlus" legal reference system. (in Russian). Accessed 2019 July 24

32. Tereshchenko, L.: Certain issues arising in court practice when applying communication secrecy rules. In: Yaroshenko, K.B. (ed.) Case Law Commentary, pp. 145–153. INFRA-M, Moscow (2016)
33. The Russian Federation Constitutional Court Ruling No. 525-O-O of October 21, 2008 "ConsultantPlus" legal reference system. (in Russian). Accessed 2019 July 24
34. The Ninth Arbitrazh Court of Appeals Judgment of August 6, 2014 in case No. A40-57559/14, "ConsultantPlus" legal reference system. (in Russian). Accessed 2019 July 24
35. The Federal Arbitrazh Court of the Moscow Circuit Judgment of March 12, 2014 in case No. A40-56142/13-130-551, "ConsultantPlus" legal reference system. (in Russian). Accessed 2019 July 24
36. The Ninth Arbitrazh Court of Appeals Judgment of November 28, 2014 in case No. A40-113991/13, "ConsultantPlus" legal reference system. (in Russian). Accessed 2019 July 24
37. The Ninth Arbitrazh Court of Appeals Judgment of May 5, 2014 in case No. A40-153867/13, "ConsultantPlus" legal reference system. (in Russian). Accessed 2019 July 24
38. The Moscow Arbitrazh Court Decision of May 19, 2014 in case No. A40-28184/14, "ConsultantPlus" legal reference system. (in Russian). Accessed 2019 July 24
39. The Russian Federation Supreme Court Plenum Judgment No. 19 of June 1, 2017, "ConsultantPlus" legal reference system. (in Russian). Accessed 2019 July 24
40. The Federal Arbitrazh Court of the Moscow Circuit Judgment of January 15, 2014 in case No. A40-56844/13-149-539, "ConsultantPlus" legal reference system. (in Russian). Accessed 2019 July 24
41. The Kurgan Oblast Court Judgment of August 15, 2015, "ConsultantPlus" legal reference system. (in Russian). Accessed 2019 July 24
42. The Eighth Arbitrazh Court of Appeals Judgment of October 12, 2016 in case No. A70-5136/2016, "ConsultantPlus" legal reference system. (in Russian). Accessed 2019 July 24
43. The Federal Arbitrazh Court of the Moscow Circuit Judgment in case no. A40-56844/13-149-539 of January 15, 2015, "ConsultantPlus" legal reference system. (in Russian). Accessed 2019 July 24
44. The Russian Federation Supreme Court Judgment No. 82-AD16-5 of October 11, 2016, "ConsultantPlus" legal reference system. (in Russian). Accessed 2019 July 24
45. The Kurgan Oblast Court Judgment No. 4A-178/2015 of August 10, 2015, "ConsultantPlus" legal reference system. (in Russian). Accessed 2019 July 24
46. The Code of the Russian Federation on Administrative Offences of December 30, 2001 No. 195-FZ, "ConsultantPlus" legal reference system. (in Russian). Accessed 2019 July 24
47. The Ninth Arbitrazh Court of Appeals Judgment in case No. A40-14902/16, "ConsultantPlus" legal reference system. (in Russian). Accessed 2019 July 24
48. The Russian Federation Supreme Court Plenum Judgment No. 8 of October 31, 1995, "ConsultantPlus" legal reference system. (in Russian). Accessed 2019 July 24
49. The Russian Federation Criminal Procedure Code of December 18, 2001 No. 174-FZ, "ConsultantPlus" legal reference system. (in Russian). Accessed 2019 July 24
50. The Federal Law of August 12, 1995 No. 144-FZ "On Intelligence and Surveillance Operations", "ConsultantPlus" legal reference system. (in Russian). Accessed 2019 July 24
51. The Federal Law of July 27, 2006 No. 152-FZ "On Personal Data", "ConsultantPlus" legal reference system. (in Russian). Accessed 2019 July 24
52. The Federal Law of July 27, 2006 No. 149-FZ "On Information, Information Technologies and on Protection of Information", "ConsultantPlus" legal reference system. (in Russian). Accessed 2019 July 24
53. The Appellate ruling of Moscow City Court of September 16, 2015 in case No. 33-30344, "ConsultantPlus" legal reference system. (in Russian). Accessed 2019 July 24

54. The Russian Federation President's Decree No. 188 of March 6, 1997 (version of July 13, 2015) "On Approving the List of Information of a Confidential Nature", "ConsultantPlus" legal reference system. (in Russian). Accessed 2019 July 24
55. The Roscomnadzor Order No. 996 "On Approval of the Requirements and Methods for Anonymization of Personal Data" of September 5, 2013, "ConsultantPlus" legal reference system. (in Russian). Accessed 2019 July 24
56. The Russian Federation Civil Code (part four) of December 18, 2006 No. 230-FZ, "ConsultantPlus" legal reference system. (in Russian). Accessed 2019 July 24
57. Bachilo, I.: An important step in regulation of information rights of citizens. Laws of Russia: experience, analysis, practice No. 11 (2006). "ConsultantPlus" legal reference system. (in Russian). Accessed 2019 July 24
58. Abrutyn, S.: Money, love, and sacredness: generalised symbolic media and the production of instrumental, affectual, and moral reality. Czech Sociol. Rev. (3), 445–471 (2015)
59. Arkhipov, V.: Premises of the concept of semantic limits of law in the context of modern informational culture. In: Informational Space: Ensuring Informational Security and Law. Collection of works, pp. 272–287. Institute of State and Law, Russian Academy of Sciences, Moscow (2018). (in Russian)
60. Arkhipov, V., Naumov, V.: Pervasive legal problems of the Internet of Things and the limits of law: Russian perspective. In: Proceedings of the Institute of State and Law of the RAS, vol. 13, no. 6, pp. 94–123 (2018)
61. Polyakova, T.: Information and legal record systems of federal state authorities: experience of creation and problems. Adm. Law Process (10), 23–30 (2015). (in Russian)
62. Savva Shipov: Deputy head of the Ministry of economic development: the perspective of smart control over business is closer than it seems (2019). http://www.cnews.ru/articles/2019-05-31_savva_shipovzamglavy_minekonomrazvitiya_perspektiva_umnogo. (in Russian). Accessed 2019 July 24

Social Networking and Media

Social Media Sentiment Analysis with Context Space Model

Anna V. Maltseva[1](✉) ⓘ, Olesia V. Makhnytkina[2] ⓘ,
Natalia E. Shilkina[1] ⓘ, and Inna A. Lizunova[2] ⓘ

[1] Saint Petersburg State University, Saint Petersburg 191124,
Russian Federation
{st801923,n.shilkina}@spbu.ru
[2] ITMO University, Saint Petersburg 197101, Russian Federation
makhnytkina@itmo.ru, inna.lizunova@gmail.com

Abstract. In this article the description of algorithm of an assessment of mood of the statement is presented with the accent on the context of user's messages in social media. The article focuses on the fact that messages containing identical sentiment objects have different meaning that affects onto the evaluation of the sentiment of the message. An additional research objective is the identification of formal criteria for assigning messages to classes "core", "periphery", "non-relevant" to denote the role of the research relevance of the object key in the message. In this article, we have given several examples of authentic messages for each group.

The method was tested on the empirical basis of more than 10,000 messages to assess the relationship of users of the social network VKontakte to the object of tonality – a form of employment "freelance". The research methodology presupposes the use of basic and additional methods of data preprocessing, data augmentation, comparative analysis of the application of classification methods. The article includes comparative description of results of application logistic regression, support vector machines, naïve Bayesian classifier, nearest neighbor, random forest.

Keywords: Sentiment-analysis · Machine learning · Social media sites · Tonality

1 Introduction

E-government as a current G2C practice deals with wide range of questions from the actual administrative issues to understanding the causes of problems in society [1–4]. Most data bases of e-government resources are not opened to researchers due to data confidentiality, so the new algorithms of statements tonality can be done on the base of opened resources data.

Currently, various services are being actively developed and introduced on the portals of state services. Therefore, the number of citizens who need to be considered is growing. An important component of monitoring the activities of various authority initiatives is also the analysis of different open sources of information, also including

A. Chugunov et al. (Eds.): EGOSE 2019, CCIS 1135, pp. 399–412, 2020.
https://doi.org/10.1007/978-3-030-39296-3_29

sites of social network. The analysis of the tonality of such messages and the identification of the object of tonality in a message allows one to classify messages into groups and distribute them to the corresponding departments and structures and evaluate emotional background of a such communication. One of the difficulties in solving this problem is the ambiguity of many common words of the Russian language, which can significantly affect the final statistics on the inclusion of opinions and identified problems on certain topics at the stage of messages' automatically processing.

Evaluation of the tonality of the text is one of the most common tasks of natural language processing. As a rule, the assessment of tonality is built around the object of tonality, relative to which the emotional assessment is expressed. In the case when reviews of a product, movie, or comments after an article about an event are considered, the object of tonality is determined unequivocally. In the case when the object of research is a certain social phenomenon, a process, when analyzing an object of tonality, one faces with difficulties. Many homonyms, for example, the word "work" may mean, on the one hand, a type of employment; on the other hand, term "work" means a course work or an occasional paper. In the study of public mood about attitudes toward celebrities, for example, the word "star" can be used as one of the descriptions of this group, which in turn also means a celestial object or a geometric figure. The object or process of interest may be described in a joke or invented history and does not actually reflect the existing reality.

Thus, it is proposed at the preliminary stage of developing a classifier for assessing tonality to separate messages into classes according to the degree of their relationship to the "true" meaning of a word, to classify messages in significance from the context in which the concept under study is used. This approach will allow one to identify groups of significant positive and negative tonality of messages accurately.

2 Related Works

There are various approaches to the analysis of public mood in social media [5]. Most of them are based on text preprocessing [6, 7] it can be consideration of language features and improvement of machine learning methods for NLP tasks [8].

Such approach is effective for processing of quite complete natural languages from (traditionally) English [9] to German, Arabic, Bengali [10], Turkish [11] or Chinese [12], Russian [13].

Among the approaches to solving the problem of assessing the tone of a message and detecting emotions, the following types of classification are distinguished: binary classification (i.e., positive and negative marks for the dataset target units), multi-class and multi-label classification. As multi-class classification approaches, we can consider those used to isolate intermediate classes, for example, adding neutral comments [14–16] or negative comments are divided into very negative, negative and weakly negative or highlighting the main emotions in a message - anger, sadness, and so on. When solving problems of identifying feelings, one of the options is to use dictionaries [17]. Analysis of raw data from social media often faces the problem of identifying of the one message to the different classes at the same time (multi-label classification), for example as expresses of anger and hard activity or refers to factually different but semantically close topics [18].

Improvement of data preprocessing methods and machine learning methods for solving the problem of sentiment analysis significantly affect the quality of the results obtained, but it also needs to consider the context in which the word object of tonality is said. Such a classification will allow one to filter messages to which the word marker is formally contained, but its meaning does not correspond to the subject of the research, this is also affected the position of the words in the text [19] and other features of texts in natural language [20]. The value in which the word is used depends largely on the social context [21].

The accent on the context component in sentiment analysis in the research of natural language processing is very actual to analyze wide number of applied problems: political rhetoric [22], opinions [23] or different emotions [24], forming of special vocabulary of affective lexicon of different groups of users [25] or understanding of representations attributed to gender-based violence [26] and many other hot social topics [27]. At the same time, formalized practices that would allow dividing message sets into groups, depending on the context, are practically absent, although such an approach may be required for analyzing messages from various specific user groups, when the meaning of word markers may differ significantly from their most common meanings.

3 Dataset

The dataset is a set of messages from the social network VKontakte, containing statements of users of the social network about freelancing. It consists of 10,000 messages, including positive, negative and neutral messages. The tone of the message was determined in accordance with the rules that allowed answering the question "How the author of the message relates to the word-marker (for example, freelance)" :

1. Positive - statement, confidence/conviction, possibility, determination, etc. In semantics, the values of the analyzed units approach the value of "GOOD" or are identical to it.
2. Neutral - information, the actual information provided in the foundations by means of language, reflecting the emotional-expressive coloring. Any advertising of freelancing and what is associated with it (as a forced but constant source of non-negative), any arguments about freelance, including advertising or anti-advertising.
   3. The evaluation or negative. Semantically, the values of the analyzed units are close to the value of "BAD", or identical to it.

Also, all messages were divided into 3 groups: "core", "periphery", "non-relevant" depending on the context in which the word "freelance" is used.

In this article we formulated several working concepts that let us to evaluate the opinion orientation (or sentiment) in a manner of "point estimate", to eliminate the non-relevant messages and to differ relevant ones to "the core" and "the periphery" messages. As usual for the sentiment-analysis of the natural language it is necessary to solve two targets: (1) to make the unique vocabularies for each specific case; (2) to increase the range of using rules. We considered that text of a message can include the individ (subjective) opinion on it directly ("the core"), but also the text of the message about the object of tonality can include the individ (subject's) opinion just formally ant its expressive/emotional meaning will relate to some other semantic objects ("the periphery"). This perspective allows us not just to evaluate the message tonality but make the pointed (direct) evaluation of the user's attitudes to the object of the tonality. And considering the place of the object of the tonality in the original message allows us to do the evaluation impartial.

The message belongs to the class "core" if the word-marker is used in its direct meaning (or 1st value from the dictionary) in the studied context (e.g., work or freelance is equal to activity that brings income or is a work like a "free artist", when an employee (this is usually a designer, copywriter or programmer) is engaged in the search for orders and clients, not working for hire and not having the need to get up every day at 7 am and play in the office), there is a demonstration of subjective opinion and/or personal experience. The message belongs to the class "core" if it directly allows to evaluate the user's opinion on the new form of employment, i.e. if the word "freelance" is used in the meaning of "labor activity", "work".

In the case of the "periphery" class, the word-marker is used in the associated knowledge within the context of the study, or any subsequent values of the dictionary beyond the 1st meaning of the word in the vocabulary of Russian language, or there is a demonstration of their affiliation to freelancing. But the author in this direction thinks/says/reports his/her opinion or reflection on the subject (formed disposition and persistent theme in the discussions). The periphery class includes messages in which the meaning of the word freelance is close to the concept of work, i.e. it is possible to indirectly assess the user's attitude to this form of employment.

Non-relevant – the word marker is used with new or remote meaning from the context of the study shades of meaning or general reasoning and as such the judgment about the freelance is not expressed. Some of the messages contain the word freelance, but do not interest the researcher, because they are fictional stories or the word freelance is used for any other purposes.

The considered dataset was collected and marked by the authors of the article with the participation of experts-linguists and labor market specialists. Examples are presented in Table 1.

Table 1. Samples of messages

Original text of message	Group
vot i ya o tom zhe, ya dlya togo chtoby puteshestvovat' ushla vo frilans. Deneg men'she, no otpuskov bol'she i v lyuboe vremya, a ne tol'ko oktyabr' i novyj god kak mne daval direktor here I am about the same, I went to freelance in order to travel. Less money, but more vacations and at any time, not just October and the new year, as the director gave me	core
a vas frilans ne zatyagivayet v beskonechnuyu rutinu, gde vy ne pomnite chisel i dney nedeli, kazhdyy den' kak pod kopirku, a zhizn' postepenno perekhodit v set'. Byli kakiye to peremeny v zhizni za posledniye 3 mesyatsa skazhem	

(continued)

Table 1. (*continued*)

Original text of message	Group
and you do not freelance draws into an endless routine, where you do not remember the numbers and days of the week, every day as a carbon paper, and life gradually goes into the network. There have been some changes in life over the past 3 months, say	
po dannym minobra, naprimer, kazhdyy chetvertyy vypusknik vuza ne trudoustroyen, a tekh komu poschastlivitsya nayti rabotu nachal'stvo starayetsya vytolknut' vo frilans, chtoby ne platit' nalogi i pensionnyye otchisleniya. No i eto yeshche ne vsya vedomstvennaya otchetnost' ne vklyuchayet tekh kto proshel obu-cheniye na platnoy osnove according to the Ministry of Industry, for example, every fourth university graduate is not employed, and those who are lucky enough to find a job are trying to push their bosses into freelancing so as not to pay taxes and pension contributions. But this is not all departmental reporting does not include those who have been trained on a fee basis	periphery
a dlya tekh kto khochet zarabatyvat' bol'shiye den'gi ya skoro opublikuyu sayty frilansa kotoryye trebuyut men'she navykov i bol'shikh zarabotkov vsem udachi but for those who want to earn big money, I will soon publish freelancing sites that require less skills and big earnings all good luck	
Vsem privet! Novaya glava moikh zametok nachinayushchego puteshestvennika posvyashchena nebol'shomu obvorozhitel'nomu ostrovu v siamskom zalive Samui, izvestnyy kurort taylanda. Vsegda s zamiraniyem serdtsa slushala i chitala istorii kak lyudi brosayut vse i yedut rabotat' frilansom i zhit' v etom zharkom solnechnom meste i dazhe pobaivalas' Hello! A new chapter of my notes for a novice traveler is devoted to a small charming island in the Siamese Bay of Samui, the famous resort of Thailand. Always with a sinking heart listened and read stories of how people give up everything and go to work as freelancing and live in this hot sunny place and even feared	non-relevant
nashli drug druga na frilans ploshchadke dlya obshcheniya. A yeshche s odnimi takimi poznakomilas' v reale, no oni uzhe zhenaty byli ran'she i drug druga tak nashli found each other on the freelance platform for communication. And with some of these met in real life, but they were already married before and each other found it	

4 Preprocessing

When solving the problem of classifying text messages, data preprocessing is of great importance. Basic data editing included lowercase text, deletion of links, IP addresses, numbers and punctuation, images, and links for images. Special attention was paid to the processing of profanity in messages, since its use, as a rule, signals the negativity of the commentary, including the methods used to correct typos in the profanity. One of the facts that complicate working with profanity is that such words are often either absent from pre-trained vector representations of words (for example, if they are trained on news texts) or have a very low frequency of occurrence. The next stage of data preparation included the removal of functional words or stop words (prepositions, conjunctions, etc.), which made it possible to reduce the dimensionality of the attribute model and take into account only words that have a meaning. Next is the morphological analysis. The normalization of words was carried out using the methods of stemming and lemmatization. This makes it possible to significantly reduce the dimension and, as a result, all significant words appearing in the document appear as signs of the document. For the implementation of stemming, the RussianStemmer module of the NLTK-package was used, for the lemmatization, the MorphAnalyzer module of the pymorphy2 package. The next step in data preparation was the construction of the attribute model, i.e. construction of some numerical model of the text. The following approaches were used to build the feature model:

Construction of the word bag model with the TF-IDF measure. The "Bag of Words" model allows you to represent a document as a multidimensional vector of words and their weights in a document, each document is a vector in multidimensional space, the coordinates correspond to the numbers of words, and the coordinate of values corresponds to the weights. TF-IDF (TF - term frequency, IDF - inverse document frequency) is a statistical measure used to assess the importance of a word in the context of a document that is part of a document collection or corpus. The weight of some words is proportional to the frequency of use of the word in the document and inversely proportional to the frequency of use of the word in all documents of the collection. 2. Use different variants of pre-trained Word2Vec vector models. The Word2Vec technology builds a multidimensional vector space where a vector is associated with each word, and the coordinates of the vectors are chosen based on the semantic proximity of words. Thus, words that are close in meaning in the space obtained are at close distances from each other. We used the Word2Vec model that was independently trained on the case under study and the pre-trained model from the "RusVectōrēs: semantic models for the Russian language" [28]. This resource contains vector models based on various corpuses (National Corpus of the Russian Language; Wikipedia; News from predominantly Russian-language news sites (about 30 million documents); Araneum Russicum Maximum; Taiga; Web: randomly selected 9 million Russian-language web pages). Vector models are available with various pre-processing options for cases, with or without deleting stop words. The advantage of using a ready-made pre-schooled Word2Vec model in comparison with independent learning of a model is that the first one was trained on more data. However, its disadvantage is that it may not contain all the words from the corpus under study.

5 Data Augmentation

Improving the quality of the constructed models allowed the use of various methods of augmentation of data:

- increasing the training set due to concatenation, i.e. pasting two comments and labeling the result of combining comment tags;

– increasing in training and test sets due to the direct and reverse translation of the text of messages from Russian into English, German, French and Spanish. For a training set, such an approach (train-time augments) makes it possible to increase its volume several times. On a test set (test-time augments), the classification algorithm is used for real comment and for three comments, which are the results of double translation. As a result, the final comment of the combined classifier is assigned to the real commentary, which corresponds to the "opinion" of the majority.

6 Methods

The following methods were used to solve the classification task: logistic regression, support vector machine, nearest neighbor method, naive Bayes classifier, and random forest.

Logistic regression solves the problem of classification by fitting data to a logistic curve. This method also allows one to estimate the posterior probabilities of the belonging of objects to classes. To implement the logistic regression, we used the sklearn package LogisticRegression.

A naive Bayes classifier is a simple probabilistic classifier based on the application of the Bayes theorem and the additional assumption that the objects being classified are described by independent signs. The advantages of this method are high speed and simplicity of the mathematical model, a small amount of data required for training, parameter estimation and classification. We used the sklearn package MultinomialNB module.

The method of nearest neighbors is based on evaluating the similarity of objects. The classifiable object belongs to the class to which most of its neighbors belong - the k nearest to it objects of the training set. In problems with two classes, the number of neighbors is taken odd so that no ambiguity situations arise when the same number of neighbors belongs to different classes. To implement this method, the KNeighborsClassifier module of the sklearn package was used.

The essence of the support vector method is to translate the source vectors into a space of higher dimension and search for a separating hyperplane in this space. The standard method for finding the best way to divide into classes is to construct two parallel hyperplanes that divide the classes. One of the advantages of this method is that it reduces to solving a quadratic programming problem in a convex domain, which always has a unique solution. In this case, optimization is much more efficient than when applying methods that solve a multi-extremal problem. Also, the SVM method finds a dividing strip of maximum width between parallel hyperplanes, which leads to a more confident classification. To implement the support vector method, the sklearn module SVC was used in the work.

To implement the support vector method, the sklearn module SVC was used in the work.

The main idea of the method is to use a large ensemble of decision trees, each of which gives a not very high quality of classification, but due to their large number, the result is good. Decision trees, in turn, are a set of rules in a consistent hierarchical structure, where each object corresponds to a single node that provides a solution. The optimal number of trees is chosen in such a way as to minimize the classifier error on the test set. The random forest was implemented using the RandomForestClassifier module of the sklearn package.

7 Evaluation

The following measures were used to assess the accuracy of the classification: precision, recall and f1-score. Precision is determined by formula (1), recall - by formula (2).

$$Precision = \frac{TP}{TP + FP} \tag{1}$$

$$Recall = \frac{TP}{TP + FN} \tag{2}$$

TP is a true positive solution, TN is a true negative solution, FP is a false positive solution, FN is a false negative solution.

Here, the precision shows the proportion of certain correctly defined positive answers from all the answers defined as positive, and recall - the proportion of certain correctly defined positive answers from all truly positive answers. The essence of this approach to assessment is a constant balancing between precision and recall, since an increase in precision leads to a decrease in recall, and vice versa.

The F-score is an estimate based on the results of an assessment of precision, recall, and is calculated using formula (3).

$$F_1 = \frac{2 \cdot Precision \cdot Recall}{Precision + Recall} \tag{3}$$

To assess the results of the experiment were used weighting by class frequency scores. The calculation of the weighted estimate for the multiclass classification is carried out according to the formula (4):

$$weigthed\ s = \frac{(s_{c1} \cdot c1) + \ldots + (s_{cn} \cdot cn)}{c1 + \ldots cn} \tag{4}$$

ci – number of instances of the i-th class, s_{c1} – some evaluation s (precision, recall or f1-score) for i-th class.

8 Results

The quality of classification models largely depends on the preprocessing methods used and the type of vector representation of words. Table 2 presents the results of the implementation of the classifier by the method of logistic regression and using various embedding methods:

- TF-IDF using tf-idf weights, vector size 8455;
- TF-IDF (LSA) using tf-idf weights and reducing the dimension using the LSA method, vector size 300;
- Word2vec using word2vec weights derived from training on dataset comments from the social network VKontakte, vector size 300;
- Word2vec using word2vec weights based on the pre-trained word2vec-engcorpora-300 model, vector size 300.

Table 2. Comparison of classification results by logistic regression

Preprocessing	Precision	Recall	f1-score
Stemming + TF-IDF	0.91	0.90	0.90
Lemmatization + TF-IDF	0.89	0.89	0.89
Stemming + TF-IDF+LSA	0,84	0,84	0,84
Stemming + Word2vec	0,43	0,43	0,43
Lemmatization + Word2vec	0,64	0,64	0,64

Thus, the best results were obtained using basic methods of preprocessing, stemming and the TF-IDF trait model. Further, experiments use this set of methods for preprocessing text messages everywhere.

Table 3 presents the results of the classification of messages of users of the social network into the classes "core", "periphery" and "non-relevant" using different methods of machine learning.

Table 3. The results of the classification of messages by machine learning methods

Method	Group	Precision	Recall	f1-score
Logistic regression	core	0,84	0,92	0,88
	periphery	0,91	0,88	0,90
	non-relevant	1,00	0,59	0,74
SVC linear	core	0,85	0,92	0,88
	periphery	0,91	0,88	0,90
	non-relevant	1,00	0,65	0,79
KNeighbors	core	0,91	0,81	0,86
	periphery	0,83	0,93	0,88
	non-relevant	0,84	0,62	0,71
MultinomialNB	core	0,85	0,89	0,87
	periphery	0,88	0,90	0,89
	non-relevant	1,00	0,38	0,55
RandomForest	core	0,83	0,85	0,84
	periphery	0,85	0,87	0,86
	non-relevant	0,95	0,62	0,75

Thus, we can conclude that the messages containing the "free-lance" lemma are indeed significantly different from each other. The highest precision is achieved for messages from the class "non-relevant", i.e. the meaning of messages that are not directly related to freelance as a form of employment differs significantly from messages from the core and periphery classes, which is confirmed by good classification accuracy results even by such simple methods as logistic regression, support vector method and naive Bayes classifier. Values of precision and recall of classifying messages from the classes "core" and "periphery" are also quite high, which means fundamental differences between the texts of messages.

The differences in the meanings of the texts of messages from the "core", "periphery" and "non-relevant" groups allow us to make the assumption that considering the messages from these classes separately will improve the quality of the text tonality assessment, also on the basis of the tone estimates of the messages and their frequency analysis it is possible to draw various conclusions about the attitude of users to the object being analyzed. For example, an assessment of the tonality of messages from the "core" group will allow evaluating the attitude to freelancing as a way of life, the form of employment, considering messages from the "periphery" group, will allow assessing the attitude to events, processes accompanying freelancer activity. Evaluation of messages from the "non-relevant" group to assess the attitude of users to an object can in most cases not be carried out, since the text of the message, as a rule, has no direct relation to the object. Let us consider the results of experiments on the construction of classifiers for the assessment of tonality throughout the dataset and separately for the groups "core", "periphery", "non-relevant" (Table 4):

Table 4. Results of tonality assessment

Method	Group	Precision	Recall	f1-score
Logistic regression	Full dataset	0,91	0,9	0,9
	core	0,86	0,86	0,85
	periphery	0,96	0,96	0,96
	non-relevant	1,00	1,00	1,00
SVC linear	full dataset	0,89	0,89	0,89
	core	0,87	0,87	0,87
	periphery	0,96	0,96	0,96
	non-relevant	1,00	1,00	1,00
KNeighbors	full dataset	0,83	0,83	0,83
	core	0,78	0,78	0,77
	periphery	0,86	0,85	0,84
	non-relevant	0,83	0,78	0,71
MultinomialNB	full dataset	0,86	0,86	0,86
	core	0,81	0,80	0,79
	periphery	0,91	0,9	0,9
	non-relevant	0,86	0,83	0,80
RandomForest	full dataset	0,86	0,86	0,86
	core	0,81	0,81	0,81
	periphery	0,91	0,91	0,91
	non-elevant	0,97	0,97	0,97

Most of the methods showed the best results in assessing the tonality of communications on the "peripheral" and "non-relevant" groups. Thus, the messages from the "non-relevant" and "periphery" groups make a significant contribution to the quality indicators of classifiers for assessing tonality throughout the dataset, while the core class that interests the researcher most is more difficult to build classification models.

9 Conclusions and Further Work

The article presents a rather effective mechanism for the classification of text messages, considering the context in which the object of assessment of tonality is used.

Pre-processing of text messages and various methods of extracting vector representations of words have become key factors in our approach. The good result of dividing messages into the classes "core", "periphery", "non-relevant" confirmed the hypothesis of a significant difference in the texts of messages containing the word freelance in the sense of "work" and messages that use this word to describe situations not related to this form. employment.

This approach allows us to further develop more accurate systems for assessing public opinion, filtering messages containing the word in the text - the object of tonality, but useless for the researcher.

In the perspective the research will be continued in two main directions: (1) development of the functionality of the research approach and the algorithms; (2) testing the approach to the data sets from the other social media specified group of users with the goal to collect more core parts of their lexicon.

Analyzing the content of the specified users' group in social media will help to detect specifics of the context space model of their language. It will provide the solving of the task of dominant-markers vocabularies (including hierarchical vocabularies) widening through the collecting of the lexical units from the messages. Collecting of such vocabularies will improve the quality of the opinion orientations evaluating in the context of the messages' object. In perspective it will be possible to find an instrument for description of language picture of the world for different types of users. Also, these results, based on the lexemes tonality would be useful for diagnostics of the level of social tension and potential readiness of people to the social changes

For developing of the functionality of the approach we plan to widen the scale for evaluating of the message tonality from three (negative, neutral, positive) to seven (strong positive, medium positive, weak positive, neutral etc.). Also, it will help to count an integral mark of users' opinion towards any object or process that will consider not only the message tonality but also its evaluation by other users (likes, dislikes, number of comments, reposts, time of the message "life"). Such indicator seems to be useful for the impartial monitoring of the changes in public moods towards the object of tonality in the messages besides it can help to analyze the mood orientation of those users that do not create any original messages but only repost or comment others.

The introduction of such a technology into information systems for analyzing public mood, evaluating the activities of public institutions will make it possible to identify significant groups of messages/that are directly related to the problem under study.

Acknowledgements. This work was financially supported by the Ministry of Education and Science of the Russian Federation, Contract 14.575.21.0178 (ID RFMEFI57518X0178).

References

1. Marzooqi, S.A., Nuaimi, E.A., Qirim, N.A.: E-governance (G2C) in the public sector: citizens acceptance to E-government systems - Dubai's case. In: Proceedings of the Second International Conference on Internet of things, Data and Cloud Computing, pp. 1–11. ACM, New York (2017). https://doi.org/10.1145/3018896.3025160
2. Al-Refaie, A., Ramadna, A., Bata, N.: Barriers to E-government adoption in Jordanian organizations from users' and employees' perspectives. Int. J. Electron. Gov. Res. **13**(1), 33–51 (2017)
3. Yusof, S.A.B.M., Abdulraheem, M.H.: Real factors which impact on decision making in the E-government. In: Proceedings, International Conference on Intelligent Systems, Modelling and Simulation, pp. 252–255. IEEE, Kuala Lumpur (2015). https://doi.org/10.1109/isms.2015.52
4. Ma, Y., Hu, S.: E-government system research based on bank of villages and towns. In: Proceedings of the 2nd International Conference on Advanced Computer Theory and Engineering, pp. 1451–1456, Cairo (2009)
5. Ravi, K., Ravi, V.: A survey on opinion mining and sentiment analysis: tasks, approaches and applications. Know. Based Syst. **89**(Supplement C), 14–46 (2015)
6. Singh, N.K., Tomar, D.S.: Comprehensive analysis of scope of negation for sentiment analysis over social media. J. Theor. Appl. Inf. Technol. **97**(6), 1704–1719 (2019)
7. Arora, M., Kansal, V.: Character level embedding with deep convolutional neural network for text normalization of unstructured data for Twitter sentiment analysis. Soc. Netw. Anal. Min. **9**(1), 1–12 (2019)
8. Zablith, F., Osman, I.H.: ReviewModus: text classification and sentiment prediction of unstructured reviews using a hybrid combination of machine learning and evaluation models. Appl. Math. Model. **71**, 569–583 (2019)
9. Attia, M., Samih, Y., Elkahky, A., Kallmeyer, L.: Multilingual multi-class sentiment classification using convolutional neural networks. In: 11th International Conference on Language Resources and Evaluation, pp. 635–640. European Language Resources Association (ELRA), Miyazaki (2019)
10. Hasan, M., Islam, I., Hasan, K.M.A.: Sentiment analysis using out of core learning. In: 2nd International Conference on Electrical, Computer and Communication Engineering, ECCE, pp. 1–6. IEEE, Cox's Bazar (2019). https://doi.org/10.1109/ecace.2019.8679298
11. Velioglu, R., Yildiz, T., Yildirim, S.: Sentiment analysis using learning approaches over emojis for Turkish tweets. In: 3rd International Conference on Computer Science and Engineering, pp. 303–307. IEEE, Sarajevo (2018). https://doi.org/10.1109/ubmk.2018.8566260

12. Zhan, X., Wang, Y., Rao, Y., Li, Q.: Learning from multi-annotator data: a noise-aware classification framework. ACM Trans. Inf. Syst. **37**(2), 1–26 (2019). https://doi.org/10.1145/3309543

13. Verkholyak, O., Karpov, A.: Combined feature representation for emotion classification from Russian speech. In: Communications in Computer and Information Science, vol. 789, pp. 68–73 (2018). https://doi.org/10.1007/978-3-319-71746-3_6

14. Öhman, E., Kajava, K.: Sentimentator: gamifying fine-grained sentiment annotation. In: CEUR Workshop Proceedings, pp. 98–110, Helsinki (2018)

15. Maltseva, A., Klebanov, A., Shilkina, N., Lyamkin, I., Mahnitkina, O.: Culture of social media interactions amongst modern students: analysis of the social network vk.com, university groups « Overheard... » with big data. In: Proceedings of the International Conference IMS-2017, pp. 11–14. ACM, New York (2017). https://doi.org/10.1145/3143699.3143712

16. Shilkina, N., et al.: Social media as a display of students' communication culture: case of educational, professional and labor verbal markers analysis. Commun. Comput. Inf. Sci. **947**, 384–397 (2019). https://doi.org/10.1007/978-3-030-13283-5_29

17. Verderber, R.F.: Communicate! Wadsworth Pub. (1993)

18. Medrouk, L., Pappa, A.: Do deep networks really need complex modules for multilingual sentiment polarity detection and domain classification? In: Proceedings of the International Joint Conference on Neural Networks. IEEE, Rio de Janeiro (2018). https://doi.org/10.1109/ijcnn.2018.8489613

19. Chen, B., Huang, Q., Chen, Y., Cheng, L., Chen, R.: Deep neural networks for multi-class sentiment classification. In: Proceedings - 20th International Conference on High Performance Computing and Communications, 16th International Conference on Smart City and 4th International Conference on Data Science and Systems, HPCC/SmartCity/DSS 2018, pp. 854–859. IEEE, Exeter (2019). https://doi.org/10.1109/hpcc/smartcity/dss.2018.00142

20. Xu, L., Qiu, J.: Unsupervised multi-class sentiment classification approach. Knowl. Organ. **46**(1), 15–32 (2019). https://doi.org/10.1016/j.dss.2014.03.004

21. Sánchez-Rada, J.F., Iglesias, C.A.: Social context in sentiment analysis: formal definition, overview of current trends and framework for comparison. Inf. Fusion **52**, 344–356 (2019). https://doi.org/10.1016/j.inffus.2019.05.003

22. Iliev, I.R., Huang, X., Gel, Y.R.: Political rhetoric through the lens of non-parametric statistics: are our legislators that different? J. Roy. Stat. Soc. Ser. A: Stat. Soc. **182**(2), 583–604 (2019). https://doi.org/10.1111/rssa.12421

23. Liao, X.-W., Liu, D.-Y., Gui, L., Cheng, X.-Q., Chen, G.-L.: Opinion retrieval method combining text conceptualization and network embedding. J. Softw. **29**(10), 2899–2914 (2018). https://doi.org/10.13328/j.cnki.jos.005548

24. Alam, F., Danieli, M., Riccardi, G.: Annotating and modeling empathy in spoken conversations. Comput. Speech Lang. **50**, 40–61 (2018). https://doi.org/10.1016/j.csl.2017.12.003

25. Li, M., Lu, Q., Long, Y.: Gui, L: Inferring affective meanings of words from word embedding. IEEE Trans. Affect. Comput. **8**(4), 443–456 (2017). https://doi.org/10.1109/TAFFC.2017.2723012

26. De La Paz, M.M., Estuar, R.E.: Using social network analysis in understanding the public discourse on gender violence: an agent-based modelling approach. In: Proceedings of the 2017 IEEE/ACM International Conference on Advances in Social Networks Analysis and Mining, ASONAM 2017, pp. 1144–1151. ACM, Sydney (2017). https://doi.org/10.1145/3110025.3120960

27. Hore, S., Bhattacharya, T.: Analyzing social trend towards girl child in India: a machine intelligence-based approach. In: Kalita, J., Balas, V.E., Borah, S., Pradhan, R. (eds.) Recent Developments in Machine Learning and Data Analytics. AISC, vol. 740, pp. 43–50. Springer, Singapore (2019). https://doi.org/10.1007/978-981-13-1280-9_4
28. RusVectōrēs: Semantic models for the Russian language. https://rusveoreores.org/ru/. Accessed 03 June 2019

Social Media Adoption and Usage in Central Banking

Dmitriy Plekhanov[✉] [iD]

Institute for Complex Strategic Studies (ICSS), Moscow, Russia
plehanov@icss.ac.ru

Abstract. The role of transparency and communications in central banking has risen significantly in recent decades. This trend accelerated with the advent of new information technologies, such as web sites and, more recently, social media, which allowed to disseminate information faster and among a larger audience. This paper presents a brief review of how central banks adopted those new communication channels over time. Main social media platforms used by central banks around the world are identified and differences among those platforms are described in terms of their application for different purposes of central banks' communication policy.

Keywords: Social media · Central banks · Web sites · Communication

1 Introduction

Central banking has changed quite dramatically in recent decades. From uncommunicative, even secretive organizations central banks moved towards increased transparency. For example, as recently as 1993, the United States' Federal Open Market Committee (FOMC) did not publicly announce its decisions about changes in the federal funds target rate after its meetings [9]. Now the Chairman of the Federal Reserve holds regular press conferences – activity which became a regular feature among world central banks. In general recently there has been steady movement in the direction of greater central bank transparency [7]. Today, there is a "general consensus among central bankers that transparency is not only an obligation for a public entity, but also a real benefit to the institution and its policies" [17]. Not only does transparency make central bank more accountable to the public, but it may also enhance the effectiveness of central banks' monetary policy [5].

Improvements in transparency of central banks coincided with dramatic technological advances. Firstly, came the World Wide Web. Since the mid-1990s, the Internet has had a revolutionary impact on everyday life, expanding access to information and increasing the speed of communication. Central banks were not lagging behind the general trend, and gradually adopted new technology. Since then websites of central banks have definitely moved from being "mildly interesting new technology" to the core of communications policy [8]. Secondly, ten years later when websites became a new norm rather than innovative approach in communication with general public, social media appeared on the stage. Although social media impact was not as strong as

© Springer Nature Switzerland AG 2020
A. Chugunov et al. (Eds.): EGOSE 2019, CCIS 1135, pp. 413–424, 2020.
https://doi.org/10.1007/978-3-030-39296-3_30

changes brought about by the Web itself, it led to another wave of transformations in the way people are communicating with each other. This fact was not left unnoticed in the central banking community. According to remarks made in 2012 by the Vice Chair of the Board of Governors Janet Yellen "if I succeed in saying anything interesting this afternoon, those words may be posted, tweeted, and blogged about even before I've left this podium" [32].

As central banks increased their presence in the web and social media networks there are natural questions one can ask: "How this presence evolved over time?" and "How central banks differ in their attitude towards various web tools and social media networks?" This paper is basically aimed at answering these questions. Moreover, monitoring of central bank websites and social media provides valuable information about the way monetary authorities communicate with the general public. One of the main results provided in this paper is the quantitative assessment of central banks' presence in social media networks, which can be considered as an additional indicator of central bank transparency. The paper is organized as follows. Section 2 reviews academic research on the use of social media by government institutions in general. Section 3 provides description of data sources and data collection process. Section 4 describes the brief history of central banks on the World Wide Web and presents a review of social media accounts and their use for the purposes of central banks' communication policy. The benefits and drawbacks of various social media platforms for the purposes of central banks' communication are presented.

2 Related Works

Social media has changed the ways in which individuals and organizations communicate and exchange information. The new technology was initially adopted in the private sector, as companies were quick to explore new opportunities and gain benefits from using social media for various business tasks such as customer relationships [13] and marketing campaigns [3, 16, 26]. In the public sector political personalities also embraced new technology quite quickly for the purposes of self-presentation and rallying support, while government institutions were actually lagging behind this trend, as the purpose and returns of social media use by institutions are not as clear as they are for political personalities and business [24]. Adoption of social media in government basically has to undergo periods of informal experimentation and constructive chaos before public organizations can finally find appropriate ways to formally incorporate social media into their day-to-day activities [23].

Academic research has showed the benefits of social media usage by the government for openness and transparency [1, 2, 29]. The use of social media by local governments and municipalities has been documented extensively [4, 15, 20, 25]. Use of Twitter and other social media channels has been found effective in crisis situations [10, 19, 28]. But there are no "one size fits all" approaches, as government institutions of different types should consider context and demand of users while trying to formulate their own social media strategy [24].

Content of social media accounts due to their open status allows to reveal communication strategies adopted by government institutions. Research on the use of social media in government has proposed the 3 category model of push, pull and networking communication to describe the type of content, which relate to the open government goals of transparency, participation and collaboration [21]. Push refers to providing information and hence transparency; pull refers to seeking feedback from stake-holders and the public at large and is associated with participation; and networking refers to more sophisticated types of online dialogue and collaboration with social media users. However, research has found that social media is most often used by government institutions to provide information, but not to engage in government-citizen conversations [14, 22, 30, 33].

Although government institutions worldwide have been increasingly adopting social media for communication and information exchange, one particular type of public institutions – central banks or monetary authorities – has not been covered by academic research on social media to date. Whereas, the issues of transparency and communication with the public are of extreme importance in the sphere of central banking, as better communication is not only considered a positive phenomenon per se for reasons of democratic legitimacy, but also is viewed as a needed prerequisite for monetary policy to be most effective [11, 18, 31]. Policy actions of central banks as well as their public announcements have drawn increasing public attention recently, as the role of central banks in regulation of financial sector and economic policy-making in general has expanded significantly after the 2008 global financial crisis [6, 27]. In this regard, the purpose of this study is to explore the question of social media adoption in central banking community, types of content generated and specific applications of social media for the purposes of central banks' communication.

3 Data

To study central banks activity on social media platforms all available online information was carefully analyzed and recorded. Information about social media use was basically gathered from the following sources: central banks websites, social media websites and online tools for social media analytics and monitoring.

Data on the website creation date was compiled from various sources including representatives of monetary authorities and national domain registrars. If no other data was available, the origin date was determined on the basis of free data "Wayback Machine" project, which provides access to collections of archived web pages dating back to the year 1996. As of January 2017 the list consisted of 177 websites of central banks and monetary institutions (including 12 regional Federal Reserve banks which were treated as separate entities in this study). The first step in analyzing central banks' social media usage was to check whether official central banks websites contained links to social media platforms and if so to which particular services. Information about official websites was drawn from the list compiled by the Bank for International Settlements (BIS). A limited number of media accounts was located from other sources, for instance, through links posted on social media platforms or websites associated with official central banks (websites of central bank museums, education portals, etc.). The authenticity of accounts was checked manually on the basis of the content produced.

Information derived from official websites allowed estimating to what extent central banks adopted social media in general and specific channels in particular. Additional data was gathered from social media accounts. By doing this, we were able to acquire more concrete information about social media accounts. For example, social media accounts can be used to find out (or at least make a guess about) the date of account creation, whether it is active or not, how often information is updated, and what type of information is disseminated. The social media services reviewed were basically the following: social networking platforms like Facebook, VKontakte (the Russian social network); the business social networks LinkedIn; the location based social network Foursquare; the microblogs Twitter, Sina Weibo (the Chinese social network); the video platforms YouTube, Livestream, and Ustream; the photo sharing applications Flickr and Instagram; and content sharing services like Pinterest. In addition, online tools for social media monitoring (such as Twitonomy, Fanpage Karma, etc.) were used to identify historical trends in social media use.

4   Results

4.1   Central Banks on the World Wide Web: A Short History

The first central banks websites were launched in the middle of the 1990s. At first this process started at a very limited pace. In the year 1996 when the BIS launched its web site its list of "Central Banks on the World Wide Web" contained only 10 names [3]. At that time it was unclear if the Web presence could be of any benefit to monetary authorities, but as Internet popularity among general public was growing with advance of personal computers, software and communication networks, central banks just could not stand on the sidelines. Soon afterwards, central bank participation in the World Wide Web was in full swing. Figure 1 presents a time series graph of the number of central bank websites. Strikingly, the results show that more than half of the current central bank websites were actually created in a 5-year period from 1995 to 1999. It is very impressive indeed that central banks were so active in adopting new technology, experimenting with it and learning how to better use this new medium to fulfill their tasks and obligations.

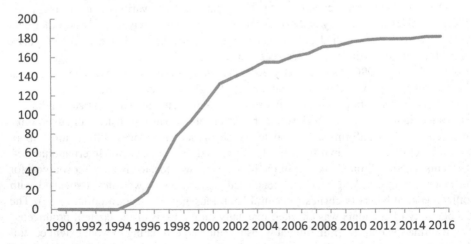

Fig. 1. Total number of central banks' websites worldwide

Surprisingly, the process of web site creation was equally distributed among various regions. It is quite natural to expect that central banks in advanced economies were the first to enter World Wide Web, but this is not the fact. Central banks in emerging markets (Asia, South America, Africa, MENA, Eastern Europe) were also presented in the World Wide Web right from the start of the new Internet era (Fig. 2). For example, during the years 1995-1998 a large number of central bank websites was launched in developing countries and transition economies such as Russia, Brazil, Argentina, Peru, Mexico, South Africa, Malaysia, etc. The initial version of central bank web sites contained very limited volume of information at that time. For example, the homepage of the Bank of Russia web site at that time had only 8 elements (links) referring to bank's history, general information, monetary policy, banking system, financial markets, press releases, publications and search engine. For comparison the current version of the web site homepage possesses more than 60 links including those providing access to a large store of macroeconomic and financial statistics, information on banking institutions, credit history, etc.

Web site is not a static thing, its design, components and structure are constantly changing to better fulfil tasks of the owner and adapt to the needs of the public. The advance of web technology also plays its part and provides new opportunities to website developers. Central bank websites are no exception. Analysis of website history was based on the free data project "Wayback Machine". Wayback Machine was used to see what previous versions of central bank websites used to look like and thus to identify how often central banks tended to change design of their websites. The analysis of archived web pages shows that central banks initially were very active in website renovation. In the early 2000s about 25–30% of central bank websites were redesigned every year. Apparently monetary authorities were experimenting with new technology, constantly making improvements into their websites.

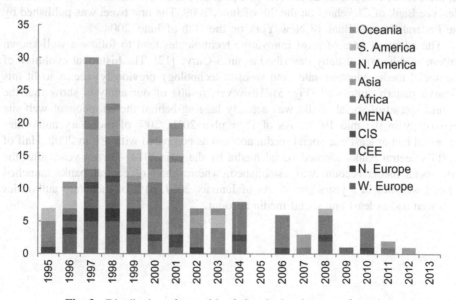

Fig. 2. Distribution of central banks' web sites by year of creation

Currently the "design change" ratio went down and became quite stable at the level of 12%, i.e. one in eight central banks change web site design every year. An average central bank changes its website design every four years. This time span seems reasonable, as regular fine-tuning is necessary to meet changing environment and new developments at monetary authorities. On the other hand, frequent changes (every 1–2 years) can be confusing and even irritating for users, because regular visitors become accustomed to website structure and content layout.

At present web sites have become indispensable tools of communications for central banks, constantly growing in volume and scope of information flows provided for the public. It is often argued that in contrast to other types of modern communication technologies, such as the use of web-sites or email service, social media applications in government entities are not initiated on the basis of top management decisions, but instead are started mostly as a kind of informal experimentation and, thus, can be slow to gain traction [7]. In case of central banks this assumption can be tested by analyzing rate of adoption of social media and comparing it with the pace of embracing web site technology by central banking community.

4.2   Central Banks Adoption of Social Media

The origin of modern social media networks can be traced back to the early 2000s. Since the mid 2000s a host of social networks have gained international prominence. The data on specific dates when monetary authorities joined social media were collected by searching social media websites for the earliest content (tweets, posts, videos, etc.) uploaded by central banks. According to the data collected, the Federal Reserve Bank of Dallas can be regarded as the first monetary institution to start using social media by uploading interview with Milton Friedman on its official YouTube channel on the 11th of November, 2007. The first post on Facebook was made by the Federal Reserve Bank of Cleveland on the 9th of June, 2009. The first tweet was published by the Federal Reserve Bank of New York on the 10th of June, 2008.

The adoption rates of most innovative technologies tend to follow a well-known pattern of diffusion, usually described as an S-Curve [12]. The historical evolution of the social media adoption rate (and website technology previously) seems to fit this S-curve pattern quite well (Fig. 3). However, results of our analysis show that the current spread of social media was actually lagging behind the adoption of web site technology in the mid 1990s. As of December 2010, 20% of monetary authorities reviewed had at least one social media account as compared with 4% in 2008. Half of world's central banks adopted social media by the year 2014 – seven years after the first social media account was established, whereas half of central banks launched official websites in 5 years period. As of January 2017, 61% of monetary authorities reviewed had at least one social media account.

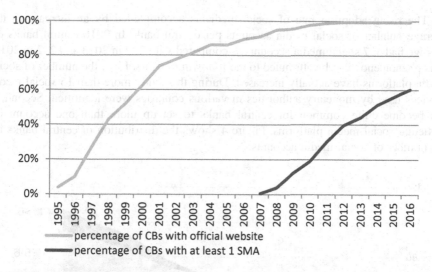

──── percentage of CBs with official website
━━━ percentage of CBs with at least 1 SMA

Fig. 3. The adoption rate of social media and web site technologies by central banks

The evolution in social media adoption has been clearly different across different regions (Table 1). North America can be considered the region with the strongest penetration rate (100%) followed by Northern Europe (88%). The emerging economies have evidently experienced lower levels of penetration, however, adoption rate among South American central banks is quite high (75%) and actually exceeds Western Europe (72%). Monetary institutions from Central and Eastern Europe and Asia are catching up steadily (67% and 61% respectively). At the same time such regions as MENA, Africa, CIS (former USSR republics) and Oceania are clearly lagging behind. But even in those regions adoption rate exceeded 30%.

Table 1. Social media adoption rate by region, %

	2008	2010	2012	2014	2016
N. America	35,7	92,9	100,0	100,0	100,0
N. Europe	0,0	50,0	87,5	100,0	87,5
S. America	3,1	21,9	46,9	62,5	75,0
W. Europe	0,0	16,7	44,4	55,6	72,2
Central&Eastern Europe	0,0	13,3	26,7	53,3	66,7
Asia	0,0	8,7	34,8	43,5	60,9
CIS	0,0	8,3	25,0	33,3	41,7
Oceania	0,0	14,3	14,3	28,6	42,9
MENA	0,0	0,0	17,6	29,4	35,3
Africa	3,0	3,0	24,2	33,3	36,4
Total	**3,9**	**19,0**	**39,7**	**51,4**	**60,3**

The rising adoption rate of social media is accompanied by an increase in the average number of social media accounts per central bank. In 2016 central banks on average had 3, 7 social media accounts as compared with 2, 9 in 2013 and 2, 2 in 2010. This phenomenon can be attributed to the following factors. First, the number of social media platforms have actually increased. During this study more than 15 social media services used by monetary authorities in various countries were identified. Second, it has become quite common for central banks to set up more than one account on particular social media platforms. Figure 4 shows the distribution of central banks by the number of social media accounts.

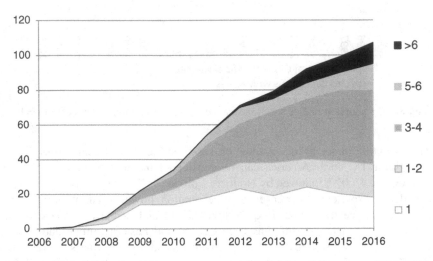

Fig. 4. Distribution of central banks by number of social media accounts, 2006–2016

Among different platforms Twitter can be considered as the most popular social media channel among central banks (Fig. 5). Some central banks use several accounts, which can be dedicated to specific topics (research, education, job announcement). Some central banks communicates only in English language, others prefer to use national language or both. In countries with several official languages (for example, Canada and Belgium) information can be duplicated and published in several accounts. Tweets are mainly used to inform the public about new statistical data, official reports, important decisions, etc. However, due to the limited size of text messages it can be difficult to use Twitter account to inform the public about unexpected decisions or to discuss thorny political issues. The risks of misunderstanding are relatively high. The previous research on the topic of social media usage by governments showed that public institutions use social media mostly for one-way (information provision) rather than two-way (online dialogue and collaboration) communication purposes [14, 22]. The sample analysis of tweets posted by central banks basically confirmed this observation, however, there is also a growing tendency among central banks to organize Q&A sessions and other activities to engage in more active communication with social media users.

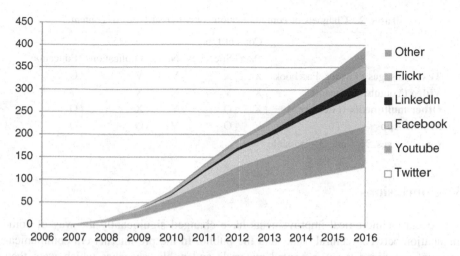

Fig. 5. Number of central banks' social media accounts by type, 2006–2016

Facebook is mainly used by central banks in North and South America. Popularity of this American social media platform in Europe is much lower: only several central banks in Central and Eastern Europe use Facebook in communications with the public. Facebook accounts can also be created in communication purposes for special events. For example, US Federal Reserve created a special Facebook account in 2013 to commemorate the centennial anniversary of the signing of the Federal Reserve Act. Central banks with currency museums have developed special accounts on money and banknotes, while those with a mandate for financial education (e.g., the Federal Reserve) created additional accounts on issues of personal finance management, financial fraud and security features of banknotes.

YouTube channels provide access to speeches/presentations of central banks' representatives, education materials and other types of visual information. This communication channel is especially useful for central banks which aim to disseminate animated and interactive presentations, explaining various aspects of central bank functions (e.g. financial stability) or economic and financial concepts. However, only about 1/3 of all central banks have YouTube accounts and less than 10% of monetary authorities post video materials on a regular basis. Users are usually restricted from making comments about videos posted on official central banks' YouTube channels. Some central banks prefer to post videos directly on their own web sites instead of using YouTube channel. In this case special web pages are created (for example Webcast, Web-TV) to provide users access to video materials. However, with the spread of social media popularity this practice seems to fade out.

All in all social media platforms provide different capabilities and content to its users. Thus, the decision of monetary authorities to adopt social media should depend on its preferences in communication process and type of content (Table 2). For example, Twitter and Facebook are better suited for news announcements and distribution of publications, while statistical data can be more effectively disseminated through mobile apps rather that existing social media platforms.

Table 2. Channels of communication for different types of content

	Content type				
	Data	Speeches	News	Publications	Education
Text messages (Twitter, Facebook)	X	X	V	V	O
Video (Youtube, Ustream)	X	V	X	X	V
Other multimedia (Flickr, etc.)	X	O	V	X	O
Mobile Apps	V	O	V	O	O

Note: V – yes, X – no, O – possible

5 Conclusions

The recent technological improvements have changed significantly the way of communication between central banks and the public. In the pre-internet era communication was organized through printed materials and public speeches which were then disseminated by the media. Use of web sites allowed to increase number of distributed materials as well as their types (research papers, reports, press releases, etc.). Web sites also provide opportunity to disseminate among general public large quantities of statistical data. The Web dramatically increased the potential target audience of central banks' messages, as central banks gradually adopted new web-based communications tools such as RSS subscription or e-mail alerts. Advance of social media provided central banks with new communication tools which allow more rapid dissemination of information and provide new types of interactions with the general public.

The following results were obtained through analysis of social media usage among central banks. Spread of social media was actually lagging behind the adoption of web site technology in the mid 1990s. The evolution in social media usage has been clearly different across different regions. North America and Northern Europe can be considered as leading regions in terms of adoption of social media. Twitter can be considered as the most popular social media channel, with some central banks creating several accounts for different content and audience (research, education, job announcements, etc.). Facebook is mainly used by central banks in North and South America, while its popularity in Europe is much lower. As social media platforms provide different capabilities and content to its users, central banks tend to use several of them, rather than limit themselves to just one social media platform. As a result, the average number of social media accounts per central bank is constantly rising. Although communication through social media is mainly used by central banks for information provision, there are also some early indications that central banks tend to become engaged in more active forms of communication with social media users, such as Q&A sessions on Twitter.

Social media platforms are rather new communication tools for public institutions in general and central banks in particular. In this paper the reported results are preliminary and describe the general trend in adoption of social media by central banks. Further research on the topic is needed to better investigate the usage of social media in the sphere of central banking, especially from the user perspective. Among the questions for further research are the following: How users react to social media messages posted by central banks (in terms of standard social media reactions such as likes, shares, etc.)? How this reaction has changed over time? Which type of content attracts more attention from the audience?

References

1. Bertot, J.C., Jaeger, P.T., Grimes, J.M.: Using ICTs to create a culture of transparency: e-Government and social media as openness and anti-corruption tools for societies. Gov. Inf. Q. **27**(3), 264–271 (2010). https://doi.org/10.1016/j.giq.2010.03.001
2. Bertot, J.C., Jaeger, P.T., Grimes, J.M.: Promoting transparency and accountability through ICTs, social media, and collaborative e-government. Transform. Gov. People Process. Policy **6**(1), 78–91 (2012). https://doi.org/10.1108/17506161211214831
3. Bogea, F., Brito, E.P.Z.: Determinants of social media adoption by large companies. J. Technol. Manag. Innov. **13**(1), 11–18 (2018). https://doi.org/10.4067/S0718-27242018000100011
4. Bonsón, E., Torres, L., Royo, S., Flores, F.: Local e-government 2.0: social media and corporate transparency in municipalities. Gov. Inf. Q. **29**, 123–132 (2012). https://doi.org/10.1016/j.giq.2011.10.001
5. Brito, S., Carrière-Swallow, Y., Gruss, B.: Disagreement about future inflation: understanding the benefits of inflation targeting and transparency. IMF Working Paper, WP/18/24 (2018)
6. Cunningham, R., Friedrich, C.: The role of central banks in promoting financial stability: an international perspective. Bank of Canada Staff Discussion Paper, No. 2016-15 (2016)
7. Dincer, N., Eichengeen, B.: Central bank transparency and independence: updates and new measures. Int. J. Cent. Bank. **10**(1), 189–253 (2014)
8. Eades, B.: The Bank on the World Wide Web. Bank of Canada Review (2001). www.bankofcanada.ca
9. Ehrmann, M., Fratzscher, M.: Transparency, disclosure and the federal reserve. ECB Working Paper Series No. 457 (2005)
10. Eriksson, M.: Lessons for crisis communication on social media: a systematic review of what research tells the practice. Int. J. Strat. Commun. **12**(5), 526–551 (2018). https://doi.org/10.1080/1553118X.2018.1510405
11. Faust, J., Svensson, L.E.: Transparency and credibility: monetary policy with unobservable goals. Int. Econ. Rev. **42**(2), 369–397 (2001). https://doi.org/10.1111/1468-2354.00114
12. Foster, R.N.: Innovation: The Attacker's Advantage. Summit Books, New York (1986)
13. Gamboa, A.M., Gonçalves, H.M.: Customer loyalty through social networks: lessons from Zara on Facebook. Bus. Horiz. **57**(6), 709–717 (2014). https://doi.org/10.1016/j.bushor.2014.07.003
14. Golbeck, J., Grimes, J.M., Rogers, A.: Twitter use by the U.S. congress. J. Am. Soc. Inf. Sci. Technol. **61**(8), 1612–1621 (2010). https://doi.org/10.1002/asi.21344
15. Guillamón, M.-D., Rios, A.-M., Gesuele, B., Metallo, C.: Factors influencing social media use in local governments: the case of Italy and Spain. Gov. Inf. Q. **33**(3), 460–471 (2016). https://doi.org/10.1016/j.giq.2016.06.005
16. Hanna, R., Rohm, A., Crittenden, V.L.: We're all connected: the power of the social media ecosystem. Bus. Horiz. **54**(3), 265–273 (2011). https://doi.org/10.1016/j.bushor.2011.01.007
17. Issing, O.: Communication, transparency, accountability: monetary policy in the twenty-first century. Rev. Fed. Reserv. Bank St. Louis (March), 65–83 (2005). https://doi.org/10.20955/r.87.65-83

18. Jeanneau, S.: Communication of monetary policy decisions by central banks: what is revealed and why. BIS Papers No. 47 (2009)
19. Kavanaugh, A.L., et al.: Social media use by government: from the routine to the critical. Gov. Inf. Q. **29**(4), 480–491 (2012). https://doi.org/10.1016/j.giq.2012.06.002
20. Lameiras, M., Silva, T., Tavares, A.: An empirical analysis of social media usage by local governments in Portugal. In: Proceedings of the 11th International Conference on Theory and Practice of Electronic Governance - ICEGOV 2018, pp. 257–268 (2018). https://doi.org/10.1145/3209415.3209503
21. Mergel, I.: The social media innovation challenge in the public sector. Inf. Polity **17**(3), 281–292 (2012). https://doi.org/10.3233/IP-2012-000281
22. Mergel, I.: Social media adoption and resulting tactics in the U.S. federal government. Gov. Inf. Q. **30**(2), 123–130 (2013). https://doi.org/10.1016/j.giq.2012.12.004
23. Mergel, I., Bretschneider, S.I.: A three-stage adoption process for social media use in government. Public Adm. Rev. **73**(3), 390–400 (2013). https://doi.org/10.1111/puar.12021
24. Mickoleit, A.: Social media use by governments: a policy primer to discuss trends, identify policy opportunities and guide decision makers. OECD Working Papers on Public Governance, No. 26 (2014). https://doi.org/10.1787/5jxrcmghmk0s-en
25. Mossberger, K., Wu, Y., Crawford, J.: Connecting citizens and local governments? Social media and interactivity in major U.S. cities. Gov. Inf. Q. **30**(4), 351–358 (2013). https://doi.org/10.1016/j.giq.2013.05.016
26. Nakara, W.A., Benmoussa, F.-Z., Jaouen, A.: Entrepreneurship and social media marketing: evidence from French small business. Int. J. Entrep. Small Bus. **16**(4), 386–405 (2012). https://doi.org/10.1504/IJESB.2012.047608
27. PwC: Central banking 2020: Ahead of the curve. https://www.pwc.com/gx/en/financial-services/pdf/cb-2020-ahead-of-the-curve.pdf
28. Sakaki, T., Okazaki, M., Matsuo, Y.: Earthquake shakes Twitter users: real-time event detection by social sensors. In: Proceedings of the 19th International Conference on World Wide Web, pp. 851–860. ACM, New York (2010). https://doi.org/10.1145/1772690.1772777
29. Song, C., Lee, J.: Citizens' use of social media in government, perceived transparency, and trust in government. Public Perform. Manag. Rev. **39**(2), 430–453 (2016). https://doi.org/10.1080/15309576.2015.1108798
30. Waters, R.D., Williams, J.M.: Squawking, tweeting, cooing, and hooting: analyzing the communication patterns of government agencies on Twitter. J. Public Aff. **11**(4), 353–363 (2011). https://doi.org/10.1002/pa.385
31. Woodford, M.: Central bank communication and policy effectiveness. NBER Working Paper No. 11898 (2005)
32. Yellen, J.L.: Revolution and evolution in central bank communications, remarks made at Haas School of Business, University of California, Berkeley (2012). https://www.federalreserve.gov/newsevents/speech/yellen20121113a.htm
33. Zheng, L., Zheng, T.: Innovation through social media in the public sector: information and interactions. Gov. Inf. Q. **31**(Suppl. 1), S106–S117 (2014). https://doi.org/10.1016/j.giq.2014.01.011

Communicative Strategies of Russian Politicians on Social Networking Site Vkontakte

Konstantin Platonov[1]([✉]) [iD] and Natalia Legostaeva[2] [iD]

[1] Center for Sociological and Internet Research,
Saint Petersburg State University, Saint Petersburg, Russia
konplatonov@gmail.com
[2] Laboratory for Research of Social-Economic and Political Processes
of Modern Society, Saint Petersburg State University, Saint Petersburg, Russia
n.legostaeva@spbu.ru

Abstract. The problem of elaboration of effective publication strategies of social media presence was not thoroughly studied in the context of Russian political communication. At the same time, this communication channel is becoming increasingly important on both Federal and regional levels as this exact channel provides broad opportunities related to communication with the audience, recruitment of new participants and receiving feedback. Based on the audience requests, politicians and press relations services build specific strategies of media presence, which could differ significantly in terms of its content and targeting.

In this research, we conduct a comparative analysis of publication strategies used by politicians of different levels on their social network accounts. Qualitative analysis is applied to the content of the posts. We use taxonomy based on definition of the key topics highlighted by every political leader and text orientation: informing, persuasion, mobilizing or interacting.

We also consider technical characteristics of strategies, such as use of video materials or external links in the posts. In order to evaluate the participation effect, we used metrics such as likes, comments and audience engagement rate. Data consolidation helped us to conclude that accounts of pro-government political leaders operate more in the informing mode and opposition use varied communicative models: informing, persuasion, and interaction in different combinations and in general are more "ingenious" in terms of content production.

The research presents the variety of communicative strategies used by Russian politicians in social networks.

Keywords: Social media · Politicians · Strategic communication · Political communication · Vkontakte · Russia

© Springer Nature Switzerland AG 2020
A. Chugunov et al. (Eds.): EGOSE 2019, CCIS 1135, pp. 425–440, 2020.
https://doi.org/10.1007/978-3-030-39296-3_31

1 Introduction

Starting from the 2000s, the media system in Russia is going through a crucial phase: a group of state mass media was actively present in the commercial sphere. Their main competitor was a group of alternative internet sources [52, p. 21]. Consequently, starting from 2014 Russian government represented by Roskomnadzor reinforced legislation related to internet and communications regulations [45]: starting from the law on "Protection of Children from Information Harmful to their Health and Development" and limiting the access to the websites of several private media sources and ending up blocking Telegram and autonomous RuNet project.

At the same time the internet was becoming very important in the lives of Russian citizens. As in January 2019, 44% of adult population of Russian Federation admitted that, in most cases, they learn news and other information from news websites and 19% – on forums, blogs and social networks [15].

In these circumstances, many political leaders use different online platforms as their informational support tools: websites and forums, mailshots and blogs, as well as social networks. And it's all despite the risks: emergence of clones [6] and false information when the account is hacked [33].

Many accounts of Russian political and public figures have already attracted a great attention not only from media sources or public, but also from researchers: among the most significant accounts, it is worth mentioning, for example, Twitter of Dmitry Medvedev [4], Twitter of Garry Kasparov [23], Instagram of Ramzan Kadyrov [37].

In the past years, Russian politicians of regional level: mayors and governors are becoming more active in the online space [36]. Having different objectives, politicians (and their press-offices) are building communication in public online space in a different way.

Apart from the fact that presence of the political leader on websites and social networks is a winning move for their strategies, the style, publication topics and direct feedback are of particular interest to researchers. Analysis of these peculiarities helps us not only define key characteristics of used publication strategies, but also to evaluate their effectiveness.

The thematic coverage and agenda appearing in the publications of various Russian politicians are extremely diverse, full of competition, and an especially rigorous confrontation is observed between pro-government and independent bloggers [13, p. 3]. Russian governors actively using personal blogs for self-presentation and legitimation are of particular interest [44]. Most comparative studies on this topic focused on individual politicians or differences across countries and regimes, but rarely focus on a systematic description of the key characteristics of communication strategies specific to the top-authors.

This research is devoted to the analysis of the key characteristics, similarities and differences of typical communication strategies implemented by Russian politicians within one online platform – the most popular Russian social networking site Vkontakte [48].

2 Related Works

In social networks, we can find a wide range of communication modes between politicians and society – from micropolitical level of family to macro policy [11]. At the same time, political communication in social networks brings together politicians' both private and professional areas of life via specific forms of addressing the audience [53].

In the Table 1 you can find studies dedicated to the investigation of political online communication on social networks. Most of the studies were conducted on Twitter social network. In the investigations of parties and political leaders' communication on Twitter and Facebook analysis of publication frequency, structure and content analysis were most commonly used.

Table 1. Researches of political leaders' communication on social networks.

Issues	Research examples: politicians/institutions – SNS
Structure of political online communications	The German Federal Diet – Twitter [43]
	USA congress – Twitter [10]
Computational propaganda, bot usage	D. Trump, H. Clinton – Twitter [3, 21]
	Brazilian politicians – Twitter [1]
	Prime Minister of Japan – Twitter [40]
Adoption/continued use of social media	Swedish and Norwegian politicians – Twitter, Facebook, websites [26]
	US politicians – Facebook [50]
Visual political communication	Singaporean parties – Instagram [22]
	Swedish politicians – Instagram [11]
Online communications strategies	Candidates in the US elections – Facebook, Twitter, Youtube, websites [34]
	The European Parliament – Facebook, Twitter, Youtube, weblogs [28]

Instagram, which "specializes in efficiently distributing visual rhetoric" [19, p. 9] occupies a special place. Artificial intelligence investigations: use of bots, anonymous accounts or spam for propaganda purposes [51] constitute a specific research area too. We need to mention that nowadays the number of descriptive studies of online strategies of Russian political leaders is relatively small.

3 Theoretical Framework

3.1 Strategy in Political Communication

Strategic communication is considered as conscious goal-oriented communication between the actors [20]. Determination to elaborate a relevant strategy, one way or another is an undeniable feature of any communicative action which supposes that actors are eager to deeply understand the situation and coordinate action plans via mechanisms of adjustment of various definitions of the situation [17, p. 86].

According to the communicative action theory, in contemporary societies, all political power is based on communicative power, which represents a "normative resource for countering the norm-free steering media of money and administrative power" [14]. For the state authorities, the mechanisms of communicative power are among the most important instruments for legitimization.

In our research, we propose several assumptions of the communicative action theory, which refer to rationality of communicators and their determination to reach an agreement in a specific situation with the audience, as well as their own political objectives. Also conceptually, we do not oppose communicative and strategic actions (as some researchers do [12]).

Together with growing complexity of social networks, the question of political actor's pertinent strategy building is becoming more relevant. It is important to understand, that the strategy is not seen as isolated, but considered in the context of established discourse, which consists of all different discussions and topics, which are created, discussed and spread both offline and online. Discourse on the online platforms, including social networks, is a part of global public discourse, which was formed under influence of the total number of discussed social and political significant issues [4].

Online communications are being actively used for agenda-setting, coverage of the leader's actions [41] and representation of public political confrontations [49]. Communicative strategies are required, on the one hand, in order to communicate information to the audience in an accessible way and, on the other hand, to influence the audience in a proper manner, increase its engagement and loyalty.

Speaking about political strategy, we must acknowledge that contemporary policy represents not only a set of persuasive, but also performance acts. The style, representation and marketing strategies play at least a similar if not a greater role than the content or even content meanings [29, p. 205]. In relation to this, when defining strategies of political leaders, we need to consider all the peculiarity of its development and production.

3.2 Strategy Taxonomy

The question concerning the classification of strategies applied by politicians (and their press-services) in online communication is complex due to their huge variety and relation to the characteristics of a given political system. Lilleker and Koc-Michalska in their research on internet communication in the European Parliament defined three leading communicative strategies: "homestyle", "impression management", and "participatory" [28]. Group of the researchers which included the same authors offered a different classification: "informing", "engaging", "mobilizing", "interacting" [27]. Similar classification models are being used in other studies [8]. Other approaches divide strategies into "intentional" and "emergent", roughly speaking, objective oriented and engagement oriented [35].

Hermans and Vergeer in their cross-national research define political leaders' strategies as personalization strategies which have three dimensions of evaluation: "professional", "home and family" and "personal preferences" [18]. Thus, there is a variety of different aspects which influence approaches to online strategies classification in political communication. In this research, we use a limited number of criteria, which we consider of greater importance. It is worth mentioning that we assume that the general political strategy of a leader corresponds with the publication strategy applied in his or her Vkontakte social network account.

Topics. Considering the diversity of political landscape represented in social networks, when investigating publication strategies, we cannot avoid topics highlighted in the politicians' accounts.

The topics of the posts are determined on the basis of generalizations of repetitive patterns in the published texts, including references to people, organizations, actual socio-economic problems, events and trends. These sets of topics represent agendas, formed by each politician's account.

Model. This criterion is related to strategic orientations and in some cases to the content style. In this dimension of strategy, we rely on differentiation scheme, which is conceptually similar to the one, suggested by Lilleker et al. [27]. However, we apply it only to the substance of texts. Combining several approaches and relying on specifics of Russian political online communication, we define 4 main communication models, characterizing the focus of content: "informing", "mobilizing", "interacting" and "persuasion" (criteria of attributing the strategy to a specific model are described in the part "Methods").

Content. Preliminary analysis showed us that, in general, accounts differ significantly in use of two specific content forms: integrated video and links. As, for example, photos and textual content are used almost universally and audio content is almost never used, we do not consider these factors as they are less important.

Metrics. As the criteria for evaluation of various publication strategies in terms of posts' effects, we use key metrics representing "public's response" in Vkontakte social network. We consider the number of likes and comments as typical reactions of users.

4   Research Questions

The objective of the research is scientifically justified description of key strategies represented by the accounts of well-known political leaders in Vkontakte social network. To reach the objective the following questions were answered:

- What are the topics which are mostly highlighted on the accounts of various political leaders?
- What are the communication models which are used on the accounts of various political leaders?
- How often are links and video materials used in the publications of various political leaders?

5 Data

As the data source for the empirical research, we used popular social network Vkontakte. This website is not only the most popular social network in Russia, but also in February 2019 was ranked as second by the average number of daily users among all Russian internet projects, exceeded only by Yandex [32].

The choice of Vkontakte social network is also based on the fact that VK API providing easy access to the data. Apart from that in this social network, many accounts of well-known Russian politicians can be easily found.

For our research, we have manually picked 23 accounts of well-known politicians of various levels, among those are both representatives of the Government of Russian Federation and regional politicians: governors, mayors, and leaders of the parties and independent leaders of the opposition.

We based the list of politicians used in the study on the ranking from project VKFaces [47], which provides information on the popular (in the sense of number of subscribers) politicians. We also included some other individuals after doing manual search. Every account has at least 8000 subscribers.

From the final list the inactive accounts were excluded. We consider politicians' accounts as a particular form of media outlets, at the same time recognizing unique features of content production and perception in the social network [25].

Based on the data description we can conclude that the accounts of the majority of politicians show activeness in a stable and regular way (Fig. 1).

Research Period. In international research practices of political online communication there is a strong bias towards the investigation of pre-electoral online campaigns periods. However, quite often another approach is implemented [e.g. 1], in which political communication is studied during standardized time period (e.g. one year). This approach allows to avoid the extremes (periods of increased publication activity) during pre-electoral campaigns and to increase the relevancy of received data with the objective to create the list of crucial for describing political online strategies indicators. For our sample, for all the accounts we have downloaded posts during one-year period (21251 posts, the period from 25.04.2018 to 25.04.2019). We have used Python script with SQLite and VK API [46] to collect the dataset.

Data shows that for the appropriateness of the further analysis and generalization of strategies and also characteristics of the audience reactions, from this sample we must exclude accounts with short existence time, the ones which have low number of posts (less than 50 during past year), and also accounts with disabled comments (D. Medvedev, N. Magdeev, A. Beglov, V. Kondratev, V. Milonov, I. Orlov, V. Medinskij). The final sample contains 16 accounts (19639 posts).

	2018									2019			
	Apr	May	Jun	Jul	Aug	Sep	Oct	Nov	Dec	Jan	Feb	Mar	Apr
Delyagin	117	843	800	813	877	769	867	926	938	739	847	874	748
ZHirinovskij	1	73	75	182	221	231	163	175	158	142	154	165	143
Kadyrov	20	136	146	120	127	94	107	93	104	81	95	106	82
Sobyanin	15	92	68	91	90	86	92	88	104	85	72	87	82
Evkurov	6	51	74	81	102	66	24	56	94	112	125	115	98
Minnihanov	6	83	89	40	90	94	101	85	76	43	67	105	61
Naval'nyj	12	37	41	23	46	38	64	63	84	56	84	81	69
Mironov	11	48	41	51	57	51	68	47	61	35	44	49	33
Milonov	1	19	24	13	56	82	58	63	59	52	30	37	26
Vorob'ev	4	48	37	56	48	38	34	37	53	37	32	38	23
Medvedev	7	19	23	25	15	27	24	28	43	33	39	44	34
Kondrat'ev	1	25	20	19	18	26	44	33	28	35	40	38	32
YAshin	10	55	26	8	12	22	24	20	34	19	26	27	28
Berdnikov	3	33	26	11	26	30	23	23	34	25	23	16	25
Zyuganov	6	14	1	14	13	42	16	9	14	27	36	50	39
Medinskij	3	10	7	3	8	16	11	28	23	43	39	38	30
Lokot'	5	32	20	17	21	16	22	13	19	18	20	15	21
Kuvshinnikov	1	15	22	21	17	14	11	12	18	22	22	20	24
YAvlinskij	4	8	8	9	4	8	8	7	8	5	11	9	5
Orlov		6	9	15	18	12	3		4	2	5	2	2
Koshin		9	12	10	8	6	5	4	2	3	2	3	6
Beglov												9	19
Magdeev		1	2			1			1	1	1		

Fig. 1. The number of posts per month during a period from 25.04.2018 to 25.04.2019. Politicians were sorted out by the overall number of posts.

6 Methods

Research methodology is based on the comparative analysis of the politicians' accounts, which are considered as typical units of observation. Comparative analysis is aimed to generalize similarities and differences of politicians' publication strategies.

Analysis of Content. Thematic scope and communication model are evaluated based on the qualitative analysis of 50 randomly selected posts on each account in sample (total subsample: 800 posts), during the process of negotiated coding and information consolidation. For each account, we distinguished several key topics covered in the posts. As the topics vary significantly, we did not provisionally list them. We attributed models to strategies based on prevalence of posts of a specific orientation.

- Informing. Focused on statement of fact, informing style.
- Mobilizing. Focused on call to "offline action" (e.g. meeting, protest action, lection).
- Interacting. Discussion or conversation focused, online feedback request, involvement of the audience without calling to action.
- Persuasion. Orientation on opinion expression, promotion of personal point of view.

One account can be attributed to several models or to none. Count of the posts with video and links materials was done manually using the same subsample.

Engagement Metrics. In order to evaluate the strategies from the audience perspective we used three indicators: the average number of views and the ratios of the number of likes and number of comments to the number of views. In addition, we use engagement rate as an indicator, which is widely used in the studies of Facebook [7].

For SNS Vkontakte, we calculated engagement rate using formula ER = ((likes + comments)/views) * 1000. As the distribution of weighted number of likes and number of comments is non-normal, we use log scales for data visualization.

7   Results

Comparison of the metrics applied to the subgroups divided according to the content use reflect some overall patterns (Table 2).

Table 2. Comparison of posts. Key metrics and content use.

	Comments/views (mean)	Likes/views (mean)	Views (mean)
Posts without video	0.0038	0.0287	14912
Posts with video	0.0035	0.0250	24588
Posts without links	0.0029	0.0281	16868
Posts with links	0.0072	0.0259	20411

The video use generally increased the number of views and affected the weighted likes and engagement rate. The links use significantly increased the number of views and weighted comments (Table 3).

Table 3. Wilcox test for integrated video and links use.

Metrics	Video use		Links use	
	p-value	W	p-value	W
ER	0.0058*	73142	0.1943	47770
Comments/views	0.4128	67394	0.0000*	32561
Likes/views	0.0094*	72671	0.1088	55397
Views	0.0000*	52882	0.0094*	58012

*p < 0.05

In general, based on engagement rate, all politicians can be divided into 3 nominal groups: high engagement rate – G. Zyuganov, I. Yashin, S. Mironov, G. Yavlinskij, medium engagement rate – Y. Evkurov and A. Navalnyj, low engagement rate – others. At the same time, we should note that some of the accounts were highly ranked for engagement rate due to the number of comments and the others due to the number of likes (Fig. 2).

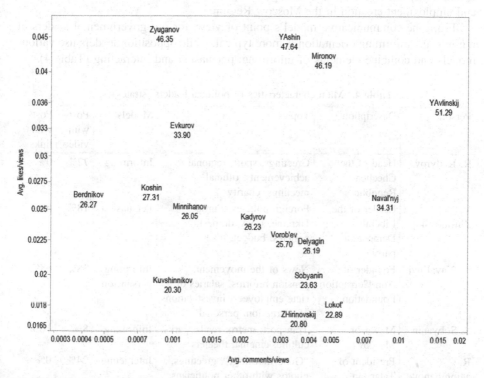

Fig. 2. Engagement rate and average weighted values of user reactions on content in politicians' accounts (log scales).

In general, high engagement rate is more typical for the politicians of federal level and opposition leaders (including systemic opposition, i.e. the representatives of Liberal Democratic, Communist and "Just Russia" parties [42]). Moreover, high engagement has little to do with the amount of posts.

Analysis of topics and models shows that politicians (or their press-services) have different approaches to account management, which can be determined by different circumstances: party or the political movement, news agenda of a city or a region, personal position, preferences and conflicts, events taking place in Russia and the world, not necessarily related to politics.

Comparison of the topic balances in different politicians' accounts showed that the highlighted problems are, first of all, influenced by membership either to pro-government bloc or opposition (systemic or independent). The accounts of the pro-government politicians (especially, heads of regions) resemble mostly as media sources: coverage of the activities, events on city/region problem solving or greetings or event coverage. Some leaders simply greet their subscribers (topic "Good morning!") on the regular basis. For the opposition leaders it is typical to cover more sensitive issues, such as the pension reform, VAT increase, relations with USA and Ukraine. Several topics reflect key issues of the regions, as the broadcasting of its solution helps to create a positive image of a politician, such as the subway in Moscow and employment creation in the Moscow Region.

From the communicative model's point of view, for pro-governmental leaders of regions, the informing orientation is more typical, while opposition leaders use various models and combine elements of informing, persuasion and interacting (Table 4).

Table 4. Main characteristics of political leaders' strategies.

Person	Description	Topics	Models	Posts with video	Posts with links
R. Kadyrov	Head of the Chechen Republic	Greetings, sport, regional achievements, official meetings, charity	Informing	72%	0%
V. Zhirinovskij	Leader of the Liberal Democratic party	Foreign policies: Europe, Ukraine, USA, domestic policies: budget, taxes	Persuasion	18%	6%
A. Naval'nyj	Founder of Anti-Corruption Foundation	News of the movement, pension reforms, salaries of state employees, investigations of corruption, personal	Informing persuasion	38%	68%
S. Sobyanin	Mayor of Moscow	Transport: metro, roads, parks, culture: cinema, theaters	Informing	8%	16%
R. Minnihanov	President of Tatarstan	"Good morning!", greetings, photos with other politicians	Interacting	24%	0%
A. Vorob'ev	Governor of Moscow Region	Manufacturing, creation of new job opportunities, health care, opening of new medical centers, improvement policies	Informing	46%	0%
G. Zyuganov	Leader of the Communist Party	General critic of state power, pension reform, VAT increase, history	Persuasion interacting	32%	22%
S. Mironov	"Just Russia" party leader	Party activities, domestic policy: pension reform, taxes	Persuasion interacting	24%	0%
A. Lokot'	Mayor of Novosibirsk	Improvement policies, infrastructure development, greetings	Informing	22%	24%
G. Yavlinskij	Leader of "Yabloko" party	Critics of state power, cherished memory of famous writers, artists, well-known writers, artists, public figures	Persuasion	28%	52%

(*continued*)

Table 4. (*continued*)

Person	Description	Topics	Models	Posts with video	Posts with links
O. Kuvshinnikov	Governor of Vologda Region	Greetings, personal memories, football world cup	Informing	22%	6%
D. Berdnikov	Mayor of Irkutsk	Greetings, building of educational institutions, development of infrastructure	Informing	0%	0%
M. Delyagin	Adviser to the head of "Just Russia" party fraction	Critics of the state power, Trump, pension reform	Persuasion	24%	98%
I. Yashin	Head of Krasnoselsky District	Critics of housing and communal services in Moscow, critics of Sobyanin	Informing Interacting	34%	26%
Y. Evkurov	Head of the Republic of Ingushetia	Tourism, infrastructure development, sport, "Good morning!"	Informing	42%	0%
I. Koshin	Deputy Minister of North Caucasus Affairs	Greetings, situation in fuel and energy complex of North Caucasus, football world cup, working missions	Persuasion	10%	2%

In varying degrees, posts with integrated video content is used in the accounts of almost all above mentioned politicians with few exceptions. In general, 27% of the posts contain video. The use of external links is less common. Only 19% of the posts contain them (these calculations have been carried out using subsample of 800 posts, 50 posts for each account). The links in most cases lead to their own websites, websites of political parties, "Youtube" and less frequently to media sources.

Generalizing communicative strategies, logic of their description can be reduced to two opposing vectors: informing on problem solving, achievements, events in the region (pro-government rhetoric) and discussion, opinion expression, position of the party or the movement (critical rhetoric). We can add a third strategy – neutral: when account just reflects image and not politician's actions or opinion.

Unique Practices. In the accounts of opposition leaders (both representatives of parliamentarian parties and independent politicians), we can find approaches which we did not find in other accounts. For example, on the page of G. Zyuganov there are posts that contain direct questions to the audience, which provokes a huge number of comments. S. Mironov uses short videos in which he answers different questions forwarded to him via Vkontakte and Internet reception.

A. Navalnyj does a huge number of reposts with press-issues and video portraying members of his movement and projects, for example, V. Milov, L. Sobol. On his account M. Delyagin uses many external links to his website delyagin.ru, which, considering the amount of content, can be viewed as a sophisticated media source.

Every fifth post of the representative of local administration I. Yashin is a repost (from different sources, for example, "Navalnyj", "Meduza", "Echo of Moscow"), such publications are used as an instrument of self-presentation of a politician and his opinion in accordance with political strategy. Probably, due to non-trivial approach many accounts of the opposition leaders ensured this high average engagement rate.

8 Discussion

Most of the described strategies of politicians are polarized within the framework of the "information-centered" – "influence centered" disposition, in some cases occupying an intermediate position [30]. It is interesting that political orientation (opposition or pro-government), however, does not always determine the dominant model, which we can see on the examples of the strategies of opposition leader I. Yashin and deputy minister I. Koshin.

A significant number of governors among active politicians in Vkontakte, combined with some similarities of their strategies, are also associated with a special pattern of their online presence: their goal is to show activity and transparency, targeting not only the mass audience, but also the Federal government [44]. At the same time, the analysis of the posts showed that the vast majority of governors, although actively addressing the audience, are not inclined to take "attempts to seem like ordinary people" [9] and to share some "personal stories".

Despite the fact that the chosen classification scheme based on models is quite appropriate, on some accounts, we can see traces of other strategies used in other researches, for example, "homestyle" and "impression management" [28].

There is a number of post metrics on Vkontakte we did not take into account. For example, A. Vorobev, R. Kadyrov, Y. Evkurov frequently use hashtags on their accounts. V. Zhirinovskij, S. Mironov and G. Zyuganov use interactive questions. Despite all the advantages of being present on social networks, many politicians still avoid using them, fearing reputational damages and close attention of media, which can be also considered as a strategy and requires an additional investigation.

Limitations. At this stage, we used a simplified scheme for classification of strategies based on two key factors: topics and models. We must admit that for the proper investigation on the classification of strategies requires a bigger number of factors.

It is important to mention that the metrics – engagement rate, "likes/views", "comments/views" do not constitute exhaustive set of indicators for evaluating all the effects of publication strategy of a political leader in the online communication.

In addition, some of the leaders significantly differ from others, that making it hard to place them into one group or another, based on our classification scheme. The number of accounts can be attributed to the category of image platforms rather than strategic communication instruments.

Further Work. Based on conducted comparative analysis, we suggest formulating scientifically proven methodology of classification of strategies which takes into consideration a system of quantitative or qualitative metrics for the complex understanding of political leaders' online communication. Further work also implies a throughout qualitative and quantitative analysis of comments in the social network.

9 Conclusion

Consolidation of data helped us to realize that accounts of the pro-government politicians operate mostly in informing mode, while opposition uses informing, persuasion and interacting, combining them in a different way and, in general, opposition is more "ingenious" in matters of account management. In most cases, the accounts of federal-level politicians and opposition leaders have higher engagement rate than pro-regime mayors and governors. We also showed that posts with video or links gain greater reach (average number of views per post). These types of content can be used to improve communicative strategies in social media. The research illustrates the variety of communicative strategies used by Russian politicians on social networks.

Despite the repetitive patterns, thematic coverage of posts is sufficiently diverse. It's worth mentioning that politicians (and their press-services) communicate in the language of the target audience, paying considerable attention to the problems that are really close to the audience, in other words, obtrusive issues [39]. This is particularly noticeable in the accounts of the most commented heads of regions.

For the independent and systemic opposition, such key topics of the federal social and political agenda as pension reform, budgeting and tax legislation proved to be extremely popular.

The "rituals" associated with greetings and conventions, which are so typical for pro-government heads of regions, can be evaluated from two positions. First, this format can produce convenient positive "newsbreaks" understandable to a broad audience. Secondly, such content allows to emphasize identity and demonstrate the intention to be close to people [2, p. 183, 38]. However, this practice is typical for European politicians too [31].

Acknowledgements. This work was funded by RFBR and EISR, project number 19-011-31651. We would like to thank our colleagues from the Center for Sociological and Internet Research of Saint Petersburg State University for guidance and support.

References

1. Arnaudo, D.: Computational propaganda in Brazil: social bots during elections. Proj. Comput. Propag. **8**, 1–39 (2017). http://blogs.oii.ox.ac.uk/politicalbots/wp-content/uploads/sites/89/2017/06/Comprop-Brazil-1.pdf. Accessed 14 May 2019
2. Azmi, A., Sylvia, I., Mardhiah, D.: Discourse analysis of politicians' social media posts. Messenger **10**(2), 174–186 (2018)
3. Bessi, A., Ferrara, E.: Social bots distort the 2016 US presidential election online discussion. First Monday **21**(11) (2016), https://ssrn.com/abstract=2982233. Accessed 14 May 2019
4. Bolgov, R., Chernov, I., Ivannikov, I., Katsy, D.: Battle in Twitter: comparative analysis of online political discourse (Cases of Macron, Trump, Putin, and Medvedev). In: Chugunov, A., Misnikov, Y., Roshchin, E., Trutnev, D. (eds.) EGOSE 2018. CCIS, vol. 947, pp. 374–383. Springer, Cham (2019). https://doi.org/10.1007/978-3-030-13283-5_28
5. Bolsover, G.: Computational propaganda in China: an alternative model of a widespread practice. Proj. Comput. Propag. **4** (2017). http://blogs.oii.ox.ac.uk/politicalbots/wp-content/uploads/sites/89/2017/06/Comprop-China.pdf. Accessed 14 May 2019

6. Bundin, M., Martynov, A.: Use of social media and blogs by federal authorities in Russia: regulation and policy. In: Proceedings of the 17th International Digital Government Research Conference on Digital Government Research, pp. 8–11. ACM, NewYork (2016)

7. Chan, M., Fassbender, K.: Evaluating public engagement for a consensus development conference. J. Palliat. Med. **21**, 1–20 (2018). https://doi.org/10.1089/jpm.2017.0390

8. Cmeciu, C., Cmeciu, D.: Web 2.0 communication and stakeholder engagement strategies: how Romanian public organizations use Facebook. Procedia - Soc. Behav. Sci. **143**, 879–883 (2014)

9. Coleman, S., Moss, G.: Governing at a distance – politicians in the blogosphere. Inf. Polity **13**(1–2), 7–20 (2008)

10. Conover, M., Ratkiewicz, J., Francisco, M., Gonçalves, B., Flammini, A., Menczer, F.: Political polarization on Twitter. In: Proceedings of the Fifth International AAAI Conference on Weblogs and Social Media. AAAI Press, Menlo Park (2011)

11. Ekman, M., Widholm, A.: Political communication in an age of visual connectivity: exploring Instagram practices among Swedish politicians. North. Light.: Film Media Stud. Yearb. **15**(1), 15–32 (2017)

12. Eriksen, E.O., Weigård, J.: Conceptualizing politics: strategic or communicative action? Scand. Polit. Stud. **20**(3), 219–241 (1997)

13. Etling, B., Alexanyan, K., Kelly, J., Faris, R., Palfrey, J.G., Gasser, U.: Public discourse in the Russian blogosphere: mapping RuNet politics and mobilization. Berkman Center Research Publication (2010)

14. Flynn, J.: Communicative power in Habermas's theory of democracy. Eur. J. Polit. Theory **3**(4), 433–454 (2004)

15. FOM. News sources and media trust, 30 January 2019. https://fom.ru/SMI-i-internet/14170. Accessed 14 May 2019

16. Froomkin, A.M.: Technologies for democracy. In: Shane, P. (ed.) Democracy Online, pp. 23–40. https://ssrn.com/abstract=2731312. Accessed 14 May 2019

17. Habermas, J.: The theory of Communicative Action: Lifeworld and System: A Critique of Functionalist Reason. Beacon Press, Boston (2003)

18. Hermans, L., Vergeer, M.: Personalization in e-campaigning: a cross-national comparison of personalization strategies used on candidate websites of 17 countries in EP elections 2009. New Media Soc. **15**(1), 72–92 (2013)

19. Holiday, S., Lewis, M.J., LaBaugh, J.L.: Are you talking to me? The socio-political visual rhetoric of the Syrian presidency's Instagram account. Southwest. Mass Commun. J. **30**(2) (2015)

20. Holtzhausen, D.: Strategic communication. The international encyclopedia of communication (2008). https://doi.org/10.1002/9781405186407

21. Howard, P.N., Bolsover, G., Kollanyi, B., Bradshaw, S., Neudert, L.-M.: Junk news and bots during the U.S. election: what were Michigan voters sharing over Twitter? Proj. Comput. Propag. **1** (2017). http://comprop.oii.ox.ac.uk/research/working-papers/junk-news-and-bots-during-the-u-s-election-what-were-michigan-voters-sharing-over-twitter/. Accessed 14 May 2019

22. Jung, Y., Tay, A., Hong, T., Ho, J., Goh, Y.H.: Politician's strategic impression management on Instagram. In: Proceedings of the 50th Hawaii International Conference on System Sciences, pp. 2195–2201 (2017). https://doi.org/10.24251/hicss.2017.265

23. Kelly, J., et al.: Mapping Russian Twitter. Berkman Center Research Publication 2012-3. https://ssrn.com/abstract=2028158. Accessed 14 May 2019

24. Kingston, J.: Nationalism and the 2014 snap election: the abe conundrum. In: Pekkanen, R.J., Scheiner, E., Reed, S.R. (eds.) Japan Decides 2014: The Japanese general election, pp. 211–225. Palgrave Macmillan, London (2016). https://doi.org/10.1057/9781137552006_17

25. Klinger, U., Svensson, J.: The emergence of network media logic in political communication: a theoretical approach. New Media Soc. **17**(8), 1241–1257 (2015)
26. Larsson, A.O., Kalsnes, B.: "Of course we are on Facebook": use and non-use of social media among Swedish and Norwegian politicians. Eur. J. Commun. **29**(6), 653–667 (2014)
27. Lilleker, D.G., Koc-Michalska, K., Schweitzer, E.J., Jacunski, M., Jackson, N., Vedel, T.: Informing, engaging, mobilizing or interacting: searching for a European model of web campaigning. Eur. J. Commun. **26**(3), 195–213 (2011)
28. Lilleker, D.G., Koc-Michalska, K.: Online political communication strategies: MEPs, e-representation, and self-representation. J. Inf. Technol. Polit. **10**(2), 190–207 (2013)
29. MacNair, B.: An Introduction to Political Communication. Routledge, London (2011)
30. Manheim, J.: Strategy in Information and Influence Campaigns: How Policy Advocates, Social Movements, Insurgent Groups, Corporations, Governments and Others Get What They Want. Routledge (2011)
31. Mattiello, E.: Reformulating political discourse: how politicians construct their identity in the Facebook era. In: XXVI AIA Conference Remediating, Rescripting, Remaking: Old and New Challenges in English Studies, Parma, pp. 12–14 (2013)
32. Mediascope. https://mediascope.net/data/. Accessed 14 May 2019
33. Miller, J.: Russian PM's Twitter hacked, posting "I resign", BBC, https://www.bbc.com/news/technology-28786683. Accessed 14 May 2019
34. Nielsen, R.K., Vaccari, C.: Do people "like" politicians on Facebook? Not really. Large-scale direct candidate-to-voter online communication as an outlier phenomenon. Int. J. Commun. **7**(24), 2333–2356 (2013)
35. Nitschke, P., Donges, P.: Intentional and emergent strategies: analyzing the motivational and structural dynamics in online communications of political interest organizations. Public Relat. Inq. **7**(3), 225–241 (2018)
36. Renz, B., Sullivan, J.: Making a connection in the provinces? Russia's tweeting governors. East Eur. Polit. **29**(2), 135–151 (2013)
37. Rodina, E., Dligach, D.: Dictator's Instagram: personal and political narratives in a Chechen leader's social network. Cauc. Surv. 1–15 (2019)
38. Rodríguez, J.L.: The interplay of greetings and promises. Pragmatics **22**(1), 167–187 (2012)
39. Rogers, E., Dearing, J.: Agenda-setting research: where has it been, where is it going? Commun. Yearb. **11**, 555–594 (1988)
40. Schäfer, F., Evert, S., Heinrich, P.: Japan's 2014 general election: political bots, right-wing internet activism and Prime Minister Shinzō Abe's hidden nationalist agenda. Big Data **5**(4), 294–309 (2017)
41. Schlæger, J., Jiang, M.: Official microblogging and social management by local governments in China. China Inf. **28**(2), 189–213 (2014)
42. Smyth, R., Sobolev, A., Soboleva, I.: A well-organized play: symbolic politics and the effect of the pro-Putin rallies. Probl. Post-Communism **60**(2), 24–39 (2013)
43. Thamm, M., Bleier, A.: When politicians tweet: a study on the members of the German Federal Diet. (2013). https://arxiv.org/abs/1305.1734. Accessed 14 May 2019
44. Toepfl, F.: Blogging for the sake of the president: the online diaries of Russian governors. Eur.-Asia Stud. **64**(8), 1435–1459 (2012)
45. Tselikov, A.: The tightening web of Russian internet regulation. Berkman Center Research Publication 2014-15 (2014). https://ssrn.com/abstract=2527603. Accessed 14 May 2019
46. VK API. https://vk.com/dev/methods. Accessed 14 May 2019
47. VKFaces. https://vkfaces.com/stars/catalog/politicians. Accessed 14 May 2019
48. VKontakte. https://vk.com/. Accessed 14 May 2019
49. Wilde, P., Michailidou, A., Trenz, H.J.: Converging on euroscepticism: online polity contestation during European parliament elections. Eur. J. Polit. Res. **4**(53), 766–783 (2014)

50. Williams, C.B., Gulati, G.J.J.: Social networks in political campaigns: Facebook and the congressional elections of 2006 and 2008. New Media Soc. **15**(1), 52–71 (2013)
51. Woolley, S.C., Howard, P.N.: Automation, algorithms, and politics. Political communication, computational propaganda, and autonomous agent – Introduction. Int. J. Commun. **10**, 4882–4890 (2016)
52. Zasoursky, I.: Media and Power in Post-Soviet Russia. Routledge, NewYork (2016)
53. van Zoonen, L., Vis, F., Mihelj, S.: Performing citizenship on YouTube: activism, satire and online debate around the anti-Islam video Fitna. Crit. Discourse Stud. **7**(4), 249–262 (2010)

Ukrainian Information Flows in the Crimean Segment of Social Media: Social Network Analysis

Elena Brodovskaya[1] ⬤, Anna Dombrovskaya[1,2] ⬤,
Artur Azarov[3(✉)] ⬤, and Dmitry Karzubov[4]

[1] Financial University under the Government of RF, Leningradsky Avenue, 49,
Moscow 125993, Russia
brodovskaya@inbox.ru
[2] Moscow State Pedagogical University, 1/1 M. Pirogovskaya,
Moscow 119991, Russia
an-doc@yandex.ru
[3] St. Petersburg Institute for Informatics and Automation of the Russian
Academy of Sciences, 39 14-th Line V.O., Saint-Petersburg, Russia
artur-azarov@yandex.ru
[4] Moscow Higher Combined Arms Command School, Golovacheva Street, 2,
Moscow 109380, Russia
karzubovdn@gmail.com

Abstract. A critical review of modern domestic and foreign studies, reflecting the characteristics of the formation of information flows by Ukrainian network leaders on the problems of development of the Crimea in the Russian Federation aiming at the disintegration and deconsolidation of the Crimean community was done. On the basis of the carried out theoretical analysis and own research experience, a unique author's method of analysis of the communication infrastructure of Ukrainian network flows, including social and media Analytics (using the online service for monitoring social media IQBuzz, total accumulated 1 000 000 relevant message), the method of social graphs (using the author's software "Social graph" carried out the structuring of intra-group and inter-group relations of the most influential Ukrainian online network communities, the strategies of network leaders in the formation of user attitudes about the development of the Russian Crimea), cognitive mapping and discourse analysis of messages of Ukrainian blogs and online network communities (1200 relevant most meaningful messages, established linguistic methods of manipulation of the consciousness of the user audience). The article is devoted to the reporting about social network analysis, highlighting Ukrainian threads about the problems of development of Crimea on the types of generated discourses (Russian aggression, the illegitimacy of the annexation of the Crimea, Sevastopol and Russia, indoctrinate the Russian citizens and the discussion of the development of the Crimean community in the context of a referendum).

Keywords: Information flows · Social media · Online content · Social network analysis

© Springer Nature Switzerland AG 2020
A. Chugunov et al. (Eds.): EGOSE 2019, CCIS 1135, pp. 441–451, 2020.
https://doi.org/10.1007/978-3-030-39296-3_32

1   Introduction

Increasingly intensive processes of expanding the Russian users audience, increasing the impact of network communications on political processes, mobilizing unconventional protest attitudes of citizens and actualize the significance of the empirical research conducted in 2018 of technological, dynamic and substantial characteristics of Ukrainian social media flows, oriented on the de-consolidation of the Crimean and the whole Russian society. Numerous world cases of the last decades, including protest activity in Russia 2011–2017 provided the status of Internet communication as a means of constructing protest, anti-government attitudes and replicating extremist behavioral strategies [4–12].

The Crimea and Sevastopol, reunited with the Russian Federation, are under significant information pressure, primarily from the Ukrainian media leaders, who are extremely active in the online environment. The social and media research carried out in the reporting period was aimed at measuring the scale and discursive characteristics of information flows created by Ukrainian network leaders that form anti-Russian attitudes among ethnic and social groups of Crimea and Sevastopol, who are experiencing relative deprivation, as well as identifying the critical communication infrastructure of Ukrainian opinion centers aimed on social destabilization and disintegration of the Crimean community [1–3].

The purpose of the article is to present the results of an analysis of the parameters of spontaneous and targeted information flows in the social media of the peninsula using the tools for automated processing of "big data" [1, 4, 8]. The following parameters were considered: the weight of the information flow; information flow dynamics; correlation of information flow and event dynamics in a real environment; socio-demographic characteristics of users; user geolocation; repertoire/main topics of information flow; orientation/objects of information flow; passive/active message character; network opinion leaders; points of view information flow; markers, triggers and patterns of non-conventional protest activity.

The practical significance of the research:

- the possibility of using the results of research in the process of organizing project-analytical sessions for employees of the Crimea and Sevastopol authorities to discuss the problems of integration of the inhabitants of Crimea and Sevastopol into the sociocultural space of the Russian Federation;
- systematization on the basis of research data of the main areas of work on the formation of a positive Russian national-state identity of the residents of Crimea and Sevastopol;
- justification of the information campaign program in the Internet space for the development of information flows that form the values of positive Russian national-state identification, positive historical identity, images of positive future development of the peninsula in the Russian Federation among Crimean residents;
- development of critical communication infrastructure of Ukrainian information flows, which serves as the basis for creating the concept of countering the decon-solidating effect of Ukrainian opinion centers in social media.

2 Research Description

The strategy of applied research was hybrid in nature and was based on a combination of quantitative and qualitative methods used to analyze information flows [1, 6, 7, 9].

The empirical model of the thesis was built on the triangulation of methods and procedures of applied research and includes:

1. Cognitive mapping of texts of Ukrainian Internet media in the Crimean segment - analysis of texts of Ukrainian Internet resources targeted at the Crimean audience for the period 2014–2018 (1200 posts), 60 blogs and network groups.
2. Discourse analysis of messages from social media users - 1200 messages from social media users which were relevant to the research topic, developing on its basis dictionaries of digital markers of message types of Ukrainian information flows in the Crimean social media segment for automated unloading of big data. Discourse analysis was also used at the stage of identifying protest metaphors and techniques for the formation of anti-Russian rhetoric in Ukrainian information flows circulating in the Crimean segment of social media.
3. Cybermetry of spontaneous and targeted information flows in social media - data sets of automated unloading of Internet content - 1 million messages from users of the VK.com, Ok.ru and Facebook networks. The method allowed to segment the Ukrainian information flows in the Crimean segment of social media, to identify their structural, informative and dynamic characteristics.
4. Construction and analysis of social graphs of online communities, that are relevant to the research topic. Analysis of the density of social connections in these communities. This method was used to determine the integration of participants and to identify the density of social connections between online communities, coordinated by Ukrainian actors.

2.1 Cybermetric Analysis Stages

Selection of groups in social media. This stage was necessary for the subsequent qualitative analysis of messages in order to form search queries. During this stage, 60 online communities were selected in total and more than 1,200 documents were analyzed. The analysis resulted in the development of search queries for uploading an array of social media posts.

Discourse analysis of the primary array. This stage was important for refining search queries and compiling dictionaries of digital markers. To identify the relevance of messages accumulated in the preliminary array, systematic sampling was used, a total of 500 messages were analyzed both in Russian-language and Ukrainian-language arrays.

Compilation of dictionaries taking into account the contexts of the analyzed subject, selected by an expert. During this stage, 5 experts - leading experts in the field of cybermetric analysis by brainstorming identified the most indicative search queries based on the results of all previous stages of work.

Automated uploading of Internet content using the developed dictionaries of markers and an online service for monitoring social media IQBuzz, totaly 1 million messages unloaded.

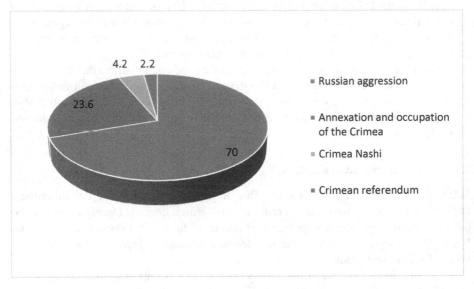

444   E. Brodovskaya et al.

Quantitative and qualitative analysis of the uploaded Internet content was carried out using automatically generated statistical reports on the technological, content and dynamic characteristics of information flows. The interpretation was made according to the criteria set by the program:

- weight of information flows;
- the dynamics of information flows;
- tag clouds - the semantic core of information flows;
- publication activity and the volume of the user audience of opinion leaders;
- distribution by gender and age of the user audience of information flows.

3 Main Results of the Research

Figure 1 shows the share of social media flows created by Ukrainian network leaders, containing different contexts conducted to the problems of the development of Crimea within the Russian Federation.

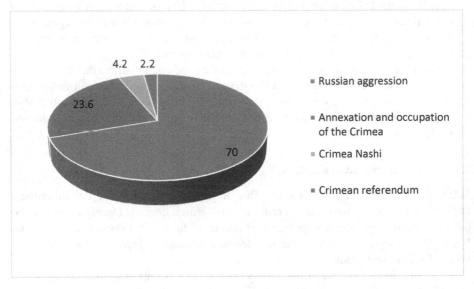

Fig. 1. The proportion of the main information flows of the Ukrainian segment of social media.

In accordance with the values that are presented in Fig. 1, the leading in distribution scale is the flow reflecting the discourse of Russia as an aggressor (70% of all accumulated relevant documents). A quarter of the entire unloaded array is a segment of messages containing references to the reunification of the Crimea and Sevastopol to Russia as acts of annexation and occupation. Statistically insignificant shares of documents include 2 types of discourse. The first of them is related to the condemnation of the Russians, who recognized the legitimacy of the reunification of the Crimea and

Sevastopol to the Russian Federation, they are marked in these reports as "Crimea Nashi", that is, people who "blindly accepted" the fact of changing the status of the state identity of the Crimean peninsula (2.2% of the total accumulated). The second of the rather unrepresentative information flows reflects the position of Ukrainian users who comprehended the fact of holding a referendum on the accession of Crimea and Sevastopol to the Russian Federation (4.2% of all relevant research documents) and which presents an alternative position regarding the positive aspects of the development of the Crimean society within Russia.

At the same time, it is quite obvious that information flows in the space of the Ukrainian segment of social media are aimed at deconsolidating and disintegrating Crimean society, messages aimed at undermining social stability and disharmonization of social relations, increasing the level of conflict in the Crimea and in general in Russian society.

3.1 Analysis of Online Communities

Large communities with the most clearly demonstrated radical rhetoric were chosen for the analyzing online communities.

The average number of links in groups was considered. This indicator shows the connectivity of the group. Group members communicate not only in a group, but also outside it. In addition, the participants in the group with the most connections form the core of the group. In a number of cases, they also become leaders of public opinion, while posting content on their pages that is similar in topic, but different in factual material from what is placed in groups. Thus, the considered groups have a fairly stable structure with the existing hierarchy of relationships. These figures are presented in Fig. 2.

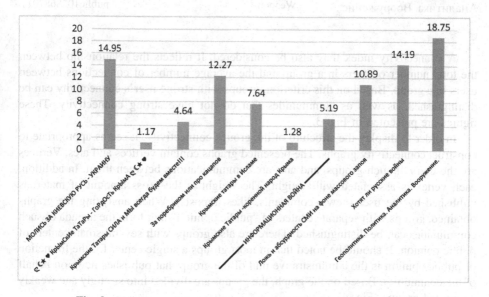

Fig. 2. Indicators of the average number of links in network groups

Group names are written in Russian, for this reason we use the native spelling, but we include the addresses of groups and its spelling in English on Table 1.

Table 1. Groups spelling translation.

Native spelling	English spelling	Group address
МОЛИСЬ ЗА КИЕВСКУЮ РУСЬ - УКРАИНУ	PRAY FOR THE KIEVAN RUS - UKRAINE	https://vk.com/club70364026
КрЫмСкИе ТаТаРы - ГоРдОсТь КрЫмА	Crimean Tatars - The Pride Of The Crimea	https://vk.com/public85015484
Крымские Татары СИЛА и МЫ всегда будем вместе!!!	Crimean Tatars are STRONG and WE will always be together!!!	https://vk.com/club82500334
За поребриком или про кацапов	Over the curb or about katsaps	https://vk.com/public99956004
Крымские татары в Исламе	Crimean Tatars in Islam	https://vk.com/crimean_islam
Крымские Татары - коренной народ Крыма	Crimean Tatars - indigenous people of Crimea	https://vk.com/public73551522
ИНФОРМАЦИОННАЯ ВОЙНА	INFORMATION WAR	https://vk.com/infowarfare
Ложь и абсурдность СМИ на фоне массового запоя	Lies and absurdity of the media against the background of a mass binge	https://vk.com/lozhsmi
Хотят ли русские войны	Do Russians want war	https://vk.com/club69583597
Геополитика. Политика. Аналитика. Вооружение.	Geopolitics. Policy. Analytics. Weapon	https://vk.com/public102868701

A connectivity index may also be considered. It reflects the relationship between the total number of users in a group and the average number of connections between users in a group. Based on this criterion, groups with strong user's connectivity can be distinguished, as well as communities that do not have strong connectivity. These figures are presented in Fig. 3.

In order to display the structure of the groups connectivity, it seems appropriate to construct connectivity graphs. The presented graphs contain vertices and arcs. Vertices are the users of such groups, and arcs are communications between them. In addition, each vertex is associated with weight. The weight is the gross amount of materials published by the user (news, comments, likes, reposts). When analyzing the graphs obtained, groups with separate centers of "public opinion" that form the agenda of such communities can be distinguished. There are also groups with several small centers of public opinion. It should be noted that in most groups a single center for the formation of public opinion is the administrative unit of the group that publishes news on behalf of the community. Based on the graph, the groups are divided into strongly and weakly connected groups (Fig. 4).

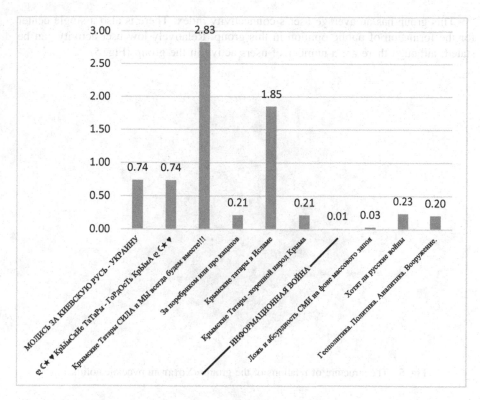

Fig. 3. Relative indicators of the average number of connections in network groups

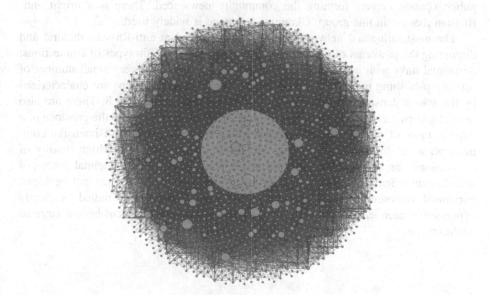

Fig. 4. The structure of relations of the group «МОЛИСЬ ЗА КИЕВСКУЮ РУСЬУКРАИНУ»

This group has an average user's connectivity index. There is also a single center for the formation of public opinion in this group. Relatively low user activity can be stated, although there are a number of users active in the group (Fig. 5).

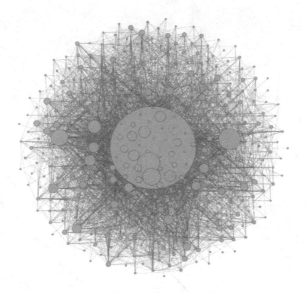

Fig. 5. The structure of relations of the group «Хотят ли русские войны»

This group has a low user's connectivity index. There is a significant number of public opinion centers forming the community news feed. There is a bright anti-Russian rhetoric in this group. Ukrainian language is widely used.

The most influential network groups that are aimed at anti-Russian rhetoric and discussing the problems of Crimea, are characterized by 2 main types of connections: horizontal links with a complete absence of clear leaders or a very small number of actively publishing messages of participants. These network groups are characterized by the lowest density of connections - on average - no more than 8. There are also several groups for which the structure of relations is characterized by the presence of a large number of opinion leaders, around which micro-societies with intensive communication are formed. These groups are distinguished by a rather high density of connections—on average, this indicator is 13. Thus, in the most influential groups of anti-Russian orientation, there are 2 types of mechanisms for disseminating ideas: horizontal, representing equal relations of like-minded people not united by clearly expressed opinion leaders and vertical, in building powerful leaders of intense targeted communication.

4 Conclusion

As a result of automated social-media and discursive analysis of Ukrainian information flows created by opinion centers on the development of Crimea as part of the Russian Federation, a logical scheme to study the communication infrastructure of data flows was identified: "Markers - triggers - message patterns of Ukrainian opinion centers on problems of the Russian Crimea."

Markers of dynamics/intensity, markers of content, markers of socio-demographic characteristics of the audience of the studied streams were developed. The speech patterns of the analyzed Ukrainian streams should be systematized in accordance with the types of data streams.

Ukrainian social and media flows, aimed at mobilizing anti-Russian sentiments among Crimean and Sevastopol users, have appeared firstly in March 2014. These flows are intensifying during periods of aggravation of the crisis situation in the South-East of Ukraine and the formation of anti-Russian rhetoric by Western politicians and media. One of the reasons for flows increasing during such periods is the emergence of additional information channels in various media covering crisis situations in South-East Ukraine, as well as the position of various political figures covering such crisis situations with anti-Russian rhetoric. The analyzed information flows are aimed at social destabilization and development of disintegration processes on the peninsula. The use of the Russian language in Ukrainian blogs indicates the calculation of their authors to have an impact on the Russian-speaking audience of the Crimea, Sevastopol and the Russian population as a whole with the aim of forming opposition movements that deconsolidate society. The most noticeable in the Ukrainian segment of the social media space are Russian-speaking flows, reflecting the discourse of "Russian aggression" and "illegitimacy" of the reunification of the Crimea, Sevastopol and Russia. Influential Ukrainian network opinion leaders most often aim at creating negative attitudes of Russian users, primarily Crimeans and Sevastopol residents, regarding the Russian government's position on the peninsula by disseminating stereotypical ideas about the actions of Russian authorities, simplifying and primitively motivating its representatives. This ensures the risk of the development of irrational, affective, unconventional attitudes among the Russian user audience. One of the means of increasing social tension is the factor of "vulnerable social groups", and, above all, ethnic communities, using the mechanisms of "stigmatization" of the situation of the Crimean Tatars, sticking "labels" of oppression of ethnic communities in Crimea and Sevastopol.

The tasks of consolidating society and overcoming the challenges of the communication space of the global network associated with the risk of social destabilization requires the use of phased resistance technology in the digital environment. First of all, it is necessary to monitor students' accounts in social networks, identify those, who are involved in extremist, nationalist and terrorist online network groups, conduct psychological and pedagogical support for such representatives of the younger generation, and carry out their digital navigation. In addition, it is important for new media, political parties, and civil society associations to form and distribute alternative constructive social and media streams that oppose arrays of messages that do not meet the goals of social development and endanger unity and accord in Russian society.

The methods of countering the destructive position revealed in the course of the analysis of social networks can be:

- the formation of a positive agenda highlighting various positive developments related to the reunification of the country. At the same time, such news should be interesting for various categories of citizens, shared in terms of age, gender and other characteristics. Moreover, to disseminate such news, the most frequently used ways of obtaining information by each category of citizens should be identified.
- analysis of user accounts that are subscribers to disintegration processes communities. First of all, the segmentation of such groups should be carried out and the real users of social networks should be singled out. Then general patterns of behavior of such users should be highlighted. Understanding the characteristics of their behavior will allow to form targeted impacts on such users, in order to draw their attention to the positive news related to the reunification of the country.

5   Research Outlook, Discussion

Prospects for research are primarily related to the development of marker dictionaries for accumulating social media reports of Ukrainian media about the problems of the development of Crimea in the Ukrainian and Crimean Tatar languages, which will allow to analyze the techniques used by Ukrainian network leaders to mobilize the disintegration attitudes of ethnic Ukrainians and ethnic Crimean Tatars and develop proposals for countering this deconsolidating influence in the network space.

The perspective of the analysis will also be a deep and wide coverage of social networks in order to identify communities that communicate in Ukrainian and Crimean Tatar languages about the problems of the Crimea and are aimed at social destabilization and development of disintegration processes on the peninsula.

Acknowledgements. This research was partially supported by RFBR, project No. 18-011-00937.

References

1. Azarov, A., Suvorova, A., Tulupyeva, T.: Changing the information system's protection level from social engineering attacks, in case of reorganizing the information system's users' structure. In: II International Scientific-Practical Conference «Fuzzy Technologies in the Industry», pp. 56–62 (2018)
2. Brodovskaya, E., Dombrovskaya, A., Pyrma, R., Sinyakov, A., Azarov, A.: The impact of digital communication on Russian youth professional culture: results of a comprehensive applied study. Monit. Public Opin.: Econ. Soc. Chang. **1**, 228–251 (2018)

3. Brodovskaya, E., Dombrovskaya, A., Karzubov, D.: Online mobilization of mass protests in Ukraine, Moldova, Armenia, and Kazakhstan (2013–2016): the results of comprehensive comparative empirical study. In: Proceedings of the International Conference on Electronic Governance and Open Society: Challenges in Eurasia (2017)
4. Dalton, R., Cain, B., Scarrow, S.: Democratic Public and Democratic Institutions. Expanding Political Opportunities in Advanced Industrial Democracies, pp. 250–275 (2003)
5. Dower, J.: War without mercy: race and power in the pacific war (1986)
6. Durkheim, E.: The Rules of Sociological Method. Trans. Solovay Sarah A., Mueller John M., ed. George E.G. Fatlin, 8th edn., 146 p. Free Press, New York (1964)
7. Edwards, D., Potter, J.: Discursive Psychology, 208 p. (1998)
8. Gamson, W., Croteau, D., Hoynes, W., Sasson, T.: Media images and the social construction of reality. Ann. Rev. Sociol. **18**, 373–393 (1992)
9. Martin, A., Wellman, B.: Social network analysis: an introduction. In: Handbook of Social Network Analysis, pp. 11–25 (2011)
10. McCarthy, J., Zald, M.: Resource mobilization and social movements: a partial theory. Am. J. Sociol. **82**, 1212–1241 (1997)
11. Polat, R.: The internet and political participation: exploring the explanatory links. Eur. J. Commun. **20**, 435–459 (2005)
12. The Network Society: From Knowledge to Policy. Center for Transatlantic Relations (2006)

Author Index

Printed in the United States
By Bookmasters